Adult Services

An Enduring Focus for Public Libraries

EDITED BY

Kathleen M. Heim

AND

Danny P. Wallace

American Library Association
CHICAGO AND LONDON 1990

Designed by Charles Bozett

Composed by Alexander Typesetting, Inc.,
Indianapolis, in Century Schoolbook
and Helvetica on a Magnafile typesetting system
and output on a Linotronic 202.

Printed on 50-pound Glatfelter, a pH-neutral
stock, and bound in Kivar 9 Linenweave
stock by Edwards Brothers, Inc.

The paper used in this publication meets the minimum requirements of American
National Standard for Information Sciences—Permanence of Paper for Printed Library
Materials, ANSI Z39.48-1984. ∞

Adult services : an enduring focus for public libraries / [edited] by
Kathleen M. Heim and Danny P. Wallace.
        p.   cm.
    Includes bibliographical references.
    ISBN 0-8389-0540-4 (alk. paper)
        1. Public libraries—Services to adults.   2. Libraries and adult
education.   I. Heim, Kathleen M.   II. Wallace, Danny P.
Z711.92.A32A37   1990   90-35122
027.6'22—dc20   CIP

Printed in the United States of America.

94 93 92 91 90   5 4 3 2 1

Dedication

to

Helen Lyman, author of many works including *Adult Education Activities in Public Libraries, Literacy and the Nation's Libraries,* and *Library Materials in Service to the Adult New Reader,* for her guidance, counsel, wisdom, and insightful evaluation;

and to

Andrew M. Hansen, Executive Director of the Reference and Adult Services Division of the American Library Association, for encouragement, patience, intelligent advice, good humor, and faith.

Contents

Acknowledgments

The Adult Services in the Eighties (ASE) project began in 1983 and ended in 1989 at Louisiana State University, School of Library and Information Science. During this time four graduate seminars were conducted for intense discussion and analysis of adult services. Participants in the seminars volunteered time for data entry and mailing. Research associates were assigned bibliographic and programming tasks.

The ASE project was far more than a study—it was a catalyst for thoughtful group interaction; it was an occasion for hard examination of the spectrum of programming and specialized services; it was a new way of looking at roles public libraries can play in a dynamic society.

Those who worked on the ASE project have assumed positions of responsibility in libraries throughout the nation. Listed below are those who worked on the ASE project along with their assigned responsibility during the project and their positions in March, 1990. To all of them I am most grateful for their generous and intelligent contributions.

> Danny P. Wallace, *Data Analysis Consultant,* Associate Dean, School of Library and Information Science, Louisiana State University, Baton Rouge
>
> J. Stuart Douglass, *Data Input and Analysis Coordinator,* Information Technologist, Texaco, Inc., Houston
>
> Joyce Meadows, *Production Supervisor,* School of Library and Information Science, Louisiana State University, Baton Rouge
>
> David M. Hovde, *ASE Coordinator, 1984–1985,* Social Science Bibliographer, Reference Librarian and Assistant Professor of Library Science, Purdue University, West Lafayette, Indiana

Donna W. Howell, *ASE Coordinator, 1988,* Government Documents/Data Services Reference Librarian, University of Georgia, Athens

Harry D. Nuttall, *ASE Coordinator, 1983–84,* Subject Specialist Librarian, Jacksonville State University, Jacksonville, Alabama

Gary O. Rolstad, *ASE Coordinator, 1985–86,* Director, St. Bernard Parish Library, Chalmette, Louisiana

Janice M. Simpson, *ASE Coordinator, 1987–88,* Director of Winn Parish Library, Winnfield, Louisiana

Connie Van Fleet, *ASE Coordinator, 1986–87,* Assistant Professor, School of Library and Information Science, Louisiana State University, Baton Rouge

Philip Hummel Arny, *Program Analysis and Data Entry,* Learning Resources Center Systems Coordinator, University of Minnesota Biomedical Library, Minneapolis

Dannie J. Ball, *Data Entry, Bibliographic Searching,* Director, Iberville Parish Library, Plaquemine, Louisiana

Anthony E. Barnes, *Data Entry, Bibliographic Searching,* Interlibrary Loan Librarian, New Orleans Public Library, New Orleans

James L. Bloom, *Programming,* Automation Librarian, Wayne County Public Library, Wayne, Michigan

Charlene C. Cain, *Data Entry, Bibliographic Searching,* Documents Librarian, Southeastern Louisiana University, Hammond

Kevin D. Cuccia, *Data Entry, Bibliographic Searching,* Science Librarian, Louisiana Tech University, Ruston

Kay Decell, *Word Processing,* Employee Relations Representative, Human Resources Division, Copolymer Rubber and Chemical Corporation, Plaquemine, Louisiana

Michele M. DeLorme, *Data Entry, Bibliographic Searching,* Librarian/Coordinator of Children's Programming, Ramsey County Public Library, Roseville, Minnesota

Gillian D. Ellern, *Program Analysis and Data Entry,* Automation Coordinator, Library, Western Carolina University, Cullowhee, North Carolina

Lolah Giamalva, *Data Entry and Bibliographic Searching,* Reference Librarian, Gloucester County Library, Sewell, New Jersey

Elizabeth A. Grice, *Bibliographic Verification,* Graduate Assistant, School of Library and Information Science, Louisiana State University, Baton Rouge

Paul G. Haschak, *Data Entry,* Night Reference Librarian, Southeastern Louisiana University, Hammond

Ann M. Hill, *Data Entry and Bibliographic Searching,* Librarian, New York Public Library, New York

Sandra M. Himel, *Bibliographic Searching,* Government Documents Librarian, University of Southwestern Louisiana, Lafayette

David H. Judell, *Data Entry, Bibliographic Searching,* Reference Librarian, Newport Beach Public Library, California

John P. McLain, *Data Consultant,* Computer Resources Coordinator, School of Library and Information Science, Louisiana State University, Baton Rouge

Dale K. McNeill, *Data Entry,* Branch Librarian, Harris County Public Library, Humble, Texas

Christopher E. Marhenke, *Data Entry and Bibliographic Searching,* Government Documents Librarian, Broward County Library, Ft. Lauderdale, Florida

Claire R. Massey, *Bibliographic Searching,* Librarian, Law Office of Heiskell, Donelson, Bearman, Adams, Williams & Kirsch, Heth, Arkansas

Kenneth Mauldin, *Data Entry, Bibliographic Searching, Labor Information Consultant,* Reference Librarian, East Baton Rouge Parish Library, Baton Rouge

Richard J. Mucklow, *Bibliographic Searching,* MBA Graduate Student at Texas Tech University, Lubbock

Connie L. Phelps, *Bibliographic Searching,* Education/Psychology and Evening Reference Librarian, University of New Orleans, New Orleans

Glenda Richardson, *Word Processing,* Student at Southeastern Louisiana University, Hammond

Patti A. Risinger, *Bibliographic Searching,* Reference Librarian, Lincoln Parish Public Library, Ruston, Louisiana

Richard J. Spector, *Data Entry,* Librarian/Computer Specialist, Follett Software Co., Santa Clara, California

Kathryn D. Watson, *Data Entry,* Consultant with Calgary Board of Education, Calgary, Alberta, Canada.

In addition, special thanks are due the Louisiana State University School of Library and Information Science Administrative Staff: Peggy Richardson, who managed fiscal arrangements; Joyce Meadows, who managed production of the final report, this book, and the bibliography; and Shirley Watson, who assisted in setting up the four ASE seminars.

Individuals who worked on the ASE project are credited either in the consulting group statement or in the lists of Reference and Adult Services officers that appear in the *Final Report*. Of particular note were the efforts of the RASD Services to Adults Committee Chairs, Neysa Eberhard, Thomas T. Jones, and Suzanne Sutton, who managed forums at ALA Annual Conferences and Midwinter Meetings.

Andrew Hansen, RASD Executive Director, was a strong supporter throughout the duration of the ASE project and offered administrative support from the division offices, intellectual support for the final monograph, and moral support as the project ambled along through the 1980s.

Herbert Bloom, senior editor, ALA Books, who shared with us his belief that professional writing is best served by rigorous thought.

Finally, as the muse of the ASE project, Helen Lyman deserves acknowledgment for her advice, encouragement, evaluative comments and wholehearted commitment to the importance of libraries in our society. Her courage and example kept us moving along.

KATHLEEN M. HEIM
Principal Investigator, Dean
School of Library and Information Science
Louisiana State University, Baton Rouge

An Overview of the Adult Services in the Eighties Project

Kathleen M. Heim

The 1983 Goal Award

In February 1983 the Services to Adults Committee of the Reference and Adult Services Division submitted a Goal Award proposal to the American Library Association to conduct a national survey of adult services. Chair Neysa Eberhard worked with Kathleen M. Heim, *RQ* editor, on proposal submission. The committee was notified in April, 1983, that it had been awarded the 1983 Bailey K. Howard Award of $5,000 to conduct the project titled, "Adult Services in the Eighties" (the ASE project).[1] Kathleen Heim was named principal investigator; as she was changing positions to assume the deanship of the School of Library and Information Science at Louisiana State University in August, 1983, the ASE project was slated to begin September 1983.

The Problem to Be Studied

"Adult services" is a term used to describe all aspects of library work with adults. The diversity of adult services defies simple codification, and current emphasis in public libraries on the planning process as a means of defining level, form, and style of services in a given community complicates any attempt to codify or provide a whole view of adult services.

It is precisely because of the current emphasis on the uniqueness of any given set of services within a specific library that the ASE project was undertaken. Diversity is a strength of adult services, but the lack of information on that diversity or areas of current and unique concentration often confounds the profession when it is asked to describe the scope of adult services for planning.

1

Trying to understand adult services as a single concept is bewildering. Typical articles in professional journals focus on a single service, such as the visually impaired elderly in Idaho or a special Hispanic information and referral center in Arizona. While these might seem to be unrelated, they are actually manifestations of the service continuum that is adult services.

No national census of adult services had been conducted since the benchmark study by Helen Lyman Smith, *Adult Education Activities in Public Libraries*, published by the American Library Association in 1954. The ASE project was intended to update work done by Lyman through presentation of data about the scope of services and compilation of bibliographic essays for key services.[2]

Phase I: Bibliography and Survey Development, 1983–1986

In September, 1983, Heim appointed Harry D. Nuttall as ASE project coordinator for 1983–1984. A bibliographic search of key adult services was undertaken to identify all items relevant to development of the emergent models. Nuttall obtained hundreds of documents, to which Heim assigned subject headings.[3] In November 1983 Heim wrote to chairs of ALA units concerned with adult services to invite their participation at an open hearing at the 1984 Midwinter Meeting of the American Library Association to solicit input on questionnaire development.

Bibliographic work continued throughout 1984, and additional hearings were conducted at the 1984 Annual Conference. Thomas T. Jones, chair of the Services to Adults Committee, presided over these sessions. A draft questionnaire was distributed to those who had attended hearings and indicated a willingness to serve on a reactor panel. David Hovde was appointed at this time to act as co-coordinator of the ASE project with Nuttall. Hovde developed questionnaire formats in several iterations.

The 1985 Midwinter Meeting brought together individuals who had registered an interest in the ASE project for a constructive session evaluating the first draft of the questionnaire. Through spring 1985 the literature review continued, and a second draft of the questionnaire was distributed. Additional field input was sought through publicity in the *RQ* feature "ASE Update" and correspondence with the ASE panel.

In fall 1985 Gary O. Rolstad was named ASE coordinator. In late December 1985 Danny P. Wallace, an information scientist who had joined the LSU/SLIS faculty, was engaged to advise on questionnaire revision. Under his supervision the questionnaire was consolidated and reduced in size to its final form.

In March 1986 a pretest of the final version of the ASE questionnaire was conducted. More refinements took place. Heim prepared a summary and context for ASE for *RQ* that included a copy of the questionnaire.[4]

Phase II: The Survey, 1986

In May 1986 the final version of the questionnaire was mailed to 1,758 library systems serving populations of 25,000 or more. Over 8,000 questionnaires were sent including one for each branch. Rolstad oversaw the mailing procedures and initiated the data-entry phase. J. Stuart Douglass, Computer Resources Coordinator at LSU/SLIS, supervised the Research Center Annex programming staff (Philip Arny, James Bloom, and Gillian Ellern) in developing input, data-check, cleanup, and "state-append" programs.

The 1986 Annual Conference occurred after the initial mailing but prior to the completion of data-entry. Rolstad organized a status report meeting at the Conference. Helen Lyman, who continued as a consultant to the ASE project during its conduct, and Suzanne Sutton, chair of the Adult Services Committee, were featured as speakers along with Heim.

In fall 1986 Connie Van Fleet was named ASE coordinator. Wallace worked with Douglass to use SPSS-PC to ascertain frequencies for each question and cross-tabulations for various sections of the data.

Two seminars enrolling LSU/SLIS research associates had been instituted during Phase II: summer 1986, LIS 7908, "Adult Services in Public Libraries" and fall 1986, LIS 7908, "Literature and Practice of Adult Services in Public Libraries."

Phase III: Data Analysis and Assimilation of Literature, 1987–1989

Wallace's final report appears in this volume as "The Character of Adult Services in the Eighties: Overview and Analysis of the ASE Questionnaire Data." As Wallace released preliminary results, Heim identified members of the Research Center Annex Consulting Group to develop essays on key adult services. Use of the extensive ASE literature files compiled during the bibliographic phase of ASE and survey findings provided the background for the essays. Van Fleet, who had been named ASE coordinator for 1986-1987, worked with Heim on a special seminar in spring 1987 to create a forum for discussion of findings and essay development: LIS 7106, "Adult Services for Special User Groups: Aging, Handicapped, Ethnic Minorities, and the Unemployed."

From 1987 through 1989 the development of the essays that grew into the chapters in this volume continued. Several authors withdrew from the project, and new authors were identified. ASE coordinators during essay development were Janice Simpson, 1987–1988 and Donna Howell, 1988, who worked with Joyce Meadows, production supervisor. Heim and Wallace edited chapters as they arrived during 1988 and 1989. In December 1989, the entire manuscript was submitted to ALA Publishing.

Key Adult Services: The Essays

The story of ASE outlined above demonstrates that large-scale research on a tight budget is time-consuming and difficult. During the process both Heim, its principal investigator, and Wallace, as its data analysis consultant, had appointments as full-time academic faculty and administrators and the ASE coordinators were full-time graduate students, yet the ASE project moved along.

Essays developed for the ASE project were intended to provide a historical context for each adult service with reference to the findings reported by Wallace. Most chapter coverage ends in 1986—the time of the ASE survey. Users of this volume should keep in mind that essays include references only to items cited and that additional citations for services used as background appear in the separate volume, *Adult Services: A Bibliography and Index*. For developments in adult services from 1987 to the present, readers should consult *Library Literature*.

HEIM: THE ENDURING FOCUS

The first essay, by Heim, examines the literature of adult services to provide a context for the service-specific essays that follow. Heim's central observation is simple and direct: *the one enduring focus of adult services is activation of resources for the community's clientele.*

Stating that the organizational structure of the American Library Association mirrors developments in U.S. librarianship, Heim summarizes the evolution of adult services within ALA. Early in this century "adult services" were subsumed in the library extension and outreach movement and by the adult education movement. It was not until the late 1930s that the nomenclature "adult services" was used. However, examination of these services continued under the rubric of "adult education" under the aegis of the ALA Education Board with support from the Ford Foundation's Fund for Adult Education (FAE). The FAE supported the American Heritage Project and the *Adult Education Activities in Public Libraries* survey, conducted by Lyman.

In 1957 the Adult Services Division was established and a separate newsletter initiated. ALA restructuring in 1972–1973 merged the ASD with the Reference Services Division. Today adult services thrive within the Reference and Adult Service division, although, as ever the case with ALA, many aspects of adult services are addressed within ALA units such as the Office of Library Outreach Services and the Public Library Association.

In her essay Heim observes that the diversity and changing nature of adult services have made theory formulation difficult. She notes that Margaret Monroe has defined the basic constructs for a theoretical framework, but that the library public services paradigm—unlike scientific paradigms—has emerged from the constructs and practices of librarianship substantiated by exploratory and survey research.

Heim offers a dialectical framework as a vantage point for understanding adult services, since dialectics help in understanding the logic of constant change. For adult service librarians to gain the correct insight to anticipate service needs, the insight is best gained by "being in the world." Services arise from special publics, not from absolutes conceptualized in the abstract by theoreticians. Future librarian involvement in adult service requires active participation to become part of synthesis, but at the same time enough flexibility and farsightedness to accept negation of outdated service styles.

WALLACE: OVERVIEW AND ANALYSIS OF THE ASE QUESTIONNAIRE DATA

Wallace outlines procedures used in conducting the ASE survey and methodologies for analysis of the data. Major categories of his analysis include "Provision of Services at No Charge," "Services Provided for a Fee," "Adult Services and *A Planning Process for Public Libraries*,"

"Regional Differences in Adult Services Provision," and "Adult Services and Demographic Differences."

General conclusions include the observation that nearly two-thirds of the services listed were provided by more than 25 percent of the respondents, suggesting that most of the services listed were usually considered important. There was also a substantial difference between the number of services provided and the use of *A Planning Process for Public Libraries*.

Regional variations were not totally consistent in differences, but overall the South lagged behind other regions in the provision of adult services. Demographic differences were not strongly related to the provision of adult services in any systematic way, although the relationships for some isolated questions and factors such as ethnicity, percentage of the community below the poverty line, or percentage of the community over retirement age bear examination.

VAN FLEET: LIFELONG LEARNING

Van Fleet's essay on lifelong learning examines the manner in which the history of the library's educational services to adults, the individualized nature of the library's approach to service provision, and strong supportive theory from other disciplines all converge at the point of a commitment to lifelong learning on the part of the public library. She views the options for library participation in the learning society as a continuum for service provision and professional attitude that moves from a traditional passive stance to a nontraditional active one. Van Fleet observes that adoption of the lifelong learning concept as an underlying philosophy for library service can focus goals and provide a continuity of service provision.

CAIN: SERVICES TO MINORITIES

Cain summarizes public library activity among minority groups, beginning with ALA's Work with the Foreign Born and continuing to today's Committee on Library Service to Minorities. She observes that the problems of providing service to ethnicultural minorities and the disadvantaged stem from complex problems of fiscal conservatism, difficulties in obtaining multilingual materials, language barriers, anglo ethnocentricity, and distrust of education institutions as vehicles for middle-class supremacy. Her careful look at key ALA documents places considerations of service to minorities in the societal context of all public library service.

DeLORME: SERVICE TO ADULT JOB-SEEKERS

DeLorme summarizes the history of public library service to people seeking vocational and career information. She examines the consolidation of information services in special collections, the cooperation of libraries with social service agencies, the provision of counseling, highlights of the ASE survey, and important issues raised by this special service.

ROLSTAD: LITERACY SERVICES

Rolstad examines the environment of federal support for literacy, summarizes the momentum of the movement in the 1980s, and provides an overview of library programs dealing with literacy education. He contends that librarians must strive toward development of an informed opinion on literacy education to help them decide whether to deploy some of the library's resources on behalf of literacy programs. The indispensable works of Helen Lyman are highlighted.

Placing responsibility at the heart of adult service provision, Rolstad argues that literacy education should be raised to a high priority if librarians' goal is to serve the broad community.

SCHNEIDER: LABOR GROUPS

Schneider provides a brief overview of the labor movement, reviews what services have been provided by libraries to labor groups, explores the question of why provide service to labor? and suggests possibilities for future services. He observes that although libraries were founded on the rhetoric of democracy, openness, equal access, and other high sounding social and political ideals, they have not always treated all patrons with equal vigor.

MOEN: THE ECONOMIC COMMUNITY

Moen sees that new imperatives exist for public libraries in times of funding crises. Major opportunities are opening for libraries as the value of information is more widely recognized by the economic community. He makes a strong case for renewed and increased efforts by librarians to serve their economic communities with the idea that service to this special population will not detract from services to other groups. Participation in serving the economic interest of the community through its efforts at economic development is serving the whole community.

BOYCE AND BOYCE: BOOKMOBILES

Bookmobiles are a significant force in the provision of public library service in the United States, with nearly 25 percent of U.S. public libraries providing bookmobile service. Aside from traditional activities, bookmobiles are commonly used for services to special groups. The most prominent of these groups are the homebound, nursing homes, migrant populations, low-income citizens and non–English-speaking minorities.

Boyce and Boyce contend that bookmobile service will continue to be an effective medium for the delivery of library services. The adult populations served by bookmobiles are those groups that otherwise would receive no library service whatsoever: the migrant, the immigrant, the elderly, the minority, the illiterate.

TUROCK: OLDER ADULTS

Turock reviews progress through three decades of library services to the older adult. She focuses on the Rutgers University Research Bureau in Library and Information Science *Update* to the 1972 *National Survey of Library Services to the Aging*. The *Update*, carried out at the same time as the ASE survey (1986), sampled 540 public libraries in communities of 25,000 or more to determine if services for older adults were characteristic of public libraries in general or better described as exemplary. Categories of service examined were: (1) extension services; (2) special resources and adjunct equipment; (3) group programs; and (4) special services that amplify traditional services.

Turock argues that too little attention has been paid by public libraries to the ways in which older adults serve as a valuable resource to our society and that there must be emphasis to transform public libraries in the 1990s.

SIMPSON: THE HANDICAPPED

Simpson defines terms relating to the disabled, summarizes governmental mandates, and describes barriers to service. She provides specific summaries of services to the blind and visually handicapped, the deaf and hearing impaired, the physically disabled, and the developmentally disabled.

Her arguments are simple: many library programs and resources are available for the disabled, but librarians need to become aware of resources and barriers to enhance effectiveness.

MARHENKE: GENEALOGY

Genealogical services are important adult services that support the study of local history and provide an avenue for instilling incentive and motivation for patrons to broaden their reading to other fields. Marhenke defines genealogy, characterizes genealogists, and describes the kind of information they require. He recognizes difficulties that information services personnel sometimes experience with genealogical patrons and calls for a better understanding.

GIAMALVA: PARENT EDUCATION

Parent education efforts in public libraries are receiving renewed attention as a result of concern about adult illiteracy, but parents need much more from libraries. Giamalva outlines the parent education movement and the involvement of the American Library Association in these efforts. She highlights successful examples of parent education programs and emphasizes linkages between libraries and the community organizations.

BARNES: PUBLIC ACCESS MICROCOMPUTERS

Barnes summarizes the development of the microcomputer and its expansion of use in the 1980s. A short history of library provision of microcomputers is provided. Barnes examines funding options for libraries that offer access to microcomputers and software. In-library access to hardware and software, circulating hardware and software, computer classes, assistance to special groups, development of local databases, sponsorship of computer clubs, bulletin boards, and online searching are explored.

Two model programs—Computer Town at Menlo Park, California, and the Personal Computer Center at the North-Pulaski Branch of the Chicago Public Library—are highlighted.

VAN FLEET AND RABER: THE PUBLIC LIBRARY AS A SOCIAL/CULTURAL INSTITUTION

Van Fleet and Raber approach the discussion of the public library as a social/cultural agency from two perspectives. They first delineate the underlying sociological foundation of the public library as a social and cultural agency and then trace the development and evolution of the library's social/cultural role in terms of operational definitions and in light of debate over nonbook and other stimulation activities.

The authors observe that the library sustains individual growth while preserving the knowledge that defines society. By acknowledging the value of the library to society, librarians obligate themselves to preserve and increase the influence of the library.

AND TO THE NINETIES

The essays on adult services presented in this volume, together with the findings of the ASE project, are intended to provide a convenient summary of the status of resources and programming for adults in libraries throughout the United States. While there has been no dearth of analysis on specific services, there has been lacking any attempt to view these services as linked on a service continuum undergirded by fundamental theories. Using the ASE project data as a unifying factor, the ASE authors have striven to identify common themes and philosophies that activate adult services.

At this writing, as librarians enter the 1990s and prepare for the 1991 White House Conference, adult services continue to manifest a robust diversity and lively intensity. The goal of this volume has been to demonstrate the strong philosophical commitment to the growth and development of adult services exhibited by U.S. librarians. This commitment has guaranteed that adult services will continue to be an enduring focus for public libraries.

Notes

1. For a complete technical report on the conduct of the Adult Services in the Eighties project including questionnaire iterations, see: Kathleen M. Heim, *Adult Services in the Eighties: Final Report Submitted to the RASD Adult Services Committee*, March 1990 (ERIC ED 316 264).
2. Kathleen M. Heim, "Adult Services in the Eighties—The ASE Project—ALA Goal Award Proposal Submitted by the Adult Services Committee of the Reference and Adult Services Division" (reprinted in *Adult Services in the Eighties: Final Report Submitted to the RASD Adult Services Committee*, March 1990).
3. Kathleen M. Heim, *Adult Services: A Bibliography and Index*. The bibliography of over 2,500 items proved too enormous for inclusion in this volume. However, so that the citations may be accessible, the entire bibliography has been submitted to the ERIC System.
4. Kathleen M. Heim, "Adult Services as Reflective of the Changing Role of the Public Library," *RQ* 26 (Winter 1986): 180–187.

CHAPTER 1

Adult Services: An Enduring Focus

Kathleen M. Heim

The enduring focus of adult services in U.S. public libraries during this century has been the active transformation of collections, resources, and staffs into programmatic responses relevant to the community served. This observation is the result of a comprehensive study of the literature of adult services including surveys and public library standards development. In this essay the literature of adult services is examined to provide the context for specific discussion of the particular services that follow.

Adult services include selection of resources for the library's collection, provisions for access to the collection including instruction in its use, and activation of use of the collection with individuals and targeted community groups.[1] Understanding adult services requires understanding public library development, since the two are inextricably linked. An understanding of the changing role of the U.S. public library is requisite to the delineation of the various focuses of adult services.[2]

What emerges from the in-depth summaries of specific adult services in this volume is a confluence of motivations, ideals, and pragmatism that undergird the delivery of adult services in general. These factors have been addressed squarely through such efforts as the Public Library Development Project manual, *Planning and Role Setting for Public Libraries.*[3] The manual crystallizes the philosophical stance that library services should be tailored to specific communities and based on local planning and decision making.[4] However, although the move toward local planning might seem to some to be a break with earlier broadly conceived definitions of service evidenced in national standards, this move actually consolidates many ideals and provides a mechanism to work through discrete influences to arrive at refined local concepts of role and mission.

11

Current thinking about library role setting is a confirmation of the viability of adult services in its many forms. As the 1986 survey of Adult Services in the Eighties demonstrates, services vary from community to community regardless of use of planning, but they vary more when planning procedures have been used.[5] The sweep of adult services in its diverse manifestations has eluded codification. Analysts have superimposed models and provided descriptions but the simple facts remain-different adult services arise to meet different community needs. *The one enduring focus of adult services is activation of resources for the community's clientele.*

Adult Services within the American Library Association

The organizational structure of the American Library Association mirrors developments in U.S. librarianship. As different concerns emerge and gain adherents a formalization through association-based affiliation occurs. While the rules governing formal recognition of issues and concerns have changed through the decades, ALA has consistently created mechanisms to ensure that an issue or concern is viable before committing resources to its inclusion within the ALA structure. Thus a summary of the evolution of adult services within ALA can provide an overview of the changing perceptions of adult services in this century.

FROM ADULT EDUCATION TO ADULT SERVICES

The underlying philosophy of adult services—which were not separately identified until the 1940s—was subsumed in the library extension and outreach movement of the early 1900s and later by the national adult education movement of the 1920s and 1930s. In her historical review of adult education, Margaret Monroe identified a variety of facets of adult library services recognized before 1920—reading guidance, adaptation of service to needs of special groups, and the library's sponsorship of education programs.[6] Van Fleet's essay on lifelong learning in this volume further illuminates the history of public library involvement in adult education.

Involvement of the American Library Association with the adult education movement was catalyzed by the publication of William S. Learned's 1924 report to the Carnegie Corporation on the potential of the public library as an agency for adult education.[7] Monroe has characterized Learned's report as a "perceptive synthesis and orderly summation of significant services already envisioned and initiated in public libraries."[8]

In 1924 ALA established a Commission on the Library and Adult Education with Carnegie Corporation funding to study the role of libraries in adult education. The Commission's report, *Libraries and Adult Education,* was issued in 1926.[9] It identified two major categories of library activities: (1) organized readers' advisory and adult education departments, and (2) programs of book distribution and library visits adapted to the needs of special groups (workers, university extension students, foreign-born, blind, inmates of hospitals and prisons).[10] Another important project of the Commission was establishment of the Subcommittee on Readable Books intended to encourage production of more books of educational value.

Continuing commitment by ALA to this broad construing of adult education as a library function is seen in the establishment in 1926 of the ALA Board on the Library and Adult Education and in the continuing publication of the quarterly bulletin, *Adult Education and the Library.*[11] The breadth of concerns dealt with by the Board is enumerated in its 1928 report, in which it noted that between 1,100 and 1,200 requests from libraries asking for advice were tallied on such diverse topics as methods for interesting groups of readers in nonfiction reading, ways to inaugurate and finance book talks, ways of meeting the problems of book supply for extension classes, material on library service for organized labor, how to bring Americanization classes in closer contact with public libraries, and classes for illiterates.[12]

The Board's extensive report in the *ALA Bulletin* demonstrates strong ALA involvement with numerous aspects of adult education, many supported by the Carnegie Corporation. These included studies of reading, establishment of a consulting service, the Reading with a Purpose project, and liaison with the American Association of Adult Education.

Some discontent with ALA's commitment to Adult Education was expressed in the 1930 report of the Activities Committee of ALA, and financial support was reduced. In its report of 1932, the Board included a statement noting, "The American Library Association has a distinct moral obligation to adult education in this country."[13] The economic depression had demonstrated ever greater needs for library participation in adult education. These sentiments were reemphasized in the 1933 report with the observation, "Man's economic extremity is indeed the library's opportunity."[14]

Headquarters support for the Board, formed by assigned staff assistants, was combined with work of library extension in the Public

Library Division under Julia Wright Merrill. This is reflected in the Board's 1934 report, which was issued as "Report on the Library and Adult Education and the Library Extension Board."[15]

The 1934 report included revised responsibilities for libraries vis-a-vis adult education, including extension to areas where library service did not exist, especially rural areas, research and experiments, and demonstrations.[16] The agencies with which liaison was maintained continued to grow. In addition to the long-standing work with the American Association for Adult Education board liaisons included the National Advisory Council on Radio in Education, the National Occupational Conferences, the Committee on Unemployed Youth, the National Education Association, and the American Country Life Association. The Adult Education and Readers' Advisers Round Table held conference programs.

In 1934 John M. Chancellor was hired at ALA headquarters as assistant in adult education—a move that Birge views as rejuvenating library adult education activities at the time the Board was embarking upon a ten-year assessment.[17] The Board's ten-year report summarized the growing importance of the adult education movement in libraries, focusing on several cumulated effects: (1) libraries became deeply conscious that the library must be one of the primary adult education agencies; (2) the growth of adult education services as exemplified by the increase in readers' advisors; (3) interaction with over seventy organizations of national scope; and (4) a program of publications, including "Reading with a Purpose" courses; the journal, *Adult Education and the Library* (1924–1930); Jennings' *Voluntary Education and the Library* and Hoit's *Books of General Interests for Today's Readers*.[18]

The years 1936 through 1940 are viewed by Monroe as a time when the profession explored the importance of moving the responsibility for adult education away from specialized service and placing it upon all professional staff serving adult readers.[19] This concern is reflected in the Board's 1937 report, which reflects on problems for examination that include the role of the library as a cultural center, access, information services and publicity.[20]

During this period the term "adult services" began to be used. Monroe notes that the term was used at the Adult Education Round Table in 1937.[21] Ernestine Rose's article, "The Need to Redirect and Unify Adult Service," argued for adult services to be as developed as has been children's services, based on community knowledge.[22]

World War II brought national concern for democracy, which was reflected in the activities of the Adult Education Board. In 1942 the

Board reported its two main efforts were assisting the ALA Post War Planning Committees to set standards to effect the social and civic intelligence of a democratic nation and to join with other national groups to establish a research commission to investigate the total educational resources needed to support democracy in America.[23]

The Board's Executive Assistant, John Chancellor, resigned in 1942, and ALA supported the Board's activities with temporary staff. In 1946 an Adult Education Section was established within the Public Library Division. The Adult Education Board languished without ALA Headquarters' support, but it regrouped in 1948 to study its functions and to develop a grant proposal to develop adult education aspects of the four-year goals and A National Plan for Library Service. This was in line with the 1948 Midwinter Council statement of policy that emphasized education of adults as a major function of libraries in order to make it difficult for anyone to remain ignorant of the great issues of our time.[24]

The Adult Education Section of the Public Library Division pursued projects similar to those that had been overseen by the Board, including preconference institutes, programs on services to the aging, services to labor, and discussion group planning.[25]

During this time ALA and the Social Science Research Council, with Carnegie Corporation support, launched the Public Library Inquiry under the direction to Robert D. Leigh to examine public library objectives, programs, structure, operations, and problems. In his discussion of services, Leigh noted:

> Service to adults in public libraries is more difficult to define in terms of an identifiable clientele with needs for specific library materials than is any other type of library service. . . . The omnibus character of the service presents difficulties but also has great advantages . . . adaptable to various individual interests and needs.[26]

Monroe observed that Leigh presented library services to adults without the specific context of adult education and that the integration of adult education objectives and methods into adult services had been achieved for the profession by 1950.[27]

The Adult Education Board, recognizing the diffusion of adult education activities throughout ALA, called a meeting of representatives of ALA divisions at the Cleveland conference in 1950. The purpose of the meeting was to focus on the need of some permanent means of providing information about current thinking and action to those working in adult education. The meeting was prompted because a Board survey of adult education activities in ALA had shown a lack of coordination, opportunistic activities among ALA units, and a "chasm between planning and representation (of ALA) in national agencies on the one hand and the line activities of individual libraries on the other."[28]

In 1951 the Ford Foundation's Fund for Adult Education (FAE) awarded $150,000 to ALA for the American Heritage Project, initially directed by Grace T. Stevenson, who also served as secretary to the Adult Education Board. The Board's 1951 report, submitted by Ruth Warncke, indicated that the Board would focus its attention on the FAE-supported American Heritage Project. The American Heritage Project lasted from 1951 to 1955, during which time 1,474 discussion groups were formed in thirty-three states to discuss political, social, and economic problems in the light of the basic documents, ideas, and experiences which constitute the American heritage.[29]

The FAE granted ALA $34,700 for a Survey of Adult Education Activities in Public libraries and Extension Agencies in 1952, and $100,000 (eventually totalling $469,000) for the development and stimulation of adult education activities in libraries to be used as subgrants to libraries in 1953. Additional support from the FAE provided funding for an Office of Adult Education at ALA to coordinate FAE-supported activities.[30]

THE EMERGENCE OF THE ADULT SERVICES CONCEPT

In 1957 the Adult Services Division (ASD) was established as a separate division in ALA. It was aimed at services to adults in all types of libraries and Eleanor Phinney served as Executive Secretary. This establishment took place after a management survey of ALA delineated two types of divisions: type-of-library and type-of-activity.

The emergence and acceptance of adult services were discussed in the "Adult Services" column of the March 1958 *ALA Bulletin,* which noted,

> The Adult Services Division inherits from the former Adult Education Section a close connection with the general adult education movement. It is essential to sustain this connection, but with increasing attention to the adult's cultural interests and use of library services for leisure hours as well as the more formally "education services."[31]

In addition, the focus on group services would be expanded to include emphasis on services to the individual.

The scope of the ASD as presented serves to exemplify the scope of adult services. These services were seen to include: (1) indirect guidance services (displays, reading lists); (2) advisory services (informed and planned reading); (3) service to organizations and groups (exhibits, reading lists, book talks, program-planning assistance); (4) library-sponsored programs (films, discussion groups, radio, television, workshops); and (5) community advisory services (conferences with other educational agencies, participation in community studies). Later in 1958 the ASD scope was expanded to include the Notable Books Council and other bibliographic projects relating to adult materials.

In 1961 the *Newsletter from the President* was launched under the aegis of president Margaret E. Monroe. The first issue included a feature on "Signs of Growth of 'Adult Services' in State and Public Libraries" that speculated that adult services became part of the organization of readers services about fifteen years earlier when the New York Public Library established its office of Adult Services in 1946.[32]

Clarification of the role of the Adult Services Division was provided by Muriel L. Fuller, president in 1963, who noted:

> In ASD our definition of adult services is limited to those library services designed to provide continuing educational, recreational, and cultural development for adults in all types of libraries. . . . Specific activities included in this definition cover indirect guidance service— displays, exhibits, booklists; advisory service to the individual; services to organizations and groups; library-sponsored programs; and cooperation with community groups. Informational, bibliographical and research activities, on the other hand, were assigned to the Reference Services Division.[33]

The Adult Services Division expanded its communication with members by establishing the *ASD Newsletter* in late 1963. At this time membership was nearly 2,000. In 1964 the *Library Service to Labor Newsletter* was incorporated in the *ASD Newsletter* to save on mailing costs and to expand the readership of each publication.

A review of ASD accomplishments appeared in 1967 upon its tenth anniversary. Short pieces were contributed by past presidents and executive secretary Phinney. Phinney summarized the Division's organizational and planning structure as well as the linkages between the earlier ALA adult education units. Projects carried out under the auspices of ASD included the Library-Community Project, the "Reading for An Age of Change" series, and work with adult illiterates.[34]

The *ASD Newsletter* steadily expanded coverage and fairly burst off its pages with lists of publications and activities. A "Checklist of Materials Available from ASD" indicated numerous publications available for the support of adult services including such diverse titles as *Books for Adults Beginning to Read, Labor, a Reading List, Literacy Activities in Public Libraries,* and *Reading Aids for the Handicapped.*[35]

In 1968 the indomitable Phinney, who had been executive secretary of both ASD and AHIL, resigned her formal affiliation with ASD. Ruth M. White, formerly ALA Headquarters Librarian, assumed the position of executive secretary. Although White served for only two and a half years, her tenure saw the adoption of "Library Rights of Adults: A Call for Action."

The "Library Rights of Adults" statement, adopted jointly by ASD and RSD in 1970, called for each adult to have the right to a "library which seeks to understand both his needs and his wants and which uses every means to satisfy them."[36] These libraries should provide wide resources, skilled staff, and efficient service.

A "Statement on Goals" adopted by the ASD Board in 1970 prioritized division goals. Commitment to the disadvantaged, aged, institutionalized, and handicapped was underscored as well as identification and support of research.[37] In June 1971 Andrew Hansen was appointed as executive secretary to both ASD and Reference Services Division (RSD) at a time when leaders of both divisions were examining goals and structures.

A joint ASD/RSD Committee on Common Concerns, which had been meeting since 1966, identified related activities and eventually recommended merger of the two divisions. Because both divisions "belong to that part of librarianship which has to do with direct service to the user" and because in many libraries there is no structural separation of service to adults into a reference department and an adult services department, merger was seen as positive.[38]

Undoubtedly the merger had outside impetus in a general ALA reorganization and straitened finances, but the memberships of both divisions approved a merger in 1972. The *ASD Newsletter* changed its name to *Adult Services* in its ninth (and last) volume, which included excellent articles on adult services in spite of the end being in sight. Of special interest to the history of adult services within ALA was its final issue, which featured "A Backward Glance: 1957–72" articles by former executive secretary Phinney and several past presidents.[39]

REFERENCE AND ADULT SERVICES

The years of transition from 1972 to 1973 were maneuvered ably by executive secretary Hansen, and copresidents Walter Allen (ASD) and Thelma K. Freides (RSD). The new Reference and Adult Services Division Bylaws reflected strong commitment to the tenets of service with the overall goal

> To stimulate and support full access to library services which are user oriented. The Division seeks actively to foster the fullest use of all media in meeting the educational, research, informational, recreational and social interests and needs of users of all types of libraries in every subject field.[40]

RQ, the RSD journal, continued quarterly publication but with an expanded scope to include all adult services in the coverage. Since the merger the journal has included columns and articles relating to adult services.

The remarkable stability of RASD since the merger in 1972 has provided a solid base of development for adult services. A good portion of this stability has been due to the steady and thoughtful leadership provided by Hansen, RASD Executive Director since 1971.

In his commentary on the twenty-fifth anniversary of *RQ,* Hansen reviewed RASD's accomplishments and noted unranked priorities that were articulated by the RASD Planning Committee in 1985. For adult services the goals included "development of services to adult user groups through techniques of planning, measurement and evaluation; publications; development of standards and guidelines; programs—ALA and regional; and surveys."[41]

Today adult services thrive within RASD, but it should be noted that some aspects of adult services—especially those with a public library focus—are addressed by the Public Library Association as well. However, the purpose of this brief overview of the positioning of adult services within ALA has not been intended to address organizational concerns but rather to help readers focus on the evolution of orientation of library services to adults within ALA.

Understanding Adult Services: A Dialectical Construct

TOWARD SYNTHESIS

Attempts to formulate a "theory" of adult services have been difficult due to the diversity and constantly changing nature of these services. As the essays in this book show quite clearly, each service examined has a rich and often turbulent history. Each service has had proponents, dissenters, ideal service models, variable funding, and different levels of professional articulation.

The problems that beset any type of consolidating theory for adult services are the same problems that surround overall definition of public library mission and goal statements. Charles McClure has stated this simply in his introduction to *Planning and Role Setting for Public Libraries*, "In spite of the multifaceted character of the nation's public libraries and the diverse communities they serve, excellence is achieved daily. . . . Excellence is a moving target."[42]

Most definers of adult services, such as Joyce Wente, move quickly from a broad-brush definition, such as "adult services has come to mean all those library services provided for the adult clientele to fill their educational, informational, cultural, and recreational library needs," to an enumeration of examples.[43]

In her presentation at a 1981 institute, Margaret E. Monroe chose to be "illustrative rather than comprehensive or definitive" as she identified significant themes relating to the future of adult services.[44] The themes Monroe explored were the importance of special publics (with service to the older adult as an example); sensitivity to new forces in society (with "leisure as a lifestyle" as an example); a new standard for quality; "impact" (with legislative information services and information and referral as examples); the role of research; and innovations as planned change.[45]

Monroe's illustrative approach, however, holds the basic constructs required for a theoretical framework and builds on her entire oeuvres. This theoretical framework was discussed by Eliza T. Dresang in her introduction to a volume of essays in Monroe's honor titled *The Service Imperative for Libraries*. Dresang noted that "the library public service paradigm, consisting of the four functions of information, instruction, guidance and stimulation, emerged gradually."[46] Further, the paradigm, unlike scientific paradigms, emerged from the constructs and practices of librarianship substantiated by exploratory and survey research, not by experimental research.

In order to be predictive about adult services, a vantage point is required that will enable these services to be considered whole. The most sensible approach is to view the entirety of these services in a dialectical framework. Simplistically stated, a dialectical framework (as used by Marx) is a method of analyzing social change. To understand the world, real human beings and their activities in the world must be considered. The dialectical relationship between humans and their environment stresses the elements that: (1) all things are in constant change; (2) the ultimate source of change is within the thing or process itself; (3) this source is the struggle of opposites, the contradiction within each thing; (4) this struggle, at nodal points, brings about qualitative changes, or leaps, so that the thing is transformed into something else; and (5) practical-critical activity resolves the contradictions.[47]

Dialectics help us to understand the logic of constant change. The internal contradictions, the struggle of opposites, is the fundamental cause of change. From point A (the thesis) to point non-A (the antithesis) come transformation and synthesis. Most writers about library service development have intuitively incorporated this framework. Emphasis on community analysis, for instance, is analogous to understanding real human beings and their activities in the world. The acceptance of diversity and the nonstatic nature of the library's public is implicit recognition of the dialectic method.

However, because adult service theorists have relied upon observation to identify paradigmatic shifts, those who look for an explanatory underpinning are left with little more than a staggering array of service examples from which to build predictive models. By suggesting a dialectical construct as a means by which to understand adult services it is easier to conceptualize future directions.

Theorizers about adult services have been clearly astute in their recognition of the import of societal forces on service as well as their reorganization of the evolutionary nature of these services. What has been missing, however, is an examination of service evolution as synthesis. Taking "library service to labor" as one example may help to clarify this point. Schneider points out in his essay in this volume, "perhaps it is time for a new perspective: 'Labor and Business—One Service for Both Revisited.' There is a generally held view of 'labor' and 'business' as two adversaries with disparate ends. They may indeed perform adversarial roles. However, 'business' in a wider context is not 'manager or owners' but rather a 'process' whereby capital and labor are managed (for a profit) to meet customer needs."

Attempting to articulate a current level of synthesis for all (or even one) adult service may seem overly ambitious in the abstract. However, as has been shown above in the review of the locus of organized action for various adult services with ALA, the national association has made a series of de facto synthetic commitments. These commitments may be manifested in various ways—personnel (a full-time staff member for adult education), publications (a newsletter on service to labor), or simply formalized association status (a section of RASD on genealogy). To the degree to which ALA's deployment of resources may be seen as legitimation of this or that service, it may be viewed as "synthesis." The factors that combine to give a service some sort of formal status include persuasive personalities (individually or in a group committed to a concern), societal pressure, outside funding, or a convergence thereof.

This is an important observation. Many assessments of movements in librarianship examine the formalized mechanisms of ALA's committee or divisional structure. This record, most often gleaned from official publications, cannot provide a comprehensive understanding of the often contradictory factors at work that moved a given service from one practiced in a few scattered libraries to one that has gained formalized status. So, even though services as addressed by ALA over the years may exhibit divergent orientations, when examined (if the records exist) as they evolved, other microlevels of diversity would be observed.

But the question here is can a dialectical construct serve to give overall understanding of adult services? From an emphasis on serving labor to an expansion of service to business or from an emphasis on Americanizing the foreign-born to celebrating ethnocultural diversity, we can certainly perceive thesis and antithesis. But do we see synthesis? If synthesis is viewed as the current established locus of a particular service, yes. But if synthesis is yet to be achieved, no. How does the adult services librarian gain the correct insight to anticipate services as needs emerge?

Surprisingly, the answer appears to lie in a continuation of the ennumerative approach—that is, by being in the world or being at the front lines, the service evolves to meet the needs. More than ever these services should arise from the special publics, not from absolutes decreed by the educated class.

In many ways public library services are the most democratic of all public goods due to the efforts of librarians to assess community needs through interaction with communities served. The testimony to this involvement is the very diversity of services. But the formalization of service styles can be in and of itself a possible restraint to the dialectic. Entrenched special interests may become self-perpetuating and require revolution on the front lines to deliver new services. While many librarians still experience longing for the days of "Great Books" discussion groups, videotape circulation has proven to be a new draw for an expanded clientele. Yet no adult service has emerged (beyond circulation) to cope with these new users.

The challenge to adult service librarians of today is a wholehearted embrace of the evolution of services both at point of service and professionwide. We must be quicker and faster to be part of the problem to continue to be part of the solution. This is not to say that librarians have been slow to do so in the past. Indeed, quite the contrary is true. The variety of services explored in this volume is testimony to involvement. But these services have tended to evolve separately and to some degree in isolation as attested to by duplicative formalization within ALA. Today literacy initiatives are so fragmented that ALA has had to create an assemblage to discover what the various units are doing. There are too many monologues.

This volume is an attempt to show commonalities in adult services and to trace the historical roots of each service. These services generate various degrees of heat and light as society at large takes up and discards causes. Are librarians helping to innovate or following societal trends? If the answer is "innovating," is this the appropriate role?

Without a construct from which to adjudge adult service development we will be either passive reactors or proscriptive doyens. Neither role is acceptable. The future of librarian involvement in adult services requires active participation in the trenches to become part of the synthesis but at the same time enough flexibility and farsightedness to accept negation of outdated service styles and a letting go as new models emerge.

Service Models for Adult Services

This volume presents the findings of the 1986 survey, "The Adult Services in the Eighties Project" (ASE project) that was commissioned by the Reference and Adult Services Division, Services to Adults Committee to provide a state-of-the-art description of the extent to which adult services are provided in U.S. public libraries serving populations of 25,000 or more.[48] Because the project was supported by RASD, a great deal of associationwide participation was sought through mailed iterations of the survey instrument and hearings held at ALA conferences. These activities are chronicled in *RQ* in the regular feature "ASE Update," which appeared from 1984 to 1988.[49]

The principal investigator for the ASE project, Kathleen M. Heim, assembled a team of research associates at the School of Library and Information Science's Research Center Annex at Louisiana State University to execute questionnaire assemblage, mailing, and data entry. Consolidation and reporting of the results appear here in Wallace's chapter, "The Character of Adult Services in the Eighties: Overview and Analysis of the ASE Questionnaire Data."

As survey analysis began it became clear that the results would give a benchmark view but that these results would be, to some degree, too static to provide a long-term effect on adult services theory building. To remedy this shortcoming, essays were commissioned to examine each service within its historical context with some reference to the ASE project findings for each service. The bibliography assembled for the ASE project was so large that a separate publication was developed and submitted to ERIC, although each essay includes appropriate references.[50] The essays that comprise the remainder of this volume were developed to provide adult services librarians with an historical perspective on the evolution of each service. Most use Helen Lyman Smith's seminal 1953 study, *Adult Education Activities in Public Libraries*—a national census of adult services—as a touchstone.[51] By comparing Lyman Smith's findings with ASE project findings (where pertinent), one can identify evolution within particularized adult services as well as adult services overall.

Notes

1. Kathleen M. Heim and Margaret E. Monroe, "Adult Services," in *ALA Encyclopedia of Library and Information Services,* 2nd ed., ed. Robert Wedgeworth (Chicago: ALA, 1986), p. 31.
2. Kathleen M. Heim, "Adult Services as Reflective of the Changing Role of the Public Library," *RQ* 26 (Winter 1986): 181.
3. Charles R. McClure et al., *Planning and Role Setting for Public Libraries: A Manual of Options and Procedures* (Chicago: ALA, 1987).
4. Ibid., p. xi.
5. See Wallace, Chapter 2 in this volume.
6. Margaret E. Monroe, *Library Adult Education: The Biography of an Idea* (New York: Scarecrow, 1963), p. 24.
7. William S. Learned, *The American Public Library and the Diffusion of Knowledge* (New York: Harcourt, Brace, 1924).
8. Monroe, *Library Adult Education,* p. 29.
9. American Library Association, Commission on the Library and Adult Education, *Libraries and Adult Education* (Chicago: ALA, 1926).
10. Monroe, *Library Adult Education,* p. 33.
11. ALA Board on the Library and Adult Education, *ALA Bulletin* 21 (July 1927): 196.
12. ALA Board on the Library and Adult Education, *ALA Bulletin* 22 (June 1928): 184–185.
13. ALA Board on the Library and Adult Education, "Adult Education in 1931" *ALA Bulletin* (April 1932): 226.
14. ALA Board on the Library and Adult Education, "Adult Education Looks to a New Era," *ALA Bulletin* (October, 1933): 434.
15. Ibid., pp. 434–438.
16. Ibid., p. 435.

17. Lynn E. Birge, *Serving Adult Learners: A Public Library Tradition* (Chicago: ALA, 1981): 50.
18. ALA Board on the Library and Adult Education, "The Library and Adult Education 1924–1934," *ALA Bulletin* 29 (June 1935): 316–323.
19. Monroe, *Library Adult Education,* p. 40.
20. ALA Adult Education Board, *ALA Bulletin* 31 (September 1937): 510–516.
21. Monroe, *Library Adult Education,* p. 75.
22. Ernestine Rose, "The Need to Redirect and Unify Adult Service," in *Helping Adults to Learn: The Library in Action,* ed. John Chancellor (Chicago: ALA, 1939), pp. 175–181.
23. ALA Adult Education Board, *ALA Bulletin* 36 (October 15, 1942): 672–674.
24. ALA Adult Education Board, *ALA Bulletin* 42 (October 15, 1948): 434.
25. ALA Public Library Division, Adult Education Section. *ALA Bulletin* 42 (September 15, 1948): 55–58.
26. Robert D. Leigh, *The Public Library in the United States* (New York: Columbia Univ. Pr., 1950), pp. 103–104.
27. Monroe, *Library Adult Education,* p. 58.
28. ALA Adult Education Board, *Proceedings* of Cleveland Conference (July 16–22, 1950), pp. 60–62.
29. Robert Ellis Lee, *Continuing Education for Adults through the American Public Library, 1833–1964* (Chicago: ALA, 1966), p. 86.
30. Grace T. Stevenson, "The ALA Adult Education Board," *ALA Bulletin* 48 (April 1954): 226–231.
31. "Adult Services," *ALA Bulletin* 52 (March 1958): 203.
32. "Signs of Growth of 'Adult Services' in State and Public Libraries," *Newsletter from the President* (March 15, 1961): 4–5.
33. Muriel L. Fuller, "Dear ASD Colleagues," *Newsletter from the President* (March 1963):1.
34. Eleanor Phinney, "Ten Years from the Vantage Point of the Executive Secretary," *ASD Newsletter* 4 (Summer 1967): 11–14.
35. "Checklist of Materials Available from ASD," *ASD Newsletter* 5 (Fall 1967): 16–17.
36. "Library Rights of Adults: A Call for Action," *ASD Newsletter* 8 (Fall 1970): 2–3.
37. "Statement on Goals," *ASD Newsletter* 8 (Winter 1971): 27–28.
38. "ASD-RSD: To Merge or Not to Merge?" *ASD Newsletter* 8 (Spring, 1971): 35–36.
39. "A Backward Glance: 1957–72," *Adult Services* 9 (Summer 1972): 29–36.
40. "Reference and Adult Services Division Proposed Bylaws," *Adult Services* 9 (Spring 1972): 25–28.
41. Andrew Hansen, "RASD: A Backward Look into the Future," *RQ* 25 (Fall 1985): 13–18.
42. Charles R. McClure et al., *Planning and Role Setting for Public Libraries: A Manual of Options and Procedures* (Chicago: ALA, 1987), p. 1.
43. Joyce Wente, "What Are 'Adult Services?'" *RQ* 18 (Spring, 1979): 231.
44. Margaret E. Monroe, "The Future for Public Library Adult Services, Opportunities and New Directions" in *Public Libraries and New Directions for Adult Services,* ed. Joan C. Durrance and Rose Vainstein (Ann Arbor, Mich.: School of Library Science, University of Michigan, 1981), p. 59.
45. Ibid., pp. 5–64.
46. Eliza T. Dresang, "The Service Paradigm" in *The Service Imperative for Libraries: Essays in Honor of Margaret E. Monroe,* ed. Gail A. Schlachter (Littleton, Colo.: Libraries Unlimited, 1982), p. 13.
47. John G. Gurley, *Challenges to Capitalism,* 3rd ed. (Reading, Mass.: Addison-Wesley, 1988), pp. 16–18.

48. Kathleen M. Heim, "Adult Services as Reflective of the Changing Role of the Public Library," *RQ* 27 (Winter 1986): 180–187.
49. "ASE Updates" by Thomas T. Jones, *RQ* 23 (Spring 1984): 294; *RQ* 24 (Fall, 1984):31; *RQ* 24 (Spring 1985): 284; Gary O. Rolstad, *RQ* 26 (Fall 1986): 18; Connie Van Fleet, *RQ* 26 (Spring 1987): 302–303; and Janice M. Simpson, *RQ* 27 (Fall, 1987): 29–30, *RQ* 27 (Spring 1988): 320–321; *RQ* 28 (Summer 1988): 477–478.
50. Kathleen M. Heim, *Adult Services: A Bibliography and Index* (June 1990), ERIC ED 316264.
51. Helen Lyman Smith, *Adult Education Activities in Public Libraries* (Chicago: ALA, 1954).

CHAPTER 2

The Character of Adult Services in the Eighties: Overview and Analysis of the ASE Questionnaire Data

Danny P. Wallace

Questionnaire Development

The study of public library adult services was discussed at the Midwinter and Annual Conference sessions of the ALA RASD Services to Adults Committee and at open meetings in 1984 and 1985.[1] In December 1984 a questionnaire based heavily on Lyman Smith's 1952–1953 survey was sent with a detailed instruction booklet to a group of interested individuals selected from the *ALA Handbook of Organization* and attendance sheets from ASE open assemblies at the 1984 ALA Midwinter Meeting.[2] Suggestions submitted by these individuals were incorporated into a second draft of the questionnaire. Changes in the second draft included elimination of the separate instruction booklet and reduction of the questionnaire from twelve pages to eight. The second draft was distributed to a similar group of concerned individuals in July 1985, and resulting comments were incorporated into a third draft. Revisions at this point further reduced the size of the questionnaire and added a question regarding use of *A Planning Process for Public Libraries*.[3]

The fourth and final version of the questionnaire represented a drastic reduction in size. An earlier section asking for "reasons your library is not providing this service" was felt to be unwieldy and was eliminated altogether. Other modifications included extensive re-wording of the questions and simplification of the instructions. The final questionnaire is included as Appendix 1 of this chapter.

Questionnaire Distribution

The goal of the survey was to gather information from all U. S. public libraries serving communities of 25,000 or more. Questionnaires were distributed to 1,758 library systems, representing more than 8,000 single unit libraries, central libraries, and branches. Systems that had not responded by July 22, 1986, were sent reminder cards. Nonrespondent systems with more than three branches were further contacted by telephone during September and October 1986.

The decision to conduct a census rather than a survey was based on the perception that adult services represent a unique and extremely diverse range of activities that could best be assessed by gathering information from as many respondents as possible. The ready avail-ability of resources for conducting and processing a census added support to the decision to take such an approach.

Processing Responses

The questionnaire was deliberately designed for a minimum of post-receipt coding. The first section required essentially no coding, al-though the second required considerable coding, which presented some processing problems discussed below. Demographic data from the *County and City Data Book* were added to each questionnaire to provide comparative information for the communities represented by the respondents.[4] Except for population, demographics were available only for the community represented by the system as a whole, not for individual communities served by branch libraries.

Data were input into an IBM Personal Computer using a program written especially for the project. Programs were used to clean and consolidate data, which were then uploaded to Louisiana State Uni-versity's IBM mainframe computer for processing by SPSS/X.

Due to the large number of responses anticipated, it was felt that extensive error correction procedures such as double data entry would be too time-consuming and too costly. Procedures built into the input program helped assure that only correct data were recorded for the major questions in section 1, but the open-ended responses to some of them in section 2 and the program descriptions were not subjected to any error control measures. Some problems with duplicate entry arose as a result of operator error; these duplicates were identified and eliminated. A sequential sampling of 112 (2.5 percent of the total) cases found errors in only five. Although this is admittedly a small sample, the sequential method used is specifically designed for such situations. It was felt that an error rate of less than 5 percent based on the sample was acceptable, and no further efforts were made to correct errors in the database. Although it cannot be assumed that the database is totally error-free, the size of the database and the apparent small incidence of error suggest that the overall integrity of the data is more than satisfactory.

Representativeness of the Responses

ASE questionnaires were distributed to a total of 1,758 library systems (for purposes of this discussion, a system is defined as a central library facility and its branches, or a "stand alone" library with no branches). Responses were received from 4,215 individual libraries representing 1,114 systems, meaning that 63 percent of the systems to whom questionnaires were sent are represented in the results.

As a means of estimating the adequacy of representation, various demographic data were collected for 1,681 of the communities to which questionnaires were sent (demographics were not available for seventy-seven communities). These demographics, drawn from the 1983 edition of the *County and City Data Book*, represent 1980 census data and include, for each community represented by a library system:

- White residents as a percentage of total population
- Black residents as a percentage of total population
- Residents of Spanish origin as a percentage of total population
- Residents of other ethnic origin (including American Indian, Eskimo, Aleut, Asian and Pacific Islander) as a percentage of total population

- Residents aged twenty-five or older who have completed at least twelve years of education as a percentage of total population
- Residents aged twenty-five or older who have completed at least sixteen years of education as a percentage of total population
- Residents aged sixty-five or older as a percentage of total population
- Families with income below the poverty level as a percentage of total population
- Per Capita income of the community
- Population of the community [5]

The population figures from the *County and City Data Book* indicate the population of the community in which the main administrative facility of the system is located. As a result, there are many systems for which this figure is substantially below the 25,000 figure used in selecting library systems for the study.

Table 1 provides a comparison of the represented ("respondents") and unrepresented ("nonrespondents") systems for each of these demographic variables and a comparison by geographic region.* Statistical analysis using t-tests indicates that for five of the demographic variables there is a significant difference between the responding and nonresponding systems in the mean value of the variable. For four of these variables—percentage of residents of Spanish origin, percentage of residents with at least a high school education, percentage of residents with at least a college education, and per capita income—the differences are small, even though statistically significant, and cannot be expected to have had any substantial influence on the results of the study.

For the fifth variable, population, the difference is both statistically significant and large—the mean population of the responding systems is nearly twice the mean of the nonresponding systems. This means that smaller communities were seriously underrepresented in the study, and that results should be interpreted in terms of this deficiency. It is not clear what effect this deficiency might have on the results. No attempt has been made to weight or scale results to compensate for this difference between the responding and nonresponding systems.

A chi-squared test used to examine the regional representation of the respondents indicated that there was a statistically significant

* Table 1 and all tables referred to herein are in Appendix 2 following this chapter.

difference between responding and nonresponding systems in terms of their distribution across four geographic regions.[6] Examination of the distribution suggests that libraries in the western region were slightly overrepresented. This difference is probably not particularly important to the results, and no attempt has been made to account for it. The overrepresentation of western libraries should, however, be kept in mind in evaluating the regional comparisons provided later in this chapter.

Analysis of Responses

Section 1 of the questionnaire asked forty-four major questions regarding public library adult services, providing for identification of a total of seventy-three services. Section 2 asked for specific information regarding successful programs. The analyses presented in this chapter will concentrate on the data supplied in response to questions in section 1. These questions can be readily divided into five major categories:

1. Provision of resource materials: displays; circulation of materials; in-library provision of materials; reading lists and bibliographies; interlibrary loan; and maintenance of resource files (questions 1 through 4, 6 through 18, 20, and 41 through 44)

2. Provision of facilities and equipment: audiovisual equipment; microcomputers; photocopiers; meeting rooms; and resources files (questions 5, 19, and 21 through 23)

3. Provision of programs: general programs (questions 24 through 27) and programming for special groups (question 34)

4. Provision of educational services: library use education (questions 28 and 29) and literacy education (questions 30 through 33)

5. Provision of external and outreach services: hospitals; prisons; retirement and nursing homes; homebound; books by mail; and bookmobile services (questions 35 through 40).

The responses of all libraries to questions 1 through 44 are summarized in Table 2. The number of services provided at no charge ranged from a minimum of 1 to a maximum of 70, with a mean (average) of 26.2 and a median (midpoint) of 25. The number of services provided for a fee ranged from a minimum of zero to a maximum of 36, with a mean of 2.1 and a median of 1. Adding the number of services provided at no charge to the number provided for a fee for each library yields a total number of services provided ranging from a minimum of 1 to a maximum of 70, with a mean of 26.8 and a median of 25.

PROVISION OF SERVICES AT NO CHARGE

Tables 3 and 4 provide listings of the services most frequently and least frequently provided at no charge. Nine services were provided at no charge by at least 75 percent of the responding libraries. These include individual and group library use instruction, displays of library and nonlibrary materials, interlibrary loan service, maintenance of community activity information files, provision of reading lists or bibliographies, referral to other agencies for literacy education, and circulation of musical records. These are all rather typical and traditional library activities, and the list includes no surprises.

The list of services provided at no charge by fewer than 25 percent of the respondents (Table 4) is much longer, and includes

> Individual or group literacy education
> Bookmobile services of any kind
> Programming for special groups, such as minorities, business persons, job seekers, genealogists, handicapped individuals, labor groups, or "other" groups
> Circulation or in-library availability of computer hardware or software
> Services to external agencies, such as hospitals, prisons, and retirement or nursing homes
> Books by mail
> Radio or cable television programming.

The common denominators of the twenty-six services least frequently provided at no charge seem to be (1) the provision of specialized services to specific groups or individuals; (2) the extension of services beyond the library; and (3) the involvement of electronic media such as radio, television, and computers.

SERVICES PROVIDED FOR A FEE

Most libraries indicated that they do charge for at least some services. The twelve services for which fees were charged by at least 2 percent of the libraries offering the service are listed in Table 5. This list is not unlike the lists that have been produced by other studies of the use of fees to support library services.[7] Not surprisingly, the provision of photocopy machines is at the top of the list, with nearly 25 percent of the libraries providing photocopiers indicating that a fee is assessed for their use. This figure is probably misleading, since many librarians may not think of coin-operated photocopy machines as constituting a service for a fee. It is probably safe to assume that a large proportion of the 2,566 libraries who indicated that photocopiers were provided at no charge are in fact providing coin-operated machines.

The eleven other services for which fees are most frequently charged include circulation of videotapes, films, and other audiovisual materials; circulation and in-library use of microcomputers and software; circulation of "other" materials; provision of meeting or conference room space; interlibrary loan service; and programming for labor groups and prisons. Five of these services—programming for labor groups, programming for prisons, circulation of microcomputers, circulation of microcomputer software, and circulation of "other" materials-are actually very uncommon services, and therefore the provision of such a service for a fee is trivial compared to the overwhelming tendency not to provide the service at all.

The remaining services fall readily into two categories—specialized services to groups or individuals, and use of electronic media. The provision of meeting or conference room space and interlibrary loan service represent specialized services to groups or individuals that do not directly benefit the library or its other patrons and that frequently involve direct charges to the library. For interlibrary loan, the direct charges are levied by lending libraries, networks, or bibliographic utilities; the number of libraries reporting fees for interlibrary loan may actually be inaccurate, since some librarians may differentiate between fees levied by them and fees imposed by lending libraries and passed on to the patron. The direct charges for meeting or conference room space involve such overhead expenses as lighting, heat, and custodial services. Charging fees for such services has an obvious rationale in the specialized nature of the service and its lack of general benefit to the library community. The provision of materials through interlibrary loan is obviously done for the benefit of individual patrons.

Circulation of videotapes, films, and audiovisual materials and provision of microcomputers for in-library use involve electronic media that are expensive to acquire, prone to damage, and in need of frequent routine maintenance and special care. For these services, the rationale for charging fees probably arises not from the specialized nature of the clientele served, but from the high cost to the library of providing such services. In many cases, the library's management might prefer to provide these services at no charge but decides that the library's budget cannot support the service without the imposition of fees.

The list of services for which very few libraries levied fees is an extensive one, and a separate listing is unnecessary. With the exception of the twelve services listed in Table 5, the major decisions facing most libraries may be related to whether a service should be offered at all, with the imposition of fees rarely considered as an option.

Adult Services and *A Planning Process* *for Public Libraries*

In 1980 ALA created a publication representing a major change in thinking with regard to the evaluation of public libraries. This publication, *A Planning Process for Public Libraries,* rejected the notion of standards set by a central authority and proposed instead that libraries and their constituents should set their own goals and objectives and engage in a systematic planning process using principles and procedures somewhat similar to those used in systems analysis. *A Planning Process for Public Libraries* has recently been superseded by *Planning and Role Setting for Public Libraries: A Manual of Options and Procedures,*[8] and its companion publications, the second edition of *Output Measures for Public Libraries*[9] and the *Public Library Data Service Statistical Report.*[10] These three works together constitute the major output of the Public Library Development Program, which was instituted with the creation within the Public Library Association of the Task Force on New Standards with the goal of revising and expanding *A Planning Process for Public Libraries* and the first edition of *Output Measures for Public Libraries.*[11]

Although there have been several commentaries on and criticisms of *A Planning Process for Public Libraries,* there appear to have been no previous efforts to determine how widespread use of the process is. One goal of the ASE project was to assess the extent to which this process has been actually employed.

Recipients of the ASE questionnaire were asked to indicate whether they had used *A Planning Process for Public Libraries,* and when they had first used it. Answers to this question were gathered for 3,969 libraries (246 respondents answered neither "yes" nor "no"; data for these 246 libraries are not included in the following analyses).

Of the 3,969 libraries for which data were available, less than one-fifth (741, or 18.7 percent) indicated that the planning process had been used. A second question asked when the process had first been used. Responses to this question revealed a potential problem: a small number of respondents (39, or 5.3 percent) supplied dates earlier than the publication date of A *Planning Process for Public Libraries*. Although it is remotely conceivable that some of these libraries were involved in the prepublication testing of the process, it is extremely unlikely that all thirty-nine were. It seems more likely that these respondents were using some set of processes other than A *Planning Process for Public Libraries*, or that they inadvertently reported the date incorrectly. Although the specific meaning of these doubtful dates is unknown, the number of libraries reporting them is small enough that the overall impact can be treated as negligible. Data for these thirty-nine libraries are included in the following analyses.

NUMBER OF SERVICES OFFERED

The mean number of services provided at no charge was 28.7 for libraries in which the planning process had been used, and 25.7 for those in which it had not been used. Although the difference is not very large, a t-test shows it to be statistically significant ($t = 5.66$, $df = 3967$, $p < .01$). The mean number of services provided for a fee was 2.1 for both those libraries in which the planning process had been used and those in which it had not been used. The mean total number of services provided was 29.3 for libraries in which the planning process had been used and 26.2 for those in which it had not been used; this difference is statistically significant ($t = 5.60$, $df = 3967$, $p < .01$). Although this relationship between use of the planning process and the number of services offered is difficult to interpret, it is at least suggestive of the possibility that the same factors that lead to use of the planning process may influence the provision of adult services.

PROVISION OF SPECIFIC SERVICES

Although the percentage of libraries providing a particular service was consistently higher for libraries that had used A *Planning Process for Public Libraries* than for those that had not, and the differences were in a number of cases statistically significant, there were very few cases in which the difference was greater than 10 percent. There were no such differences in the provision of facilities and equipment, educational services, or external and outreach services.

Although there were statistically significant differences between libraries that had employed the planning process and those that had not for thirteen of the twenty-two questions in the resource materials category, they differed substantially in their responses to only one: "Does your library maintain a human resources file?" Only 420 libraries that had used the planning process (56.7 percent) provided this service, versus 1,488 libraries that had not used the process (46.1 percent).

One of the general programming questions produced a difference that was both statistically significant and substantial. Libraries that had used the planning process were more likely to report that book talks or reviews were provided than were those that had not used the planning process (62.5 percent vs. 52.9 percent). Libraries that had used the planning process also were more prominent than those that had not in the provision of programming for job seekers (30.0 percent vs. 18.6 percent) and parents (48.4 percent vs. 34.9 percent).

CONCLUSIONS

Although only a minority of the respondents reported having made use of *A Planning Process for Public Libraries,* there does appear to be some relationship between its use and the number and scope of services offered. For all but five questions, the percentage of respondents reporting that a particular service was provided was greater for libraries that had used the planning process than for those that had not. On the other hand, the differences were statistically significant for only about half the questions, and were deemed substantial for a much smaller number of questions. Furthermore, there is no evidence to suggest any sort of causal link in either direction between the provision of adult services and use of *A Planning Process for Public Libraries.*

It might be speculated that those libraries using the planning process are those that are big enough or wealthy enough to support its use. Although specific data regarding the sizes and budgets of libraries were not gathered for this study, the populations of the communities in which the libraries are located and the average incomes of the households in those communities can be taken as rough indicators of size and wealth. Analysis using t-tests indicates that there is not a statistically significant relationship between use of the planning process and either of these factors. There are, in fact, no meaningful relationships between use of the planning process and any of the demographic variables for which data were gathered.[12]

Regional Differences in Adult Services Provision

A potentially important set of issues is that of whether the provision of public library services to adults differs according to the location and demographic characteristics of the community. To address these issues, demographic data were gathered as described above. For ease of geographic comparison, the libraries from which data were gathered were grouped into four geographic regions, using the regional divisions established by the U. S. Bureau of the Census as found in the *County and City Data Book*. Although any grouping of states into regions is inherently arbitrary, the grouping used has the advantage of being sanctioned by an agency of the federal government, and has been used in several previous studies of libraries. A comparison of the questionnaire data for the differences among the four regions is provided in Table 6.

Regional differences in the responses to individual questions were examined using the chi-squared test of independence. This test revealed statistically significant differences for all but two questions: provision of materials on demand to hospitals and provision of programming as a part of bookmobile service. Statistical significance, however, does not necessarily imply practical significance or ease of interpretation. As a rule of thumb for determining whether regional differences were of practical as well as statistical significance, it was assumed for this analysis that a difference was probably meaningful if the percentage of libraries providing a particular service at no charge varied among the regions by more than 10 percent. For question 4 (Does your library circulate books in multiple copies for group use?), for instance, the percentage of libraries indicating that the service was provided varied from 32.6 percent for the South to 44.1 percent for the North. Since this variation is greater than 10 percent, a discussion of the difference is included in this chapter. For questions for which the difference between the greatest and least percentage is 10 or less, no discussion has been provided. This admittedly ad hoc approach was adopted as a means of providing consistency in the analysis. Reference to the tables and to other chapters provides information regarding other relationships.

NUMBER OF SERVICES PROVIDED

The mean number of services provided at no charge was 28.1 for libraries in the North region, 24.4 for libraries in the South, 26.5 for the Central region, and 25.7 for the West. One-way analysis of variance indicated that the differences among the means were statistically significant, and a Scheffé post-hoc test showed that the major source of the difference was that the mean for the South was significantly lower than the mean for any of the other three regions. The mean number of services provided for a fee was 2.3 for the North, 1.6 for the South, 2.4 for the Central region, and 2.1 for the West. Again, one-way analysis of variance indicated that the differences were significant. The Scheffe test revealed that the mean for the South was significantly lower than the means for the North and Central regions, but not significantly different than the mean for the West. Although these differences were statistically significant, it is difficult to attach any practical significance to them. The difference in means between the greatest and least means was only 3.7 for services provided at no charge, and .8 for services provided for a fee.

Comparison of the four regions may provide useful clues regarding geographic variations, but the comparisons must be interpreted carefully. In many cases, variations within a particular region may be as meaningful as variations among the four regions. This is exemplified by Table 7, which provides a breakdown of the mean number of services provided at no charge, mean number provided for a fee, and total number provided for each state. It can be seen that the differences in means for individual states within a region were for every region greater than the overall differences among the regions. Furthermore, there were undoubtedly even greater differences among individual libraries within each state. Nonetheless, comparison of the four geographic regions does provide a convenient way of estimating regional trends.

PROVISION OF RESOURCE MATERIALS

The most notable differences in the provision of primary resources relate to the circulation of books for group use; circulation of musical and spoken records and tapes; circulation of audiovisual materials and films; circulation of "other" resources; reading lists and bibliographies; in-library provision of microcomputer software; maintenance of information on community activities; maintenance of human resources files; and maintenance of "other" resource files.

Circulation of books for group use was somewhat more prevalent in the North and Central regions than in the South and West: 44.1 percent of the libraries in the North provided this service, compared to 42.5 percent of those in the Central region, 37.1 percent of those in the West, and 32.6 percent of those in the South.

Circulation of musical records was also most common among libraries in the North (87.9 percent) and Central (82.6 percent) regions, and least common among libraries in the South (74.7 percent) and West (73.8 percent). The same pattern applies to circulation of spoken records (83.1 percent for North, 75 percent for Central, 69.1 percent for South, 70 percent for West). Circulation of audiotapes was most common in the West—67.7 percent of Western libraries circulated musical tapes, compared to 64.3 percent of libraries in the North, 55.6 percent of libraries in the Central region, and 53.5 percent of Southern libraries. The corresponding figures for circulation of spoken tapes were 77.2 percent for Western libraries, 73.6 percent for the North, 67.5 percent for Central, and 65.1 percent for South.

There was little variation among the North (59 percent), South (56.1 percent) and Central (54.8 percent) regions with regard to circulation of audiovisual materials, but all were substantially above the West (48.4 percent). The same general pattern held for the circulation of films, with 56.8 percent of the libraries in the North, 49.3 percent of those in the South, and 44.3 percent of Central libraries reporting provision of this service at no charge, compared to only 32.6 percent of libraries in the West.

Microcomputer software for in-library use was provided by only 20 percent of the respondents, and any comments on the provision of this service must be interpreted accordingly. There was, however, a rather clear regional trend: 24.5 percent of Northern libraries, 25.1 percent of Central libraries, and 23.7 percent of the respondents from the West indicated that this service was provided. The corresponding figure for the South was 13.4 percent, indicating that this particular service was much less common in the South than elsewhere.

Maintenance of information on community activities was also least common in the South, with 75.6 percent of the libraries in that region reporting provision of this service as opposed to 89.2 percent of the Western respondents, 87.9 percent of the libraries in the North, and 84.7 percent of Central libraries. The same trend was even more apparent for the maintenance of human resource files (58.2 percent for North, 58.3 percent for West, 47.8 percent for Central, 38 percent for South). The percentages for maintenance of human resources files are of particular interest, since only 48.2 percent of all respondents indicated that such files were maintained; the influence of the responses for the South on the total response is very apparent.

PROVISION OF FACILITIES AND EQUIPMENT

In-library provision of audiovisual equipment was least common in the West (52.1 percent), with the North, Central and South regions reporting very similar figures of 61.5 percent, 61.3 percent, and 62 percent, respectively. In-library provision of microcomputers, not surprisingly, followed the general pattern of provision of in-library microcomputer software: the North, Central, and West reported 23.4 percent, 25.4 percent, and 23.1 percent; the South was much lower, with 13.9 percent.

The provision of meeting or conference room space varied considerably: this service was most common in the North, with 71 percent of its libraries reporting the service. The Central and Southern regions were somewhat less likely to provide meeting rooms, with figures of 64 percent and 60.9 percent. Libraries in the West were least likely to provide this service, with 56.8 percent reporting that it was provided.

PROVISION OF PROGRAMS

Two of the questions addressing general programming activities— provision of book talks or reviews and provision of live programs— revealed apparently substantial regional differences. In both cases, the North, Central, and West regions were roughly comparable, and the South lagged somewhat behind. For the provision of book talks or reviews, the figures were 56.4 percent for the North, 60.6 percent for Central libraries, 57.8 percent for the West, and 48.7 percent for the South. Live programs were provided by 80.1 percent of libraries in the North, 75.5 percent of those in the Central region, and 75.6 percent of Western libraries, compared to 68.4 percent of libraries in the South.

Substantial regional differences were found for four of the listed categories of programming for special groups: job seekers, older adults, parents, and minority groups. Consideration of these differences, however, must be tempered by the fact that 1,969 libraries (44.3 percent) indicated that they did not provide any programming to special groups, and an additional 1,112 libraries (25 percent) indicated that they provided such programming for only one or two groups. For most of the subquestions under question 34, an overwhelming majority of respondents checked "do not provide."

Job seekers were most frequently provided programming by libraries in the North (32.3 percent), with libraries in the Central, South, and West regions reporting 21.7 percent, 16.6 percent, and 18.7 percent, respectively. Programming for older adults was also most common in the North (48.1 percent), with 40.3 percent of Central libraries, 35.4 percent of libraries in the South, and 31.1 percent of Western libraries reporting programming for this group. This corresponds roughly to the differences among the regions in number of residents aged sixty-five or over as a percentage of total community population, for which the means were 13.0 percent for the North, 12.8 percent for the South, 11.8 for the Central region, and 11.0 percent for the West. Based on percentage of residents aged sixty-five or over, however, it would be expected that services to older adults would be more prevalent in the South that in the Central region, which was not found to be true.

The North also dominated the distribution of programming for parents, with 48.8 percent of the respondents from that region reporting that such programming was provided. The corresponding figures for the South, Central and Western regions were 31.8 percent, 40.6 percent, and 36.8 percent.

The South and Central regions lagged somewhat behind the other regions in the provision of programming for minority groups. The North and West recorded figures of 13.8 percent and 15.6 percent, but only 9.8 percent of respondents in the South and 10.5 percent of respondents in the Central region reported that programming for minority groups was provided. It is interesting to compare these figures to the overall distribution of the nation's minority population. According to the *County and City Data Book,* in 1980 minority groups made up 13.6 percent of the population of the North, 11.2 percent of the population of the Central region, 18.5 percent of the population of the West, and 21.6 percent of the population of the South. Although the absolute meaning of the differences in minority population and the percentage of libraries providing services to minorities is difficult to assess, the lack of minority programming in the region with the highest minority population seems to be worthy of attention. This disparity could be a function of the general tendency of the libraries in the South to provide fewer services, and particularly few programming services. It could also be the case that the higher proportion of minority residents makes deliberate programming for minority groups less important, since attendants at most programs may be minority group members. This is a finding that certainly needs further exploration than is allowed for by the results of the ASE questionnaire.

PROVISION OF EDUCATIONAL SERVICES

No substantial regional differences were found with regard to library use instruction, which was a nearly universal service. Group literacy education services were provided by only 647 respondents (15.4 percent), and there were no noticeable regional differences among these 647 libraries. Substantial differences did exist for the provision of individual literacy education, literacy education facilities, and literacy education referral.

Individual literacy education at no charge was provided by 1,036 (24.6 percent) of the responding libraries. Nearly a third of these (324 or 31.3 percent) were in the West, and 32.3 percent of all the libraries in the West reported provision of this service. Individual literacy education was provided by 28.9 percent of libraries in the North, 18.2 percent of libraries in the Central region, and 21.9 percent of South libraries.

A total of 2,214 libraries (52.5 percent) provided facilities for literacy education at no charge. The regional distribution for this service indicates that it was provided by 63.4 percent of libraries in the North, 47.7 percent of those in the South, 52.8 percent of the respondents from the Central region, and 53 percent of West region libraries.

The most frequently provided literacy service was referral to another agency, which was provided by 3,381 libraries (80.2 percent). The provision of this service by region varied from 85.5 percent for libraries in the West to 75.1 percent for the South, with 84 percent for the North, and 80.6 percent for the Central region.

PROVISION OF EXTERNAL AND OUTREACH SERVICES

The external and outreach services for which there were apparent regional differences include provision of services to retirement and nursing homes, materials for the homebound, and bookmobile services.

The only geographic area for which more than half of the respondents indicated that services were provided to retirement and nursing homes was the Central region, with 55.1 percent of the respondents in that region reporting that such services were provided. The corresponding figures for the North, South, and West were 49.2 percent, 43.5 percent, and 40.1 percent, respectively. The same general pattern held for all services to retirement and nursing homes (materials on demand, deposit collections, and programming), with the services being most frequently provided in the Central region and least common in the West. This pattern corresponds roughly to the distribution of the nation's aging population. According to the 1987 *Statistical Abstract of the United States*, the percentage of residents aged sixty-five or older was 13.2 for the North, 12.3 percent for the Central region, 11.8 percent for the South, and 10.5 percent for the West.[13]

Materials for the homebound were provided by more than half the libraries in the Central (52.7 percent) and West (54.3 percent) geographic regions, and by nearly half of those in the North (49.7 percent). A much lower 38 percent of libraries in the South reported that this service was provided.

Bookmobile services were provided by about a fourth of the respondents (1,014, or 24.1 percent). The percentages for libraries in the South, Central and West regions tended to be very similar for all the bookmobile services identified, with the North lagging substantially behind. Bookmobile services were provided by 27.2 percent of Southern libraries, 24.4 percent of libraries in the Central region, and 24.2 percent of those in the West, but only 15.7 percent of the respondents in the North indicated that bookmobile services were provided. The differences were not as substantial for the provision of individual bookmobile services.

CONCLUSIONS

The differences described above, and further examination of the data presented in Table 6, indicate a clear trend. The number of services provided was least for the South, and when there were substantial differences among the regions in the provision of a service, it was most frequently the case that the South trailed the other regions. Of the twenty-six services for which substantial regional differences were noted, the percentage of libraries providing service was least for the South for fourteen services (53.8 percent). This difference is especially noticeable for new services such as the provision of electronic media and programming for special groups. The specific reasons for this cannot be determined from the data available here, but may be related to the long-term economic depression of many of the southern states.

Adult Services and Demographic Differences

In addition to the regional variations, differences in various demographic characteristics were examined to provide an indication of what factors might influence the provision of adult services. These figures represent only the community in which the main administrative facility of the library or library system is located, and data for seventy-seven communities were not available at all. This means that the demographic differences discussed below are applicable only to the 1,681 communities for which data were available. These demographics, which were drawn from the 1983 edition of the *County and City Data Book* and represent 1980 census data, include, for each community represented by a library or system:

> White residents as a percentage of total population
> Black residents as a percentage of total population
> Residents of Spanish origin as a percentage of total population
> Residents of other ethnic origin (including American Indian, Eskimo, Aleut, Asian and Pacific Islander) as a percentage of total population
> Residents aged twenty-five or older who have completed at least twelve years of education as a percentage of total population
> Residents aged twenty-five or older who have completed at least sixteen years of education as a percentage of total population
> Residents aged sixty-five or older as a percentage of total population
> Families with income below the poverty level as a percentage of total population
> Per capita income of the community
> Population of the community

The relationships between these demographic characteristics and the services identified on the questionnaire were examined using appropriate statistical tests. The most frequently used test was one-way analysis of variance, which was used to determine whether the mean value for a specific demographic characteristic was statistically related to whether a particular service was provided at no charge, not provided, or provided for a fee. For population served, then, the question addressed by one-way analysis of variance was "are there significant differences in the mean sizes among the communities served by libraries that provide a particular service at no charge, those that do not provide it at all, and those that provide the service for a fee?"

As with the previous discussions, relationships have been discussed here only when they appear to be of practical as well as statistical significance. As an arbitrary means of determining whether a relationship was of apparent practical significance, it was decided that the differences in groups would be deemed worthy of discussion if there was a difference in means of more than 10 percent for those demographic characteristics that were measured in percentages, a difference in mean per capita income of more than $1,000, or a difference in mean population of more than 10,000. These cutting points are deliberately conservative; that is, they were chosen on the assumption that incorrectly concluding that a relationship is not meaningful is potentially less harmful than incorrectly concluding that a relationship is meaningful. In a few instances, a substantial difference between groups existed, but one of the groups consisted of only one or two libraries. These cases are not discussed here, since a difference based on such a small group is clearly of questionable validity.

For convenience in comparison, Tables 8 through 17 divide all the demographic characteristics except population into two categories: those communities with values above the median for the entire population, and those with values below the median. For population, a quartile division was used. These divisions were used only for convenience in presenting the data in tabular form, and cannot be used to draw accurate conclusions regarding the relationships among the demographic characteristics and responses to the questionnaire.

NUMBER OF SERVICES OFFERED

It might be speculated that the number of services a library provides is closely related to factors such as the size of the community it serves and the socioeconomic makeup of its populace. A library serving a relatively affluent community, for instance, might be expected to provide more services than one serving a poorer community. It might also be expected that libraries in large communities might provide more services than those serving smaller communities. Similar speculations could be made regarding the relationship between population or socioeconomic factors and the tendency to charge fees for services. The relationships among the demographic characteristics and the numbers of services provided were examined by computing Pearson correlation coefficients. No meaningful relationships were observed. It does not, therefore, appear to be the case that there was any systematic relationship between any of the demographic characteristics and the sheer number of adult services provided, either at no charge or for a fee.

PROVIDING SPECIFIC SERVICES

Four of the demographic characteristics were related in a statistically significant and apparently meaningful way to the provision of specific services. These four characteristics were (1) the percentage of residents with at least twelve years of education; (2) the percentage of residents with at least sixteen years of education; (3) per capita income; and (4) population.

Educational Level

The percentage of residents with at least twelve years of education was found to be meaningfully related to two specific services, both of which relate to the circulation of audio recordings. The mean percentages for the circulation of spoken records were 66.7 percent for the 1,020 libraries that reported providing the service at no charge, 63.7 percent for the 103 libraries that did not provide the service, and 75.4 percent for the 13 libraries charging a fee for the service. The mean percentage was 67.4 for libraries providing musical tapes at no charge (815 libraries represented), 64.1 for libraries not providing the service (314 libraries), and 77.9 for libraries charging a fee for the service (7 libraries). The mean percentage of residents with the equivalent of a college education was also found to be related to this service: the percentages were 16.9 percent for the 804 libraries that provided the service at no charge, 15 percent for the 311 libraries not providing the service, and 27 percent for the 7 libraries charging a fee for the circulation of such items.

Examination of the relationship between educational level and other services reveals a less striking but similar pattern, and suggests that certain services are most prevalent in libraries with relatively well-educated target populations and that the educational level of communities in which fees are charged has a tendency to be greater than those in which these services are provided at no charge. It is not clear what this really implies, and a definitive conclusion cannot be reached without further information. It may be the case that a well-educated populace has a greater appreciation of library services and either demands a greater variety of services or provides a greater level of funding for library services. Similarly, it may be the case that a better educated populace is more willing to accept the instigation of fees for library services.

Per Capita Income

Per capita income appears to be meaningfully related to five specific services. As was true for the percentage of residents with the equivalent of a high school education, the most noticeable relationship between per capita income and provision of specific services had to do with the circulation of audio recordings. The mean per capita income for libraries circulating spoken records for a fee was $8,977 (fourteen libraries reporting), which was significantly greater than the figures of $7,329 for the 1,073 libraries that provided the service at no charge, and $6,903 for the 106 libraries not providing the service at all. The means for the circulation of musical tapes were $10,127 for the eight libraries that charged a fee, $7,425 for 853 libraries not charging fees, and $6,943 for the 332 libraries not providing the service. The differences for circulation of musical records and spoken tapes were similar, although not as great. It can be concluded from these figures that libraries in a handful of relatively wealthy communities charge fees for circulation of audio recordings, while most libraries do not charge fees, and libraries in the poorest communities do not circulate audio recordings at all. The differences in mean per capita income between libraries not charging fees and libraries not providing the service, however, were not statistically significant for the circulation of records, although they were significant for the circulation of tapes.

A similar set of figures exists for the circulation of videotapes: the mean per capita income was $8,606 for the 148 libraries that charged fees, $7,290 for the 679 libraries that provided the service at no charge, and $6,841 for the 366 libraries not providing the service. The mean for libraries not providing the service was significantly lower than the means for libraries in the other two categories.

The final two services that were related to per capita income were the availability of photocopiers and the provision of meeting or conference room space. The mean per capita income for libraries charging for the use of photocopying machines was $7,553 (355 libraries), as opposed to $7,222 for libraries providing the service at no charge (817 libraries), and $6,573 for libraries not providing photocopiers at all (twenty-one libraries). Libraries in relatively afflu-ent communities were also most likely to charge fees for meeting or conference room space. The mean per capita income for libraries charging fees was $8,139 (91 libraries), while the mean for libraries not charging a fee was $7,270 (936 libraries), and the mean for libraries not providing the service was $7,078 (166 libraries).

Similar comments could be made for a variety of other services for which the relationship between provision of service and per capita income was less meaningful. The general conclusion that can be drawn about the relationship between per capita income and the provision of specific services is that libraries in the least affluent communities tend not to provide some services at all, while those in communities whose residents are potentially best able to pay extra fees tend to charge such fees. Furthermore, the differences that appear to be most meaningful relate to less traditional services that may carry rather high investment costs.

Population

The population of the community in which the library is located was found to be meaningfully related to the provision of ten services, most of which involve the provision of programming or other services for special population groups. These ten services were provision of book talks or reviews, presentation of cable television programs, provision of group literacy education, provision of programming for business, provision of programming for handicapped, provision of programming for job seekers, provision of programming for older adults, provision of programming for other special groups, provision of services to prisons, and provision of books by mail. For all ten services, the mean population was significantly greater for libraries providing the service at no charge than for those not providing the service. The mean population for libraries providing the service for a fee was quite variable, and of little interest, since very few libraries charged fees for any of the ten services. The differences in population means for the ten services are summarized in Table 18. Almost all of these are services that are not provided by a majority of the responding libraries. The exceptions are the provision of book talks and reviews, which was provided at no charge by 73 percent of the 1,113 libraries for which population data were available, and provision of programming for older adults, which was provided at no charge by 51 percent of the respondents for whom data were available. Most of the other services that were oriented toward special groups exhibited population differences that were substantial even though not statistically significant. It seems clear from these figures that programming for special population groups is strongly related to the population of the community served. Apparently, libraries in larger communities are either better prepared to serve special groups, or feel a greater need to do so.

Other Demographic Relationships

In addition to the three demographic characteristics that appear to be systematically related to the provision of adult services, there were a few isolated relationships that are of special interest. One of these involves the relationship between ethnicity and the provision of services to minority groups. As might be expected, programming for minority groups was more prevalent in communities with a relatively high minority population. The percentage of the community represented by nonwhite residents was 20.93 for libraries that provided programming for minorities, but was a much lower 12.88 for libraries that did not. Although this difference was interesting and was statistically significant ($t = 3.98$, df $= 260$, $p < .01$), it must be kept in mind that only 12 percent of the respondents to the questionnaire provided any programming for minorities.

Slightly more than one-third of the respondents indicated that programming was organized for older adults. It might be expected that programming for older adults would be more prevalent in communities with a relatively high percentage of adults beyond retirement age. Somewhat surprisingly, the provision of programming for older adults was not found to be related to the percentage of older adults living in the community. The percentage was 12.3 for libraries that do provide such programming, and 12.2 for those that do not (the mean for all respondents was 12.2); this difference was trivial, and was very far from being statistically significant.

CONCLUSIONS

There does not appear to be any overwhelming or universal relationship between a community's demographic characteristics and the provision of public library adult services. The relationships summarized above, however, are suggestive of a set of trends that should perhaps be subjected to further exploration. These trends involve the relationships between the provision of public services and the educational level of the population served, the per capita income of the population served, and the size of the population served. Although the data do not support any firm conclusions regarding these trends, there is some indication that libraries in larger communities serving relatively well-educated and relatively wealthy populations may provide a greater diversity of adult services, if not a greater number of services.

Summary of the ASE Questionnaire Data

The results of the ASE study are difficult to summarize or condense, because they represent a great diversity in response and in the demographic characteristics of the libraries that responded. There are, however, some general statements that can be made without overly compromising the inherent variability of the data.

Although the adult services most frequently provided by the respondents appear to be rather traditional and mostly passive in nature (Table 3), nearly two-thirds of the services listed on the questionnaire were provided by more than 25 percent of the respondents. This suggests that most of the services listed are generally considered important, and that there is a considerable diversity in the range of services provided by most libraries. At the same time, the list of services least frequently provided (Table 4) may be viewed as an indicator of potential problem areas.

Two aspects of this list may be of particular concern. Although literacy is generally seen as a national problem of crisis proportions, neither group nor individual literacy education was provided by a very substantial proportion of the respondents. The figures do represent an upward change from 1952 to 1953, when Lyman Smith's study reported that only 6.5 of the respondents provided "fundamental reading instruction," but the 1986 figures of 15.4 percent providing group instruction and 24.6 percent providing individual instruction still seem rather disappointing.[14]

A second area of concern is the low frequency of provision of microcomputer hardware and software. This is probably explained by the relatively high costs associated with such services, but failure to adopt an active role as microcomputer access centers may put libraries in the position of being excluded from an important arena of activity.

The imposition of fees for services appears to be a widespread practice, but one that sees only limited application in individual libraries. Very few libraries reported charging fees for more than one or two services, and those services for which fees were charged are for the most part those that benefit individuals or special groups rather than the community as a whole. Although the data gathered for the ASE study cannot shed any direct light on administrative decision-making processes, there is perhaps some support for the conclusion that most decisions regarding adult services revolve around whether a service will be provided at all rather than whether a charge will be levied.

Although a distinct minority of responding libraries reported having used *A Planning Process for Public Libraries,* there did appear to be some fairly substantial differences between those libraries that had used the planning process and those that had not. Those that had used the process offered more services overall than those that had not, and were more likely to offer nearly all of the individually identified services as well. Available data suggest that this is not a function of library size, but do not provide any definitive explanation for the differences. It may be that the use of the planning process is itself an indirect service, and that its use fits into whatever general set of circumstances leads to the provision of a greater number and variety of public services.

The differences among geographic regions are not totally consistent, but overall the South appears to lag behind the other regions in the provision of adult services. The average number of services provided is least for the South, and the South is most frequently ranked fourth among the regions in provision of specific services. Those services that are commonly provided in the South are for the most part quite traditional, and services involving electronic media and specific population groups are a rarity in the South. These findings cannot be explained within the context of the data gathered for the ASE study and must be tempered by an appreciation for the differences among the individual states that comprise the four regions. It does, however, seem fairly safe to speculate that the historically depressed state of the South's economy is in some way related to the results of the ASE study.

Demographic differences other than geographic location do not appear to be very strongly related to the provision of public library adult services, although there may be some influence exerted by the size, educational level and per capita income of the community served by the library. There do not appear to be any systematic relationships between the provision of adult services and such community factors as ethnicity, percentage of the community below the poverty line, or percentage of the community above retirement age, although the relationships for some isolated questions are of interest.

In the report for her 1952–53 study of adult education activities in public libraries, Lyman Smith went to great lengths to emphasize the "fact-finding" nature of the study.[15] The same caveat should be applied to any attempt at interpreting and evaluating the results of the ASE study. Although the purpose of gathering demographic data and applying statistical tests was to explore relationships between responses to the questionnaire and possible influencing factors, any statement of possible cause and effect situations must be treated as quite speculative. It is hoped that the results of the ASE study may provide some clues as to possible problem areas in the provision of adult services in public libraries, and act as a source of impetus for further in-depth study of the complex situations behind the results.

Notes

1. For a complete technical report on the conduct of the Adult Services in the Eighties project, including questionnaire iterations, see Kathleen M. Heim, *Adult Services in the Eighties: Final Report Submitted to the RASD Adult Services Committee*, March 1990 (ERIC ED 316 264).
2. Helen Lyman Smith, *Adult Education Activities in Public Libraries* (Chicago: ALA, 1954).
3. Vernon E. Palmour, Marcia C. Bellassai, and Nancy V. DeWath, *A Planning Process for Public Libraries* (Chicago: ALA, 1980).
4. U.S. Bureau of the Census, *County and City Data Book, 1983,* (Washington, D.C.: U.S. Government Printing Office, 1983).
5. The population figures from the *County and City Data Book* indicate the population of the community in which the main administrative facility of the system is located. As a result, there are many systems for which this figure is substantially below the 25,000 figure used in selecting library systems for the study.
6. The regions identified for this study are those used by the U.S. Bureau of the Census, as indicated in the *County and City Data Book*. The states included in each region are as follows:

    North: Maine, Vermont, New Hampshire, New York, Massachusetts, Connecticut, Rhode Island, New Jersey, Pennsylvania

    South: Texas, Oklahoma, Arkansas, Louisiana, Mississippi, Alabama, Tennessee, Kentucky, West Virginia, Maryland, Delaware, Virginia, North Carolina, South Carolina, Georgia, Florida, District of Columbia

    Central: North Dakota, South Dakota, Nebraska, Minnesota, Iowa, Kansas, Missouri, Wisconsin, Michigan, Illinois, Indiana, Ohio

    West: Oregon, Washington, Idaho, Montana, California, Nevada, Wyoming, Utah, Colorado, Arizona, New Mexico, Alaska, Hawaii.

7. See, for instance, National Commission on Libraries and Information Science, "The Role of Fees in Supporting Library and Information Services in Public and Academic Libraries," *Collection Building* 8 (1986): 3–17.
8. Charles R. McClure et al., *Planning and Role Setting for Public Libraries: A Manual of Options and Procedures* (Chicago: ALA, 1987).
9. Nancy Van House et al., *Output Measures for Public Libraries: A Manual of Standardized Procedures*, 2nd ed. (Chicago: ALA, 1987).
10. Public Library Association, *Public Library Data Service Statistical Report, 88* (Chicago: Public Library Association, ALA, 1988).
11. Kathleen Mehaffey Balcom, "To Concentrate and Strengthen: The Promise of the Public Library Development Project," *Library Journal* 111 (June 15, 1986): 37.
12. It should be kept in mind that demographic data were available only for the community in which the main library is located.
13. *Statistical Abstract of the United States* (Washington, D.C.: U.S. Government Printing Office, 1987), p. 23.
14. Lyman Smith, p. 17.
15. Ibid., p. 63.

Appendixes

1. SURVEY QUESTIONNAIRE

1 *Directions*

Below is a list of library services to adults. Circle "Y" if your library provides; circle "N" if it does not. If fees are charged circle "Y" in column three.

Does Your Library . . . ?	Provide	Do Not Provide	Fees Charged
1. Display within the library exhibits based on materials owned by the library.	Y	N	Y
2. Display within the library exhibits based on non-library materials.	Y	N	Y
3. Display outside the library exhibits based on materials owned by the library.	Y	N	Y
4. Circulate books in multiple copies for group use.	Y	N	Y
5. Circulate microcomputers.	Y	N	Y
6. Circulate microcomputer software.	Y	N	Y
7. Circulate musical records.	Y	N	Y
8. Circulate spoken records.	Y	N	Y
9. Circulate musical tapes.	Y	N	Y
10. Circulate spoken tapes.	Y	N	Y
11. Circulate AV materials.	Y	N	Y
12. Circulate films.	Y	N	Y
13. Circulate videotapes.	Y	N	Y
14. Circulate other (list) _____.	Y	N	Y
15. Circulate other (list) _____.	Y	N	Y
16. Circulate other (list) _____.	Y	N	Y
17. Provide reading lists or bibliographies.	Y	N	Y
18. Provide interlibrary loan services.	Y	N	Y
19. Provide AV equipment for in-library use.	Y	N	Y
20. Provide microcomputer software for in-library use.	Y	N	Y
21. Provide microcomputers for in-library use.	Y	N	Y
22. Provide meeting or conference room space.	Y	N	Y
23. Provide photocopy machines.	Y	N	Y
24. Present book talks/reviews.	Y	N	Y

Does Your Library . . . ?	Provide	Do Not Provide	Fees Charged
25. Present live programs.	Y	N	Y
26. Present radio programs.	Y	N	Y
27. Present cable TV programs.	Y	N	Y
28. Provide instruction to groups on library use.	Y	N	Y
29. Provide instruction to individuals on library use.	Y	N	Y
30. Provide literacy education to groups.	Y	N	Y
31. Provide literacy education to individuals.	Y	N	Y
32. Provide facilities for literacy education.	Y	N	Y
33. Provide referral to another agency for literacy education.	Y	N	Y
34. Organize programming for special groups.			
a. Business.	Y	N	Y
b. Genealogists.	Y	N	Y
c. Handicapped.	Y	N	Y
d. Job seekers.	Y	N	Y
e. Labor groups.	Y	N	Y
f. Older adults.	Y	N	Y
g. Parents.	Y	N	Y
h. Minority (list).			
1._____.	Y	N	Y
2._____.	Y	N	Y
3._____.	Y	N	Y
i. Other (list).			
1._____.	Y	N	Y
2._____.	Y	N	Y
3._____.	Y	N	Y
35. Provide to hospitals.	Y	N	Y
a. Materials on demand.	Y	N	Y
b. Deposit collections.	Y	N	Y
c. Programming.	Y	N	Y
36. Provide to prisons.	Y	N	Y
a. Materials on demand.	Y	N	Y
b. Deposit collections.	Y	N	Y
c. Programming.	Y	N	Y
37. Provide to retirement/nursing homes.	Y	N	Y
a. Materials on demand.	Y	N	Y
b. Deposit collections.	Y	N	Y
c. Programming.	Y	N	Y

Does Your Library . . . ?	Provide	Do Not Provide	Fees Charged		Does Your Library . . . ?	Provide	Do Not Provide	Fees Charged
38. Provide materials to homebound.	Y	N	Y		42. Maintain information about media resources other than those owned by the library.	Y	N	Y
39. Provide books by mail.	Y	N	Y					
40. Provide bookmobile service.	Y	N	Y		43. Maintain a human resources file.	Y	N	Y
a. Materials on demand.	Y	N	Y					
b. Programming.	Y	N	Y		44. Maintain other resource files (list).	Y	N	Y
c. Publicize central library programming.	Y	N	Y		a._____.	Y	N	Y
					b._____.	Y	N	Y
41. Maintain information on community activities.	Y	N	Y		c._____.	Y	N	Y
					d._____.	Y	N	Y

2 We want to learn the details of key adult services programs offered by your library in 1985. On the grid below please indicate titles of up to five programs and answer specific questions as in the example. We are interested in the entire range of possible programs such as concerts, literary discussion groups, adult learners assistance, career information programs, microcomputer instruction, genealogy programs, programs aimed at special groups (such as minorities, the handicapped, older adults, labor groups), literacy programs and parent education programs. Since *you* are to select the programs that *you* feel were the most important or successful we are certain that there will be many surprises and that your input will make this part of the ASE project an exciting contribution to the story of today's public library adult services. Thank you for your attention and time!

Background on Each Activity
(Use N/A if Question Does Not Apply or DK if You Don't Know)

Title of Program	1. What was the subject with which the activity was concerned?	2. What was the purpose of the activity?	3. What agencies cooperated in this activity?	4. If externally funded what was the source of these funds?	5. Is this an ongoing activity?	6. How long has this activity been operational?
Example: "Vietnamese-English Course"	English as a 2nd Language	Education	Board of Education	Board of Education	YES	2 yrs

Background on Each Activity
(Use N/A if Question Does Not Apply or DK if You Don't Know)

Title of Program	7. Who were the typical participants? (men, women, labor groups, minority groups, etc.)	8. What was the estimated number of participants? (if ongoing give average)	9. Where held? (library or other location)	10. Who conducted the program?	11. How were programs publicized?	12. What evaluation methods were used?
(Example: "Vietnamese-English Course")	Job Seekers	18	Library	Community volunteers	Radio and direct mail	Questionnaire

2. TABLES

Table 1. COMPARISON OF RESPONDENTS TO NONRESPONDENTS.

CHARACTERISTIC	MEAN FOR RESPONDENTS	MEAN FOR NONRESPONDENTS
Percentage of white residents	85.5	84.7
Percentage of black residents	13.2	14.9
Percentage of hispanic residents	5.5	7.2*
Percentage of residents of other ethnic origin	2.4	2.8
Percentage of residents with at least twelve years' education	66.6	64.7*
Percentage of residents with at least sixteen years' education	16.5	15.1*
Percentage of residents aged sixty-five or older	12.2	12.7
Percentage of households below poverty level	10.5	10.9
Per capita income	$7,305.57	$7,090.90*
Population of community	114,550	63,404*

*A t-test indicates that the difference between the two means are statistically significant at the .05 level.

Table 2. QUESTIONNAIRE RESPONSES, ALL LIBRARIES.

Does Your Library:	NUMBER OF LIBRARIES	PERCENT
1. Display within the library exhibits based on materials owned by the library?		
Provide	3803	90.2
Do not provide	410	9.7
Fees charged	1	0.1
2. Display within the library exhibits based on non-library materials?		
Provide	3166	75.1
Do not provide	1045	24.8
Fees charged	3	0.1
3. Display outside the library exhibits based on materials owned by the library?		
Provide	1224	29.0
Do not provide	2990	71.0
Fees charged	0	0.0
4. Circulate books in multiple copies for group use?		
Provide	1591	37.8
Do not provide	2622	62.2
Fees charged	1	0.0
5. Circulate microcomputers?		
Provide	117	2.8
Do not provide	4080	96.8
Fees charged	17	0.4
6. Circulate microcomputer software?		
Provide	175	4.2
Do not provide	4034	95.7
Fees charged	5	0.1
7. Circulate musical records?		
Provide	3302	78.4
Do not provide	875	20.8
Fees charged	37	0.9
8. Circulate spoken records?		
Provide	3069	72.8
Do not provide	1112	26.4
Fees charged	33	0.8
9. Circulate musical tapes?		
Provide	2487	59.0
Do not provide	1702	40.4
Fees charged	25	0.6

Table 2. QUESTIONNAIRE RESPONSES, ALL LIBRARIES. (Continued)

Does Your Library:	NUMBER OF LIBRARIES	PERCENT
10. Circulate spoken tapes?		
Provide	2943	69.8
Do not provide	1236	29.3
Fees charged	35	0.8
11. Circulate AV materials?		
Provide	2293	54.4
Do not provide	1840	43.7
Fees charged	81	1.9
12. Circulate films?		
Provide	1910	45.3
Do not provide	2152	51.1
Fees charged	152	3.6
13. Circulate videotapes?		
Provide	1590	37.7
Do not provide	2366	56.1
Fees charged	258	6.1
14. - 16. Circulate other?		
Provide	1499	35.6
Do not provide	2639	62.6
Fees charged	76	1.8
17. Provide reading lists or bibliographies?		
Provide	3380	80.2
Do not provide	830	19.7
Fees charged	4	0.1
18. Provide interlibrary loan service?		
Provide	3715	88.2
Do not provide	289	6.9
Fees charged	210	5.0
19. Provide AV equipment for in-library use?		
Provide	2503	59.4
Do not provide	1694	40.2
Fees charged	17	0.4
20. Provide microcomputer software for in-library use?		
Provide	854	20.3
Do not provide	3343	79.3
Fees charged	17	0.4
21. Provide microcomputers for in-library use?		
Provide	853	20.2
Do not provide	3284	77.9
Fees charged	77	1.8

Table 2. QUESTIONNAIRE RESPONSES, ALL LIBRARIES. (Continued)

Does Your Library:	NUMBER OF LIBRARIES	PERCENT
22. Provide meeting or conference room space?		
Provide	2620	62.2
Do not provide	1434	34.0
Fees charged	160	3.8
23. Provide photocopy machines?		
Provide	2566	60.9
Do not provide	805	19.1
Fees charged	843	20.0
24. Present book talks/review?		
Provide	2311	54.8
Do not provide	1896	45.0
Fees charged	7	0.2
25. Present live programs?		
Provide	3100	73.6
Do not provide	1111	26.4
Fees charged	3	0.1
26. Present radio programs?		
Provide	347	8.2
Do not provide	3865	91.7
Fees charged	2	0.0
27. Present cable TV programs?		
Provide	405	9.6
Do not provide	3806	90.3
Fees charged	3	0.1
28. Provide instruction to groups on library use?		
Provide	3493	82.9
Do not provide	720	17.1
Fees charged	1	0.0
29. Provide instruction to individuals on library use?		
Provide	3959	93.9
Do not provide	254	6.0
Fees charged	1	0.0
30. Provide literacy education to groups?		
Provide	647	15.4
Do not provide	3563	84.6
Fees charged	4	0.1
31. Provide literacy education to individuals?		
Provide	1036	24.6
Do not provide	3176	75.4
Fees charged	2	0.0

Table 2. QUESTIONNAIRE RESPONSES, ALL LIBRARIES. (Continued)

Does Your Library:	NUMBER OF LIBRARIES	PERCENT
32. Provide facilities for literacy education?		
Provide	2214	52.5
Do not provide	1997	47.4
Fees charged	3	0.1
33. Provide referral to another agency for literacy education?		
Provide	3381	80.2
Do not provide	832	19.7
Fees charged	1	0.0
34. Organize programming for special groups:		
a. Business?		
Provide	968	23.0
Do not provide	3233	76.7
Fees charged	14	0.3
b. Genealogists?		
Provide	853	20.2
Do not provide	3353	79.6
Fees charged	8	0.2
c. Handicapped?		
Provide	648	15.4
Do not provide	3557	84.4
Fees charged	9	0.2
d. Job seekers?		
Provide	872	20.7
Do not provide	3335	79.1
Fees charged	7	0.2
e. Labor groups?		
Provide	226	5.4
Do not provide	3979	94.4
Fees charged	9	0.2
f. Older adults?		
Provide	1579	37.5
Do not provide	2629	62.4
Fees charged	6	0.1
g. Parents?		
Provide	1587	37.7
Do not provide	2621	62.2
Fees charged	6	0.1
h. Minorities?		
Provide	504	12.0
Do not provide	3711	88.0
Fees charged	0	0.4
i. Other?		
Provide	360	8.5
Do not provide	3852	91.4
Fees charged	2	0.1

Table 2. QUESTIONNAIRE RESPONSES, ALL LIBRARIES. (Continued)

Does Your Library:	NUMBER OF LIBRARIES	PERCENT
35. Provide to hospitals:		
Provide	848	20.1
Do not provide	3363	79.8
Fees charged	3	0.1
a. Materials on demand?		
Provide	797	18.9
Do not provide	3413	81.0
Fees charged	4	0.1
b. Deposit collections?		
Provide	311	7.6
Do not provide	3758	92.3
Fees charged	4	0.1
c. Programming?		
Provide	165	3.9
Do not provide	4046	96.0
Fees charged	3	0.1
36. Provide to prisons:		
Provide	690	16.4
Do not provide	3519	83.5
Fees charged	5	0.1
a. Materials on demand?		
Provide	634	15.0
Do not provide	3576	84.9
Fees charged	4	0.1
b. Deposit collections?		
Provide	450	10.7
Do not provide	3761	89.3
Fees charged	3	0.1
c. Programming?		
Provide	130	3.1
Do not provide	4081	96.8
Fees charged	3	0.1
37. Provide to retirement/nursing homes:		
Provide	1962	49.6
Do not provide	2248	53.3
Fees charged	4	0.1
a. Materials on demand?		
Provide	1808	42.9
Do not provide	2403	57.0
Fees charged	4	0.1

Table 2. QUESTIONNAIRE RESPONSES, ALL LIBRARIES. (Continued)

Does Your Library:	NUMBER OF LIBRARIES	PERCENT
37. Provide to retirement/nursing homes: (Continued)		
b. Deposit collections?		
Provide	1129	26.8
Do not provide	3084	73.2
Fees charged	2	0.0
c. Programming?		
Provide	818	19.4
Do not provide	3392	80.5
Fees charged	5	0.1
38. Provide materials to homebound:		
Provide	1986	47.1
Do not provide	2225	52.8
Fees charged	4	0.1
39. Provide books by mail?		
Provide	702	16.7
Do not provide	3706	83.3
Fees charged	10	0.2
40. Provide bookmobile service?		
Provide	1014	24.1
Do not provide	3197	75.8
Fees charged	4	0.1
a. Materials on demand?		
Provide	987	23.4
Do not provide	3224	76.5
Fees charged	4	0.1
b. Programming?		
Provide	415	9.8
Do not provide	3796	90.1
Fees charged	3	0.1
c. Publicize central library programming?		
Provide	1298	30.8
Do not provide	2914	69.1
Fees charged	3	0.1
41. Maintain information on community activities?		
Provide	3493	82.9
Do not provide	719	17.1
Fees charged	3	0.1

Table 2. QUESTIONNAIRE RESPONSES, ALL LIBRARIES. (Continued)

Does Your Library:	NUMBER OF LIBRARIES	PERCENT
42. Maintain information about media resources other than those owned by the library?		
Provide	2735	64.9
Do not provide	1477	35.0
Fees charged	3	0.1
43. Maintain a human resources file?		
Provide	2032	48.2
Do not provide	2179	51.7
Fees charged	4	0.1
44. Maintain other resources files?		
Provide	1222	29.0
Do not provide	2991	79.0
Fees charged	2	0.1

TABLE 3. SERVICES MOST FREQUENTLY PROVIDED AT NO CHARGE

SERVICE	QUESTION NUMBER	NUMBER OF LIBRARIES	PERCENT
Individual library use instruction	29	3959	93.9
Displays of library materials	1	3803	90.2
Interlibrary loan service	18	3715	88.2
Community activity information	41	3493	82.9
Group library use instruction	28	3493	82.9
Literacy education referral	32	3381	80.2
Reading lists or bibliographies	17	3380	80.2
Circulation of musical records	7	3302	78.4
Displays of nonlibrary materials	2	3166	75.1

TABLE 4. SERVICES LEAST FREQUENTLY PROVIDED AT NO CHARGE

SERVICE	QUESTION NUMBER	NUMBER OF LIBRARIES	PERCENT
Individual literacy education	31	1036	24.6
Bookmobile service	40	1014	24.1
Bookmobile materials on demand	40a	987	23.4
Programming for business	34a	968	23.0
Programming for job seekers	34d	872	20.7
Microcomputer software for in-library use	20	854	20.3
Microcomputers for in-library use	21	853	20.2
Programming for genealogists	34b	853	20.2
Service to hospitals	35	848	20.1
Programming for retirement/nursing homes	37c	818	19.4
Materials on demand for hospitals	35a	797	18.9
Books by mail	39	702	16.7
Services to prisons	36	690	16.4
Programming for handicapped	34c	648	15.4
Group literacy education	30	647	15.4
Materials on demand for prisons	36a	634	15.0
Programming for minorities	34h	504	12.0
Deposit collections for prisons	36b	450	10.7
Bookmobile programming	40b	415	9.8
Cable TV programs	27	405	9.6
Programming for "other" groups	34i	360	8.5
Radio programs	26	347	8.2
Deposit collections for hospitals	35b	311	7.6
Programming for labor groups	34e	226	5.4
Circulation of microcomputer software	6	175	4.2
Programming for hospitals	35c	165	3.9
Programming for prisons	36c	130	3.1
Circulation of microcomputers	5	117	2.8

Table 5. SERVICES MOST FREQUENTLY PROVIDED FOR A FEE

SERVICE	QUESTION NUMBER	NUMBER OF LIBRARIES PROVIDING	NUMBER PROVIDING FOR A FEE	PERCENT
Photocopy machines	23	3409	843	24.7
Circulation of videotapes	13	1848	258	14.0
Circulation of microcomputers	5	134	17	12.7
Microcomputers for in-library use	21	930	77	8.3
Circulation of films	12	2062	152	7.4
Meeting or conference room space	22	2780	160	5.8
Interlibrary loan service	18	3925	210	5.4
Circulation of "other" materials	14	1575	76	4.8
Programming for labor groups	34e	235	9	3.8
Circulation of AV materials	11	2374	81	3.4
Circulation of microcomputer software	6	180	5	2.7
Programming for prisons	36c	133	3	2.3

Table 6. RESPONSES BY GEOGRAPHIC REGION

Does Your Library:	NORTH		SOUTH		CENTRAL		WEST	
	NUMBER OF LIBRARIES	PERCENT	NUMBER OF LIBRARIES	PERCENT	NUMBER OF LIBRARIES	PERCENT	NUMBER OF LIBRARIES	PERCENT
1. Display within the library exhibits based on materials owned by the library?								
Provide	601	93.3	1378	87.2	914	92.5	910	90.8
Do not provide	42	6.5	202	12.8	74	7.5	92	9.2
Fees charged	1	0.2	0	0.0	0	0.0	0	0.0
2. Display within the library exhibits based on non-library materials?								
Provide	510	79.2	1167	73.9	719	72.8	770	76.8
Do not provide	133	20.7	412	26.1	268	27.1	232	23.2
Fees charged	1	0.2	1	0.1	1	0.1	0	0.0
3. Display outside the library exhibits based on materials owned by the library?								
Provide	181	28.1	426	27.0	344	34.8	273	27.2
Do not provide	463	71.9	1154	73.0	644	65.2	729	72.8
Fees charged	0	0.0	0	0.0	0	0.0	0	0.0
4. Circulate books in multiple copies for group use?								
Provide	284	44.1	515	32.6	420	42.5	372	37.1
Do not provide	359	55.7	1065	67.4	568	57.5	630	62.9
Fees charged	1	0.2	0	0.0	0	0.0	0	0.0

Table 6. RESPONSES BY GEOGRAPHIC REGION (Continued)

Does Your Library:	NORTH		SOUTH		CENTRAL		WEST	
	NUMBER OF LIBRARIES	PERCENT	NUMBER OF LIBRARIES	PERCENT	NUMBER OF LIBRARIES	PERCENT	NUMBER OF LIBRARIES	PERCENT
5. Circulate microcomputers?								
Provide	44	6.8	34	2.2	28	2.8	11	1.1
Do not provide	596	92.5	1542	97.6	951	96.3	991	98.9
Fees charged	5	0.7	4	0.2	9	0.9	0	0.0
6. Circulate microcomputer software?								
Provide	27	4.2	60	3.8	67	6.8	21	2.1
Do not provide	615	95.5	1201	96.2	918	92.9	981	97.9
Fees charged	2	0.3	0	0.0	3	0.3	0	0.0
7. Circulate musical records?								
Provide	566	87.9	1181	74.7	816	82.6	739	73.8
Do not provide	76	11.8	399	25.3	146	14.8	254	25.3
Fees charged	2	0.3	0	0.0	26	2.6	9	0.9
8. Circulate spoken records?								
Provide	535	83.1	1092	69.1	741	75.0	701	70.0
Do not provide	108	16.8	488	30.9	223	22.6	293	29.2
Fees charged	1	0.2	0	0.0	24	2.4	8	0.8
9. Circulate musical tapes?								
Provide	414	64.3	846	53.5	549	55.6	678	67.7
Do not provide	229	35.6	734	46.5	423	42.8	316	31.5
Fees charged	1	0.2	0	0.0	16	1.6	8	0.8

Table 6. RESPONSES BY GEOGRAPHIC REGION (Continued)

Does Your Library:	NORTH		SOUTH		CENTRAL		WEST	
	NUMBER OF LIBRARIES	PERCENT	NUMBER OF LIBRARIES	PERCENT	NUMBER OF LIBRARIES	PERCENT	NUMBER OF LIBRARIES	PERCENT
10. Circulate spoken tapes?								
Provide	474	73.6	1028	65.1	667	67.5	774	77.2
Do not provide	168	26.1	551	34.9	300	30.4	217	21.7
Fees charged	2	0.3	1	0.1	21	2.1	11	1.1
11. Circulate AV materials?								
Provide	380	59.0	887	56.1	541	54.8	485	48.4
Do not provide	254	39.4	682	43.2	404	40.9	500	49.9
Fees charged	10	1.6	11	0.7	43	4.4	17	1.7
12. Circulate films?								
Provide	366	56.8	779	49.3	438	44.3	327	32.6
Do not provide	265	41.1	769	48.7	474	48.0	644	64.3
Fees charged	13	2.0	32	2.0	76	7.7	34	3.1
13. Circulate videotapes?								
Provide	275	42.7	554	35.1	399	40.4	362	36.1
Do not provide	318	49.4	1009	63.9	449	45.4	590	58.9
Fees charged	51	7.9	17	1.1	140	14.2	50	5.0
14 – 16. Circulate other?								
Provide	290	45.0	533	33.7	325	32.9	351	35.0
Do not provide	346	53.7	1038	65.7	608	61.5	647	64.6
Fees charged	8	1.2	9	0.6	55	5.6	4	0.4

Table 6. RESPONSES BY GEOGRAPHIC REGION (Continued)

Does Your Library:	NORTH		SOUTH		CENTRAL		WEST	
	NUMBER OF LIBRARIES	PERCENT	NUMBER OF LIBRARIES	PERCENT	NUMBER OF LIBRARIES	PERCENT	NUMBER OF LIBRARIES	PERCENT
17. Provide reading lists or bibliographies?								
Provide	535	83.1	1172	74.2	818	82.8	855	85.3
Do not provide	106	16.5	408	25.8	169	17.1	147	14.7
Fees charged	3	0.5	0	0.0	1	0.1	0	0.0
18. Provide interlibrary loan service?								
Provide	599	93.0	1370	86.7	875	88.6	871	86.9
Do not provide	28	4.3	155	9.8	66	6.7	40	4.0
Fees charged	17	2.6	55	3.5	47	4.8	91	9.1
19. Provide AV equipment for in-library use?								
Provide	396	61.5	979	62.0	606	61.3	522	52.1
Do not provide	244	37.9	600	38.0	376	38.1	474	47.3
Fees charged	4	0.6	1	0.1	6	0.6	6	0.6
20. Provide microcomputer software for in-library use?								
Provide	158	24.5	211	13.4	248	25.1	237	23.7
Do not provide	482	74.8	1367	86.5	735	74.4	759	75.7
Fees charged	4	0.6	2	0.1	5	0.5	6	0.6
21. Provide microcomputers for in-library use?								
Provide	151	23.4	220	13.9	251	25.4	231	23.1
Do not provide	473	73.4	1346	85.2	719	72.8	746	74.5
Fees charged	20	3.1	14	0.9	18	1.8	25	2.5

Table 6. RESPONSES BY GEOGRAPHIC REGION (Continued)

Does Your Library:	NORTH		SOUTH		CENTRAL		WEST	
	NUMBER OF LIBRARIES	PERCENT	NUMBER OF LIBRARIES	PERCENT	NUMBER OF LIBRARIES	PERCENT	NUMBER OF LIBRARIES	PERCENT
22. Provide meeting or conference room space?								
Provide	457	71.0	962	60.9	632	64.0	569	56.8
Do not provide	161	25.0	583	36.9	307	31.1	383	38.2
Fees charged	26	4.0	35	2.2	49	5.0	50	5.0
23. Provide photocopy machines?								
Provide	427	66.3	944	59.7	553	56.0	642	64.1
Do not provide	84	13.0	356	22.5	165	16.7	200	20.0
Fees charged	133	20.7	280	17.7	270	27.3	160	16.0
24. Present book talks/reviews?								
Provide	363	56.4	770	48.7	599	60.6	579	57.8
Do not provide	280	43.5	808	51.1	387	39.2	421	42.0
Fees charged	1	0.2	2	0.1	2	0.2	2	0.2
25. Present live programs?								
Provide	516	80.1	1080	68.4	746	75.5	758	75.6
Do not provide	127	19.7	499	31.6	241	24.4	244	24.4
Fees charged	1	0.2	1	0.1	1	0.1	0	0.0
26. Present radio programs?								
Provide	36	5.6	148	9.4	113	11.4	50	5.0
Do not provide	607	94.3	1432	90.6	875	88.6	951	94.9
Fees charged	1	0.2	0	0.0	0	0.0	1	0.1

Table 6. RESPONSES BY GEOGRAPHIC REGION (Continued)

Does Your Library:	NORTH NUMBER OF LIBRARIES	PERCENT	SOUTH NUMBER OF LIBRARIES	PERCENT	CENTRAL NUMBER OF LIBRARIES	PERCENT	WEST NUMBER OF LIBRARIES	PERCENT
27. Present cable TV programs?								
Provide	74	11.5	93	5.9	104	10.5	134	13.4
Do not provide	569	88.4	1486	94.1	884	89.5	867	86.5
Fees charged	1	0.2	1	0.1	0	0.0	1	0.1
28. Provide instruction to groups on library use?								
Provide	540	83.9	1253	79.3	859	86.9	841	83.9
Do not provide	103	16.0	327	20.7	129	13.1	161	16.1
Fees charged	1	0.2	0	0.0	0	0.0	0	0.0
29. Provide instruction to individuals on library use?								
Provide	595	92.4	1486	94.1	923	93.4	955	95.3
Do not provide	48	7.5	94	5.9	65	6.6	47	4.7
Fees charged	1	0.2	0	0.0	0	0.0	0	0.0
30. Provide literacy education to groups?								
Provide	99	15.4	226	14.3	129	13.1	193	19.3
Do not provide	543	84.3	1353	85.6	859	86.9	808	80.6
Fees charged	2	0.3	1	0.1	0	0.0	1	0.1
31. Provide literacy education to individuals?								
Provide	186	28.9	346	21.9	180	18.2	324	32.3
Do not provide	457	71.0	1233	78.0	808	81.8	678	67.7
Fees charged	1	0.2	1	0.1	0	0.0	0	0.0

Table 6. RESPONSES BY GEOGRAPHIC REGION (Continued)

Does Your Library:	NORTH		SOUTH		CENTRAL		WEST	
	NUMBER OF LIBRARIES	PERCENT	NUMBER OF LIBRARIES	PERCENT	NUMBER OF LIBRARIES	PERCENT	NUMBER OF LIBRARIES	PERCENT
32. Provide facilities for literacy education?								
Provide	408	63.4	753	47.7	522	52.8	531	53.0
Do not provide	235	36.5	826	52.3	465	47.1	471	47.0
Fees charged	1	0.2	1	0.1	1	0.1	0	0.0
33. Provide referral to another agency for literacy education?								
Provide	541	84.0	1187	75.1	796	80.6	857	85.5
Do not provide	102	15.8	393	24.9	192	19.4	145	14.5
Fees charged	1	0.2	0	0.0	0	0.0	0	0.0
34. Organize programming for special groups:								
a. Business?								
Provide	163	25.3	341	21.6	234	23.7	230	23.0
Do not provide	476	73.9	1236	78.2	755	76.3	766	76.4
Fees charged	5	0.8	3	0.2	0	0.0	6	0.6
b. Genealogists?								
Provide	108	16.8	347	22.0	200	20.2	198	19.8
Do not provide	533	82.8	1231	77.9	786	79.6	803	80.1
Fees charged	3	0.5	2	0.1	2	0.2	1	0.1
c. Handicapped?								
Provide	104	16.1	251	15.9	151	15.3	142	14.2
Do not provide	534	82.9	1328	84.1	837	84.7	858	85.6
Fees charged	6	0.9	1	0.1	0	0.0	2	0.2

Table 6. RESPONSES BY GEOGRAPHIC REGION (Continued)

	NORTH		SOUTH		CENTRAL		WEST	
Does Your Library:	NUMBER OF LIBRARIES	PERCENT	NUMBER OF LIBRARIES	PERCENT	NUMBER OF LIBRARIES	PERCENT	NUMBER OF LIBRARIES	PERCENT
34. Organize programming for special groups: (Continued)								
d. Job seekers?								
Provide	208	32.3	263	16.6	214	21.7	187	18.7
Do not provide	431	66.9	1316	83.3	774	78.3	814	81.2
Fees charged	5	0.8	1	0.1	0	0.0	1	0.1
e. Labor groups?								
Provide	35	5.4	47	3.0	57	5.8	87	8.7
Do not provide	604	94.2	1532	97.0	931	94.2	912	91.0
Fees charged	5	0.8	1	0.1	0	0.0	3	0.3
f. Older adults?								
Provide	310	48.1	569	35.4	398	40.3	312	31.1
Do not provide	331	51.4	1020	64.6	589	59.6	689	68.8
Fees charged	3	0.5	1	0.1	1	0.1	1	0.1
g. Parents?								
Provide	314	48.8	503	31.8	401	40.6	369	36.8
Do not provide	325	50.5	1076	68.1	587	59.4	633	63.2
Fees charged	5	0.8	1	0.1	0	0.0	0	0.0
h. Minorities?								
Provide	89	13.8	155	9.8	104	10.5	156	15.6
Do not provide	555	86.2	1425	90.2	884	89.5	846	84.4
Fees charged	0	0.0	0	0.0	0	0.0	0	0.0

Table 6. RESPONSES BY GEOGRAPHIC REGION (Continued)

Does Your Library:	NORTH		SOUTH		CENTRAL		WEST	
	NUMBER OF LIBRARIES	PERCENT	NUMBER OF LIBRARIES	PERCENT	NUMBER OF LIBRARIES	PERCENT	NUMBER OF LIBRARIES	PERCENT
34. Organize programming for special groups: (Continued) i. Other?								
Provide	67	10.4	139	8.8	86	8.7	68	6.8
Do not provide	577	89.6	1441	91.2	901	91.2	933	93.1
Fees charged	0	0.0	0	0.0	1	0.1	1	0.1
35. Provide to hospitals:								
Provide	119	18.5	328	20.8	220	22.3	181	18.1
Do not provide	525	81.5	1249	79.1	768	77.7	821	81.9
Fees charged	0	0.0	3	0.2	0	0.0	0	0.0
a. Materials on demand?								
Provide	118	18.3	305	19.3	197	19.9	177	17.7
Do not provide	526	81.7	1272	80.5	790	80.0	825	82.3
Fees charged	0	0.0	3	0.2	1	0.1	0	0.0
b. Deposit collections?								
Provide	42	6.6	138	9.2	74	7.9	57	5.7
Do not provide	597	93.4	1355	90.6	867	92.0	939	94.3
Fees charged	0	0.0	3	0.2	1	0.1	0	0.0
c. Programming?								
Provide	21	3.3	66	4.2	52	5.3	26	2.6
Do not provide	623	96.7	1511	95.6	936	94.7	976	97.4
Fees charged	0	0.0	3	0.2	0	0.0	0	0.0

Table 6. RESPONSES BY GEOGRAPHIC REGION (Continued)

Does Your Library:	NORTH		SOUTH		CENTRAL		WEST	
	NUMBER OF LIBRARIES	PERCENT	NUMBER OF LIBRARIES	PERCENT	NUMBER OF LIBRARIES	PERCENT	NUMBER OF LIBRARIES	PERCENT
36. Provide to prisons:								
Provide	66	10.2	299	18.9	153	15.5	172	17.2
Do not provide	578	89.8	1277	80.8	835	84.5	829	82.7
Fees charged	0	0.0	4	0.3	0	0.0	1	0.1
a. Materials on demand?								
Provide	72	11.2	273	17.3	119	12.0	170	17.0
Do not provide	572	88.8	1303	82.5	869	88.0	832	83.0
Fees charged	0	0.0	4	0.3	0	0.0	0	0.0
b. Deposit collections?								
Provide	39	6.1	198	12.5	91	9.2	122	12.2
Do not provide	605	93.9	1379	87.3	897	90.8	880	87.8
Fees charged	0	0.0	3	0.2	0	0.0	0	0.0
c. Programming?								
Provide	11	1.7	44	2.8	12	1.2	63	6.3
Do not provide	633	98.3	1533	97.0	976	98.8	939	93.7
Fees charged	0	0.0	3	0.2	0	0.0	0	0.0
37. Provide to retirement/nursing homes:								
Provide	317	49.2	687	43.5	544	55.1	414	41.3
Do not provide	325	50.5	891	56.4	444	44.9	588	58.7
Fees charged	2	0.3	2	0.1	0	0.0	0	0.0

Table 6. RESPONSES BY GEOGRAPHIC REGION (Continued)

Does Your Library:	NORTH NUMBER OF LIBRARIES	PERCENT	SOUTH NUMBER OF LIBRARIES	PERCENT	CENTRAL NUMBER OF LIBRARIES	PERCENT	WEST NUMBER OF LIBRARIES	PERCENT
37. Provide to retirement/nursing homes: (Continued)								
a. Materials on demand?								
Provide	301	46.7	620	39.2	485	49.0	402	40.1
Do not provide	342	53.1	958	60.6	503	50.9	600	59.9
Fees charged	1	0.2	2	0.1	1	0.1	0	0.0
b. Deposit collections?								
Provide	210	32.6	351	22.2	343	34.7	225	22.5
Do not provide	434	67.4	1227	77.7	646	65.3	777	77.5
Fees charged	0	0.0	2	0.1	0	0.0	0	0.0
c. Programming?								
Provide	126	19.6	326	20.6	229	23.2	137	13.7
Do not provide	517	80.3	1251	79.2	759	76.7	865	86.3
Fees charged	1	0.2	3	0.2	1	0.1	0	0.0
38. Provide materials to homebound?								
Provide	320	49.7	601	38.0	521	52.7	544	54.3
Do not provide	324	50.3	975	61.7	468	47.3	458	45.7
Fees charged	0	0.0	4	0.3	0	0.0	0	0.0
39. Provide books by mail?								
Provide	104	16.1	213	13.5	185	18.7	200	20.0
Do not provide	538	83.5	1362	86.2	802	81.1	801	79.9
Fees charged	2	0.3	5	0.3	2	0.2	1	0.1

Table 6. RESPONSES BY GEOGRAPHIC REGION (Continued)

Does Your Library:	NORTH		SOUTH		CENTRAL		WEST	
	NUMBER OF LIBRARIES	PERCENT	NUMBER OF LIBRARIES	PERCENT	NUMBER OF LIBRARIES	PERCENT	NUMBER OF LIBRARIES	PERCENT
40. Provide bookmobile service?								
Provide	101	15.7	430	27.2	241	24.4	242	24.2
Do not provide	543	84.3	1147	72.6	747	75.5	760	75.8
Fees charged	0	0.0	3	0.2	1	0.1	0	0.0
a. Materials on demand?								
Provide	111	17.2	400	25.3	238	24.1	238	23.8
Do not provide	533	82.8	1176	74.4	751	75.9	764	76.2
Fees charged	0	0.0	4	0.3	0	0.0	0	0.0
b. Programming?								
Provide	30	4.7	145	9.2	121	12.2	119	11.9
Do not provide	614	95.3	1432	90.6	867	87.7	883	88.1
Fees charged	0	0.0	3	0.2	0	0.0	0	0.0
c. Publicize central library programming?								
Provide	169	26.2	507	32.1	304	30.7	318	31.7
Do not provide	475	73.8	1070	67.7	685	69.3	684	68.3
Fees charged	0	0.0	3	0.2	0	0.0	0	0.0
41. Maintain information on community activities?								
Provide	566	87.9	1195	75.6	838	84.7	894	89.2
Do not provide	77	12.0	384	24.3	151	15.3	107	10.7
Fees charged	1	0.2	1	0.1	0	0.0	1	0.1

Table 6. RESPONSES BY GEOGRAPHIC REGION (Continued)

Does Your Library:	NORTH		SOUTH		CENTRAL		WEST	
	NUMBER OF LIBRARIES	PERCENT	NUMBER OF LIBRARIES	PERCENT	NUMBER OF LIBRARIES	PERCENT	NUMBER OF LIBRARIES	PERCENT
42. Maintain information about media resources other than those owned by the library?								
Provide	445	69.1	965	61.1	658	66.5	667	66.6
Do not provide	198	30.7	613	38.8	331	33.5	335	33.4
Fees charged	1	0.2	2	0.1	0	0.0	0	0.0
43. Maintain a human resources file?								
Provide	375	58.2	600	38.0	473	47.8	584	58.3
Do not provide	267	41.5	978	61.9	516	52.2	463	41.6
Fees charged	2	0.3	2	0.1	0	0.0	0	0.0
44. Maintain other resource files?								
Provide	219	34.0	406	25.7	295	30.0	302	30.1
Do not provide	424	65.8	1173	74.2	693	70.0	700	69.9
Fees charged	1	0.2	1	0.1	0	0.0	0	0.0

Table 7. MEAN NUMBER OF SERVICES, BY STATE.

REGION	STATE	NUMBER OF LIBRARIES	MEAN NUMBER OF SERVICES PROVIDED		
			AT NO CHARGE	FOR A FEE	TOTAL
All Libraries		4215	26	2	27
North		644	29	2	29
	Connecticut	48	29	2	30
	Massachusetts	88	30	2	31
	Maine	6	22	2	22
	New Hampshire	4	26	1	26
	New Jersey	123	25	2	26
	New York	197	33	3	33
	Pennsylvania	165	25	2	26
	Rhode Island	12	32	1	32
	Vermont	1	43	-	43
South		1580	25	2	25
	Alabama	84	22	2	23
	Arkansas	26	16	1	17
	Delaware	7	25	-	25
	Florida	164	29	1	29
	Georgia	216	22	2	22
	Kentucky	74	26	1	26
	Louisiana	179	18	3	18
	Maryland	101	30	2	30
	Mississippi	129	25	1	25
	North Carolina	143	24	2	25
	Oklahoma	59	27	2	28
	South Carolina	82	23	1	24
	Tennessee	42	18	1	18
	Texas	130	30	2	30
	Virginia	101	28	2	29
	West Virginia	43	24	2	25

Table 7. MEAN NUMBER OF SERVICES, BY STATE. (Continued)

REGION	STATE	NUMBER OF LIBRARIES	AT NO CHARGE	MEAN NUMBER OF SERVICES PROVIDED FOR A FEE	TOTAL
Central		989	27	2	28
	Illinois	120	28	2	29
	Indiana	111	29	1	29
	Iowa	26	38	2	39
	Kansas	33	26	1	26
	Michigan	118	27	5	29
	Minnesota	105	28	2	29
	Missouri	91	24	3	25
	Nebraska	17	28	2	28
	North Dakota	4	35	-	35
	Ohio	277	25	2	26
	South Dakota	10	16	1	17
	Wisconsin	77	29	2	29
West		1002	27	2	27
	Alaska	001	21	5	26
	Arizona	42	30	1	30
	California	601	28	2	28
	Colorado	80	26	2	26
	Hawaii	37	26	1	26
	Idaho	9	25	2	26
	Montana	16	26	2	26
	Nevada	19	24	3	25
	New Mexico	18	24	2	25
	Oregon	54	20	2	20
	Utah	11	34	4	35
	Washington	94	26	1	26
	Wyoming	20	24	3	24

Table 8. QUESTIONNAIRE RESPONSE BY WHITE RESIDENTS AS A PERCENTAGE OF TOTAL RESIDENTS (POPULATION MEDIAN = 91 PERCENT).

Does Your Library:	BELOW MEDIAN		ABOVE MEDIAN	
	NUMBER OF LIBRARIES	PERCENT	NUMBER OF LIBRARIES	PERCENT
1. Display within the library exhibits based on materials owned by the library?				
Provide	529	96.4	566	97.1
Do not provide	20	3.6	17	2.9
Fees charged	0	0.0	0	0.0
2. Display within the library exhibits based on non-library materials?				
Provide	499	90.9	527	90.4
Do not provide	50	9.1	56	9.6
Fees charged	0	0.0	0	0.0
3. Display outside the library exhibits based on materials owned by the library?				
Provide	248	45.2	225	38.6
Do not provide	301	45.7	358	61.4
Fees charged	0	0.0	0	0.0
4. Circulate books in multiple copies for group use?				
Provide	220	40.1	250	42.9
Do not provide	329	59.9	333	57.1
Fees charged	0	0.0	0	0.0
5. Circulate microcomputers?				
Provide	27	4.9	40	6.9
Do not provide	520	94.7	536	91.9
Fees charged	2	0.4	7	1.2
6. Circulate microcomputer software?				
Provide	43	7.8	68	11.7
Do not provide	503	91.6	514	88.2
Fees charged	3	0.5	1	0.2
7. Circulate musical records?				
Provide	491	89.4	544	93.3
Do not provide	50	9.1	31	5.3
Fees charged	8	1.5	8	1.4
8. Circulate spoken records?				
Provide	488	88.9	529	90.7
Do not provide	55	10.0	47	8.1
Fees charged	6	1.1	7	1.2

Table 8. QUESTIONNAIRE RESPONSE BY WHITE RESIDENTS AS A PERCENTAGE OF
TOTAL RESIDENTS (POPULATION MEDIAN = 91 PERCENT). (Continued)

Does Your Library:	BELOW MEDIAN		ABOVE MEDIAN	
	NUMBER OF LIBRARIES	PERCENT	NUMBER OF LIBRARIES	PERCENT
9. Circulate musical tapes?				
Provide	385	70.1	428	73.4
Do not provide	160	29.1	152	26.1
Fees charged	4	0.7	3	0.5
10. Circulate spoken tapes?				
Provide	477	86.9	517	88.7
Do not provide	66	12.0	62	10.6
Fees charged	6	1.1	4	0.7
11. Circulate AV materials?				
Provide	447	81.4	475	81.5
Do not provide	92	16.8	89	15.3
Fees charged	10	1.8	19	3.3
12. Circulate films?				
Provide	382	69.6	411	70.5
Do not provide	135	24.6	124	21.3
Fees charged	32	5.8	48	8.2
13. Circulate videotapes?				
Provide	315	57.4	334	57.3
Do not provide	191	34.8	157	26.9
Fees charged	43	7.8	92	15.8
14 – 16. Circulate other?				
Provide	304	55.3	334	57.3
Do not provide	227	41.3	225	38.6
Fees charged	18	3.4	24	4.1
17. Provide reading lists or bibliographies?				
Provide	486	88.5	512	87.8
Do not provide	63	11.5	70	12.0
Fees charged	0	0.0	1	0.2
18. Provide interlibrary loan service?				
Provide	506	92.2	531	91.1
Do not provide	5	0.9	7	1.2
Fees charged	38	6.9	45	7.7
19. Provide AV equipment for in-library use?				
Provide	445	81.1	485	83.2
Do not provide	99	18.0	90	15.4
Fees charged	5	0.9	8	1.4

Table 8. QUESTIONNAIRE RESPONSE BY WHITE RESIDENTS AS A PERCENTAGE OF TOTAL RESIDENTS (POPULATION MEDIAN = 91 PERCENT). (Continued)

Does Your Library:	BELOW MEDIAN		ABOVE MEDIAN	
	NUMBER OF LIBRARIES	PERCENT	NUMBER OF LIBRARIES	PERCENT
20. Provide microcomputer software for in-library use?				
Provide	177	32.2	225	38.6
Do not provide	367	66.8	353	60.5
Fees charged	5	0.9	5	0.9
21. Provide microcomputers for in-library use?				
Provide	174	31.7	218	37.4
Do not provide	356	64.8	336	57.6
Fees charged	19	3.5	29	5.0
22. Provide meeting or conference room space?				
Provide	434	79.1	457	78.4
Do not provide	79	14.4	77	13.2
Fees charged	36	6.6	49	8.4
23. Provide photocopy machines?				
Provide	388	70.7	390	66.9
Do not provide	11	2.0	8	1.4
Fees charged	150	27.3	185	31.7
24. Present book talks/reviews?				
Provide	400	72.9	424	72.7
Do not provide	148	27.0	157	26.9
Fees charged	1	0.2	2	0.3
25. Present live programs?				
Provide	475	86.5	483	82.8
Do not provide	73	13.3	100	17.2
Fees charged	1	0.2	0	0.0
26. Present radio programs?				
Provide	120	21.9	94	16.1
Do not provide	429	78.1	489	83.9
Fees charged	0	0.0	0	0.0
27. Present cable TV programs?				
Provide	92	16.8	111	19.0
Do not provide	456	83.1	477	81.0
Fees charged	1	0.2	0	0.0

Table 8. QUESTIONNAIRE RESPONSE BY WHITE RESIDENTS AS A PERCENTAGE OF
TOTAL RESIDENTS (POPULATION MEDIAN = 91 PERCENT). (Continued)

	BELOW MEDIAN		ABOVE MEDIAN	
Does Your Library:	NUMBER OF LIBRARIES	PERCENT	NUMBER OF LIBRARIES	PERCENT
28. Provide instruction to groups on library use?				
Provide	506	92.2	538	92.3
Do not provide	43	7.8	45	7.7
Fees charged	0	0.0	0	0.0
29. Provide instruction to individuals on library use?				
Provide	517	94.2	555	95.2
Do not provide	32	5.8	28	4.8
Fees charged	0	0.0	0	0.0
30. Provide literacy education to groups?				
Provide	110	20.0	113	19.4
Do not provide	438	79.8	470	80.6
Fees charged	1	0.2	0	0.0
31. Provide literacy education to individuals?				
Provide	179	32.6	162	27.8
Do not provide	369	67.2	421	72.2
Fees charged	1	0.2	0	0.0
32. Provide facilities for literacy education?				
Provide	383	69.8	386	66.2
Do not provide	165	30.1	196	33.6
Fees charged	1	0.2	1	0.2
33. Provide referral to another agency for literacy education?				
Provide	477	86.9	503	86.3
Do not provide	72	13.1	80	13.7
Fees charged	0	0.0	0	0.0
34. Organize programming for special groups:				
a. Business?				
Provide	218	39.7	243	41.6
Do not provide	327	59.6	339	58.0
Fees charged	4	0.8	2	0.3
b. Genealogists?				
Provide	245	44.6	238	40.8
Do not provide	302	55.0	344	59.0
Fees charged	2	0.4	1	0.2

Table 8. QUESTIONNAIRE RESPONSE BY WHITE RESIDENTS AS A PERCENTAGE OF TOTAL RESIDENTS (POPULATION MEDIAN = 91 PERCENT). (Continued)

Does Your Library:		BELOW MEDIAN		ABOVE MEDIAN	
		NUMBER OF LIBRARIES	PERCENT	NUMBER OF LIBRARIES	PERCENT
34. Organize programming for special groups: (Continued)					
c. Handicapped?					
	Provide	149	27.1	145	24.9
	Do not provide	399	72.7	437	75.0
	Fees charged	1	0.2	1	0.2
d. Job seekers?					
	Provide	163	29.7	191	32.8
	Do not provide	385	70.1	392	67.2
	Fees charged	1	0.2	0	0.0
e. Labor groups?					
	Provide	36	6.6	46	7.9
	Do not provide	510	92.9	537	92.1
	Fees charged	3	0.5	0	0.0
f. Older adults?					
	Provide	292	53.2	290	49.7
	Do not provide	256	46.6	293	50.3
	Fees charged	1	0.2	0	0.0
g. Parents?					
	Provide	274	49.9	317	54.4
	Do not provide	274	49.9	266	45.6
	Fees charged	1	0.2	0	0.0
h. Minorities?					
	Provide	119	21.7	42	7.2
	Do not provide	430	78.3	541	92.8
	Fees charged	0	0.0	0	0.0
i. Other?					
	Provide	74	13.5	68	11.7
	Do not provide	474	86.3	514	88.2
	Fees charged	1	0.2	1	0.1
35. Provide to hospitals:					
	Provide	199	36.2	223	38.3
	Do not provide	350	63.8	360	61.7
	Fees charged	0	0.0	0	0.0
a. Materials on demand?					
	Provide	171	31.1	191	32.8
	Do not provide	377	68.7	392	67.2
	Fees charged	1	0.2	0	0.0

Table 8. QUESTIONNAIRE RESPONSE BY WHITE RESIDENTS AS A PERCENTAGE OF
TOTAL RESIDENTS (POPULATION MEDIAN = 91 PERCENT). (Continued)

Does Your Library:		BELOW MEDIAN		ABOVE MEDIAN	
		NUMBER OF LIBRARIES	PERCENT	NUMBER OF LIBRARIES	PERCENT
35. Provide to hospitals: (Continued)					
b. Deposit collections?					
	Provide	81	15.8	93	16.4
	Do not provide	431	84.0	473	83.6
	Fees charged	1	0.2	0	0.0
c. Programming?					
	Provide	44	8.0	36	6.2
	Do not provide	505	92.0	547	93.8
	Fees charged	0	0.0	0	0.0
36. Provide to prisons:					
	Provide	210	38.3	176	30.2
	Do not provide	339	61.7	406	69.6
	Fees charged	0	0.0	1	0.2
a. Materials on demand?					
	Provide	183	33.3	153	26.2
	Do not provide	366	66.7	430	73.8
	Fees charged	0	0.0	0	0.0
b. Deposit collections?					
	Provide	149	27.1	110	18.9
	Do not provide	400	72.9	473	81.1
	Fees charged	0	0.0	0	0.0
c. Programming?					
	Provide	27	4.9	19	3.3
	Do not provide	522	95.1	564	96.7
	Fees charged	0	0.0	0	0.0
37. Provide to retirement/nursing homes:					
	Provide	395	71.9	442	75.8
	Do not provide	154	28.1	141	24.2
	Fees charged	0	0.0	0	0.0
a. Materials on demand?					
	Provide	384	69.9	411	70.4
	Do not provide	165	30.1	173	29.6
	Fees charged	0	0.0	0	0.0
b. Deposit collections?					
	Provide	243	44.3	315	53.9
	Do not provide	306	55.7	269	46.1
	Fees charged	0	0.0	0	0.0

Table 8. QUESTIONNAIRE RESPONSE BY WHITE RESIDENTS AS A PERCENTAGE OF
TOTAL RESIDENTS (POPULATION MEDIAN = 91 PERCENT). (Continued)

Does Your Library:	BELOW MEDIAN		ABOVE MEDIAN	
	NUMBER OF LIBRARIES	PERCENT	NUMBER OF LIBRARIES	PERCENT
37. Provide to retirement/nursing homes: (Continued) c. Programming?				
Provide	188	34.2	176	30.1
Do not provide	360	65.6	408	69.9
Fees charged	1	0.2	0	0.0
38. Provide materials to homebound?				
Provide	345	62.8	424	72.6
Do not provide	204	37.2	160	27.4
Fees charged	0	0.0	0	0.0
39. Provide books by mail?				
Provide	134	24.4	144	24.7
Do not provide	415	75.6	438	75.0
Fees charged	0	0.0	2	0.3
40. Provide bookmobile service?				
Provide	244	44.4	212	36.3
Do not provide	305	55.6	371	63.5
Fees charged	0	0.0	1	0.2
a. Materials on demand?				
Provide	245	44.6	208	35.6
Do not provide	303	55.2	376	64.4
Fees charged	1	0.2	0	0.0
b. Programming?				
Provide	93	16.9	88	15.1
Do not provide	456	83.1	495	84.8
Fees charged	0	0.0	0	0.0
c. Publicize central library programming?				
Provide	234	42.6	201	34.4
Do not provide	315	57.4	383	65.6
Fees charged	0	0.0	0	0.0
41. Maintain information on community activities?				
Provide	477	86.9	514	88.0
Do not provide	72	13.1	70	12.0
Fees charged	0	0.0	0	0.0

Table 8. QUESTIONNAIRE RESPONSE BY WHITE RESIDENTS AS A PERCENTAGE OF TOTAL RESIDENTS (POPULATION MEDIAN = 91 PERCENT). (Continued)

Does Your Library:	BELOW MEDIAN		ABOVE MEDIAN	
	NUMBER OF LIBRARIES	PERCENT	NUMBER OF LIBRARIES	PERCENT
42. Maintain information about media resources other than those owned by the library?				
Provide	434	79.1	472	80.8
Do not provide	115	20.9	111	19.0
Fees charged	0	0.0	1	0.2
43. Maintain a human resources file?				
Provide	337	61.4	346	59.2
Do not provide	212	38.6	238	40.8
Fees charged	0	0.0	0	0.0
44. Maintain other resource files?				
Provide	230	41.9	236	40.5
Do not provide	319	58.1	346	59.3
Fees charged	0	0.0	1	0.2

Table 9. QUESTIONNAIRE RESPONSE BY BLACK RESIDENTS AS A PERCENTAGE OF TOTAL RESIDENTS (POPULATION MEDIAN = 7 PERCENT).

Does Your Library:	BELOW MEDIAN		ABOVE MEDIAN	
	NUMBER OF LIBRARIES	PERCENT	NUMBER OF LIBRARIES	PERCENT
1. Display within the library exhibits based on materials owned by the library?				
Provide	449	97.6	473	96.1
Do not provide	11	2.4	19	3.9
Fees charged	0	0.0	0	0.0
2. Display within the library exhibits based on non-library materials?				
Provide	418	90.9	450	91.5
Do not provide	42	9.1	42	8.5
Fees charged	0	0.0	0	0.0
3. Display outside the library exhibits based on materials owned by the library?				
Provide	177	38.5	225	45.7
Do not provide	283	61.5	267	54.3
Fees charged	0	0.0	0	0.0
4. Circulate books in multiple copies for group use?				
Provide	180	39.1	206	41.9
Do not provide	280	60.9	286	58.1
Fees charged	0	0.0	0	0.0
5. Circulate microcomputers?				
Provide	33	7.2	24	4.9
Do not provide	421	91.5	466	94.7
Fees charged	6	1.3	2	0.4
6. Circulate microcomputer software?				
Provide	50	10.9	37	7.5
Do not provide	410	89.1	452	91.9
Fees charged	0	0.0	3	0.6
7. Circulate musical records?				
Provide	427	92.8	439	89.2
Do not provide	25	5.4	47	9.6
Fees charged	8	1.7	6	1.2
8. Circulate spoken records?				
Provide	420	91.3	437	88.8
Do not provide	33	7.2	50	10.2
Fees charged	7	1.5	5	1.0

Table 9. QUESTIONNAIRE RESPONSE BY BLACK RESIDENTS
AS A PERCENTAGE OF TOTAL RESIDENTS (POPULATION MEDIAN = 7
PERCENT). (Continued)

Does Your Library:		BELOW MEDIAN		ABOVE MEDIAN	
		NUMBER OF LIBRARIES	PERCENT	NUMBER OF LIBRARIES	PERCENT
9. Circulate musical tapes?					
	Provide	355	77.2	329	66.9
	Do not provide	101	22.0	160	32.5
	Fees charged	4	0.9	3	0.6
10. Circulate spoken tapes?					
	Provide	413	89.8	420	85.4
	Do not provide	42	9.1	67	13.6
	Fees charged	5	1.1	5	1.0
11. Circulate AV materials?					
	Provide	379	82.4	405	82.3
	Do not provide	66	14.3	80	16.3
	Fees charged	15	3.3	7	1.4
12. Circulate films?					
	Provide	317	68.9	349	70.9
	Do not provide	102	22.2	117	23.8
	Fees charged	41	8.9	26	5.3
13. Circulate videotapes?					
	Provide	258	56.1	286	58.1
	Do not provide	125	27.2	172	35.0
	Fees charged	77	16.7	34	6.9
14 – 16. Circulate other?					
	Provide	270	38.7	270	54.9
	Do not provide	172	37.4	206	41.9
	Fees charged	18	3.9	16	3.3
17. Provide reading lists or bibliographies?					
	Provide	408	88.7	432	87.8
	Do not provide	51	11.1	60	12.2
	Fees charged	1	0.2	0	0.0
18. Provide interlibrary loan service?					
	Provide	416	90.4	459	93.3
	Do not provide	4	0.9	7	1.4
	Fees charged	40	8.7	26	5.3
19. Provide AV equipment for in-library use?					
	Provide	376	81.7	404	82.1
	Do not provide	79	17.2	84	17.1
	Fees charged	5	1.1	4	0.8

Table 9. QUESTIONNAIRE RESPONSE BY BLACK RESIDENTS
AS A PERCENTAGE OF TOTAL RESIDENTS (POPULATION MEDIAN = 7
PERCENT). (Continued)

Does Your Library:	BELOW MEDIAN		ABOVE MEDIAN	
	NUMBER OF LIBRARIES	PERCENT	NUMBER OF LIBRARIES	PERCENT
20. Provide microcomputer software for in-library use?				
Provide	181	39.3	159	32.3
Do not provide	275	59.8	330	67.1
Fees charged	4	0.9	3	0.6
21. Provide mircocomputers for in-library use?				
Provide	173	37.6	155	31.5
Do not provide	264	57.4	323	65.7
Fees charged	23	5.0	14	2.8
22. Provide meeting or conference room space?				
Provide	351	76.3	393	79.9
Do not provide	63	13.7	71	14.4
Fees charged	46	10.0	28	5.7
23. Provide photocopy machines?				
Provide	307	66.7	347	70.5
Do not provide	5	1.1	11	2.2
Fees charged	148	32.2	134	27.2
24. Present book talks/reviews?				
Provide	328	71.3	364	74.0
Do not provide	131	28.5	127	25.8
Fees charged	1	0.2	1	0.2
25. Present live programs?				
Provide	388	84.3	425	86.4
Do not provide	72	15.7	66	13.4
Fees charged	0	0.0	1	0.2
26. Present radio programs?				
Provide	72	15.7	113	23.0
Do not provide	388	84.3	379	77.0
Fees charged	0	0.0	0	0.0
27. Present cable TV programs?				
Provide	97	21.1	76	15.4
Do not provide	363	78.9	415	84.3
Fees charged	0	0.0	1	0.2

Table 9. QUESTIONNAIRE RESPONSE BY BLACK RESIDENTS
AS A PERCENTAGE OF TOTAL RESIDENTS (POPULATION MEDIAN = 7
PERCENT). (Continued)

	BELOW MEDIAN		ABOVE MEDIAN	
Does Your Library:	NUMBER OF LIBRARIES	PERCENT	NUMBER OF LIBRARIES	PERCENT
28. Provide instruction to groups on library use?				
Provide	430	93.5	449	91.3
Do not provide	30	6.5	43	8.7
Fees charged	0	0.0	0	0.0
29. Provide instruction to individuals on library use?				
Provide	439	95.4	465	94.5
Do not provide	21	4.6	27	5.5
Fees charged	0	0.0	0	0.0
30. Provide literacy education to groups?				
Provide	90	19.6	102	20.7
Do not provide	370	80.4	389	79.1
Fees charged	0	0.0	1	0.2
31. Provide literacy education to individuals?				
Provide	137	29.8	157	31.9
Do not provide	323	70.2	334	67.9
Fees charged	0	0.0	1	0.2
32. Provide facilities for literacy education?				
Provide	321	69.8	342	69.5
Do not provide	138	30.0	149	30.3
Fees charged	1	0.2	1	0.2
33. Provide referral to another agency for literacy education?				
Provide	409	88.9	426	86.6
Do not provide	51	11.1	66	13.4
Fees charged	0	0.0	0	0.0
34. Organize programming for special groups:				
a. Business?				
Provide	193	42.0	196	39.8
Do not provide	265	57.6	292	59.3
Fees charged	2	0.4	4	0.8
b. Genealogists?				
Provide	177	38.5	231	47.0
Do not provide	282	61.3	259	52.6
Fees charged	1	0.2	2	0.4

Table 9. QUESTIONNAIRE RESPONSE BY BLACK RESIDENTS
AS A PERCENTAGE OF TOTAL RESIDENTS (POPULATION MEDIAN = 7
PERCENT). (Continued)

Does Your Library:		BELOW MEDIAN		ABOVE MEDIAN	
		NUMBER OF LIBRARIES	PERCENT	NUMBER OF LIBRARIES	PERCENT
34. Organize programming for special groups: (Continued)					
c. Handicapped?					
	Provide	116	25.2	138	28.0
	Do not provide	343	74.6	353	71.7
	Fees charged	1	0.2	1	0.2
d. Job seekers?					
	Provide	154	33.5	147	29.9
	Do not provide	306	66.5	344	69.9
	Fees charged	0	0.0	1	0.2
e. Labor groups?					
	Provide	33	7.2	28	5.7
	Do not provide	427	92.8	461	93.7
	Fees charged	0	0.0	3	0.6
f. Older adults?					
	Provide	219	47.6	270	54.9
	Do not provide	241	52.4	221	44.9
	Fees charged	0	0.0	1	0.2
g. Parents?					
	Provide	242	52.6	251	51.0
	Do not provide	218	47.4	240	48.8
	Fees charged	0	0.0	1	0.2
h. Minorities?					
	Provide	52	11.3	96	19.5
	Do not provide	408	88.7	396	80.5
	Fees charged	0	0.0	0	0.0
i. Other?					
	Provide	62	13.5	67	13.6
	Do not provide	396	86.1	425	86.4
	Fees charged	2	0.4	0	0.0
35. Provide to hospitals:					
	Provide	163	35.4	193	39.2
	Do not provide	297	64.6	299	60.8
	Fees charged	0	0.0	0	0.0
a. Materials on demand?					
	Provide	132	28.7	163	33.1
	Do not provide	328	71.3	328	66.7
	Fees charged	0	0.0	1	0.2

Table 9. QUESTIONNAIRE RESPONSE BY BLACK RESIDENTS
AS A PERCENTAGE OF TOTAL RESIDENTS (POPULATION MEDIAN = 7
PERCENT). (Continued)

Does Your Library:		BELOW MEDIAN		ABOVE MEDIAN	
		NUMBER OF LIBRARIES	PERCENT	NUMBER OF LIBRARIES	PERCENT
35. Provide to hospitals: (Continued)					
b. Deposit collections?					
	Provide	69	15.4	82	18.1
	Do not provide	379	84.6	370	81.7
	Fees charged	0	0.0	1	0.2
c. Programming?					
	Provide	31	6.7	41	8.3
	Do not provide	429	93.3	451	91.7
	Fees charged	0	0.0	0	0.0
36. Provide to prisons:					
	Provide	138	30.0	194	39.4
	Do not provide	322	70.0	298	60.6
	Fees charged	0	0.0	0	0.0
a. Materials on demand?					
	Provide	117	25.4	164	33.3
	Do not provide	343	74.6	328	66.7
	Fees charged	0	0.0	0	0.0
b. Deposit collections?					
	Provide	96	20.9	133	27.0
	Do not provide	364	79.1	359	73.0
	Fees charged	0	0.0	0	0.0
c. Programming?					
	Provide	18	3.9	25	5.1
	Do not provide	442	96.1	467	94.9
	Fees charged	0	0.0	0	0.0
37. Provide to retirement/nursing homes:					
	Provide	341	74.1	354	72.0
	Do not provide	119	25.9	138	28.0
	Fees charged	0	0.0	0	0.0
a. Materials on demand?					
	Provide	319	69.3	340	69.1
	Do not provide	141	30.7	152	30.9
	Fees charged	0	0.0	0	0.0
b. Deposit collections?					
	Provide	233	50.7	223	45.3
	Do not provide	227	49.3	269	54.7
	Fees charged	0	0.0	0	0.0

Table 9. QUESTIONNAIRE RESPONSE BY BLACK RESIDENTS
AS A PERCENTAGE OF TOTAL RESIDENTS (POPULATION MEDIAN = 7
PERCENT). (Continued)

Does Your Library:	BELOW MEDIAN		ABOVE MEDIAN	
	NUMBER OF LIBRARIES	PERCENT	NUMBER OF LIBRARIES	PERCENT
37. Provide to retirement/nursing homes: (Continued)				
c. Programming?				
Provide	137	29.8	179	36.4
Do not provide	323	70.2	312	63.4
Fees charged	0	0.0	1	0.2
38. Provide materials to homebound?				
Provide	327	71.1	305	62.0
Do not provide	133	28.9	187	38.0
Fees charged	0	0.0	0	0.0
39. Provide books by mail?				
Provide	110	23.9	119	24.2
Do not provide	350	76.1	372	75.6
Fees charged	0	0.0	1	0.2
40. Provide bookmobile service?				
Provide	175	38.0	221	44.9
Do not provide	285	62.0	271	55.1
Fees charged	0	0.0	0	0.0
a. Materials on demand?				
Provide	173	37.6	223	45.3
Do not provide	287	62.4	268	54.5
Fees charged	0	0.0	1	0.2
b. Programming?				
Provide	69	15.0	84	17.1
Do not provide	391	85.0	408	82.9
Fees charged	0	0.0	0	0.0
c. Publicize central library programming?				
Provide	168	36.5	207	42.1
Do not provide	292	63.5	285	57.9
Fees charged	0	0.0	0	0.0
41. Maintain information on community activities?				
Provide	408	88.7	421	85.6
Do not provide	52	11.3	71	14.4
Fees charged	0	0.0	0	0.0

Table 9. QUESTIONNAIRE RESPONSE BY BLACK RESIDENTS
AS A PERCENTAGE OF TOTAL RESIDENTS (POPULATION MEDIAN = 7
PERCENT). (Continued)

Does Your Library:	BELOW MEDIAN		ABOVE MEDIAN	
	NUMBER OF LIBRARIES	PERCENT	NUMBER OF LIBRARIES	PERCENT
42. Maintain information about media re-sources other than those owned by the library?				
Provide	372	80.9	386	78.5
Do not provide	87	18.9	106	21.5
Fees charged	1	0.2	0	0.0
43. Maintain a human resources file?				
Provide	286	62.2	293	59.6
Do not provide	174	37.8	199	40.4
Fees charged	0	0.0	0	0.0
44. Maintain other resource files?				
Provide	200	43.5	202	41.1
Do not provide	259	56.3	290	58.9
Fees charged	1	0.2	0	0.0

Table 10. QUESTIONNAIRE RESPONSE BY RESIDENTS OF HISPANIC ORIGIN
AS A PERCENTAGE OF TOTAL RESIDENTS
(POPULATION MEDIAN = 1 PERCENT).

Does Your Library:	BELOW MEDIAN		ABOVE MEDIAN	
	NUMBER OF LIBRARIES	PERCENT	NUMBER OF LIBRARIES	PERCENT
1. Display within the library exhibits based on materials owned by the library?				
Provide	403	96.0	542	97.1
Do not provide	17	4.0	16	2.9
Fees charged	0	0.0	0	0.0
2. Display within the library exhibits based on non-library materials?				
Provide	367	87.4	524	93.9
Do not provide	53	12.6	34	6.1
Fees charged	0	0.0	0	0.0
3. Display outside the library exhibits based on materials owned by the library?				
Provide	182	43.3	227	40.7
Do not provide	238	56.7	331	59.3
Fees charged	0	0.0	0	0.0
4. Circulate books in multiple copies for group use?				
Provide	172	41.0	233	41.8
Do not provide	248	59.0	325	58.2
Fees charged	0	0.0	0	0.0
5. Circulate microcomputers?				
Provide	23	5.5	35	6.3
Do not provide	393	93.6	519	93.0
Fees charged	4	1.0	4	0.7
6. Circulate microcomputer software?				
Provide	42	10.0	52	9.3
Do not provide	377	89.8	503	90.1
Fees charged	1	0.2	3	0.5
7. Circulate musical records?				
Provide	386	91.9	511	91.6
Do not provide	29	6.9	39	7.0
Fees charged	5	1.2	8	1.4
8. Circulate spoken records?				
Provide	377	89.8	510	91.4
Do not provide	39	9.3	41	7.3
Fees charged	4	1.0	7	1.3

Table 10. QUESTIONNAIRE RESPONSE BY RESIDENTS OF HISPANIC ORIGIN
AS A PERCENTAGE OF TOTAL RESIDENTS
(POPULATION MEDIAN = 1 PERCENT). (Continued)

Does Your Library:		BELOW MEDIAN		ABOVE MEDIAN	
		NUMBER OF LIBRARIES	PERCENT	NUMBER OF LIBRARIES	PERCENT
9. Circulate musical tapes?					
	Provide	293	69.8	421	75.4
	Do not provide	126	30.0	132	23.7
	Fees charged	1	0.2	5	0.9
10. Circulate spoken tapes?					
	Provide	364	86.7	502	90.0
	Do not provide	54	12.9	49	8.8
	Fees charged	2	0.5	7	1.3
11. Circulate AV materials?					
	Provide	353	84.0	444	79.6
	Do not provide	60	14.3	96	17.2
	Fees charged	7	1.7	18	3.2
12. Circulate films?					
	Provide	310	73.8	376	67.4
	Do not provide	81	19.3	144	25.8
	Fees charged	29	6.9	38	6.8
13. Circulate videotapes?					
	Provide	236	56.2	327	58.6
	Do not provide	134	31.9	162	29.0
	Fees charged	50	11.9	69	12.4
14 – 16. Circulate other?					
	Provide	231	55.0	329	59.0
	Do not provide	171	40.7	212	38.0
	Fees charged	18	4.3	17	3.0
17. Provide reading lists or bibliographies?					
	Provide	366	87.1	502	90.0
	Do not provide	53	12.6	56	10.0
	Fees charged	1	0.2	0	0.0
18. Provide interlibrary loan service?					
	Provide	389	92.6	508	91.0
	Do not provide	7	1.7	2	0.4
	Fees charged	24	5.7	48	8.6
19. Provide AV equipment for in-library use?					
	Provide	356	84.8	442	79.2
	Do not provide	61	14.5	107	19.2
	Fees charged	3	0.7	9	1.6

Table 10. QUESTIONNAIRE RESPONSE BY RESIDENTS OF HISPANIC ORIGIN
AS A PERCENTAGE OF TOTAL RESIDENTS
(POPULATION MEDIAN = 1 PERCENT). (Continued)

Does Your Library:	BELOW MEDIAN		ABOVE MEDIAN	
	NUMBER OF LIBRARIES	PERCENT	NUMBER OF LIBRARIES	PERCENT
20. Provide microcomputer software for in-library use?				
Provide	141	33.6	210	37.6
Do not provide	274	65.2	343	61.5
Fees charged	5	1.2	5	0.9
21. Provide microcomputers for in-library use?				
Provide	137	32.6	202	36.2
Do not provide	267	63.6	328	58.8
Fees charged	16	3.8	28	5.0
22. Provide meeting or conference room space?				
Provide	336	80.0	435	78.0
Do not provide	55	13.1	77	13.8
Fees charged	29	6.9	46	8.2
23. Provide photocopy machines?				
Provide	281	66.9	394	70.6
Do not provide	9	2.1	8	1.4
Fees charged	130	31.0	156	28.0
24. Present book talks/reviews?				
Provide	312	74.3	409	73.3
Do not provide	107	25.5	147	26.3
Fees charged	1	0.2	2	0.4
25. Present live programs?				
Provide	347	82.6	485	86.9
Do not provide	72	17.1	73	13.1
Fees charged	1	0.2	0	0.0
26. Present radio programs?				
Provide	79	18.8	95	17.0
Do not provide	341	81.2	463	83.0
Fees charged	1	0.2	0	0.0
27. Present cable TV programs?				
Provide	74	17.6	110	19.7
Do not provide	345	82.1	448	80.3
Fees charged	0	0.0	0	0.0

Table 10. QUESTIONNAIRE RESPONSE BY RESIDENTS OF HISPANIC ORIGIN
AS A PERCENTAGE OF TOTAL RESIDENTS
(POPULATION MEDIAN = 1 PERCENT). (Continued)

Does Your Library:		BELOW MEDIAN		ABOVE MEDIAN	
		NUMBER OF LIBRARIES	PERCENT	NUMBER OF LIBRARIES	PERCENT
28. Provide instruction to groups on library use?					
	Provide	379	90.2	523	93.7
	Do not provide	41	9.8	35	6.3
	Fees charged	0	0.0	0	0.0
29. Provide instruction to individuals on library use?					
	Provide	398	94.8	531	95.2
	Do not provide	23	5.2	27	4.8
	Fees charged	0	0.0	0	0.0
30. Provide literacy education to groups?					
	Provide	79	18.8	119	21.3
	Do not provide	340	81.0	439	78.7
	Fees charged	1	0.2	0	0.0
31. Provide literacy education to individuals?					
	Provide	106	25.2	197	35.3
	Do not provide	313	74.5	361	64.7
	Fees charged	1	0.2	0	0.0
32. Provide facilities for literacy education?					
	Provide	278	66.2	394	70.6
	Do not provide	140	33.3	164	29.4
	Fees charged	2	0.5	0	0.0
33. Provide referral to another agency for literacy education?					
	Provide	363	86.4	491	88.0
	Do not provide	57	13.6	67	12.0
	Fees charged	0	0.0	0	0.0
34. Organize programming for special groups: a. Business?					
	Provide	168	40.0	240	43.0
	Do not provide	251	59.8	313	56.1
	Fees charged	1	0.2	5	0.9
b. Genealogists?					
	Provide	198	47.1	218	39.1
	Do not provide	221	52.6	339	60.8
	Fees charged	1	0.2	1	0.2

Table 10. QUESTIONNAIRE RESPONSE BY RESIDENTS OF HISPANIC ORIGIN
AS A PERCENTAGE OF TOTAL RESIDENTS
(POPULATION MEDIAN = 1 PERCENT). (Continued)

Does Your Library:		BELOW MEDIAN		ABOVE MEDIAN	
		NUMBER OF LIBRARIES	PERCENT	NUMBER OF LIBRARIES	PERCENT
34. Organize programming for special groups: (Continued)					
c. Handicapped?					
	Provide	110	26.2	143	25.6
	Do not provide	310	73.8	414	74.2
	Fees charged	0	0.0	1	0.2
d. Job seekers?					
	Provide	122	29.0	197	35.3
	Do not provide	298	71.0	360	64.5
	Fees charged	0	0.0	1	0.2
e. Labor groups?					
	Provide	31	7.4	38	6.8
	Do not provide	388	92.4	518	92.8
	Fees charged	1	0.2	2	0.4
f. Older adults?					
	Provide	220	52.4	294	52.7
	Do not provide	200	47.6	263	47.1
	Fees charged	0	0.0	1	0.2
g. Parents?					
	Provide	214	51.0	304	54.5
	Do not provide	206	49.0	253	45.3
	Fees charged	0	0.0	1	0.2
h. Minorities?					
	Provide	43	10.2	105	18.8
	Do not provide	377	89.8	453	81.2
	Fees charged	0	0.0	0	0.0
i. Other?					
	Provide	47	11.2	83	14.9
	Do not provide	373	88.8	475	85.1
	Fees charged	0	0.0	0	0.0
35. Provide to hospitals:					
	Provide	169	40.2	190	34.1
	Do not provide	251	59.8	368	65.9
	Fees charged	0	0.0	0	0.0
a. Materials on demand?					
	Provide	140	33.0	162	29.0
	Do not provide	280	66.7	395	70.8
	Fees charged	0	0.0	1	0.2

Table 10. QUESTIONNAIRE RESPONSE BY RESIDENTS OF HISPANIC ORIGIN
AS A PERCENTAGE OF TOTAL RESIDENTS
(POPULATION MEDIAN = 1 PERCENT). (Continued)

Does Your Library:	BELOW MEDIAN		ABOVE MEDIAN	
	NUMBER OF LIBRARIES	PERCENT	NUMBER OF LIBRARIES	PERCENT
35. Provide to hospitals: (Continued)				
b. Deposit collections?				
Provide	78	20.1	73	13.4
Do not provide	310	79.9	471	86.4
Fees charged	0	0.0	1	0.2
c. Programming?				
Provide	35	8.3	36	6.5
Do not provide	385	91.7	522	93.5
Fees charged	0	0.0	0	0.0
36. Provide to prisons:				
Provide	145	34.5	170	30.5
Do not provide	275	65.5	387	69.4
Fees charged	0	0.0	1	0.2
a. Materials on demand?				
Provide	121	28.8	149	26.7
Do not provide	299	71.2	409	73.3
Fees charged	0	0.0	0	0.0
b. Deposit collections?				
Provide	100	23.8	112	20.1
Do not provide	320	76.2	446	79.9
Fees charged	0	0.0	0	0.0
c. Programming?				
Provide	16	3.8	25	4.5
Do not provide	404	96.2	533	95.5
Fees charged	0	0.0	0	0.0
37. Provide to retirement/nursing homes:				
Provide	314	74.8	397	71.1
Do not provide	106	25.2	161	28.9
Fees charged	0	0.0	0	0.0
a. Materials on demand?				
Provide	296	70.5	381	68.3
Do not provide	124	29.5	177	31.7
Fees charged	0	0.0	0	0.0
b. Deposit collections?				
Provide	228	54.3	237	42.5
Do not provide	192	45.7	321	57.5
Fees charged	0	0.0	0	0.0

Table 10. QUESTIONNAIRE RESPONSE BY RESIDENTS OF HISPANIC ORIGIN
AS A PERCENTAGE OF TOTAL RESIDENTS
(POPULATION MEDIAN = 1 PERCENT). (Continued)

Does Your Library:		BELOW MEDIAN		ABOVE MEDIAN	
		NUMBER OF LIBRARIES	PERCENT	NUMBER OF LIBRARIES	PERCENT
37. Provide to retirement/nursing homes: (Continued)					
c. Programming?					
	Provide	150	35.7	174	31.2
	Do not provide	269	64.0	384	68.8
	Fees charged	1	0.2	0	0.0
38. Provide materials to homebound?					
	Provide	282	67.1	374	67.0
	Do not provide	138	32.9	184	33.0
	Fees charged	0	0.0	0	0.0
39. Provide books by mail?					
	Provide	100	23.8	137	24.6
	Do not provide	319	76.0	421	75.4
	Fees charged	1	0.2	0	0.0
40. Provide bookmobile service?					
	Provide	179	42.6	193	34.6
	Do not provide	240	57.1	365	65.4
	Fees charged	1	0.2	0	0.0
a. Materials on demand?					
	Provide	183	43.6	190	34.1
	Do not provide	237	56.4	367	65.8
	Fees charged	0	0.0	1	0.2
b. Programming?					
	Provide	74	16.9	75	13.4
	Do not provide	349	83.1	483	86.6
	Fees charged	0	0.0	0	0.0
c. Publicize central library programming?					
	Provide	176	41.9	184	33.0
	Do not provide	244	58.1	374	67.0
	Fees charged	0	0.0	0	0.0
41. Maintain information on community activities?					
	Provide	349	83.1	512	91.8
	Do not provide	71	16.9	46	8.2
	Fees charged	0	0.0	0	0.0

Table 10. QUESTIONNAIRE RESPONSE BY RESIDENTS OF HISPANIC ORIGIN
AS A PERCENTAGE OF TOTAL RESIDENTS
(POPULATION MEDIAN = 1 PERCENT). (Continued)

Does Your Library:	BELOW MEDIAN		ABOVE MEDIAN	
	NUMBER OF LIBRARIES	PERCENT	NUMBER OF LIBRARIES	PERCENT
42. Maintain information about media re-sources other than those owned by the library?				
Provide	325	77.4	459	82.3
Do not provide	95	22.6	98	17.6
Fees charged	0	0.0	1	0.2
43. Maintain a human resources file?				
Provide	240	57.1	369	66.1
Do not provide	180	42.9	189	33.9
Fees charged	0	0.0	0	0.0
44. Maintain other resource files?				
Provide	168	40.0	244	43.7
Do not provide	251	59.8	314	56.3
Fees charged	1	0.2	0	0.0

Table 11. QUESTIONNAIRE RESPONSE BY RESIDENTS OF OTHER ETHNIC ORIGIN
AS A PERCENTAGE OF TOTAL RESIDENTS
(POPULATION MEDIAN = 1 PERCENT).

Does Your Library:	BELOW MEDIAN		ABOVE MEDIAN	
	NUMBER OF LIBRARIES	PERCENT	NUMBER OF LIBRARIES	PERCENT
1. Display within the library exhibits based on materials owned by the library?				
Provide	411	96.9	277	96.5
Do not provide	13	3.1	10	3.5
Fees charged	0	0.0	0	0.0
2. Display within the library exhibits based on non-library materials?				
Provide	383	90.3	268	93.4
Do not provide	41	9.7	19	6.6
Fees charged	0	0.0	0	0.0
3. Display outside the library exhibits based on materials owned by the library?				
Provide	190	43.9	120	41.8
Do not provide	238	56.1	167	58.2
Fees charged	0	0.0	0	0.0
4. Circulate books in multiple copies for group use?				
Provide	186	43.9	120	41.8
Do not provide	238	56.1	167	58.2
Fees charged	0	0.0	0	0.0
5. Circulate microcomputers?				
Provide	24	5.7	15	5.2
Do not provide	398	93.9	270	94.1
Fees charged	2	0.4	2	0.7
6. Circulate microcomputer software?				
Provide	47	11.1	24	8.4
Do not provide	375	88.4	261	90.9
Fees charged	2	0.5	2	0.7
7. Circulate musical records?				
Provide	396	93.4	254	88.5
Do not provide	25	5.9	24	8.4
Fees charged	3	0.7	9	3.1
8. Circulate spoken records?				
Provide	385	90.8	256	89.2
Do not provide	36	8.5	24	8.4
Fees charged	3	0.7	7	2.4

Table 11. QUESTIONNAIRE RESPONSE BY RESIDENTS OF OTHER ETHNIC ORIGIN
AS A PERCENTAGE OF TOTAL RESIDENTS
(POPULATION MEDIAN = 1 PERCENT). (Continued)

Does Your Library:	BELOW MEDIAN		ABOVE MEDIAN	
	NUMBER OF LIBRARIES	PERCENT	NUMBER OF LIBRARIES	PERCENT
9. Circulate musical tapes?				
Provide	302	71.2	217	75.6
Do not provide	122	28.8	64	22.3
Fees charged	0	0.0	6	2.1
10. Circulate spoken tapes?				
Provide	372	87.8	263	91.6
Do not provide	50	11.8	18	6.3
Fees charged	2	0.5	6	2.1
11. Circulate AV materials?				
Provide	355	83.7	213	74.2
Do not provide	62	14.6	58	20.2
Fees charged	7	1.7	16	5.6
12. Circulate films?				
Provide	322	75.9	164	57.1
Do not provide	78	18.4	97	33.8
Fees charged	24	5.7	26	9.1
13. Circulate videotapes?				
Provide	263	62.0	153	53.3
Do not provide	116	27.4	88	30.7
Fees charged	45	10.6	46	16.0
14 – 16. Circulate other?				
Provide	256	60.4	164	57.1
Do not provide	150	35.4	115	40.1
Fees charged	18	4.2	8	2.8
17. Provide reading lists or bibliographies?				
Provide	376	88.7	265	92.3
Do not provide	47	11.1	22	7.7
Fees charged	1	0.2	0	0.0
18. Provide interlibrary loan service?				
Provide	393	92.7	256	89.2
Do not provide	4	0.9	2	0.7
Fees charged	27	6.4	29	10.1
19. Provide AV equipment for in-library use?				
Provide	341	80.4	228	79.4
Do not provide	78	18.4	54	18.8
Fees charged	5	1.2	5	1.7

Table 11. QUESTIONNAIRE RESPONSE BY RESIDENTS OF OTHER ETHNIC ORIGIN
AS A PERCENTAGE OF TOTAL RESIDENTS
(POPULATION MEDIAN = 1 PERCENT). (Continued)

Does Your Library:	BELOW MEDIAN		ABOVE MEDIAN	
	NUMBER OF LIBRARIES	PERCENT	NUMBER OF LIBRARIES	PERCENT
20. Provide microcomputer software for in-library use?				
Provide	163	38.4	107	37.3
Do not provide	259	61.1	176	61.3
Fees charged	2	0.5	4	1.4
21. Provide microcomputers for in-library use?				
Provide	159	37.5	103	35.9
Do not provide	246	58.0	171	59.6
Fees charged	19	4.5	13	4.5
22. Provide meeting or conference room space?				
Provide	339	80.0	216	75.3
Do not provide	56	13.2	41	14.3
Fees charged	29	6.8	30	10.5
23. Provide photocopy machines?				
Provide	299	70.5	190	66.2
Do not provide	7	1.7	6	2.1
Fees charged	118	27.8	91	31.7
24. Present book talks/reviews?				
Provide	319	75.2	212	73.9
Do not provide	105	24.8	73	25.4
Fees charged	0	0.0	2	0.7
25. Present live programs?				
Provide	361	85.1	251	87.5
Do not provide	63	14.9	36	12.5
Fees charged	0	0.0	0	0.0
26. Present radio programs?				
Provide	73	17.2	49	17.1
Do not provide	351	82.8	238	82.9
Fees charged	0	0.0	0	0.0
27. Present cable TV programs?				
Provide	70	16.5	67	23.3
Do not provide	354	83.5	220	76.7
Fees charged	0	0.0	0	0.0

Table 11. QUESTIONNAIRE RESPONSE BY RESIDENTS OF OTHER ETHNIC ORIGIN
AS A PERCENTAGE OF TOTAL RESIDENTS
(POPULATION MEDIAN = 1 PERCENT). (Continued)

Does Your Library:	BELOW MEDIAN		ABOVE MEDIAN	
	NUMBER OF LIBRARIES	PERCENT	NUMBER OF LIBRARIES	PERCENT
28. Provide instruction to groups on library use?				
Provide	390	92.0	271	94.4
Do not provide	34	8.0	16	5.6
Fees charged	0	0.0	0	0.0
29. Provide instruction to individuals on library use?				
Provide	404	95.3	274	95.5
Do not provide	20	4.7	13	4.5
Fees charged	0	0.0	0	0.0
30. Provide literacy education to groups?				
Provide	81	19.1	59	20.6
Do not provide	343	80.9	228	79.4
Fees charged	0	0.0	0	0.0
31. Provide literacy education to individuals?				
Provide	115	27.1	99	34.5
Do not provide	309	72.9	188	65.5
Fees charged	0	0.0	0	0.0
32. Provide facilities for literacy education?				
Provide	298	70.3	196	68.3
Do not provide	126	29.7	90	31.4
Fees charged	0	0.0	1	0.3
33. Provide referral to another agency for literacy education?				
Provide	374	88.2	256	89.2
Do not provide	50	11.8	31	10.8
Fees charged	0	0.0	0	0.0
34. Organize programming for special groups:				
a. Business?				
Provide	181	42.6	128	44.6
Do not provide	243	57.2	155	54.0
Fees charged	1	0.2	4	1.4
b. Genealogists?				
Provide	193	45.5	104	36.2
Do not provide	231	54.5	181	63.1
Fees charged	0	0.0	2	0.7

Table 11. QUESTIONNAIRE RESPONSE BY RESIDENTS OF OTHER ETHNIC ORIGIN
AS A PERCENTAGE OF TOTAL RESIDENTS
(POPULATION MEDIAN = 1 PERCENT). (Continued)

Does Your Library:		BELOW MEDIAN		ABOVE MEDIAN	
		NUMBER OF LIBRARIES	PERCENT	NUMBER OF LIBRARIES	PERCENT
34. Organize programming for special groups: (Continued)					
c. Handicapped?					
	Provide	111	26.2	71	24.7
	Do not provide	312	73.6	216	75.3
	Fees charged	1	0.2	0	0.0
d. Job seekers?					
	Provide	149	35.1	97	33.8
	Do not provide	274	64.6	190	66.2
	Fees charged	1	0.2	0	0.0
e. Labor groups?					
	Provide	39	9.2	21	7.3
	Do not provide	384	90.6	265	92.3
	Fees charged	1	0.2	1	0.3
f. Older adults?					
	Provide	225	53.1	155	54.0
	Do not provide	198	46.7	132	46.0
	Fees charged	1	0.2	0	0.0
g. Parents?					
	Provide	232	54.7	159	55.4
	Do not provide	191	45.0	128	44.6
	Fees charged	1	0.2	0	0.0
h. Minorities?					
	Provide	65	15.3	53	18.5
	Do not provide	359	84.7	234	81.5
	Fees charged	0	0.0	0	0.0
i. Other?					
	Provide	52	12.3	40	13.9
	Do not provide	372	87.7	247	86.1
	Fees charged	0	0.0	0	0.0
35. Provide to hospitals:					
	Provide	154	36.3	94	32.8
	Do not provide	270	63.7	193	67.2
	Fees charged	0	0.0	0	0.0
a. Materials on demand?					
	Provide	133	31.4	83	28.9
	Do not provide	291	68.6	203	70.7
	Fees charged	0	0.0	1	0.3

Table 11. QUESTIONNAIRE RESPONSE BY RESIDENTS OF OTHER ETHNIC ORIGIN
AS A PERCENTAGE OF TOTAL RESIDENTS
(POPULATION MEDIAN = 1 PERCENT). (Continued)

Does Your Library:		BELOW MEDIAN		ABOVE MEDIAN	
		NUMBER OF LIBRARIES	PERCENT	NUMBER OF LIBRARIES	PERCENT
35. Provide to hospitals: (Continued)					
b. Deposit collections?					
	Provide	66	15.6	36	12.5
	Do not provide	358	84.4	250	87.1
	Fees charged	0	0.0	1	0.3
c. Programming?					
	Provide	30	7.1	14	4.9
	Do not provide	394	92.9	273	95.1
	Fees charged	0	0.2	0	0.0
36. Provide to prisons:					
	Provide	135	31.8	95	33.1
	Do not provide	289	68.2	191	66.6
	Fees charged	0	0.0	1	0.3
a. Materials on demand?					
	Provide	107	25.2	91	31.7
	Do not provide	317	74.8	196	68.3
	Fees charged	0	0.0	0	0.0
b. Deposit collections?					
	Provide	98	23.1	62	21.6
	Do not provide	326	76.9	225	78.4
	Fees charged	0	0.0	0	0.0
c. Programming?					
	Provide	17	4.0	15	5.2
	Do not provide	407	96.0	272	94.8
	Fees charged	0	0.0	0	0.0
37. Provide to retirement/nursing homes:					
	Provide	318	75.0	199	69.3
	Do not provide	106	25.0	88	30.7
	Fees charged	0	0.0	0	0.0
a. Materials on demand?					
	Provide	303	71.3	195	67.9
	Do not provide	122	28.7	92	32.1
	Fees charged	0	0.0	0	0.0
b. Deposit collections?					
	Provide	231	54.4	117	40.8
	Do not provide	194	45.6	170	59.2
	Fees charged	0	0.0	0	0.0

Table 11. QUESTIONNAIRE RESPONSE BY RESIDENTS OF OTHER ETHNIC ORIGIN
AS A PERCENTAGE OF TOTAL RESIDENTS
(POPULATION MEDIAN = 1 PERCENT). (Continued)

Does Your Library:	BELOW MEDIAN		ABOVE MEDIAN	
	NUMBER OF LIBRARIES	PERCENT	NUMBER OF LIBRARIES	PERCENT
37. Provide to retirement/nursing homes: (Continued)				
c. Programming?				
Provide	145	34.1	984	29.3
Do not provide	280	65.9	202	70.4
Fees charged	0	0.0	1	0.3
38. Provide materials to homebound?				
Provide	286	67.3	202	70.4
Do not provide	139	32.7	85	29.6
Fees charged	0	0.0	0	0.0
39. Provide books by mail?				
Provide	109	25.6	75	26.1
Do not provide	316	74.4	212	73.9
Fees charged	0	0.0	0	0.0
40. Provide bookmobile service?				
Provide	170	40.0	106	36.9
Do not provide	255	60.0	181	63.1
Fees charged	0	0.0	0	0.0
a. Materials on demand?				
Provide	169	39.8	102	35.5
Do not provide	255	60.0	185	64.5
Fees charged	1	0.2	0	0.0
b. Programming?				
Provide	75	17.7	44	15.3
Do not provide	349	82.3	243	84.7
Fees charged	0	0.0	0	0.0
c. Publicize central library programming?				
Provide	171	40.2	99	34.5
Do not provide	254	59.8	188	65.5
Fees charged	0	0.0	0	0.0
41. Maintain information on community activities?				
Provide	372	87.5	266	92.7
Do not provide	53	12.5	21	7.3
Fees charged	0	0.0	0	0.0

Table 11. QUESTIONNAIRE RESPONSE BY RESIDENTS OF OTHER ETHNIC ORIGIN
AS A PERCENTAGE OF TOTAL RESIDENTS
(POPULATION MEDIAN = 1 PERCENT). (Continued)

Does Your Library:	BELOW MEDIAN		ABOVE MEDIAN	
	NUMBER OF LIBRARIES	PERCENT	NUMBER OF LIBRARIES	PERCENT
42. Maintain information about media resources other than those owned by the library?				
Provide	339	79.8	241	84.0
Do not provide	86	20.2	45	15.7
Fees charged	0	0.0	1	0.3
43. Maintain a human resources file?				
Provide	270	63.5	195	67.9
Do not provide	155	36.5	92	32.1
Fees charged	0	0.0	0	0.0
44. Maintain other resource files?				
Provide	183	43.1	138	48.1
Do not provide	242	56.9	149	51.9
Fees charged	0	0.0	0	0.0

Table 12. QUESTIONNAIRE RESPONSE BY RESIDENTS HAVING COMPLETED AT LEAST
TWELVE YEARS OF EDUCATION AS A PERCENTAGE OF TOTAL RESIDENTS
(POPULATION MEDIAN = 66 PERCENT).

Does Your Library:	BELOW MEDIAN		ABOVE MEDIAN	
	NUMBER OF LIBRARIES	PERCENT	NUMBER OF LIBRARIES	PERCENT
1. Display within the library exhibits based on materials owned by the library?				
Provide	516	95.9	583	97.5
Do not provide	22	4.1	15	2.5
Fees charged	0	0.0	0	0.0
2. Display within the library exhibits based on non-library materials?				
Provide	486	90.3	543	90.8
Do not provide	52	9.7	55	9.2
Fees charged	0	0.0	0	0.0
3. Display outside the library exhibits based on materials owned by the library?				
Provide	230	42.8	243	40.6
Do not provide	308	57.2	355	59.4
Fees charged	0	0.0	0	0.0
4. Circulate books in multiple copies for group use?				
Provide	215	40.0	255	42.6
Do not provide	323	60.0	343	57.4
Fees charged	0	0.0	0	0.0
5. Circulate microcomputers?				
Provide	27	5.0	40	6.7
Do not provide	508	94.4	552	92.3
Fees charged	3	0.6	6	1.0
6. Circulate microcomputer software?				
Provide	44	8.2	68	11.4
Do not provide	491	91.3	529	88.5
Fees charged	3	0.6	1	0.2
7. Circulate musical records?				
Provide	493	91.6	545	91.1
Do not provide	42	7.8	40	6.7
Fees charged	3	0.6	13	2.2
8. Circulate spoken records?				
Provide	477	88.7	543	90.8
Do not provide	58	10.8	45	7.5
Fees charged	3	0.6	10	1.7

Table 12. QUESTIONNAIRE RESPONSE BY RESIDENTS HAVING COMPLETED AT LEAST TWELVE YEARS OF EDUCATION AS A PERCENTAGE OF TOTAL RESIDENTS (POPULATION MEDIAN = 66 PERCENT). (Continued)

Does Your Library:	BELOW MEDIAN		ABOVE MEDIAN	
	NUMBER OF LIBRARIES	PERCENT	NUMBER OF LIBRARIES	PERCENT
9. Circulate musical tapes?				
Provide	359	66.7	456	76.3
Do not provide	178	33.1	136	22.7
Fees charged	1	0.2	6	1.0
10. Circulate spoken tapes?				
Provide	449	83.5	549	91.8
Do not provide	86	16.0	42	7.0
Fees charged	3	0.6	7	1.2
11. Circulate AV materials?				
Provide	446	82.9	479	80.1
Do not provide	84	15.6	98	16.4
Fees charged	8	1.5	21	3.5
12. Circulate films?				
Provide	389	72.3	405	67.7
Do not provide	115	21.4	147	24.6
Fees charged	34	6.3	46	7.7
13. Circulate videotapes?				
Provide	311	57.8	340	56.9
Do not provide	188	34.9	161	26.9
Fees charged	39	7.2	97	16.2
14 – 16. Circulate other?				
Provide	270	50.2	369	61.7
Do not provide	247	45.9	208	34.8
Fees charged	21	3.9	21	3.5
17. Provide reading lists or bibliographies?				
Provide	456	84.8	546	91.3
Do not provide	82	15.2	51	8.5
Fees charged	0	0.0	1	0.2
18. Provide interlibrary loan service?				
Provide	497	92.4	542	90.6
Do not provide	7	1.3	6	1.0
Fees charged	34	6.3	50	8.4
19. Provide AV equipment for in-library use?				
Provide	451	83.8	482	80.6
Do not provide	83	15.4	107	17.9
Fees charged	4	0.7	9	1.5

Table 12. QUESTIONNAIRE RESPONSE BY RESIDENTS HAVING COMPLETED AT LEAST TWELVE YEARS OF EDUCATION AS A PERCENTAGE OF TOTAL RESIDENTS (POPULATION MEDIAN = 66 PERCENT). (Continued)

Does Your Library:	BELOW MEDIAN		ABOVE MEDIAN	
	NUMBER OF LIBRARIES	PERCENT	NUMBER OF LIBRARIES	PERCENT
20. Provide microcomputer software for in-library use?				
Provide	153	28.4	251	42.0
Do not provide	381	70.8	341	57.0
Fees charged	4	0.7	6	1.0
21. Provide microcomputers for in-library use?				
Provide	151	28.1	243	40.6
Do not provide	371	69.0	323	54.0
Fees charged	16	3.0	32	5.4
22. Provide meeting or conference room space?				
Provide	429	79.7	465	77.8
Do not provide	71	13.2	86	14.4
Fees charged	38	7.1	47	7.9
23. Provide photocopy machines?				
Provide	376	69.9	405	67.7
Do not provide	12	2.2	8	1.3
Fees charged	150	27.9	185	30.9
24. Present book talks/reviews?				
Provide	378	70.3	449	75.1
Do not provide	159	29.6	147	24.6
Fees charged	1	0.2	2	0.3
25. Present live programs?				
Provide	444	82.5	516	86.3
Do not provide	93	17.3	82	13.7
Fees charged	1	0.2	0	0.0
26. Present radio programs?				
Provide	119	22.1	95	15.9
Do not provide	419	77.9	503	84.1
Fees charged	0	0.0	0	0.0
27. Present cable TV programs?				
Provide	70	13.0	133	22.2
Do not provide	467	86.8	465	77.8
Fees charged	1	0.2	0	0.0

Table 12. QUESTIONNAIRE RESPONSE BY RESIDENTS HAVING COMPLETED AT LEAST TWELVE YEARS OF EDUCATION AS A PERCENTAGE OF TOTAL RESIDENTS (POPULATION MEDIAN = 66 PERCENT). (Continued)

Does Your Library:	BELOW MEDIAN		ABOVE MEDIAN	
	NUMBER OF LIBRARIES	PERCENT	NUMBER OF LIBRARIES	PERCENT
28. Provide instruction to groups on library use?				
Provide	495	92.0	552	92.3
Do not provide	43	8.0	46	7.7
Fees charged	0	0.0	0	0.0
29. Provide instruction to individuals on library use?				
Provide	505	93.9	571	95.5
Do not provide	33	6.1	27	4.5
Fees charged	0	0.0	0	0.0
30. Provide literacy education to groups?				
Provide	118	21.9	106	17.7
Do not provide	419	77.9	492	82.3
Fees charged	1	0.2	0	0.0
31. Provide literacy education to individuals?				
Provide	174	32.3	168	28.1
Do not provide	363	67.5	430	71.9
Fees charged	1	0.2	0	0.0
32. Provide facilities for literacy education?				
Provide	371	69.0	400	66.9
Do not provide	166	30.9	197	32.9
Fees charged	1	0.2	1	0.2
33. Provide referral to another agency for literacy education?				
Provide	442	82.2	541	90.5
Do not provide	96	17.8	57	9.5
Fees charged	0	0.0	0	0.0
34. Organize programming for special groups:				
a. Business?				
Provide	181	33.6	280	46.8
Do not provide	355	65.9	315	52.7
Fees charged	3	0.6	3	0.5
b. Genealogists?				
Provide	244	45.4	239	40.0
Do not provide	292	54.3	358	59.9
Fees charged	2	0.4	1	0.2

Table 12. QUESTIONNAIRE RESPONSE BY RESIDENTS HAVING COMPLETED AT LEAST
TWELVE YEARS OF EDUCATION AS A PERCENTAGE OF TOTAL RESIDENTS
(POPULATION MEDIAN = 66 PERCENT). (Continued)

Does Your Library:		BELOW MEDIAN		ABOVE MEDIAN	
		NUMBER OF LIBRARIES	PERCENT	NUMBER OF LIBRARIES	PERCENT
34. Organize programming for special groups: (Continued)					
c. Handicapped?					
	Provide	152	27.1	156	24.5
	Do not provide	408	72.7	480	75.4
	Fees charged	1	0.2	1	0.2
d. Job seekers?					
	Provide	139	25.8	215	36.0
	Do not provide	398	74.0	383	64.0
	Fees charged	1	0.2	0	0.0
e. Labor groups?					
	Provide	33	6.1	49	8.2
	Do not provide	503	93.5	548	91.6
	Fees charged	2	0.4	1	0.2
f. Older adults?					
	Provide	261	48.5	322	53.8
	Do not provide	276	51.3	276	46.2
	Fees charged	1	0.2	0	0.0
g. Parents?					
	Provide	242	45.0	351	58.7
	Do not provide	295	54.8	247	41.3
	Fees charged	1	0.2	0	0.0
h. Minorities?					
	Provide	86	16.0	75	12.5
	Do not provide	452	84.0	523	87.5
	Fees charged	0	0.0	0	0.0
i. Other?					
	Provide	59	11.0	83	14.2
	Do not provide	478	88.8	499	85.6
	Fees charged	1	0.2	1	0.2
35. Provide to hospitals:					
	Provide	220	40.9	203	33.9
	Do not provide	318	59.1	395	66.1
	Fees charged	0	0.0	0	0.0
a. Materials on demand?					
	Provide	188	34.9	175	29.3
	Do not provide	350	65.1	422	70.6
	Fees charged	0	0.0	1	0.2

Table 12. QUESTIONNAIRE RESPONSE BY RESIDENTS HAVING COMPLETED AT LEAST TWELVE YEARS OF EDUCATION AS A PERCENTAGE OF TOTAL RESIDENTS (POPULATION MEDIAN = 66 PERCENT). (Continued)

		BELOW MEDIAN		ABOVE MEDIAN	
Does Your Library:		NUMBER OF LIBRARIES	PERCENT	NUMBER OF LIBRARIES	PERCENT
35. Provide to hospitals: (Continued)					
b. Deposit collections?					
	Provide	95	19.0	80	13.7
	Do not provide	405	81.0	502	86.1
	Fees charged	0	0.0	1	0.2
c. Programming?					
	Provide	48	8.9	32	5.4
	Do not provide	490	91.1	566	94.6
	Fees charged	0	0.0	0	0.0
36. Provide to prisons:					
	Provide	222	41.3	164	27.4
	Do not provide	316	58.7	433	72.4
	Fees charged	0	0.0	1	0.2
a. Materials on demand?					
	Provide	187	34.8	149	24.9
	Do not provide	351	65.2	449	75.1
	Fees charged	0	0.0	0	0.0
b. Deposit collections?					
	Provide	150	27.9	109	18.2
	Do not provide	388	72.1	489	81.8
	Fees charged	0	0.0	0	0.0
c. Programming?					
	Provide	22	4.1	24	4.0
	Do not provide	516	95.9	574	96.0
	Fees charged	0	0.0	0	0.0
37. Provide to retirement/nursing homes?					
	Provide	399	74.2	440	73.6
	Do not provide	139	25.8	158	26.4
	Fees charged	0	0.0	0	0.0
a. Materials on demand?					
	Provide	372	69.0	425	71.1
	Do not provide	167	31.0	173	28.9
	Fees charged	0	0.0	0	0.0
b. Deposit collections?					
	Provide	258	47.9	300	50.2
	Do not provide	281	52.1	298	49.8
	Fees charged	0	0.0	0	0.0

Table 12. QUESTIONNAIRE RESPONSE BY RESIDENTS HAVING COMPLETED AT LEAST
TWELVE YEARS OF EDUCATION AS A PERCENTAGE OF TOTAL RESIDENTS
(POPULATION MEDIAN = 66 PERCENT). (Continued)

Does Your Library:	BELOW MEDIAN		ABOVE MEDIAN	
	NUMBER OF LIBRARIES	PERCENT	NUMBER OF LIBRARIES	PERCENT
37. Provide to retirement/nursing homes: (Continued) c. Programming?				
Provide	186	34.5	178	29.8
Do not provide	353	65.5	419	70.1
Fees charged	0	0.0	1	0.2
38. Provide materials to homebound?				
Provide	350	64.9	421	70.4
Do not provide	189	35.1	177	29.6
Fees charged	0	0.0	0	0.0
39. Provide books by mail?				
Provide	133	24.7	145	24.2
Do not provide	405	75.1	452	75.6
Fees charged	1	0.2	1	0.2
40. Provide bookmobile service?				
Provide	262	48.6	194	32.4
Do not provide	277	51.4	403	67.4
Fees charged	0	0.0	1	0.2
a. Materials on demand?				
Provide	259	48.1	194	32.4
Do not provide	280	51.9	403	67.4
Fees charged	0	0.0	1	0.2
b. Programming?				
Provide	97	18.0	84	14.0
Do not provide	441	81.8	514	86.0
Fees charged	1	0.2	0	0.0
c. Publicize central library programming?				
Provide	237	44.0	199	33.3
Do not provide	302	56.0	399	66.7
Fees charged	0	0.0	0	0.0
41. Maintain information on community activities?				
Provide	437	81.1	557	93.1
Do not provide	102	18.9	41	6.9
Fees charged	0	0.0	0	0.0

Table 12.   QUESTIONNAIRE RESPONSE BY RESIDENTS HAVING COMPLETED AT LEAST
TWELVE YEARS OF EDUCATION AS A PERCENTAGE OF TOTAL RESIDENTS
(POPULATION MEDIAN = 66 PERCENT). (Continued)

Does Your Library:	BELOW MEDIAN		ABOVE MEDIAN	
	NUMBER OF LIBRARIES	PERCENT	NUMBER OF LIBRARIES	PERCENT
42. Maintain information about media resources other than those owned by the library?				
Provide	407	75.5	501	83.8
Do not provide	132	24.5	96	16.1
Fees charged	0	0.0	1	0.2
43. Maintain a human resources file?				
Provide	294	54.4	391	65.4
Do not provide	245	45.5	207	34.6
Fees charged	0	0.0	0	0.0
44. Maintain other resource files?				
Provide	204	37.9	262	44.9
Do not provide	334	62.1	320	54.9
Fees charged	0	0.0	1	0.2

Table 13. QUESTIONNAIRE RESPONSE BY RESIDENTS HAVING COMPLETED AT LEAST SIXTEEN YEARS OF EDUCATION AS A PERCENTAGE OF TOTAL RESIDENTS (POPULATION MEDIAN = 14 PERCENT).

Does Your Library:	BELOW MEDIAN		ABOVE MEDIAN	
	NUMBER OF LIBRARIES	PERCENT	NUMBER OF LIBRARIES	PERCENT
1. Display within the library exhibits based on materials owned by the library?				
Provide	472	95.2	613	97.9
Do not provide	24	4.8	13	2.1
Fees charged	0	0.0	0	0.0
2. Display within the library exhibits based on non-library materials?				
Provide	447	90.1	572	91.3
Do not provide	49	9.9	54	8.6
Fees charged	0	0.0	0	0.0
3. Display outside the library exhibits based on materials owned by the library?				
Provide	207	41.7	261	41.7
Do not provide	289	58.3	365	58.3
Fees charged	0	0.0	0	0.0
4. Circulate books in multiple copies for group use?				
Provide	192	38.7	274	43.8
Do not provide	304	61.3	352	56.2
Fees charged	0	0.0	0	0.0
5. Circulate microcomputers?				
Provide	23	4.6	43	6.9
Do not provide	470	94.8	577	92.2
Fees charged	3	0.6	6	1.1
6. Circulate microcomputer software?				
Provide	41	8.3	67	10.7
Do not provide	453	91.3	557	89.0
Fees charged	2	0.4	2	0.3
7. Circulate musical records?				
Provide	458	92.3	567	90.6
Do not provide	35	7.1	47	7.3
Fees charged	3	0.6	13	2.1
8. Circulate spoken records?				
Provide	438	88.3	569	90.9
Do not provide	55	11.1	47	7.2
Fees charged	3	0.6	10	1.6

Table 13. QUESTIONNAIRE RESPONSE BY RESIDENTS HAVING COMPLETED AT LEAST SIXTEEN YEARS OF EDUCATION AS A PERCENTAGE OF TOTAL RESIDENTS (POPULATION MEDIAN = 14 PERCENT). (Continued)

Does Your Library:	BELOW MEDIAN		ABOVE MEDIAN	
	NUMBER OF LIBRARIES	PERCENT	NUMBER OF LIBRARIES	PERCENT
9. Circulate musical tapes?				
Provide	335	67.5	469	74.9
Do not provide	160	32.3	151	24.1
Fees charged	1	0.2	6	1.0
10. Circulate spoken tapes?				
Provide	413	83.3	572	91.4
Do not provide	80	16.1	47	7.5
Fees charged	3	0.6	7	1.1
11. Circulate AV materials?				
Provide	409	82.5	503	80.4
Do not provide	78	15.7	103	16.5
Fees charged	9	1.8	20	3.2
12. Circulate films?				
Provide	352	71.0	432	69.0
Do not provide	109	22.0	149	23.8
Fees charged	35	7.1	45	7.2
13. Circulate videotapes?				
Provide	283	57.1	360	57.5
Do not provide	169	34.1	175	28.0
Fees charged	44	8.9	91	14.5
14 – 16. Circulate other?				
Provide	240	48.4	392	62.6
Do not provide	238	48.0	210	33.5
Fees charged	18	3.6	24	3.8
17. Provide reading lists or bibliographies?				
Provide	414	83.5	575	91.9
Do not provide	82	16.5	50	8.0
Fees charged	0	0.0	1	0.2
18. Provide interlibrary loan service?				
Provide	451	90.9	577	92.2
Do not provide	7	1.4	5	0.8
Fees charged	38	7.7	44	7.0
19. Provide AV equipment for in-library use?				
Provide	410	82.7	511	81.6
Do not provide	83	16.7	105	16.8
Fees charged	3	0.6	10	1.6

Table 13. QUESTIONNAIRE RESPONSE BY RESIDENTS HAVING COMPLETED AT LEAST SIXTEEN YEARS OF EDUCATION AS A PERCENTAGE OF TOTAL RESIDENTS (POPULATION MEDIAN = 14 PERCENT). (Continued)

Does Your Library:	BELOW MEDIAN		ABOVE MEDIAN	
	NUMBER OF LIBRARIES	PERCENT	NUMBER OF LIBRARIES	PERCENT
20. Provide microcomputer software for in-library use?				
Provide	142	28.6	254	40.6
Do not provide	350	70.6	367	58.6
Fees charged	4	0.8	5	0.8
21. Provide microcomputers for in-library use?				
Provide	144	29.0	242	38.7
Do not provide	339	68.3	350	55.9
Fees charged	13	2.6	34	5.4
22. Provide meeting or conference room space?				
Provide	391	78.8	493	78.8
Do not provide	73	14.7	80	12.8
Fees charged	32	6.5	53	8.5
23. Provide photocopy machines?				
Provide	342	69.0	429	68.5
Do not provide	12	2.4	7	1.1
Fees charged	142	28.6	190	30.4
24. Present book talks/reviews?				
Provide	343	69.2	472	75.4
Do not provide	151	30.4	153	24.4
Fees charged	2	0.4	1	0.2
25. Present live programs?				
Provide	400	80.6	552	88.2
Do not provide	95	19.2	74	11.8
Fees charged	1	0.2	0	0.0
26. Present radio programs?				
Provide	113	22.8	99	15.8
Do not provide	383	77.2	527	84.8
Fees charged	0	0.0	0	0.0
27. Present cable TV programs?				
Provide	64	12.9	138	22.0
Do not provide	431	86.9	488	78.0
Fees charged	1	0.2	0	0.0

Table 13. QUESTIONNAIRE RESPONSE BY RESIDENTS HAVING COMPLETED AT LEAST SIXTEEN YEARS OF EDUCATION AS A PERCENTAGE OF TOTAL RESIDENTS (POPULATION MEDIAN = 14 PERCENT). (Continued)

Does Your Library:	BELOW MEDIAN		ABOVE MEDIAN	
	NUMBER OF LIBRARIES	PERCENT	NUMBER OF LIBRARIES	PERCENT
28. Provide instruction to groups on library use?				
Provide	459	92.5	575	91.9
Do not provide	37	7.5	51	8.1
Fees charged	0	0.0	0	0.0
29. Provide instruction to individuals on library use?				
Provide	466	94.0	596	95.2
Do not provide	30	6.0	30	4.8
Fees charged	0	0.0	0	0.0
30. Provide literacy education to groups?				
Provide	111	22.4	107	17.1
Do not provide	384	77.4	519	82.9
Fees charged	1	0.2	0	0.0
31. Provide literacy education to individuals?				
Provide	152	30.6	184	29.4
Do not provide	343	69.2	442	70.6
Fees charged	1	0.2	0	0.0
32. Provide facilities for literacy education?				
Provide	335	67.5	426	68.1
Do not provide	160	32.3	199	31.8
Fees charged	1	0.2	1	0.2
33. Provide referral to another agency for literacy education?				
Provide	408	82.3	562	89.8
Do not provide	88	17.7	64	10.2
Fees charged	0	0.0	0	0.0
34. Organize programming for special groups:				
a. Business?				
Provide	165	33.2	292	46.6
Do not provide	330	66.4	330	52.7
Fees charged	2	0.4	4	0.6
b. Genealogists?				
Provide	225	45.4	255	40.7
Do not provide	269	54.2	370	59.1
Fees charged	2	0.4	1	0.2

Table 13. QUESTIONNAIRE RESPONSE BY RESIDENTS HAVING COMPLETED AT LEAST SIXTEEN YEARS OF EDUCATION AS A PERCENTAGE OF TOTAL RESIDENTS (POPULATION MEDIAN = 14 PERCENT). (Continued)

Does Your Library:		BELOW MEDIAN		ABOVE MEDIAN	
		NUMBER OF LIBRARIES	PERCENT	NUMBER OF LIBRARIES	PERCENT
34. Organize programming for special groups: (Continued)					
c. Handicapped?					
	Provide	126	25.4	166	26.5
	Do not provide	369	74.4	459	73.3
	Fees charged	1	0.2	1	0.2
d. Job seekers?					
	Provide	125	25.2	225	35.9
	Do not provide	371	74.8	400	63.9
	Fees charged	0	0.0	1	0.2
e. Labor groups?					
	Provide	31	6.3	51	8.1
	Do not provide	465	93.8	572	91.4
	Fees charged	0	0.0	3	0.5
f. Older adults?					
	Provide	232	46.8	347	55.4
	Do not provide	264	53.2	278	44.4
	Fees charged	0	0.0	1	0.2
g. Parents?					
	Provide	228	46.0	360	57.5
	Do not provide	268	54.0	265	42.3
	Fees charged	0	0.0	1	0.2
h. Minorities?					
	Provide	70	14.1	90	14.4
	Do not provide	426	85.9	536	85.6
	Fees charged	0	0.0	0	0.0
i. Other?					
	Provide	49	9.9	93	14.9
	Do not provide	446	89.9	532	85.0
	Fees charged	1	0.2	1	0.2
35. Provide to hospitals:					
	Provide	213	42.9	206	32.9
	Do not provide	283	57.1	420	67.1
	Fees charged	0	0.0	0	0.0
a. Materials on demand?					
	Provide	185	37.3	174	27.8
	Do not provide	311	62.7	451	72.0
	Fees charged	0	0.0	1	0.2

Table 13. QUESTIONNAIRE RESPONSE BY RESIDENTS HAVING COMPLETED AT LEAST SIXTEEN YEARS OF EDUCATION AS A PERCENTAGE OF TOTAL RESIDENTS (POPULATION MEDIAN = 14 PERCENT). (Continued)

Does Your Library:		BELOW MEDIAN		ABOVE MEDIAN	
		NUMBER OF LIBRARIES	PERCENT	NUMBER OF LIBRARIES	PERCENT
35. Provide to hospitals: (Continued)					
b. Deposit collections?					
	Provide	85	18.2	88	14.6
	Do not provide	381	81.8	514	85.2
	Fees charged	0	0.0	1	0.2
c. Programming?					
	Provide	36	7.3	43	6.9
	Do not provide	460	92.7	583	93.1
	Fees charged	0	0.0	0	0.0
36. Provide to prisons:					
	Provide	212	42.7	171	27.3
	Do not provide	284	57.3	454	72.5
	Fees charged	0	0.0	1	0.2
a. Materials on demand?					
	Provide	181	36.5	154	24.6
	Do not provide	315	63.5	472	75.4
	Fees charged	0	0.0	0	0.0
b. Deposit collections?					
	Provide	139	28.0	117	18.7
	Do not provide	357	72.0	509	81.3
	Fees charged	0	0.0	0	0.0
c. Programming?					
	Provide	16	3.2	29	4.6
	Do not provide	480	96.8	597	95.4
	Fees charged	0	0.0	0	0.0
37. Provide to retirement/nursing homes:					
	Provide	379	76.4	450	71.9
	Do not provide	117	23.6	176	28.1
	Fees charged	0	0.0	0	0.0
a. Materials on demand?					
	Provide	359	72.2	429	68.5
	Do not provide	138	27.8	197	31.5
	Fees charged	0	0.0	0	0.0
b. Deposit collections?					
	Provide	253	50.9	299	47.8
	Do not provide	244	49.1	327	52.2
	Fees charged	0	0.0	0	0.0

Table 13. QUESTIONNAIRE RESPONSE BY RESIDENTS HAVING COMPLETED AT LEAST SIXTEEN YEARS OF EDUCATION AS A PERCENTAGE OF TOTAL RESIDENTS (POPULATION MEDIAN = 14 PERCENT). (Continued)

Does Your Library:	BELOW MEDIAN		ABOVE MEDIAN	
	NUMBER OF LIBRARIES	PERCENT	NUMBER OF LIBRARIES	PERCENT
37. Provide to retirement/nursing homes: (Continued)				
c. Programming?				
Provide	159	32.0	202	32.3
Do not provide	338	68.0	423	67.6
Fees charged	0	0.0	1	0.2
38. Provide materials to homebound?				
Provide	333	67.0	430	68.7
Do not provide	164	33.0	196	31.3
Fees charged	0	0.0	0	0.0
39. Provide books by mail?				
Provide	128	25.8	148	23.6
Do not provide	368	74.0	478	76.4
Fees charged	1	0.2	0	0.0
40. Provide bookmobile service?				
Provide	239	48.1	213	34.0
Do not provide	258	51.9	412	65.8
Fees charged	0	0.0	1	0.2
a. Materials on demand?				
Provide	237	47.7	212	33.9
Do not provide	260	52.3	413	66.0
Fees charged	0	0.0	1	0.2
b. Programming?				
Provide	92	18.5	88	14.1
Do not provide	404	81.3	538	85.9
Fees charged	0	0.0	0	0.0
c. Publicize central library programming?				
Provide	218	43.9	213	34.0
Do not provide	279	56.1	413	66.0
Fees charged	0	0.0	0	0.0
41. Maintain information on community activities?				
Provide	408	82.1	576	92.0
Do not provide	89	17.9	50	8.0
Fees charged	0	0.0	0	0.0

Table 13. QUESTIONNAIRE RESPONSE BY RESIDENTS HAVING COMPLETED AT LEAST
SIXTEEN YEARS OF EDUCATION AS A PERCENTAGE OF TOTAL RESIDENTS
(POPULATION MEDIAN = 14 PERCENT). (Continued)

Does Your Library:	BELOW MEDIAN		ABOVE MEDIAN	
	NUMBER OF LIBRARIES	PERCENT	NUMBER OF LIBRARIES	PERCENT
42. Maintain information about media resources other than those owned by the library?				
Provide	375	75.5	524	83.7
Do not provide	122	24.5	101	16.1
Fees charged	0	0.0	1	0.2
43. Maintain a human resources file?				
Provide	263	52.9	418	66.8
Do not provide	234	47.1	208	33.2
Fees charged	0	0.0	0	0.0
44. Maintain other resource files?				
Provide	174	35.1	290	46.3
Do not provide	322	64.9	335	53.5
Fees charged	0	0.0	1	0.2

Table 14. QUESTIONNAIRE RESPONSE BY RESIDENTS AGED SIXTY-FIVE OR OLDER
AS A PERCENTAGE OF TOTAL RESIDENTS
(POPULATION MEDIAN = 12 PERCENT).

Does Your Library:	BELOW MEDIAN		ABOVE MEDIAN	
	NUMBER OF LIBRARIES	PERCENT	NUMBER OF LIBRARIES	PERCENT
1. Display within the library exhibits based on materials owned by the library?				
Provide	518	96.3	578	97.1
Do not provide	20	3.7	17	2.9
Fees charged	0	0.0	0	0.0
2. Display within the library exhibits based on non-library materials?				
Provide	485	90.1	542	91.1
Do not provide	53	9.9	53	8.9
Fees charged	0	0.0	0	0.0
3. Display outside the library exhibits based on materials owned by the library?				
Provide	225	41.8	247	41.5
Do not provide	313	58.2	348	58.5
Fees charged	0	0.0	0	0.0
4. Circulate books in multiple copies for group use?				
Provide	229	42.6	241	40.5
Do not provide	309	57.4	354	59.5
Fees charged	0	0.0	0	0.0
5. Circulate microcomputers?				
Provide	34	6.3	32	5.4
Do not provide	496	92.2	562	94.5
Fees charged	8	1.5	1	0.2
6. Circulate microcomputer software?				
Provide	51	9.5	61	10.3
Do not provide	485	90.1	532	89.6
Fees charged	2	0.4	2	0.3
7. Circulate musical records?				
Provide	494	91.8	541	90.9
Do not provide	38	7.1	44	7.4
Fees charged	6	1.1	10	1.7
8. Circulate spoken records?				
Provide	492	91.4	525	88.2
Do not provide	41	7.6	62	10.4
Fees charged	5	0.9	8	1.3

Table 14. QUESTIONNAIRE RESPONSE BY RESIDENTS AGED SIXTY-FIVE OR OLDER
AS A PERCENTAGE OF TOTAL RESIDENTS
(POPULATION MEDIAN = 12 PERCENT). (Continued)

Does Your Library:	BELOW MEDIAN		ABOVE MEDIAN	
	NUMBER OF LIBRARIES	PERCENT	NUMBER OF LIBRARIES	PERCENT
9. Circulate musical tapes?				
Provide	386	71.7	426	71.6
Do not provide	150	27.9	164	27.6
Fees charged	2	0.4	5	0.8
10. Circulate spoken tapes?				
Provide	485	90.1	510	85.7
Do not provide	49	9.1	79	13.3
Fees charged	4	0.7	6	1.0
11. Circulate AV materials?				
Provide	432	80.3	491	82.5
Do not provide	89	16.5	92	15.5
Fees charged	17	3.2	12	2.0
12. Circulate films?				
Provide	374	69.5	417	70.1
Do not provide	124	23.0	138	23.2
Fees charged	40	7.4	40	6.7
13. Circulate videotapes?				
Provide	311	57.8	338	56.8
Do not provide	158	29.4	190	31.9
Fees charged	69	12.8	67	11.3
14 – 16. Circulate other?				
Provide	310	57.6	328	55.1
Do not provide	203	37.7	250	42.0
Fees charged	25	4.7	17	2.9
17. Provide reading lists or bibliographies?				
Provide	485	90.1	514	86.4
Do not provide	52	9.7	81	13.6
Fees charged	1	0.2	0	0.0
18. Provide interlibrary loan service?				
Provide	484	90.0	552	92.8
Do not provide	7	1.3	6	1.0
Fees charged	47	8.7	37	6.2
19. Provide AV equipment for in-library use?				
Provide	439	81.6	491	82.5
Do not provide	90	16.7	100	16.8
Fees charged	9	1.7	4	0.7

Table 14. QUESTIONNAIRE RESPONSE BY RESIDENTS AGED SIXTY-FIVE OR OLDER
AS A PERCENTAGE OF TOTAL RESIDENTS
(POPULATION MEDIAN = 12 PERCENT). (Continued)

Does Your Library:	BELOW MEDIAN		ABOVE MEDIAN	
	NUMBER OF LIBRARIES	PERCENT	NUMBER OF LIBRARIES	PERCENT
20. Provide microcomputer software for in-library use?				
Provide	191	35.5	212	35.6
Do not provide	344	63.9	376	63.2
Fees charged	3	0.6	7	1.2
21. Provide microcomputers for in-library use?				
Provide	190	35.3	203	34.1
Do not provide	328	61.0	364	61.2
Fees charged	20	3.7	28	4.7
22. Provide meeting or conference room space?				
Provide	424	78.8	468	78.7
Do not provide	76	14.1	81	13.6
Fees charged	38	7.1	46	7.7
23. Provide photocopy machines?				
Provide	371	69.0	409	68.7
Do not provide	11	2.0	9	1.5
Fees charged	156	29.0	177	29.7
24. Present book talks/reviews?				
Provide	379	70.4	445	74.8
Do not provide	158	29.4	148	24.9
Fees charged	1	0.2	2	0.3
25. Present live programs?				
Provide	452	84.0	505	84.9
Do not provide	85	15.8	90	15.1
Fees charged	1	0.2	0	0.0
26. Present radio programs?				
Provide	79	14.7	134	22.5
Do not provide	459	85.3	461	77.5
Fees charged	0	0.0	0	0.0
27. Present cable TV programs?				
Provide	102	19.0	101	17.0
Do not provide	435	80.9	494	83.0
Fees charged	1	0.2	0	0.0

Table 14. QUESTIONNAIRE RESPONSE BY RESIDENTS AGED SIXTY-FIVE OR OLDER
AS A PERCENTAGE OF TOTAL RESIDENTS
(POPULATION MEDIAN = 12 PERCENT). (Continued)

Does Your Library:	BELOW MEDIAN		ABOVE MEDIAN	
	NUMBER OF LIBRARIES	PERCENT	NUMBER OF LIBRARIES	PERCENT
28. Provide instruction to groups on library use?				
Provide	497	92.4	547	91.9
Do not provide	41	7.6	48	8.1
Fees charged	0	0.0	0	0.0
29. Provide instruction to individuals on library use?				
Provide	515	95.7	558	93.8
Do not provide	23	4.3	37	6.2
Fees charged	0	0.0	0	0.0
30. Provide literacy education to groups?				
Provide	101	18.8	122	20.5
Do not provide	436	81.0	473	79.5
Fees charged	1	0.2	0	0.0
31. Provide literacy education to individuals?				
Provide	154	28.6	187	31.4
Do not provide	383	71.2	408	68.6
Fees charged	1	0.2	0	0.0
32. Provide facilities for literacy education?				
Provide	354	65.8	416	69.9
Do not provide	182	33.8	179	30.1
Fees charged	2	0.4	0	0.0
33. Provide referral to another agency for literacy education?				
Provide	474	88.1	506	85.0
Do not provide	64	11.9	89	15.0
Fees charged	0	0.0	0	0.0
34. Organize programming for special groups:				
a. Business?				
Provide	218	40.5	241	40.4
Do not provide	317	58.9	352	59.1
Fees charged	3	0.6	3	0.6
b. Genealogists?				
Provide	233	43.3	248	41.7
Do not provide	304	56.5	345	58.0
Fees charged	1	0.2	2	0.3

Table 14. QUESTIONNAIRE RESPONSE BY RESIDENTS AGED SIXTY-FIVE OR OLDER
AS A PERCENTAGE OF TOTAL RESIDENTS
(POPULATION MEDIAN = 12 PERCENT). (Continued)

Does Your Library:		BELOW MEDIAN		ABOVE MEDIAN	
		NUMBER OF LIBRARIES	PERCENT	NUMBER OF LIBRARIES	PERCENT
34. Organize programming for special groups: (Continued)					
c. Handicapped?					
	Provide	127	23.6	165	27.7
	Do not provide	410	76.2	429	72.1
	Fees charged	1	0.2	1	0.2
d. Job seekers?					
	Provide	169	31.4	184	30.9
	Do not provide	368	68.4	411	69.1
	Fees charged	1	0.2	0	0.0
e. Labor groups?					
	Provide	31	5.8	51	8.6
	Do not provide	505	93.9	543	91.3
	Fees charged	2	0.4	1	0.2
f. Older adults?					
	Provide	277	51.5	303	50.9
	Do not provide	260	48.3	292	49.1
	Fees charged	1	0.2	0	0.0
g. Parents?					
	Provide	296	55.0	296	49.7
	Do not provide	241	44.8	299	50.3
	Fees charged	1	0.2	0	0.0
h. Minorities?					
	Provide	70	13.0	90	15.1
	Do not provide	468	87.0	505	84.9
	Fees charged	0	0.0	0	0.0
i. Other?					
	Provide	70	13.0	72	12.1
	Do not provide	466	86.6	523	87.9
	Fees charged	2	0.4	0	0.0
35. Provide to hospitals:					
	Provide	196	36.4	226	38.0
	Do not provide	342	63.6	369	62.0
	Fees charged	0	0.0	0	0.0
a. Materials on demand?					
	Provide	166	30.9	197	33.1
	Do not provide	372	69.1	397	66.7
	Fees charged	0	0.0	1	0.2

Table 14. QUESTIONNAIRE RESPONSE BY RESIDENTS AGED SIXTY-FIVE OR OLDER
AS A PERCENTAGE OF TOTAL RESIDENTS
(POPULATION MEDIAN = 12 PERCENT). (Continued)

Does Your Library:		BELOW MEDIAN		ABOVE MEDIAN	
		NUMBER OF LIBRARIES	PERCENT	NUMBER OF LIBRARIES	PERCENT
35. Provide to hospitals: (Continued)					
b. Deposit collections?					
	Provide	79	15.2	95	17.0
	Do not provide	441	84.8	464	82.9
	Fees charged	0	0.0	1	0.2
c. Programming?					
	Provide	28	5.2	52	8.7
	Do not provide	510	94.8	543	91.3
	Fees charged	0	0.0	0	0.0
36. Provide to prisons:					
	Provide	184	34.2	200	33.6
	Do not provide	353	65.6	395	66.4
	Fees charged	1	0.2	0	0.0
a. Materials on demand?					
	Provide	154	28.6	181	30.4
	Do not provide	384	71.4	414	69.6
	Fees charged	0	0.0	0	0.0
b. Deposit collections?					
	Provide	127	23.6	131	22.0
	Do not provide	411	76.4	464	78.0
	Fees charged	0	0.0	0	0.0
c. Programming?					
	Provide	18	3.3	28	4.7
	Do not provide	520	96.7	567	95.3
	Fees charged	0	0.0	0	0.0
37. Provide to retirement/nursing homes:					
	Provide	401	74.5	435	73.1
	Do not provide	137	25.5	160	26.9
	Fees charged	0	0.0	0	0.0
a. Materials on demand?					
	Provide	379	70.4	415	69.6
	Do not provide	159	29.6	181	30.4
	Fees charged	0	0.0	0	0.0
b. Deposit collections?					
	Provide	248	46.1	308	51.7
	Do not provide	290	53.9	288	48.3
	Fees charged	0	0.0	0	0.0

Table 14. QUESTIONNAIRE RESPONSE BY RESIDENTS AGED SIXTY-FIVE OR OLDER
AS A PERCENTAGE OF TOTAL RESIDENTS
(POPULATION MEDIAN = 12 PERCENT). (Continued)

Does Your Library:	BELOW MEDIAN		ABOVE MEDIAN	
	NUMBER OF LIBRARIES	PERCENT	NUMBER OF LIBRARIES	PERCENT
37. Provide to retirement/nursing homes: (Continued)				
c. Programming?				
Provide	183	34.0	179	30.0
Do not provide	355	66.0	416	69.8
Fees charged	0	0.0	1	0.2
38. Provide materials to homebound?				
Provide	366	68.0	403	67.6
Do not provide	172	32.0	193	32.4
Fees charged	0	0.0	0	0.0
39. Provide books by mail?				
Provide	116	21.6	160	26.8
Do not provide	421	78.3	435	73.0
Fees charged	1	0.2	1	0.2
40. Provide bookmobile service?				
Provide	221	41.1	234	39.3
Do not provide	317	58.9	361	60.6
Fees charged	0	0.0	1	0.2
a. Materials on demand?				
Provide	216	40.1	236	39.6
Do not provide	321	59.7	360	60.4
Fees charged	1	0.2	0	0.0
b. Programming?				
Provide	84	15.6	96	16.1
Do not provide	454	84.4	499	83.7
Fees charged	0	0.0	0	0.0
c. Publicize central library programming?				
Provide	213	39.6	222	37.2
Do not provide	325	60.4	374	62.8
Fees charged	0	0.0	0	0.0
41. Maintain information on community activities?				
Provide	482	89.6	510	85.6
Do not provide	56	10.4	86	14.4
Fees charged	0	0.0	0	0.0

Table 14. QUESTIONNAIRE RESPONSE BY RESIDENTS AGED SIXTY-FIVE OR OLDER
AS A PERCENTAGE OF TOTAL RESIDENTS
(POPULATION MEDIAN = 12 PERCENT). (Continued)

Does Your Library:	BELOW MEDIAN		ABOVE MEDIAN	
	NUMBER OF LIBRARIES	PERCENT	NUMBER OF LIBRARIES	PERCENT
42. Maintain information about media resources other than those owned by the library?				
Provide	445	82.7	461	77.3
Do not provide	92	17.1	135	22.7
Fees charged	1	0.2	0	0.0
43. Maintain a human resources file?				
Provide	338	62.8	345	57.9
Do not provide	200	37.2	251	42.1
Fees charged	0	0.0	0	0.0
44. Maintain other resource files?				
Provide	239	44.4	227	38.2
Do not provide	298	55.4	368	61.8
Fees charged	1	0.2	0	0.0

Table 15. QUESTIONNAIRE RESPONSES BY HOUSEHOLDS BELOW POVERTY LEVEL
AS A PERCENTAGE OF TOTAL HOUSEHOLDS
(POPULATION MEDIAN = 9 PERCENT).

Does Your Library:	BELOW MEDIAN		ABOVE MEDIAN	
	NUMBER OF LIBRARIES	PERCENT	NUMBER OF LIBRARIES	PERCENT
1. Display within the library exhibits based on materials owned by the library?				
Provide	495	98.0	601	95.7
Do not provide	10	2.0	27	4.3
Fees charged	0	0.0	0	0.0
2. Display within the library exhibits based on non-library materials?				
Provide	461	91.3	565	90.0
Do not provide	44	8.7	63	10.0
Fees charged	0	0.0	0	0.0
3. Display outside the library exhibits based on materials owned by the library?				
Provide	204	40.4	267	42.5
Do not provide	301	59.6	361	57.5
Fees charged	0	0.0	0	0.0
4. Circulate books in multiple copies for group use?				
Provide	225	44.6	243	38.7
Do not provide	280	55.4	385	61.3
Fees charged	0	0.0	0	0.0
5. Circulate microcomputers?				
Provide	37	7.3	30	4.8
Do not provide	459	90.9	598	95.2
Fees charged	9	1.8	0	0.0
6. Circulate microcomputer software?				
Provide	65	12.9	47	7.5
Do not provide	438	86.7	579	92.2
Fees charged	2	0.4	2	0.3
7. Circulate musical records?				
Provide	466	92.3	570	90.8
Do not provide	29	5.7	52	8.3
Fees charged	10	2.0	6	1.0
8. Circulate spoken records?				
Provide	462	91.5	556	88.5
Do not provide	35	6.9	67	10.7
Fees charged	8	1.6	5	0.8

Table 15. QUESTIONNAIRE RESPONSES BY HOUSEHOLDS BELOW POVERTY LEVEL
AS A PERCENTAGE OF TOTAL HOUSEHOLDS
(POPULATION MEDIAN = 9 PERCENT). (Continued)

Does Your Library:	BELOW MEDIAN		ABOVE MEDIAN	
	NUMBER OF LIBRARIES	PERCENT	NUMBER OF LIBRARIES	PERCENT
9. Circulate musical tapes?				
Provide	376	74.5	436	69.4
Do not provide	125	24.8	189	30.1
Fees charged	4	0.8	3	0.5
10. Circulate spoken tapes?				
Provide	459	90.9	536	85.4
Do not provide	41	8.1	87	13.9
Fees charged	5	1.0	5	0.8
11. Circulate AV materials?				
Provide	411	81.4	512	81.5
Do not provide	75	14.9	106	16.9
Fees charged	19	3.8	10	1.6
12. Circulate films?				
Provide	353	69.9	440	70.1
Do not provide	106	21.0	155	24.7
Fees charged	46	9.1	33	5.3
13. Circulate videotapes?				
Provide	301	59.6	348	55.4
Do not provide	110	21.8	239	38.1
Fees charged	94	18.6	41	6.5
14 – 16. Circulate other?				
Provide	325	64.3	314	50.0
Do not provide	150	31.3	294	46.8
Fees charged	22	4.4	20	3.2
17. Provide reading lists or bibliographies?				
Provide	462	91.5	537	85.5
Do not provide	42	8.3	91	14.5
Fees charged	1	0.2	0	0.0
18. Provide interlibrary loan service?				
Provide	463	91.7	574	91.4
Do not provide	3	0.6	10	1.6
Fees charged	39	7.7	44	7.0
19. Provide AV equipment for in-library use?				
Provide	411	81.4	519	82.6
Do not provide	87	17.2	103	16.4
Fees charged	7	1.4	6	1.0

Table 15. QUESTIONNAIRE RESPONSES BY HOUSEHOLDS BELOW POVERTY LEVEL
AS A PERCENTAGE OF TOTAL HOUSEHOLDS
(POPULATION MEDIAN = 9 PERCENT). (Continued)

Does Your Library:	BELOW MEDIAN		ABOVE MEDIAN	
	NUMBER OF LIBRARIES	PERCENT	NUMBER OF LIBRARIES	PERCENT
20. Provide microcomputer software for in-library use?				
Provide	212	42.0	192	30.6
Do not provide	289	57.2	430	68.5
Fees charged	4	0.8	6	1.0
21. Provide microcomputers for in-library use?				
Provide	202	40.0	192	30.6
Do not provide	275	54.5	416	66.2
Fees charged	28	5.5	20	3.2
22. Provide meeting or conference room space?				
Provide	402	79.6	490	78.0
Do not provide	57	11.3	99	15.8
Fees charged	46	9.1	39	6.2
23. Provide photocopy machines?				
Provide	335	66.3	445	70.9
Do not provide	5	1.0	15	2.4
Fees charged	165	32.7	168	26.8
24. Present book talks/reviews?				
Provide	367	72.7	460	73.2
Do not provide	135	26.7	168	26.8
Fees charged	3	0.6	0	0.0
25. Present live programs?				
Provide	432	85.5	527	83.9
Do not provide	73	14.5	100	15.9
Fees charged	0	0.0	1	0.2
26. Present radio programs?				
Provide	78	15.4	136	21.7
Do not provide	427	84.6	492	78.3
Fees charged	0	0.0	0	0.0
27. Present cable TV programs?				
Provide	124	24.6	79	12.6
Do not provide	381	75.4	548	87.3
Fees charged	0	0.0	1	0.2

Table 15. QUESTIONNAIRE RESPONSES BY HOUSEHOLDS BELOW POVERTY LEVEL
AS A PERCENTAGE OF TOTAL HOUSEHOLDS
(POPULATION MEDIAN = 9 PERCENT). (Continued)

Does Your Library:	BELOW MEDIAN		ABOVE MEDIAN	
	NUMBER OF LIBRARIES	PERCENT	NUMBER OF LIBRARIES	PERCENT
28. Provide instruction to groups on library use?				
Provide	469	92.9	575	91.6
Do not provide	36	7.1	53	8.4
Fees charged	0	0.0	0	0.0
29. Provide instruction to individuals on library use?				
Provide	481	95.2	592	94.3
Do not provide	24	4.8	36	5.7
Fees charged	0	0.0	0	0.0
30. Provide literacy education to groups?				
Provide	91	18.0	133	21.2
Do not provide	414	82.0	494	78.7
Fees charged	0	0.0	1	0.2
31. Provide literacy education to individuals?				
Provide	145	28.7	196	31.2
Do not provide	360	71.3	431	68.6
Fees charged	0	0.0	1	0.2
32. Provide facilities for literacy education?				
Provide	346	68.5	423	67.4
Do not provide	158	31.3	204	32.5
Fees charged	1	0.2	1	0.2
33. Provide referral to another agency for literacy education?				
Provide	450	89.1	531	84.6
Do not provide	55	10.9	97	15.4
Fees charged	0	0.0	0	0.0
34. Organize programming for special groups: a. Business?				
Provide	237	46.9	222	35.3
Do not provide	266	52.7	403	64.1
Fees charged	2	0.4	4	0.6
b. Genealogists?				
Provide	201	39.8	282	44.9
Do not provide	304	60.2	343	54.6
Fees charged	0	0.0	3	0.5

Table 15. QUESTIONNAIRE RESPONSES BY HOUSEHOLDS BELOW POVERTY LEVEL
AS A PERCENTAGE OF TOTAL HOUSEHOLDS
(POPULATION MEDIAN = 9 PERCENT). (Continued)

Does Your Library:		BELOW MEDIAN		ABOVE MEDIAN	
		NUMBER OF LIBRARIES	PERCENT	NUMBER OF LIBRARIES	PERCENT
34. Organize programming for special groups: (Continued)					
c. Handicapped?					
	Provide	114	22.6	180	28.7
	Do not provide	391	77.4	446	71.0
	Fees charged	0	0.0	2	0.3
d. Job seekers?					
	Provide	180	35.6	173	27.5
	Do not provide	325	64.4	454	72.3
	Fees charged	0	0.0	1	0.2
e. Labor groups?					
	Provide	40	7.9	42	6.7
	Do not provide	465	92.1	583	92.8
	Fees charged	0	0.0	3	0.5
f. Older adults?					
	Provide	273	54.1	308	49.0
	Do not provide	232	45.9	319	50.8
	Fees charged	0	0.0	1	0.2
g. Parents?					
	Provide	293	58.0	299	47.6
	Do not provide	212	42.0	328	52.2
	Fees charged	0	0.0	1	0.2
h. Minorities?					
	Provide	55	10.9	106	16.9
	Do not provide	450	89.1	573	91.2
	Fees charged	0	0.0	0	0.0
i. Other?					
	Provide	64	12.7	77	12.3
	Do not provide	439	86.9	551	87.7
	Fees charged	2	0.4	0	0.0
35. Provide to hospitals:					
	Provide	170	33.7	253	40.3
	Do not provide	335	66.3	375	59.7
	Fees charged	0	0.0	0	0.0
a. Materials on demand?					
	Provide	149	29.5	213	33.9
	Do not provide	356	70.5	414	65.9
	Fees charged	0	0.0	1	0.2

Table 15. QUESTIONNAIRE RESPONSES BY HOUSEHOLDS BELOW POVERTY LEVEL
AS A PERCENTAGE OF TOTAL HOUSEHOLDS
(POPULATION MEDIAN = 9 PERCENT). (Continued)

Does Your Library:		BELOW MEDIAN		ABOVE MEDIAN	
		NUMBER OF LIBRARIES	PERCENT	NUMBER OF LIBRARIES	PERCENT
35. Provide to hospitals: (Continued)					
b. Deposit collections?					
	Provide	61	12.4	114	19.4
	Do not provide	432	87.6	472	80.4
	Fees charged	0	0.0	1	0.2
c. Programming?					
	Provide	29	5.7	51	8.1
	Do not provide	476	94.3	577	91.9
	Fees charged	0	0.0	0	0.0
36. Provide to prisons:					
	Provide	139	27.5	247	39.3
	Do not provide	365	72.3	381	60.7
	Fees charged	1	0.2	0	0.0
a. Materials on demand?					
	Provide	123	24.4	212	33.8
	Do not provide	382	75.6	416	66.2
	Fees charged	0	0.0	0	0.0
b. Deposit collections?					
	Provide	94	18.6	165	26.3
	Do not provide	411	81.4	463	73.7
	Fees charged	0	0.0	0	0.0
c. Programming?					
	Provide	24	4.8	22	3.5
	Do not provide	481	95.2	606	96.5
	Fees charged	0	0.0	0	0.0
37. Provide to retirement/nursing homes:					
	Provide	379	75.0	457	72.8
	Do not provide	126	25.0	171	27.2
	Fees charged	0	0.0	0	0.0
a. Materials on demand?					
	Provide	363	71.9	431	68.5
	Do not provide	142	28.1	198	31.5
	Fees charged	0	0.0	0	0.0
b. Deposit collections?					
	Provide	267	52.9	288	45.8
	Do not provide	238	47.1	341	54.2
	Fees charged	0	0.0	0	0.0

Table 15. QUESTIONNAIRE RESPONSES BY HOUSEHOLDS BELOW POVERTY LEVEL
AS A PERCENTAGE OF TOTAL HOUSEHOLDS
(POPULATION MEDIAN = 9 PERCENT). (Continued)

Does Your Library:	BELOW MEDIAN		ABOVE MEDIAN	
	NUMBER OF LIBRARIES	PERCENT	NUMBER OF LIBRARIES	PERCENT
37. Provide to retirement/nursing homes: (Continued)				
c. Programming?				
Provide	158	31.3	205	32.6
Do not provide	346	68.5	424	67.4
Fees charged	1	0.2	0	0.0
38. Provide materials to homebound?				
Provide	370	73.3	398	63.3
Do not provide	135	26.7	231	36.7
Fees charged	0	0.0	0	0.0
39. Provide books by mail?				
Provide	122	24.2	155	24.6
Do not provide	382	75.6	473	75.2
Fees charged	1	0.2	1	0.2
40. Provide bookmobile service?				
Provide	182	36.0	272	43.2
Do not provide	322	63.8	357	56.8
Fees charged	1	0.2	0	0.0
a. Materials on demand?				
Provide	178	35.2	273	43.4
Do not provide	327	64.8	355	56.4
Fees charged	0	0.0	1	0.2
b. Programming?				
Provide	82	16.2	99	15.7
Do not provide	423	83.8	529	84.1
Fees charged	0	0.0	1	0.2
c. Publicize central library programming?				
Provide	174	34.5	261	41.5
Do not provide	331	65.5	368	58.5
Fees charged	0	0.0	0	0.0
41. Maintain information on community activities?				
Provide	472	93.5	520	82.7
Do not provide	33	6.5	109	17.3
Fees charged	0	0.0	0	0.0

Table 15. QUESTIONNAIRE RESPONSES BY HOUSEHOLDS BELOW POVERTY LEVEL
AS A PERCENTAGE OF TOTAL HOUSEHOLDS
(POPULATION MEDIAN = 9 PERCENT). (Continued)

Does Your Library:	BELOW MEDIAN		ABOVE MEDIAN	
	NUMBER OF LIBRARIES	PERCENT	NUMBER OF LIBRARIES	PERCENT
42. Maintain information about media resources other than those owned by the library?				
Provide	428	84.8	478	76.0
Do not provide	76	15.0	151	24.0
Fees charged	1	0.2	0	0.0
43. Maintain a human resources file?				
Provide	332	65.7	352	56.0
Do not provide	173	34.3	277	44.0
Fees charged	0	0.0	0	0.0
44. Maintain other resource files?				
Provide	220	43.6	244	38.9
Do not provide	284	56.2	384	61.1
Fees charged	1	0.2	0	0.0

Table 16. QUESTIONNAIRE RESPONSES BY PER CAPITA INCOME AS A PERCENTAGE
OF TOTAL RESIDENTS
(POPULATION MEDIAN = $7,016)

Does Your Library:	BELOW MEDIAN		ABOVE MEDIAN	
	NUMBER OF LIBRARIES	PERCENT	NUMBER OF LIBRARIES	PERCENT
1. Display within the library exhibits based on materials owned by the library?				
Provide	540	95.4	557	98.1
Do not provide	26	4.6	11	1.9
Fees charged	0	0.0	0	0.0
2. Display within the library exhibits based on non-library materials?				
Provide	510	90.1	517	91.0
Do not provide	56	9.9	51	9.0
Fees charged	0	0.0	0	0.0
3. Display outside the library exhibits based on materials owned by the library?				
Provide	247	43.6	226	39.8
Do not provide	319	56.4	342	60.2
Fees charged	0	0.0	0	0.0
4. Circulate books in multiple copies for group use?				
Provide	214	37.8	255	44.9
Do not provide	352	62.2	313	55.1
Fees charged	0	0.0	0	0.0
5. Circulate microcomputers?				
Provide	29	5.1	37	6.5
Do not provide	536	94.7	523	92.1
Fees charged	1	0.2	8	1.4
6. Circulate microcomputer software?				
Provide	46	8.1	65	11.4
Do not provide	518	91.5	501	88.2
Fees charged	2	0.4	2	0.4
7. Circulate musical records?				
Provide	519	91.7	517	91.0
Do not provide	42	7.4	40	7.0
Fees charged	5	0.9	11	1.9
8. Circulate spoken records?				
Provide	501	88.5	517	91.0
Do not provide	60	10.6	43	7.6
Fees charged	5	0.9	8	1.4

Table 16. QUESTIONNAIRE RESPONSES BY PER CAPITA INCOME AS A PERCENTAGE
OF TOTAL RESIDENTS
(POPULATION MEDIAN = $7,016) (Continued)

Does Your Library:	BELOW MEDIAN		ABOVE MEDIAN	
	NUMBER OF LIBRARIES	PERCENT	NUMBER OF LIBRARIES	PERCENT
9. Circulate musical tapes?				
Provide	384	67.8	430	75.7
Do not provide	180	31.8	133	23.4
Fees charged	2	0.4	5	0.9
10. Circulate spoken tapes?				
Provide	479	84.6	517	91.0
Do not provide	83	14.7	45	7.9
Fees charged	4	0.7	6	1.1
11. Circulate AV materials?				
Provide	470	83.0	454	79.9
Do not provide	85	15.0	96	16.9
Fees charged	11	1.9	18	3.2
12. Circulate films?				
Provide	397	70.1	396	69.7
Do not provide	133	23.5	128	22.5
Fees charged	36	6.4	44	7.7
13. Circulate videotapes?				
Provide	316	55.8	333	58.6
Do not provide	207	36.6	142	25.0
Fees charged	43	7.6	93	16.4
14 – 16. Circulate other?				
Provide	288	50.9	349	61.4
Do not provide	258	45.6	197	36.7
Fees charged	20	3.5	22	3.9
17. Provide reading lists or bibliographies?				
Provide	483	85.3	518	91.2
Do not provide	83	14.7	49	8.6
Fees charged	0	0.0	1	0.2
18. Provide interlibrary loan service?				
Provide	516	91.2	521	91.7
Do not provide	8	1.4	5	0.9
Fees charged	42	7.4	42	7.4
19. Provide AV equipment for in-library use?				
Provide	478	84.5	454	79.9
Do not provide	83	14.7	106	18.7
Fees charged	5	0.9	8	1.4

Table 16. QUESTIONNAIRE RESPONSES BY PER CAPITA INCOME AS A PERCENTAGE
OF TOTAL RESIDENTS
(POPULATION MEDIAN = $7,016) (Continued)

Does Your Library:	BELOW MEDIAN		ABOVE MEDIAN	
	NUMBER OF LIBRARIES	PERCENT	NUMBER OF LIBRARIES	PERCENT
20. Provide microcomputer software for in-library use?				
Provide	164	29.0	239	42.1
Do not provide	399	70.5	322	56.7
Fees charged	3	0.5	7	1.2
21. Provide microcomputers for in-library use?				
Provide	169	29.9	224	39.4
Do not provide	384	67.8	309	54.4
Fees charged	13	2.3	35	6.2
22. Provide meeting or conference room space?				
Provide	447	79.0	446	78.5
Do not provide	85	15.0	71	12.5
Fees charged	34	6.0	51	9.0
23. Provide photocopy machines?				
Provide	398	70.3	381	67.1
Do not provide	12	2.1	8	1.4
Fees charged	156	27.6	179	31.5
24. Present book talks/reviews?				
Provide	400	70.7	426	75.0
Do not provide	166	29.3	139	24.5
Fees charged	0	0.0	3	0.5
25. Present live programs?				
Provide	458	80.9	501	88.2
Do not provide	107	18.9	67	11.8
Fees charged	1	0.2	0	0.0
26. Present radio programs?				
Provide	119	21.0	95	16.7
Do not provide	447	79.0	473	83.3
Fees charged	0	0.0	0	0.0
27. Present cable TV programs?				
Provide	58	10.2	144	25.4
Do not provide	507	89.6	424	74.6
Fees charged	1	0.2	0	0.0

Table 16. QUESTIONNAIRE RESPONSES BY PER CAPITA INCOME AS A PERCENTAGE
OF TOTAL RESIDENTS
(POPULATION MEDIAN = $7,016) (Continued)

Does Your Library:		BELOW MEDIAN		ABOVE MEDIAN	
		NUMBER OF LIBRARIES	PERCENT	NUMBER OF LIBRARIES	PERCENT
28. Provide instruction to groups on library use?					
	Provide	527	93.1	519	91.4
	Do not provide	39	6.9	49	8.6
	Fees charged	0	0.0	0	0.0
29. Provide instruction to individuals on library use?					
	Provide	535	94.5	539	94.9
	Do not provide	31	5.5	29	5.1
	Fees charged	0	0.0	0	0.0
30. Provide literacy education to groups?					
	Provide	117	20.7	106	18.7
	Do not provide	448	79.2	462	81.3
	Fees charged	1	0.2	0	0.0
31. Provide literacy education to individuals?					
	Provide	172	30.4	169	29.8
	Do not provide	393	69.4	399	70.2
	Fees charged	1	0.2	0	0.0
32. Provide facilities for literacy education?					
	Provide	379	67.0	391	68.8
	Do not provide	186	32.9	176	31.0
	Fees charged	1	0.2	1	0.2
33. Provide referral to another agency for literacy education?					
	Provide	472	83.4	509	89.6
	Do not provide	94	16.6	59	10.4
	Fees charged	0	0.0	0	0.0
34. Organize programming for special groups: a. Business?					
	Provide	192	33.9	267	47.0
	Do not provide	373	65.8	297	52.3
	Fees charged	2	0.4	4	0.7
b. Genealogists?					
	Provide	254	44.9	227	40.0
	Do not provide	309	54.6	341	60.0
	Fees charged	3	0.5	0	0.0

Table 16. QUESTIONNAIRE RESPONSES BY PER CAPITA INCOME AS A PERCENTAGE
OF TOTAL RESIDENTS
(POPULATION MEDIAN = $7,016) (Continued)

Does Your Library:		BELOW MEDIAN		ABOVE MEDIAN	
		NUMBER OF LIBRARIES	PERCENT	NUMBER OF LIBRARIES	PERCENT
34. Organize programming for special groups: (Continued)					
c. Handicapped?					
	Provide	153	27.0	140	24.6
	Do not provide	412	72.8	427	75.2
	Fees charged	1	0.2	1	0.2
d. Job seekers?					
	Provide	149	26.3	204	35.9
	Do not provide	417	73.7	363	63.9
	Fees charged	0	0.0	1	0.2
e. Labor groups?					
	Provide	40	7.1	41	7.2
	Do not provide	525	92.8	525	92.4
	Fees charged	1	0.2	2	0.4
f. Older adults?					
	Provide	270	47.7	312	54.9
	Do not provide	296	52.3	255	44.9
	Fees charged	0	0.0	1	0.2
g. Parents?					
	Provide	260	45.9	333	58.6
	Do not provide	306	54.1	234	41.2
	Fees charged	0	0.0	1	0.2
h. Minorities?					
	Provide	83	14.7	77	13.6
	Do not provide	483	85.3	491	86.4
	Fees charged	0	0.0	0	0.0
i. Other?					
	Provide	59	10.6	83	14.6
	Do not provide	496	89.2	484	85.2
	Fees charged	1	0.2	1	0.2
35. Provide to hospitals:					
	Provide	233	41.2	190	32.7
	Do not provide	333	58.8	378	66.5
	Fees charged	0	0.0	0	0.0
a. Materials on demand?					
	Provide	195	34.5	168	29.6
	Do not provide	370	65.4	400	70.4
	Fees charged	1	0.2	0	0.0

Table 16. QUESTIONNAIRE RESPONSES BY PER CAPITA INCOME AS A PERCENTAGE
OF TOTAL RESIDENTS
(POPULATION MEDIAN = $7,016) (Continued)

Does Your Library:		BELOW MEDIAN		ABOVE MEDIAN	
		NUMBER OF LIBRARIES	PERCENT	NUMBER OF LIBRARIES	PERCENT
35. Provide to hospitals: (Continued)					
b. Deposit collections?					
	Provide	100	18.9	75	13.6
	Do not provide	428	80.9	477	86.4
	Fees charged	1	0.2	0	0.0
c. Programming?					
	Provide	49	8.7	31	5.5
	Do not provide	517	91.3	537	94.5
	Fees charged	0	0.0	0	0.0
36. Provide to prisons:					
	Provide	237	41.9	148	26.1
	Do not provide	329	58.1	419	73.8
	Fees charged	0	0.0	1	0.2
a. Materials on demand?					
	Provide	196	34.6	139	24.5
	Do not provide	370	65.4	429	75.5
	Fees charged	0	0.0	0	0.0
b. Deposit collections?					
	Provide	159	28.1	99	17.4
	Do not provide	407	71.9	469	82.6
	Fees charged	0	0.0	0	0.0
c. Programming?					
	Provide	23	4.1	23	4.0
	Do not provide	543	95.9	545	96.0
	Fees charged	0	0.0	0	0.0
37. Provide to retirement/nursing homes:					
	Provide	422	74.6	415	73.1
	Do not provide	144	25.4	153	26.9
	Fees charged	0	0.0	0	0.0
a. Materials on demand?					
	Provide	400	70.5	395	69.5
	Do not provide	167	29.5	173	30.5
	Fees charged	0	0.0	0	0.0
b. Deposit collections?					
	Provide	277	48.9	281	49.5
	Do not provide	290	51.1	287	50.5
	Fees charged	0	0.0	0	0.0

Table 16. QUESTIONNAIRE RESPONSES BY PER CAPITA INCOME AS A PERCENTAGE
OF TOTAL RESIDENTS
(POPULATION MEDIAN = $7,016) (Continued)

Does Your Library:		BELOW MEDIAN		ABOVE MEDIAN	
		NUMBER OF LIBRARIES	PERCENT	NUMBER OF LIBRARIES	PERCENT
37. Provide to retirement/nursing homes: (Continued) c. Programming?					
	Provide	187	33.0	177	31.2
	Do not provide	380	67.0	390	68.7
	Fees charged	0	0.0	1	0.2
38. Provide materials to homebound?					
	Provide	366	65.4	403	71.0
	Do not provide	201	35.4	165	29.0
	Fees charged	0	0.0	0	0.0
39. Provide books by mail?					
	Provide	143	25.2	135	23.8
	Do not provide	422	74.4	433	76.2
	Fees charged	2	0.4	0	0.0
40. Provide bookmobile service?					
	Provide	269	47.4	186	32.7
	Do not provide	298	52.6	381	67.1
	Fees charged	0	0.0	1	0.2
a. Materials on demand?					
	Provide	268	47.3	184	32.4
	Do not provide	298	52.6	384	67.6
	Fees charged	1	0.2	0	0.0
b. Programming?					
	Provide	101	17.8	80	14.1
	Do not provide	465	82.0	488	85.9
	Fees charged	1	0.2	0	0.0
c. Publicize central library programming?					
	Provide	249	43.9	186	32.7
	Do not provide	318	56.1	382	67.3
	Fees charged	0	0.0	0	0.0
41. Maintain information on community activities?					
	Provide	461	81.3	531	93.5
	Do not provide	106	18.7	37	6.5
	Fees charged	0	0.0	0	0.0

Table 16. QUESTIONNAIRE RESPONSES BY PER CAPITA INCOME AS A PERCENTAGE
OF TOTAL RESIDENTS
(POPULATION MEDIAN = $7,016) (Continued)

	BELOW MEDIAN		ABOVE MEDIAN	
Does Your Library:	NUMBER OF LIBRARIES	PERCENT	NUMBER OF LIBRARIES	PERCENT
42. Maintain information about media re- sources other than those owned by the library?				
Provide	427	75.3	480	84.5
Do not provide	140	24.7	87	15.3
Fees charged	0	0.0	1	0.2
43. Maintain a human resources file?				
Provide	302	53.3	383	67.4
Do not provide	265	46.7	185	32.6
Fees charged	0	0.0	0	0.0
44. Maintain other resource files?				
Provide	209	36.9	257	45.2
Do not provide	357	63.1	310	54.6
Fees charged	0	0.0	1	0.2

Table 17. RESPONSES BY POPULATION GROUP

Does Your Library:	26,049 OR LESS NUMBER OF LIBRARIES	PERCENT	26,050 TO 43,244 NUMBER OF LIBRARIES	PERCENT	43,245 TO 92,573 NUMBER OF LIBRARIES	PERCENT	MORE THAN 92,573 NUMBER OF LIBRARIES	PERCENT
1. Display within the library exhibits based on materials owned by the library?								
Provide	275	97.5	273	98.2	264	95.7	267	96.4
Do not provide	7	2.5	5	1.8	12	4.3	10	3.6
Fees charged	0	0.0	0	0.0	0	0.0	0	0.0
2. Display within the library exhibits based on non-library materials?								
Provide	253	89.7	258	92.8	249	90.2	251	90.6
Do not provide	29	10.3	20	7.2	27	9.8	26	9.4
Fees charged	0	0.0	0	0.0	0	0.0		
3. Display outside the library exhibits based on materials owned by the library?								
Provide	105	37.2	90	32.4	111	40.2	163	58.8
Do not provide	177	62.8	188	67.6	165	59.8	114	41.2
Fees charged	0	0.0	0	0.0	0	0.0	0	0.0
4. Circulate books in multiple copies for group use?								
Provide	116	41.1	122	43.9	101	36.6	125	45.1
Do not provide	166	58.9	156	56.1	175	63.4	152	54.9
Fees charged	0	0.0	0	0.0	0	0.0	0	0.0

Table 17. RESPONSES BY POPULATION GROUP (Continued)

Does Your Library:	26,049 OR LESS		26,050 TO 43,244		43,245 TO 92,573		MORE THAN 92,573	
	NUMBER OF LIBRARIES	PERCENT	NUMBER OF LIBRARIES	PERCENT	NUMBER OF LIBRARIES	PERCENT	NUMBER OF LIBRARIES	PERCENT
5. Circulate microcomputers?								
Provide	21	7.4	22	7.9	11	4.0	12	4.3
Do not provide	259	91.8	254	91.4	261	94.6	264	95.3
Fees charged	2	0.7	2	0.7	4	1.4	1	0.4
6. Circulate microcomputer software?								
Provide	24	8.5	32	11.5	28	10.1	26	9.4
Do not provide	256	90.8	245	88.1	247	89.5	251	90.6
Fees charged	2	0.7	1	0.4	1	0.4	0	0.0
7. Circulate musical records?								
Provide	259	91.8	260	93.5	257	93.1	245	88.4
Do not provide	22	7.8	13	4.7	15	5.4	26	9.4
Fees charged	1	0.4	5	1.8	4	1.4	6	2.2
8. Circulate spoken records?								
Provide	253	89.7	249	89.6	255	92.4	246	88.8
Do not provide	28	9.9	25	9.0	18	6.5	26	9.4
Fees charged	1	0.4	4	1.4	3	1.1	5	1.8
9. Circulate musical tapes?								
Provide	208	73.8	202	72.7	189	68.5	203	73.3
Do not provide	74	26.2	73	26.3	86	31.2	71	25.6
Fees charged	0	0.0	3	1.1	1	0.4	3	1.1

Table 17. RESPONSES BY POPULATION GROUP (Continued)

Does Your Library:	26,049 OR LESS		26,050 TO 43,244		43,245 TO 92,573		MORE THAN 92,573	
	NUMBER OF LIBRARIES	PERCENT	NUMBER OF LIBRARIES	PERCENT	NUMBER OF LIBRARIES	PERCENT	NUMBER OF LIBRARIES	PERCENT
10. Circulate spoken tapes?								
Provide	247	87.6	244	87.8	245	88.8	242	87.4
Do not provide	34	12.1	31	11.2	29	10.5	31	11.2
Fees charged	1	0.4	3	1.1	2	0.7	4	1.4
11. Circulate AV materials?								
Provide	233	82.6	233	83.8	220	79.7	224	80.9
Do not provide	44	15.6	33	11.9	49	17.8	48	17.3
Fees charged	5	1.8	12	4.3	7	2.5	5	1.8
12. Circulate films?								
Provide	200	70.9	196	70.5	193	69.9	191	69.0
Do not provide	68	24.1	63	22.7	59	21.4	64	23.1
Fees charged	14	5.0	19	6.8	24	8.7	22	7.9
13. Circulate videotapes?								
Provide	156	55.3	154	55.4	163	59.1	167	60.3
Do not provide	98	34.8	86	30.9	80	29.0	75	27.1
Fees charged	28	9.9	38	13.7	33	12.0	35	12.6
14 – 16. Circulate other?								
Provide	140	49.6	175	62.9	153	55.4	161	58.1
Do not provide	130	46.1	94	33.8	112	40.6	107	38.6
Fees charged	12	4.3	9	3.2	11	4.0	9	3.2

Table 17. RESPONSES BY POPULATION GROUP (Continued)

Does Your Library:	26,049 OR LESS		26,050 TO 43,244		43,245 TO 92,573		MORE THAN 92,573	
	NUMBER OF LIBRARIES	PERCENT	NUMBER OF LIBRARIES	PERCENT	NUMBER OF LIBRARIES	PERCENT	NUMBER OF LIBRARIES	PERCENT
17. Provide reading lists or bibliographies?								
Provide	244	86.5	244	87.8	245	88.8	251	90.6
Do not provide	38	13.5	34	12.2	31	11.2	25	9.0
Fees charged	0	0.0	0	0.0	0	0.0	1	0.4
18. Provide interlibrary loan service?								
Provide	255	90.4	253	91.0	254	92.0	257	92.8
Do not provide	3	1.1	2	0.7	3	1.1	2	0.7
Fees charged	24	8.5	23	8.3	19	6.9	18	6.5
19. Provide AV equipment for in-library use?								
Provide	232	82.3	234	84.2	230	83.3	219	79.1
Do not provide	49	17.4	38	13.7	42	15.2	56	20.2
Fees charged	1	0.4	6	2.2	4	1.4	2	0.7
20. Provide microcomputer software for in-library use?								
Provide	98	34.8	96	34.5	104	37.7	99	35.7
Do not provide	183	64.9	179	64.4	168	60.9	176	63.5
Fees charged	1	0.4	3	1.1	4	1.4	2	0.7
21. Provide microcomputers for in-library use?								
Provide	102	36.2	91	32.7	99	35.9	95	34.3
Do not provide	172	61.0	173	62.2	163	59.1	170	61.4
Fees charged	8	2.8	14	5.0	14	5.1	12	4.3

Table 17. RESPONSES BY POPULATION GROUP (Continued)

Does Your Library:	26,049 OR LESS		26,050 TO 43,244		43,245 TO 92,573		MORE THAN 92,573	
	NUMBER OF LIBRARIES	PERCENT	NUMBER OF LIBRARIES	PERCENT	NUMBER OF LIBRARIES	PERCENT	NUMBER OF LIBRARIES	PERCENT
22. Provide meeting or conference room space?								
Provide	223	79.1	221	79.5	223	80.8	210	75.8
Do not provide	43	15.2	37	13.3	28	10.1	44	15.9
Fees charged	16	5.7	20	7.2	25	9.1	23	8.3
23. Provide photocopy machines?								
Provide	206	73.0	187	67.3	184	66.7	186	67.1
Do not provide	2	0.7	3	1.1	4	1.4	10	3.6
Fees charged	74	26.2	88	31.7	88	31.9	81	29.2
24. Present book talks/reviews?								
Provide	194	68.8	201	72.3	201	72.8	217	78.3
Do not provide	87	30.9	77	27.7	74	26.8	59	21.3
Fees charged	1	0.4	0	0.0	1	0.4	1	0.4
25. Present live programs?								
Provide	231	81.9	249	89.6	218	79.0	244	88.1
Do not provide	51	18.1	29	10.4	57	20.7	33	11.9
Fees charged	0	0.0	0	0.0	1	0.4	0	0.0
26. Present radio programs?								
Provide	51	18.1	51	18.3	44	15.9	62	22.4
Do not provide	231	81.9	227	81.7	232	84.1	215	77.6
Fees charged	0	0.0	0	0.0	0	0.0	0	0.0

Table 17. RESPONSES BY POPULATION GROUP (Continued)

Does Your Library:	26,049 OR LESS		26,050 TO 43,244		43,245 TO 92,573		MORE THAN 92,573	
	NUMBER OF LIBRARIES	PERCENT	NUMBER OF LIBRARIES	PERCENT	NUMBER OF LIBRARIES	PERCENT	NUMBER OF LIBRARIES	PERCENT
27. Present cable TV programs?								
Provide	36	12.8	49	17.6	51	18.5	65	23.5
Do not provide	246	87.2	229	82.4	224	81.2	212	76.5
Fees charged	0	0.0	0	0.0	1	0.4	0	0.0
28. Provide instruction to groups on library use?								
Provide	250	88.7	265	95.3	255	92.4	258	93.1
Do not provide	32	11.3	13	4.7	21	7.6	19	6.9
Fees charged	0	0.0	0	0.0	0	0.0	0	0.0
29. Provide instruction to individuals on library use?								
Provide	262	92.9	268	96.4	262	94.9	264	95.3
Do not provide	20	7.1	10	3.6	14	5.1	13	4.7
Fees charged	0	0.0	0	0.0	0	0.0	0	0.0
30. Provide literacy education to groups?								
Provide	57	20.2	53	19.1	55	19.9	55	19.9
Do not provide	225	79.8	225	80.9	220	79.7	222	80.1
Fees charged	0	0.0	0	0.0	1	0.4	0	0.0
31. Provide literacy education to individuals?								
Provide	97	34.4	74	26.6	80	29.0	84	30.3
Do not provide	185	65.6	204	73.4	195	70.7	193	60.7
Fees charged	0	0.0	0	0.0	1	0.4	0	0.0

Table 17. RESPONSES BY POPULATION GROUP (Continued)

Does Your Library:	26,049 OR LESS		26,050 TO 43,244		43,245 TO 92,573		MORE THAN 92,573	
	NUMBER OF LIBRARIES	PERCENT	NUMBER OF LIBRARIES	PERCENT	NUMBER OF LIBRARIES	PERCENT	NUMBER OF LIBRARIES	PERCENT
32. Provide facilities for literacy education?								
Provide	192	68.1	181	65.1	184	66.7	197	71.1
Do not provide	90	31.9	96	34.5	91	33.0	80	28.9
Fees charged	0	0.0	1	0.4	1	0.4	0	0.0
33. Provide referral to another agency for literacy education?								
Provide	233	82.6	247	88.8	236	85.5	250	90.3
Do not provide	49	17.4	31	11.2	40	14.5	27	9.7
Fees charged	0	0.0	0	0.0	0	0.0	0	0.0
34. Organize programming for special groups:								
a. Business?								
Provide	100	35.5	117	42.1	109	39.4	126	45.5
Do not provide	181	64.2	160	57.6	168	60.6	147	53.1
Fees charged	1	0.4	1	0.4	0	0.0	4	1.4
b. Genealogists?								
Provide	110	39.0	119	42.8	117	42.4	128	46.2
Do not provide	172	61.0	157	56.5	158	57.2	149	53.8
Fees charged	0	0.0	2	0.7	1	0.4	0	0.0

Table 17. RESPONSES BY POPULATION GROUP (Continued)

Does Your Library:	26,049 OR LESS		26,050 TO 43,244		43,245 TO 92,573		MORE THAN 92,573	
	NUMBER OF LIBRARIES	PERCENT	NUMBER OF LIBRARIES	PERCENT	NUMBER OF LIBRARIES	PERCENT	NUMBER OF LIBRARIES	PERCENT
34. Organize programming for special groups: (Continued)								
c. Handicapped?								
Provide	69	24.5	63	22.7	77	27.9	80	28.9
Do not provide	212	75.2	215	77.3	199	72.1	196	70.8
Fees charged	1	0.4	0	0.0	0	0.0	1	0.4
d. Job seekers?								
Provide	78	27.7	86	30.9	79	28.6	106	38.3
Do not provide	204	72.3	192	69.1	197	71.4	170	61.4
Fees charged	0	0.0	0	0.0	0	0.0	1	0.4
e. Labor groups?								
Provide	17	6.0	17	6.1	20	7.2	26	9.4
Do not provide	265	94.0	261	93.9	255	92.4	249	89.9
Fees charged	0	0.0	0	0.0	1	0.4	2	0.7
f. Older adults?								
Provide	126	44.7	154	55.4	137	49.6	153	55.2
Do not provide	156	55.3	124	44.6	139	50.4	123	44.4
Fees charged	0	0.0	0	0.0	0	0.0	1	0.4
g. Parents?								
Provide	145	51.4	159	57.2	134	48.6	149	53.8
Do not provide	137	48.6	119	42.8	142	51.4	127	45.8
Fees charged	0	0.0	0	0.0	0	0.0	1	0.4

Table 17. RESPONSES BY POPULATION GROUP (Continued)

Does Your Library:	26,049 OR LESS		26,050 TO 43,244		43,245 TO 92,573		MORE THAN 92,573	
	NUMBER OF LIBRARIES	PERCENT	NUMBER OF LIBRARIES	PERCENT	NUMBER OF LIBRARIES	PERCENT	NUMBER OF LIBRARIES	PERCENT
34. Organize programming for special groups: (Continued)								
h. Minorities?								
Provide	26	9.2	34	12.2	37	13.4	62	22.4
Do not provide	256	90.8	244	87.8	239	86.6	215	77.6
Fees charged	0	0.0	0	0.0	0	0.0	0	0.0
i. Other?								
Provide	25	8.9	40	14.4	31	11.2	47	17.0
Do not provide	257	91.1	237	82.3	245	88.8	229	82.7
Fees charged	0	0.0	1	0.3	0	0.0	1	0.3
35. Provide to hospitals:								
Provide	99	35.1	111	39.9	107	38.8	98	35.4
Do not provide	183	64.9	167	60.1	169	61.2	179	64.6
Fees charged	0	0.0	0	0.0	0	0.0	0	0.0
a. Materials on demand?								
Provide	92	32.6	94	33.8	92	33.3	76	27.4
Do not provide	190	67.4	184	66.2	184	66.7	200	72.2
Fees charged	0	0.0	0	0.0	0	0.0	1	0.4
b. Deposit collections?								
Provide	36	13.5	49	18.4	43	16.5	46	17.4
Do not provide	231	86.5	218	81.6	218	83.5	218	82.3
Fees charged	0	0.0	0	0.0	0	0.0	1	0.4

Table 17. RESPONSES BY POPULATION GROUP (Continued)

Does Your Library:	26,049 OR LESS		26,050 TO 43,244		43,245 TO 92,573		MORE THAN 92,573	
	NUMBER OF LIBRARIES	PERCENT	NUMBER OF LIBRARIES	PERCENT	NUMBER OF LIBRARIES	PERCENT	NUMBER OF LIBRARIES	PERCENT
35. Provide to hospitals: (Continued)								
c. Programming?								
Provide	20	7.1	23	8.3	20	7.2	17	6.1
Do not provide	262	92.9	255	91.7	256	92.8	260	93.9
Fees charged	0	0.0	0	0.0	0	0.0	0	0.0
36. Provide to prisons:								
Provide	85	30.1	78	28.1	99	35.9	119	43.0
Do not provide	197	69.9	199	71.6	177	64.1	158	57.0
Fees charged	0	0.0	1	0.4	0	0.0	0	0.0
a. Materials on demand?								
Provide	75	26.6	78	28.1	80	29.0	96	34.7
Do not provide	207	73.4	200	71.9	196	71.0	181	65.3
Fees charged	0	0.0	0	0.0	0	0.0	0	0.0
b. Deposit collections?								
Provide	49	17.4	53	19.1	62	22.5	93	33.6
Do not provide	233	82.6	225	80.9	214	77.5	184	66.4
Fees charged	0	0.0	0	0.0	0	0.0	0	0.0
c. Programming?								
Provide	7	2.5	11	4.0	6	2.2	21	7.6
Do not provide	275	97.5	267	96.0	270	97.8	256	92.4
Fees charged	0	0.0	0	0.0	0	0.0	0	0.0

Table 17. RESPONSES BY POPULATION GROUP (Continued)

Does Your Library:	26,049 OR LESS		26,050 TO 43,244		43,245 TO 92,573		MORE THAN 92,573	
	NUMBER OF LIBRARIES	PERCENT	NUMBER OF LIBRARIES	PERCENT	NUMBER OF LIBRARIES	PERCENT	NUMBER OF LIBRARIES	PERCENT
37. Provide to retirement/nursing homes:								
Provide	217	77.0	201	72.3	219	79.3	194	70.0
Do not provide	65	23.0	77	27.7	57	20.7	83	30.0
Fees charged	0	0.0	0	0.0	0	0.0	0	0.0
a. Materials on demand?								
Provide	203	72.0	196	70.5	206	74.4	183	66.1
Do not provide	79	28.0	82	29.5	71	25.6	94	33.9
Fees charged	0	0.0	0	0.0	0	0.0	0	0.0
b. Deposit collections?								
Provide	145	51.4	122	43.9	141	50.9	141	50.9
Do not provide	137	48.6	156	56.1	136	49.1	131	47.3
Fees charged	0	0.0	0	0.0	0	0.0	0	0.0
c. Programming?								
Provide	89	31.6	88	31.7	90	32.5	92	33.2
Do not provide	193	68.4	190	68.3	186	67.1	185	66.8
Fees charged	0	0.0	0	0.0	1	0.4	0	0.0
38. Provide materials to homebound?								
Provide	195	69.1	190	68.3	199	71.8	175	63.2
Do not provide	87	30.9	88	31.7	78	28.2	102	36.8
Fees charged	0	0.0	0	0.0	0	0.0	0	0.0

Table 17. RESPONSES BY POPULATION GROUP (Continued)

Does Your Library:	26,049 OR LESS		26,050 TO 43,244		43,245 TO 92,573		MORE THAN 92,573	
	NUMBER OF LIBRARIES	PERCENT	NUMBER OF LIBRARIES	PERCENT	NUMBER OF LIBRARIES	PERCENT	NUMBER OF LIBRARIES	PERCENT
39. Provide books by mail?								
Provide	69	24.5	54	19.4	66	23.8	83	30.0
Do not provide	212	75.2	224	80.6	210	75.8	194	70.0
Fees charged	1	0.4	0	0.0	1	0.4	0	0.0
40. Provide bookmobile service?								
Provide	98	34.8	87	31.3	122	44.0	140	50.5
Do not provide	183	64.9	191	68.7	155	56.0	137	49.5
Fees charged	1	0.4	0	0.0	0	0.0	0	0.0
a. Materials on demand?								
Provide	101	35.8	87	31.3	122	44.0	135	48.7
Do not provide	181	64.2	191	68.7	154	55.6	142	51.3
Fees charged	0	0.0	0	0.0	1	0.4	0	0.0
b. Programming?								
Provide	31	11.0	33	11.9	54	19.5	60	21.7
Do not provide	251	89.0	245	88.1	222	80.1	217	78.3
Fees charged	0	0.0	0	0.0	1	0.4	0	0.0
c. Publicize central library programming?								
Provide	90	31.9	90	32.4	115	41.5	133	48.0
Do not provide	192	68.1	188	67.6	162	58.5	144	52.0
Fees charged	0	0.0	0	0.0	0	0.0	0	0.0

Table 17. RESPONSES BY POPULATION GROUP (Continued)

Does Your Library:	26,049 OR LESS		26,050 TO 43,244		43,245 TO 92,573		MORE THAN 92,573	
	NUMBER OF LIBRARIES	PERCENT	NUMBER OF LIBRARIES	PERCENT	NUMBER OF LIBRARIES	PERCENT	NUMBER OF LIBRARIES	PERCENT
41. Maintain information on community activities?								
Provide	231	81.9	250	89.9	240	86.6	254	91.7
Do not provide	51	18.1	28	10.1	37	13.4	23	8.3
Fees charged	0	0.0	0	0.09	0	0.0	0	0.0
42. Maintain information about media resources other than those owned by the library?								
Provide	212	75.2	234	84.2	218	78.7	230	83.0
Do not provide	70	24.8	43	15.5	59	21.3	47	17.0
Fees charged	0	0.0	1	0.4	0	0.0	0	0.0
43. Maintain a human resources file?								
Provide	155	55.0	175	62.9	159	57.4	186	67.1
Do not provide	127	45.0	103	37.1	118	42.6	91	32.9
Fees charged	0	0.0	0	0.0	0	0.0	0	0.0
44. Maintain other resource files?								
Provide	93	33.0	126	45.3	116	42.0	128	46.2
Do not provide	189	67.0	152	54.7	159	57.6	149	53.8
Fees charged	0	0.0	0	0.0	1	0.4	0	0.0

Table 18. SERVICES MEANINGFULLY RELATED TO POPULATION
OF COMMUNITY SERVED (NUMBERS OF LIBRARIES ARE IN
PARENTHESES).

	Provided at No Charge	Not Provided	Provided for a Fee
Provision of book talks/reviews	132,533 (813)	78,669 (297)	65,581 (3)
Presentation of cable TV programs	191,671 (201)	101,836 (911)	53,361 (1)
Provision of group literacy education	171,706 (220)	104,674 (892)	53,361 (1)
Provision of programming for business	154,560 (452)	91,933 (656)	179,716 (6)
Provision of programming for handicapped	181,599 (289)	95,665 (822)	62,572 (2)
Provision of programming for job seekers	187,591 (349)	86,234 (763)	118,102 (1)
Provision of programming for older adults	146,377 (570)	87,714 (542)	118,102 (1)
Provision of programming for other special groups	168,383 (143)	57,253 (968)	414,796 (2)
Provision of services to prisons	158,322 (381)	97,092 (731)	39,590 (1)
Provision of books by mail	201,067 (272)	90,986 (840)	27,116 (2)

CHAPTER 3

Lifelong Learning Theory and the Provision of Adult Services

Connie Van Fleet

Lifelong Learning: Definition and Context

Lifelong learning is a concept that was conceived and developed in the 1970s in recognition of the need to approach learning, education, individual growth, and personal development as part of a holistic philosophy. The term encompasses all phases of adult education and adult learning and is intended to serve as a broad-based theoretical framework that may accommodate all facets of the human being's need to change and grow.[1] Lifelong learning may not be defined in terms of a set of discrete services. It is, rather, an all-inclusive philosophy that influences every phase of library service. For the purposes of this paper, lifelong learning will be discussed primarily in its relation to adult services provision. The value of the concept, however, is in its recognition of the cumulative effect of learning throughout the lifespan. Awareness of the interrelationships of learning for all service groups, regardless of age or previous educational achievement serves as a basis for every facet of library service.

The concept of lifelong learning has its genesis in the growth of adult education study in the 1960s. Although Knowles was instrumental in drawing attention to the educational needs of adults, his focus at that time was in distinguishing the characteristics and needs of adult learners from those generally addressed by traditional education methods.[2] A comprehensive and generally accepted definition of adult education was slow in coming to the field of education, as was recognition of adult education as a separate discipline. It is not surprising, then, that defining adult education has been problematic for the library profession for decades. This lack has hampered efforts to formulate a conceptual basis upon which to build. Smith noted that "adult education from the library point of view . . . defies definition. . . . It breaks across institutional and organizational lines. It resists evaluation and presents difficulties for research."[3]

Many theorists in the field of adult education have put forth definitions. International cooperation has resulted in a common ground for beginning discussion. The Education Committee of the Organization for Economic Cooperation and Development asserted that

> Adult education refers to any activity or programme deliberately designed by a providing agent to satisfy any learning need that may be experienced at any stage in his life by a person who is over the normal school-leaving age and no longer a full-time student. Its ambit spans non-vocational, vocational, general formal, non-formal, and community education and is not restricted to any academic level.[4]

This definition includes several points characteristic of adult education theory. While the subject matter and formats are varied, they are generally purposefully designed by a third party. This emphasis on organization and interaction between teacher and learner is common in discussions of adult education. The 1976 General Conference of UNESCO issued a statement that typified international thought:

> The term adult education denotes the entire body of organized educational processes, whatever the content, level, and method, whether formal or otherwise, whether they prolong or replace initial education in schools, colleges, and universities as well as in apprenticeships, whereby persons regarded as adult by the society to which they belong develop their abilities, enrich their knowledge, improve their technical or professional qualifications, or turn them in a new direction and bring about changes in their attitudes or behaviors in the two-fold perspective of full personal development and participation in balanced and independent social, economic, and cultural development.[5]

In the 1970s, the trend was to emphasize adult learning, rather than adult education. Some theorists were concerned that emphasis in the seventies on structured classroom activities would lead to an "overcredentialed society," and felt that more attention should be paid to learners who planned their own activities and instituted their own criteria.[6] Surveys indicated that adult learning in unstructured situations was much more widespread than had previously been realized.

Earlier research focused on adults who participated in organized classes, with the finding that 12 to 31 percent of adults in the United States engaged in learning activities.[7] Later studies by Tough and Penland were based on an expanded perception of adult learning, and emphasized independent, informal learning. As a result of this new perspective, a much larger percentage of adults (79 to 98 percent) were found to engage in learning activities on a regular basis.[8]

Adult education tends to emphasize the teacher-student relationship and carries with it connotations of organized, externally directed activity, while the concept of adult learning focuses on the independence of the learner. Surveys such as those conducted by Penland and Tough in the early seventies indicate that many adults undertake learning projects on their own, and in many cases tend to avoid structured classroom settings.[9] Of primary importance is the learner-centered focus implied by the term. Learning is seen as a characteristic of the learner, rather than a commodity supplied by a teacher. Adult learning theory emphasizes the responsibility of learners in planning and fulfilling their goals. The objective is for the learner to become more independent and self-motivated. As Cross notes, "There is a continuum of freedom and self-direction implied in this use of the term."[10] The teacher, then, has a secondary role—as a facilitator, not a giver of knowledge.[11] This role may be one that will be more readily accepted by librarians, as it is more in harmony with the traditional view of librarians as skilled and sympathetic intermediaries between people and resources, and may help to overcome the traditional bias against librarian as teacher.

The most recent conceptual paradigm, supported by observers in many disciplines from economics to psychology, emphasizes lifelong learning. This philosophy incorporates the ideas of both adult learning and adult education, but gives a broader perspective. It recognizes that the attitudes and skills of adults are based on childhood development, and that the growth and attitudes of a society reflect the personal development of its individual members. While recommendations for developing and implementing the "learning society" often identify particular groups to be served, the focus is first and foremost on the individual. Services are to be provided to the individual regardless of educational attainment, skill level, socioeconomic condition, or age. The Education Amendments of 1976 (to the Adult Education Act 1966) define lifelong learning as including, but not restricted to:

> Adult basic education, continuing education, independent study, agricultural education, business education and labor education, oc-

cupational education and job training programs, parent education, postsecondary education, preretirement and education for older and retired people, remedial education, special educational programs for groups or for individuals with special needs, and also educational activities designed to upgrade occupational and professional skills, to assist business, public agencies, and other organizations in the use of innovation and research results, and to serve family needs and personal development.[12]

While the Act includes a vast array of services and programs for a wide variety of purposes, it is limited to adults. The more common concept of lifelong learning applies to people of every age and has broad implications for preparatory education as well. The Lifelong Learning Project, formed under the auspices of this Act, stated:

The goal of lifelong learning is the enhancement and expansion of learning opportunities for all social groups and ages in American society. Lifelong learning is a desirable way both to reform the current general arrangements for education and to create alternatives to the learning opportunities already available through the existing educational system.[13]

Results of the Adult Services in the Eighties survey support the notion that public libraries, to a very large degree, are already providing services to support lifelong learning. Specialized programming and the provision of a wide variety of formats and services indicate an awareness on the part of librarians throughout the country that the library's role in adult learning is a vital one. What has traditionally been lacking is "a unifying background of theory."[14] As is common with many practice-oriented disciplines, theory is often based upon a body of practice, rather than practice growing from a broad theoretical background. The history of the library's educational services to adults, the individualized nature of the library's approach to service, the evidence of the library's ongoing commitment to service provision, and strong supportive theory from other disciplines all converge at the point of a commitment to lifelong learning on the part of the public library. As Houle observed in 1946, "a public librarian or any other educator needs some principles which he can accept and which will provide the position where he may stand to look at the activities of the library."[15]

Nearly forty years later, Birge argued that one of the problems hampering librarians was that they had "never developed a coherent philosophy of educational service."[16] Peterson sees lifelong learning as a "conceptual framework for conceiving, planning, implementing, and coordinating activities designed to facilitate learning by all

Americans throughout their lifetimes."[17] As educators, public policy-makers, business people and sociologists develop a strong commitment to lifelong learning, librarians can join this coalition and at last find that "common statement of belief" that has been lacking in our profession.[18]

Adult Education as a Rationale for the Establishment of the Public Library

Many reasons have been recorded for the foundation and growth of public libraries in the United States. While economic ability and local pride played an important part, many other factors directly related to universal education and civic participation offered a philosophical basis. Lee notes that "the public library was the first tax-supported agency established in the United States for the informal education of adults. It was organized specifically to provide a means by which mature individuals could continue to learn through their own efforts."[19] Obviously then, lifelong learning theory and the underlying foundations of the public library have much in common: both recognize the importance of continuing, universal education for vocational and personal development.

Although the early public library made no provision for children's services, library service was seen as part of an educational continuum, with formal education providing but the first step. The 1852 Report to the Boston Public Library states one of the primary arguments offered by lifelong learning proponents today:

> Although the school and even the college and the university are, as all thoughtful persons are well aware, but the first stages in education, the public makes no provision for carrying on the great work. . . . The trustees submit, that all the reasons which exist for furnishing the means of elementary education, at the public expense, apply in an equal degree to a reasonable provision to aid and encourage the acquisition of the knowledge required to complete a preparation for active life or to perform its duties.[20]

During the nineteenth century, a profound belief existed in the capacity of ordinary people to advance themselves through self-education and improvement.[21] Formal educational opportunities were limited, but lyceums and institutes were plentiful. Josiah Holbrook founded the Society for Mutual Education, popularly known as the American Lyceum. This Lyceum movement gave impetus to continuing education and "demonstrated the feasibility of an integrated national system of local groups organized primarily for adult education purposes."[22] The desire for vocational improvement was visible in the mechanics' and apprentices' libraries, modeled after the British workers' institutes and established to provide for "the intellectual development of the artisan."[23]

The establishment of the public library was inextricably linked to the move for universal public education. Public education was seen as a way to preserve democracy through an informed citizenry, to provide skilled workers, to alleviate social inequities, and to cure many of the social ills of the day. "The goal was a better society, the barrier was ignorance, and the means—public education."[24] However, this philosophy also rested on the ideal of initiative and personal responsibility. The means were provided, and individuals were expected to show independence and initiative. The public librarian's duty, therefore, was to collect books, to preserve and care for them, and to make them available to the library's patrons. These early years were spent in building collections and developing ways to organize them to fullest advantage.

DEVELOPMENT AND GROWTH OF THE PUBLIC LIBRARY, 1850–1890

The establishment of the Boston Public Library in 1854 marked the beginning of remarkable growth for the public library. By 1876, when the United States Office of Education issued its report, most large cities had established libraries. A burgeoning adult education movement was evidenced by the growth of the Chautauqua movement, university extension, and the organization of clubs and societies for intellectual pursuits.[25] The American Library Association, formed in 1876, explored the importance of the educational work of the library, debated the inclusion of popular novels in public library collections, and explored efficient methods for collecting and organizing library materials.[26] Library leaders from Josiah P. Quincy in 1876 through Henry Munson Utley in 1895 expressed the importance of the library in offering educational services.[27] While there were many who agreed with them, there was by no means a consensus. Many did not recognize the library as an educational agency. Additionally, many of those whom the library had been called upon to help through free access to books were prohibited from taking full advantage of the opportunity, either because of circumstances (children were often called upon to work rather than attend school), or because of the failure of the public school to provide an adequate foundation.[28]

Recognition of these problems led to a growing sense of responsibility among librarians. The primary duties for the librarian still lay in the organization and conservation of the collection. By the late 1880s, however, collections were larger and diverse, and a few librarians were beginning to see assistance to readers as part of their professional responsibility.

EXPANSION OF SERVICES, 1891–1940

The 1890s marked the beginnings of outreach and expansion of library services. The importance of personal assistance to readers was emphasized by Brett in his presidential address at the 1897 ALA Conference, in which he stated that "the personal influence of librarians who assisted and advised readers was the most potent factor in molding community reading."[29] As awareness of the personal assistance service grew, other objectives began to vie for money and attention. It was during this period that the reference objective was initiated, and that the recreational objective, while still controversial, was gaining recognition. All of these services—the provision of personal assistance, recreational reading, and reference service—were indicative of the library's growing commitment to reach out into the community. Outreach services were evidence of this attempt to meet the unique needs of each community. Recognition of their changing environment and clientele, a sincere concern for their patrons, and a growing professionalism led librarians to consider the role of the library in a societal context. Winsor noted: "there can be no such thing as a model collection so long as communities differ and individuality survives."[30] This community service model made librarians particularly sensitive to the influx of unskilled rural workers and immigrants to urban areas in the early 1900s. The educational needs of these segments of the population were obvious, and the library initiated services to meet them.

In 1912, E. A. Hardy published "The Special Activities of the Library in Relation to Education," in which a variety of educational activities were discussed and all found appropriate and worthwhile.[31] Readers' advisory services, which involved personal interviews and the preparation of individualized learning plans, came to be accepted as "the cornerstone of public library service to the community," and as "the greatest contribution of public libraries to the adult education movement of the first half of the twentieth century."[32] The purpose was to offer direct, personalized help over an extended period of time through the provision of an individualized plan of study and through

referrals to formal classes and educational institutions. The personalized plan and ongoing interaction differentiated the learner's advisory service from reference service, which tended to be impersonal,
of short duration, and in response to an immediate, very specific need.

Except for those well-defined outreach programs to immigrants,
adult education programs often ranked behind recreational and
informational functions of the library. Not only were reader advisory
services expensive in regards to staff time, they did not produce the
impressive circulation figures of recreational materials or the statistics of reference service. It was only as a result of the energizing effect
of the Library War Service Program, which provided library service to
soldiers and sailors during World War I, that librarians began to
reconsider the importance of service to the individual reader.[33]
Largely as a result of the involvement with the Library War Service
Program, the ALA Enlarged Program was adopted by the ALA
Executive Board in 1920. Among the activities proposed were: (1)
provision of lists and reading courses for adult learners; (2) services to
institutions; (3) services to immigrants; (4) services for the blind; (5)
library extension; and (6) a survey of libraries.[34] Although the program could not be implemented because of lack of funding, it did
establish priorities and concerns of the profession at that time.

As a result of this renewed interest in the readers' advisory service,
many librarians began to perceive the adult education function as the
most important for the public library. In 1924, William S. Learned, a
member of the staff of the Carnegie Foundation for the Advancement
of Teaching, published the report, *The American Public Library and
the Diffusion of Knowledge*.[35] It proposed a detailed and systematic
plan for establishing the dominance of the educational objective of the
public library. Learned was convinced of the inevitability of the
central role of the library in the education of the community, provided
that the collection was supplemented with knowledgeable and concerned professionals. He anticipated skepticism, but asserted "that a
free community book exchange . . . destined to be transformed into an
active intelligence center through the addition of a competent staff of
scholars trained in fitting books to human needs, is an idea as dimly
perceived today as was the free library itself seventy-five years ago."[36]
While the report created a good deal of controversy, it also provoked
professional thinking and emphasized the importance of individualized service. Between 1928 and 1935, the number of libraries
offering personalized service grew from twenty-five to forty-eight.

The interaction of personal service and service to immigrants and
unschooled adults led to an increased concern by librarians about the

types of materials and services they were able to offer. In 1924, the ALA Executive Board appointed the Commission on the Library and Adult Education (funded by a grant from the Carnegie Corporation). The Subcommittee on Readable Books, formed in 1925, grew from the Commission's concern over the lack of suitable books for beginning adult readers. Subsequent studies of adult reading were used to improve readers' advisory services. Over the next ten years, several reports on readable books were published, and in 1936 the Readability Laboratory was established at Teachers College, Columbia University.

To serve the general reader, the Commission, with a grant from the Carnegie Corporation, prepared a series of pamphlets titled "Reading with a Purpose." Designed to be used in conjunction with the readers' advisory service, the pamphlets were prepared by subject specialists who provided an introductory essay and short bibliography. The series was enormously popular, and over 850,000 copies of the pamphlets were sold between 1925 and 1931.[37]

In 1926, the ALA Commission on the Library and Adult Education published *Libraries and Adult Education*, in which it maintained that "each public library had an inherent duty to assume an active role in adult education."[38] One of the most important ways that the library could fulfill this role was through the provision of readers' advisory services. The profession was not in agreement on the Commission's findings. Some librarians felt that adult education was for those who could already function independently in the library setting, and not for that undereducated segment of society that many others seemed so intent on serving. The sentiment was that instruction was an inappropriate role for a librarian who, after all, was not a teacher.[39]

In spite of these objections, the readers' advisory service continued to grow throughout the 1920s and 1930s. Lee notes three phases.[40] The first, 1922 through 1926, represented an experimental stage for the service, during which it was initiated in seven urban libraries. It was seen as an "extra" service and was provided by a special readers' guidance librarian. The second phase, from 1927 to 1935, saw a growth in the service whose quality had been enhanced by numerous studies on adult reading. The number of libraries offering readers' advisory service grew from 25 in 1930 to 44 in 1935. The growth in number is attributed to the increased number of professional librarians, the increased demand created by the Depression, and the reading studies. The third phase, 1936 through 1940, saw the departmentalization of the service. The readers' adviser function was split among subject specialists within the library. During this time, readers' advisory service received unprecedented attention in the professional literature.

Birge notes this departmentalization as the beginning of the eclipse of the readers' advisory service.[41] The service was less visible when it was absorbed into various departments, and subject specialists were more oriented to reference work than the prolonged personal contact involved in readers' adviser work. The beginning of World War II resulted in a decrease in leisure time and subsequent diminished demand for the service. Administrators questioned the service because it was costly, and lack of training opportunities resulted in inconsistent quality of service.[42] Professionally, interest had grown in the provision of group services, which reached more people for less money.[43]

The commitment to adult education remained strong within the profession. Alvin Johnson's report, prepared at the request of the American Association of Adult Education and funded by the Carnegie Corporation, was issued in 1938 as *The Public Library—A People's University*.[44] Johnson proposed that a dynamic plan of action to establish the educational prominence of the public library was the optimal approach. Although most librarians agreed that the public library should have some educational objective, they were not in agreement as to how aggressive they should be in fulfilling the educational role, nor as to which methods would prove most appropriate. By 1938, both the ALA Adult Education Board and the ALA Adult Education Roundtable found that although individualized readers' advisory services were the preferred method of adult education, discussion groups and other methods were acceptable.[45] Work being done in the adult education field tended to support the importance of group dynamics in learning.[46] Given these factors—the costliness of readers' advisory services, the departmentalization of the library, professional acceptance, and supportive theory from adult education—it is understandable that administrators began to lean toward group service and cooperative support as a means to fulfill the library's educational function.

CIVIC ENLIGHTENMENT AND THE WANING OF THE EDUCATIONAL OBJECTIVE, 1941–1959

With the close of World War II, the library's educational commitment was supported by the profession's awareness of the need to supply unbiased information to the citizens of an increasingly complex and threatening world. The dawn of the cold war brought home the recognition of the need to understand political issues on a globalscale. Born of this awareness were two important projects. The Great Issues program (1948) and the ALA American Heritage Project (1951) were both designed to give adults the opportunity to discuss the important issues of the day: inflation, civil rights, organized labor, and American and Soviet relations.[47]

The library profession at this time was forced into a more aggressive political stance. While the United States government was extolling the virtues of democracy over communist authoritarianism, it increasingly encroached upon the civil rights of its citizens. It was a time of fear and distrust characterized by McCarthyism, congressional investigations, and loyalty programs. ALA reacted by reaffirming the Library Bill of Rights, which provided for access to information and the rights of the reader. In 1952 and 1953 ALA sponsored two Intellectual Freedom Institutes.[48]

The Public Library Inquiry (undertaken in 1947 by ALA and the Social Science Research Council) recommended that libraries "provide opportunity and encouragement for people of all ages to educate themselves continuously."[49] The report, entitled *The Public Library in the United States*, created a furor by stating that public libraries should focus their educational efforts on the small but select segment of the population who could appreciate them.[50] *Post-War Standards for Public Libraries* suggested that particular emphasis should be placed on the educational function of the public library, particularly in the area of public affairs.[51]

Throughout the 1950s, the adult education goal remained, although it took a secondary role to recreational and informational services. The ALA Fund for Adult Education was instrumental in many important projects that underscored the desirability of adult education in public libraries and the strong commitment to this goal in some libraries. Among these were the American Heritage Project; the Survey of Adult Education in Public Libraries, which studied the provision of adult education services in public libraries; the Adult Education Subgrant Project, which helped to develop programs for adult education; and the Allerton Park Conference, which afforded an opportunity for library school educators and public library administrators to discuss adult education activities.[52] The Library Community Project, 1955 to 1960, also funded by the Fund for Adult Education, was particularly important. Its purpose was to aid in developing long-term adult education programs using a community needs analysis approach.[53] In 1956, ALA's *Public Library Service: A Guide to Evaluation with Minimum Standards* prescribed three main objectives for public libraries: education, information, and recreation.[54] In 1957, the Library Services Act was passed, marking the first federal program of assistance to public libraries. The Act was designed to provide service to rural populations underserved by libraries, and to stimulate the use of state and local funds by providing federal matching funds. Between 1957 and 1963, over $42 million in federal funds and $94 million in matching state and local funds had been spent.[55] The Adult Services Division of ALA was established in 1957, and in 1958 the Division formed the Committee on Bibliography of Library Adult Education. The nation celebrated the first National Library Week in 1958.

This period, while it witnessed a decline in personalized educational services, was characterized by a growth in educational services offered to groups, either by the library or in cooperation with other community agencies. Although the informational and recreational roles of the library gained prominence, there were many who continued to stress the importance of the public library's educational opportunities, and who worked to provide services to support the educational goal.

SOCIOLOGICAL AWARENESS, 1960–1987

Library activities of the past two decades have given credence to Shera's assertion that the library is primarily a reactive social agency, reflecting the values and trends of society.[56] The renewed emphasis within the library community on provision of service to the traditionally underserved—particularly ethnic minorities and the poor—developed as a result of federal concern and public awareness of these groups. The Johnson administration's War on Poverty and the Civil Rights movement had enormous impact on the country as a whole, and on libraries and educational institutions in particular. Once again, education was viewed as the solution to society's major problems: poverty and inequality.

A logical extension of this growing sociological awareness was the move toward outreach services and community analysis as part of the planning agenda. Aware of a professional as well as a moral obligation to meet the needs of all members of society, and equally cognizant of the fact that strong leadership would be required, the ALA took steps toward self-study and formalizing the profession's stand on equal treatment for all. In 1961, the ALA Council passed an amendment to the Library Bill of Rights proposed by the ALA Committee on Civil Rights. It stated: "The rights of an individual to the use of a library should not be denied or abridged because of his race, religion, national origin or political views."[57] *Access to Public Libraries,* the ALA study of possible inequities in public library service because of race, student status, lack of foreign language resources or inequitable regional distribution of resources was published in 1963. Where the findings found discrimination, moves were made to equalize opportunity.[58]

The Library Services Act (1957) was expanded in scope and renamed in 1964 as the new Library Services and Construction Act (LSCA). The LSCA broadened the scope of the earlier Act to include grants to underserved urban as well as rural areas and to provide funds for construction of library buildings. The Economic Opportunity Act (1964) made provision for combating the lack of education that was seen as a major cause of poverty. Under this law, libraries could serve as community educational resource centers.[59]

The importance of reaching out into the community became primary to many librarians. Storefront libraries represented a commitment to adult learning by offering adult basic education services, English language courses, services to seniors and to blacks, consumer information, civil service training information, and vocational information. The Neighborhood Library Center of New Haven was typical. The funding for the Center, established in 1964, came from the Ford Foundation and the Office of Economic Opportunity through a local action group called Community Progress, Inc.[60] The federal government recognized the importance of early childhood development and supported programs such as Headstart. As the importance of these early learning opportunities was demonstrated, libraries increased their services to children. The library was beginning to assume the role of a center for lifelong learning. Unfortunately, no underlying body of principle gave a strong foundation to this trend.

Many individual projects were undertaken to demonstrate better ways to fulfill the educational objective which had taken precedence during the sixties. Librarians were reassured of the importance of their role in society, and of the potential impact of the library. Although readers' advisory services were no longer as common as they once were, there was continued evidence of interest in the service. In 1960, the ALA Small Library Project published *Reader's Guidance in a Small Public Library* by Helen Lyman.[61] In the same year the "Reading for an Age of Change" project, sponsored by ALA's Adult Service Division and funded by a Carnegie Grant produced guides on current topics. (The grant was renewed in 1963).[62] The Institute on Reader Guidance was conducted at the University of

Wisconsin Library School in cooperation with the Adult Services Division of ALA. Once again, there was a link between interest in personalized reader service and in the provision of suitable materials.

In 1963 ALA established the Committee on Reading Improvement in Adults, which published *Service to Adult Illiterates: Guidelines for Librarians.*[63] The Public Library Association's Committee on Services to the Functionally Illiterate issued a policy statement in 1965 which claimed that "responsibility to undereducated persons grows from recognition of the public library's major social role as a change agent."[64] The Committee on Reading Improvement for Adults and the Public Library Association sponsored a two-day workshop on Books for Adults Beginning to Read (1966), and in 1967 the Free Library of Philadelphia established its Reader Development Program.[65] The program was marked by its successful interagency communication and the development of bibliographies of suitable materials. Between 1967 and 1972, Helen Lyman conducted a research project that produced two important guides for evaluating materials for beginning or poor readers: *Reading and the New Adult Reader*[66] and *Literacy and the Nation's Libraries.*[67]

The enactment of two more far-reaching pieces of legislation in the mid-sixties was evidence of continued federal support and concern. The Higher Education Act (1965) and the Elementary and Secondary Education Act (1965) served as bases for future important legislation. Title III of the 1966 amendments to the Elementary and Secondary Education Act created the Adult Education Act. The 1974 Amendments to the Higher Education Act created the Special Projects Act, and Title I of the 1976 amendments created the Lifelong Learning (or Mondale) Act. In 1978, Penland published his seminal work, *Self-Planned Learning in America.*[68] Support was provided through a grant from the Library Research and Demonstration Branch, Office of Libraries and Learning Resources, U.S. Office of Education, under Title IIB of the Higher Education Act.[69] These laws supplied impetus for needed research and project development, as well as firmly establishing education as a primary concern of this nation.

As a result of the shifting national demographics of the seventies (such as fewer college-age students, more women returning to work, job changes) and the upheaval on college campuses, many institutions began to explore alternative curricula and formats, including credit for experience or prior knowledge. In recognition of this, the College Entrance Examination Board developed the College Level Examination Program that enabled students to receive college credit for successful performance on an examination. The Board, in conjunction with the

Council on Library Resources and the National Endowment for the Humanities, planned and initiated the Dallas Public Library Independent Study Project. The project studied the effectiveness of a cooperative program of the Dallas Public Library and Southern Methodist University in helping adults acquire formal credit for independent study.

In 1972, after having studied the results of the Dallas project, the Board established its Office of Library Independent Study and Guidance Projects. The purpose of the Office was to assist public libraries in providing services to independent learners. It established the Adult Independent Learning Project, an extension of the Dallas project, in which libraries offered learners' advisory services as well as educational brokering. In 1976, the Consortium of Public Library Innovation was established to spread these learners' advisory ideas after the end of the College Board Project. Although the original purpose was to conduct workshops in appropriate techniques and methods, the Consortium's focus shifted to working for data systems and strategies for more effective administration of the brokering services.[70] By 1977, several libraries had expanded their educational and career information and referral services.[71] Lifelong Learning Centers had been established in Pennsylvania at Reading and Philadelphia. Westchester (N.Y.) had developed the Westchester Hotline, and Winston-Salem was offering the service as part of the ACE (Adult Continuing Education) Project.

The 1979 White House Conference on Library and Information Services was devoted to policy issues on five themes, one of which was lifelong learning. Several resolutions pertained to the library's role in the learning society, and the establishment of information and referral centers was specifically mandated. The resolution called for federal funding of incentive grants to establish the centers in cooperation with other community agencies, and for libraries to engage in an "aggressive public awareness effort to promote the utilization of libraries and information and referral centers."[72] A specific mandate was issued "to provide such service at centers for independent learning bringing such services to those not served."[73] The conference also set forth a basic philosophy of service: "that all learners, regardless of age, residence (including institutions), race, disability, ethnic or cultural background, should have continuing access to the information and material necessary to cope with the increasing complexity of our changing social, economic, and technological environment."[74]

In the years since the conference, there is some evidence of an attempt to realize the propositions set forth.[75] Incentive grants awarded under LSCA Title I have been forthcoming, and the specific language of that title has been modified to include information and referral centers. The Detroit "TIP" program and the Memphis CI&R were established under Title IIB of the Higher Education Act. The Freedom to Read Foundation has been established and has been active in promoting equal access and combating censorship.

By the end of the 1970s, public concern had shifted. Campus unrest, changing mores, concern over inflation and the economy had taken priority, and a decline in educational commitment was in evidence. Balancing the budget and increasing expenditures on defense were more important than continuing social reform programs. This trend has continued through the 1980s, exemplified by the Reagan administration's consistent opposition to renewal and funding for the Library Services and Construction Act. Taxpayers on a local level have been less willing to support public services, and many programs that were instituted in the sixties and early seventies have been eliminated in the face of budget cuts and declining federal support. Birge sees this declining visibility and dwindling support as a result of the lack of an integrated, dynamic commitment to learners' advisory and adult education services.[76] As long as these types of services are viewed as extras, rather than vital parts of the library's service mandate, they will continue to be at risk.

Nauratil observes that many librarians see the eighties as a time for retrenchment, not expansion and innovation.[77] As evidence of growing indifference to the plight of nontraditional clientele—those effectively disenfranchised because of age, race, lack of educational achievement, poverty, or institutionalization—she points out that the number of citations listed under the heading "Libraries and Social and Economic Problems" in *Library Literature* plummeted from well over one hundred in the mid-seventies to less than a third of that number by the mid-eighties.[78]

Despite the apparent trend toward federal government indifference and cutbacks on the local level, there is evidence of the pressing need for the library to become involved dynamically in lifelong learning and to develop a philosophy of public library service that promotes this educational goal. Congress has repeatedly overridden presidential vetoes to ensure funds for the continuance of the LSCA. The publication of *A Nation at Risk* has called national attention to the need for an improved system of public education, one which adopts the concept of a learning society.[79] *Libraries and the Learning Society: Papers in Response to "A Nation at Risk"* points out that the library's goals and resources are already attuned to this need, and makes recommendations to ensure that the library take a more active and vital part in creating a learning society.[80] The Education for Economic Security Act, passed in 1984, gives recognition to the economic impact of a poorly educated populace.

Literature from other disciplines indicates a growing concern for a people ill-prepared to meet the demands of a society that requires constant change and adjustment, and a growing recognition for the need to establish a network of educational opportunities that will meet the individual's needs at every stage of development. The report of the Commission on Non-Traditional Study stated that "the aim of public libraries to provide unlimited knowledge is in total harmony with the aim of non-traditional education: to provide unlimited opportunity. The possibility for joining the two should not be permitted to pass by quietly."[81]

Recent Trends in Education

FINDINGS ABOUT ADULT LEARNERS

Perhaps the most startling finding from recent experimentation in the educational field is the pervasiveness of adult learning activities. When adult learning was examined in the more traditional sense, taking into account only formal, organized activities, participation rates for adults ranged from 12 to 31 percent.[82] Tough, who explored adult learning by studying independent learning projects, found that 98 percent of adults participated in some learning activity over a year's time span, and that less than 1 percent of those were undertaken for credit.[83] More conservative estimates have placed activity as low as 79 percent, which still represents a vast majority of adults.[84]

Why do adults undertake learning activities? Tough's study found a variety of reasons:

1. To prepare for a job, or to update skills
2. To cope with specific job-related problems
3. To deal with home and personal responsibilities
4. To upgrade a broad area of competence
5. To occupy leisure
6. To satisfy curiosity about a particular subject.[85]

These are extensions of Knowles's ideas that learning is undertaken by the individual to "prevent obsolescence" of skills and knowledge and to enhance the individual's self-development.[86] He observed that "a society in which machinery is doing more and more of the work of man requires a citizenry capable of performing increasingly complicated occupational roles and capable of creatively using more leisure time."[87]

The surveys by Penland and Tough indicate that many more adults take part in independent, self-initiated projects than in organized activities. While some of the causes are situational (transportation, money, childcare), the primary reason appears to be dispositional.[88] That is, while external factors act as barriers to participation in structured activities, most adults simply prefer to learn independently. Penland's study listed reasons adults seem to prefer learning independently:

1. Preference for setting one's own pace
2. Preference for using one's own style of learning
3. Desire to keep the activity flexible and easy to change
4. Desire to control the structure of the project
5. Lack of awareness of classes in the desired subject
6. Desire to learn immediately (rather than wait for a class)
7. Lack of time for formalized class
8. Dislike of classroom setting
9. Lack of money
10. Lack of transportation.[89]

He noted that adults "often feel a strong need to establish the pace and control the character of their learning experiences," and that those reasons were most often cited as the reason for avoiding formal classes.[90] In light of these findings, it is only logical that "the goal of the learning society is to make adults stronger, more self-motivated and self-directed learners."[91]

The concept of andragogy postulated and codified by Knowles is largely responsible for the new way of looking at education and learning that has formed the basis for lifelong learning theory.[92] Knowles observed that the ways in which adults approached learning were vastly different from the traditional methods found in formal institutions of education. Although originally seen as a way of differentiating between the teaching of children and the teaching of adults, the pedagogy-andragogy dichotomy came to be viewed as simply two different teaching methods, either of which might be appropriate for any age learner, depending on the individual.

The two models are on opposite ends of a continuum that moves from teacher dependency to self-direction and motivation. The teacher ultimately becomes a facilitator of knowledge, rather than an instructor or controller. The andragogical model recognizes that the individual has an accumulated store of knowledge and experience to bring to the learning situation, and tends to employ experiential, active teaching methods rather than passive ones. Learning in the pedagogical model tends to be subject-centered with a delayed application, while in the andragogical model a problem-centered approach with immediate application is seen as more relevant. Studies of adult learners tend to support this last assumption. Generally, adults seem to emphasize learning that is useful and applied. They tend to be problem-centered and goal-oriented, and are generally more apt to engage in acquiring knowledge which they view as utilitarian.[93]

In summary, then, recent educational thought has put the emphasis on the individual learner. Studies have found that a large percentage of the adult population engages in learning activities and that they generally prefer to pursue them at their own pace and in their own way. The current trend is to recognize that "learning is the active, not the passive part of the process."[94] "Learning is an internal process" and adults "are motivated to engage in learning to the extent that they feel a need to learn and perceive a personal goal that learning will help to achieve."[95]

THE GROWTH OF NONTRADITIONAL STUDY

Recognition of the individuality of the learner leads to the growth of a variety of opportunities. Gardner notes that "if we are to do justice to individual differences, if we are to provide suitable education . . . then we must cultivate diversity in our higher education system to correspond to the diversity of the clientele."[96] More attempts were being made to provide educational opportunities to fulfill a wide variety of needs for a remarkably heterogeneous clientele.

In reaction to the student activism of the 1960s and the economic realities of a declining student population, colleges and universities began "to move toward loosening their conventions regarding the terms, places, mechanisms, and content of postsecondary education."[97] Changes in course content and degree requirements were made in response to student demands for a more relevant and individualized education. Remedial, vocational, and basic skills courses were offered for the educationally disadvantaged, and administrative changes were made in an attempt to meet the needs of different segments of the population. These changes provided for scheduling and location options, including evening and weekend courses, and sometimes made provision for self-paced learning. Students could gain credit for off-campus courses, whether through extension, work, or at-home study. Innovative teaching methods included distance teaching, independent study, teaching cassettes, computer based courses, and learning contracts. Older students could gain college credit by exam, for life experience, or proven competency in an area. Student services were expanded to include guidance and educational assistance, including remedial assistance, basic education, and psychological support.[98] Although some of these innovative programs have been discontinued, there remain a vast array of nontraditional services offered through higher education.

Many options exist outside of the university setting, and more adults are taking advantage of them. Knox finds that the higher level of educational attainment among adults and the pressures of change result in more adults participating in continuing education.[99] As a result, he notes that there are many independent providers, and this makes it difficult for the potential student to make the most appropriate choice.

Darkenwald and Merriam list the wide variety of organizations offering educational programs.[100] Among community-based agencies he finds learning exchanges, free universities, and private literacy groups. Libraries and museums offer substantial contributions. Other independent agencies with educational concerns are private vocational, trade, and business schools, and correspondence courses. Churches and synagogues offer adult education programs, over a quarter of which deal with nonreligious subjects. The Red Cross and YMCAs offer many different types of programming. Public schools have become increasingly involved in adult education as evidenced by the growth of GED and adult basic education courses offered. Community colleges offer a broad spectrum of courses from vocational to recreational, with or without credit. Darkenwald and Merriam point out the contribution of the cooperative extension service, calling it "the world's largest publicly supported informal adult education and development organization."[101] His assertion is supported by the Adult Services in the Eighties project, in which cooperative extension was frequently listed as a sponsor or cosponsor of library programming. Business organizations have become increasingly involved in employee education and training, and this trend will be discussed later in this chapter. The federal government has traditionally supplied training and educational opportunities for both military and civilian employees. A very recent trend is the proliferation of short courses and workshops offered to the public by hospitals and medical centers.

Given this broad array of services, it would seem that the learning society is firmly in place. The very diversity of the offerings, while an asset, is also a major problem. Learners cannot find their way through the maze to the program that will prove most effective for them. Those who most need to avail themselves of the opportunities provided may be the least able to negotiate the tangle of credit or not-for-credit, free or costly, long-term or short-term, recreational or vocational, and advanced or beginner offerings of government, community, work, church, or college-sponsored offerings. "The critical element for stimulating the learning society lies in the effectiveness of the matching process."[102] In recognition of this situation, and of the importance of that "missing link" between learners and resources, much emphasis has been given to the fairly new concept of educational brokering.[103]

THE GROWTH OF EDUCATIONAL BROKERING

In the face of this overwhelming variety of educational options, it was found that the learner needed "reliable help from a neutral source in finding his or her way to a program that suited his educational level, financial condition, and life situation."[104] Between 1973 and 1978, over 300 new programs or agencies were established for adult guidance and counseling.[105] "A number of state and federal funding programs were instituted and a new theme in public policy agendas emerged: the lifelong learning concept."[106]

Heffernan identified and discussed factors that led to the increased popularity and availability of educational brokering services.[107] The first was foundation support for development and demonstration projects. The Ford Foundation, Carnegie Corporation, and Kellogg Foundation were all instrumental in supplying funds for projects such as the Regional Learning Service (Syracuse, 1971–1972), the National Center for Education Brokering, and OPTIONS Inc. (Columbus, Ohio, 1978). Foundation support gave agencies the financial freedom to develop innovative programming, as well as the credibility needed to attract other funding.

The Career Education Project (1972), developed and run by the Education Development Center of Newton, Massachusetts, until 1975 represented a "major research-and-development effort in the career-education area."[108] While the project made a major impact on the clients and demonstrated the value of phone counseling, it lost much of its value because of poor dissemination of the findings.

The establishment of the Fund for the Improvement of Postsecondary Education (FIPSE) in 1973 was "central to the developing identity and focus of the brokering movement."[109] Although the fund sponsored a broad range of innovative educational programs, it did not have the funding to support independent agencies long enough for them to achieve stability. As a result, FIPSE began to support programs in established organizations, but had difficulty in ensuring neutrality and a client-centered focus under those conditions.[110]

Heffernan viewed the expansion of library-based learners' advisory programs in the 1970s as significant to the expansion of the education brokering concept.[111] "Libraries are client and community oriented and are institutionally neutral, characteristics that have made them natural settings for educational-brokering services."[112] The Adult Independent Learners Project and the Consortium of Public Library Innovation (previously discussed), as well as the Higher Education Learners' Advisory Services (HELAS) of the New York state library system and the Lifelong Learning Centers programs of Philadelphia and Reading, Pennsylvania, provided valuable examples of the effectiveness of educational brokering in action. Unfortunately, after special funding was withdrawn, public libraries were unable "to absorb even the most moderate time and dollar expenses," although it was shown that add-on costs for the services were minimal.[113]

Amendments to the Higher Education Act of 1965 were important to the development of educational brokering. The 1972 amendments established Educational Opportunity Centers to provide information on financial and academic assistance programs, to assist with admissions and financial aid applications, and to offer counseling and tutorial services.[114] In 1976, Title I, Part A of HEA was amended to assist colleges and universities in strengthening community service programs. Brokering services were one of the methods for carrying out this charge. Educational Information Centers were authorized by 1976 amendments to Title IV. This provision was particularly important, as it established the principle of accessible career and educational information, it recognized the value of diverse agencies and settings, it supported the use of cooperation, networking, and existing resources, and it strengthened the link between educational and occupational concerns.[115]

Statewide career-information systems were established by the Department of Labor in 1974 to offer information on careers and requirements, employment opportunities, and educational and training resources. The Association of Computer Based Systems for Career Information (ACSCI) grew from the project. Its purpose was to form a national consortium for "accreditation, training, and technical assistance."[116] In 1978, control passed to the National Occupation Information Coordinating Committee.

The National Center for Educational Brokering, supported by FIPSE, fees, publications, and projects with the National Manpower Institute, was founded in 1976. It published *Educational Brokering: A New Service for Adult Learners*, as well as a monthly bulletin. The Center sponsored workshops, published an annual directory, acted as a publications clearinghouse, and sent information to state and federal legislative bodies.[117] The National Occupational Information Coordination Committee was established in 1977 under the Vocational Education Act of 1963 (as amended 1976) to serve as "the chief coordinating agency for the development of a national occupational-information system" in coordinating job information from the data banks of the Departments of Labor and Health, Education, and Welfare, including the Employment and Training Administration and the Bureau of Labor Statistics.[118]

Interest in education brokering continues to grow. Cross sees brokering as the link between learners and resources, and identifies three functions: helping the learner to define goals, helping the learner to select experiences, and helping the learner to gain access to opportunities.[119] Models employed in educational brokering appear to fulfill these goals. Following a study of clients of diverse brokering services, Heffernan found that

> Despite difference in measures, inferences about causality, appropriateness of services, and a host of other sources of variance, the majority of the educational brokering clients surveyed indicated that they were specifically and positively affected by their contact with the agency. Between 64 and 99.3 percent of the clients studied experienced tangible, positive changes following their counseling, information, or referral contacts.[120]

GROWTH OF CONCERN OVER TRADITIONAL PREPARATORY EDUCATION

Concern over the quality of education in public school systems has grown over the past several years. *A Nation at Risk* called attention to the failings of the traditional system in preparing students to develop personally and to compete in the marketplace.[121] Functional illiteracy has caused widespread concern and a major, nationwide campaign to combat the problem has emerged. The dropout rate is high and unemployment among the young and undereducated is epidemic. Businesses report an inability to find qualified applicants to fill positions, and worry about competing in the world market. Many observers place the responsibility for these problems squarely on the public school system and its inability to formulate an effective plan of action. Additionally, these deficiencies have an even greater impact on minorities and the poor, and tend to exacerbate the problem of the increasing gaps between the haves and the have-nots in the information society. The implications for a society that values information are clear: those "who do not possess the levels of skill, literacy, and training essential to this new era will be effectively disenfranchised."[122] Adler points out that "We are politically a classless society. Our citizenry as a whole is our ruling class. We should, therefore, be an educationally classless society."[123]

The importance of the lifelong learning concept is in its recognition of the impact of early schooling on adult life. *A Nation at Risk* asserts that "educational reform should focus on the goal of creating a Learning Society."[124] Because of constant change and the resultant needs for adaptation and growth, emphasis needs to be given to the preparatory nature of school. Formal education establishes the attitudes and develops the skills which will enable the individual to continue to grow and develop. "The simple fact is that education institutions, even at their best, cannot turn out fully educated men and women."[125]

Suggestions have been made for restructuring the educational system to better serve the goals of the learning society and the best interests of the students. McLuhan states that it is time for a new philosophy of education. "The classroom is now in a vital struggle for survival with the immensely persuasive 'outside' world created by new informational media. Education must shift from instruction, from imposing of stencils, to discovery, to probing and exploration and to the recognition of the language of forms."[126] In the Paideia Proposal, Adler suggests that schools concentrate on improving the mind in three ways: "(1) by the acquisition of organized knowledge; (2) by the development of intellectual skills; and (3) by the enlargement of understanding, insight, and aesthetic appreciation."[127] This theme is repeated over and over again: in light of accelerating innovation and rapid obsolescence, it is impossible to predict, far less teach, all the necessary skills and knowledge requisite for a successful life. "So it is no longer functional to define education as a process of transmitting what is known. It must now be defined as a lifelong process of continuing inquiry. And so the most important learning of all—for both children and adults—is learning how to learn."[128]

Educational trends discussed—findings about adult learners, the growth of nontraditional study, the development of educational brokering services, and the recognition of the need for a more effective educational system—support the principles of lifelong learning. Lifelong learning encompasses all forms of learning, both formal and informal. It recognizes and respects individual differences and needs. It does not begin and end with school, but encompasses a lifetime of activity. It offers a "democratization of education," by promoting "flexibility and an abundance of content, study materials, study techniques, and learning occasions."[129] This concept, then, can form the foundation for more effective learning opportunities for individuals at every stage of life.

Trends in Sociology

Sociologists have noted several trends that will have a major impact on American society. Chief among these are demographic and occupational shifts and the rapid changes in personal, work and societal relationships.

The dramatic shift toward an older population has led to a reassessment of adults and their capabilities. "In all of history, there have never been as many old people, either numerically or proportionally as now."[130] As the baby boomers have come of age, there has been a concurrent "greying of America." In 1982, over 11 percent of the population of the United States was over sixty-five years old, and the trend toward an older population will continue.[131]

The educational attainment of people in the United States is rising. While in 1940 the average number of school years completed by people 25 and over was 8.6, in 1979 it was 12.5.[132] The implications for lifelong learning are obvious. The more education people have, the more they are likely to acquire. Conversely, this trend tends to emphasize the gap between the well-educated and the undereducated.

The changing status of women is impacting on educational institutions and the work force. While in 1950, only 25.8 percent of married women entered the work force, in 1979 the percentage approached 50 percent.[133] Additionally, fewer women are marrying, and those who do are marrying later, divorcing more often, and having fewer children. As heads of households, women are entering the labor force in increased numbers.[134] Unfortunately, although women's salaries are generally lower than men's, their costs of working are generally higher when one considers hidden costs such as child care and convenience services.[135] While single mothers and women reentering the job market are most likely to need additional education, they are often the least likely to be able to overcome the situational barriers imposed by lack of funds, transportation, or child care facilities.[136]

Another phenomenon that has attracted attention and underscores the need for continual vocational education is the tendency of Americans to change jobs and occupational categories. Not only do people tend to move from one job to another more frequently, there is an amazing growth in the number who change from one occupation to another.[137] The National Manpower Institute reports that "about 1.3 million people in this country move each year from one major occupational area to another under circumstances requiring significant retraining or education in order to make this change."[138]

Perhaps the most disconcerting and certainly the most unacceptable change is the growing number of economically disenfranchised people in this country. Street people, bag ladies, the unemployed, and the homeless are drawing increased national attention. They are symptomatic of a society that has failed to make adequate provision for opportunities for self-development for its citizens.

Change in society is becoming increasingly rapid and adaptation more complex. The interdependency of disciplines, of nations, of ecological and personal relationships has made understanding them increasingly difficult. The 1970s saw a breakdown of institutions and a growing distrust in the ability of traditional systems to solve the problems confronting society.[139] The 1980s has been a decade of turbulence created by crisis following upon crisis: pollution, the energy shortage, population growth, the threat of nuclear war, and terrorism. The amount of information grows, but its production only adds to an increasing feeling of being overwhelmed by change out of control, rather than supplying solutions to pressing problems. Knowledge continues to grow at an enormous pace, and is becoming more complex and specialized.[140] As technological change has grown, it has "become increasingly more pervasive. Changes whose impacts might have been contained in particular industries, in particular regions or in particular aspects of life, now penetrate all industries, all regions, and all of life."[141]

Virtually everything seems to be changing so quickly that it is impossible to keep up. Society and all of its institutions are in a state of continual transformation. Toffler calls the resulting psychological impact "future shock."[142] Schon calls this phenomenon "the loss of the stable state."[143] He proposes that we deal with it by learning to "understand, guide, influence and manage these transformations.

... The task which the loss of the stable state makes imperative for the person, for our institutions, for our society as a whole, is to learn about learning."[144]

Trends from Psychology

The impact of this atmosphere of change has psychological as well as sociological implications. Schon has noted that there is a sense that "the anchors of personal identity are everywhere being eroded."[145] McLuhan called for a radical change in thinking and the educational system, asserting that "Our 'Age of Anxiety' is, in great part, the result of trying to do today's job with yesterday's tools—with yesterday's concepts."[146] Knowles observed that in spite of all the problems facing modern men and women, "a strong case can be made for the proposition that the greatest danger to the survival of civilization is . . . the underlying cause of them all, the accelerating obsolescence of man. The evidence is mounting that man's ability to cope with a changing world is lagging farther and farther behind the changing world."[147]

Humanistic psychologists see lifelong learning as a means for the individual to become open to change and to "live in existential fashion," growing from experience rather than being threatened by it.[148] Rogers feels that the most important learning is "the learning of the process of learning, a continuing openness to experience and incorporation into oneself of the process of change."[149] Through this openness and learning, the individual can achieve self-actualization, personal development of the highest degree.[150]

The impact of humanistic psychology on Knowles's theory of andragogy is clear. Humanists emphasize the importance of experiential learning, of relevance to the individual learner, of respect for the individuality of the learner, of the move toward self-motivation and direction, and of the relationship of the facilitator and the learner. Rogers underscores the importance of the personal contact between facilitator and learner, and characterizes the successful facilitator as one who "accepts both the intellectual content and the emotionalized attitudes [of the learner] endeavoring to give each aspect the approximate degree of emphasis which it has for the individual."[151]

Recognition of this interplay between the cognitive and affective domains characterizes the humanistic philosophy towards education. The need to incorporate the right brain capabilities (intuition and creativity) into the traditional left brain curriculum (logic, cognition, reasoning) is emphasized.[152] After conducting a review of recent research, Harman was forced to conclude that "the potentialities of creative/intuitive problem-solving and choice guidance are far vaster than is ordinarily assumed."[153] These findings tend to support the recent cry for a move from a mechanistic to a more holistic view in problem solving on a global scale.[154] The need to develop these skills is echoed in both the educational field (Adler) and in the corporate world (Naisbitt).[155]

Another supportive contribution to lifelong learning theory is the notion of the adult as a developing organism which passes through continual transition. Sheehy developed the idea that adults pass through certain predictable stages throughout the lifespan.[156] Gross noted that "adulthood is not a plateau on which the personality formed by earlier experiences is merely played out against changing circumstances."[157] The notion of change is tied irrevocably to development and learning.

Recent studies have discovered that "age has no veto power over learning."[158] Contrary to some earlier findings, age has been shown to affect learning ability less than other factors such as motivation, interest, and perceived relevance.[159] Cropley finds that there is no homogeneous group of older learners, and that the individual learning styles evidenced during this time of life require the same diversity of method and format as in earlier years.[160] Catell theorizes that there are two types of intelligence: fluid, which is genetically based and neurophysiologically bound, and crystallized, which is dependent upon experience and accumulated knowledge. Although fluid intelligence tends to decrease after early adulthood, crystallized intelligence tends to increase, so that performance can remain relatively stable throughout most of adulthood.[161] In essence, these and other studies support the conclusion that a "major aspect of educational reform should consist of redistributing educational programs throughout the life-span."[162]

These trends in psychological study tend to reinforce the importance of the lifelong learning concept. They establish the need for a change mechanism, whether because of vast sociological change or because of personal change created by the developmental stages. Humanistic theories on the nature of effective learning situations form the basis for andragogy and adult learning theory. While psychologists have underscored the needs of adults, they have also gathered evidence that reveals that intellectual capabilities do not diminish with age and that individuals may take advantage of the benefits of a learning society throughout most of their adult years.

Trends in Business

"Knowledge, learning, information, and skilled intelligence are the new raw materials of international commerce and are today spreading throughout the world as vigorously as miracle drugs, synthetic fertilizers and blue jeans did earlier."[163] The challenge of global economic competition has forced companies to examine their traditional structures and values. Two elements necessary for social change are at work today in the corporate world: the development of "new humanistic values and global economic imperatives."[164]

Observers have noted societal trends at work that erode the more traditional business structures and which are forcing the "reinventing of the corporation."[165] America's industrial society has shifted to an information society. The result is that value is now placed on human creativity and intellectual capability, rather than raw materials.[166] The majority of workers who will be in the work force in the year 2000 are already there.[167] As the baby boomers mature, and fewer new employees enter the work force, a seller's market will exist for workers, resulting in a new competition to hire and keep the best employees.[168] Jobs are growing increasingly complex as technology eliminates repetitive and menial work.[169] Middle management jobs are disappearing as the computer takes over those tasks.[170] "The continuing entrepreneurial revolution" is forcing companies to "transform employees into capitalists and stockholders."[171] The emergence of a diverse work force, particularly of women, is forcing innovation in scheduling, benefits, and values.[172] Finally, "the plethora of governmental regulations that require corporations to provide training in a multitude of areas related to occupational safety, quality assurance, and compliance with various legislative mandates related to environmental protection, consumer rights, affirmative action, and so on" is forcing a realization of the value and rights of employees.[173] The thrust of these trends leads to one conclusion: "in the new information society, human capital has replaced dollar capital as the strategic resource. People and profits are inexorably linked."[174]

Recognition of the value of the human resource has led corporations to engage in educational activities on a massive scale. Opportunities for continuing education are motivated by the need to create an environment that will attract, hold, and develop the best employees as well as to prevent obsolescence and to train employees in basic skills. Educational opportunities for managers, supervisors, scientists, and other professionals are generally broader in subject content, while those for lower-level employees tend to be more closely job-related, although they may include general studies for basic education and high school equivalency exams.[175] Companies may establish their own educational programming, or supply tuition or leave time in support of outside activities. The widespread acceptance of the educational function has led to the observation that "universities are becoming more like businesses, and corporations are becoming more like universities of lifelong learning."[176] The Carnegie Foundation reports that:

> At least eighteen corporations and associations award academic degrees, and eight more will by 1988.
>
> Wang, Northrop corporation, Arthur Anderson, and Humana offer master's degrees to both the public and employees.
>
> Over 400 campuses and educational buildings are owned by companies like Xerox, IBM, and Control Data.
>
> IBM spends over $700 million a year on employee education.[177]

Nearly all large corporations have full-time staff to develop educational and training programs, with high tech companies having the highest rate of participation. Tektronix Corporation (Oregon) reported that 85 percent of the firm's 15,000 employees had taken part in some sort of company-supported educational activity.[178] Labor unions offer members apprenticeship training, general education courses, and labor studies. Twenty-five percent of the two hundred national and international unions have education departments.[179]

The growing concern over credentials and continuing education is evidence of two factors: the rapid obsolescence of professional training and consumer disenchantment with professionals.[180] Public demands for increased accountability are apparent in the growing number of malpractice suits against professionals in medicine, law, and other fields. Professional recognition of the need for continual updating of skills and the desire for a way to restore the public's trust have led to examination of methods for meeting those needs. Options include mandated formal continuing education, periodic redetermination of competence (testing), and self-guided study. Professional associations are attempting to formulate effective ways to ensure continued competency and many offer educational courses. The American Institute of Architects offers 60 courses a year, the American Management Association offers some 3200 programs a year (with over 100,000 people participating), and the American Society of Mechanical Engineers offers 100 courses yearly.[181]

Some professions award Continuing Education Units (CEU), credit gained for professional education, as a means of recognizing continued professional interest and growth. Some are beginning to require the accumulation of these credits to maintain certification. Most professionals are becoming aware that "degree obsolescence is today's way of life. The 'half-life' of knowledge in any given profession may now be as little as two to three years. The degree, in short, is today the beginning of the education of a professional."[182]

Corporations are becoming aware of "the mismatch between our education system and the needs of the new information society. . . . The corporations' need for skilled, well-educated graduates is sparking an unprecedented alliance between business and the schools."[183]

This problem has led to increased corporate interest and support for public schools. The Boston Alliance, a contract between Boston area businesses and local high school students, is a successful example. Dropout rates have been cut substantially, the number of students entering college is up, and unemployment among minority students has declined as a result of the business community's promise to find jobs and financial aid for those students who stayed in school. The White House Office of Private Sector Initiatives has identified 10,000 corporations involved with 20,000 schools through similar "adopt-a-school" programs.[184]

Some observers feel that the traditional educational system is simply not suited to today's society. Adler advocates vocational training in the schools, not in the traditional, restrictive sense, but as a development of a broad range of skills for adaptation and innovation.[185] Naisbitt underscores the importance of a new approach by suggesting that the three R's of reading, writing, and arithmetic be replace by TLC (thinking, learning, creating).[186] Maslow suggests that the most effective goals of education are "self-actualization" and "the discovery of identity and the discovery of vocation."[187] He suggests that "finding one's identity is almost synonymous with finding one's career."[188] Obviously this theory compels schools to provide the student with the opportunity to develop a concept of career and vocation broad enough to adapt to change and innovation:

> Today's education system—the one some reformers want to elevate to a level of excellence—was never meant to serve the needs of today's information society; it was custom-made to fit the industrial society—a time when it made sense to treat everyone the same. Uniformity, control, centralization in the factory and in management were the ideals of industrial society. Individuality, creativity, the ability to think for one's self—the values we treasure now—were hardly considered assets. . . . What good does it do us to achieve excellence in an education system that no longer fits society?[189]

The Library as the Logical Meeting Point

The lifelong learning concept has gained recognition and support from trends in many other disciplines. The recognition of the value and pervasiveness of adult learning, the growth of nontraditional educational formats and consequent development of educational brokering have persuaded leaders in the field of education to support the concept of lifelong learning, and to study its implications in preparatory education as well as for postsecondary studies.

Sociologists recognize the impact of frequent, inescapable change on both institutions and individuals, and find that an ability to learn and adapt throughout the lifespan are important in coping with this change. Psychologists recognize the growing sense of alienation and helplessness in the face of this change and the need for an effective coping mechanism. The humanist view of adults as growing, developing human beings has gained credence throughout the profession, and additional studies have documented the adult's desire and capacity to learn. Businesses have recognized the challenge of the world economy and the need to develop human resources through continued education and improved preparatory education. The complexity of political decision making, the dynamic dangerous impact of the media in this area, and the vital importance of a knowledgeable citizenry all point to the support and development of a learning society. The importance of developing a learning society to deal with change, to promote individual growth and to produce competitive businesses is becoming widely accepted.

The fundamental characteristics of the public library serve to underscore its suitability as an integral part of the learning society. The Commission on Non-Traditional Study found that "the public library should be strengthened to become a far more powerful instrument for nontraditional education than is now the case. . . . It is a free institution where the individual has open access to great quantities of information. It exists in great numbers, possesses the materials of knowledge, has a public service staff, and is a referral point to other resources within the educational network."[190]

The library has vast resources already in place. There are close to 10,000 public library systems, and 1,300 of those maintain an additional 4,900 branches. The total book holdings alone are in excess of 319 million. In recent years more than 850 million circulations have been transacted with more than 50 million borrowers.[191] It is typical for advocates of readers' advisory services to point out that costs of these services and of educational brokering services are comparatively low since most of the staff and resources necessary are already available in public libraries.[192]

The neutrality of library service is an important asset to adult learners. They are allowed to pursue their own courses and to reach their own conclusions. "Our best public libraries are characterized by the spirit of tolerance essential to real adult education."[193] The extension of this neutrality to educational brokering services is of equal importance. The "institutionally neutral" stance of the library allows it to put the needs of the user before those of any particular organization.[194]

Public libraries have vast experience in linking individuals and resources. Already in place is a staff experienced in accessing information, locating sources, organizing activities with other agencies, and linking patrons with these resources. As a matter of course, the public library already organizes and conducts group learning activities and facilitates the adult education activities of other agencies.[195] This linking activity cannot be overemphasized. "There is little point in having resources and methods available if the person is not aware of them, or lacks sufficient information to choose wisely. They [public libraries] have the distinction of being one of the very few institutions already providing such services to adult learners."[196]

In tune with the most basic tenet of lifelong learning, the library continues to emphasize services to the individual as it has throughout its history.[197] As Houle notes, "One mode of service, the provision of the means of learning for the independent student, is accepted by all public librarians as essentially and inherently at the core of their institution's educational service."[198] The library's recognition of the wide diversity of its clientele is evidenced in its provision of service for all age groups, of services to ethnic minorities, of services to handicapped persons, and of service to provide for the development of a wide variety of interests.

The library is the "single institution that freely provides continuing education" once the learner has completed secondary school, and the "only major educational institution with a mandate covering the entire lifespan of its clients."[199] This provision of random access to learning resources is a primary advantage of the public library.[200] As Kurland notes, "a strong program of parent and family education should be a cornerstone of strong lifelong learning strategy. . . . Lifelong learning means that learning begins with life itself. If every child is given a good start . . . then the probability that we will come closer to the goal of equality will be increased."[201]

To be effective, learning opportunities must provide for three directions of growth. Learning must be perpendicular in providing for growth throughout the lifespan; it must be horizontal in that it is interdisciplinary; and it must be interior, in that it accommodates a series of needs from the most basic to the most sublime.[202] The public library incorporates opportunities for all types of growth in its basic service agenda.

The basic components of an effective agency for the learning society are all present in the public library. Learning resources, both material and human, are already in place, in convenient locations and accessible at convenient times. The library is institutionally neutral, and traditionally has recognized the importance of personalized service to the individual. Its services span the entire range of ages and educational levels. Librarians are skilled and experienced in linking learners with resources, both within the library and within the community. The library is a logical focal point for the learning society. "It appears to be a question of doing the same things that we have always done, but doing them with more awareness, more forethought, more conviction and more zest."[203]

Options for the Public Library

Society's recognition of the value of lifelong learning for every segment of the population compels the library profession to examine its role in the learning society. A closer alliance with other institutions and a focus on the educational goal are vital for the growth and survival of the public library.[204] Recent reductions in funding have caused some libraries to begin a period of retrenchment, while other librarians reason that innovation and expansion of educational service are the means of securing a more dynamic and indispensable role in society.[205] "Libraries may have to become more effective in demonstrating what they return for the tax dollar, i.e., through programs that contribute to the community's economic base: literacy, child care and nutrition, family planning."[206] The importance of the educational role cannot be overstated in a society that values learning. This function of the library may of necessity take precedence over other recreational functions if funding is limited. "Without the educational role, public libraries seem just another community amenity, like community swimming pools or parks."[207]

Options for fulfilling the educational goal are diverse and vary from library to library, depending on a number of factors. The presence of other counseling services in the community, the abilities and attitudes of library staff and administration, the importance of education to community leaders, the needs of learners, and the resources available will influence the nature of services offered. While styles and methods may vary, however, "the road to greatness for the public library comes from undertaking tasks which will make it more and more significant in the life of people. It should do what little it can at the start and then gradually gain strength as it helps individuals to grow and society to reconstruct itself."[208]

The options for library participation in the learning society may be viewed as a continuum for service provision and professional attitude that moves from a traditional, passive stance to a nontraditional, active one. The term "traditional" applies to the prevailing philosophy accepted within the profession. Throughout library history, there have been those farsighted few who advocated more dynamic action in fulfilling the educational role, but their ideas have often been ignored or discarded by the profession as a whole. Innovative programs often remain isolated examples, and are discontinued when special funding disappears, evidence of the superficiality of commitment. Birge suggests that the most widely accepted traditional activities are those which "require the least active intervention in the learning process and personal involvement with the learner," while programs requiring more personal involvement and intervention are less readily integrated into the library's agenda.[209]

At one end of the service continuum is the simple provision of support materials for the independent learner. This service allows the librarian to concentrate on materials acquisition, and requires a minimum of interaction between the user and librarian. This is not to suggest that effective collection development is not a vital fundamental function of the library, or that it does not require effective action from the librarian. Provision of materials requires efficient networking for interlibrary loan, anticipation of user needs, and organization for easy access. It is, however, a most basic service, and requires very little personal involvement with the individual learner.

Moving along the continuum, the library may add support services for the education activities of other agencies. These services include provision of materials, meeting facilities, and bibliographies or study guides. More active support may lead to interagency cooperation and services. While the interaction and initiative required for organizing these activities may be dynamic, the librarian is nevertheless removed from personal interaction with the learner.

Incorporation of independent library programming for groups moves forward on the continuum toward more active fulfillment of the educational goal. Programming for groups has been widely accepted since the end of World War II. Group programming gained popularity because it efficiently utilized existing resources, reaching a much larger clientele at less cost, and because use of those resources could be justified by the attendance figures produced. Individualized readers' advisory services were not only more costly in terms of staff time, it was difficult to interpret the impact of diverting resources to fulfill the advisory function. While services to groups moves forward on the continuum, group instruction incorporates a degree of distance. The lack of personal interaction may be another reason for wide acceptance of group services within the profession.

The above types of service provision are widely accepted as fundamental to the library's educational objective.[210] They require the least amount of interaction between librarian and patron. Librarians are confident of their abilities in the areas of acquisition and organization, while they are uneasy about counseling and advising.[211] These traditional services are valuable and form a strong foundation for the library's services, but they do not realize the library's full potential in facilitating learning in today's society. Thresher places services on a continuum that moves from information provision to information and referral services to advising and counseling.[212] The services become more involving (in terms of time and energy) for both librarian and learner, increasingly individualized and personalized for the learner, and more effective in linking the learner with a broad array of resources. If the library is to secure a leadership role, it must initiate and commit to those activities for which it is uniquely suited.

Readers' advisory services and educational brokering, both of which require a step beyond information and referral to advising and counseling, are two options for this dynamic participation in the learning society. The historic concern of the library profession for the individual is of primary importance in today's society, and serves to underscore the suitability of the public library as a center for the independent learner. "As technological advances force greater depersonalization of many aspects of community public service, the library has the opportunity to reemphasize its long tradition of concern for the individual."[213] The primacy of the individual, in effect, makes the library institutionally neutral. While diverse learning opportunities have evolved, the library remains unbiased in its institutional stance.

The objective is to find the best alternative for the learner, not to support any particular learning program. By providing for individualized planning within the library (readers' advisory), and by acting as a clearinghouse for other learning opportunities in the community, the librarian may effectively work with patrons to discover and meet their learning needs.

Margaret Monroe extended the continuum one step beyond full involvement with the individual learner. She suggested a model that moves from provision of requested materials to a collaborative approach to the independent community learning center and ultimately to a "community task force style."[214] The public library would not merely provide individuals with information to cope with a changing world, but participate in problem solving and policy formulation in cooperation with other community agencies. This paradigm may represent not so much a revolution in attitude as an evolution of "the library's developing program in support of independent study and the concept of a learning society."[215]

Obstacles to Public Library Leadership in the Learning Society

Although the basic qualities of the public library make it uniquely suited to assume a role of leadership in the learning society, it is possible that this opportunity will go unfulfilled. Four basic obstacles may prevent effective participation in lifelong learning: (1) librarians' reluctance to assume a nontraditional role; (2) poor public perception of the library's function; (3) lack of resources; and (4) the absence of an underlying philosophy to serve as a basis for coherent planning. Librarians tend to be uncomfortable with a role that requires advising and counseling. Birge noted that the profession tends to accept services that require a minimum of involvement and interaction.[216] Thresher, in her analysis of the findings of the Adult Independent Learner Project, found that "nearly all librarians felt that they were not qualified and could not be trained on-the-job to function as counselors."[217]

Some of this concern may arise from a poor understanding of adult learning theory. It appears that librarians, influenced by traditional concepts of teachers and students, tend to assume too much responsibility for planning and outcome of learners' projects. Seymour found that librarians were far more enthusiastic and confident about personalized learning services when they recognized the patron's responsibility in planning and ultimately carrying out their individual learning plans.[218] Adult learning theory emphasizes the role of teacher as facilitator, not instructor, and recognizes the learning experience as an equal partnership. Resistance in the library profession may be due to a perception of adult education as "a didactic form of instruction . . . violating the cherished freedom and flexibility of good public library practice."[219] Those who perceive adult education in this vein overlook fundamental concepts of lifelong learning that enable the librarian to act as partner, not as director, and that enable the learner to move toward self-motivation and independence.

In spite of this supporting theory, there is every possibility that the profession will be reluctant to accept a more active role in adult learning. "Neither AIL [Adult Independent Learning Project]–Nationwide or AIL–New York State proved that librarians, as a professional group, were willing to expand their helping roles to function as learners' advisors."[220] While some may view this resistance to change as a professional characteristic, historians recognize the desire to maintain the status quo as a much more widespread phenomenon. "Given the power of gravity, custom and fear, the dead weight of inertia, of orthodoxy and of complacency, the tasks of persuading majorities to accept innovations remain forever formidable. What counts in the end is the subversion of old ideas by the changing environment."[221] Changes in society point to the adoption of a new library role in the learning society. The degree to which librarians will recognize, accept, and adapt to these changes may well determine the survival of the public library as a vital institution.

Poor public perception of the services and functions of the public library tends to lead to underuse and poor support for services. Libraries are largely overlooked as educational institutions. Penland, in his study of independent learners, found that although the vast majority of adults participate in some sort of self-planned learning activity, only 60 percent have ever used the library, and only 14 percent use the library regularly. He concludes that the library is "not generally perceived as a significant source of help."[222] While the Commission on Non-Traditional Study suggested that libraries could be central to the establishment of a learning society, it also found that "public libraries have too long been regarded as passive conveyors of information or recreation, available when needed, but not playing, or expected to play, active roles in the educational process. Their vast capabilities have often been ignored."[223]

This lack of recognition of the value of library services and potential undermines funding. Heffernan noted that libraries were ideal sites for educational brokering services because resources were, for the most part, already in place and add-on costs were minimal. Yet brokering services have not become widespread in public libraries for several reasons: (1) staff members are already overworked and when special funding stops, other responsibilities take priority; (2) the library is unable "to absorb even the most moderate time and dollar expenses;" and (3) "even though library-based counseling services do get heavy use when they are in operation, they still cannot depend on user fees for support."[224] Changing the public perception of the value of libraries is vital if adequate funding is to be secured. Birge points to the need to develop a total program of adult education activities with specific goals and objectives. Not only would a coherent well-planned program more efficiently utilize existing resources, it would improve the library's image as a focused, dynamic institution.[225]

Over forty years ago, Houle suggested that instead of stating goals in terms of resources, the library should develop goals focused on what it hoped to accomplish.[226] In 1939, the ALA Adult Education Board recognized the need for librarians to take a more dynamic part in "stimulating intellectual curiosity and reading interest" and in advancing "the educational and cultural objective of the nation and the community."[227] The Board's emphasis was important because it created an awareness of the educational nature of services and encouraged libraries to promote their services to the public as educational opportunities.[228] Again, the focus was on what the library perceived as its goal, and not on quantification of materials and programming. Activities are made more significant if viewed in relation to "objectives and principles of continuity and interaction."[229]

Adoption of the lifelong learning concept as an underlying philosophy for library service can focus goals and provide a continuity of service provision. As long as adult learning activities are viewed as discrete services instead of part of a conceptual whole, the library will be plagued by segmentation. If these activities can be seen as part of a unified adult learning program, and if that program can be viewed as part of a lifelong continuum that includes services to children and young adults, a focused educational goal can be presented to the public. Unfortunately, while the educational goal of the library has some enthusiastic and dedicated supporters, "the underlying philosophical structure and other means for implementation are either weak or absent."[230] Many authors have urged the adoption of a basic philosophy of educational service in the library. Zweizig underscored this need in *Alliance for Excellence: The Library Response to "A Nation at Risk"* by linking the educational goal to funding and public support.[231] It would appear that little progress has been made in spite of these admonitions. In 1938, Alvin Johnson observed:

> If the need is recognized the services can be found. But little or no progress can be made in this direction so long as the libraries regard adult education as incidental to 'coverage,' and so long as libraries are so cramped in their resources that they cannot consider seriously any service that cannot from the outset produce impressive statistical results.[232]

The lifelong learning concept can provide the necessary theoretical framework. It is widely accepted in other disciplines and uniquely suited to library service. The library profession cannot allow traditional and largely internal obstacles to prevent active participation and leadership in the learning society.

Notes

1. James R. Broschart, *Lifelong Learning in the Nation's Third Century: A Synthesis of Selected Manuscripts about the Education of Adults in the United States* (Washington, D.C.: GPO, 1977), p.37; K. Patricia Cross, *The Missing Link: Connecting Adult Learners to Learning Resources* (New York: College Entrance Examination Board, 1978), p. 7; Gordon G. Darkenwald and Sharon B. Merriam, *Adult Education: Foundations and Practice* (New York: Harper & Row, 1982), pp. 11–13; William J. Hilton, "Lifelong Learning," in *The Future of Education: Policy Issues and Challenges,* ed. Kathryn Cirincione-Coles (Beverly Hills, Calif.: Sage, 1981), p. 196; Norman D. Kurland, "A National Strategy for Lifelong Learning," *Phi Delta Kappan* 59 (February 1978): 385–389.
2. Malcolm S. Knowles, *The Modern Practice of Adult Education,* revised and updated (Chicago: Association Pr., 1980), pp. 40-59.
3. Helen Lyman Smith, "Spotlight on Adult Education," *ALA Bulletin* 47 (May 1953): 191.
4. Broschart, *Lifelong Learning,* p. 12.
5. Darkenwald and Merriam, *Adult Education,* p. 11.
6. Cross, *The Missing Link,* p. 2.
7. Ibid., p. 1.
8. Patrick Penland, "Adult Self-Planned Learning," *Public Libraries* 17 (Summer 1978): 6–7; Allen Tough, *The Adult's Learning Projects: A Fresh Approach to Theory and Practice in Adult Learning,* 2nd ed. (Austin, Texas: Learning Concepts, 1979), p. 18.
9. Penland, "Adult Self-Planned Learning," p. 6; Tough, p. 19.
10. Cross, *The Missing Link,* p. 4.
11. Darlene Weingand, *Reflections of Tomorrow: Lifelong Learning and the Public Library, A Delphi Study* (Madison, Wis.: Derby Associates, 1980), p. 35.
12. 1976 Education Amendments (Lifelong Learning Act), Higher Education Act, Title I-B, *Statutes at Large,* vol. 90, sec. 132 (1976), *U.S. Code,* vol. 20, 1015a.
13. Lifelong Learning Project, Penelope L. Richardson, coordinator, *Lifelong Learning and Public Policy* (Washington, D.C.: GPO, 1978), p. 47.
14. Weingand, *Reflections of Tomorrow,* p. 31.
15. Cyril O. Houle, "A Basic Philosophy of Library Service for Adult Education, Part I," *Library Journal* 71 (November 1, 1946): 1513.

16. Lynn Birge, *Serving Adult Learners: A Public Library Tradition* (Chicago: ALA, 1981), p. 4.
17. Richard E. Peterson and Associates, *Lifelong Learning in America* (San Francisco: Jossey-Bass, 1979), p. 5.
18. Houle, "A Basic Philosophy," p. 1601.
19. Robert E. Lee, *Continuing Education for Adults through the American Public Library, 1833–1964* (Chicago: ALA, 1966), p. 1.
20. Ibid., pp. 7–8.
21. Jessie H. Shera, *Foundations of the Public Library: The Origins of the Public Library Movement in New England, 1629–1855* (1949; reprint Hamden, Conn.: Shoe String, 1974), p. 226.
22. Weingand, *Reflections of Tomorrow,* p. 3.
23. Shera, *Foundations of the Public Library,* p. 230.
24. Lee, *Continuing Education for Adults,* p. 10.
25. Birge, *Serving Adult Learners,* p. 9.
26. Lee, *Continuing Education for Adults,* p. 16.
27. Ibid., pp. 16–17.
28. Ibid., p. 18.
29. Ibid., p. 23.
30. Ibid., p. 29.
31. E. A. Hardy, "The Special Activities of the Library in Relation to Education," in Birge, *Serving Adult Learners,* p. 9.
32. Birge, *Serving Adult Learners,* p. 33.
33. Lee, *Continuing Education for Adults,* pp. 43–44.
34. Ibid., p. 46.
35. Williams S. Learned, *The American Public Library and the Diffusion of Knowledge* (New York: Harcourt, Brace, 1924).
36. Ibid., p. 56.
37. Lee, *Continuing Education for Adults,* p. 50.
38. Ibid., p. 51.
39. Birge, *Serving Adult Learners,* p. 5.
40. Lee, *Continuing Education for Adults,* p. 57.
41. Birge, *Serving Adult Learners,* pp. 68–70.
42. Lee, *Continuing Education for Adults,* p. 60.
43. Ibid., p. 61.
44. Alvin Johnson, *The Public Library—A People's University* (New York: American Assn. for Adult Education, 1938).
45. Lee, *Continuing Education for Adults,* pp. 68–69.
46. Ibid., p. 73.
47. Birge, *Serving Adult Learners,* p. 64.
48. Lee, *Continuing Education for Adults,* p. 74.
49. Ibid., p. 76.
50. Ibid., p. 79.
51. Ibid., p. 75.
52. Ibid., p. 88.
53. Birge, *Serving Adult Learners,* p. 79.
54. American Library Association, *Public Library Service: A Guide to Evaluation with Minimum Standards* (Chicago: ALA, 1956).
55. Lee, *Continuing Education for Adults,* p. 92.
56. Shera, *Foundations of the Public Library,* p. 248.
57. Lee, *Continuing Education for Adults,* p. 90.

58. Ibid., pp. 91–93.
59. Ibid., p. 98.
60. James M. Heffernan, *Educational and Career Services for Adults* (Lexington, Mass.: Heath, 1981), p. 49.
61. Helen Lyman, *Reader's Advisory in a Small Public Library* (Chicago: ALA Library Administrative Division, Small Libraries Project, 1962).
62. Lee, *Continuing Education for Adults,* p. 99.
63. Birge, *Serving Adult Learners,* p. 108.
64. Ibid., p. 110.
65. Ibid.
66. Helen Lyman, *Reading and the New Adult Reader* (Chicago: ALA, 1976).
67. Helen Lyman, *Literacy and the Nation's Libraries* (Chicago, ALA, 1977).
68. Penland, "Adult Self-Planned Learning," p. 6.
69. Ibid.
70. Heffernan, *Educational and Career Services,* p. 47.
71. Whitney North Seymour, Jr., ed., *The Changing Role of Public Libraries: Background Papers from the White House Conference* (Metuchen, N.J.: Scarecrow, 1980), pp. 28–33.
72. The White House Conference on Library and Information Services 1979, *Resolutions* (Washington, D.C.: GPO, 1979), p. 7.
73. Ibid., p. 10.
74. Ibid.
75. The White House Conference on Library and Information Service Task Force, *Five Year Review of Progress Made toward Implementation of the Resolutions Adopted at the 1979 White House Conference on Library and Information Service* (Washington, D.C.: GPO, 1984), pp. 3–5.
76. Birge, *Serving Adult Learners,* p. 4.
77. Marcia J. Nauratil, *Public Libraries and Nontraditional Clienteles: The Politics of Special Services* (Westport, Conn.: Greenwood, 1985), p. ix.
78. Ibid.
79. The National Commission on Excellence in Education, *A Nation at Risk: The Full Account* (Cambridge, Mass.: USA Research, 1984).
80. American Library Association, *Libraries and the Learning Society: Papers in Response to "A Nation at Risk"* (Chicago: ALA, 1984).
81. Samuel B. Gould, Chairman of the Commission on Non-Traditional Study, *Diversity by Design* (San Francisco: Jossey-Bass, 1978), p. 85.
82. Cross, *The Missing Link,* p. 1.
83. Tough, *The Adult's Learning Projects,* p. 18.
84. Cross, *The Missing Link,* p. 1.
85. Tough, *The Adult's Learning Projects,* p. 32.
86. Knowles, *Modern Practice,* pp. 28–29.
87. Ibid., p. 36.
88. Cross, *The Missing Link,* pp. 44–45.
89. Tough, *The Adult's Learning Projects,* p. 39.
90. Penland, "Adult Self-Planned Learning," p. 6.
91. Cross, *The Missing Link,* p. 4.
92. Knowles, *Modern Practice,* p. 43.
93. Tough, *The Adult's Learning Projects,* p. 39.
94. J. Roby Kidd, *How Adults Learn* (New York: Association Pr., 1959), p. 15.
95. Knowles, *Modern Practice,* p. 55.
96. John W. Gardner, *Excellence: Can We Be Equal and Excellent Too?* (New York: Harper & Row, 1961), p. 77.

97. Heffernan, *Educational and Career Services*, p. 8.
98. Ibid., p. 9.
99. Alan B. Knox, "Counseling and Information Needs of Adult Learners," in *Adult Learners, Learning, and Public Libraries*, ed. Elizabeth Burge, *Library Trends* 31 (Spring 1983): 564–565.
100. Darkenwald and Merriam, *Adult Education*, p. 155.
101. Ibid., p. 164.
102. Cross, *The Missing Link*, p. 46.
103. Ibid., pp. 8–10.
104. Seymour, *The Changing Role*, p. 33.
105. Heffernan, *Educational and Career Services*, pp. 39–40.
106. Ibid., p. 40.
107. Ibid.
108. Ibid., p. 42.
109. Ibid., p. 44.
110. Ibid., pp. 44–47.
111. Ibid., pp. 47–48.
112. Ibid., p. 47.
113. Ibid., p. 48.
114. Ibid., pp. 49–50.
115. Ibid., pp. 57–60.
116. Ibid., p. 55.
117. Ibid., p. 56.
118. Ibid., p. 60.
119. Cross, *The Missing Link* pp. 9–10.
120. Heffernan, *Educational and Career Services*, p. 132.
121. The National Commission on Excellence in Education, *A Nation at Risk*.
122. Ibid., p. 7.
123. Mortimer J. Adler, *The Paideia Proposal: An Educational Manifesto* (New York: Macmillan, 1982), p. 5.
124. National Commission on Excellence in Education, *A Nation at Risk*, p. 17.
125. Adler, *The Paideia Proposal*, p. 9.
126. Marshall McLuhan and Quentin Fiore, *The Medium Is the Massage* (New York: Random House, 1967), p. 100.
127. Adler, *The Paideia Proposal*, p. 22.
128. Knowles, *Modern Practice*, p. 41.
129. Broschart, *Lifelong Learning*, p. 37.
130. Nauratil, *Public Libraries*, p. 52.
131. Ibid.
132. Darkenwald and Merriam, *Adult Education*, p. 5.
133. Ibid.
134. Lifelong Learning Project, *Lifelong Learning*, p. 34.
135. Ibid.
136. Ibid., p. 35.
137. Darkenwald and Merriam, *Adult Education*, p. 5.
138. Ibid.
139. Harold G. Shane, "Global Developments and Educational Consequences," in *The Future of Education: Policy Issues and Challenges*, ed. Kathryn Cirincione-Coles (Beverly Hills: Sage, 1981), p. 253.
140. Darkenwald and Merriam, *Adult Education*, p. 4.
141. Donald A. Schon, *Beyond the Stable State* (New York: Norton, 1971), p. 24.
142. Alvin Toffler, *Future Shock* (New York: Bantam, 1970).
143. Schon, *Beyond the Stable State*, p. 30.

144. Ibid.
145. Ibid., p. 22.
146. McLuhan, *The Medium Is the Message*, p. 9.
147. Malcolm Knowles, *The Adult Learner: A Neglected Species,* 3rd ed. (Houston: Gulf, 1984), pp. 180–181.
148. Carl Rogers, *Freedom to Learn for the 80s* (Columbus: Merrill, 1983), p. 283.
149. Carl Rogers, *Freedom to Learn* (Columbus: Merrill, 1979), p. 163.
150. Darkenwald and Merriam, *Adult Education,* p. 80.
151. Rogers, *Freedom to Learn,* pp. 164–165.
152. Rogers, *Freedom to Learn for the 80s,* p. 2.
153. Willis W. Harman, "Recent Psychological and Psychic Research: Implications for Science and Society," in *The Future of Education: Policy Issues and Challenges,* ed. Kathryn Cirincione-Coles (Beverly Hills: Sage, 1981), p. 218.
154. Knowles, *Adult Learner,* p. 180.
155. Adler, *The Paideia Proposal,* p. 22; John Naisbitt and Patricia Aburdene, *Reinventing the Corporation: Transforming Your Job and Your Company for the New Information Society* (New York: Warner, 1985), p. 55.
156. Gail Sheehy, *Passages: Predictable Crises of Adult Life* (New York: Dutton, 1976).
157. Ronald Gross, *The Lifelong Learner* (New York: Simon & Schuster, 1977), p. 57.
158. Kidd, *How Adults Learn,* p. 90.
159. Ibid.
160. A. J. Cropley, *Lifelong Education: A Psychological Analysis* (New York: Pergamon, 1977), p. 94.
161. Darkenwald and Merriam, *Adult Education,* p. 107.
162. Ibid., p. 109.
163. National Commission on Excellence in Education, *A Nation at Risk,* p. 7.
164. Naisbitt and Aburdene, *Reinventing the Corporation,* p. 2.
165. Ibid.
166. Darkenwald and Merriam, *Adult Education,* p. 170.
167. National Commission on Excellence in Education, *Adult Education,* p. 4.
168. Naisbitt and Aburdene, *Reinventing the Corporation,* p. 6.
169. Darkenwald and Merriam, *Adult Education,* p. 170.
170. Naisbitt and Aburdene, *Reinventing the Corporation,* p. 6.
171. Ibid.
172. Ibid., p. 7.
173. Darkenwald and Merriam, *Adult Education,* p. 170.
174. Naisbitt and Aburdene, *Reinventing the Corporation,* p. 4.
175. Darkenwald and Merriam, *Adult Education,* pp. 170–171.
176. Naisbitt and Aburdene, *Reinventing the Corporation,* p. 165.
177. Ibid., pp. 166–167.
178. Darkenwald and Merriam, *Adult Education,* p. 173.
179. Ibid., p. 175.
180. Phillip E. Frandson, "Continuing Education for the Professions," *Serving Personal and Community Needs through Adult Education,* ed. Edgar J. Boone et al. (San Francisco: Jossey-Bass, 1980), p. 75.
181. Naisbitt and Aburdene, *Reinventing the Corporation,* p. 169.
182. Frandson, "Continuing Education," p. 61.
183. Naisbitt and Aburdene, *Reinventing the Corporation,* p. 6.
184. Ibid., p. 148.
185. Adler, *The Paideia Proposal,* p. 17.
186. Naisbitt and Aburdene, *Reinventing the Corporation,* p. 120.
187. Darkenwald and Merriam, *Adult Education,* p. 80.

188. Ibid.
189. Naisbitt and Aburdene, *Reinventing the Corporation,* p. 120.
190. Gould, *Diversity by Design,* pp. 82–83.
191. Ibid.
192. Birge, *Serving Adult Learners,* p. 135; Heffernan, *Educational and Career Services,* p. 48.
193. Johnson, *The Public Library,* p. 29.
194. Seymour, *The Changing Role,* p. 27; Patrick R. Penland, "Client-Centered Librarians," *Public Libraries* 21 (Summer 1982): 47.
195. Darkenwald and Merriam, *Adult Education,* p. 166.
196. Joan Neehall and Alan Tough, "Fostering Intentional Changes Among Adults," in *Adult Learners, Learning, and Public Libraries* ed. Elizabeth J. Burge, *Library Trends* 31 (Spring 1983): 550.
197. Birge, *Serving Adult Learners,* p. 4; Penland, "Client-Centered Librarians," p. 45; Douglas L. Zweizig, "Public Libraries and Excellence: The Public Library Response to *A Nation at Risk,*" in *Libraries and the Learning Society: Papers in Response to "A Nation at Risk"* (Chicago: ALA, 1984), p. 107.
198. Cyril O. Houle, "Seven Adult Educational Roles of the Public Library," in *As Much to Learn as to Teach: Essays in Honor of Lester Asheim,* ed. Joel M. Lee and Beth A. Hamilton (Hamden, Conn.: Linnet, 1979), p. 97.
199. J. Roby Kidd, "Learning and Libraries: Competencies for Full Participation," in *Adult Learners, Learning and Public Libraries* ed. Elizabeth J. Burge, *Library Trends* 31 (Spring 1983): 531–532; Zweizig, "Public Libraries," p. 92.
200. Weingand, *Reflections of Tomorrow,* p. 35.
201. Norman D. Kurland, "A National Strategy for Lifelong Learning," *Phi Delta Kappan* 59 (February 1978): 386.
202. General Conference of UNESCO, "Recommendations on Adult Education," (1976) in Kidd, "Learning and Libraries," p. 531.
203. Houle, "A Basic Philosophy," p. 1602.
204. Samuel B. Gould, "Independent Learning and the Future Role of Public Libraries," in *ALA Yearbook of Library—1976,* ed. Robert Wedgeworth (Chicago: ALA, 1977); Nauratil, *Public Libraries,* p. 15; Zweizig, "Public Libraries," p. 98.
205. Nauratil, *Public Libraries,* p. 15; Herbert White, "Public Libraries and the Political Process," *Library Journal* 111 (June 15, 1986): 50.
206. Zweizig, "Public Libraries," p. 100.
207. Ibid., p. 95.
208. Houle, "A Basic Philosophy," p. 1604.
209. Birge, *Serving Adult Learners,* p. 3.
210. Ibid.
211. Ibid., p. 4; Seymour, *The Changing Role,* pp. 24-25.
212. Jacquelyn Thresher, "The 1970s—Decade of the Adult Learner," in *Public Libraries and New Directions for Adult Services* ed. Joan C. Durrance and Rose Vainstein (Ann Arbor: School of Library Science, University of Michigan, 1981), p. 38.
213. Birge, *Serving Adult Learners,* p. 4.
214. Margaret E. Monroe, "A Conceptual Framework for the Public Library as a Community Learning Center for Independent Study," *Library Quarterly* 46 (January 1976): 56–58.
215. Ibid.
216. Birge, *Serving Adult Learners,* p. 4.
217. Thresher, "The 1970s," p. 40.
218. Seymour, *The Changing Role,* pp. 24–25.
219. Houle, "Seven Adult Educational Roles," p. 95.

220. Thresher, "The 1970s," p. 39.
221. Arthur M. Schlesinger, Jr., *The Cycles of American History* (Boston: Houghton Mifflin, 1986), p. 426.
222. Penland, "Adult Self-Planned Learning," p. 6.
223. Gould, "Diversity," pp. 82–83.
224. Heffernan, *Educational and Career Services,* p. 48.
225. Birge, *Serving Adult Learners,* p. 4.
226. Houle, "A Basic Philosophy," pp. 15–16.
227. American Library Association Council, "A National Plan for Libraries," *ALA Bulletin* 33 (February 1939): 140.
228. Birge, *Serving Adult Learners,* p. 51.
229. Houle, "Basic Philosophy," p. 1602.
230. Weingand, *Reflections of Tomorrow,* p. 27.
231. Zweizig, "Public Libraries," pp. 94–95.
232. Johnson, *The Public Library,* p. 35.

CHAPTER 4

Public Library Service to Minorities

Charlene Cain

The public library's roots as an institution dedicated to serving this nation's citizenry date from the middle of the nineteenth century. Since that time the library's constituency has been redefined each time the social milieu has changed.

There are approximately 46 million individuals belonging to the Native American, Asian, Black, and Spanish-speaking minorities residing in the United States.[1] By the year 2000 that figure is expected to reach 77 million, or 29 percent of the projected total population of the United States. By 2025 these groups are expected to comprise 35 percent of the population.[2] These percentages do not take into account the invisible masses of illegal immigrants who travel this country as migrant workers and who resist assimilation, as any recordkeeping of their activities may result in deportation.[3] Librarians' social responsibility is a serious one, especially if it is accepted that, "historically, libraries have been inhospitable to minorities."[4]

The democratic ideal under scrutiny is whether librarians are willing to act upon the fact that the contributions of the four major minorities impact significantly upon the political, social, and economic climate of the United States.

Librarians have often written of "the disadvantaged," "the unserved," "the culturally deprived," "the economically disfranchised," lumping many members of diverse groups together because of economic poverty[5] and their disinterest in the world of books.[6] Outreach is a service style involving direct interaction between librarians and elements of diverse communities outside library buildings. The correctness of these special services has been the subject of much debate.

A seminal article in the examination of the library's place in the social milieu is Monroe's "The Cultural Role of the Public Library," in

212

which she defines folk and ethnic culture as "focused on the unique or characteristic popular culture of distinctive peoples, with such traditions in the arts, festivals, clothing, and food being part of the appreciation of cultural differences."

Programming based upon cultural diversity requires coplanning with community groups and is therefore often practiced by branches rather than central libraries.[7]

Some writers maintain that special services to groups detract from the other recognized functions of the public library. The methods by which libraries activate their clienteles impact significantly upon the other service functions of information provision, guidance, and library instruction. This activation is commonly referred to as stimulation, defined in its broadest sense as "any activity which prompts members of a library's actual or potential user community to make use of that library's human or material resources."[8] The form that stimulation takes is dictated by the social milieu.[9] In an essay on stimulation in *The Service Imperative*, Heim explicates the Stimulation Continuum model. Heim defines two levels of the continuum— "indirect," which are services developed to serve the library's entire constituency, and "direct," or services based on individual needs. Two modes characterize each level—public relations followed by the "creation of a climate for use," which takes the form of library "commitment to fostering an environment in which matters of individual and community concern may be addressed."[10] Heim points out that the commitment must fit the needs of the constituencies within the community served. Outreach is the term most often used in the past twenty years in regard to fostering library use by the disadvantaged.[11] Librarians who write of service to ethnic groups without emphasizing economic status dwell upon the concept of ethnic pluralism, a term that refers to "a variety of ethnic minorities, each of which wants equality of opportunity in addition to a group identity that will be accepted by other groups in society."[12] Without an understanding of an ethnic group's distinguishing behavior patterns, including both the cognitive and emotional aspects, the library's attempts to activate its ethnic clientele will be useless.[13]

Writers recommend that librarians must work within the social structure of the group to be served, learning its customs, diversities, and most importantly, its language. The motivating factor behind this intense commitment is that as individuals use library facilities, they are first drawn into a world of information resources,[14] then a system fostering self-education,[15] and finally a universe providing intellectual stimulation.[16] Much as this entails an alteration of patrons' attitudes, it also requires the library itself to change to meet the challenges of activating patrons and then sustaining their involvement. It is the purpose of this essay to examine how the literature of librarianship and public library service have reflected those changes.

Historical Background

Historically, librarians have viewed their agencies as pillars of the democratic society. As Shera has pointed out, the movement for tax-supported libraries was based upon at least four factors:

> (a) A growing awareness of the ordinary man and his importance to the group, (b) the conviction that universal literacy is essential to an enlightened people, (c) a belief in the practical value of technical studies, and (d) an enthusiasm for education for its own sake.[17]

Though some writers embrace the picture of the library as the institution where the "common man" may find a welcome atmosphere for self-education,[18] others dispute what they consider the romanticism of that view. As Martin has noted, little hard evidence exists that masses of less educated individuals actually used the public library for this purpose.[19] As a tax-supported institution, the library justified its existence by providing the services and materials demanded by its visible constituency. That group tended to be educated and economically advantaged; the public library evolved into an institution tailored to serve the propertied middle class.[20] Nonetheless, librarians have long been responsive to the needs of immigrants. Although the public library is well-known as the institution which assisted in the assimilation of immigrants at the turn of the century, the work of many public librarians with the "foreign born" between the two world wars is less often addressed. According to McMullen, librarians' sensitivity to acculturation developed in the social milieu following World War I, when it was noted that about one quarter of the male population in America of voting age was born abroad and fewer than one-half of these men were naturalized citizens.[21] A campaign to Americanize these individuals began, supported by libraries offering materials for naturalization classes.[22] The American Library Association's Committee on Work with the Foreign Born became active in the 1920s, disseminating bibliographies of foreign language books popular among immigrants and later working with the Foreign Language Information Service to distribute useful government information.[23] Although the Committee remained active through the Second World War, outside factors contributed to the decline in library services to the foreign born. The Immigration Law of 1924 set quotas; the Depression cut the numbers of immigrants still further "by removing the economic incentive and the wherewithal for coming."[24]

Through the thirties and forties librarians grew less involved with the foreign born. McMullen speculates that this may be because the last wave of Europeans who immigrated just prior to or after World War II assimilated rather quickly, making use of programs set up earlier in the century. Additionally, immigration levels never returned to those of earlier in the century, and social attitudes had changed to the point that "'Americanization' was no longer considered necessary for the national health."[25]

At about the time that the Americanization ideal lost its impetus in public libraries, a long-deferred cause emerged. "The sleeping giant" of black civil rights awareness awoke with vigor in the 1930s, advanced gradually in the 1940s, and accelerated in the 1950s.[26] It had long been taken for granted that what were considered as rights by most Americans were frequently considered privileges for blacks, especially in the South. The legal fiction of "separate but equal" facilities established under *Plessy vs. Ferguson* in 1896 would continue for several years, but the concept was truly little more than moot in view of the outright denial of access exercised by many southern libraries. Eliza Atkins Gleason conducted a survey of library services from 1939 to 1940 as research for her doctorate at the University of Chicago.[27] Her findings, published as *The Southern Negro in the Public Library* in 1941, showed discriminatory practice in southern library services. Some maintained separate facilities; others provided services exclusively to whites. Gleason concluded that only one-fifth of the nearly nine million blacks in the thirteen southern states received any library service at all.[28]

Meanwhile, national attitudes toward the deprived took their cue from the "psychiatric world view" popular in the 1940s. As Nauratil notes:

> This ideology, developed as a means of meeting the occupational and advancement needs of the newly emerging professional class, did not seek to determine the social causes of social, medical, educational and economic problems, but assigned psychological diagnoses to individuals afflicted with these problems.[29]

These attitudes did not do much toward encouraging services to the poverty-stricken, possibly because most librarians felt unqualified to deal with supposed psychiatric problems.

Adding to the confusion toward services for the deprived were the opposing viewpoints espoused by the library profession during the

1940s. Heim points out that the 1943 *Post-War Standards for Public Libraries* and *A National Plan for Public Library Service* (issued in 1948) both emphasized the correctness of activity aimed at stimulation to use, even displaying an early orientation toward what would later be called outreach. The *National Plan* also stressed the need for library book selection oriented toward providing leadership in arousing community discussion of public issues.[30]

These standards, which arose from a national environmental context emphasizing the preservation of democracy, were overshadowed by the publications of the Public Library Inquiry. In researching one area of the Inquiry's interest, Leigh consolidated the objectives of the *Post War Standards*, the *National Plan* and the *Four Year Goals*, mailing the final version to a variety of librarians with the request that they critique its accuracy in regard to the reality of public library service.[31] Leigh's interpretation of the responses led him to conclusions that undermined much of the substance of the official standards. Contrasting the idealism of "library faith" of the standards to the "stubborn realities" of library work,[32] Leigh narrowed the objectives of stimulation to activation of the library's most visible clientele, the educated and economically advantaged.[33] Because the publications of the Public Library Inquiry defined "many of the formative constructs with which American librarians would be working through the fifties," Heim describes them as having "partially blunted the fairly egalitarian tenets" of the National Plan.[34] Harris notes that "librarians in general reacted negatively" to Leigh's findings regarding the library's "natural audience," but attributes this to "their fear of public disapproval."[35] Other writers believe that librarians, acting in faith that their basic mission of service to all would come to fruition in the very near future, postponed concern for the disadvantaged.[36]

It is difficult to draw substantive conclusions regarding the state of library service to the disadvantaged from Helen Lyman Smith's survey, *Adult Education Activities in Public Libraries*, as most of the findings are couched in generic terms. As the terminology of the survey shows, by 1954 librarians were still dwelling upon the foreign born in discussions of service to ethnic groups. Only 153 libraries out of a total of 1,692 offered services to the foreign born, which ranked fifteenth of the twenty community groups delineated in responses to the questionnaire. Intercultural agencies ranked slightly higher; 287 libraries reported having worked with them.[37] As to the objectives of these programs, Lyman Smith noted, "Least frequently mentioned were: to inform about the library, to serve a special group, to reach individuals, to help other agencies or groups achieve educational objectives."[38] Not surprisingly, considering the time period, the vast majority of the libraries surveyed clung to books and booklike materials in provision of service to community groups.[39]

THE 1950s: ERA OF THE DEMOCRATIC IDEAL

Lyman Smith's findings support the idea that by the 1950s democracy had replaced Americanization as the societal context for public library service. American heritage programming ranked third among the public libraries' own successful programs and activities. This emphasis on democratic ideals is interesting because in 1954 an event of powerful significance in American history took place. This was, of course, the landmark Supreme Court decision *Brown vs. the Board of Education of Topeka, Kansas*, which dismissed forever the fiction that separate facilities could ever be considered equal.

Data concerning southern library service during the period following *Brown* can be found in Bell's work, *Library Service in Thirteen Southern States, 1954–1962*. Bell sent questionnaires to 448 libraries, of which 269 replied. The survey confirmed that integrated library service had grown in the South, for thirteen states provided it. At the time of Eliza Atkins Gleason's study in 1941 only four states provided such service from main libraries.[40] The study says little about outreach, or even stimulation in its broadest sense, mainly containing straight reportage of librarians' responses in regard to the status of integration and availability of services to blacks.

A similar inattention to stimulation is reflected in the standards document issued in 1956, *Public Library Service: A Guide to Evaluation, with Minimum Standards*. As Heim notes, this document depicts the librarian as passive, "translating, explaining, or leading discussions, but not telling or suggesting what should be investigated." Heim characterizes the 1956 *Standards* as strongly influenced by the Public Library Inquiry findings, "which set forth the business of running the library quite precisely but focused in the main on the library institution rather than the community of users and potential users."[41]

Interestingly, two years after these standards were issued, the first thrust of the Brooklyn Public Library's systemwide outreach services began. Experience gleaned from this adult reading improvement program later led Eleanor T. Smith, Coordinator of Adult Services at the Brooklyn Public, to remark that the greatest obstacle in the program was furnishing high interest, low vocabulary books for adults, since such were few.[42] As "an attempt to build a bridge between library and community through personalized response to individuals in single or group situations," Brooklyn's program was truly a model for outreach in its most fundamental sense. From the beginning the program was centered around the work of the community coordinator, whose purpose was to accommodate the special needs of individual neighborhoods.[43] The advent of this innovative program, coupled with the passage of the Library Services Act in 1956, which legislated the first direct federal funding for libraries, signaled that great things lay ahead. Times, and attitudes, were changing.

THE 1960s: DECADE OF SOCIOLOGICAL PROBING AND ACTIVISM

The 1960s began as a time of sociological probing. During the period prior to the onset of the War on Poverty program, library literature concentrated on barriers to physical access by blacks, which still took the form of segregated facilities in the South. The emphasis tended to be placed on services to urban blacks and Appalachian whites, although McMullen points out that it was about this time that the influx of Cubans fleeing Castro's regime required the Miami Public Library to increase both its Spanish-language collection and its Spanish-speaking staff.[44] He also notes that New York City's Spanish population had grown to 1.6 million by 1960, providing the impetus for the South Bronx project, which will be discussed later in this essay.[45]

In *The Evolution of Library Outreach 1960–75 and Its Effect on Reader Services*, Weibel analyzes the literature of the early sixties as having "looked inward, building primarily on itself" and focusing on

> First, service to the poor through provision of more and relevant materials and an intensification of accepted library reader service activities; second, the extension of services into the community through active participation of library staff in the life of the community—an emphasis on the reader-services function of creating a climate for use; and third, a change in the role of the public library—an extension of the creation of a climate for use to political and social considerations beyond the library.[46]

In 1963, librarians were startled out of complacency by the International Research Association's study, *Access to Public Libraries*. The survey provided evidence of outright denial of access to blacks in five states of the deep South as well as proof of the existence of lesser barriers in the rest of that region. Expected as this information was by librarians, many were outraged by the study's charge that indirect discrimination existed in libraries across the United States.[47] As a result, research methods used to compile the study were challenged.[48] Other writers, such as Parker, defended the findings, noting that insidious discrimination in the North resulted in an emphasis on the construction of more branches for the suburbs than for inner city areas inhabited primarily by blacks.[49]

It was during this period of hot debate that the federal government began its War on Poverty program with a flurry of legislation designed to alleviate the crippling severity of poverty identified by social scientists. The legal foundation for activity during this era was the Civil Rights Act of 1964, the passage of which "marked the end of the era of legal and formal discrimination against Negroes and created important new machinery for combating covert discrimination and unequal treatment."[50]

The Economic Opportunity Act of 1964 was the first shot fired in the War on Poverty. It authorized many programs with which librarians became involved, including: (1) the Job Corps, which provided young people with vocational training in urban centers operated by universities and private corporations, and remedial education in rural conservation centers run by the federal government;[51] (2) Neighborhood Youth Corps and College Work Study Programs, which supplied part-time work experience for young people from low-income families so that they would be able to remain in school;[52] (3) Community Action Programs, which funded community-staffed organizations aimed at mobilizing local resources to alleviate poverty;[53] (4) VISTA (Volunteers in Service to America), which trained highly motivated young people to work with migrant laborers as "the domestic version of the Peace Corps";[54] and (5) Project Headstart, which provided as much as 90 percent funding for local preschool development centers dedicated to igniting a love of books in economically deprived children alienated from the world of learning.[55]

It should be noted that in taking advantage of the funding for these programs, libraries were required to cooperate with governmental agencies and community groups. This official, external stimulus toward outreach had the additional influence of being a source of funding for many of the services that public librarians were on record as having wished to provide.[56]

Another important War on Poverty innovation was the Model Cities Act, directed by the Department of Housing and Urban Development. The program was designed to streamline activation of resources by consolidating use of federal housing, education, and manpower programs. Political accountability for success or failure came from the fact that responsibility was shared between the city government and neighborhoods. If the public library as an urban institution was sometimes ignored by Model City planners, authors have attributed as much blame to librarians' passivity as to the planners' ignorance.[57]

Finally, the War on Poverty's most direct influence on librarians' approach to the stimulation function came with the increase of federal funding resulting from the 1964 transformation of the Library Services Act into the Library Services and Construction Act. As Nauratil notes, one of the primary functions of the LSCA was to assist states in improvement of library services to the disadvantaged and to other needy groups and to revitalize the major urban libraries.[58]

Urban library constituencies had changed during the 1950s; responding to the needs of inner-city dwellers would present a challenge to librarians documented time and again in the literature of the War on Poverty. These changes wreaked havoc on traditional urban services, as Lacy observed in *Libraries at Large*:

> The migration of displaced agricultural laborers to central cities of metropolitan areas was paralleled by a migration of more prosperous families from the central cities to the suburbs. . . . These parallel population movements produced a truly revolutionary change in the character of nearly all major cities, redefining the clientele of all their services, greatly increasing the demands for those services, and reducing or limiting the financial resources to support them.[59]

There is a healthy anger in library literature during this period, much of which is directed at traditional passivity in librarianship as it related to the sweeping changes in America's cities. The writings of Conant,[60] Corrigan,[61] and Jordan,[62] among many others, describe the era of "white dispersion" and "black containment." Conant, in particular, contrasts the complacent mindset evolving from the range of choices available to suburban whites with the militancy and psychological ghettoization of urban blacks.[63]

With additional funding, a wealth of literature, and a growing sense of activism, librarians set out to fight the War on Poverty with their most basic tool of aggression, "Books as Weapons." Weibel has identified four service models utilized during the period, cautioning that the positions occupied on the outreach continuum are differentiated by emphasis either on the community or the library as the determining force in defining services.[64] The first style emphasizes traditional library services relevant to community needs; the second involves a creative approach to community life participation in which human interaction is considered more important than library materials; the third accentuates communication with clientele in the storefront library setting; and the fourth builds outreach programs through coordinated action with other agencies.[65] This last style may be contrasted with public library activity of the previous decade, when library planning and leadership in community programming ranked 18.5 in the list of adult education activities surveyed by Helen Lyman Smith.[66]

Other trends evident in the literature include a growing emphasis on neighborhood recruitment for professional and nonprofessional positions. In 1954, Lyman Smith noted that among in-house adult education programs, 55 percent were conducted by volunteers or subject specialists from the community; she questioned whether the 15.5 percent of responding libraries that did not provide such services due to lack of qualified library personnel had explored the possibility of lay recruitment.[67] Perhaps librarians were listening, for findings from a 1968 American Library Association survey led writers to conclude "it may well be that the greatest contribution libraries are making to the war on poverty is the employment of indigenous personnel."[68]

Writers urged librarians to explore a creative approach to client interaction as well as nontraditional library materials in programming for the disadvantaged. For example, in "San Francisco: Down These Meaningful Streets," Bennette described the innovative Fillmore Street Reference Project, where personnel transported boxes of books to corners frequented by street people, set the boxes on the hoods of cars, and loaned them out without stopping to process them according to traditional library circulation methods. The purpose was to "lure street people into the world of information," not into the library.[69] Even more radically, Moses declared "The day of the deified book is over," urging librarians to use whatever materials were available to activate clientele.[70] The importance of drawing individuals into the world of information meant that librarians had to provide the formats people wanted. Paperbacks distributed in storefront libraries and film showings on street corners were just two methods of stimulating clientele. As Moon noted in an article examining the High John experiment, the library's moral imperative did not lie in providing "good books" so much as in hooking the patron on reading.[71] The ultimate aim was for the library to become so integral to the community that perception of it as an institution by and for the well-to-do would disappear.

High John was a library education experiment originated by the University of Maryland's School of Library and Information Services, wherein the library submerged so deeply into the Fairmount Heights, Maryland, community that it lost much of the veneer that most individuals identify as library-esque. The atmosphere was casual and homey; there were no labels, no card catalog or classification scheme.

All the book and magazine covers faced outward on slanted shelves to encourage browsing. Anyone could check out books—a totally egalitarian atmosphere.[72] Although the experiment failed, due in part to the fact that the library staff was entirely white, it has continued to be the best-known example from the "anything that works" school of outreach.[73]

The prestigious Bank Street College of Education's study included the Brooklyn Public Library Community Coordinator Project (an excellent example of "a system-wide effort to decentralize library policy selectively to accommodate differences between neighborhoods"[74]) and the North Manhattan Project of the New York Public Library (which embodied the relevant traditional style identified by Weibel as focusing on "excellent service . . . as all that was needed to draw the community to the library"[75]).

An interesting mixture of these modes is found in the work of the Enoch Pratt Free Library, as described in *Baltimore Reaches Out*. Its author, Lowell Martin, a proponent of getting back to basics in serving the underprivileged,[76] also recognized the importance of "experiments in neighborhood extension."[77] These experiments included storefront libraries and frequent book wagon stops in neighborhoods.[78] Nonetheless, Martin did not place his greatest hope with adult education activities, noting that "any realistic library program for the disadvantaged will stress the opportunity with children."[79] The important point was to try whatever might work, as Martin noted:

> It would be pie-in-the-sky to expect a mass response to this or any other reading program for the undereducated. But the test is not whether this effort reforms the world but whether it opens the way back from that "other America" for those who have the potential to journey.[80]

The *Minimum Standards for Public Library Systems*, issued in 1966, is not very reflective of the spirited work being carried out in urban areas. Although it shows a marked sensitivity to the stimulation function of library service, the document emphasizes institutional, rather than community-oriented definition of services.[81] Indeed, the democratic ideal of an informed citizenry takes a back seat in the 1966 *Standards*. As Heim observed, "The library is seen as a source of important information on issues rather than a catalyst to cause the public to think about these issues."[82]

In 1967 ALA's Special Committee on Freedom of Access to Libraries reported on its survey of public libraries. The report contained a series of recommendations regarding location of facilities for minority groups, adequacy of materials, educational programs for librarians dealing with ethnic groups, and recruitment of minorities.[83] The Committee perceived a definite improvement in access since 1960,[84] but noted that librarians were more concerned with access from an operational than from a legal viewpoint.[85] Its final recommendation was that provision of library services to the culturally disadvantaged and underprivileged become a major goal of ALA for as long as might be necessary.[86]

In 1968, the ALA Council established the Coordinating Committee on Library Service to the Disadvantaged, which issued a study the following year of public libraries serving populations over 15,000.[87] The study concluded that "a very small proportion of the public libraries of the nation are participating in library programs to the disadvantaged; and of these, over half participate in no more than two programs."[88] Its findings supported the idea that most special work with the disadvantaged took place in urban areas. Most personnel added for such programming were found to be indigenous to the area; the numbers of professional staff hired for planning were usually increased only in libraries serving populations of 100,000 or more.[89]

Although this study provides evidence that some libraries were taking advantage of LSCA and Economic Opportunity Community Action Program grants (totalling $4 million), not enough was being done.[90] As the decade neared its end, the nation's attention turned more and more to the Vietnam Conflict. In 1969, President Nixon put an end to the War on Poverty by cutting out the primary funding that still existed when short-term grants had ended. The era of plenty ended before librarians could make the mark that so many had hoped for, and as Edwin Castagna remarked in 1967, the profession would be judged

> Because if as librarians, we do not reach out to all the unserved people within our country during this tortured time of troubles, we will have failed to grasp one of the biggest opportunities libraries have had. If we fail, we will have earned the disdain of our successors, and we will have betrayed our public trust as essential agents in our nation's apparatus for education in its broadest sense.[91]

In retrospect, such a judgment would be too harsh, for there is evidence that many had worked diligently, especially in urban libraries. A new era had begun, wherein activism would be the environmental context, and librarians would build upon the lessons of the sixties.

1969 TO THE PRESENT: COPING WITH SOCIETAL CHANGE

Weibel characterizes the period from 1969 to 1974 as one of "closure and legitimation." In this transitional period, attention shifted to "specific client group definition" and planning for provision of services based on perceptions of unique needs.[92] Far from being apathetic, writers now began to develop a philosophical infrastructure on which to base future planning. Lacy saw that an "emerging library responsibility" for the 1970s would be "to play a role in the reintegration into society of groups now largely isolated and excluded by their lacks in education and training."[93] Lacy foresaw the role that technology had only begun to play in the disfranchisement of groups still marginally included in society.[94] Monroe analyzed the outreach styles employed by public libraries and devised a conceptual framework for growth in her seminal study, "Reader Services to the Disadvantaged in Inner Cities."[95] Major Owens called for action in serving the poor and powerless, noting that "knowledge of the right facts at the right time is a form of power,"[96] and that "the library and its services must be a natural extension . . . of the mother community."[97] Allie Beth Martin's *A Strategy for Public Library Change* focused on the importance of both the public relations mode and the creation of a climate for use as proper efforts in activation of clientele.[98]

Owens's key article regarding the role of libraries in the struggle for black civil rights was followed by others expanding upon the impor- tance of activism. Bundy, one of the originators of the High John experiment, called for advocacy service to ghetto patrons, "initiated . . . to get information to where it is needed at a time it is critically needed in an effort which puts it directly and immediately in challenge of an established insitution's manner of proceeding with clients."[99] E. J. Josey blasted southern libraries for "coddling segregation" and provided evidence (gathered by ALA's Black Caucus in cooperation with local chapters of the NAACP) that many had serviced private segregated schools established to circumvent desegregation orders.[100] Black librarians took another step forward in the bicentennial year when ALA elected its first black president, Clara Stanton Jones.[101]

As Weibel observed, librarians' perceptions of the disadvantaged expanded more and more to include the other three predominant ethnic groups identified at the beginning of this essay. Farrington described the state of library service to Native Americans as a problem of illiteracy resulting from a highly sophisticated culture with a non-book tradition, a situation worsened by an unusual language barrier.[102] Cunningham examined funding for Native American services, describing pursuit of Johnson-O'Malley financing as "an exercise in a Kafka-like nightmare."[103]

At the same time that these authors were venting their frustration on behalf of Native Americans, services to the Spanish-speaking were making great strides in the New York area with the South Bronx Project. Originally funded by an LSCA grant to provide service to eight primarily Puerto Rican neighborhoods, its innovative information and referral service recruited interested neighborhood residents as a means to maintain contacts with influential individuals and institutions.[104] Another LSCA grant, this one to aid Mexican-Americans, established La Biblioteca Latinoamerica, a library in the San Francisco bay area. When the grant ran out in 1973, the Oakland Public absorbed the library as one of its branches.[105] Even at this date, it was already apparent that recruitment of Spanish-speaking and Native Americans to library staffs was less than it should have been, given their availability in the pool of college graduates.[106]

On the negative side, special services to Asian Americans were a very long time in coming. For years Asian language collections could be found only in large Chinatowns such as those in San Francisco and New York.[107] The arrival of large numbers of Vietnamese increased awareness of needs, but innovations in service were scarce until the late seventies.

Awareness of the rural poor as a service clientele progressed with the creation of the Appalachian Adult Education Center (AAEC), which began at Morehead (Kentucky) State University as an effort to encourage literacy by accentuating its necessity as a survival skill.[108] The center recruited library commitment by issuing a series of free publications on methods of providing service to undereducated adults. The AAEC worked with public libraries in Alabama, South Carolina, West Virginia, Ohio, Tennessee, Georgia, and Mississippi to negate factors which undermine adult education services; it used information gained through this experience to develop guidelines which asked hard questions about the library's ability to dedicate materials and staffing to instruction, resource files, and stimulation.[109] It is notable that the National Indian Education Association later used these AAEC publications to form guidelines of its own.[110]

The concept of literacy as a skill necessary to survival also begins to appear in literature on service to migrant workers during this period. In 1973 Zonligt conducted a survey of services available to seasonal and migrant farmworkers in the Northwest.[111] His findings led him to advocate the creation of Survival Information Centers within community public libraries.[112] Zonligt recommended sensitivity to the social isolation felt by migrants and encouraged employment of librarians with backgrounds similar to this clientele as factors essential to the success of programming.[113] As a social institution, the Survival Information Center would cooperate with other agencies to seek out and serve migrant informational needs,[114] concentrating on providing tutorial assistance in English as a second language, consumer information, and job skill requirements.[115]

Attitudes toward the disadvantaged began to change as sociological studies shifted perspective from the "psychiatric world view" prominent in the forties to a "culture of poverty" ideology. The culture of poverty concept attributes those character defects supposedly to blame for economic disadvantagement to environmental inadequacies.[116] Providing the basic necessities to the poor may, in the short run, alleviate the problem as perceived by the culture of poverty school of thought, but, as Nauratil notes, "access to economic and political power" through information provision is the real key to changing lives.[117] The librarian is seen as the keeper of that key.

Along with an awareness of the need to provide basic informational necessities to minorities, it was becoming more and more of an issue that too few members of ethnocultural groups were being afforded the opportunity of careers in librarianship.[118] From 1972 to 1974, the Illinois Minorities Manpower Project (IMMP), a joint effort of the ALA Office for Library Personnel Resources (OLPR) and the Illinois State Library, functioned under OLPR Minority Recruitment Specialist, Marilyn Salazar. The project recruited the enrollment of ten minority group representatives living in Illinois as students in library education programs.[119] IMMP's recommendations included encouragement of state libraries to develop minority recruitment programs based on the IMMP model, as well as surveys of other library entities to identify manpower utilization. Noting that since the demise of the ALA Office for Recruitment no official entity oversaw minority recruitment, one of its primary recommendations was the creation of a task force for that purpose.[120] This became ALA's Minority Recruitment Task Force, discussed later in this essay.

During the early seventies, librarians' traditional neutrality in regard to discussion of public issues, encouraged by the tone of the 1966 *Standards*, began to give way somewhat to advocacy and a demand for autonomy. It was affirmed that social responsibility lies not only in passive provision of materials, but in unabashed stimulation, as Monroe puts it:

> The library profession must be free to sustain and develop the climate of the community for the use of libraries, library resources, and library services. Unless the library practitioners exercise this professional prerogative in sustaining the exploration of information, ideas,

and creative experience from all forms of media, librarianship falls short of its obligation to society, as well as to individuals.[121]

The concept of information and referral services, first developed by Kahn in 1966, was a new style of information provision based upon individual need.[122] The Detroit Public Library adapted the concept for its own use, as did the Enoch Pratt Free Library. According to Detroit's Director, Clara Stanton Jones, creation of "The Information Place" followed the prevailing social milieu in "a natural evolution"[123] that transformed it into "an information searching organization, dependent not only upon its own accumulated print resources, but upon its ability to search outside its walls for 'non-book' information as well . . ."[124] The moral imperative was clear, as Jones went on to say, "It is impossible to remain alive without responding to the force of a worldwide social revolution that already has the momentum of two decades behind it!"[125]

It would be unfair to paint this period as one in which librarians reached some kind of consensus regarding the correctness of the library's role in this social revolution. Some writers, such as Berry, found the library programs of the War on Poverty era "an enlightened, if irrelevant effort" rendered ineffective by lack of support.[126] Longtime critic of outreach services, Ervin J. Gaines questioned the ability of libraries to shoulder the financial burden of projects best left to social welfare agencies.[127] At least one other writer disputed the validity of Gaines's comments regarding outreach, implying that his approach to this subject is reactionary by comparing it to the philosophy of the Public Library Inquiry.[128]

During the seventies the public library's role shifted once more, and "understanding change, the context for a post-industrial society" became a primary concern. The United States was changing from a commodity-based to an information-based society.[129] How were the undereducated to deal with this new trick of history? The problem has been called information poverty, a term used by Childers in 1975 in reference to shared characteristics among the poor that "constitute barriers to their felt need for information, their search for it, their acceptance of it, or their use of it."[130] Not all authors accept the information poverty concept. Nauratil sees this ideology as another form of the "culture of poverty" trap:

> Concentrating on this type of information service . . . not only betrays our adherence to the view that the poor are responsible for their own poverty—material and informational—but contributes to their continued oppression. Directing the energies of the poor toward more efficient maintenance of their present situation can, consciously or

unconsciously, deflect those energies from their struggle for economic, political, and social rights."[131]

Whatever its long-term implications, the concept of information poverty revitalized focus on specific client groups. In 1980, the American Library Association's Office for Library Service to the Disadvantaged became the Office for Library Outreach Service (OLOS);[132] today its purview includes promotion of services to all minority groups, the economically disadvantaged, the illiterate, and "those isolated by cultural differences." OLOS also supplies technical assistance and other information to libraries involved in provision of these services.[133]

ALA has formed committees to deal with specific client groups as well. These include the Council on Minority Concerns, designed to protect the interests of minority librarians and serve as a liaison with other ALA offices and committees.[134] The Task Force on Minority Recruitment plans and implements a "national recruitment campaign in cooperation with other ALA units," filling "specializations where shortages are evident."[135] As a source of information on ethnic collections, the Ethnic Materials Information Exchange Round Table works closely with OLOS for the improvement of outreach services.[136] The Multilingual Library Service Committee, a standing unit of the Public Library Association, disseminates information on multilingual collections, advises on the viability of networking, and coordinates activities for foreign language services.[137] The Reference and Adult Services Division has its own Committee on Library Services to the Spanish-speaking, which seeks to improve library services for that client group.[138]

In addition to these groups, several autonomous library organizations serving ethnic groups have affiliated with ALA. These include the American Indian Library Association (AILA), the Asian/Pacific American Librarians Association (APALA),[139] the Black Caucus, the Chinese-American Librarians Association (CALA),[140] REFORMA (the National Association to Promote Library Services to the Spanish Speaking), and the Ukrainian Library Association of America.[141]

ALA has set special goals for library service to Native Americans by affiliating with the National Indian Education Association. Together, the associations "support guidelines designed to meet the informational needs and to purvey and promote the rich cultural heritage of American Indians." This is done by encouraging library recruitment of Native Americans, encouraging "sensitivity to cultural and social components existent in individual Indian communities," and promoting "a bicultural view of history and culture."[142]

The library community is listening. To promote the library as an information source for the 10,000 American Indians living in its vicinity, the Milwaukee Public Library established the Native American Library Project under an LSCA grant. Planners of the project included representatives from ten Indian agencies in the city, as well as public officials and librarians.[143] In addition to this cooperation with other civic agencies, the coordinator, a Native American, visits community agencies, attends meetings, and publicizes the project. It is thought that the success enjoyed by the project has much to do with the coordinator's ethnicity, another testament that employment of indigenous personnel is a cornerstone to successful outreach programs.[144]

The Milwaukee Public project also educates librarians in the need for sensitivity to the differences within seemingly homogeneous groups, another recurring theme in literature dealing with service to ethnic groups. This emphasis on sensitivity is also found in the writing of Robert P. Haro. In *Developing Library and Information Services for Americans of Hispanic Origin*, Haro meticulously defined the varied groups that Anglo librarians sweepingly refer to as "Hispanics." He discussed the cultural differences and unique service needs of Puerto Ricans, Mexican-Americans, Cubans, and Latinos— always emphasizing the historic importance of the Hispanic experience in the United States.[145]

A third theme often found in recent literature is the importance of networking in the provision of multilingual materials, an activity overseen on the national level by the PLA Multilingual Library Service Committee. One cooperative purchasing and processing program is Hispanex (Hispanic Information Exchange), which began in 1977 as the Spanish Catalog Project under the auspices of the California State Library. After the project grew into a statewide Spanish language union catalog, emphasis moved to the development of a bibliographic database to support integrated library operations.[146] Hispanex also supports a journal providing reviews of Spanish language and bilingual materials[147] and a press for development of reference materials for U. S. Hispanics.[148]

Another networking effort underway is Project ASIA (Asian Shared Information and Acquisition), a networking activity designed to facilitate the reading and information needs of California's Vietnamese, Chinese, Korean, and Japanese communities.[149] Project Asia has a centralized staff which selects, acquires, and catalogs books in the four Asian languages spoken by these communities,[150] entering all records into the RLIN database.[151] In addition to its technical services, the project functions as a communications liaison with local and statewide Asian educational and cultural groups; it also maintains professional contacts with library organizations dealing with Asian concerns.[152] Project ASIA has experienced financial difficulties in that its original LSCA funding has run out and the participating libraries must pick up the substantial costs of the operation.[153] The project is also plagued by the same problems constantly voiced in writings about multilingual collections: finding librarians who know the necessary languages;[154] dealing with special vendors;[155] and handling an enormous load of original cataloging.[156]

In consideration of the library profession's inattention to the needs of Asian Americans, the National Commission on Library and Information Science funded, upon the recommendation of its Task Force on Library and Information Services to Cultural Minorities, a survey conducted by APALA of the library and information needs of this group.[157] The APALA survey findings indicate that although about half of the responding libraries attempt to reach out to this constituency, they are hampered by the same problems encountered by practitioners of Project ASIA. It is interesting that the other half of the libraries surveyed do not seem to perceive the importance of creation of a climate for use in regard to Asian American patrons. As the authors of the report point out:

> It is easy to deduce from an apparent lack of demand a corresponding lack of need, and conclude that a needs assessment was unnecessary. It is much more difficult—but ultimately more rewarding—to dig deeper, to try to discern why people are not making their needs known.[158]

As the 1970s came to a close, the American Library Association issued *The Public Library Mission Statement and Its Imperatives for Service.* Highly egalitarian in tone, the *Mission Statement* defines the library's role in the face of sweeping societal change as

> An agency that guides the user at all levels to the most significant and relevant materials, and that actively brings every person—regardless of age, education, language, religion, ethnic and cultural background, and mental and physical health—into effective contact with the human record. It is an agency to help people be realistic, to plan rather than panic in the face of a world that may be vastly altered.[159]

For librarians to live up to this definition, two of Monroe's models for cultural programming must be incorporated into library programming. The library must (1) provide "a network of cultural outreach centers for the community"; and (2) "stimulate consideration of public issues in the light of humanistic values, building such values into the everyday culture of our society."[160] It seems likely that the public library's goals as a cultural center will prove ineffective unless its staff also develops the qualities for library practitioners outlined by Monroe. These qualities are "a capacity and willingness to be a vital part of the community" and the ability to deal effectively with individuals from every walk of life.[161] Both requirements are given credence by the evidence in library literature of the success of programs that involved library personnel of ethnic origin, urged sensitivity to bicultural values, and emphasized community contacts.

The 1979 White House Conference on Library and Information Services addressed many of the prevalent issues discussed as barriers to library use by ethnic minorities and the disadvantaged. These included resolutions concerning the need for information policy designed to enhance access to information, as it was thought that levying of fees for library services would hinder access by persons who could not afford to pay.[162] Resolution A-5 affirmed that "libraries and information services are obligated to reach out to all persons," while A-6 emphasized the need for "training of professionals in human relations, effective use of public relations, and marketing techniques necessary to increase public usage of library services."[163] The Conference also addressed minority needs in Special Constituent Concerns Resolution D-4:

> Whereas, the Nation's people are rich in cultural and ethnic diversity,
> Therefore be it resolved, that library collections and personnel training shall include a special emphasis on the indigenous ethnic populations of the local community they serve, and
> Be it further resolved, that collections and staff training be developed with the participation and assistance of representatives from the indigenous ethnic population of the local community, and
> Be it further resolved, that categorical grants be made available to school, public, and academic libraries to accomplish these goals.[164]

At the same time that librarians were evaluating their own profession for tendencies toward racism and sexism, the United States Department of Education was taking stock of its priorities for the rest of the twentieth century. The product of this effort, *A Nation at Risk*, articulated the concept of the Learning Society:

> A commitment to a set of values and to a system of education that affords all members an opportunity to stretch their minds to full capacity, from early childhood through adulthood, learning more as the world changes.[165]

It is interesting that although *A Nation at Risk* emphasized egalitarianism, individual learning, continuing education, and information access—concerns prominent in library literature for decades—the report's treatment of libraries in the education process is fleeting.

Distressed by this omission, librarians replied with *Realities: Educational Reform in a Learning Society*. This statement by the ALA Task Force on Excellence in Education included two concepts focal to stimulation of nontraditional clienteles: (1) "people in a learning society need libraries throughout their lives"; and (2) "public support of libraries is an investment in people and communities."[166] The Department of Education responded with *Alliance for Excellence: Librarians Respond to "A Nation at Risk,"* a report which this time affirmed both the centrality of libraries in the education process and the partnership between librarians and educators.[167]

In the aftermath of the White House Conference there were objections by some librarians that the resolutions made did not address ethnocultural needs with any specificity and did not take into account the wide range of cultural diversity in the United States.[168] The NCLIS established its Task Force on Library and Information Service to Cultural Minorities in 1980 for this reason.[169] During the ALA Annual Conference at San Francisco in 1981, testimony was taken from twenty-two persons committed to strengthening library services to minorities in an effort to obtain current information on the status of such services.[170] The Task Force's report, issued in 1983, concentrated on "institutional racism" in library education and professional recruitment, programs significant to cultural minorities, availability and quality of materials and resources, and funding.[171] The report characterizes institutional racism as the most destructive barrier to minority participation in continuing education.[172] It also examines programs significant to cultural minorities, affirming the centrality of the stimulation function in public libraries, especially in regard to I & R services and technology.[173] The Task Force found that lack of computer literacy is a barrier in the information seeking patterns of minorities, noting that "libraries have a strong responsibility to the community to assist in bridging the gap between technology and the library's community."[174] Availability of materials, networking, and barriers to access in the form of censorship and user fees are integral issues in the Report. The Task Force characterizes censorship as one of the most insidious forms of access denial, comparing its impact to that of segregation in southern libraries. User fees are also seen as a means to deny service, for they place a barrier between information and the economically disadvantaged.[175]

Testimony presented at the Task Force hearings established that funding for special services often comes from federal sources; the advent of "Reaganomics" has meant severe cutbacks in these sources and a corresponding decrease in public library services.[176] The report quite logically points out that "since minorities are taxpayers and have a right to library services and programming, it makes good educational and political sense for libraries to factor them into their budgeting plans."[177]

Although NCLIS endorsed the majority of the Task Force's forty-two recommendations, it declined to support eight of them. These include recommendations that urge both ALA and the Special Libraries Association to conduct special studies of racial, ethnic, and sexual composition of personnel (recommendations 7 and 8);[178] that enjoin publishers to remove stereotypical images of ethnocultural minorities from their materials but encourage production of works by minority authors (30 and 31);[179] and that exert pressure on states to specify that certain percentages of block grant allocations be used to provide services based on minority library and information needs (38).[180] Recommendations 5, 25, and 37 relate to de facto denial of access resulting from user fees, insufficient staffing to provide assistance, and the lack of multilingual collections.[181] In most cases NCLIS refused to support the recommendations because it felt implementation was beyond its purview. In other cases, such as the statement on removal of stereotypical images, the Commission found the wording unclear and did not wish to endorse a recommendation that it felt advocated censorship. In the case of user fees, it was felt that further study of the matter was warranted before a final decision could be made.[182]

In the wake of the controversy surrounding the NCLIS rejection of the eight Task Force recommendations, the ALA Executive Board created the President's Committee on Library Services to Minorities. The Committee reviewed the Task Force Report and formulated an action document for ALA which became *Equity at Issue: Library Services to the Nation's Major Minority Groups*.[183] It endorsed all forty-two Task Force recommendations, requesting that the rejected statements be reconsidered by NCLIS under the provision that they would be "revised to remove any perceived conflict with intellectual freedom."[184] As an action document, *Equity at Issue* provides specific methods of implementing the Task Force recommendations, including items to be addressed by the next White House Conference on Library and Information Services.[185] This document was reviewed by a broad cross-section of ALA, including the Executive Board, Council, divisions, round tables, and minority caucuses. The President's Committee used the responses to formulate a revised action document (renumbered 1985–86 Council Document 30), which contains twenty-two recommendations for ALA consideration, each one correlated to NCLIS Task Force recommendations and current ALA policy stipulations.[186] During the Midwinter 1987 meeting, the Committee on Minority Concerns presented an implementation plan for *Equity at Issue*, requesting that each of the twenty-two recommendations be prioritized according to its correspondence to one or more of the ALA priority areas and goals.[187]

The immediacy of the need to take action is driven home by the *Report of the Commission on Freedom and Equality of Access to Information*, better known as the Lacy Report. This document scrutinizes the propriety of library response to overwhelming societal change—an issue that returns this essay to its starting point. The Lacy Report explores the evolution of the United States from a commodity-based to an information-based society.[188] It endorses the time-honored role of libraries "in assuring that all Americans have ready, effective access to the full range of information resources that are essential to meaningful participation in modern life."[189] The report is deeply concerned with the complex problem of illiteracy as it is exacerbated by the growing ubiquity of technology in information access. It foresees that library systems will be "in a unique position to provide a continuum of literacy training, spanning both print and electronic media, to a broad cross-section of society."[190]

It seems that librarianship has traveled very far and over many roads to return to the same question librarians have debated for most of this century: What is the extent of the public library's social responsibility? The only conclusive answer seems to be that the fabric of the library profession is so closely intertwined with society that its responsiblities must be defined by and must keep pace with the needs of society. The authors of *Equity at Issue, 1985–86*, assert that the current climate of fiscal and social conservatism is evidence that national attitudes regarding the plight of minorities are shifting toward indifference and antipathy.[191] If this is so, the role of the public library will continue to be debated. Is it to be an institution of middle class culture, or an arsenal of democracy?

Analysis of the ASE Data

A full analysis of the ASE data appears in Wallace's chapter (page 27). Data reported here are derived from tables in that chapter. Certain parts of the ASE questionnaire, especially question 34h about organized programming for minorities and the third page, were designed to elicit information regarding public library services to minorities. The form did not contain direct questions regarding the status of services to the disadvantaged, and very few libraries indicated that such programming was offered.

There are caveats that must be observed in the analysis of the ASE data. Some libraries located in areas having large ethnic populations may not have responded to question 34h simply because ethnic peoples make up the majority of their clientele. Those located in areas with relatively small ethnic populations may not have responded because they lacked the personnel or fiscal resources to provide programming based on special cultural needs. Indeed, many of the returned questionnaires contained handwritten notes from librarians lamenting such limitations. For these reasons, and because it is assumed that any resident of the United States is free to use his or her local public library, this essay will analyze data based on responses from those libraries that indicated a special emphasis on stimulation of ethnic clientele either by responding to question 34h or by listing specific minority-oriented programming on the third page of the questionnaire.

Development of the ASE questionnaire is described in detail with all iterations in *Adult Services in the Eighties: Final Report* by Kathleen M. Heim, ERIC Documentation Reproduction System, 1990 (ED 316 264).

Table 1 presents the libraries indicating special programming for minorities by region as well as the percentage of minorities living in each region. As Wallace points out in his summary of the ASE data, the absolute meaning of the difference in minority population and the percentage of libraries providing services to minorities is difficult to assess, but the lack of programming for minorities in the South is worthy of attention. The disparity could be a function of the general tendency of libraries in the South to provide fewer services. It could also be that the higher proportion of minority residents may make deliberate programming for minority groups less important since attendants at most programs may be minority group members. The majority of programming for Native Americans, Asians, and Hispanics takes place in California (Native American, 52; Asian, 9; Hispanic, 52). States

Table 1. LIBRARIES OFFERING PROGRAMMING FOR MINORITIES BY REGION.

| | PROVIDE | | DO NOT PROVIDE | | PERCENTAGE OF MINORITIES |
	NUMBER	PERCENTAGE	NUMBER	PERCENTAGE	IN REGIONAL POPULATION
North	89	13.8	555	86.2	13.6
South	155	9.8	1425	90.2	21.6
Central	104	10.5	884	89.5	11.2
West	156	15.6	846	84.4	18.5

reporting ten or more libraries offering programming to blacks include California (12 libraries); Florida (13); Georgia (10); Illinois (13); North Carolina (13); New York (13); and Ohio (13).

A tabulation of responses to page three of the ASE questionnaire discloses that 291 library programs designed for minorities were initiated in 1985. Of these, 110 focused on black history, culture, and issues. Hispanic culture, especially food and music, was the subject of twenty-eight more. Twenty-four programs centered on Asian concerns and six on Native American culture. There were seventy-two programs offering instruction in English as a second language (ESL), usually cosponsored by local boards of education and colleges, or funded through LSCA grants. (Many of these ESL programs were designed for specific minorities, especially Hispanics and Asians.) Finally, libraries organized eighteen programs based on general ethnic concerns—including multicultural understanding, business operation, tax help, genealogical research, and political issues. Those states which offered ten or more programs either for specific minorities or based on minority concerns include California (66 libraries), New York (27), Illinois (27), Texas (26), and Massachusetts (11).

Conclusion

The figures obtained by analysis of the ASE data have a limited utility in the study of public library services to ethnocultural minorities; a survey solely for this purpose is long overdue. Certain points can be made based upon the ASE findings, however. Only 504 libraries out of the 4,215 responding institutions reported programming aimed at activation of minority clienteles. Although these figures do not record the unfulfilled aspirations librarians may have regarding provision of such programming, they do bespeak of neglect for special minority needs. Both the ASE data and the projected population figures of the four major minority groups cited at the beginning of this essay support the assertion that libraries must do more to assist in the education of ethnocultural groups.

Libraries have come a long way from the days of the Lyman Smith survey, when minority groups were spoken of in terms of the "foreign born." Librarians no longer cling only to books and book-like materials. Indeed, those items that librarians indicated nearly twenty years ago were needed in serving the disadvantaged, such as bilingual materials and sources containing nonstereotypical treatment of minority groups,[192] are becoming more readily available, though not in the numbers one might wish. Additionally, innovations in traditional services, such as provision of reading lists, could take the form of "action bibliographies," which were called for by Major Owens in 1970 as a means to help informationally impoverished clienteles cope with modern problems.[193]

The creation of community resource files and provision of information and referral services are steps in the right direction, but progress has continued to be slow despite the passage of nearly seventeen years since publication of the Owens article. Such progress may require librarians to become advocates for the information poor, and as of this writing, advocacy is still a matter for debate.

The problems of providing service to ethnocultural minorities and the disadvantaged stem from complex problems of fiscal conservatism, difficulties in obtaining multilingual materials, staff shortages, language barriers, anglo ethnocentricity, and distrust of educational institutions as vehicles for middle class supremacy. Despite millions of words written on the subject, a multitude of actions taken in the struggle, and greater awareness of the library's role in the context of today's sociopolitical environment, the same questions of social responsibility continue to be debated by each new generation of librarians.

Notes

1. National Commission on Library and Information Science, *Report of the Task Force on Library and Information Services to Cultural Minorities* (Washington, D.C.: NCLIS, 1983), p. xii.
2. Ibid.
3. Rachael Naismith, "The Moveable Library: Serving Migrant Farm Workers," *Wilson Library Bulletin* 57 (March 1983): 573.

4. American Library Association, President's Committee on Library Service to Minorities, *Equity at Issue: Library Services to the Nation's Four Major Minority Groups, 1985–86,* 1985–86 Council Document #30, June 1986, p. 5.

5. Thirty-four million Americans fall into the category labeled as living below the poverty level. U.S. Bureau of the Census, *Statistical Abstract of the United States: 1984,* 104th ed. (Washington, D.C.: GPO, 1985), p. 471.

6. During the mid sixties, psychologist Kenneth Clark urged librarians not to label their minority clienteles as disadvantaged, but to concentrate on the individual worth of each human being. See Kenneth B. Clark, "A Role for Librarians in the Relevant War against Poverty," *Wilson Library Bulletin* 40 (September 1965): 42–47.

7. Margaret E. Monroe, "The Cultural Role of the Public Library," in *Advances in Librarianship,* ed. Michael H. Harris (New York: Academic Pr., 1981), vol. 2, pp. 5–6.

8. Kathleen M. Heim, "Stimulation," in *The Service Imperative for Libraries: Essays in Honor of Margaret E. Monroe,* ed. Gail A. Schlachter (Littleton, Colo.: Libraries Unlimited, 1982), p. 120.

9. Ibid., p. 143.

10. Ibid., p. 120.

11. Ibid.

12. David Cohen, "Ethnicity in Librarianship: A Rationale for Multiethnic Library Services in a Heterogeneous Society," *Library Trends* 29 (Fall 1980): 179.

13. Ibid., p. 185.

14. See Major Owens, "A Model Library for Community Action," *Library Journal* 95 (May 1, 1970): 1703–1704.

15. Ibid., p. 1701.

16. Monroe, "The Cultural Role," p. 3.

17. Jesse H. Shera, *Foundations of the Public Library: The Origins of the Public Library Movement in New England: 1629–1855* (Chicago: Univ. of Chicago Pr., 1949): 221–222.

18. Alvin Johnson, *The Public Library—the People's University* (Washington, D.C.: Amer. Assn. for Adult Education, 1938), p. 27.

19. Lowell A. Martin, *Baltimore Reaches Out: Library Service to the Disadvantaged,* Deiches Fund Studies of Public Library Service, no. 3 (Baltimore: Enoch Pratt Free Library, June 1967), p. 16.

20. Marilyn Salazar, *Illinois Minorities Manpower Project, Final Report* (Chicago: ALA, 1976), p. 89.

21. Haynes McMullen, "Service to Ethnic Minorities Other than Afro-Americans and American Indians," in *A Century of Service: Librarianship in the United States and Canada,* eds. Sidney L. Jackson, Eleanor B. Herling, and E. J. Josey (Chicago: ALA, 1976), p. 48.

22. Ibid., p. 49.

23. Ibid., p. 51.

24. Ibid., p. 54.

25. Ibid., pp. 56–57.

26. See A. P. Marshall, "Service to Afro-Americans," in *A Century of Service.*

27. Gleason was the first black American to receive a Ph.D. in librarianship. Marcia J. Nauratil, *Public Libraries and Nontraditional Clienteles: The Politics of Special Services,* no. 8 in *New Directions in Librarianship* (Westport, Conn.: Greenwood, 1985), p. 112.

28. Eliza Atkins Gleason, *The Southern Negro and the Public Library* (Chicago: Univ. of Chicago Pr., 1941): 21–22, as cited by A. P. Marshall, "Service to Afro Americans," pp. 69–70.

29. Nauratil, *Nontraditional Clienteles*, p. 24.

30. Heim, "Stimulation," p. 125.

31. Robert D. Leigh, *The Public Library in the United States* (New York: Columbia Univ. Pr., 1950), p. 15.

32. Ibid., p. 20.

33. Ibid., p. 48.

34. Heim, "Stimulation," p. 126.

35. Michael H. Harris, "The Role of the Public Library in American Life: A Speculative Essay" (Occasional Paper no. 117, University of Illinois Graduate School of Library Science, Urbana-Champaign, January 1975), p. 20.

36. Nauratil, *Nontraditional Clienteles*, p. 31.

37. Helen Lyman Smith, *Adult Education Activities in Public Libraries* (Chicago: ALA, 1954), p. 38.

38. Ibid., p. 40.

39. Ibid., p. 51. Later, librarians would emphasize the use of nontraditional materials to draw in disadvantaged nonusers. Clara S. Jones, *Reflections on Library Service to the Disadvantaged, A Talk Delivered at the 92nd Annual Conference of the American Library Association, June 27, 1973*, Office of Library Service to the Disadvantaged, publication no. 1 (Chicago: ALA, 1974), p. 12.

40. Bernice Lloyd Bell, "Public Library Integration in Thirteen Southern States," *Library Journal* 88 (December 15, 1963): 4713.

41. Heim, "Stimulation," pp. 127–128.

42. Eleanor T. Smith, "Public Library Service to the Economically and Culturally Deprived: A Profile of the Brooklyn Public Library," in *The Library Reaches Out: Reports on Library Service and Community Relations by Some Leading American Librarians*, eds. Kate Coplan and Edwin Castagna (New York: Oceana, 1965), p. 222.

43. Kathleen Weibel, *The Evolution of Library Outreach 1960–1975 and Its Effect on Reader Services* (Occasional Paper no. 156, University of Illinois Graduate School of Library and Information Science, Urbana-Champaign, December 1982), p. 16.

44. Ibid., p. 7.

45. McMullen, "Service to Ethnic Minorities," p. 56.

46. Weibel, "Evolution of Library Outreach," p. 13.

47. International Research Associates, *Access to Public Libraries* (Chicago: ALA, 1963), p. 59.

48. Weibel, "Evolution of Library Outreach," p. 12.

49. Thomas F. Parker, "Can We Afford to Ignore the Negro?" *Library Journal* 88 (December 15, 1963): 4716. See also Herbert J. Gans, "The Access Survey from the Social Scientist's Viewpoint," *Wilson Library Bulletin* 38 (December 1963): 366–368 ff.

50. Casper LeRoy Jordan, "Library Service to Black Americans," *Library Trends* 20 (October 1971): 274.

51. Anne M. Dalzell, *The Role of the Public Library in Serving the Culturally Deprived: A Bibliographic Essay* (Master's thesis, School of Library Science, Catholic University of America, Washington, D.C., March 1966), p. 28.

52. Ibid., p. 29. Dalzell points out that the Neighborhood Youth Corps programs were advantageous for libraries in that the provision of paying jobs for young people

advanced the latter's appreciation of community service and freed librarians to do specialized work.

53. Ibid.
54. Ibid., pp. 29–30.
55. Ibid., p. 30.
56. Respondents to the Lyman Smith survey in 1954 listed many adult education services they would have liked to provide, but were unable to, primarily because of lack of funding (Lyman Smith, *Adult Education Activities,* pp. 18–23).
57. N. Beckman, "The Metropolitan Area: Coherence Versus Chaos," *Wilson Library Bulletin* 43 (January 1969): 443.
58. Nauratil, *Nontraditional Clienteles,* p. 31.
59. Dan Lacy, "Social Change and the Library: 1945–1980," in *Libraries at Large: Tradition, Innovation, and the National Interest,* eds. Douglas M. Knight and E. Shepley Nourse (New York: Bowker, 1969), p. 5.
60. Ralph W. Conant, "Black Power in Urban America," *Library Journal* 93 (May 15, 1963):1963–1967.
61. Nancy W. Corrigan, "The Urban Negro and the Library," in *The Library's Public Revisited,* ed. Mary Lee Bundy and Sylvia Goodstein (University of Maryland, School of Library and Information Science, 1967), pp. 32–45.
62. Jordan, "Library Services to Black Americans," pp. 271–279.
63. Conant, "Black Power in Urban America," pp. 1964–1965.
64. Weibel, "Evolution of Library Outreach," p. 14.
65. Ibid., pp. 14–19.
66. Lyman Smith, *Adult Education Activities,* p. 41.
67. Ibid., p. 66.
68. American Library Association Committee on Economic Opportunity Programs, *Library Service to the Disadvantaged: A Study Based on Responses to Questionnaires from Public Libraries Serving Populations of Over 15,000* (Chicago: ALA, 1969), p. 56.
69. Guy Bennette, "San Francisco: Down These Meaningful Streets," *Wilson Library Bulletin* 43 (May 1969): 872. Note that this concept fits into Weibel's storefront communication and community life participation models of outreach service.
70. Richard Moses, "The Training of Librarians to Serve the Unserved," in *Library Service to the Unserved—Papers presented at a Library Conference Held at the University of Wisconsin—Milwaukee School of Library and Information Science, November 16–18, 1967* Library and Information Science Studies, no. 2, ed. Laurence L. Sherill (New York: Bowker, 1970), p. 74.
71. Eric E. Moon, "High John: Report on a Unique Experiment in Maryland Designed to Initiate Change in Public Library Service and in Library Education," *Library Journal* 93 (January 15, 1968): 150.
72. Ibid.
73. Eleanor Frances Brown, *Library Service to the Disadvantaged* (Metuchen, N.J.: Scarecrow, Inc., 1971), p. 501. Again, the employment of indigenous personnel was perceived as integral to the success of a project.
74. Weibel, "Evolution of Library Outreach," p. 16.
75. Ibid., p. 14.
76. See Lowell A. Martin, "Our Own Modest Genius," *Wilson Library Bulletin* 43 (May 1969): 851–853.
77. Martin, *Baltimore Reaches Out,* p. 51.
78. Ibid.

79. Ibid., p. 42.
80. Ibid., p. 51.
81. Heim, "Stimulation," p. 128.
82. Ibid., p. 129.
83. "Special Committee on Freedom of Access to Libraries," *ALA Bulletin* 62 (July 1968): 883–887.
84. Ibid.
85. Ibid.
86. Ibid.
87. See American Library Association, *Library Service to the Disadvantaged.*
88. Ibid., p. 56.
89. Ibid.
90. Ibid., p. 59.
91. Edwin Castagna, "A Troubled Mixture: Our Attitudes toward the Unserved as Librarians in a Professional Capacity," in *Library Service to the Unserved*, p. 15.
92. Weibel, "Evolution of Library Outreach," pp. 20–21.
93. Lacy, "Social Change and the Library," *Libraries at Large*, p. 18.
94. Ibid., p. 7.
95. Margaret E. Monroe, "Reader Services to the Disadvantaged in Inner Cities," in *Advances in Librarianship* (1971), vol. 2, pp. 253–274.
96. Owens, "A Model Library," p. 1703.
97. Ibid., p. 1704.
98. Allie Beth Martin, *A Strategy for Public Library Change: Proposed Public Library Goals—Feasibility Study* (Public Library Association, American Library Association, 1972).
99. Mary Lee Bundy, "Urban Information and Public Libraries: A Design for Service," *Library Journal* 97 (January 1972): 167.
100. E. J. Josey, "The Case for ALA Action: Coddling Segregation," *Library Journal* 96 (May 15, 1971): 1778.
101. Jessie Carney Smith, "Library Services to Ethnic Groups: Blacks," *ALA Yearbook*, 1977, p. 119.
102. William H. Farrington, "Statewide Outreach: Desert Booktrails to Indians," *Wilson Library Bulletin* 43 (May 1969): 864–876.
103. William D. Cunningham, "The Changing Environment and Changing Institution: Indian Project of the Northeast Kansas Library System," *Library Trends* 20 (October 1971): 381.
104. Rachael Naismith, "Outreach Services to Hispanics," *Illinois Libraries* 64, no. 7 (September 1982): 964.
105. Ibid.
106. Salazar, *Illinois Minorities Manpower Project*, p. 87.
107. Nauratil, p. 116.
108. Weibel, "Evolution of Library Outreach," pp. 22–23.
109. Priscilla Gotsick, "The Role of the Library Helping Undereducated Adults," *Catholic Library World* 47 (February 1976): 283–284.
110. "Office of Library Service to the Disadvantaged," *ALA Yearbook*, 1976, pp. 150–151.
111. Martin J. Zonligt, *Library Service to Farmworkers: The Need for a Survival Information Center*, 1974, p. v.
112. Ibid., p. 17.
113. Ibid.
114. Ibid.

115. Ibid., p. 18.
116. Nauratil, *Nontraditional Clienteles*, p. 24.
117. Ibid., pp. 25–26.
118. Title II-B of the Higher Education Act (1965) funds programs in library training and research. This legislation, along with LSCA, has been a major financial resource for minority recruitment. Both have been "sorely underfunded over the past decade." President's Committee on Library Services to Minorities, *Equity at Issue*, 1985–86, p. 17.
119. Salazar, *Illinois Minorities Manpower Project*, p. vii.
120. Ibid., p. 87.
121. Monroe, "Reader Services to the Disadvantaged," p. 272.
122. See Alfred Kahn, *Neighborhood Information Centers* (New York: Columbia University School of Social Work, 1966).
123. Jones, *Reflections on Library Service to the Disadvantaged*, p. 8.
124. Ibid., p. 12.
125. Ibid., p. 8.
126. John Berry, "Service: Social or Reference?" *Library Journal* 94 (April 15, 1969): 1563.
127. Ervin T. Gaines, "The Large Municipal Library as a Network" *Library Quarterly* (January 1969): 417. See also Ervin J. Gaines, (Vantage Point/Opinion) "Let's Return to Traditional Library Service: Facing the Failure of Social Experimentation," *Wilson Library Bulletin* 55 (September 1980): 50–53 ff.
128. Heim, "Stimulation," p. 142.
129. Ibid., p. 131.
130. Thomas Childers, *The Information-Poor in America* (Metuchen, N. J.: Scarecrow, 1975), p. 32.
131. Nauratil, *Nontraditional Clienteles*, p. 29.
132. Heim, "Stimulation," p. 147.
133. American Library Association, *ALA Handbook of Organization, 1987/1988* (Chicago: ALA, 1987), p. 186.
134. Ibid., p. 19.
135. Ibid., p. 17.
136. Ibid., p. 160.
137. Ibid., p. 112.
138. Ibid., p. 127.
139. Ibid., p. 176.
140. Ibid.
141. Ibid.
142. Ibid., p. 237.
143. Gail Brown, "Native American Library Project: Milwaukee Public Library," *Wisconsin Library Bulletin* 77 (Summer 1981): 83.
144. Ibid., p. 84.
145. Robert P. Haro, *Developing Library and Information Services for Americans of Hispanic Origin* (Metuchen, N.J.: Scarecrow, 1981).
146. Brian Aveney and Vivian Pisano, "Hispanex: Serving Libraries Serving Hispanics," *Wilson Library Bulletin* 59 (March 1985): 453.
147. Ibid., p. 454.
148. Ibid., p. 455.
149. Russell G. Fischer, "Project Asia: California Public Libraries Serving the Asian Community," *Library Journal* 111 (March 1986): 62.

150. Ibid.
151. Ibid., p. 64.
152. Ibid., p. 62.
153. Ibid., p. 64.
154. Ibid., pp. 62–63.
155. Ibid.
156. Ibid.
157. NCLIS, Task Force on Library and Information Services to Cultural Minorities, *Report*, p. xi.
158. Henry C. Chang and Suzine Har-Nicolescu, "Needs Assessment Study of Library Information Service for Asian American Community Members in the United States," Appendix I in NCLIS, Task Force on Library and Information Services to Cultural Minorities, *Report*, p. 81.
159. Heim, "Stimulation," p. 133.
160. Monroe, "The Cultural Role of the Public Library," p. 13.
161. Ibid., p. 10.
162. The White House Conference on Library and Information Services, *The Final Report: Summary* (Washington, D.C.: White House Conference on Library and Information Services, 1979), p. 8.
163. Ibid., pp. 11–12.
164. Ibid., p. 47.
165. National Commission on Excellence in Education, *A Nation at Risk: The Imperative for Educational Reform* (Washington, D.C.: GPO, 1983), pp. 13–14.
166. Virginia H. Mathews, "Implementing *Alliance for Excellence* and *Realities: Libraries' Partnership in a Learning Society*," *Bowker Annual 1985* (New York: Bowker, 1985), pp. 81–82.
167. Ibid., p. 84.
168. Haro, *Developing Library and Information Services*, p. 225.
169. NCLIS, Task Force on Library and Information Services to Cultural Minorities, *Report*, p. x.
170. National Commission on Libraries and Information Science, Task Force on Library and Information Services to Cultural Minorities, *Hearings Held at the American Library Association Annual Conference, San Francisco, California, 1981*, p. v.
171. NCLIS, Task Force on Library and Information Services to Cultural Minorities, *Report*, pp. xiv–xv.
172. Ibid., p. xiv.
173. Ibid.
174. Ibid., pp. 37–38.
175. Ibid., p. 51.
176. Ibid., pp. 68–69.
177. Ibid.
178. Ibid., p. vi.
179. Ibid.
180. Ibid., p. vii.
181. Ibid.
182. Ibid., pp. v–viii.
183. ALA President's Committee on Library Services to Minorities, *Equity at Issue: Library Services to the Nation's Major Minority Groups, 1985*, 1984-1985 Council Document #40.

184. Ibid., p. 16.
185. Ibid., pp. 18–20.
186. President's Committee on Library Services to Minorities, *Equity at Issue, 1985–86,* p. 8.
187. Committee on Minority Concerns, Report to the Council, Midwinter 1987, 1986–1986 Council Document #19, p. 3.
188. Dan M. Lacy, *Freedom and Equality of Access to Information—A Report to the American Library Association by the Commission on Freedom and Equality of Access to Information* (Chicago: ALA, 1986), p. 105.
189. Ibid., p. 107.
190. Ibid., p. 105.
191. President's Committee on Library Services to Minorities, *Equity at Issue, 1985–86,* p. 5.
192. American Library Association, *Library Service to the Disadvantaged,* p. 28.
193. Owens, "A Model Library for Community Action," p. 1703.

CHAPTER 5

Literacy Services in Public Libraries

Gary O. Rolstad

Few library issues have stirred as much literature, as much emotion, as much controversy, as much effort, and overall as rich a recent history as has the issue of literacy services in America's public libraries. The overlap of literacy services with other concerns such as the educational role of the library, or the gap between services to the affluent and services to the disadvantaged, may be the major underlying issue. Another issue is that the very population to be served is the group that is the least vocal, the least empowered, and the least involved in the process at any stage of service delivery.

Nevertheless, there is vocal advocacy among librarians who have developed creative and devoted programs for illiterates; there are coalitions spearheaded by librarians; there are commitments by library systems, state libraries, and professional library organizations that mean an increase in library services to illiterates. The purpose of this chapter is to examine the environment of federal support, the momentum of the 1980s, and the current status of library programs dealing with literacy education.

Definitions

There has been much discussion about the varying definitions of illiteracy. The programs that have arisen to deal with illiteracy are extremely varied as well. The need to define a population to be served is certainly a logical one. Yet, no one has shown that a precise definition of illiteracy aids the establishment or continuation of an overall library program. A discussion of the prevailing definitions will help form a context for discussing this service.

245

The broad definition of the illiterate as one who cannot read or write tends to minimize the severity of the problem, because so many citizens read at very poor levels. Many who can write only their names or read just well enough to interpret street signs and other basic symbols seem to cope with most of their environment, but their lack of literacy skills may severely limit opportunities to improve their socioeconomic situation.[1] From this understanding of the need to cope with everyday problems developed the phrase "functionally illiterate."

The level at which a person can read a newspaper was a popular watershed in the sixties. UNESCO, the U.S. Census, and the U.S. Army used as a standard a fifth-grade level of reading. An eighth-grade level reading ability was once considered literate. Some say the complexity of our world requires a twelfth-grade level of reading. The issue is clouded by the assumption on the part of others that computer skills are or will be basic literacy skills.[2] In 1987, ALA President Margaret Chisholm created a Commission on Information Literacy. The final report of the Commission states, "To be information literate, a person must be able to recognize when information is needed and have the ability to locate, evaluate, and use effectively the needed information."[3]

Grade level indicators are vague at best. Helen Lyman pointed out that "important skills for the adult are communication (reading, writing, speaking, listening); computation; problem solving; and interpersonal relations."[4] Adult Performance Level (APL) was a measure introduced by the University of Texas in 1975 that "identified 65 reading-and-writing-related tasks that its designers felt adult Americans should be able to perform such as reading job notices, filling out job application forms, addressing envelopes, and reading road signs."[5] Harvard's David Harman tells us that social, cultural, and economic realities form a different context for the issue of illiteracy. He states, "Literacy levels in the United States cannot be determined by a universal national standard."[6] Harman's *Literacy: A National Dilemma*, provides a good discussion of the contextual problems in defining illiteracy.[7]

Perhaps the difficulty in coping with the breadth of the problem has flowed from the inconsistency of definition. There is certainly little doubt that illiteracy leaves a mark that, if not always clearly defined, is indelible and painful to society. Jonathan Kozol noted that there is a cycle of illiteracy; the children of minority, poor, and nonreading parents are far more likely to slip into an undereducated future even though they begin public education as do other children.[8] The poor stay poor, and the gap between rich and poor is the subject of newspaper articles and library documents, such as *Report of the ALA Commission on Freedom and Equality of Access to Information*, better known as the Lacy Report. Declaring the continued primacy of print despite all the electronic information available to society, this report stated that literacy is the "key skill for acquiring information."[9]

The Commission declared that "there has not even been recognition of the important problems and enormous opportunities to broaden the flow of information to everyone."[10] The Commission eloquently stated that "the needs of much of the population cannot be expressed as a demand in the marketplace that will evoke the information services needed."[11] This leaves it gravely incumbent upon librarians to recognize the needs of illiterate citizens and to maintain the democratic nature of access to information in the public library because this freedom may be disappearing elsewhere.

Some say it is the marketplace itself that suffers when the work force is low in reading skills. The Business Council for Effective Literacy has documented incidents of error caused by lack of reading skills that cost employers huge sums of money. *Workforce 2000*, a study from the Department of Labor, estimates that most jobs available between now and the year 2000 will require a post-secondary education.[12] This also means that the tens of millions who are estimated to lack basic reading and writing skills are shut off from improving themselves.

The educational system may or may not be the problem; this is not for librarians to say. Many argue that the cycle must end through improvement in the schools. By ensuring that all children become capable readers, the elimination of illiterate adults is therefore just a generation away. That effort is not underway, and the huge number of potential library users who could benefit from even the most modest literacy effort in the public library needs access to such programs. Literacy efforts for adults in public libraries may mean a greater future for libraries just as does a population of university-trained youngsters.

Adult Services

Where does literacy education fit in the context of adult services? If libraries have goals to serve the broad community, the pervasive problem of illiteracy should raise the priority of a service program in the area of literacy education to an important level. No community, regardless of affluence or average level of education, is without a population of illiterate adults. In communities such as Columbus, Ohio, one estimate is that 88,000—or about one fifth-of their citizens are illiterate.[13] From Queens County in New York City the estimate is that 350,000 adults over the age of sixteen are functionally illiterate.[14] Minnesota's governor estimates that about 671,000 resident adults cannot read.[15] As an institution of lifelong learning, the library is uniquely qualified to be a resource and proactive force in literacy education. Libraries have materials and physical space; librarians have the knowledge and ability to refer users to sources of information and assistance through coalition and referral (to other materials and agencies); and there is the potential for librarians and library staff to initiate programs, coordinate support, and provide continuity to such a service. This is a basic service that can make a difference in people's lives.

The broad spectrum of adult services ultimately flows from the prism of community understanding and involvement. Lyman stated:

> Librarians must identify the interests and needs of adults and adult groups, evaluate and find suitable materials for use by adults, cooperate with other agencies and organizations, and respect the rights of adults to the service and to a part in making decisions about the nature of the service.[16]

Adult services as a whole developed slowly and diversified gradually beginning in the 1920s. Robert Ellis Lee observed that librarians considered adult education in general a special service.[17] Monroe noted, "Book service to special groups within the community led to the librarian's active concern for joint community action as a solution to their [the group's] problems."[18] The development of literacy services, especially since the 1960s, was similar. Initial efforts were conservative compared to the in-depth activity undertaken by some librarians today. Service began with the provision of high-interest and low-vocabulary materials, or through the referral of adult new readers to adult education efforts in the community.

A Review of the Literature

Three areas of literature provide valuable information about the scope, stigma, and strategies of literacy education. Popular literature, for example, frequently addresses the global or national problem of illiteracy. Newspapers, news magazines, and widely sold books tell of the blight that is illiteracy. There are often emotional appeals, like

Jonathan Kozol's *Illiterate America*,[19] an updated, companion volume to his earlier *Prisoners of Silence: Breaking the Bonds of Illiteracy*.[20] A popular author and educator, Kozol showed the persistence of the cycle of illiteracy despite efforts by the government and devoted organizations to intervene. He laid heavy blame on the government and faulted the school system as well. Kozol's mention of libraries is brief, but he stated in a *Wilson Library Bulletin* article that "librarians have a natural, perhaps inevitable, stake in something that is so close to their own work and their professional concern."[21]

Librarians have long struggled with the notion of what their role in the general area of education should be; the specific nature of their role in the campaign against illiteracy has been difficult as well. The mainstream library literature provides evidence of an ongoing debate as to whether librarians are attempting a teaching role for which they are not trained. Librarians should be familiar with Margaret E. Monroe's *Library Adult Education*; its broad and historical viewpoint has great relevancy for later developments and for current understanding of the role of public libraries in any educational area. Monroe referred to a "climate of criticism and dispute," especially following the commitment of the Carnegie Corporation to adult education in the 1920s.[22] Although librarians had been involved in numerous activities related to adult education before this period, the attention of the profession was much greater and aggressive stands were taken on the issue. ALA's Adult Education Board provided strong leadership and received extensive funds from educational foundations.[23] But, especially around 1950, there were articulate opponents along the way. John Cotton Dana and Jesse Shera attacked the ideas as well as the commitment of some librarians to adult education.[24]

Another cogent review of this controversy of role is a work by Lynn Birge, *Serving Adult Learners: A Public Library Tradition*. Birge's descriptive issue-oriented account would benefit any librarian seeking a contextual and philosophical background in the broader area of adult education in public libraries. One chapter, "Special Readers," deals more specifically with service to the illiterate population. Birge observed that there was "little evidence in the late 1970's that the majority of librarians were persuaded that service to illiterates was a priority concern for librarians."[25]

Historically, literacy efforts tended to be educational programs such as those the New York Public Library provided for immigrants in the late nineteenth and early twentieth centuries. Eleanor Touhey Smith noted there is "no evidence that public libraries considered they had any role to play in [illiterates'] education until the National War on Poverty was begun by the Federal government in the 1960s."[26] Early programs were more properly English as a Second Language classes. Monroe qualified them further by saying libraries "sponsored rather than conducted" them.[27] When Helen Lyman Smith wrote *Adult Education Activities in Public Libraries* for ALA in 1954, two services were identified in the area of reading instruction. Under the category of "Training" services, librarians were asked whether they provided "fundamental instruction" or "remedial reading instruction." Other reading services identified in Lyman Smith's adult education questionnaire may have overlapped slightly with literacy education, but not in detail enough to be analyzed in relation to the four items in the Adult Services in the Eighties questionnaire discussed later in this chapter. The questions asked by Lyman Smith drew comments from librarians such as, "Don't think it is part of library service; should be done by schools." Another terse comment was, "I regret (that) libraries must train."[28]

John Berry raised questions in a 1966 article in which he noted there are "serious doubts about the role of libraries in education for literacy":

> Are librarians even qualified to evaluate the very special material for this audience? Is the library really a meaningful institution to a ghetto illiterate? Will he come there? Is there any material currently available that will do the multiple job of helping the adult read better, attract him to books and libraries, and help him relate to the society?[29]

In a more recent work Marcia Nauritil agrees with Birge that provision of reading instruction service "has been generally resisted by the profession."[30] But any notion that resistance to literacy service in public libraries is of historical interest only needs consideration of Thomas Ballard's recent declarations, worth quoting at length:

> Illiteracy is now the focus of national attention and public libraries seem almost desperate to be prominent in the attempt to teach people to read. But is this a reasonable use of our resources? Given the near helplessness of persons in our society that cannot read, there can be no question about the social value of successful efforts in this direction. Nonetheless, public libraries were never intended to educate anyone directly. They exist to support the schools, which have this primary responsibility, and to provide resources that would allow individuals to pursue further education on their own should they choose to do so . . . . The fight against illiteracy is even more labor intensive than general education . . . . It should be obvious that public libraries, given their present resources, must be minor participants in the effort to reduce

adult illiteracy. . . . We have lots of books. The adult illiterate, however, does not need lots of books but rather one book or at most, several. When he or she is no longer illiterate our large book collections may be of use . . . . The problem of illiteracy . . . is an example of the kind of activity that public libraries should avoid. Other than a willingness to accommodate volunteer tutors and their pupils at times when their activities would not bother our regular library users, such projects are inappropriate . . . . We must not be diverted by a misplaced sense of "social responsibility" into wasting resources on projects that are almost certain to disappear without a trace within a few years.[31]

The imprimatur of ALA as a publisher was attached to this work only a few months prior to another ALA publication, *Libraries and Literacy: A Planning Manual* by Debra Wilcox Johnson, in 1987.[32]

The Advocates

Work by Bernice MacDonald of New York Public Library in the mid-sixties became a starting point for a new era of service. Funded with a grant from the Adult Services Division of ALA, MacDonald sought to find out what literacy education efforts existed in American public libraries. Although some library involvement was found, in-depth programs were rare; actual literacy teaching centers were operating in only three libraries.

MacDonald's published study, *Literacy Activities in Public Libraries*,[33] collected information about services in specific areas such as reading aloud to groups. She also asked the question, "Is it the library's job to teach?" Monroe summarized MacDonald's conclusions: "It is the library's job to supply materials and space for classes, recruit students, and follow up with reading guidance and information service to the adult new literates."[34]

In 1972 the proceedings of a seminar, "Public Library Service to the Illiterate Adult," included papers that dealt with library materials for the adult new reader and discussed successful methods and programs such as those accomplished at the Free Library of Philadelphia and in Southern Appalachian public libraries.[35] U.S. Department of Health, Education and Welfare funds under the Title IIB portion of the Library Services and Construction Act supported the seminar.

Three important works from the research of Helen Lyman emerged in the seventies. The presses of ALA produced all three, beginning in 1973 with *Library Materials in Service to the Adult New Reader*.[36] This book is the result of five years of study by Lyman in response to the growing demand for adult new reader materials; it provides much information about reading levels and teaching techniques so that librarians can have an understanding of the larger dynamic of reading skills. *Reading and the Adult New Reader* followed in 1976.[37] Finally, *Literacy and the Nation's Libraries*, published in 1977, provided a culmination.

Literacy and the Nation's Libraries is an informative planning manual that discussed the importance of literacy education, reading, and the whole process of developing a library service. Lyman showed that literacy education is a logical public library program, and it is the result of a basic analysis of a community.[38] Within the larger educational role of all public libraries, service to illiterates is a basic service, not an overextension of service.

Other library literature that demonstrated new concern for the topic of literacy education included special issues of several well-known journals. *Drexel Library Quarterly* (October 1978), *Public Libraries* (September 1985), and *Library Trends* (Fall 1986) are among the journals that devoted an issue to illiteracy.

Some research studies are discussed below when the data from the Adult Services in the Eighties questionnaire are analyzed. Themes from these studies and other library literature shed some light on the progress of library service to the illiterate segment of the population. For example, out of the White House Conference on Library and Information Science from 1979 came a group of recommendations to develop successful literacy programs, including professional awareness, cooperation with a variety of agencies, and adequate funding. Even if the role of the library issue moved toward resolution, it is still stated that "some reordering of library priorities will be necessary if libraries are to make a substantial contribution to new literacy programs."[39]

Another listing of library priorities was the subject of an ALA member survey in 1985. Of sixteen identified areas of interest, literacy/illiteracy ranked fourteenth. But in a list of thirty-two areas of action identified as of primary importance, literacy service was not included.[40]

Role of the Federal Government

The federal government's first literacy program was for military personnel in the first World War; similar efforts were made in World War II. Not until the 1960s, however, was attention focused on the lack of reading skills in the adult general population.

In 1962 the Manpower Development and Training provided government-funded educational and vocational programs for unemployed youth. Many program participants were illiterate, so an amendment allowed for the provision of adult basic education. The Economic Opportunity Act of 1964 allotted direct funds for literacy education.

The Library Services and Construction Act of 1964 is particularly important because it provided funds for services to the economically and socially disadvantaged, handicapped, homebound, and institutionalized adults as well as for further service to rural areas. The Adult Basic Education Act passed in 1966 encouraged adult education programs. This provided funds directly to literacy programs for those adults with less than an eighth-grade education. Birge told how this was important for libraries:

> The Adult Education Act of 1966 was particularly instrumental in facilitating library service to the undereducated, for one of the greatest problems had always been means to reach this group of potential users. With the formation of many adult basic education classes, libraries finally had access to large groups of new readers, as well as the possibility of cooperating with other agencies in the war on illiteracy.[41]

In 1971, the Nixon administration established the Right to Read Program with the goal of overcoming illiteracy in the United States in ten years. It was discontinued six years later (obviously short of its goal), but some research and pilot reading programs were established. During these years, the National Reading Improvement Program was begun.

The Adult Basic Education Act was reauthorized in 1983. In the Fall of 1983, the government announced the Adult Literacy Initiative (ALI), including an eight-item action plan. Only one item was funded; five proposals regarding private sector involvement were, according to Kozol, "insubstantial gestures."[42] Part of the effort promoted college credit for volunteer literacy training (as well as suggesting that all federal employees be volunteers). The ALI has quietly faded away, although the U.S. Department of Education continues to "consolidate federal activities and promote coalition building among the many organizations concerned about illiteracy."[43]

Kozol stated that the "placebo effect" that something was being done was a typical example of the lack of commitment on the part of the federal government.[44] Some of the private sector interest was absorbed into the Coalition for Literacy as discussed below. Kozol was also skeptical about coalitions, believing:

> Even with an open-minded willingness to find our allies where they may appear, we should recognize the fragile nature of such coalitions,

as well as their susceptibility to government cooption fostered in part by niceties of social behavior which the established nature of this sort of coalition can too easily enforce as the accepted level of debate.[45]

In 1984, the Library Literacy Program, Title VI of LSCA, authorized grants to state and local public libraries for literacy projects. Funds totaling $5 million were made available in 1986. Altogether, 239 projects received grants ranging from $1,500 to $25,000. Forty-six states were represented; 22 state libraries and 217 local libraries designed projects that included a wide variety of services. Funds were used to recruit tutors, or to target special groups like Native Americans or older Americans. A public awareness campaign was the focus of one project; parental involvement was devised in another; computer-assisted instruction was begun in several of the projects.[46] Projects from the libraries funded in fiscal 1987, the second year of the LSCA Title VI, show similar and expanded diversity: 245 grants totaling $5 million were awarded to 230 local public libraries and 15 state libraries.

Coalition building, public awareness campaigns, training programs, collection development, employment oriented efforts, rural outreach, and other methods were summarized. The two summary reports from the Office of Educational Research and Improvement, U.S. Department of Education provide ideas for planners of new or expanded services.[47] Kozol argued that the number served by the various efforts of the government is insignificant.[48] For example, federal support to the Coalition for Literacy in 1985 was a mere $50,000 in the total U.S. budget of $1 trillion. The Reagan administration wanted to eliminate the National Commission on Library and Information Science, which is responsible for identification of the illiteracy problem for the purposes of library action. The belief persists that state and local governments are better equipped to deal with such a problem and that private business would contribute adequate support.

The Coalition Era

ALA spearheaded the founding of the Coalition for Literacy in 1981. The coalition grew out of the need for professional commitment to literacy service and out of the recognized need to work with national and community organizations and businesses in order to be effective. By 1977, Lyman had identified three roles for libraries in the provision of literacy services: education, collaboration, and community awareness. She recognized the problems inherent in collaborative efforts, but library services, she reminds us, "cut across every educational agency and institution."[49] In the case of literacy service, the funding issue was and is a crucial one. Jean Coleman, as Executive Director of the ALA Office for Library Outreach Services from 1978 through 1987, provided leadership that melded the focus of eleven groups that formed the Coalition for Literacy:

> American Association for Adult and Continuing Education
> American Association of Advertising Agencies
> American Library Association
> Contact, Inc.
> B. Dalton Bookseller
> International Reading Association
> Laubach Literacy International
> Literacy Volunteers of America
> National Advisory Council on Adult Education
> National Commission of Libraries and Information Science
> National Council of State Directors of Adult Education

Start-up funds came from a Department of Education award of $50,000. The three stated objectives of the coalition were to:

1. Increase awareness of the illiteracy problem through an advertising campaign.
2. Provide a toll-free and mail referral service through Contact Literacy, Inc., Lincoln, Nebraska.
3. Raise funds for additional public awareness.[50]

The coalition successfully expanded over the next several years, gaining funds and cooperation from the Corporation for Public Broadcasting and the American Broadcasting Corporation (ABC-TV); the Gannet Corporation; B. Dalton Booksellers (B. Dalton has since left the coalition but maintains an active interest in funding literacy education efforts, including cooperation with libraries); the Business Council for Effective Literacy; the MacArthur Foundation, and other institutions, totaling over three-fourths of a million dollars.

Chiefly an advertising campaign, the coalition has nevertheless probably had an influence on the decision of librarians to take an active role in providing some new literacy service in the recent period, admittedly along with other factors, as discussed in the section regarding activity after 1981.

The coalition's "Literacy Contact Center" had received over 400,000 calls from interested trainers and students as of July 1988.[51] The advertising campaign has garnered approximately $32 million in media time and space, according to one estimate.[52]

Continuing amendments to the Adult Education Act redefine legislative authority toward the state level. A program called Even Start is a new "family literacy" effort still in an evaluative stage. Dollar General, a retail discount chain, has donated advertising time to recruiting literacy trainers, and contact points are in the stores themselves. The Florida Bar Association donated $29,000 to the Florida Literacy Coalition to help produce radio and television announcements about literacy education programs.[53] All of these have connections to public libraries, which are eligible for the monies involved, or that become the next institution in the training effort itself. The public library can at least measure some success from its expanding identity and involvement in various types of grass roots and local efforts.

ALA has provided recognition of efforts in literacy services. The Public Library Association (PLA, a division of ALA) and the American Library Trustee Association (ALTA, also a division of ALA) sponsor annual awards for contributions in the fight against illiteracy. There is a PLA State Education and Literacy Services Committee.

The ALA Policy Manual (Section Two, 50.7) includes two paragraphs on "Literacy and the Role of Libraries and State Library Agencies."

> The American Library Association supports the achievement of national literacy through educational activities utilizing the historical and cultural experience of libraries and librarians.
> The American Library Association urges state library agencies to address the problems of illiteracy and give high priority to solutions in their short- and long-range plans for library development and the use of federal and state funds.[54]

At the ALA Annual Conference in Dallas in June 1989, the first ALA Literacy Assembly convened to review the policy statements and to help support the goals of national efforts, such as the coalition, and to "establish a focal point" within the association beyond unit membership committees."[55]

The *ALA Yearbook* carries an annual article and mentions developments in research, funding, and commitment in areas of literacy education.[56] What the coalition represented was the notion raised by many over the course of many years and throughout the development of other socially oriented services that awareness was the key issue.

ASE and Literacy

The questions posed in the Lyman Smith survey are different from those asked in the ASE survey. The evolution of some services is evident; some questions asked in the early 1950s are unnecessary; some new questions asked were necessary for the ASE questionnaire. The variety of services in the ASE survey is greater, but so is the direction—the arm of the library is longer and more geared toward problems and issues. Because of the perceived immediacy of some of the problems and in light of the social importance of the issues, it is little wonder that hundreds and even thousands of librarians are motivated to attempt creative efforts, as enumerated and reported in the ASE survey.

Only a few studies have sought to determine the extent of literacy services in public libraries. Lyman Smith's 1954 survey of Adult Education Services included only two queries that fell into the category of literacy service.[57] Question 18 tallied the number of libraries providing "fundamental reading instruction," and question 19 dealt with "remedial reading instruction." Of thirty-seven services in this study, these ranked thirty-second and thirty-fourth in frequency, respectively. Of 1,692 respondents to the Adult Education Services questionnaire, 110 (6.5 percent) provided fundamental reading instruction; 94 (5.5 percent) provided remedial reading instruction.[58] When queried about which programs librarians would like to provide, the rankings of the same thirty-seven services were slightly higher: twenty-ninth and twenty-third, respectively, but the percentages, 9.9 and 8.1 percent, were still low. Clearly, the actual provision of these services was minimal, and the priority for the services was only slightly greater.[59]

In the early 1950s, according to the results of the Lyman Smith survey, smaller libraries tended to be more likely to offer the two identified reading services. Lyman Smith showed that among five groups of libraries listed by population served, those libraries serving 5,000 to 10,000 persons were more likely to provide "fundamental reading instruction" or "remedial reading instruction," as shown in Table 1.[60]

Table 1. PERCENTAGES OF LIBRARIES PROVIDING READING INSTRUCTION, BY SIZE OF POPULATION SERVED.

	100,000+	25,000–99,000	10,000–25,000	5,000–10,000	STATE LIBRARIES
Fundamental Reading Instruction	3.6%	4.5%	4.9%	9.0%	7.1%
Remedial Reading Instruction	3.6	4.7	5.1	6.5	7.1

Illiterates as a community group were undefined as far as the Lyman Smith survey was concerned. Despite some of the above percentages, "television programs" was the only service ranked below these two, and 1954 was, quite simply, an age before mass television.

The Contract Research Center (CRC) produced a study published by the U.S. Department of Education in May, 1981, entitled *Libraries in Literacy.*[61] This "State of the Art Manuscript" was later summarized in *Library and Information Science Research* by Esther Gottlieb Smith.[62] The CRC sampled 160 public libraries, gaining responses from 121 to questions about library characteristics, reasons for involvement or noninvolvement in literacy education, and staff attitudes toward the idea of service to illiterates.[63] The data are different both from the Lyman Smith study and from the ASE information, but some very interesting points are made that are backed by hard data.

The CRC found that awareness of need for literacy education and the appropriateness of the library to provide this need were the greatest incentives for public librarians to become involved.[64] The chief barrier to involvement was found to be the perception of librarians that literacy education was not "within the scope of services librarians usually provide."[65] Three of Lyman Smith's questions, though not exactly the same, are comparable to questions asked about specific type of literacy service similar to those in the ASE Survey as described in Wallace's chapter in this volume. The questions and responses are summarized below.[66]

Libraries in Literacy	*Adult Services in the Eighties*
1. Provide space for literacy education classes: 57 out of 121, or 47.1 percent	1. Provide facilities for literacy education: 2214 out of 4214, or 52.5 percent
2. Provide one-on-one literacy tutorial sessions: 49 out of 121, or 40.5 percent	2. Provide literacy education to individuals: 1036 out of 4214, or 24.6 percent
3. Provide information and referral services on and to available literacy education programs: 49 out of 121, or 40.5 percent	3. Provide referral to another agency for literacy education: 3381 out of 4214, or 80.2 percent

There are some caveats both about these numbers and the comparability of the questions from one survey to the other. In the CRC survey, the seventy-nine nonrespondents might be libraries that are not active in literacy education in various ways, because this survey dealt primarily with literacy education; that is, librarians are probably less likely to respond about things they do not do. The ASE survey was broad in scope, and nonrespondents could have been motivated to decline for any of a number of reasons rather than simply because they did not engage in any literacy activity. The CRC study used a figure of 52.3 percent (64 out of 121) to describe the proportion of libraries attempting some type of service in 1980 (the actual period of distribution and data from the survey).[67] ASE data indicated a number somewhat greater than 80.2 percent (the number providing at least a referral service), a larger and very encouraging figure to those who believe librarians should be involved with some type of literacy service.

Another reason the CRC data are interesting is because the data come from the period immediately preceding the founding of the Coalition for Literacy. Although correlation is not causality, the ASE survey reports additional data that suggests the Coalition has had some impact on librarians' decisions to provide some level of service. This conclusion comes from the final section of the ASE survey, wherein librarians were asked to describe five of the most successful programs provided in their library during 1985.

Librarians featured literacy education programs 210 times on the third page of the ASE survey. Most programs—173 of 210, or 82.4 percent—involved a coalition with a group outside the library. Most programs were less than five years old. Again, the Coalition for Literacy was founded in 1981. Although leaders such as Lyman had acknowledged the importance and probable necessity of working together with other community groups to provide literacy service from the library, these numbers nevertheless record a great interest in this type of service, and this interest occurred after an ALA initiative to heighten awareness and encourage participation. In a report to the 1988 PLA conference, Debra Wilcox Johnson stated that one-half of the libraries studied by the Wisconsin Literacy Project (a nationwide sampling similar to the CRC survey, collecting data during 1986 and 1987, and scheduled for publication in May 1988) had programs that began after 1984.[68]

The ASE data also provide an interesting national overview that shows no great variation among the various regions, or even from state to state. Involvement in some sort of literacy education program can be found in libraries in every state. The well-known statewide programs that began in California, Texas, New York, and Tennessee are no longer unique nor isolated from other efforts. Librarians in state libraries, for example, have become experienced coordinators of funds and activities. The State Library of Ohio produced an Occasional Paper called "The

Public Library and Literacy: A Community Based Approach," a manual that would help anyone ready to start a program or to organize their thoughts about implementation of literacy service.[69]

Programs described on the third page of the ASE questionnaire show the diversity in method of literacy education services. Also shown are common threads and reiteration of techniques identified in the literature. In Union, Mississippi, the library helped sixty-one adult nonreaders in a program that began in 1984. The coalition of support included the State Department of Education, the Governor's Office, and an advocacy group called Action. Conducting the effort were community volunteers. Nonreaders were attracted through radio, television, and even door-to-door contacts.

The Greater Indianapolis (Indiana) Literacy League cooperated with the local library system to develop a program that drew sixty participants each month. In Newport, Kentucky, an estimated 200 participated in a literacy effort of the North Kentucky Regional Office of the State Library. LSCA funds started an effort in Hyatts-ville, Maryland, that led to a "community network" in which various agencies helped publicize the literacy program, recruit volunteers, and provide meeting sites so that seventy people enrolled to learn to read.

The agency that is the common thread of these efforts, be they local or statewide, is the public library. Sometimes the initial efforts to increase awareness, develop coalitions, raise funds, find space, gather materials, train tutors, and coordinate and implement these necessities are intense, and the momentum is begun so that diminishing returns are realized. The ultimate return is the adult new reader whose newfound skills are tied to the local public library. They are the real grassroots of future support.

ASE Questions

The responses to four literacy services questions from the Adult Services in the Eighties survey are worthy of an additional look.

QUESTION 30

Does your library provide literacy education to groups?

Provide	647	15.4%
Do not provide	3563	84.6%
Fees charged	4	0.1%

QUESTION 31

Does your library provide literacy education to individuals?

Provide	1036	24.6%
Do not provide	3176	75.4%
Fees charged	2	0.0%

QUESTION 32

Does your library provide facilities for literacy education?

Provide	2214	52.5%
Do not provide	1997	47.4%
Fees charged	3	0.1%

QUESTION 33

Does your library provide referral to another agency for literacy education?

Provide	3381	80.2%
Do not provide	832	19.7%
Fees charged	1	0.0%

In question 33, the 80 percent of libraries able to provide literacy education referral is a very important figure. This is evidence that the overwhelming majority of librarians are aware of the widespread problem of illiteracy.

The responses to the other three questions might be interpreted to indicate that librarians are doing what they can to facilitate some sort of service that helps adult nonreaders. The one-fourth that are providing some sort of individual instruction, in question 31, is even reason for notice—"fundamental reading instruction" was available from only 6.5 percent of the respondents to the Lyman Smith study 33 years before.[70]

Librarians may interpret these questions slightly differently; this is true with any survey. But the heightened level of advocacy is clear from these numbers and from the fact that 210 libraries further highlighted a literacy education program in the final portion of the survey. Librarians in 1986 seemed to perceive literacy education as a noteworthy, viable, and many times, successful service.

Summary

The Adult Services in the Eighties questionnaire does not resolve the dilemmas of literacy services in public libraries. However, the numbers demonstrate the widespread provision of some level of service and also seem to indicate a growth pattern. The barriers of inadequate awareness, poor funding, and resistant attitudes continue. There are still many good reasons why librarians cannot provide or expand the services they provide in their libraries. But public awareness (much of it thanks to librarians), private and government support, and greater acceptance of socially proactive efforts by community librarians have developed.

Librarians must nevertheless strive for an informed opinion on literacy education to help them decide whether to deploy some of the library's resources on behalf of literacy programs. For background on adult education, specifically in libraries, the contributions of Monroe and Lee are general but informative and occasionally inspiring works that librarians should consider. Good summaries of the issues and complexities are provided by Birge and Nauritil. The national scene is presented in works by Kozol, and recently by the Department of Education in a recommended work available from the Government Printing Office: *Illiteracy in America: Extent, Causes, and Suggested Solutions*, compiled by the Literacy Committee of the National Advisory Council on Adult Education, which included David Harman.[71]

ALA's *Libraries and Literacy: A Planning Manual* approaches the practical side of a librarian's considerations and deliberations. This outline really leads to the indispensable works of Helen Lyman, particularly *Literacy and the Nation's Libraries*, also published by ALA. Although twelve years old, it stands as *the* volume for the shelf of a library considering, planning, or undertaking a literacy education endeavor of any kind.

In Queens Borough Public Library (the borough's largest literacy provider), the touching results of a literacy program were manifest in a brief speech from Sarah White to the Board of Estimate and the City Council. She eloquently testified and documented the value of the literacy service through the example of her own participation, wherein she became a reader. She then asked the officials to restore the proposed cuts to the library budget for the 1989 fiscal year. Her success became the library's.[72]

The key for librarians in the nineties is to be aware of their situations and their choices and to have at hand information resources that can help them intelligently plan how to use material resources in the years ahead. The issues that will affect the services they strive to provide are many. Some of these issues affect the creation, promotion, devotion, or expansion of literacy services in public libraries. Some of the issues are about librarians themselves. Librarians are an important human resource who can effect change, just as those who are provided a service, like Sarah White, can effect change in ourselves and in our institutions.

Notes

1. Edward Fiske, "National Policy Urged to Combat Illiteracy," *New York Times*, September 8, 1988, A12.
2. For a discussion on this issue see, for example, Benjamin M. Campaine, *Information Technology and Cultural Change: Toward a New Literacy?* (Cambridge, Mass.: Center for Information Policy Research, Harvard University, 1984), passim.
3. American Library Association Presidential Commission on Information Literacy, *Final Report* (Chicago: ALA, 1989), p. 1.
4. Helen Lyman, *Literacy and the Nation's Libraries* (Chicago: ALA, 1977), p. 14.
5. David Harman, *Literacy: A National Dilemma* (Cambridge, Mass.: Adult Education Company, 1987), pp. 7–8.
6. Ibid., p. 36.
7. Ibid., especially chapters 1 (pp. 1–11) and 3 (pp. 29–45).
8. Jonathan Kozol, *Illiterate America* (New York: New American Library, 1985), pp. 62–69.
9. Commission of Freedom and Equality of Access to Information, *Freedom and Equality of Access to Information: A Report to the American Library Association* (Chicago: ALA, 1986), p. 1.
10. Ibid., p. 13.
11. Ibid., p. 12.
12. Rick Gladstone, "Illiteracy Poses Economic Threat," Champaign (Ill.) *News-Gazette* sec. C., p. 1 and 5.
13. Joe Fowler, Interview by Author, Columbus, Ohio, February 26, 1988.
14. Queens Borough Public Library Press Release, August 23, 1988, Jamaica, N.Y., p. 1.
15. Proclamation, State of Minnesota, July 21, 1986, p. 1.
16. Lyman, *Literacy and the Nation's Libraries*, p. 74.
17. Robert Ellis Lee, *Continuing Education for Adults through the American Public Library* (Chicago: ALA, 1966), pp. 16–17.
18. Margaret E. Monroe, *Library Adult Education: The Biography of an Idea* (New York: Scarecrow, 1963), pp. 57–59.
19. Jonathan Kozol, *Illiterate America* (New York: New American Library, 1985).
20. Jonathan Kozol, *Prisoners of Silence: Breaking the Bonds of Illiteracy in the United States* (New York: Continuum, 1980).
21. Jonathan Kozol, "How We Can Win: A Plan to Reach and Teach Twenty-five Million Illiterate Adults," *Wilson Library Bulletin* 54 (June, 1980): 124.
22. Monroe, *Library Adult Education*, p. 4.
23. Ibid., p. 2.
24. Ibid., p. 19.

25. Lynn Birge, *Serving Adult Learners: A Public Library Tradition* (Chicago: ALA, 1981), pp. 114–115.

26. Eleanor Touhey Smith, "Advocates for Literacy: The Library Situation," *Catholic Library World*, 52 (Sept. 1980): 66.

27. Margaret E. Monroe, "The Evolution of Literacy Programs in the Context of Library Adult Education," *Library Trends,* 35 (Fall, 1986): 199–200.

28. Helen Lyman Smith, *Adult Education Activities in Public Libraries* (Chicago: ALA, 1954), p. 7.

29. John Berry, "Editorial," *Library Journal* 91 (August 1966): 1344.

30. Marcia Nauritil, *Public Libraries and Nontraditional Clientele* (Westport, Conn.: Greenwood, 1985), p. 94.

31. Thomas Ballard, *Failure of Resource Sharing in Public Libraries and Alternative Strategies for Services* (Chicago: ALA, 1986), pp. 270–272.

32. Debra Wilcox Johnson, *Libraries and Literacy: A Planning Manual* (Chicago: ALA, 1987).

33. Bernice McDonald, *Literacy Activities in Public Libraries* (Chicago: ALA, 1964).

34. Quoted in Monroe, *Library Adult Education*, p. 200.

35. Genevieve Casey, ed., *Public Library Service to the Illiterate Adult* (Detroit: Wayne State University, 1972).

36. Helen Lyman, *Library Materials in Service to the Adult New Reader* (Chicago: ALA, 1973).

37. Helen Lyman, *Reading and the Adult New Reader* (Chicago: ALA, 1976.)

38. Helen Lyman, *Literacy and the Nation's Libraries* (Chicago: ALA, 1977).

39. National Commission of Libraries and Information Science, *Libraries and Literacy: A Theme Conference Summary*, (Washington: NCLIS, 1979), p. 4.

40. Roger Parent, ed., *American Library Association Yearbook of Library and Information Services '86* (Chicago: ALA, 1987), p. 19.

41. Birge, *Serving Adult Learners*, p. 107.

42. Kozol, *Illiterate America*, p. 51.

43. Coalition for Literacy, *Campaign Report* (Chicago: ALA, 1988), p. 5.

44. Kozol, *Illiterate America*, p. 51.

45. Ibid., p. 52.

46. Office of Educational Research and Improvement, *Library Programs LSCA VI: Library Literacy Program Analysis of Funded Projects 1986* (U.S. Department of Education, 1987).

47. Office of Educational Research and Improvement, *Library Programs LSCA VI: Library Literacy Program Analysis of Funded Projects 1987* (U.S. Department of Education, 1988).

48. Kozol, *Illiterate America*, pp. 41–42.

49. Lyman, *Literacy and the Nation's Libraries*, p. 27.

50. Coalition for Literacy, *Campaign Report*, p. 5.

51. Contact Literacy Center, *Written Word*, July 1988, p. 1.

52. Coalition for Literacy, *Campaign Report*, p. 5.

53. U.S. Department of Education, *The Update*, July 1988, p. 1.

54. *ALA Handbook of Organization*, ed. Patricia Scarry (Chicago: ALA, 1988), p. 234.

55. Kenneth Yamashita (Chair, Advisory Committee of Office of Library Outreach Services), letter to Norman Horrocks (Committee on Organization) (Chicago: ALA, 1989), p. 2.

56. See, for example, the "Libraries and Adult Literacy" section of the *ALA Yearbook of Library and Information Services 1988* (Chicago: ALA, 1988), pp. 1–7.

57. Lyman Smith, *Adult Education Activities*, p. 80.
58. Ibid., p. 17.
59. Ibid., p. 21.
60. Ibid., p. 25.
61. Contract Research Center, *Libraries in Literacy*, Volume 1 (Washington, D.C.: U.S. Department of Education, Office of Library and Learning Technologies, 1981).
62. Esther Gottlieb Smith, "Literacy Education Gap: The Involvement of Public Libraries in Literacy Education," *Library and Information Science Research* 6 (Jan.–March 1984), p. 81.
63. Ibid., p. 85.
64. Ibid., p. 79.
65. Ibid., p. 80.
66. Ibid., p. 82.
67. Ibid., p. 80.
68. Debra Wilcox Johnson, Report at Public Library Association Conference, Pittsburgh, Penn., April 1988.
69. Roger Szudy, *Public Library and Literacy: A Community-Based Approach* (Columbus: The State Library of Ohio, 1988).
70. Lyman, *Literacy and the Nation's Libraries*, p. 17.
71. Literacy Commission, National Advisory Council on Adult Education, *Illiteracy in America: Extent, Causes, and Suggested Solutions* (Washington, D.C.: U.S. Department of Education, 1987).
72. Queens Borough Public Library, "News for Staff" 3, no. 15 (May 31, 1988): 1

CHAPTER 6

Public Library Service to Adult Job Seekers

Michele DeLorme

Public libraries have a long history of serving the vocational and educational needs of their communities, as outlined in Van Fleet's chapter on lifelong learning. This chapter traces the development of services to adult job seekers in public libraries from 1950 to the present. It covers: (1) the consolidation of information sources in special collections; (2) the cooperation of public libraries with social service agencies to provide services to job seekers; (3) the provision by public libraries of counseling services for job seekers; (4) highlights of the ASE Study; and (5) issues of library service that have been raised by this provision.

Definition of Terms

"Service" in the context of job-seeking has a number of different definitions. Public libraries have included materials for job seekers in their collections for decades. The 1934 edition of *Library Literature* uses "vocational guidance" as a subject heading, and the 1934 *Standard Catalog for Public Libraries* recommends thirty titles of a vocational nature for public libraries to include in their collections.[1,2] Simply making such material available may be seen as a primitive form of service, albeit passive, since selection might be viewed as a de facto decision to organize collections with emphasis for different client groups. "Service" in this chapter, however, means the active promotion of the use of vocational materials in the collection. Librarians have encouraged the use of vocational materials through a variety of methods. A library may offer a single event to promote materials (for example, a three-hour resume-writing workshop offered once every two months); a series of events linked by a theme (a program series of four workshops—resume writing, assertiveness training, interviewing, salary negotiation); a special collection that is prominently identified; or cooperative programs with other municipal, state, or federal agencies. Cooperative programs may span years, and generally enable the public library to offer programs that might not be possible using only library resources.

The terms "vocational material" and "materials for job seekers" are equivalent. They encompass a wide variety of materials, including those about job-seeking skills and information about education, occupations, or careers. The term "job seekers," includes people over eighteen who are unemployed, seeking a career change, underemployed, or entering the job market for the first time. Those under the age of eighteen are not considered in this chapter, though the public library may serve them, because they are also served by school libraries and because they do not fall in to the category of "adults."

Rationale for Services to Job Seekers

One aspect of the mission of the public library is to collect and organize information so it is retrievable, then to disseminate that information to the community it serves, according to the community's needs. Where does library service to job seekers fit in this definition? Obviously, creating a special collection of materials fits this definition since it involves organizing material so that it is easily retrievable. The Robbins Library of Arlington, Massachusetts, found that setting up an Employment and Education Center greatly increased the use of materials in these areas and made more efficient use of staff time.[3]

But what about libraries that offer programs to build job-seeking skills, display lists of job openings, or offer career counseling to their patrons? Are these activities truly within the scope of the library's mission? At one time, librarians believed that they were not. In 1964, Katherine O'Brien, coordinator of adult services at the New York Public Library, is quoted as saying that libraries would be "willing partners, but cannot be leaders" in helping to educate the economically depressed and socially disadvantaged.[4] Edward B. Gold, in a 1968 article about distributive education (D.E.), wrote:

> D.E. and marketing instructors differ on how helpful the librarian can—or should—be. Some feel the . . . field is so specialized that only

they—the teachers—can make purchasing decisions. Others are equally sure that librarians can supplement their own efforts.[5]

Gold, manager of Fairchild Publications' book and visuals divisions at the time, viewed the librarian in the first two roles of the library mission—collecting and organizing information—but had no expectation of the librarian being active in disseminating information. In direct contrast, E. J. Josey made the following statement in the 1981 *ALA Yearbook*: "Programming to meet the needs of all segments of the library's constituency, including reaching out to nonusers and going beyond the call of duty to shore up services to regular users, remains an indispensable element of library service."[6]

If vigorous outreach is viewed as a function of the public library's goal of disseminating information, questions still remain about the appropriateness of the activities listed above. Teaching job-seeking skills and maintaining lists of job openings are functions of state employment agencies, and few librarians are trained as career counselors. Are librarians involving themselves in activities better left to other agencies whose personnel have the expertise to carry them out?

For the most part, librarians have been very aware of the problems in usurping the role of other public agencies. In a *Library Journal* article about New York State's Education and Job Information Centers, Tarin and Shapiro point out that "Many agencies base their survival on certain levels of client participation. They may, therefore, perceive the EJIC (Education and Job Information Center) as encroaching on their relationship with the public." They continue:

> New York EJIC librarians have avoided some turf battles by trying not to needlessly duplicate specific services provided by others, by making appropriate referrals, and by inviting agency personnel into the library to make presentations and use the resources.[7]

Nor are library services to job seekers always regarded as a threat by other agencies. Laurana Tucker Campanaro effectively summarizes the value of the public library to the Office of Women's Services, County of Nassau (New York):

> For a community outreach program to be effective, it had to be close to the community it wanted to reach. The local library was selected as the ideal place [to house an adult career counseling program] because it satisfied this and several other criteria. It usually is located in the heart of the community and usually within easy access for most members of the community. The library also provides a quiet relaxed atmosphere and does not have the stigma attached to it that a governmental office may have. The wealth of job, career, and educational resource material in a library provided another bonus.[8]

The assumption by librarians of the role of counselor is a controversial action. Sara Fine, Director of the Institute on Career Collections Development and Counseling conducted at the University of Pittsburgh by its Graduate School of Library and Information Science, advocates the role of the librarian as counselor. She states,"While the skills taught at this Institute are fundamental to the counseling profession, they are not the sole prerogative of professional counselors."[9] She later expanded on this statement:

> Career counseling has traditionally been viewed as the prerogative of "career counselors," with professionals trained in specific areas and theories and charged with the professional responsibility to provide career guidance. But a major limitation in the effective delivery of career guidance is that while counseling professionals may be highly skilled in counseling, they are generally untrained and unskilled in handling the vast amounts of information available.[10]

David A. Rouse, of the Business and Information Center of the Chicago Public Library, disagrees with the concept of librarian as counselor. He states:

> Sarah Fine . . . makes a strong case for the librarian as counselor. Unfortunately, many or most librarians do not have the skills, training, or predisposition to counsel. Poor advice and guidance is more damaging than none. It is certainly much more important for the librarian to know the collection and be able to assess the level of the request.[11]

Although the provision of highly individualized and focused service for job seekers continues as an area of debate, public libraries appear to have become more aware of and responsive to the job-seeking information needs of the communities they serve. The establishment of counseling and education brokering has often been in cooperation with other community agencies or has been in response to the lack of such services in a community. A history of the development of services to job seekers and a description of exemplary programs suggest that providing counseling and education brokering to patrons is not only possible for the public library but also appropriate and that it will continue to be a crucial function in the 1990s.

History

Service to job seekers is not a recent phenomenon in public libraries. During the Depression in the 1930s and in the postwar years of the 1940s, public libraries offered services to job seekers.[12,13] Public libraries provided special collections of vocational and job-seeking information, cooperated with social service organizations to serve job seekers, and even offered in-house counseling. During the 1950s, due to the affluence of the decade and to the relatively low unemployment rate, these services as represented in the literature fell into obscurity. It was not until high unemployment was again a significant social factor that writing about services to job seekers reappeared in the literature.

Helen Lyman Smith, in her survey, *Adult Education Activities in Public Libraries*, dealt with services prior to 1950.[14] This paper covers the period since 1950. A literature search covering the years 1950 through 1987 was conducted using *Library Literature*. Few citations were found for the years 1950 through 1966. The unemployment rate in the early 1950s was low, which may explain why there was little about services to job seekers reported during this period. During the mid-1950s and through the early 1960s, unemployment increased, yet the literature showed little response to this increase, with no citations between 1959 and 1964. There is an increase in citations in the literature after 1968, and the number of citations increases steadily through 1985. It is not until 1977, however, that the literature documents services as defined above in any great quantity. Indeed, of citations about *services* to job seekers, approximately 80 percent appeared between 1977 and 1985.

The 1960s and the Ohio Model

In 1967 Ethel Madge Hutcherson conducted a national survey among public library directors about how the library could meet the needs of adult job seekers.[15] Of seven services perceived as desirable by more than 75 percent of the administrators, the first five related to the type of materials that belong in a library collection. The sixth service was cooperating with other agencies to provide materials. The seventh was focused on the training and retraining of library personnel. The combination of belief in the library's responsibility to provide materials to job seekers, and the desirability of cooperating with other agencies provided the background for services to job seekers at this time.

An outstanding example of the thinking of the late sixties was presented in 1968 by Evelyn Levy, Library Supervisor, Community Action Program at the Enoch Pratt Free Library, at the BOOKS/JOBS Conference. Levy delineated a "Library Service to the Un- and

Under-employed" and outlined Enoch Pratt's outreach program for the unemployed.[16] The library worked with several job-training programs in Baltimore. Each Community Action Center was provided job opportunity books, which were placed in "library rooms" staffed by library aides from a welfare work experience program.[17]

OHIO

In 1968, Ohio launched its BOOKS/JOBS Program, "the first library outreach program for the unemployed to be conducted statewide."[18] Using Library Services and Construction Act funds, the State Library of Ohio and the Ohio Bureau of Employment Services jointly sponsored the program, which had three specific aims: (1) to provide libraries with more information and greater understanding of the needs of the unemployed; (2) to develop effective communication between libraries and agencies that deal directly with job seekers; and (3) to assist in providing materials.[19] The first part of the program offered a core collection of sixteen books and pamphlets to each library in Ohio. Once a library had requested and received the core collection, it was eligible to request funds for supplementary materials. "Funds were allocated to counties in proportion to the number of unemployed persons who had registered with the Bureau of Employment Services."[20] The third part of the program provided funds for special projects.[21]

The Bellaire, Barnesville, St. Clairsville, and Martins Ferry Public Libraries in Belmont County established a job information network and specialized collections for job-training programs and for individuals.[22] Laurel Krieg, librarian of the Martins Ferry Public Library, said that the main benefit of the Belmont County project was the cooperative spirit that grew among the librarians. "This was the first time our four libraries had worked together," she said, "and it was a revelation to me how successful it was."[23]

In Cuyahoga County the Cleveland Public Library established a center for audiovisual materials to be used by libraries of Cuyahoga County and other agencies and produced a seventeen-minute sound film, "A Whole New World."[24] The library presented a day-long Job Film Fair for librarians, job counselors, social workers, and businessmen to promote the use of the audiovisual collection.[25]

The Ohio Library Association Junior Members Round Table in Cincinnati trained local library aides to assist readers in using collections that were placed in Neighborhood Centers.[26] When the BOOKS/JOBS support ended, the Cincinnati Public Library provided funds to continue operation of four of the Neighborhood Center libraries and three community center collections.[27]

In Franklin County the Columbus Public Library operated a Jobmobile in cooperation with the Ohio Bureau of Employment Services. The Columbus Public Library also provided neighborhood collections of books and materials and expanded its film collection.[28] The Mansfield Public Library in Richland County established an employment information library in the Opportunities Industrialization Center Office, that provided training programs for hard core unemployed.[29]

The Akron Public Library in Summit County developed its audiovisual collection and services, particularly those for community agencies working in the jobs and vocational information field, including business firms developing job training programs.[30] The Akron project, which appeared to be the only one that gained the interest and support of business, offered film and filmstrip programs on subjects such as getting and holding a job, health, consumer education, and the economic and political factors leading to unemployment.[31]

In Scioto County the Portsmouth Public Library established collections of printed and audiovisual materials in Opportunity and Adult Education centers.[32] Counselors at the BES office in Portsmouth made extensive use of the BOOKS/JOBS materials, especially films and filmstrips.[33]

In Stark County the Canton, Alliance and Massilon Public Libraries established Job information Centers in neighborhood centers for informal use by individuals and as support of tutoring programs.[34] The program was coordinated by a librarian attached to the County OEO office with assistance of sponsoring libraries.[35]

The Ohio BOOKS/JOBS program demonstrated that the public library could be of use to the staffs and clients of social welfare agencies.[36] Most of the project evaluations emphasized the value of the links forged among libraries, the State Library, and between libraries and other community service agencies.

The BOOKS/JOBS program could have been improved by increased staffing on both the state level and the local level. A. J. Goldwyn, associate dean of Case Western Reserve Library School, suggested that "instead of 70 percent for materials and 30 percent for staff, the percentages might have been reversed."[37] An example of the effects of the lack of funds for staff is the Stark County BOOKS/JOBS Project. The project set up Job Resource Areas in six community action centers. Each Center employed an OEO aide who had responsibility for many duties, including taking care of the Job Resource Area. At the outset, the aides received training at the local public library. Some of the aides spent very little of their time and effort on the resources collections, however, in part because of their many other duties.[38]

Koons attributed the relatively low amount of use in some centers in part to this lack of adequate staffing.[39] Another problem in large libraries was that while specialists at headquarter libraries worked closely with community agencies, in many cases there was little involvement on the part of branch libraries, though branch libraries were the nearest "community library" for many job seekers.[40]

In evaluation of the BOOKS/JOBS Program, Joseph F. Shubert wrote:

> Although individual projects within communities have ranged from solid success to complete failure, the program has accomplished its three aims. Some Ohio librarians do have more information and greater understanding of the needs of the unemployed. Effective communication has been developed between many libraries and agencies dealing with job seekers. And large quantities of current materials have been acquired.[41]

The turbulent decade of the 1960s saw the beginnings of a trend toward updating and placing materials for job seekers in special collections, either in libraries or in community centers. As exemplified in Ohio, public librarians recognized the need to serve job seekers through cooperation with other community agencies, becoming active participants in promoting the use of information for job seekers rather than passive collectors of such information.

The 1970s and the New York Model

In the 1970s, many libraries, including the Seattle (Washington) Public Library[42] and the District of Columbia Public Library,[43] placed their information for job seekers in special collections and continued to devise new methods of service.

In 1972, the New Mexico Economic Security Commission requested the State Library's aid in disseminating job information. The state library set up a program through which job information was distributed via bookmobile.[44] Also in 1972, the Cleveland Public Library participated in the Action in Manpower (AIMS/Jobs) program by hiring thirty clerical and semiclerical workers through the program.[45] In 1975, the Bossier (Louisiana) Parish Library cooperated with the Louisiana State Employment Service by displaying the Service's Job Bank Book in the library daily.[46] In 1977, the Lawrence (Massachusetts) Public Library was chosen to house a computer offering the Massachusetts Occupational Information System, which provided information on occupations, schools, apprenticeships, and CETA programs, and which included a self-assessment questionnaire that patrons could use to explore their career interests.[47]

In August 1977, *Library Journal* announced that the Free Library of Philadelphia had set up Lifelong Learning Centers in seven of its branches.[48] The centers offered assistance to adults in career and educational planning—also known as educational brokering.[49] Those doing the counseling were not librarians, but persons with appropriate backgrounds in guidance and counseling.[50] According to Marge Pacer, the Lifelong Learning Center was one of twenty-four libraries across the nation offering educational brokering at this time.[51]

New York State provided support for education and job information centers for more than a decade. The state had already adopted the Adult Independent Learner Project by the early 1970s, which created a favorable climate for the establishment of adult learner services in public libraries.[52] In 1972, the Yonkers Library started the first Job Information Center in the state, which "created interest in other parts of the state and, under the leadership of the New York State Library, Library Services and Construction Act funds were made available in 1975 to establish a network of these centers."[53] Thus, in the mid-1970s job information centers were established in the Schnectady County Library,[54] the Hempstead Public Library,[55] the West Islip Public Library,[56] the Buffalo and Erie County Public Library,[57] and the Bethlehem Public Library (inter alia).[58] In mid-1976,[59] the Nassau County Office of Women's Services developed a project to provide career counseling for citizens of Nassau and Suffolk Counties in New York, called the Long Island Regional Advisory Council on Higher Education (LIRACHE).[60] LIRACHE provided educational and vocational counseling in eleven libraries in the two counties. The counselors were candidates for graduate degrees in counselor education and were available for individual counseling approximately eight hours per week at each library.[61]

In September 1977, *Wilson Library Bulletin* reported that the Higher Education Library Advisory Service of the Queens Borough Public Library offered individual consultation on resuming education, upgrading job skills, and changing careers.[62] According to the report, the librarian was doing the counseling.

In the 1970s public libraries continued to provide special collections to serve job seekers. A major difference from the 1960s was that, rather than cooperating with other social agencies by placing collections outside the library, the emphasis was on offering expanded services to job seekers in the library, with the cooperation of other social agencies. By the end of the 1970s, some libraries had begun to offer more than information to job seekers by adding counseling to their services.

The 1980s

In 1980 there was a sharp increase in the U.S. national unemployment rate, up from 5.8 percent in 1979 to 7.1 percent in 1980[63] to 9.7 percent in 1982, the highest since 1950.[64] The literature shows increased efforts by librarians to meet the needs of job seekers. New York State continued to put a strong emphasis on the development of services to job seekers through the Education Information Centers Program, a jointly sponsored project of the New York State Education Department and the State Library, that had begun in the late 1970s. "Virtually every one of the state's twenty-two public library systems has at least one location with a resource center designated to provide this type of information."[65] Services for job seekers offered in New York's libraries are many and varied.

The LIRACHE Project in Nassau and Suffolk counties ended in June of 1978. To fill the void, the Nassau Library System and the Suffolk Cooperative Library System created the Library Career Counseling program.[66] By pooling money and sharing costs, the two systems hired a full-time counseling professional to supervise the project. The cost of career counseling was met with LSCA funds to pay two-thirds of professional counselor's salaries, and the other third was provided by the local library.[67] In 1980 twenty-five libraries offered a total of 3,850 counseling hours to adult patrons.[68] In 1981, when LSCA funds were reduced, Suffolk County "decided not to share the bi-county aspect of counseling coordination. Nassau was able to maintain the counseling coordinator's services on a contract basis."[69] All but one local library in Nassau County voted to contribute a larger share for the counselors' salaries.

In July of 1980, a Comprehensive Employment and Training Act (CETA) grant established EIC/LEARN (Library Employment Assistance Reinforcement Network) in New York State.[70] "LEARN's goal was to enhance the CETA experience by improving the capability of CETA clients to search for and use employment and education information."[71] Although LEARN's life was short—July 1980 to September 1981:

> It managed to (1) train over 3,100 CETA-eligible persons to increase their awareness of and ability to use the resources of library-based

education and job information; (2) establish relationships with almost 200 agencies to support LEARN activities and create a referral network; (3) develop original information sources and materials and expand existing collections to provide a more in-depth resource for disadvantaged adults; (4) find the means to extend LEARN-inspired services, in five of the ten locations, beyond the life of the CETA grant.[72]

The Westchester Library System (WLS), like other library systems in New York, participated in a statewide public library effort to provide services for the adult learner and jobseeker. The first of New York's Job Information Centers was established in the Westchester Library System at Yonkers in 1972.[73] By 1978, WLS had well-developed services for job seekers and adult independent learners, but had recognized that those using the services needed more than information.[74] In 1979 the Westchester Library System and the New York State School of Industrial and Labor Relations "were awarded a two-year W. K. Kellogg Foundation grant to design and develop a library-based service for adults interested in career change, job advancement, and/or obtaining further education."[75] WLS and NYSSILR designed the Westchester Education Brokering Service (WEBS), capitalizing on the strengths of both institutions. WEBS defined "brokering" as

> A process which links adults to the vast array of learning opportunities and resources. Brokers present their clients with the full range of educational alternatives and help them choose as well as gain access to the program/opportunity most appropriate to their individual needs. Brokers are neutral to the choices made by clients.[76]

Such collaboration among professionals from different disciplines to strive toward a common good provided a fresh approach to complex problems. The target group of blue-collar, clerical and service workers was agreed upon, and brokering provided by individuals who had returned to school as adults, many selected from the target population. Counselors with master's degrees were hired to work five to ten hours per week, and all staff had to complete a twenty-two–hour WEBS training program.[77]

Group counseling, the primary focus of the WEBS program, was provided through a fifteen-hour Career Development Seminar. In the seminar, clients develop action plans to attain the goals they set for themselves, and learn a process which they can use on their own when again confronted with a career change.[78]

Ohio's public libraries attempted to meet patron needs in a variety of ways. The Cuyahoga County Public Library instituted Project PLACE (Public Library Adult and Career Education), offering regular workshops related to job seeking, as well as in-depth career reference consultations.[79] The Public Library of Youngstown and Mahoning County used a 1983 $6099 LSCA grant to buy books for the seven Job Markets it maintains. The funds were needed to buy materials to meet the heavy demand for practice test books, resume guides, job interview handbooks, and career planning books.[80] In 1983 the Lorain (Ohio) Public Library, in response to a 20 percent unemployment rate, instituted Project ACTION (Adult Career and Training Information for Occupation Needs) to meet the career information needs of Lorain's citizens.[81] The first step in the project was to create a collection of current resources.[82] "The other facets of Project ACTION are the individual consultations and workshops offered by Tari Kratt, project specialist, and Project Director [Martin] Jaffe."[83]

In 1980, the Spokane Public Library was designated an Educational Information Center.[84] Volunteers from the Washington State Employment Security Office provided career counseling at the EIC to 339 adults in October of 1982.[85] Services provided by the EIC include skills assessment, occupational counseling, labor market information, resume writing, interview techniques, and tips on coping with unemployment.[86] The Junior League, in addition to providing the help of ten volunteers, granted the Spokane Public Library $26,734 to pay the salary of a library technical assistant for three years.[87]

In June of 1987, an ALA news release reported that the Public Library Association (PLA), a division of ALA, was awarded a grant by the W. K. Kellogg Foundation to create a network among the public library-based Education Information Centers (EICs) already aided by the Kellogg Foundation.[88] The goals of the PLA/EIC program are to ensure the development and delivery of educational information that is comprehensive, impartial, and accurate; provide equal access to information and counseling service for all residents, with a special outreach to adults who are handicapped, disadvantaged and geographically isolated; and support the use of existing institutions and agencies providing information and counseling services and promote cooperation among them.[89]

The PLA/EIC project consists of the PLA/EIC National Coordinating Office and a National EIC Advisory Committee. The EIC coordinating office is designed to foster networking among the Kellogg-funded sites. Networking will be facilitated by periodic meetings of EIC site staff and through a number of other methods including the project's newsletter, the *EIC Linkletter*, which will report on training and evaluation activities, program ideas and tips, news from various EICs, methods of improving EIC services, and a variety of other topics.[90]

The New York EICs can provide the library field with valuable information about how they work and who uses them. Most who have gone to an EIC in New York are women, and most have at least some college education. The typical user may be underemployed; that is, she or he may be working, but not in a satisfying or rewarding job. About 20 percent are unemployed.

Users came to an EIC because they needed information about jobs (56 percent), had trouble deciding on a career goal (38 percent), were confused about their future (36 percent), or needed information about college (36 percent). (Totals add to more than 100 percent because of multiple responses.) Most came away with new information of value to them (81 percent) or became more aware of their own interests and abilities (51 percent). Some became clearer about their goals (46 percent), received support to do something about their situation (34 percent), or began to feel better about what they were doing for themselves (32 percent). Nearly all of them (97 percent) felt that the EIC had been either very or somewhat useful to them.[91]

This national level recognition of the importance of services to job seekers indicates that education and job information centers have become an integral part of public library service in the 1980s. The provision of job counseling and education brokering in public libraries has been a pragmatic response to the needs of job seekers. The philosophical ramifications of these services raise issues that engage public librarians in lively debate.

The ASE Data

To determine the level of service provided to adult job seekers, the ASE questionnaire asked specifically if organized programming was provided to job seekers. Information about individual programs was gained from the third page of the survey where librarians were asked to list specific programs they provided, cooperation with other agencies, targeted audience, duration of the program, and average attendance. The data appear in Table 1.

Table 1. LIBRARIES PROVIDING SERVICES TO ADULT JOB SEEKERS.

REGION	PROVIDES	DOES NOT PROVIDE	FEES CHARGED
North	208 (32.3%)	431 (66.9%)	5 (.8%)
South	263 (16.6%)	1316 (83.3%)	1 (.1%)
Central	214 (21.7%)	774 (78.3%)	0 (0%)
West	187 (18.7%)	814 (81.2%)	1 (.1%)

Of the 4,207 responding libraries, 876 (20.7 percent) provided programming for adult job seekers. Only seven (.7 percent) of that number charged fees in connection with these programs. The North and Central regions reported higher percentages of programs provided.

The types of programming reported for adult job seekers included resume workshops, interview skills training, displaced homemaker career counseling, and others. These programs were generally ongoing efforts and reflect a relatively high level of cooperation between the libraries and other organizations. For example, the Lane Public Library in Hamilton, Ohio, had two ongoing programs in conjunction with the Ohio Department of Education, Ohio Department of Human Services, and the Job Training Partnership Act (JTPA) Authority. These programs, "New Horizons for Displaced Homemakers" and "Job Club," had been active for five years and three years respectively and had an average combined patron participation of 450.

In addition to programming that specifically targeted adult job seekers, many other programs served that group as part of a larger audience. Examples include computer skills, small business start-up seminars, family budgeting and debt counseling, and stress management. Perhaps the largest group of unemployed patrons are served by adult basic education and adult literacy programs. Some 28.9 percent of the responding libraries provide literacy education to individuals directly, 52.5 percent provide literacy education facilities, and 80.2 percent provide patron referral to other agencies for literacy education. This is a significant service to this group since persons with poor communication skills, reading, and writing generally constitute a large percentage of the total unemployed.

Conclusion

Results of the ASE survey indicate that the provision of information and services to job seekers is of concern to librarians throughout the nation. It seems clear from the literature review that the Educational Information Center (EIC) is likely to provide the model for such services well into the 1990s (and perhaps beyond).

EICs offer a proactive approach to service provision. In addition to relevant materials and referrals, they offer individualized attention in assessing personal skills, setting career goals, and establishing strategies to achieve those goals. The impetus given to the establishment and spread of EICs by the Kellogg Foundation should not be understated. Support from the Foundation continues in the form of funding for national dissemination of information about EICs, evaluation of services, networking, and research. Continued cooperation between the Public Library Association and the Foundation may be the final step in popularizing educational information centers and integrating the provision of services to job seekers into the realm of "basic library service."

Notes

1. *Library Literature* 1933–1935 (New York: Wilson, 1936), p. 419.
2. *Standard Catalog for Public Libraries*, 1st ed. (New York: Wilson, 1934), pp. 276–279.
3. "Popular Job Information Center Also Saves Staff Time," *Library Journal* 109 (March 1984): 416.
4. " 'War on Poverty': Book Publishing's Role in Adult Education, Job Retraining," *Publisher's Weekly* 185 (February 17, 1964): 45.
5. Edward B. Gold, "Relevance: A Job, a Future, a Sense of Dignity," *Library Journal* 93 (December 15, 1968): 4706.
6. E. J. Josey, "Social Responsibilities," in *The ALA Yearbook* (Chicago: ALA, 1982), p. 260.
7. Patricia Tarin and Barbara Shapiro, "Learning, Jobs, and the Quality of Life," *Library Journal* 106 (December 15, 1981): 2367.
8. Laura Tucker Campanero, "The Long Island Regional Advisory Council," *The Bookmark* 37 (Spring 1978): 96.
9. Sara Fine, ed., *Developing Career Information Centers* (New York: Neal-Shuman, 1980), p. 3.
10. Ibid., p. 47–48.
11. David A. Rouse, "Help Wanted: The Job Searcher and the Librarian," *Illinois Libraries* 65 (October 1983): 521.
12. John S. Morgan, "Books and the Unemployed," *The Library Association Record* 38 (April 1936): 144–147.
13. William Allen, "Occupational Library Materials," *Library Journal* 71 (September 15, 1946): 1187–1189.
14. Helen Lyman Smith, *Adult Education Activities in Public Libraries* (Chicago: ALA, 1954).
15. Ethel Madge Hutcherson, "The Role of the Public Library in Retraining People Displaced by Technological Change," *Florida Libraries* 18 (September 1967): 17.
16. Evelyn Levy, "Library Service to the Un- and Under-Employed," *Ohio Library Association Bulletin* 38 (April 1968): 18.
17. Ibid., p. 22.
18. Joseph F. Shubert and Edwin C. Dowlin, "Ohio's BOOKS/JOBS Program," *Library Journal* 95 (October 1970): 3239.
19. Ibid.
20. Ibid., p. 3240.
21. "Library Board Approves Eight BOOKS/JOBS Projects." *Ohio Library Association Bulletin* 38 (July 1968): 4.

22. Shubert and Dowlin, "Ohio's BOOKS/JOBS Program," p. 3243.
23. Ibid., p. 3242.
24. Ibid., p. 3243.
25. Ibid., p. 3241.
26. Ibid., p. 3243.
27. Ibid., p. 3242.
28. Ibid., p. 3243.
29. Ibid.
30. Ibid.
31. Ibid., p. 3241.
32. Ibid., p. 3243.
33. Ibid., p. 3242.
34. Ibid., p. 3243.
35. Ibid., p. 3242.
36. Ibid.
37. Ibid.
38. "BOOKS/JOBS Program in Ohio," *American Library Association Bulletin* 63 (June 1969):741.
39. Ibid., p. 742.
40. Shubert and Dowlin, "Ohio's BOOKS/JOBS Program," p. 3242.
41. Ibid.
42. Arthur S. Meyers, "Libraries Serve the Unemployed," *RQ* 24 (Fall 1968): 28.
43. Ibid., p. 29.
44. "Libraries across the Nation Tackle Unemployment Crisis," *Library Journal* 95 (April 1, 1972): 1227.
45. Ibid.
46. Lynda M. Netherlands, "Job Bank Service," *Louisiana Library Association Bulletin* 37 (Winter 1975): 104.
47. "Education and Job Information: Two Tales," *Wilson Library Bulletin* 54 (September 1977): 19.
48. "Career Help in New York; Lifelong Learning in Pa." *Library Journal* 102 (August 1977):1551.
49. Marge Pacer, "Lifelong Learning Center," *Catholic Library World* 51 (July 1979): 21.
50. Ibid.
51. Ibid.
52. Tarin and Shapiro, "Learning, Jobs, and the Quality of Life," p. 2368.
53. Ibid.
54. Meyers, "Libraries Serve the Unemployed," p. 28.
55. Ibid., p. 29.
56. Catherine M. Skelly, "Job Information Center," *Catholic Library World* 52 (December 1980): 236.
57. "Job Services and Information Centers Run by Libraries," *Library Journal* 101 (May 15, 1976): 1174.
58. Meyers, "Libraries Serve the Unemployed," p. 29.
59. Campanero, "The Long Island Regional Advisory Council," p. 96.
60. Ibid.
61. Ibid.
62. "Education and Job Information," p. 19.
63. U.S. Department of Labor, Bureau of Labor Statistics, *Handbook of Labor Statistics*, Bulletin 2217 (June 1985): 64.

64. Ibid.
65. Tarin and Shapiro, "Learning, Jobs, and the Quality of Life," p. 2365.
66. Dorothy Puryear, "The Adult Independent Learner Program in Nassau Library System," *The Bookmark* 40 (Spring 1982): 146.
67. Ibid., p. 147.
68. Ibid., p. 148.
69. Ibid.
70. Patricia Tarin and Joanne Genovese. "Learning Together—Libraries and CETA Cooperate in Training Disadvantaged Adults," *The Bookmark* 49 (Spring 1982): 131.
71. Ibid., p. 132.
72. Ibid., p. 131.
73. Jacquelyn Thresher, "WEBS (Westchester Education Brokering Service): An Overview of a Two-year Public Library-University Collaboration," *The Bookmark* 40 (Spring 1982): 135.
74. Ibid., p. 136.
75. Ibid., p. 135.
76. Ibid., p. 136.
77. Ibid., p. 137.
78. Ibid.
79. Carol Ann Desch, "Meeting the Challenge: Adult Job Seekers in the Public Library," *RQ* 23 (Spring 1984): 279.
80. Ibid.
81. Martin Elliot Jaffe, "Project ACTION: Meeting the Challenge of the 1980s . . . and Beyond," *Ohio Library Association Bulletin* 54 (April 1984): 24.
82. Ibid., p. 25.
83. Ibid.
84. "Spokane Library Hosts Employment Counselors," *Library Journal* 108 (January 15, 1983): 86.
85. Ibid.
86. Ibid.
87. Ibid.
88. "W. K. Kellogg Foundation Grant to Public Library Association," *American Library Association News Release* (June 1987): 1.
89. Barbara Flynn, "A Brief History of EIC's," *EIC Linkletter* 1, no. 2 (Winter 1988): 1.
90. Joan C. Durrance and James Nelson, "Educational Information Centers Invest in People," *Public Libraries* 26 (Winter 1987): 155.
91. Joan Durrance and James Nelson, "Educational Information Centers Invest in People," *Public Libraries* 26 (Winter 1987): 153–156., citing Marilyn Jacobsen, *New York State Education Information Centers Program: Summative Evaluation Report* (Albany: New York State Education Department, 1984).

CHAPTER 7

Library Service to Labor Groups

D. W. Schneider

"I consider it important, indeed urgently necessary, for intellectual workers to get together, both to protect their economic status and . . . to secure their influence in the political field."

Albert Einstein

The labor movement in the United States has been one of high ideals, colorful leaders, boisterous confrontations, and social change. From the very founding of the Nation, laborers, sometimes conscripted and often peopled from waves of immigrants, have provided the muscle and sweat that has built America. The history of the public libraries indicates that services to "the laboring classes" were often the cause celebre for their founding.[1]

Yet with labor groups as their "foundation," public libraries have established relatively few programs to provide services to labor groups. This chapter presents a brief overview of the labor movement, reviews what services have been provided for labor groups, explores the question of why provide service to labor, and finally attempts to explore the possibilities of future services.

The literature of library service to labor groups is confused and confusing, relatively small and often repetitive. The confusion in the literature lies in the ambiguity of the term "library service" when used as the antecedent to *labor*. In responses to surveys and in the writings about service to labor, there is often confusion in targeting the audience—should it be labor groups (or unions), union workers, all blue-collar workers, all nonmanagement workers, and so on?[2] Many articles, especially those dealing with the history of public libraries, are concerned with services to the working class without regard to union status or affiliation. Articles that are directed to the topic often deal very narrowly with service directed specifically at union leaders or union membership.

Excluding library history that speaks of workers in passing, the body of literature dealing specifically with library union services is small. Oko laments this fact and its repercussion:

Throughout the literature there are many references to the fact that there is so little literature in this field of library service and that the field while continuing to develop slowly has not taken its deserved place either in libraries or in library school curricula.[3]

Oko states further:

The need for more literature in the field is pointed up by the fact that, although more than 2500 copies of the *Guide*[4] were initially published, continued demand requires that it be reprinted. It is also significant that all the literature on the subject is of an ephemeral nature and frequently not available.[5]

In an attempt to fill this gap in library literature Oko and Downey wrote a manual entitled *Library Service to Labor*, which has become the classic in the field.[6] Additionally, the Joint Committee on Library Service to Labor Groups (a joint ALA and AFL–CIO committee established to further library service to labor groups) published *Developing a Public Library Service to Labor Groups* (the *Guide* above) and the *Library Service to Labor Newsletter* from 1948 to 1970. One library school thesis written in 1941 and several additional theses written in the early 1950s, before Oko and Downey expressed their concerns, can be considered serious contributions to the literature in library service to labor.[7]

Only a handful of articles has been written on this subject; in the last twenty-five years, fewer than fifty relevant citations have appeared in *Library Literature*; of these, seven were citations to the *ALA Yearbook*; seven were labor bibliographies and four pertained to labor archives. The decline in materials on service to labor is highlighted further by the omission of the subject in two recent reference publications: (1) after appearing regularly as a subject in the *ALA Yearbook* from 1976 to 1986, there was no heading under "Labor Groups, Library Service to" in either the 1987 or the 1988 *ALA Yearbook*; and (2) although the *Encyclopedia of Library and Information Science* (1968) contained an extensive article by Roberta McBride on library service to labor groups,[8] neither the first (1980) nor the second (1986) editions of the *ALA World Encyclopedia of Library and Information Science* made mention of this library service.[9]

Because the body of literature is small, much of it is repetitive, i.e., quoting and requoting the few existent articles and pieces. The Oko and Downey work is a collection of articles intended to be a manual offering guidance and examples for those seeking to provide library service to labor groups. It is a comprehensive collection and in turn is cited frequently as the source of many articles.

Literature size may be a chicken-and-egg phenomena; there is a small body of literature because not very many libraries provide service to labor groups, and not very many libraries provide that service because it is not reflected in the literature as important.[10] One thing the literature does suggest, however, is that librarians are unaware of labor history[11] or the information needs of labor.[12]

The remainder of this chapter will attempt (1) to point to some important trends in labor history; (2) to outline library service to labor groups up to the present; and (3) to suggest some future directions that library service might take to provide and extend library service to an important segment of the public that needs information.

Labor Movement Overview

A quick perusal of the terms, names, events, and acts listed in Table 1 will probably elicit a nod of familiarity from most readers. Almost everyone has been introduced to most of these terms in a high school civics or American history class. Unless one has engaged in additional study or done specific reading in labor history, however, it is doubtful whether many readers have a coherent understanding of the unity or progression of these terms, or how they relate to the labor movement and to the progression of American history.

A nodding acquaintance with the aims and accomplishments of the labor movement is not sufficient preparation for provision of service to labor. McBride concludes in her article in *The Encyclopedia of Library and Information Science*, "The labor public is best reached through the labor structure, and therefore the librarian in charge of such service must be familiar with and sympathetic to labor and its goals."[13] Albertson points out, "One of the principal reasons given for the failure of the public library to develop service to labor groups is the lack of leadership and personnel trained in working with labor" and, by extension, the lack of familiarity and empathy with the labor movement.[14] In 1984 there were 19.8 million men and women, 16.1 percent of the labor force, in the United States who were members of organized labor.[15] These union members represent a large and important segment of the public library's constituency. Every librarian should have some sense of the contribution this constituency has made to the American economic system and the nature of their needs for library service. A very brief outline of the American labor movement follows.[16]

Table 1. NAMES, EVENTS, CONCEPTS RELEVANT TO AMERICAN LABOR HISTORY

PREREVOLUTIONARY	Uriah Stephens	John L. Lewis
Indentured labor	Samuel Gompers	Child labor laws
Redemption	Daniel de Leon	River Rouge strike
Guild system	Pinkertons	Taft-Hartley Act
Licensed trades	Haymarket Square (Chicago)	Right-to-work
Bakers strike (New York, 1741)	Pullman strike	Prevailing wage
REVOLUTION TO CIVIL WAR	Homestead strike	Teamsters
Construction strike (1791)	**1900 TO MID-1930s**	Harry Bridges
Slavery	Industrial Workers of the World (Wobblies)	Gus Hall
Utopian experiments	Joe Hill	Eugene McCarthy
Trade associations	Congress of Industrial Organizations (CIO)	McCarthyism
Interchangeable parts	Mass production	**1956 TO PRESENT**
Business cycles	Labor Adjustment Committee	George Meany
Robert Owen	**1935–1955**	Walter Reuther
Rappites	Great Depression	Service economy
CIVIL WAR TO 1900	Davis-Bacon Act	American Federation of State, County and Municipal Employees (AFSCME)
Robber Barons	Franklin Delano Roosevelt	Concession bargaining
Monopoly	New Deal	Multi-national conglomerates
Antitrust	Sherman Act	Professional Air Traffic Controllers Organization (PATCO)
Cartel	Clayton Act	Ronald Reagan
American Federation of Labor (AFL)	National Labor Relations Act (NLRA)	Trickle down economy
Craft unions	Collective bargaining	Import quotas
Industrial unions	Wagner Act	Robotization
National Labor Union	Norris–La Guardia Act	Japanese management
Eugene V. Debs	National Industrial Recovery Act	
Knights of Labor	National Labor Relations Board (NLRB)	

WHAT ARE LABOR UNIONS?

Howard M. Wachtel states in *Labor and the Economy,* "Almost from the first day that large groups of individuals were hired as employees, attempts have been made by workers to join together for collective protection and influence over the conditions of work."[17] Frank Tannenbaum writes about the reason for this tendency to join together:

> In terms of the individual, the labor union returns the worker to his "society." It gives him a fellowship, a part in a drama that he can understand, and life takes a meaning once again because he shares a value system common to others.[18]

The institutional form of labor organization is the labor union. The definition of trade union was given simply by Sidney and Beatrice Webb as a "continuous association of wage-earners for the purpose of maintaining or improving the conditions of their working lives."[19] Alan Belfour restates the purposes and goals as follows:

> The purpose of unions is to get for employees what they could not get without one. Major goals of unions are (1) to improve employee wages and benefits, (2) to assure fair treatment of employees in the workplace, and (3) to allow employees input on decisions affecting them.[20]

These definitions and goals for labor unions seem quite simple and straightforward, yet labor unions are complex. The history of their struggle for the improvement of the quality of life and economic well being of the working class often has been marked with confrontation, corruption, and violence.

THE BEGINNINGS OF THE LABOR MOVEMENT IN AMERICA

The earliest methods for securing laborers in America before the Revolutionary War were through systems of indentured labor, redemption, and slavery. All of these systems had elements of involuntary association and master-servant relationships. A guild system and a system of licensed trades developed for indentured workers once they had earned their freedom. Wachtel states that work stoppages for withholding services rarely occurred during this period. The earliest recorded strike was by the bakers in New York City in 1741.[21] This strike, ironically, was a "municipal" strike by the bakers against licensing fees imposed by the city.

Between the Revolutionary and the Civil Wars two dominant themes prevailed in this period of labor history:

1. Emerging embryonic forms of labor organization, along with capital's response to those work stoppages
2. Attempts by workers to escape the factory system by organizing various forms of agricultural utopian societies.[22]

The Rappites of New Harmony, Indiana, and Brook Farm were representative of the many experiments that failed; the Amana and Oneida communities were exceptions that went on to become flourishing manufacturing concerns.

America's massive industrialization began in full force at the end of the Civil War. In 1820 only 28 percent of the work force was listed as working in nonfarm activities; by 1860 the percent of farm to nonfarm workers was about equal. By the time the 1880 census was taken, more of the workforce was engaged in nonfarm than farm employment.[23] This period of rapid industrialization was characterized by the following labor developments:

First great wave of *economic* concentration

Development of craft unions, industrial unions and general worker unions

American Federation of Labor (AFL) was founded in 1886; Samuel Gompers was first president

More than ten national unions were founded before 1868

Vast numbers of immigrants came to the United States filling the great labor need of industrialization

The American labor movement became influenced, though not totally dominated by, socialist trade unionists, e.g., Eugene V. Debbs and Daniel de Leon

The frontier closed, bringing to an end the period of great land migration.[24]

This period of labor-capital relationship was one of ideological, political, and in many cases physical conflict. In 1885 there were 695 work stoppages; in 1886, 1,572. Many of these strikes resulted in intervention by the dreaded Pinkertons (members of a professional, private security force). Some of the strikes, such as the Haymarket Square in Chicago, the Pullman, and the Homestead, became rallying cries for increased unionization during the early part of the twentieth century.

THE LABOR MOVEMENT; 1900–MID-1930s

Trade union membership grew rapidly during the early part of the twentieth century. In 1900 union membership was 440,000 (2.7 percent of the labor force); by 1934 it had grown to 3,700,000 (7.2 percent of the labor force). In 1900 the American Federation of Labor (AFL) was the predominant union, challenged only by the Industrial Workers of the World, referred to as the Wobblies. In contrast to the AFL, which concentrated its organizing efforts on craft unions, the Wobblies organized the employed and the unemployed, hoboes, derelicts, lumberjacks, and segments of America that had been largely ignored in other organizing efforts. The Wobblies had for all practical purposes ceased to exist by the end of the First World War, primarily because of their opposition to the international conflict.

The government needed the cooperation of labor during World War I to meet its war efforts, and the AFL gained widespread acceptance during this period. In 1916 the Council of National Defense was established and Samuel Gompers was appointed to it. The Labor Adjustment Committee was established in 1917 to mediate disputes between management and labor; Gompers was generally accepted as the spokesman of American labor. After the first World War and into the 1930s, mass production industries that used semiskilled and unskilled laborers, such as the auto industry, grew to become dominant forces in the American economy. Union membership, however, which had grown steadily during the early part of the century, declined rapidly after 1920.[25] The death of Gompers in 1924, the Great Depression, and the decreasing need for craft unions were some of the major reasons for the drop in union membership.

INDUSTRIAL UNIONIZATION: 1930s to 1950s

Wachtel states, "The Great Depression and the New Deal permanently established government in the economy. And labor was no exception to this general historical change in the United States."[26] The AFL championed the policies of the New Deal and favored stronger legislation to regulate management and labor relations. A change in the public attitude toward labor in the 1930s led to a series of important pieces of labor legislation that granted legal status to unions for the first time. This legislation included the Norris–La Guardia Act, the National Industrial Recovery Act, and the National Labor Relations Act (Wagner Act), which established the National Labor Relations Board (NLRB). Although portions of the Wagner Act were eventually declared unconstitutional, two important provisions remained:

> Legal union status through a provision that required employers to recognize a union and negotiate with it after a properly held election

Provision that NLRB had the right to conduct representational elections among employees in a bargaining unit to determine exclusive union representation.[27]

The exclusive representation clause of the act led to the hotly debated issue between the AFL craft unions and the emerging industrial unions over what constituted a bargaining unit.

This issue of jurisdiction constituted the tone and tenor of the labor movement during this time and through the mid-1950s. In 1933 the AFL began in earnest to organize the mass production industries. But in 1935, at its annual convention, the AFL rejected a recommendation of its Committee for Industrial Organization, led by John L. Lewis of the United Mine Workers, to move it toward support of industrial unionism (industrywide unions for steel, autos, trucking, and so on). Within a year the Committee was expelled from the AFL and was reconstituted as the Congress of Industrial Organizations (CIO).

The CIO invested huge sums of money in political campaigns and industrial organizational efforts.[28] Aided by money and the new organizing tactic of the sitdown strike, whereby the employees simply refused to leave a factory, the CIO successfully organized employees in the auto, steel, textile, rubber, and electrical machinery industries. These organizing efforts led to rapid growth in labor unionization as union membership increased from 3.7 million members in 1935 to 5.8 million two years later, and from 6.7 percent to 12.9 percent of the labor force respectively.[29]

The organizing efforts continued through the end of the decade and through World War II, sometimes with violent results, such as the River Rouge battle to organize the Ford Motor Company. Wachtel suggests that "the war years . . . marked the zenith of labor's strength in the American economy."[30] After the Second World War unions grew slowly but no longer commanded the influence they had during the New Deal and the war years.

The unions had cooperated with the war effort, but after the war a series of strikes occurred in support of their pent-up demands for higher wages and better working conditions. This period of labor unrest led to the passage of the Taft-Hartley Act in 1947, which restricted labor's ability to organize new sectors of the economy.

The attitude of Americans toward labor was also changing at this time: The Taft-Hartley Act . . . symbolized a changed attitude of the public toward labor. Although never cherished in most households in the United States, labor had nevertheless managed to acquire a sympathetic following of far more people during the New Deal than it has ever been able to muster since that period. The Taft-Hartley Act . . . indicated a transformation of that attitude. The act had enough support in Congress to be passed over President Truman's veto.[31]

UNION CONSOLIDATION AND CHANGES: MID-1950s TO THE PRESENT

In 1955, under the leadership of George Meany of the AFL and Walter Reuther of the CIO, the two labor federations merged to form the AFL-CIO. In 1953 union membership peaked at 26 percent of the total workforce and the percentage has declined steadily since that time. From 1953 to 1984, however, the total number of workers belonging to unions increased from 16.3 million to 18.3 million members.[32]

The inability of organized labor to maintain its percentage of the workforce is due in part to the changing economic structure of the United States. Since the end of World War II, there has been a shift from the production of goods to the provision of services. The production industries have traditionally included manufacturing, mining, and construction, while service industries include transportation, trade, finance, insurance, real estate, services, and all government. The service provision sector of the workforce grew from 57.9 percent in 1957 to 75 percent in 1986.[33] Much of this growth has taken place in government and in quasiprofessional employment groups, such as computer services. Unions have traditionally been less influential in the service-provision sector, excluding the public employee sector.[34]

The decline of smoke-stack industries as the predominant force in the economy, the increase in two-income families, and the increase in the unionization of public employees have all led to a gender shift in the labor force and in union membership. Shank states, "Today, seven of ten women age twenty-five to fifty-four are members of the labor force, as are the majority of mothers—even mothers of very young children."[35] She contrasts this 70 percent participation rate today to only 36.8 percent in 1950. This increase in participation of women in the labor force has led to increased female union membership; in the years between 1970 and 1972, for example, half of all new members of the AFL-CIO were women.[36]

Much of this increase was due to expansion of government employment, where women are well represented; public employee union membership increased sevenfold from 1962 to 1972.[37] Increased participation of women in the labor force and in unions comes about at a time when union influence is declining.

The changes in the structure of the American and international economy are affecting labor's ability to maintain its previous strength and influence. Multinational conglomerates, the decline of the dollar, the increasing number of women entering the labor force, the rise of Japan as a major industrial country (with its "Japanese management system"), automation and robotization, and the investment of labor's own pension funds (over which unions have little say or legal control) have led to new labor-management bargaining stances.[38] Consensus bargaining has led to union retrenchments and concessions at the bargaining table in many industries (such as steel, auto, and airlines) and has resulted in the giving up of previously negotiated wages and fringe benefits.

Ironically, some of the labor movement's own successes have led to a lessening of its influence:

> Acceptance of public employee unionization (which generally have "no strike" provisions in their contracts) has led to large increases in labor membership (see above) but little strategic influence.
>
> Legalization of unions as legitimate bargaining units has reduced the zeal and idealism, and thus some of the dynamics and cause celebre, of the union movement.
>
> Success in getting worker's wages raised and hours reduced has led to the "middle classification" of the labor force and a concomitant lessening for labor movement concerns.[39,40]

Labor groups are affected not only by their success, but also by hard demographic facts. The Bureau of Labor Statistics projects that there will be a slowdown in the rate of growth in the labor force for the period 1986 to 2000. The bureau predicts that only 21 million jobs (18 percent) will be added during that fourteen-year period, stating further:

> Not only is the labor force expected to continue to slow in rate of increase . . . but it is projected to become increasingly minority and female.[41]

Different occupational groups will be affected in differing ways as a new pattern of the labor market develops:

> Five occupational groups are projected to experience faster than average employment growth . . . technicians, service workers, professional workers, sales workers and executive and managerial employees . . . . Only two groups—farming, forestry, and fishing workers and private household workers—are expected to have absolute declines. Three broad occupational groups are expected to experience below average growth: precision production, craft, and repair workers; administrative support workers, including clerical; and operators, fabricators, and laborers.[42]

It is precisely in these "below average growth" occupational groups that labor unions have historically found their growth and strength. It can be assumed from these data that in the future union membership will decline as a percentage of the American labor force.

A discussion of the labor movement cannot be concluded without mention of some of labor's failures. Labor suffers from a grave image problem. The specters of violence against management and itself, questionable patriotism, and corruption have plagued it. Hardhats at factory gates with clubs, the disappearance of Jimmy Hoffa, socialist opposition to World War I, communist union members before the McCarthy hearings, mobster labor leaders before Kefauver, and pension fund and construction industry scandals have created an image of labor that has overshadowed the great impact the labor movement has made on the working lives of the laboring class and on the economic well-being of all Americans. Silvia Goodstein states:

> Others have pointed out that the American trade-union movement is less of the dedicated cause today and to many of its followers and supporters it has lost some of its glamour, prestige, and moral effectiveness. Its public image has been tarnished; and as far as the public generally is concerned, labor now is just another pressure group. These attitudes both within and without the labor movement have tended to isolate it from the mainstream of American intellectual life. Much of the movement's old rough and tumble vigor is gone; there is institutional inertia where there once was vitality and forward movement. Labor boasts of more maturity and responsibility; compared with the past, this is essentially conservatism.[43]

The old image, which persists in the minds of many librarians today, has also been a factor in the support libraries and librarians have provided to labor groups.[44] Reports of labor's continued corrupt activities and associations with organized crime that appear in the press unfortunately do little to dispel this unsavory image.[45]

While labor groups may have an image problem, business and industry do not. Almost every public library of any size proudly carries on its service to business. The history of American business—such episodes as indentured servitude, child labor, the outrages of Upton Sinclair's *The Octopus*, the Robber Barons, pyramiding, insider trading, defense contract overrides, and industrial espionage notwithstanding—appears to provide no deterrent to needed service. It appears that the unlawful actions in business are assigned to a few unscrupulous businessmen, while the sins of labor leaders are passed on to their organizations (for generations). One could assume that the public relations of business are much more effective than those of labor, that the librarians who provide service are more tolerant of business foibles, that librarians are ignorant of the importance and contributions of their labor constituencies, or that through class, status, or education (or lack thereof), librarians have no empathy for the information needs of labor. In any case, business has received a degree of library service never offered or provided to labor groups.

Overview of Library Service to Labor

Although the exact date and location of the founding of the first public library in the United States are open to debate by librarians and historians, "sooner or later they all converge on Boston, for everyone agrees that it was the establishment of the Boston Public Library which really heralded the beginnings of the public library movement."[46] Soltow points out, however, that:

> Many years before free public libraries existed, a large number of employers and employees realized that there was a valid relationship between reading and general material prosperity. One example is seen in the establishment of the early mechanics' and apprentices' libraries started by small entrepreneurs in order to provide practical education for their employees. Another example is the rise of factory libraries frequently found throughout textile communities in the nineteenth century.[47]

Though the company owners were providing libraries for both practical and philanthropic motives, the working conditions of that period of industrialization would indicate that owners were "acting also in response to current attack on industrialism and factory conditions."[48]

A good example of this type of public factory library was the Pacific Mills Library at Lawrence, Massachusetts. Its stated purpose was "to elevate and enlighten the minds of these operatives," more than two-thirds of whom were of foreign birth in 1857.[49] This library was for the sole benefit of the Pacific Mills employees, all of whom were assessed one cent a week to insure the maintenance of library and lecture facilities.[50] Many of these types of libraries formed the nuclei for libraries that went on to become public in the more conventional sense.

There was a great surge in the founding of public libraries between the 1850s and 1890s. Borden cites as contributing factors to this growth:

The great increase in leisure among the most populous class of society made the public library a necessity. By and large the rapid multiplication of libraries between 1850 and 1890 was synchronous with the labor movement and the achievement of shorter working hours. Whether or not the connection between the two movements was visible to the people of that day, it appears clear in retrospect that such a connection existed.[51]

It is difficult to believe from a present-day perspective, considering the general educational level of the day and given the technological development of the period, that the great increase in leisure would have spawned any great growth in library formation.

However, by 1890 librarians "conceived it as their special mission to bring the library to the industrial employee."[52] Often their methods of outreach resembled those of today:

Librarians distributed pamphlets and book lists among employees as they left the mill; they sent circulars to manufacturers requesting them to encourage their workers to use the public libraries; and they placed borrowers' application forms at strategic locations in the mills.[53]

Librarians put forward their institution as a worthy substitute for schools, which many people had not been able to attend for very long "owing to circumstances."[54] This concept of workingman's university or people's university was put forth as a theme in many of the speeches at the dedication ceremonies of these new libraries, and the concept of the libraries being for the workers was often expressed. Carnegie libraries were "almost always dedicated with the hope 'that the masses of workingmen and women . . . would remember that this is their library . . . .' "[55]

The millions of dollars that Carnegie gave to libraries were responsible in great part for the rapid growth of public libraries during this period. But rather than welcoming with open arms these gifts to the working people, many labor activists bit the hand that was trying to forcefeed them. "It was the reception of Carnegie grants and the funds contributed locally to 'match' them that brought on the first rift between laborers as a class and the public libraries."[56]

Samuel Gompers did not believe that any man could "do full justice to labor and at the same time amass so large a fortune." But Gompers was a pragmatist and when asked by a union in Toronto, Canada, about accepting a Carnegie gift, he wrote:

Yes, accept his library, organize the workers, secure better conditions and, particularly, reduction in hours of labor, and then the workers will have the chance and leisure in which to read books.[57]

If Gompers said yes, Eugene V. Debs "cried 'shame' upon the workers who had uncritically accepted gifts 'from the hands of Andrew Carnegie, red with the blood of their slain comrades.' " Debs went on to say:

> We want libraries, and we will have them in glorious abundance when Capitalism is abolished and workingmen are no longer robbed by the philanthropic pirates of the Carnegie class . . . . Then the library will be, as it should be, a noble temple dedicated to culture and symbolizing the virtue of the people.[58]

As pointed out above, the time after the Civil War was a time of large-scale immigration, rapid industrialization, and increased unionization of workers. Although in later years labor was to become a supporter of libraries and urge union members to become active on local library committees,[59] there remained for many years a skepticism and reluctance on the part of workers to accept the public library as theirs.

Although early public libraries purported to be democratic institutions and workers' universities, workers visiting them often were not made to feel welcome, and their interests often were rarely represented on public library boards. Harris states:

> The selection of men for the boards of American public libraries was rarely an exercise in democracy. The trustee was generally male, "past his prime," white, Protestant, well-educated, wealthy, a member of the social elite, and usually a member of a profession or a business executive.

This elitism is still apparent to anyone examining the nature of public library boards. Indeed, anyone familiar with the attitudes and motives of those who were generally appointed to guide the development of America's public libraries should not be at all surprised at the fact that these same libraries were characteristically inflexible, coldly authoritarian, and elitist.[60]

Coldly authoritarian and elitist libraries were not appealing to workers. Just before the turn of the century the Boston Public Library reported having 72,000 card holders; only 702 were classed as laborers (less than 1 percent).[61] The residual concept of elitism makes public libraries unappealing to many of the working class even today.

The practice of selective trustees has continued through to more recent times, despite the fact that the AFL passed resolutions at its conventions of 1922 and 1938 advocating increased participation and representation of union members on library boards. Goshkin found in her 1940 study that out of thirty-seven libraries surveyed, having combined board membership of 338, only ten members, about 3 percent, were labor members.[62] Nothing has appeared in the library literature since that study to indicate that labor representation on library boards has increased significantly.

Although labor participation on public library boards did not increase as hoped for by George Meany, increases in services to labor did occur. "The workers' education movement of the early 1920s acted as a catalyst to further library services to labor groups."[63] The public library served as a source of supplementary reading for these educational programs. Sullivan points out:

> The more correct term . . . is an informational program since their aim is two-fold: the indoctrination of union tenets into workers and liaison between the union and cooperating groups, including of course the public library.[64]

Many librarians may be uncomfortable with the term *indoctrination*, as it seems to be at odds with their concepts of democratic institutions, access to information on all sides of issues, censorship, and intellectual freedom. It may be that a concern over building labor collections for union groups, by the nature of their own narrowly focused informational programs, has been a factor in sparse representation of labor materials in library collections and the inactive pursuit of labor as a patron group.

"It may be also that the mission of liaison is a main cause of the confusion that has arisen concerning the unionization of library employees and the work of the library with union groups."[65] Possibly well-educated, mostly middle-class, library managers have been concerned that services to labor groups would lead to library unionization—the staff would become whom they associated with (although this does not seem to be a concern with service to other special groups such as the unemployed, the blind and physically handicapped, minorities, etc.). Sullivan goes on to say that librarians have attempted to compensate for this concern by seeking "a great deal more social intelligence" which could lead toward a "more liberal attitude toward laboring men as individuals and toward trade unions as such."[66]

Most public libraries have not made an effort to extend service to labor groups, but during the 1940s some notable exceptions occurred. Dorothy Kuhn Oko, a librarian at the New York Public Library,

> was responsible for single-handedly building an outstanding service to labor unions, both city- and statewide. From fewer than two hundred books housed in an alcove in the sub-basement of the New York Public Library, the collection grew to many thousands. The Labor Education

Service became part of the library's Business and Industrial Department and served a wide network of New York State unions.[67]

In 1943 Boston Public Library established a special library service to trade unions at the request of the Boston Central Labor Union. Another program was established in Newark Public Library in the 1940s, implemented by the efforts of Dorothy Bendix.

Partially as a result of the success of these programs and the dedication and leadership capabilities of the principal librarians involved, and in part because "librarians realized they could have a worthwhile ally in the trade unions," a proposal was made to the American Library Association to appoint a joint committee on labor.[68] The proposal was made in July, 1945, for the

> appointment of a joint committee representing the American Federation of Labor, the Congress of Industrial Organizations, the Grand Lodge Brotherhood of Railroad Trainmen, and the American Library Association.[69]

In October, 1945, the Executive Board of ALA authorized the president of the association to appoint such a committee. Objectives for the committee were suggested in December, 1946:

1. The provision of adequate source material in research collections on various phases of the labor movement in this country and abroad.
2. The operation of a joint program of education of local librarians and local labor leaders in the various fields in which cooperation is desirable; including the designation of one or two libraries for experimental work in labor education.
3. The provision through libraries of objective and timely materials to secure public understanding of labor problems.
4. The adequate provision of library materials for the use of labor organizations.
5. The encouragement of greater library use by working people in general.[70]

Later the objectives were synthesized to a statement of functions, which was approved by ALA in June, 1948:

> To discover ways of encouraging and assisting public libraries to develop specialized library services which will be useful to labor groups.[71]

The Joint Committee was made a standing committee in July, 1950, and its functions were made the responsibility of the Adult Education Division (presently Reference and Adult Services) Division in January, 1957.

One of the first major contributions the Joint Committee was to make to labor service was the publication of a newsletter, *Library Service to Labor*, which was issued from 1948 to the spring of 1970. It served as the major platform for communicating to those directly interested and to those librarians who might not be familiar with the importance, possibilities, and practical methods of providing service to labor groups. The newsletter chronicled the Joint Committee's ALA meetings (published minutes of Annual and Midwinter sessions) and published: case histories;[72] issue bibliographies ("Equal Employment Opportunity," "Youth Facing the World of Work," "The Migratory Farm Worker," etc.); source lists for general and reference labor collections; samples of successful library-labor programs (library and conference exhibits, deposit collections, book discussion groups, union recreation programs, election day activities, etc.); and news about persons and events of interest to labor librarians and educators. ALA received cries of "outrage" when it ceased funding the newsletter in 1970;[73] nothing of comparative value has emerged to replace this fruitful source of library-union communication.[74]

In addition to the newsletter the Joint Committee published guides and pamphlets pertaining to establishing and developing library services to labor.[75]

In spite of the increased interest in and concern for labor, evidenced by the formation of the Joint Committee and the publication of its newsletter, service to labor groups was a special service being provided by very, very few libraries in the United States. "From the early 1930s through the mid-1950s no more than twelve public libraries actually carried on a continuing service to labor."[76] Downey indicates that library service to labor increased throughout the next decade but then fell into decline:

> Probably one of the periods of most active service existed in the 1950s to the mid-1960s at a time when the American Library Association Joint Committee on Library Service to Labor Groups was most active in pressing for such services. Since that time, there has been a decline in services, particularly at the public library level, with the disappearance of special services for labor from such noted libraries as the New York Public Library and the Detroit Public Library, where significant library and information services had been available.[77]

Results of two surveys sponsored by the Joint Committee (1967, and 1976) and a census of Adult Services in the Eighties (ASE) conducted by the Reference and Adult Services Division of the American Library Association (1985) corroborate this level of service.[78] Soltow points out that while twenty-two libraries reported having a particular staff assigned to work with labor groups, the 1976 survey indicates that this figure had dropped to fourteen.[79]

The magnitude, scope, and targeted population of the two Joint Committee surveys were quite different from the ASE census.[80] The 1967 and the 1976 surveys were designed specifically to determine levels of service to labor and contained open-ended questions for specific comment on labor service. Besides the obvious fact that the quantity of labor service had declined between the two surveys, one of the most disturbing observations was that "many statements indicated the librarian's mistrust of unions."[81] Imhoff and Brandwein summarized this mood for the provision of "little service" by the statement of one librarian:

> We need to know what they need; we also need to have some indication that the materials will be *used*. The truth is, if people had been coming in asking for labor services we would have had them by now.[82]

In the ASE census, only question 34e out of forty-four questions measured labor service.[83] Table 2 displays responses to question 34e broken down by region. The data indicate that only 5.4 percent of the public libraries responding provided service to labor groups. This low figure contrasts to the level of organized programming provided by responding libraries to other special groups: business (23 percent); genealogists (20.2 percent); handicapped (15.4 percent); job seekers (20.7 percent); older adults (37.3 percent); parents (37.7 percent); minorities (12 percent); and other (8.5 percent).[84] The number of responses indicating a fee service for labor groups is too small to be significant.[85]

The data in Table 2 also indicate that while the North and Central regions surveyed provide service to labor groups on or close to the national mean, the level of service in the South (3 percent) is much lower, and in the West (8.7 percent) much higher.[86] It could be speculated that number and assertivness of unions, level of support

Table 2. ORGANIZED PROGRAM FOR LABOR GROUPS

	NORTH		SOUTH		CENTRAL		WEST		TOTAL	
	NUMBER	PERCENT	NUMBER	PERCENT	NUMBER	PERCENT	NUMBER	PERCENT	NUMBER	PERCENT
Provide	5	5.4	47	3.0	57	5.8	87	8.7	226	5.4
Do Not Provide	604	94.2	1532	97.0	931	94.2	912	91.0	3979	94.4
Fees Charged	9	0.2	5	0.8	1	0.1	0	0.0	3	0.3

for public libraries, strength of right-to-work legislation, social consciousness of librarians, public perception or acceptance of unions, and so on could be causes for this regional disparity. However, to date no studies have been undertaken to make such a determination.

The statement that seems to epitomize library service to labor groups is, "while some public libraries have done an admirable job serving labor's needs, *precious few have*."[87] The survey results certainly confirm that few libraries do indeed provide service to labor. It can be questioned if service to labor groups is as high as reported, since there is generally some confusion when dealing with the terms labor (to mean all workers—wage earners) and labor groups (referring to organized workers or to union organizations). The reason that few libraries provide organized programs to labor groups may be because they do not understand why they should provide service to unions or how such service can be incorporated effectively into already extended service programming.

Why Service to Labor Groups?

Should a public library provide programmed service to special groups whose primary membership is voluntary? If so, to which groups and at what expenditure of resources? A variety of such groups readily comes to mind: veterans' groups (American Legion, VFW); civic clubs (Rotary, League of Women Voters); conservation groups (Sierra Club, Audubon Society); political organizations (Young Americans for Freedom, Libertarians); religious denominations and organizations; and so on. To this list of groups whose members choose to join could be added labor unions. In fact, public libraries do provide information, facilities and other services to many of these groups as a regular part of their adult programing.

The ASE questionnaire was divided into five parts to conduct the census of public library service: (1) provision of resource materials; (2) provision of facilities and equipment; (3) provisions of programs; (4) provision of educational services; and (5) provision of external and outreach services. In addition to labor groups, other groups specifically identified in part three that could be considered voluntary were business and genealogists. Job seekers were also identified, but it is assumed that this group is primarily made up of involuntarily unemployed. Since programmed service was provided to business and genealogists in 23 percent and 20.2 percent respectively of the librar-

ies that responded, it appears that volunteerism is a moot consideration in the identification of special groups meriting programmed
service.

Volunteerism aside, what are some of the bases for service to labor
groups? One of these bases is spelled out in the introduction to the
Standards for Adult Services in Libraries:

> Indeed we would hope that we would take advantage of our develop-
> ing abilities to recognize and isolate groups for whom we can plan a
> specific approach to their library needs. Service to labor, to the aged, to
> the blind, to the hospitalized, and to other exceptions to the general,
> will allow us . . . to see more clearly the common approaches needed,
> while at the same time permitting us to plan more significantly for the
> uncommon attributes of various groups.[88]

In this standard labor is specifically targeted as one of the exceptions to the general. The precedence of service to labor is an historic
one and "attention to 'special publics' has been an organizing principle for the planning of adult services, from its work with labor and
foreign-born at the beginning of the 20th century."[89] In many communities "labor is one of the largest, and in a sense one of the most
homogenous groups."[90] It should be noted further "that although
organized labor comprises only about one-third of the total number of
wage and salary earners, it does have a significant impact on the
entire labor market, establishing patterns of employment terms and
conditions for large groups of unorganized workers."[91] In addition to
the numerical importance of organized labor, Downey goes on to
stress its "impact" on and legitimacy in society:

> Trade unionism is a major institution in the United States, having
> significant impact on the economy. Moveover, national policy accepts
> collective bargaining as a basis for dealing with labor-management
> relations. It is, therefore, in the public interest to have a well-informed
> group of workers, able to function effectively in society.[92]

Few economists or labor historians would argue the impact, either
economic or social, that unions have had on American history. It
would appear, however, from the comments received on the 1976
survey and from other sources that the rationale for the provisions of
service to labor groups may well depend upon the perception and
understanding that individual librarians have of labor and their
acceptance of the legitimacy of labor's aims.[93] This perception, once
one of violence and struggle, may be becoming modified today. Not
many years ago unions and strikes conjured up an image of dirty-
faced, club-swinging bullies in overalls confronting company guards

at picket lines (River Rouge, Michigan, and Pullman, Illinois). Today's strikes present a new violence, a more personalized manifestation; they affect our senses and sensibilities (the smell of garbage in Philadelphia), our families (the closing of schools in Chicago), and our daily routines (the loss of Sunday football and the interruption of the new fall TV season).

With these changing images also comes a change in the profile of labor groups: union members are now better educated, better paid, and increasingly female, minority, white collar, and professional.[94] It is perhaps time to ask whether the services offered to groups at the beginning of the twentieth century are needed or appropriate to today's union members.

The types of services traditionally offered to labor groups have been discussed previously in this paper.[95] Downey states:

> The specific library and information services objectives for labor, in priority order should be:
> 1. Provide collective bargaining information to assist labor in its employer-employee relations.
> 2. Provide information on the development of labor and trade union principles and practices so that labor may be better informed on its heritage and have the ability to perform more effectively in relation to organizational objectives.
> 3. Provide information on economic and social problems as they affect the interests of labor, such as international trade, civil rights, race relations, and housing, so that, in gaining a better understanding of society, labor may contribute to the solution of society's problems.
> 4. Provide individual labor people with the information necessary to make them better informed citizens of their communities and to assist them in their life-long education programs so that they may enjoy full development of their personalities and an improvement in the quality of their lives.[96]

In his introduction Downey mentions the confusing use of the term labor (for employees, labor force, labor movement) and defines laborers for his purposes to be "those men and women, both blue collar and white collar, who are attached in some way to the organized labor movement."[97] This confusion, noted earlier, is prevalent throughout the literature dealing with library history, adult services, and service to labor. Downey states that information needs "vary with the individuals and their functional roles in the labor organization."[98] It would appear that when addressing the needs of labor, organized labor can be separated into two distinct categories: rank and file, and union officials. Although in some cases this demarcation is not clearcut, most of the time the information needed to carry on union business would be quite different from the library services that would be useful to rank and file union members. It is when addressing the library needs of labor in the context of the rank and file that unionists become synonymous with workers, employees, labor force, etc. The questions become: Are rank and file needs different from other workers, what are these differences, and how can the public library serve them.

If we look at Downey's specific library and information services outlined above, it would seem that only provision of information on the development of labor and union principles and practices would be specific to union employees. It can be questioned whether it is the library's function to provide educational matter on this subject or whether it is the unions' responsibility to provide the materials it needs for its indoctrination programs. The educational role of the library can be questioned, but not its role to provide accurate, unbiased, and accessible information on the wide variety of topics needed by its clientele. There should be no question that materials on labor principles, practices, and history should be present in every public library. Books on labor organizations, on labor history, and about prominent persons in the labor movement should be collected routinely as part of a wider collection development policy, at various reading levels, in the depth and scope that represents programmatic demand, and in sufficient breadth to cover all sides of the labor question (including right-to-work, socialist labor perspectives, and so on). The library should promote this collection as it would any other special topical collection, with special displays, book talks, topical discussion groups, topical reading lists, and so on.

The provision of information on economic and social problems as they affect the interest of labor, item 3 on Downey's list, is not really labor union specific. Employers, union officials, rank and file members, and citizens in general have a need for both general information and hard data on this subject. This type of information should be collected as part of any general program to make patrons better informed on economic or social matters and is not too distinct for the fourth priority.

Downey's fourth priority, provision of information for the making of better citizens, is certainly not labor specific. Indeed, services and collections that encourage "good citizenship" are primary objectives for all areas of public library service—children's, young adults, and adult.

In addition to these broad classifications of labor information priorities, other more specific library service needs for labor groups have been identified, such as running effective meetings, improving communication skills, and the need for meeting space. Again, these needs generally are not labor specific, but rather library services that should be made available to labor with the same openness provided to other library constituencies.

The first information priority, collective bargaining information, is more specifically an information need of union leaders, i.e., the information required by the union (the organization as a bargaining unit) to carry on its primary function of representing its members in labor negotiations. These types of information are economic, legal, industrial, financial, demographic, social, and as pointed out by Munn,[99] generally not different from those information needs of business managers with whom they negotiate. According to the results of the ASE survey, 23 percent of the reporting libraries had programmed services to business; it can be assumed that if union leaders were informed and encouraged, this could become a service to labor too.

In view of the changing nature of the labor movement,[100] the changing characteristics of the labor market[101] and the lack of "success" libraries have had in providing library service to labor groups,[102] it is perhaps time to reevaluate the thrust of library service to labor groups. Once the dichotomy of the term labor group can be accepted, it can be assumed that many of labor's information needs can be met through existing programs.

As indicated by the ASE survey, many public libraries already have in place services and programs targeting minorities, parents, job seekers, literacy, and so on in addition to the regular collections, facilities, and information services. These programs are available for union group participation as well as to other patrons as a part of libraries' broader programming. It is questionable, given the middle-class status of today's rank and file union members, whether union members identify themselves very closely with their union association or see themselves as a group to be targeted for labor service.[103] Membership, however, does serve as a channel of identification.

History and the hard facts of library surveys have borne out the realization that libraries have not been successful in reaching out to labor groups. Given today's environment of cheap and available paperback books (fiction and nonfiction), cable TV programming, the thirty-second spot commercial, and the home personal computer (with modem), labor groups and all adults have a wide variety of sources to meet their information needs. Also given the funding situation of most public libraries, it would appear a prudent and economical strategy to program rank and file labor needs in with other adult programs. However, it should be remembered that labor groups, because they are organized, present a large and identifiable group of potential patrons that should be informed of and recruited for library programs. The success of using unions as conduits (using their meetings, membership lists, and social functions as a channel to their membership) to identify and reach out to patrons for other programs was demonstrated by the Washington County (Pennsylvania) Library System in a program to identify job seekers.[104]

Service to union officials, the other identifiable component of "labor groups," is perhaps the service area in which public libraries can make the most significant impact with little redirection of resources. The importance of collective bargaining is stated by Wachtel:

> The collective bargaining process is an important social institution in American life. It should not be seen only in its narrow context as a means by which unions extract concessions from management. In a profound sense the collective bargaining agreement is the cornerstone on which the entire edifice of economic welfare is built for the American worker.[105]

Because of the importance of collective bargaining "it is, therefore, in the public interest to have a well-informed group of workers, able to function effectively in society."[106]

It is perhaps time for a new perspective: "Labor and Business—One Service for Both Revisited."[107] There is a generally held view of labor and business as two adversaries with disparate ends. They may indeed perform adversarial roles. However, business in a wider context is not management or owners but rather a *process* whereby capital and labor are managed (for a profit) to meet customer needs. Labor as a component of the process has many of the same information needs as business managers.

Russell Munn, who was responsible for establishing the first public library reference division to include "Labor" in its name,[108] points out in his 1951 article[109] the resources necessary for and advantages of providing a single service to both labor and business. At the bargaining table and for day-to-day awareness, their information needs are almost identical.

Although business collections have always been there for labor to use, labor has not been a primary user, for several reasons: (1) signage—collections have always been labeled "business" or "business and industry"; (2) orientation—labor leaders have tended to be rank and file oriented and less library or information directed; (3) outreach—business has historically been targeted for service and informed of its availability, not so for labor; (4) publication—business associations and publishers (more numerous than labor's) produce large quantities of identifiable business-oriented materials; and (5) library staffing—by education and social inclination librarians have more easily identified with business. Public libraries could overcome most of these restraints on incorporating labor information needs into their business programs with a few simple steps:

> First, change the sign. "Labor" should become an integral and ostentatious part of the business, labor, and industry service.
>
> Second, train staff. This might mean in many cases merely reorienting staff to think in terms of labor information needs and having them gain perspective through increased understanding of labor history and goals.
>
> Third, reach out. Survey the patrons, make contact, inform them of the service, and follow up.
>
> Fourth, supplement collections. After surveying the patrons, it may be found that information on specific unions, trades or industries is lacking. It may be necessary to purchase or move materials from other parts of the collection.
>
> Fifth, reemphasize the professional nature of the client-patron privilege. This will be necessary for maintaining the confidence of both labor and management while providing service and information for both sides of an issue.

None of these actions should require great expenditures on the part of public libraries. Yet, the incorporation of labor services into traditional business services would go a long way towards providing equal information to both sides of the bargaining table. After all, both sides are the library's public.

Summary

Although founded on the rhetoric of democracy, openness, equal access, and other such high-sounding social and political ideals, libraries have not always treated all patrons equally, nor sought to serve them with equal vigor. Members of labor groups, partly because of their image, partly because of a passive seeking of library service, and partly because of the social and educational background of library trustees and librarians, have as a patron class been served with benign neglect.

Even though declining as a percentage of the total labor force, union membership continues to grow in numbers annually and will continue to do so well into the next century. As an identifiable and organized class of citizens, union members provide an excellent opportunity for libraries to identify and communicate their variety of adult programs.

Rank and file members and union leaders both have information needs that should be served by their libraries. It is time libraries cast out prejudices and images of the past and move with deliberate speed to incorporate service to labor into their regular library programming in a separate or integrated way.

History depicts the labor movement in the United States as confrontational and stormy, although very important to social and economic progress. Libraries, since their founding, have targeted labor as a primary patron class. The services provided and the success in attracting labor as patrons have been limited. If labor groups are considered to be made up of rank and file and of union officials, both groups will be served more effectively in the future through incorporating their library service needs into existing programs and increasing efforts to inform them of available services.

Notes

1. Sidney Ditzion, *Arsenals of a Democratic Culture* (Chicago: ALA, 1947), pp. 112ff.
2. Wallace points out that although "labor groups" was not defined in the ASE survey, on pages 1 and 3, the responses seem to indicate that "in most cases" the term was assumed to mean organized labor (Chapter 2 in this volume).
3. Dorothy Kuhn Oko and Bernard F. Downey, *Library Service to Labor* (New York: Scarecrow, 1963), p. 2.
4. ALA Joint Committee, *Guide for Developing a Public Library Service to Labor* (Chicago: ALA, 1958).
5. Oko and Downey, *Library Service to Labor,* p. 2.
6. Ibid.
7. Ida Goshin, *Public Library Cooperation with Labor Organizations,* thesis for the degree of Master of Science. Faculty of Library Service, Columbia University, 1941; Erma Albertson, *Trends in Library Adult Education with Special Emphasis on Work with Labor Groups,* thesis for the degree of Master of Librarianship. University of Washington, 1952; Richard Bruce Engen, *Working People and Their Relationship to the Public Library,* thesis for the degree of Master of Librarianship. University of Washington, 1953; Bernard Poll, *Working People and Their Relationship to the American Public Library: History and Analysis,* thesis submitted for the degree of Master of Librarianship. University of Washington, 1953; Margaret Anne Sullivan, *Work of Public Libraries with Trade Unions in the United States,* dissertation submitted for the degree of Master of Science in Library Science. Catholic University of America, 1953.
8. *Encyclopedia of Library and Information Science,* eds. Allan Kent and Harold Lancour (New York: Dekker, 1968).
9. *ALA World Encyclopedia of Library and Information Science,* 2nd ed. (Chicago: ALA, 1986).

10. Table 2 indicates that only 5.4 percent of the public libraries responding to the ASE survey provided service to labor.

11. Kathleen Imhoff and Larry Brandwein, "Labor Collections and Services in Public Libraries throughout the United States, 1976," *RQ* 17 (Winter, 1977): 149ff.

12. Bernard F. Downey, "Library and Information Service Needs of Labor," in *Library and Information Needs of the Nation: Proceedings of a Conference on the Occupational, Ethnic, and Other Groups in the United States* (Washington, D.C.: GPO, 1974) p. 108.

13. Roberta McBride, "Labor Groups, Library Service to," *Encyclopedia of Library and Information Science* (Chicago: ALA, 1968), vol. 14, p. 29.

14. Albertson, *Trends in Library Adult Education*, p. 43. Albertson was less than prophetic, however, in her next statement, "There are indications, however, that the leadership is coming into being."

15. Leo Troy and Neil Sheflin, *Union Sourcebook: Membership, Structure, Finance, Directory*, 1st ed. (West Orange, N.J.: Industrial Relations Data and Information Services, 1985), p. 1–1.

16. More thorough and comprehensive histories of labor can be obtained from: Henry Pelling, *American Labor* (Chicago: Univ. of Chicago Pr., 1960); Joseph G. Rayback, *History of American Labor* (New York: Free Pr., 1966); Howard M. Wachtel, *Labor and the Economy* (Orlando, Fla.: Academic Pr., Inc., 1984).

17. Wachtel, *Labor and the Economy*, p. 361.

18. Frank Tannenbaum, *A Philosophy of Labor* (New York: Knopf, 1951), p. 10.

19. Sidney and Beatrice Webb, *The History of Trade Unionism*, revised ed., extended to 1920 (London: Longmans, Green & Co., 1926), p. 1. The Webbs state in a footnote on this page: "In the first edition we said 'of their employment.' This has been objected to as implying that Trade Unions have always contemplated a perpetual continuance of the capitalist or wage-system. No such implication was intended. Trade Unions have, at various dates during the past century at any rate, frequently had aspirations towards a revolutionary change in social and economic relations."

20. Alan Belfour, *Union-Management Relations in a Changing Economy* (Englewood Cliffs, N.J.: Prentice-Hall, 1987), p. 2.

21. Wachtel, *Labor and the Economy*, p. 364.

22. Ibid., p. 365.

23. U.S. Department of Commerce, *Historical Statistics* (Washington, D.C.: GPO, 1975), p. 134.

24. Wachtel, *Labor and the Economy*, p. 368.

25. Ibid., p. 375.

26. Ibid., p. 376.

27. Ibid., p. 377.

28. Pelling, *American Labor*, p. 166. He points out that the CIO contributed $700,000 to the Roosevelt re-election campaign of 1936 as contrasted to only $95,000 contributed to political campaigns by the AFL over the previous thirty years.

29. Wachtel, *Labor and the Economy*, p. 379.

30. Ibid., p. 380.

31. Ibid.

32. Troy and Sheflin, *Union Sourcebook*, pp. 3–20.

33. *Statistical Abstract of the United States, 1988* (Washington, D.C.: GPO, 1987), table 642. The *Abstract* listed 24,681,000 workers in "goods related" employment and 74,930,000 in "service related" in 1986.

34. Wachtel, *Labor and the Economy,* p. 383. Total government employment was 6.4 million in 1950 and had grown to 16.2 million by 1980. Membership in the largest public employee union, American Federation of State, County and Municipal Employees (AFSCME), has grown from 281,000 in 1964 to about 1.1 million in 1980 (almost 400 percent).

35. Susan E. Shank, "Women and the Labor Market: The Link Grows Stronger," *Monthly Labor Review* (March, 1988) p.3. Shank goes on to project this participation rate to 80.8 percent by the year 2000.

36. Barbara Wertheimer and Anne Nelson, "The American Woman at Work," *Personnel Management* (March, 1974): 22.

37. Virginia Bergquist, "Women's Participation in Labor Organizations," *Monthly Labor Review* (October, 1974): 3. The role of women in the labor force and the potential of their unionization is discussed further in Catherine Samuels, *The Forgotten Five Million: Women in Public Employment* (Brooklyn: Women's Action Alliance, Inc., 1975), pp. 239–275.

38. "Over $200 billion in pension fund capital comes from combined deferred savings of 19 million union members and the public employee funds of the sixteen states that make up the northeast/midwest corridor. . . . The banks, in turn, have used these capital assets to shift jobs and production to the Sunbelt and overseas, thus crippling organized labor and the northern economics of the United States." Jeremy Rifkin and Randy Barber, *The North Will Rise Again: Pensions, Politics and Power in the 1980s* (Boston: Beacon, 1978), pp. 10–11.

39. "Most union members today consider themselves part of the middle class, evidence little sense of responsibility towards unorganized workers, and are often critical of welfare and other government programs to provide aid to the less fortunate." Richard Scheuch, *Labor in the American Economy* (New York: Harper & Row, 1981), p. 305.

40. The results of this success are stated further by Sumner Slichter:
    "Now success has put business unionism in the position where merely being practical prevents it from having adequate social objectives. Hence, unionism needs to transform itself—to escape the results of success by embracing new goals, by becoming a champion of new and better social and economic institutions than we now possess and by becoming an instrument for achieving these new and better institutions." ("The Position of Trade Unions in the American Economy," in Michael Harrington and Paul Jacobs, *Labor in a Free Society* (Berkeley, Calif.: Univ. of California Pr., 1960), pp. 43–44.)

41. Ronald E. Kutscher, "Overview and Implications of the Projections to 2000," *Monthly Labor Review* (September, 1987): 3.

42. Kutscher, "Overview and Implications," p. 5.

43. Silvia Goodstein, "Labor and Libraries," in Mary Lee Bundy and Sylvia Goodstein, eds., *The Library's Public Revisited,* Student Contribution Series, Number 1 (School of Library and Information Science, University of Maryland, 1967), p. 52.

44. Many statements indicated the librarian's mistrust of unions. One librarian stated, " . . . unions will ruin the United States. This library does not wish to assist in our country's downfall." Kathleen Imhoff and Larry Brandwein, "Labor Collections and Services in Public Libraries throughout the United States, 1976," *RQ* 17 (Winter, 1977): 156.

45. "The Commission (Commission on Organized Crime appointed by President Reagan) . . . charged that mobsters are 'increasingly using labor unions as a tool

to obtain monopoly power in some industries.' It said the Teamsters, the International Longshoremen's Association, the Hotel Employees and Restaurant Employees International Union and Laborers' International Union are all 'substantially influenced and/or controlled by organized crime'." (*Time* (January 27, 1986): 22.)

46. Michael Harris, "The Purpose of the American Library; A Revisionist Interpretation of History," *Library Journal* 98 (September 15, 1973): 2510.
47. Martha Jane Soltow, "Public Libraries' Service to Organized Labor: An Overview," *RQ* 24 (Winter, 1984): 163.
48. Ditzion, *Arsenals of a Democratic Culture,* p. 111.
49. Ibid.
50. Ibid.
51. A. K. Borden, "The Sociological Beginnings of the Library Movement," *Library Quarterly* 1 (July, 1931): 278.
52. Ditzion, *Arsenals of a Democratic Culture,* p. 118.
53. Soltow, "Public Libraries' Service," pp. 163–164.
54. Ditzion, *Arsenals of a Democratic Culture,* p. 118.
55. Ibid., p. 114.
56. Sullivan, *Work of Public Libraries,* p. 9.
57. *Iowa Library Commission Quarterly,* III (April, 1903): 32.
58. Eugene V. Debs, "Crimes of Carnegie," letter, *The People* (April 7, 1901) in Ditzion, *Arsenals of a Democratic Culture,* pp. 162–163.
59. "In 1945 George Meany, then secretary-treasurer of the AFL, urged America's union members to help improve the quality of libraries by becoming active on local library committees. He stated in a News release from AFL-CIO (March 14, 1945) 'Adequate libraries are an essential part of the educational and recreational opportunity which we provide our selves in America . . . They can help us to achieve a fuller life and to become better citizens and better trade unionists'," in Soltow, "Public Libraries' Service," p. 164.
60. Harris, "The Purpose of the American Library," p. 2511.
61. Sullivan, *Work of Public Libraries,* p. 10.
62. Ida Goshkin, *Public Library Cooperation with Labor Organizations*, thesis for Master of Science, School of Library Service, Columbia University, 1941, pp. 44–45.
63. Soltow, "Public Libraries' Service," p. 164. Soltow quotes Lawrence Rogin's description of labor education:
    "The branch of adult education that attempts to meet workers' educational needs and interests as these arise out of the participation in unions. It is education directed toward action. Its programs are intended to enable workers to function more effectively as unionists, to help them understand society and fulfill their obligations as citizens, and to promote individual development." (Lawrence Rogin and Margorie Rachlin, *Labor Education in United States* (New York: Scarecrow, 1968), p. 1.)
64. Sullivan, *Work of Public Libraries,* p. 11.
65. Ibid.
66. Ibid., pp. 11–12.
67. Soltow, "Public Libraries' Service," p. 166.
68. Ibid., p. 165. Imhoff and Brandwein, while reporting on the results of the Joint Committee 1976 Survey, observed that the high number of responses on how librarians viewed labor-library cooperation were "indicative of the fact that most libraries were more interested in what labor could do for them than in what they

could do for labor." (Kathleen Imhoff and Larry Brandwein, "Labor Collections and Services in Public Libraries throughout the United States, 1976," *RQ* 17 (Winter, 1977): 154.)

69. Roberta McBride, "Joint Committee on Library Service to Labor Groups: An Organizational Chronology," *Library Service to Labor* (Summer, 1961): 1.

70. Ibid.

71. Ibid.

72. Between November 1948 and May 1949, the *Newsletter* published the case histories of the Akron Public Library, Boston Public Library, Milwaukee Public Library, New York Public Library and the Newark Public Library. The Joint Committee, through ALA, published a pamphlet entitled *Public Library Service to Labor Groups* (Chicago: ALA, 1950) that was a collection of these case studies. These case studies were also reprinted in Oko and Downey, *Library Service to Labor*, pp. 267–299.

73. Albert K. Herling, Director of Public Relations of the Bakery and Confectionery Workers' International Union of America (and then member of the Joint Committee) published an extensive letter in *American Libraries* expressing a "deep consternation and . . . sense of outrage at the action taken" by ALA. (*American Libraries* 1 (November, 1970): 934–935.)

74. A recent periodical, *Labor's Heritage* (Quarterly of the George Meany Memorial Archives, vol. 1, no. 1, January 1989) has articles and new items pertaining to labor archives; the first issue did not deal with other aspects of library service to labor groups.

75. Some of the more recent publications, all published by ALA, included: *Developing Library Service to Labor Groups* (1967); *Labor: A Reading List* (1967); *Library Resources for Union Research Activities* (1968); *Library Service to Labor Groups; A Guide for Action* (1989).

76. Joseph Mire, *Labor Education* (Madison, Wis.: Inter-University Education Committee, 1956), p. 158.

77. Bernard F. Downey, "Library and Information Service Needs of Labor," in *Library and Information Needs of the Nation: Proceedings of a Conference on the Occupational, Ethnic, and Other Groups in the United States* (Washington, D.C.: GPO, 1974), p. 108.

78. The results of the 1967 questionnaire were reported on by: Lawrence Rogin and Margorie Rachlin, *Labor Education in the United States* (Washington, D.C.: National Institute of Labor Education, American University, 1968) and the results of the 1976 survey were reported on by Kathleen Imhoff and Larry Brandwein, "Labor Collections and Services in Public Libraries throughout the United States, 1976," *RQ* 17 (Winter, 1977): 149–158.

79. The results of the ASE survey are reported by Wallace in Chapter 2.

80. In 1967, 950 surveys were sent to public libraries with annual book budgets of $10,000 or more; 384 were returned (40.4 percent). In 1976, 723 questionnaires were mailed to public libraries in cities of 10,000 or more or having a central labor council; 385 were returned (53.2 percent). The ASE census mailed 1,758 questionnaires to public libraries serving 25,000 or more; responses were received from 4,215 individual libraries representing 1,114 (63.4 percent of the systems queried).

81. Imhoff and Brandwein, *Labor Collections*, p. 156.

82. Ibid.

83. Question 34d provided a response of programs for job seekers, a special library service sometimes provided within the context of service to labor.

84. Wallace, Chapter 2.

85. Ibid.
86. The breakdown of states listed in each region may be found in Wallace, Chapter 2. When discussing "significant" differences in the responses to question 34, Wallace does not mention Question 34e, Labor Groups.
87. Soltow, *Public Libraries' Service,* p. 167. Emphasis added.
88. Agatha L. Klein, "Serving the Exceptional Adult," *Minnesota Libraries* (Autumn, 1967): 64.
89. Kathleen M. Heim, "Adult Services," in *ALA World Encyclopedia of Library and Information Services,* 2nd ed. (Chicago: ALA, 1986), p. 32.
90. *Developing Library Service to Labor Groups,* Joint Committee on Library Service to Labor Groups (Chicago: ALA, 1967), p. 1.
91. Downey, *Library and Information,* p. 105.
92. Ibid.
93. The basic aims are considered to be (1) improvement in wages; (2) improvement in working conditions; and (3) increased control over their working conditions (Belfour, *Union Management Relations,* p. 2).
94. Kutscher, "Overview and Implications," p. 3.
95. The most comprehensive collection of examples of service to labor groups can be found in Oko and Downey (1963) and in the *Newsletter* for the years 1963 to 1970.
96. Downey, *Library and Information,* p. 8.
97. Ibid., p. 105. He notes on the same page, "Note should be taken that an increasing number of professional and public employee associations now engage in collective bargaining."
98. Ibid., p.107. He identifies rank and file members, staff representatives, and local union officials as having "specific information needs."
99. Russell Munn, "Labor and Business—One Service for Both," *Library Journal* 76 (July, 1951): 1087–1090.
100. "Union leaders do not generate the enthusiasm associated with popular causes; few of the rising generation were fired in the crucible of overt industrial conflict, and many leaders appear to be prototypes of our pluralistic society's 'organization man'." (Scheuch, *Labor in the American Economy,* p. 305).
101. Kutscher, "Overview and Implications," p. 3.
102. The "success" (lack thereof) is brought into focus by the ASE survey, which points out how few libraries provide this service.
103. "The growth, relatively and absolutely, of the white-collar labor force; the shortening of the workweek and the concomitant increase in leisure time; the larger number of more educated persons in the population; and the protection afforded significant portions of the labor force by private health and welfare programs and social security have contributed to the middle-class orientation of American workers." (Scheuch, *Labor in the American Economy,* p. 305.)
104. Peter G. Sullivan, "Service to Labor: A New Beginning," *Linkletter* (Summer, 1988): 2–3. *Linkletter* is a newsletter published by PLA/EIC National Coordinating Office, ISSN 0895-8475.
105. Wachtel, *Labor and the Economy,* p. 410.
106. Downey, *Library and Information,* p. 106.
107. Russell Munn put forth this idea in "Labor and Business—One Service for Both," *Library Journal* (July, 1951), in Oko and Downey, *Library Service to Labor,* pp. 109–116.
108. "Business and Labor Service" was a division of the Akron, Ohio, Main Library.
109. Munn, "Labor and Business," in Oko and Downey, *"Library Service to Labor,"* pp. 109–116.

CHAPTER 8

Bookmobiles and Adult Services

Bert R. Boyce and Judith I. Boyce

What is a bookmobile? In the first monograph on bookmobile service, Brown begins with this definition:

> The term "bookmobile" means literally "books in motion." Whenever books are taken out of the four walls of a library building and transported to the areas in which the people live, so that they are given an opportunity to select what they will read, even though the choice may be limited, we have the rudiments of what today we call "bookmobile service."[1]

More specifically today, bookmobiles are vehicles that provide outreach services to user populations presumed to be unable for some reason to make regular visits to a permanent library facility. The reason is often distance. A large portion of bookmobile service is made to rural parts of a library's service area that are far from the buildings housing its collections and staff. Bookmobiles are also used to provide on-site collections and library services to schools that would otherwise have no such services. They are used to bring special collections into ethnic communities. They are used to provide outreach services to the elderly and the homebound.

We limit our discussion of bookmobile service here to vehicles that transport a collection of some size and function like small branch libraries at their stops. The typical bookmobile of this sort carries an average of 2500 volumes.[2] It usually is a vehicle constructed from a van, recreational vehicle, bus, truck, or tractor trailer.[3] It should be remembered, however, that many libraries provide outreach service to special groups with staff members utilizing small vans, station wagons, and automobiles. These employees often provide readers' advisory services as well as delivery of requested materials. These are common and important services, and are more often than not adult services; but while they are certainly bookmobiles by Brown's definition, they are not discussed in this chapter.

314

A Brief History of Bookmobile Services

The rudiments of today's bookmobile service were instituted before the turn of the century—books were circulated from canal boats in Washington, D.C.; in the Kentucky and Tennessee mountains, pack mules served the same purpose; and reading rooms were occasionally set up in railroad cars for the benefit of railroad workers and their families. It was 1905 when Mary Titcomb, librarian of the Washington County Free Library, Hagerstown, Maryland, originated the idea of a wagon designed especially to provide direct book service to rural areas. The first bookmobile was a horse-drawn, converted spring wagon with a black, boxlike body that held 250 books.[4] It served an area of 500 square miles, taking four days to make one round trip.

The first house-to-house bookmobile service was instituted in 1916 by the Plainfield Public Library, Plainfield, Indiana.[5] Serving special populations was the purpose of another pioneer bookmobile service begun by the Hibbing Public Library, Hibbing, Minnesota in 1919.[6] The Hibbing bookmobile served iron mining villages and temporary camps. The miners represented many different nationalities, so the bookmobile, with a capacity of 1600 volumes, transported books in English, Croatian, Finnish, French, German, Greek, Italian, Norwegian, Polish, Portuguese, Russian, Serbian, Slovenian, Spanish, and Swedish. Bookmobile service in urban areas is reported to have begun as early as 1933 to supplement the branches and subbranches of the New York Public Library. Known as the Richmond Regional Traveling Library, the service operated on Staten Island and in the Richmond Borough of New York City.[7]

The successful bookmobile services that these libraries pioneered both spawned and piqued the interest of librarians all over the country. By 1937 there were sixty bookmobiles providing service in the United States, the majority in the South.[8] At that time North Carolina was the leader in the provision of bookmobile services. In the early 1950s many urban libraries adopted bookmobiles, because of their mobility and economy, to serve areas that were not within reasonable walking distance of a branch or main library.[9,10] Their stops were either at schools or community locations on streets, in housing projects, or at shopping centers. Juvenile materials accounted for the majority of items circulated through these mobile libraries.

The number of bookmobiles in service grew to 603 in 1950, and to 919 by 1956. Nearly half of these were in the southern states. In 1953 Kentucky's successful statewide bookmobile service began with tremendous grassroots support when groups of Kentucky citizens bought 100 bookmobiles and stocked them with gift books collected through an all-time record book drive.[11] The Library Services Act of 1956 and the Library Services and Construction Act of 1959 made it possible for many libraries to proceed with projects involving bookmobiles. Most of the 200 projects under the Library Services Act in 1959 employed bookmobiles.[12] The national total reached 1400 by 1963, and approached 2000 in 1965.[13]

In 1950 twenty-six of Louisiana's thirty-one established parish library systems had bookmobile service.[14] The bookmobile played an integral role in the Louisiana State Library's effort (1925–1968) to establish demonstration public library systems in each of the state's sixty-four parishes. In 1971 the bookmobile reached its service zenith in Louisiana. That year seventy-eight bookmobiles served fifty-five parishes and accounted for 23 percent of the total public library circulation.[15]

The height of bookmobile utilization came in the early 1970s. The dramatic increase in gasoline prices later in this decade caused many libraries to reconsider the cost effectiveness of the service and drop it. Probably the most impressive change during these years was a move away from regular service to schools.

Mobile Ideas 84–85 contained a directory of 968 public library systems that in 1984 provided bookmobile service in 47 states, Guam, and Puerto Rico.[16]

Bookmobiles as a Service Mechanism

The debate over the service and cost effectiveness of the bookmobile has gone on for decades.[17–22] Arguments against the bookmobile are these: (1) because of space limitations, bookmobile collections must be relatively small, reference materials inadequate, facilities such as tables and chairs cannot be provided for on-site research and study, and programming efforts are restricted; (2) because of their mobile intent, bookmobiles provide less public service time at their scheduled stops than is provided at fixed library locations; (3) because of their mechanical nature and inclination to break down, bookmobiles do not serve as reliable service outlets; and (4) the initial cost of the bookmobile and its maintenance and operation are perceived as higher than that of fixed service outlets or other outreach alternatives such as books-by-mail.

While there is certainly an element of truth in each of these contentions, it is possible to present counterarguments. There is little that can be done about physical space limitations, and the bookmobile is unlikely to become a major area for study and research. However, both reference and programming, while perhaps restricted, can certainly be effectively carried out with proper planning and effort.

It is often possible for the bookmobile to draw upon the resources of the main library in real time in order to answer reference questions. It is also true that, just as 20 percent of a library's collection accounts for 80 percent of its circulation, a relatively small portion of its reference collection can be used to answer a large portion of its reference questions. If one has an atlas, a dictionary, a world almanac, statistical abstracts, an encyclopedia, a thesaurus, and access to the main library catalog (whether it is in book form, microform, or electronic) along with a solid understanding of their use, a great deal can be accomplished.

While the collection will be small, it can be modified readily for each service circuit. If a reader interest survey is conducted and kept up to date, there is no reason that the collection cannot reflect the needs and desires of the population it serves. If properly managed, the bookmobile collection can better reflect the needs of its patrons than can many small fixed branches whose collections contain a large number of unused and obsolete volumes. Bookmobiles do not have weeding problems, since what does not circulate is likely to be quickly replaced with what does.[23]

The use of other space is always a possibility for bookmobile programs. Arrangements can be made for the use of churches, schools, and public rooms of various kinds, with the bookmobile providing the staff and materials. Bookmobiles can and do carry motion picture projectors and VCRs. In good weather it is always possible to extend an awning, spread a ground cloth, and conduct a children's storytelling session. All that is necessary for sound and effective bookmobile programming is a well-trained staff and careful planning and coordination.

It is indeed true that the bookmobile, because of its schedule requirements, is usually not available to the public at any one site for as many hours per week as most small branch libraries.[24] Nevertheless, if the bookmobile schedule is well publicized and maintained with consistency, and if the stops have been planned for the public's convenience according to location, safety, and time of day, people will use the bookmobile to meet their reading needs.

Many libraries have failed to adjust their bookmobile schedules to accommodate the majority of adults who work outside the home during the day. The rise in the popularity of take-home meals and home entertainment with VCRs indicates a current trend to stay at home once the workday ends. Early evening neighborhood stops might well better serve the working adult. Such scheduling combined with another natural advantage over the branch library—the proximity of the bookmobile stop to the patron's home or a shopping center that he or she frequents—can give the bookmobile an advantage as a service. Accessibility and visibility are strong determinants of library usage.

Reliable bookmobile service is the result of many factors, not the least of which are the vehicle and its mechanical components, the regularity and thoroughness of vehicle maintenance, the bookmobile driver's road ability, and the competence of the mechanics who service the vehicle. Of utmost importance in planning for a bookmobile purchase is the establishment of expected performance criteria and the careful consideration of possible vehicle components that meet those criteria. Bookmobiles carry heavy loads, over a variety of road conditions, and through sweltering summers and frigid winters. Their routes may consist of many short house stops or any variety of longer community stops. Whatever the route, length of stop, or load carried, the bookmobile vehicle must tolerate and stand up under much abuse. If performance criteria are ignored, the engine and the electrical power source configuration may be incompatible with the route and service needs. Careful and proper design and good engineering are crucial for avoiding ongoing maintenance problems. A careful planning process prior to any purchase is essential. Horror stories abound.[25] For a detailed discussion of the purchasing process one may refer to Boyce and Boyce.[26,27]

Finding mechanics willing and qualified to keep the bookmobile running and to maintain and repair its generator (if that is the electrical power source) is not an easy task. Without regular and competent maintenance the vehicle cannot be expected to be dependable. Trained drivers who understand the importance of routine vehicle maintenance and who practice good driving habits can do much to extend vehicle life. While it is certainly the case that mechanical failures can interrupt bookmobile service, there is no need for them to be a regular occurrence. Careful maintenance, an ongoing relationship of mutual trust with a qualified mechanic, and regular staff training are crucial to overcoming problems of reliability.

It is unclear whether bookmobiles are a more expensive service mechanism than other methods of outreach service. As Healy says, "The many cousins of bookmobiles—deposit collections, reading centers, substandard libraries run by volunteers, book trailers—are just as costly as bookmobiles, inferior in service rendered, and not as flexible."[28] The rise in gasoline prices has made some change in the equation, but comparable cost figures are very difficult to obtain and current studies unavailable in the literature.

In 1955 Little reported great difficulty in obtaining useful data from the libraries on the costs of bookmobile operations.[29] In 1973 Jacobsen found that in terms of cost per items circulated the bookmobile service provided by the State Library Commission of Utah was slightly more expensive than that in thirty-three rural libraries. On the other hand, bookmobiles generated considerably more use per item held and circulated more items per capita.[30] Studies of bookmobile costs vs. the costs of books-by-mail are generally flawed by the lack of available standardized costs of operation. They seem, however, to show that cost per circulation is lower for the bookmobiles than for books-by-mail and that the potential for additional services by bookmobiles is much greater.[31,32] The Vavrek survey found circulation costs from the bookmobile to be lower than either books-by-mail or circulation through a headquarters library.[33] Books-by-mail service involves considerable recordkeeping in order to avoid sending the same books over and over again to a patron.

While one cannot make definitive statements about comparative costs, one can see the need for standardized cost reporting.

Current Use

Bookmobiles are a significant force in the provision of public library service in the United States. Data from the ASE project indicate that 1,014 of the 4,215 responding libraries provide bookmobile service. It seems safe to believe that nearly 25 percent of public libraries in the United States are currently making use of bookmobiles. The study also indicates that 10 percent of public libraries provide some sort of programming from their bookmobiles and nearly all libraries with bookmobile service will provide materials on demand through their bookmobile. Forty-seven percent of the responding public libraries provide materials to the homebound and service to retirement and nursing homes. Under the broadest definition, delivery of materials in this fashion could be considered bookmobile service as well.

Age and community income do not seem to be significant factors in whether or not a library provides bookmobile service. The larger the population served by a public library, however, the more likely it is that bookmobile service will be provided. The ASE data indicate that

20 percent of libraries with a service community below 25,050 provide bookmobile service. Thirty-one percent of libraries serving a population between 26,050 and 43,245, 44 percent of libraries serving between 43,245 and 92,574, and 50 percent of those libraries serving more than 92,574 provide such service. If one assumes that bookmobile service is relatively rare in large metropolitan areas, one can deduce that bookmobile service is very common indeed in libraries with a large geographical service area.

Only 17 percent of responding libraries provide books-by-mail service. As service community population increases, so does the percentage of the libraries providing this service. On the other hand, percentages of libraries providing service to the homebound and nursing homes peak in the middle population ranges and tail off in communities of over 92,574.

In 1984 the top five states in terms of the number of library systems providing bookmobile service were Kentucky with 119, North Carolina with 63, Ohio with 54, California with 44, and Louisiana with 41. To understand the impact of bookmobiles on library circulation, some statistics from public libraries in Louisiana may be useful. In 1986 Louisiana bookmobiles circulated an average of 31,239 volumes, while branch libraries averaged 23,514 circulations. For that year forty-six bookmobiles generated 10 percent of the total public library circulation, while 314 library branches generated 50 percent.[34] The bookmobile was a viable and indeed important channel of library service in the 1980s. There is every reason to believe that it will continue to be so until at least the turn of the century.

The Scope of Bookmobile Service

What follows addresses bookmobile services to adult populations, but it is important to make clear that a large portion of bookmobile activities are focused on children (preschool to twelve years). Bookmobiles are used most by children: juvenile materials account for a third of bookmobile circulation. The high children's use is due to the services bookmobiles offer to preschool and elementary schools. Summer reading clubs and story hours, film programs, in-school storytelling, library instruction, book talks, and holiday programs are services that bookmobiles often provide.[35]

Adult Services by Bookmobile

Library service to adults in the bookmobile environment is not significantly different in function from that of a branch library. Bookmobile collections are divided between fiction and nonfiction in response to community interest. At least 40 percent of bookmobile collections are typically adult books.

It is relatively unusual for a librarian with a master's degree to work on board the bookmobile. Vavrek suggests that 17 percent are so qualified.[36] It cannot be expected that bookmobile staff will have had significant training in reader's advisory or reference services. One can expect that they will be regularly called on to carry out these functions. This implies the need for ongoing staff training in both these functions and particularly in recognizing which problems can be handled immediately on board and which should be referred to the main library for resolution.

Aside from traditional activities bookmobiles are commonly used for services to special groups. The most prominent among these are service to the homebound, service to those in nursing homes, and service to migrant populations, low-income citizens, and non–English-speaking minorities. In Washington, D.C., the public library, its Division for the Blind and Handicapped, provides full library service and programs for the inner city elderly by means of a bookmobile. This bookmobile, which entered service in 1983, has a capacity for 2500 volumes and carries a collection consisting of large print books, regular print books, braille magazines, records, community information, and magnifying lenses. It has been equipped with a wheelchair lift and a retractable step to provide the elderly patron ease of access. The bookmobile's fourteen service points are located throughout all eight of the city's wards; it does not stop at recreation or senior citizen daycare centers, but serves retirement and nursing homes and homes providing a combination of nursing, partial care, and retirement facilities. Each site is visited for two hours on a biweekly schedule: one hour at each stop is devoted to programming.

The low-key programs are tailored to each site and are planned three months in advance with the assistance of site personnel. Prepackaged programs by BiFokal Productions, Inc., are used to facilitate the elderly patron's conversation and the discussion of life experiences. Photograph albums depicting themes such as family life and transportation are the program materials. Along this same line local history programs are put together, again to encourage conversation and interaction. Newspaper clippings, historical pictures of local settings, letters, and so on are used. Local organizations, agencies, and museums are asked to provide programs, lectures, and tours.[37]

In Indiana the Vigo County Public Library used a mediamobile (a bookmobile outfitted with media resources) to provide year-round service to low-income citizens in the Office of Economic Opportunity Community Center areas of Terre Haute and outlying communities. The project was designed to encourage users to plan and develop their own educational programs. While the program was generally considered successful, the report of the evaluation team states, "As far as adults were concerned, we could find no observable nor expressed changes which could be related to an increased capacity to earn or learn." Certainly information resources were made available to groups where they had been practically unknown.[38]

In Louisiana adult programming from bookmobiles may include reading clubs and films directed to nursing home residents, prison inmates, and visitors to senior citizen centers. Deposit book collections at community centers (29 percent), book delivery by mail (29 percent), and door-to-door library delivery for shut-ins (68 percent) are among the services that bookmobile departments provide.[39]

In 1973 the U.S. Office of Education funded demonstration projects in several states to show the value of interrelating library services and basic education services for disadvantaged adults. In all of these demonstrations bookmobiles played the key role in providing educational materials to support adult education centers.[40,41,42]

Several public library systems in California have developed successful bookmobile services to migrant workers and foreign-born residents. In Los Angeles the Inner City Bookmobile Unit has, since 1966, provided materials in five languages to more than thirty communities cut off from branch library service by freeways and complex terrain as well as by poverty and language. The bookmobile can be particularly effective in minority communities. "Even today, library buildings can seem formidable to blacks and other minorities who have not enjoyed a long history of pleasant relationships with public services. . . . Informality is one of the greatest advantages bookmobiles can offer. 'They don't have high columns or fancy archways or carved doors . . . they just roll into the neighborhood, fling open their side panels and blend into the surroundings, just like the bread trucks and fruit vendors people remember from their youth.'"[43]

The San Joaquin Library System has effectively used bookmobiles to serve migrant labor camps and more permanent Mexican-American communities. They have found children and young adults easy to attract but adults more difficult. Sending free Mexican periodicals home with children and showing Spanish language films have been effective means of reaching the adult population.[44] Migrants, particularly those who are illegal aliens, do not have a tradition of free public library service and are wary of governmental institutions. "If migrant workers are provided access to information in a milieu of respect and comfort by library professionals and paraprofessionals who understand their language and culture, they will have the opportunity to cope more effectively."[45] The bookmobile has proven particularly effective in providing this milieu.

New Technologies

Librarians have been slower in applying new technologies to bookmobile services than to stationary library facilities. The electronic revolution is moving forward in all library environments and will come to the bookmobile as well. Bookmobiles are a practical environment for the operation of microcomputer-based systems, and several such circulation systems exist. Some have been designed as backup for large integrated library automation systems, and these are particularly well-suited to the mobile environment since their files can be easily incorporated into the main library file at the end of each day. The possibility of real-time use of the main library system for circulation control is also a possibility if communication channels are available. This would require either land-line telephones at each stop, cellular telephones—a new technology which will soon be universally available—or perhaps data packet radio, a technology specially designed for transmitting electronic data outside the telephone system.

Should such remote access technology be available, not only the headquarters library circulation system but its online catalog could easily be accessible from bookmobile units. The large storage capacity of microcomputer controlled optical disc systems will make it possible for the bookmobile to have the headquarters library catalog without the necessity of communication capability. The catalog, of course, could also be available in a book or microform format.

Many public libraries are making microcomputer equipment and software available for patron use. While space limitations make any large number of such stations unlikely in the bookmobile environment, a single patron work station is a possibility. Motion pictures are not an uncommon medium for conducting bookmobile programs. There is every reason to expect that the use of video tapes in this manner will rapidly increase. In fact, it seems likely that bookmobiles may well begin carrying collections of videotaped material. It is estimated that by 1990, 67.3 percent (63.3 million) of U.S. households will have at least one VCR.[46]

Librarians now report that people who have never been to the public library before are coming in to borrow videos where they are available. Once inside they become interested in the library's other collections, services, and programs. While there is currently no solid research indicating that the availability of videos increases circulation and a preliminary study has suggested that circulation of videos and circulation of other materials are not related,[47] there is a large body of anecdotal evidence to suggest that there is a relationship.

Communication channels to the main library, whether by citizens band radio, cellular telephone, or land line, bring the headquarters library's reference resources to the bookmobile patron. If one adds a microcomputer and modem, on site online searching becomes a possibility. Many such systems now claim to be easily searchable by the end user or patron.

One additional piece of technology which should always be considered is a device to make the bookmobile accessible to patrons who are physically handicapped. Ramps and chair lifts are currently the only available possibilities. Due to storage problems, ramps are not normally carried on the vehicle though they may be available at certain regular stops. Chair lifts, both electrical and manual, are beginning to appear. Electric chair lifts are expensive ($10,000) and may not be regarded with confidence by handicapped patrons.

The Future of the Bookmobile for Adult Services

The bookmobile has been an effective medium for the delivery of library services for over eighty years. There is no reason to think that it will not continue to be. While bookmobile service is not cheap, and true cost figures are very difficult to obtain, there is little reason to think that such service is not cost-effective. The adult user populations served by bookmobiles are just those groups that which otherwise would receive no library service whatsoever. These populations—the migrant, the immigrant, the elderly, the minority, and the illiterate—are increasing. It also seems likely that currently available advances in technology can greatly expand the service and programming potentials of the bookmobile.

Outreach service will not survive without careful nurturing. Just as stationary library operations require constant planning, careful budgeting, skillful material selection, clever programming, and dedicated, highly trained personnel, so do bookmobiles. The responsibilities of the outreach coordinator are great, but above all else she or he must strive to see that the on-board staff are highly motivated, well aware of the needs of their service community, and highly trained not only in driving skills and in the use of new technology as it is added to their vehicles, but most importantly in developing a close working relationship with the public they serve.

Notes

1. Eleanor Frances Brown, *Bookmobiles and Bookmobile Service* (Metuchen, N.J.: Scarecrow, 1967) p. 13.
2. Bernard Vavrek, "The Rural Bookmobile: Going Strong after Eighty Years," *A National Bookmobile Survey Conducted in 1985* (available from the author).
3. Judith I. Boyce, and Bert R. Boyce, "Buying Your Bookmobile," *Wilson Library Bulletin* 62 (February 1988): 51–56.
4. Brown, Bookmobiles, p. 14.
5. Ibid., p. 18.
6. Ibid., p. 20.
7. Dorothy Nourse Pitman, "A Wagon Load of Books," *Wilson Library Bulletin* 29 (June 1955): 779.
8. Brown, *Bookmobiles*, p. 28.
9. G. I. Will, "Bookmobiles and the Municipal Library?" *Library Journal* 81 (September 15, 1956): 1955–1956.
10. Dallas R. Shawkey, "Reaching Out: Bookmobile Service in Brooklyn," *ALA Bulletin* (September 1957): 612–617.
11. Gretchen Kneif Schenk, "Extending Library Service," *Wilson Library* Bulletin (April 1962): 684.
12. Brown, *Bookmobiles*, p. 35.
13. Ibid., p. 32.
14. Margaret Dixon and Nantelle Gittinger, *The First Twenty-five Years of the Louisiana State Library: 1925–1950*. (Baton Rouge, La.: Louisiana State Library, 1950) p. 11.
15. Judith I. Boyce, "On the Road Again: The Character of Bookmobile Service in Louisiana," *LLA Bulletin*, 48 (Fall 1985): p. 61.
16. *Mobile Ideas 84–85*, ed. Mary Tutlon (Chicago: ALA, 1985), pp. 73–86.
17. Alex Boyd and James Benson, "By Mail or Mobile Unit?—Developing Programs for Extending Library Services," *Public Libraries* 20, no. 3 (Fall 1981): 67–69.
18. Carol Hole, "Bad News/Good News on the Horns of the Bookmobile Dilemma," *Keystone* 11, no. 2 (April/May 1982): 1–5.
19. John J. Philip, "No Bits, No Bytes, but Plenty of Library Service: Bookmobile Service in Ohio," *Ohio Library Association Bulletin* 55 (July 1985): pp. 20–22.
20. Stewart W. Smith, "Potentialities and Capabilities of Bookmobiles for Library Service," *Library Trends* 9 (January 1961): 296–302.
21. Vavrek, *The Rural Bookmobile*.
22. Will, "Bookmobiles and the Municipal Library?" p. 1955.
23. Smith, "Potentialities and Capabilities," p. 297.
24. Ibid., p. 296.
25. Eugene Healy, "Bookmobiles: A Somewhat Closer Look," *American Libraries* 22 (January, 1971): 72–78.
26. Judith I. Boyce and Bert R. Boyce. "The Bookmobile Selection Process," in *The Book Stops Here: New Directions for Bookmobile Service*, ed. Catherine Alloway (Metuchen, N.J.: Scarecrow, 1990), in press.
27. Boyce and Boyce, "Buying Your Bookmobile," pp. 51–56.
28. Healy, "Bookmobiles."
29. Minnie J. Little, "Budgeting the Operation Cost of Bookmobiles," *Library Trends* 9 (January 1961): 337–349.
30. Brent N. Jacobsen, "Rural Bookmobile Service: Efficiency and Effectiveness," master's project, Brigham Young University, 1973, 52 pp.

31. Diane Friese, *Evaluation of Public Library Bookmobile Service in Rural Areas in Comparison to a Books-by-Mail Service*, 1976, 30pp., ED125633.
32. Boyd and Benson, "By-Mail or Mobile Unit?" pp. 67–69.
33. Vavrek, *The Rural Bookmobile.*
34. Office of the State Library. *Public Libraries in Louisiana: Statistical Report, 1986* (Baton Rouge, La.: State Library, 1987), p.7.
35. Boyce, "On the Road Again," pp. 62–65.
36. Vavrek, *The Rural Bookmobile.*
37. From an address delivered by Wanda Cox to the Third Annual National Bookmobile Conference in Columbus, Ohio, June 1987.
38. Edward N. Howard, "POME and the Mediamobile," *Catholic Library World* 46, no. 9 (April 1975): 384–387.
39. Boyce, "On the Road Again."
40. Phyllis MacVicar, *A Demonstration of the Interrelating of Library and Basic Education Services for Disadvantaged Adults*, June 1973, 77pp., ED087401.
41. Roland Jones, *A Demonstration of the Interrelating of Library and Basic Education Services for Disadvantaged Adults. Final Report, Kentucky Model Center*, June 1973, 252pp., ED087399.
42. Ann Gwin, *A Demonstration of the Interrelating of Library and Basic Education Services for Disadvantaged Adults. Final Report, Alabama Model Center*, June 1973, 135pp., ED087398.
43. Judith Wagner, "Spanish on Friday, Japanese on Saturday," *American Education* 16, no. 8 (October 1980): 49–57.
44. Mary B. Reynolds, "La Biblioteca Ambulante," *Wilson Library Bulletin*, Vol. 44, No. (March 1970) p. 767.
45. Rachael Naismith, "The Moveable Library: Serving Migrant Farm Workers," *Wilson Library Bulletin* 57, no. 7 (March 1983): 575.
46. "Prerecorded Video Sell-Through Market Explodes," *Chain Store Age* 63, no. 1 (January 1987): 29.
47. Connie Van Fleet, "Public Library Video Pilot Project," unpublished report, Indiana University, 1988.

CHAPTER 9

Public Library Service
to the Economic Community

William E. Moen

A public library has, at the heart of its mission, service to the community. The multitude of services offered by a library is a reflection of the many and diverse groups within the community. Business and industry, or more broadly speaking, the economic community, are a special population within the general community served by the library. This important segment of the general community has special information needs.

This chapter offers an historical overview of the development of library service to business and the economic community. In addition, components of successful service to this special population are shown in the writings of major figures in library service to business, notably John Cotton Dana, Marian Manley, and more recently, Raymond Holt.

New imperatives exist for public libraries in times of funding crises and major opportunities are opening for these same libraries as the value of information is more widely recognized by the economic community. As part of its service to the economic community, the library can claim a role for itself in local economic development and position itself more strongly as the information center of the community. Libraries from Portland, Oregon, and Denver, Colorado, to Canton, Illinois, and the state library of North Carolina have discovered recently the needs of the economic community and their responsibilities to serve them. The ASE study data show that large numbers of libraries see the importance of special programming geared to the information needs of business groups. The chapter attempts to present a strong case for renewed and increased efforts by libraries to serve their economic communities with the idea that service to this special population will not detract from

327

services to other groups. Service to the economic community should help strengthen the economy of the community so library service to all may flourish.

The early period of American public library development reveals the concern of libraries with services to educate and edify the people who, in the latter half of the nineteenth century, were moving in ever-increasing numbers to urban areas. Part of the libraries' interest in providing such services rested in humanitarian considerations, but another aspect was founded in libraries' understanding that they had a role to play in the economic life of their communities. With this understanding, libraries began to answer the question of why they should offer information services to business and industry. From the establishment of mechanics' and apprentices' libraries to the subsequent era of the free public library, employers and employees "accepted a functional relationship between reading and general material prosperity."[1] The history of public library services to the economic community shows libraries attempting to figure out the form, extent, and mechanism for the delivery of library services to the economic community. Yet today, the how and why questions of public library services to business continue to be raised by the library community.

A related issue in the history of library services to business was, and still is today, who the possible audiences for such library services were. Industrial workers, mechanics, apprentices, professionals, and business owners were served by the library with the idea that economic prosperity would be attained if the workers as well as the business owners could have access to information and knowledge leading to improvements in skill and productivity. Yet as the twentieth century began, the emphasis of library service to business and industry shifted to the information needs of the commercial organizations rather than focusing on the needs of workers within those organizations who might be attempting to improve their own skill levels.

As in the case of why library service should be provided to the economic community, librarians today are also discussing to whom to extend information services. Not only have library services to labor and the unemployed been separated from general services to business and industry, the separation of the economic interests from community interests causes members of the community and members of the library profession itself to question the advisability of special library services to businesses that could otherwise afford to pay for the information they need and from which profits will be built. In the nineteenth century, the scope of public libraries was general, yet they "achieved their greatest development in industrial and trading communities" and "their special virtues in distributing economic and technical information were frequently singled out" as reasons for their success and the financial support they received.[2]

At the time when public libraries began in the United States, librarians seemed to see a more clear connection between the welfare of commercial concerns and the general welfare of the community. Much of what would be considered adult literacy training and adult education efforts by public libraries in the second half of the nineteenth century was offered because libraries recognized the connection between reading abilities, general skills, and technical knowledge and the general material prosperity of the community. The sizes of municipalities, the ownership of the commercial enterprises, a more obvious interdependence among the citizenry, and a sense that what was good for the economic interests was good for the community accounted for librarians' broader understanding of the makeup of their service population.

Wendell Berry, describing a contemporary Amish community, discussed the interrelation and intimate connection of community and economy and touched upon a connection between economic interests and community interest that may have fueled public library services to the various members of business and industry:

> The community accomplished the productive work that is necessary for any economy; the economy supports and preserves the land and the people. The economy cannot prey on the community because it is not alienated from the community; it is the community. . . . With the Amish, economy is not merely a function of community; the community and the economy are virtually the same.[3]

Similarly, the public library, in serving workers and commercial enterprises in the nineteenth century, acted as if there was little disparity between the interests of the community and the local economic interests. Needless to say, nineteenth-century communities in the United States were not as homogenous nor as coherent as an Amish community. The public libraries were well aware, however, of the importance of the economy to the community.

While public libraries in the nineteenth century were attempting to serve general educational functions in regard to workers, the beginning of the twentieth century witnessed libraries offering their business and economic community clientele practical knowledge that would assist both in production and in decision making.

In his major writings on the economic considerations and economic impact of information, Machlup distinguished five classes of knowledge: practical knowledge; intellectual knowledge; small-talk and pastime knowledge; spiritual knowledge; and unwanted knowledge. All five categories are supplied by the public library in the course of normal operations. The first type of knowledge detailed by Machlup is of primary concern to the economic community; following is his description and subcategories of practical knowledge:

> Useful in the knower's work, his decisions, his actions; can be subdivided according to his activities, into a) Professional knowledge, b) Business knowledge, c) Workman's knowledge, d) Political knowledge, e) Household knowledge, and f) Other practical knowledge.[4]

The first type of knowledge, practical knowledge, is wanted by the members of the economic community. The first three subdivisions of practical knowledge relate directly to the economic sphere. These people want information in order to do something or as a basis for deciding something. This type of information consists of specific facts, statistics, or anything that can be used to produce an item, an action, or a decision. It is purely instrumental knowledge, not knowledge for its own sake. With a clear sense of the kind of knowledge needed by the economic community, the library will come to understand a third major component, namely the class of knowledge, in its service to the economic community.

The why, how, and what of public library service to the economic community have been discussed for over 100 years. Even with such attention by the library community, a library consultant in California reported in a 1971 study of library business services in Pomona and Pasadena that all was not bright for services to the economic community.

> During the past two decades, public libraries have launched numerous outreach programs intended to reach the "unserved" in our society. At least one group has been largely overlooked in this missionary effort—the businessman! While they may not qualify as "deprived" in the socioeconomic sense, representatives of business and industry constitute a significant group whose unfilled information requirements must place them in the vanguard of the "unserved."[5]

Librarians must at least be aware of the implications of Holt's findings for their libraries. Public libraries rely upon healthy local, state, and national economic conditions. The tax base that supports most public libraries is directly related to economic conditions. Add to this the fact that taxes are collected to some extent from most businesses and industries. Should these groups within the community not receive some attention from the public libraries in return for the taxes they pay?

Library service to the economic community has existed nearly since the beginning of public libraries in this country. Prior to the public library movement, subscription libraries and mechanics' and apprentices' libraries as well as factory libraries filled an information and educational need for the rising industrial classes in the United States. Now however, business and industry, according to Holt, are one of the least served of the special populations of the library's community.

Public librarians often feel inadequate to the task of providing information or the expertise needed by businesses and industry that comprise the economic community. Often there is the attitude that it is not completely appropriate for the library to offer special services for businesses whose primary concern is private profit. There are probably librarians who don't even consider the connection between the library and the economic community. Several voices have begun to speak again in favor of an activist stand by the public library in the economic life and particularly the economic development of their community. Voices in the past have often spoken to the need for public libraries to offer special services or good reference services and collections to the businesses and industries of a town or city. A brief look at the history of such public library services, notwithstanding the differences in circumstances between then and now, reveals concepts, attitudes toward service, procedures, and processes that can serve as a foundation for public library services to the economic community in the 1990s and beyond.

A Brief History

The public library movement during the nineteenth century in the United States attempted primarily humanitarian, educational, and vocational activities. Not the least among the services offered were those addressing the needs of workers and industrial employees. Often the mechanics and apprentices served in the public libraries were the same people running and managing the factories of that time. Increasing industrialization was changing the landscape of American society. Economic needs and motivations toward prosperity drove libraries to offer members of the economic community information and knowledge to make the individuals more skillful, the enterprises more productive and competitive, and finally the society more prosperous. "The mechanic and artisan saw in the library a means of making themselves more proficient, thereby increasing their wage-earning power. The entrepreneur could envisage a better product and a consequently higher profit."[6] The ideas and concepts of library service that developed in the later years of the nineteenth century set the stage for John Cotton Dana, considered by many to be the father of modern library service to business.

Dana formulated thoughts on the responsibility of the library to serve the members of the economic community during the years he managed a public library in Denver.

> I noted that the vast majority of business men in the community, men in stores, factories, insurance and real estate offices, and the like; owners, operators, managers, promoters, public officials, agents, contractors, builders, foremen, bench workers, mechanics, etc.—I noted that most of these men of affairs never used the library or called on it only for novels and an occasional book of history, travel and the like.[7]

Dana noted as well the "vast extent" of the material available that related closely to those activities that could be designated as business. From his observations, few members of the business community were knowledgeable of this material. He decided, on the basis of his experiences in Denver, "that when the opportunity could be found, or made, I would try to open in a large city a business branch in the city's business center."[8]

That opportunity came for Dana while he was in charge of the Newark, N.J., public library. In 1904 he opened the doors to the Business Branch of the Public Library of Newark. The branch was housed in a small storefront location in the Newark's commercial and office center. By 1913, the library had developed a large and current collection useful to the business clientele.

> Its resources include 13,000 books, maps of more than 1,000 cities, towns, states and countries of all parts of the world, 700 directories, which cover many thousand different towns and countries and scores of occupations; the latest publications of cities, counties and states on subjects of interest to Newark and New Jersey, ninety house organs, sixty trade union papers, ninety business periodicals, sixty municipal and local development journals; many volumes of statistics; a collection of the catalogs of 3,000 Newark manufacturers, very fully indexed; a good collection of modern fiction and of general literature.[9]

In addition to the collection of materials, other services to the patrons included:

> A special telephone service which connects it in an instant with the lending and reference center of the main library, or with its technical or school or art or fiction or order departments or with the central office; and—a messenger service through which it can get from the main library's collection of 180,000 volumes, in thirty minutes if need be, anything a patron calls for which the branch itself cannot supply.

Dana's example of library service to business existed within a concept of general library service in which he perceived the public library as "eager to be of use in a practical and everyday way to the citizens of the community."[10] He also felt the library had a responsibility to the business community and that members of that community should "know your own library and ask it to help you and your fellow citizens in promoting your business and developing your city."[11] In 1910, a pamphlet entitled *The Business Branch* was published. Written by Dana, it stimulated interest in the development of library services to business in other public libraries throughout the country as well as guiding them in establishing such a service.

The Business Branch of the Newark Public Library was an example of just one form library service to business could take. Although it was a prototype in many respects, especially in the areas of collection development with an emphasis on the need for currency in the collection, marketing, and publicity, and the special service orientation to a segment of the community that demanded and respected promptness and efficiency, the branch library option as a separate unit as in the Newark case was not the only one being developed. Some branches were located in local chamber of commerce offices, or combined with municipal reference services and located in or near the city hall. Another configuration of service to business was to establish a department or unit within the main building of the library. In this form, business was frequently combined with other subjects such as technology, science or industry to constitute a department.[12]

During the second decade of the century a number of other public libraries, primarily in major metropolitan areas, initiated special service to business. The New York Public Library established the Economics Division of its Reference Department in 1911. Combined business and technology departments were started by public libraries in Fort Wayne, Indiana, and Portland, Oregon, in 1913. The Minneapolis Business and Municipal Branch followed Newark's example and established the second separate branch to offer services to business in 1916.[13]

Marian C. Manley, Business Branch librarian of the Newark Public Library, conducted two surveys of public library services to business. The first one, in 1930, collected data on 109 public libraries in the nation's larger cities. The second, in 1942, looked at approximately 115 libraries and their services to business. As evidenced in the reports of the libraries cooperating in the surveys, the question for many libraries was not in the establishment of the service, but rather in the form and manner it could be developed most successfully. Two publications by Manley, *Business and the Public Library: Steps in Successful Cooperation* and *Public Library Service to Business: A Comparative Study of Its Development in Cities of 70,000 and More* document the existing public library services to business.[14]

In 1940, Manley wrote of the two paths of business library development: "Business library development in the last thirty years has followed two roads—the relatively few selective business collections maintained by public libraries, and the many specialized collections in business corporations, directed by special librarians."[15] A large number of businesses and corporations continue to possess libraries for their internal use. Although economic conditions have forced some corporations to close their libraries and turn toward public library collections for their information needs, Manley's observations still hold today.

Manley uncovered in her surveys some common problems faced by libraries in their information services to the economic community. Throughout the current literature on library services to business, these same concerns are discussed almost fifty years later, namely the libraries' limited resources and the problem of publicizing the information available at or through the library to the economic community. Manley almost assumes the inevitable problem associated with limited funds, but sees the librarian as having the responsibility to get the business person's attention for what the library has to offer.

> The two major difficulties to be met are first, the usual limitations of staff and funds, and second, the business man's concentration on the problems and possibilities in his immediate field of activity. To break through that concentration and attract his attention to an institution with information that will save him time and trouble is the job of the business department librarian. Not once, but many times, must the matter be brought before him in various ways.[16]

Manley presented not only the common problems libraries faced in providing service to business, but included as well the concepts, procedures, resources, and policies these libraries had developed to deal with their problems. In addition, Manley gave expression to the broader context within which service to business occurs. As noted above, the libraries' role in the economic life of the community was recognized as important from the early days of the public library movement. Manley continued to articulate the importance for the community of its public library offering service to businesses and industry.

> With service to business, the library shows its consciousness of the economic problems of the community. It takes its place as an agency through whose use these problems may be more swiftly solved. It serves all equally by maintaining a public collection of information only available privately at great cost. It recognizes that along with spiritual and cultural

growth should economic welfare be fostered. The library that serves the community must meet its economic needs.[17]

From the late 1940s through the mid-1960s, libraries exhibited a continuing interest in offering services to business. Also library organizations and agencies encouraged such service. As one example, the ALA Council adopted a four-point program in 1946 that recognized the potential role of libraries in the economic life of the country. To develop their potential role, ALA urged libraries to "ascertain areas for community economic opportunity, define the extent of library service, discover sources through which library service may be supplemented, and by a positive program through all media and channels, inform the community of the library's role and resources."[18]

The number of libraries offering services to business, from Dana in Newark to the libraries surveyed by Manley, expanded in the second and third decades of this century, but this growth was interrupted by the Depression and World War II and did not resume in the period after the war. In a survey in the early 1950s, approximately seventy public libraries were identified as having established specialized business service.[19] Later in the decade, the Library Services Branch of the U.S. Office of Education listed sixty-five public library systems with a "separately organized service to business." Only seven of the sixty-five public libraries, however, served populations under 100,000.[20] And the listing of services offered, collection development policies, and concepts and attitudes underlying the services were not much different than the services Manley wrote about twenty years or more earlier. However, there were still discussions about the nature of the services to be offered and the mechanism for delivery of the services.

In a study of business services in the early 1950s, Fenner discussed in more detail the means of delivering the services. Two basic options for the delivery of services existed, and each had positive aspects. One option was the branch library, as epitomized by the Newark Business Branch. The other was the model of a specialized department in the main library. The branch library could be located close to the center of the business community. During the early part of the century, business and industrial concerns were often located in central areas of the town or city. In the later decades of the century, business, commerce, and industry spread far and wide, and were dispersed throughout a municipality. The option of establishing a department or unit within the main building of the library had the large benefit that a patron could have access to all the resources of the library at one location for quick and easy reference. There was also less need to duplicate certain aspects of the collection. Library service to business was based on two distinguishing features, the materials selected for the collection and the special group to be served. In the branch business library, patrons were primarily drawn from the ranks of white-collar workers. A department existing in the main library building served a more diversified group that might include housewives and students as well as those who would patronize a branch business library, namely, white-collar, professional and managerial, skilled worker, and unskilled worker groups.[21]

In the U.S. Office of Education survey of public libraries offering specialized services to business, Vainstein reported a list of the essentials for good public library service to business. She distilled the following essentials from studying the literature and from information about existing programs: (1) the collection should cover the five "m's": management, men, materials, markets, and money; (2) service should be immediate, objective and current; (3) business trends and interests should be anticipated; (4) community contacts should be close as well as diverse to provide that essential supplement to public library resources—referral and consultation; and (5) publicity should be continuous and specific, and advantage should be taken of all media of communication.[22]

If Dana's Newark Public Library Business Branch offered a prototype for library service to business that conditioned such service for over sixty years, a project in the latter 1960s in California pointed libraries in a direction for the planning and development of such library services and expanding the notion of sharing resources of a number of libraries to serve the information needs of the economic community. Conducted by Meyer and Rostvold and funded by money from Title I, Library Services and Construction Act, the study focused on a "market analysis of the business firms in the Pasadena and Pomona areas, with respect to their needs, habits, and desires concerning their acquisition and utilization of the information they require in the course of their world."[23] While the Meyer and Rostvold study systematically explored and analyzed the needs of the economic community and also profiled and inventoried the members of this community, the need for such knowledge to serve the information needs of industry and business had been recognized by many of the people involved in attempting to satisfy such information needs.

Thirty years prior to the Meyer and Rostvold study, Anne F. Leidendeker, librarian of the science and industry department at Los Angeles Public Library, stated the case for understanding the market in a 1930 report of the Business and Technology Section in the *Bulletin of the American Library Association.*

> The first need is to know what businesses are in the community. Who are the business men? Then, how may you reach them to make them acquainted with printed material in their particular field? Now to get business men to use our special collections, we must, first of all, know our community and be aware of possible need trends. We need also to check our resources against business changes, both past and anticipated, in the community.[24]

The analysis of the community and development of resources cited by Leidendeker are two of the three basic actions on the part of the library in establishing a service for business. Closely related to these activities are efforts at publicizing the service. Getting the people to know and use the resources requires a major commitment and effort. "We have distributed book lists, published information on our outstanding patents' collection, given talks to various groups, and stressed our holdings in special fields and in government documents."[25] The goal is to understand the information needs, make the possible clientele aware of the library as a place to satisfy the needs, and have the materials on hand to fill the information requirements of the clientele. "And because we were able to serve a specific need, they [the business men] were 'pricked' to 'think library'."[26]

The Meyer and Rostvold study in Pomona and Pasadena is an example of comprehensive planning prior to the implementation of a particular library service. Taking a cue from the business community it hoped to survey, the study referred to itself as a "market analysis of the economic community's needs, habits, and desires concerning their acquisition and utilization of information required in their work."[27] A large library considering the establishment of a business service would be advised to understand the economic community and the role and capacity of itself in the delivery of needed services. The Meyer and Rostvold study is one example of a way to proceed in the planning and preparation of a business service. In that analysis and study, the researchers looked at the information needs and sources of supply, the use of the public library by businessmen, the role of the public library in serving the economic community, evaluation of the public library, methods of support from the economic community, cooperative relationships required for total library resources, and the implementation of a service in staff and budget requirements.

Although the study was specific to Pomona and Pasadena, some of the key recommendations are worth noting for the broad view of public library service to the economic community. The public library should be the first point of contact for the business person who needs information and whose company's information resources are inadequate to meet the need. Furthermore, the public library as the community's library should be the coordinator of the library resources in a community, pulling together information resources of academic, special, and public libraries in an area.

The public library should also take on some of the attributes previously associated with the special library—namely, the service provided should be personalized, flexible, time-saving and user-oriented. There must be an active program, carried on vigorously, to acquaint the economic community with the library's services and facilities. An advisory committee consisting of members of the community should be established to advise the library on matters of selection, policies, and procedures and to represent the library to the economic community. As well as efforts at stimulating the economic community in use of the library and its resources for its own information needs, the library must also stimulate financial and other kinds of support from the community, and the library objectives should be reexamined to see that resources are allocated properly.[28]

In consideration of financial resources needed and available to fund expanded services to the economic community, the Meyer and Rostvold study investigated methods of financial support including the use of user fees. The issue of fees for service is complicated and has a special problem in connection with the service under discussion. Shortly after Meyer and Rostvold concluded their study and recommendations, and the Pomona and Pasadena service was undertaken, the public library in Minneapolis began a new library service to the economic community— one that was set up on the basis of charging the customer for the specialized services provided.

In 1972, INFORM (Information for Minnesota) was established as a "cooperative library endeavor patterned to provide library research on a custom-designed, reimbursement basis to business and industry."[29] Personalized service, packaging the information to the customer's needs, as well as timeliness, convenience, confidentiality, and flexibility were hallmarks of the INFORM service. What INFORM offered went beyond what Dana offered in the Newark library, but not outside of the scope he would have approved. INFORM moved library service to the economic community into the arena of the information broker. Minneapolis was not the only library choosing the user fee route to support the specialized reference services for business. In 1975, the Houston Public Library set up a fee-based reference service called Business Information Service to satisfy the specialized information needs of businesses, government agencies and other organizations.[30]

Public librarians, as part of their normal duties and services, offer value-added information to their patrons. Almost any of the adult services a library decides to offer is a value-added service. The library that offers special service to business is offering a distinctly value-added information service. Value-added information can take a number of forms, including book lists, telephone reference service, a clippings file, a newsletter, or online searching. Should library service to the economic community be seen in a separate and different light simply because of the segment of the community being served?

The question of fees will not go away. Whether the question is asked in the black and white form of "fee or free?" or whether other sources of funding for the library and, in particular, library services to business are pursued, the decision will be made by the individual library. No library services or materials come free. Instead, there has been an indirect payment for those materials and services the library has offered in the past—usually in the form of taxes paid. The rub comes when discussing the special services and who will pick up the tab for such things. Malcolm J. Campbell, author of the *Manual of Business Library Practice*, stated that he has no difficulty in justifying the public provision of business information. The question, however, for Campbell and many others, is to what extent can specialized services be provided? "Should public libraries be prepared to face the question of direct payment by users for services beyond some point?"[31]

Ideally, the public library would offer all services, basic and specialized (however one defines basic or specialized), without additional charges or fees. Trezza expressed this idea in an article on equal opportunity of access. Basic to his remarks is the idea of public library services as public goods. Trezza suggested that the use of a planning process involving representatives of the various communities within the community will be effective in deciding the services and levels of services to be provided by the public library. With an understanding of the community, its needs, and resources, decisions can be made on the charging of fees. Planning and community analysis involves the entire community.

> The decision can then be based on the public good concept, not the economic commodity concept. The commitment to public good requires the library to constantly improve the quality of services, the effective use of technology, and the efficiency of the operations with the goal of eliminating all fees. This approach, or philosophy, increases the chance of meeting the challenge of equal opportunity of access for all. The librarian can defend the library priority—the fair-share concept based on the public good.[32]

New Imperatives for Service to the Economic Community

In the economic dislocations of the 1970s and 1980s, one of the priorities of many U.S. communities—large and small—has been the local economic development initiative. Economic development has been a continuing activity and process in U.S. communities in the last 100 years. In the past few decades many communities have adopted a proactive attitude toward economic development that leaves less to the vagaries of choices by businesses and industry. Community leaders felt that with appropriate marketing and research, businesses and industries could be enticed into making favorable relocation decisions. In many cases, these communities focused on economic development because of their legitimate fear that further decline in their economic base could severely affect the health and continued existence of their communities.

The attempt to recruit businesses to a community often is made based on information collected and developed by an economic development agency or committee. The community is marketing itself on the basis of the resources it can offer to members of the potential economic community. A good school system, good roads and transportation access, financial and communication resources are touted as positive reasons why new businesses should open, industries should relocate, and the federal government should open a research facility in a particular community. The library prides itself on being an important element in a community, but how often do the recruitment brochures actually proclaim the resources of the library as a compelling reason for relocation of businesses? Yet it is the library that could offer so much in the way of information resources and information access to these same businesses.

By the mid-1980s, examples of public library service to the economic community in North Carolina, Illinois, and Oregon offer evidence that the library needs to be more than an adjunct to the economic community, not only offering services to it but also being a player in economic development and an integral partner in the economic growth of an area. The North Carolina State Library is developing the North Carolina Information Network, attempting an application of network services to the nonlibrary community, in particular to the business community. Looking at libraries from the perspective and language of economists, staff at the State Library saw the need to put in place an "information infrastructure," parallel to the infrastructures of transportation, finance and communications. "Information dissemination, like finance and transportation, is one of the underpinnings of economic development."[33] Without committing itself to the establishment of direct fees to support information dissemination, North Carolina saw the importance of serving the economic community for the good of library services across the board. "Local businesses need to be taught the value and use of information in their daily operations. It will be especially necessary to begin to teach businesses the cost of information services. When a positive cost-benefit relationship for the use of information is seen by a business person, a realistic pricing of these services can be developed by the library and willingly paid by the businesses, either by means of direct fees or through increased local government support."[34]

At the Parlin-Ingersoll Library in Canton, Illinois, the attitude exists that active participation in economic development of the local community is an essential role that must be developed if the library is to establish itself as the information center for the community. "Libraries need to assume a more positive, aggressive posture towards economic development by assisting in any concerted community effort."[35] This library compiled a promotional folder with important information about the city of Canton, the low cost of doing business there, labor cost, taxes, and other information needed for recruiting new businesses to the city and other aspects of economic development. As with North Carolina and other places where the public library works with the economic community to answer information needs, the Canton library sees a direct relationship between its efforts at economic development and the community support it receives.

The library is likely to benefit from a more healthy economy when its efforts in economic development are appreciated and when the connection is made between the library's role in economic development and its service to the general community.

> Any progress the community makes towards revitalizing the economic infrastructure stands to benefit the library . . . more jobs mean more people, more discretionary income, and most important for libraries, more tax revenues. It's quite simple. We serve ourselves by serving our citizens. We serve our citizens by serving as partners in economic development.[36]

One relatively new development in the library's role in the economic community is being undertaken by the Multnomah County Library in Oregon. Its service, the Federal Government Procurement Center, is a resource center to help local businesses get federal contracts. Established in 1986 with LSCA funding, the center offers information on government markets and bidding procedures as well as industry, military, and federal standards and specifications. In its first year of operation, an estimated $14 million in new business was brought into the state.[37]

The brief historical overview offered evidence that library service to business has been a concern of public libraries since at least the beginning of the public library movement in the middle of the nineteenth century. In addition, the evidence revealed a connection between library service to business and the fulfillment of the library's obligation to serve all members of the community. Librarians often felt the need to promote and educate the economic community of the usefulness of the library's resources for making informed business and commercial decisions. Running through the descriptions of various libraries' services over the years, the library often saw the benefits that accrued to it because of its contribution to the economic health of the local community. The more visibility the library can establish for itself in the community, especially in the eyes of those often responsible for making civic and tax decisions in the community, the more support the library could expect to receive on the basis of serving the information needs of the economic community. Walkey, in discussing the Business Information Services offered by the Milwaukee Public Library, summarized in a threefold philosophy much of what the history of library services to business reveals: "the business community is largely unaware of the library's potential; information is an exploitable commodity; and an informed business community increasingly will support its library in a variety of ways."[38]

Herbert White candidly spoke to the matter in a "White Papers" column in 1986: the library "must find a way to make itself and its activities indispensable to the work and life habits of a wider constituency, particularly of those who make the decisions which control our resources."[39] As much as some would say that library service to business is too expensive for their libraries, those libraries that have established such services and people such as McGinn from North Carolina, Wilson from Canton, Walkey from Milwaukee, and White would likely claim that a library cannot afford not to offer service specifically to the economic community.

A survey undertaken by the ALA Office for Research in 1986 collected specific information on services offered by public libraries to businesses as well as what businesses offered to the library. The survey covered all libraries serving populations of 500,000 or more. In addition, a random sample of libraries serving populations 25,000 and over was also surveyed.[40] Only 2 percent of the 551 libraries responding had a separate business branch, 34 percent had business departments, yet many more libraries offered business-related services. Nearly 90 percent collect business directories; over 80 percent carry sources of investment information; and one-third offered database searching services (11 percent charging a fee for this service).[41]

The questionnaire also asked for information about reciprocal actions from businesses. More than three-quarters of the libraries responding said that individual or groups in the business community had donated funds to the library. Over 43 percent claimed they received help with sponsorship of programs. Businessperson's Friends of the Library groups existed in 3.1 percent of the responding libraries.[42]

These numbers suggest strongly that public libraries are active in their service to the economic community. *Bringing in Business: Promotion Guide for Libraries and Librarians* contains the data relating to business service from the ALA survey, as well as containing helpful information that shows the breadth and depth of services being offered to the economic community by public libraries.

While professionals in the field attempt to implement new practices regarding public library services to the economic community, one group within a professional organization is attempting to offer support for business reference services. In 1987, the Reference and Adult Services Division (RASD) of the American Library Association established the Business Reference and Services Section (BRASS). A Business Reference Service Committee had existed since 1964, but the increasing need for business reference services information and programming was the impetus to establish a section within RASD. Among other things, section status allows Annual Conference programs. BRASS membership will come primarily from public and academic libraries. The Section will be a focal point for the discussion of issues and concerns, e.g., what is the relationship between the library and the business community? It will also be a forum for the discussion of innovative programs and the needs of business.[43]

One might easily and persuasively argue that the needs of the economic community from the early to midpoint of the century were simpler and were such that the local public library could, in the course of its operation, provide services to the business and economic interests. Yet the look back at the history shows that the libraries that offered special services to businesses did so with an accompanying special effort. Well-planned or not, well-executed or not, the attempts by these public libraries to serve the economic community took a special effort, a special attention to a particular segment of the local community.

One difference with the current situation and the circumstance surrounding the service to business in previous eras is that now consumers and users of business, scientific, and technical information can choose their information from many different sources. People involved in the economic community can choose from information brokers, dial-up reference and document delivery services, and expensive but available online database vendors. Business and industry may consider the cost effectiveness of these various sources, yet when information is needed for making an important investment or other business decision, actual money cost may be less important than efficient delivery, appropriate packaging, and ease of acquisition. The public library is in competition, whether it wants to recognize that or not, with other information providers. In the large majority of cases, the public libraries have come up short in the delivery of appropriate services to the economic community. When looking at the data collected in the ASE survey and interpreting its meaning, one immediately questions whether the low number of libraries providing special programming for business means there is little demand for such programming because the businesses are going elsewhere for their information, or whether it is just a matter of the library choosing not to allocate its resources in that direction.

ASE Survey Findings

A number of questions in the ASE study could be considered to relate to library services to business, but question 34 asked directly for responses from those libraries that offer specific programming for special groups.[44] Part A of question 34 asked whether the libraries polled offered programming to business. Of those responding, 968 libraries or 23.0 percent indicated that they provide programming to business. In the broader context of the economic community, answers to questions 34d and 34e could be considered as programming organized for the economic community. In addition, libraries answering questions relating to circulation of microcomputer software, reading lists or bibliographies, interlibrary loan service, microcomputers and software for in-library use, and maintenance of resource files could be providing these services and materials in conjunction with their library services to business.

Comparing the number of libraries providing programming to business in the ASE survey with the number of libraries counted in the Library Service Branch of the U.S. Office of Education survey in the late 1950s and early 1960s, we can see a very large increase. One would be cautioned from making too many claims from a comparison with the ASE data, however. The extent of programming to business that is represented by the libraries saying that they are providing such programming is not completely certain. Yet, it seems likely that after twenty-five or more years of federal government funding through LSCA, a much larger number of libraries would be offering service to business than did so in 1959.

When looking at responses to the ASE questionnaire that listed specific programs offered to businesses, it seems possible that the large number of libraries reporting organized programming for business do not necessarily have ongoing services to business or the economic community in any systematic fashion. Yet, it is important to note that libraries, often in cooperation with business groups and organizations— and with individual members of the business community—are providing important educational sessions for people in business. Often the reported programs consider the issues of opening a new small business. Business computer applications and uses and programs on investing and investments also appeared often in the reports of special programming.

Summary

During the late 1970s and into the 1980s, public libraries were facing increased demands for their services. Some of this demand occurred as a result of the outreach efforts of the previous decade. The increased demands were combined with funding decreases, loss of tax revenue from the erosion of the tax base, and an inability or unwillingness to see library service as a basic service as are other community services. The library offered services to children, to the elderly, to the homebound, to minorities, to the handicapped, and to those needing literacy training, all important services geared to various special populations in the community. Yet an important special group was not fully served by the public library, namely the economic community. Members of this community were in a position often to make funding decisions at the community level, and they were also integrally involved in the enhancement or decline of the tax bases in a community. Even so, the public library, as the literature review shows and the ASE data presents, did not reach out significantly to serve this special group of the community.

Libraries and librarians offer very legitimate concerns and questions about public services being put to the use of private profit and gain. Many times there is a sense that businesses should pay for special services for the simple reason that they are able to or are already paying for transactions with information brokers. The library may need to consider alternate methods of funding service to this group and be willing to be aggressive in the pursuit of such clients. Alternate funding could include fees for services, requests for grants from specific businesses, or other methods. As one alternative to either direct fees for service or indirect payment through taxes, the Denver Public Library offers specialized library services to the United Bank of Denver in exchange of a contribution to library income.[45] There may be good reasons why the library, no matter its constrained budget, should finance such a service to the economic community from appropriated funds initially.

While understanding in a larger framework the economic community of which it is a part and whose information needs it can serve, the library also needs to see that through its efforts at economic development, it is serving the whole community. The economic interest of the community and the community the library serves needn't be in conflict. It would be naive to think that all parts and elements of the economic community have the whole community at heart when business decisions are made. The library must pursue an educational function as part of its basic information services to the economic community to alert specific business and industrial interests in the community of their reciprocal responsibility to the community.

New views of the economic community might be needed to bring more public libraries to a willingness to serve such an element of the larger community. The increasing awareness that information in various forms and formats has economic value can be one basis on which to build the imperative for library service to business and industry. The tax base and its good health, have a direct connection to library funding. By positioning itself in the modes and methods of economic development, by understanding in a broad way the economic community, and by marketing the valuable information contained in the collection it houses, the library can begin to have the conceptual and theoretical basis for pursuing this service to this special group of the community.

Notes

1. Sidney Herbert Ditzion, *Arsenals of a Democratic Culture: A Social History of the American Public Library Movement in New England and the Middle States from 1850 to 1900* (Chicago: ALA, 1947), p. 110.

2. Ibid., p. 118.

3. Wendell Berry, *Home Economics: Fourteen Essays* (San Francisco: North Point Pr., 1987), p. 189.

4. Fritz Malchup, *Knowledge: Its Creation, Distribution, and Economic Significance*, vol. 1: *Knowledge and Knowledge Production* (Princeton, N.J.: Princeton Univ. Pr., 1980), p. 108.

5. Raymond M. Holt, *Focusing Library Services on the Economic Community: An Evaluation of a LSCA Demonstration Project in Pasadena and Pomona* (Del Mar, Calif.: Holt, 1971), p. i.

6. Ditzion, *Arsenals of a Democratic Culture*, p. 119.

7. John Cotton Dana, *Libraries: Addresses and Essays* (reprint of 1916 edition; Freeport, N.Y.: Books for Libraries Pr., 1966), p. 216.

8. Ibid., p. 218.
9. Ibid., p. 214.
10. Ibid., p. 212.
11. Ibid., p. 213.
12. "Specialized Services to Business and Industry in Florida Public Libraries," *Florida Libraries* 19 (March 1968): 21.
13. "Specialized Services to Business and Industry in Florida Public Libraries," *Florida Libraries* 19 (March 1968): 21; Edward H. Fenner, "Business Services in Public Libraries," *Special Libraries* 44 (July/August 1953): 223.
14. Marian C. Manley, ed., *Business and the Public Library: Steps in Successful Cooperation*, (New York: Special Libraries Assn., 1940); Marian C. Manley, *Public Library Service to Business: A Comparative Study of its Development in Cities of 70,000 and More* (Newark, N.J.: The Public Library, 1942).
15. Manley, *Business and the Public Library*, p. 14; also see Marydee Ojala, "Public Library Business Collections and New Reference Technologies," *Special Libraries* 74 (April 1983): 144.
16. Ibid., p. 16.
17. Manley, *Public Library Service*, p. 49.
18. Rose Vainstein, "Public Library Service to Business," *Library Journal* 84 (May 1, 1959): 1403.
19. Fenner, "Business Services," p. 222.
20. Vainstein, "Public Library Service," p. 1402.
21. Fenner, "Business Services," pp. 224, 226.
22. Vainstein, "Public Library Service," pp. 1402–1403.
23. Robert S. Meyer and Gerhard N. Rostvold, *The Library and the Economic Community: A Market Analysis of Information Needs of Business and Industry in the Communities of Pasadena and Pomona, California* (Sacramento: California State Library, 1969), from the transmittal letter in the report, no page number.
24. Anne F. Leidendeker, "Why Business Men Use Special Collections of the Public Library," *Bulletin of the American Library Association* 32 (October 15, 1938): 854–855.
25. Ibid., p. 855.
26. Ibid.
27. Meyer and Rostvold, *The Library and the Economic Community*, p. 6.
28. Ibid., p. iv.
29. Zella J. Shannon, "Public Library Service to the Corporate Community," *Special Libraries* 65 (January 1974): 29.
30. "Service to Business: The Fee Question," *Library Journal* 100 (June 15, 1975): 1182.
31. Malcolm J. Campbell, "Running Dogs in the Ref?" *New Library World* 77 (December 1976): 233.
32. Alphonse F. Trezza, "Equal Opportunity of Access: A Responsibility and Challenge," *Government Publications Review* 13 (1986): 52.
33. Howard F. McGinn, Jr., "The North Carolina Information Network: A Vital Cog in Economic Development," *North Carolina Libraries* 44 (Fall 1986): 175.
34. Howard McGinn, "Information Networking and Economic Development," *Wilson Library Bulletin* 62 (November 1987): 31.
35. W. Randall Wilson, "Partners in Economic Development," *Library Journal* 111 (March 15, 1986): 34.
36. Ibid.
37. "Procurement Center Adds Services in Oregon," *Library Journal* 111 (November 15, 1986): 26; "Multnomah County Attracts $14 Million in Contracts," *Wilson Library Bulletin* 62 (November 1987): 14.

38. Elizabeth M. Walkey, "The Making of . . . a Business Information Service," *Wisconsin Library Bulletin* 71 (May/June 1975): 126.
39. Herbert S. White, "White Papers: Public Libraries and the Political Process," *Library Journal* 111 (June 15, 1986): 50.
40. American Library Association, Office for Research, "ALA Survey of Public Library Service: A Summary Report, March 1987" (Chicago: ALA, 1987).
41. American Library Association, Public Information Office, *Bringing in Business: Promotion Guide for Libraries and Librarians* (Chicago: ALA, 1987), p. 4–5.
42. Ibid.
43. Gerald Gill, "Business Reference: Reaching Out for the Brass Ring," in "Current Issues in Reference and Adult Services," *RQ* 27 (Winter 1987): 171–174.
44. For data collected by the ASE survey, see chapter 2.
45. "Bank to Pay Denver Public for Library Services," *Library Journal* 110 (February 1, 1985): 28

CHAPTER 10

Serving Older Adults

Betty J. Turock

The demographic shift with the most profound implications for future adult services is the aging of the U.S. population. In 1988 approximately one in eight Americans was sixty-five years and over, an increase of 3.6 million, or 14 percent, since 1980, and compared to the five percent increase for those under 65.[1]

While in 1900, older adults accounted for 4.1 percent of the total U.S. inhabitants; by 1988 their number had tripled and comprised 12.1 percent, a rise of over nine times from 3.1 million to 29.2 million. During 1987 approximately 2.1 million persons celebrated their sixty-fifth birthday, at the rate of 5,900 per day. Since 1.5 million people over sixty-five died in the same time period, the result was a net increase of 630,000 for 1988 or 1,750 new older adults each day.[2]

This pattern of rapid growth is predicted to continue, slowing somewhat in the 1990s because of the relatively small number of babies born during the Great Depression. When the baby boom generation reaches 65, that slowing will give way to the most intense period of increase. Forecasts show that by 2030, 65 million Americans will have become older adults—21.2 percent of the nation's population, or two and one-half times their total in 1980. In fact, if current fertility and immigration levels remain stable, the only age groups to experience significant growth in the next century will be those past 65.[3]

Advocacy for Aging Spurs Library Attention

Interest in aging—the process of change that takes place during the life cycle—is as old as history, but gerontology, which studies the biological and behavioral aspects of life-span changes, was not recognized as an

349

independent field until the 1940s. As the number of elders began to soar and attention to aging heightened, library and information services designated to meet the special needs of the elderly emerged. The movement dates back over forty-five years to the establishment of the Adult Education Department of the Cleveland Public Library, and the inauguration of the department's Live Long and Like It Library Club for men and women over sixty. An unqualified success, the club led to the initiation of similar programs all over the country.[4]

Progress Through Three Decades

It was 1959, however, before sufficient advocacy on behalf of older adults resulted in Harry S. Truman convening the National Conference on Aging, which recommended the first White House Conference on the Aging (WHCOA). Since then, in each decade, the WHCOA has spurred progress in legislation and a multiplicity of services for elders. The 1961 Conference was a significant factor in the subsequent enactment of the Older Americans Act (OAA)—a program of entitlements designed to assist elders by providing funds for services, training, and research in many fields, including librarianship. From 1966 to 1988, appropriations for the Act grew from $6.5 million to $1.53 billion.[5]

The Administration on Aging (AOA), now under the aegis of the Department of Health and Human Services, was established as a direct outcome of OAA, Title II, while Title III formed the organizational structure for the network on aging which links the AOA with State and Area Agencies on Aging throughout the country. A 1978 amendment to the OAA, important for libraries, requires the AOA's Area Agencies on Aging to establish and maintain information and referral services if they are not otherwise available in the community.[6]

Preparations for the 1959 and 1961 conferences on aging stepped up library interest in serving elders. ALA formally expanded its Adult Education Board to the Adult Services Division and appointed the first Committee on Library Service to the Aging. At the request of the Office of Education, this committee undertook a survey of library services to the elderly. The study results, released in 1957, revealed that, while libraries were offering some services to the aging, the three leading the list—in order of frequency—were (1) supplying books; (2) providing services to shut-ins; and (3) working with other agencies.[7]

Beginning in the mid-1960s, Congress approved other legislation of crucial importance to increasing library service for older adults. The

1964 amendment to the Library Services and Construction Act (LSCA) added funding to alter the physical structure of libraries to meet the needs of the physically handicapped, many of whom were elderly. LSCA's Title I became the major source for the initiation of library programs responsive to the aging. This legislation was equally successful in increasing the availability of large-print collections and services. In 1966 the amended Pratt-Smott Act provided another ongoing impetus for bringing a wide range of materials not only to the blind, but also to thousands of citizens—including older adults—who, although not legally blind, were unable to use conventional books because of physically disabling conditions.

The burgeoning work associated with serving elders required special training. The final piece of legislation passed in the 1960s supporting library services for the aging was Title II-B of the Higher Education Act, Library Career Training and Library Research Demonstration. Enacted in 1965, the program funded workshops, institutes, and research programs that began to break ground toward the development of leadership capability in the profession.[8]

For the second WHCOA in 1971, "The Library's Responsibility to the Aging," a position paper prepared for the 1961 sessions by ALA's Adult Services Division, was updated. The National Survey of Library Services to the Aging, conducted under the joint auspices of the U.S. Office of Education and the Cleveland Public Library and supported by the Higher Education Act (HEA), Title III, was contracted to the research firm of Booz, Allen & Hamilton. The data from that investigation comprised the last comprehensive compilation on the status of library services for older adults until 1985.[9]

Ultimately, the 1970s saw the development of new programs that responded to issues identified in the National Survey. ALA's renamed Library Services to the Aging Population Committee continued to address elder needs as part of the association's Reference and Adult Services Division (RASD). In 1976, a new section, Library Services to the Impaired Elderly (LSIE), was added within ALA's Association of Specialized and Cooperative Library Agencies (ASCLA) to focus on outreach and to supplement the emphasis on reference services of the RASD committee.

But the major recommendation for libraries arising from the 1971 WHCOA—an amendment to LSCA creating Title IV, Older Readers Service, which passed into law on May 10, 1973—was less successful. It proposed to carry out a program of grants for the states: to train librarians to work with the elderly; conduct special programs for the elderly; purchase special library materials for use by the elderly; and pay for the services of elderly persons who wished to work as assistants on programs for their peers. That title was never funded.[10]

Within the current decade, the library field looked forward to another White House Conference on Aging and presented copies of it and the Association's 1975 statement "Guidelines for Library Service to an Aging Population" for conferencewide distribution. Position papers, commissioned by the U.S. Department of Education, were prepared by Virginia H. Mathews[11] and Betty J. Turock.[12] Recommendations from WHCOA 1981, supporting specific funding for library services for elders, served to stimulate inclusion of the Older Readers Act provisions in Title I, LSCA when that legislation was re-authorized in 1984.

Over the past forty-five years librarians have had the opportunity to become increasingly cognizant of their role in the provision of education and information for an aging population. Older adults are currently second only to those thirty-five to fifty-four in their political activity. Couple the growing number of elders with their amalgamation into a political force and implications for the continued fiscal support of libraries in the decades ahead are obvious.

ASE Findings

The Adult Services in the Eighties survey provided information on the relative percentages of libraries offering programs to special groups. Programming for older adults outstripped programming to all other groups except parents, with 37.5 percent of responding libraries indicating targeted programming for older adults. The narrative program descriptions listed 140 programs aimed at the older adults, and "Consumer and Community Information," "Tax Help," "Booktalks and Discussions," "Entertainment," and "Health" ranked highest.[13] The ASE data provide information about the status of services to older adults among the broad spectrum of adult services and are useful for gaining a perspective on where these services stand in comparison to other services.

Update 1988

To transform the library to better serve older adults in the 1990s, we must first document the status of service today. The 1972 *National Survey* data, collected from 244 libraries, revealed that:

1. Services to the aging had not developed at a pace consistent with the increase in the number of persons sixty-five and older in the nation and commensurate with the increase in national interest in the needs and problems of the aging.
2. About two-thirds of the public libraries gave the aging a low priority compared to other groups in the population.
3. Funds for services to the aging constituted less than 1 percent of the budgets of public libraries.
4. Staffing of services for the aging was minimal.
5. Lack of recognition of services to the aging in local library plans, programs and organizational structures inhibited the development of adequate services.[14]

To determine progress, the Research Bureau in Library and Information Science at Rutgers University—with funding from the Department of Education—began to update the facts. Although older adult services have been the subject of several regional investigations,[15,16] and were included as part of the ASE Project from RASD's Services to Adults Committee,[17] no in-depth systematic review had been undertaken in close to fifteen years specifically directed at this segment of the population.

COLLECTING THE FACTS

The major definitions by which data were collected for the *National Survey* were retained. Older adults were described chronologically as those sixty-five years of age and over. As in its predecessor, service for older adults was denoted as any library offering (1) which was developed specifically for the aging, or (2) in which 50 percent of the participants were sixty-five and older. This eliminated services provided routinely, such as general circulation and reference.

The *Update* was conducted in two phases. In Phase I, begun during 1984, the 390 libraries that comprised the 1971 study population were surveyed once again. In addition, State Librarians, Administrative Librarians in the U.S. Department of Education's Division of Library Programs who are the LSCA program Officers, and other leaders in services for the aging across the United States were asked to help identify libraries currently offering elder services that were not nominated in 1971. LSCA records were examined and a literature review conducted to assist in the task.[18-37] These combined efforts led to the identification of 618 sites that were then solicited for input.

In Phase II, completed in 1986, a random sample of 540 public libraries in communities with populations of 25,000 or more was drawn from the *American Library Directory* to determine whether services for older adults in the nominated libraries were characteristic of public libraries in general or whether they were better described as exemplary.

Information was gathered on four categories of service, the first three of which were part of the *National Survey;* the fourth was added in 1984. These categories were:

1. Extension services are activities that increase access to materials for elders who cannot conveniently use library facilities because of impaired mobility and other barriers—in other words, delivery systems, such as books-by-mail, bookmobiles, personal home or bedside delivery, subbranches or deposit collections in service centers, nursing homes, and apartments for the aging.
2. Special resources are materials and adjunct equipment for those older adults who experience disabilities that interfere with the use of standard media, e.g., large print book, talking books, reading aids.
3. Group programs are activities held either within the library or in places where the aging congregate—nutrition sites, service centers, drop-in centers, and homes for the aging.
4. Special services are activities targeted for older adults that amplify traditional services, e.g., information and referral (I&R), oral history, and lifelong learning.

To inventory the volume and variety of current services, specific programs were enumerated under the four categories and librarians were asked to check those provided; to denote their inclusive dates; and, if terminated, to provide the reason for that action. Information was also collected on organizational support.

EXTENT OF SERVICE

Based on the 331 libraries responding to Phase I and the 325 responding to Phase II, what are the scope and extent of library services for older adults as we prepare to enter the 1990s?

Trends over the past decade illustrate that the development of new services hit a high water mark in the mid-seventies. As in the *National Survey,* libraries in urban and suburban communities are far more likely to provide programs than their rural counterparts, despite the fact that the greatest proportion of older adults reside in less densely populated areas.

Table 1 depicts the variety and frequency of offerings from libraries reporting services.

Table 1. SERVICES CURRENTLY OFFERED OLDER ADULTS THROUGH PUBLIC LIBRARIES REPORTING.

Services	LIBRARIES OFFERING PHASE I	% (n = 318)	LIBRARIES OFFERING PHASE II	% (n = 275)
1. Extension				
Delivery to Institutions	167	53	98	36
Bookmobile: Standard entrance	105	33	42	15
Hydraulic lift	11	3	4	1
Deposit Collections: Senior Centers	114	36	36	13
Senior Housing	129	41	38	14
Nursing Homes	153	48	69	25
Books and Media by Mail	76	24	44	16
Homebound Services	167	53	106	39
Other	3	1	2	.7
2. Special Resources				
Large Print Books	288	91	232	84
Talking Books	186	58	151	55
Magnifying Devices	188	59	107	39
Ceiling Projectors	18	6	11	4
Page Turners	22	7	6	2
Kurzweil Reading Machines	29	9	9	3
Telecommunication Devices for the Deaf	81	25	19	7
Close Captioned Viewing Adaptors	28	9	8	3
Other	63	20	3	.1

Table 1. SERVICES CURRENTLY OFFERED OLDER ADULTS THROUGH PUBLIC LIBRARIES REPORTING. (Continued)

Services	LIBRARIES OFFERING PHASE I	% (n = 318)	LIBRARIES OFFERING PHASE II	% (n = 275)
3. Programs inside the Library				
Clubs	52	16	32	12
Films and Film Programs	105	33	48	17
Live Artists	33	10	30	11
Lectures	64	20	53	19
Book Talks	55	17	45	16
Discussion Groups	47	15	40	15
Art Exhibits	82	26	53	19
Other	18	6	2	.7
4. Programs outside the Library				
Clubs	29	9	17	6
Film and Film Programs	100	36	37	13
Live Artists	5	2	5	2
Lectures	32	11	19	7
Book Talks	89	30	45	16
Discussion Groups	22	7	6	2
Art Exhibits	8	3	3	1
Other	32	10	2	.7
5. Special Services				
Information and Referral	12	4	1	.3
Information from Online Databases	46	14	18	7

Table 1. SERVICES CURRENTLY OFFERED OLDER ADULTS THROUGH PUBLIC LIBRARIES REPORTING. (Continued)

Services	LIBRARIES OFFERING PHASE I	% (n = 318)	LIBRARIES OFFERING PHASE II	% (n = 275)
5. Special Services (Continued)				
Oral History	50	16	38	14
Genealogy	125	39	88	32
Local History	121	38	89	32
Bibliotherapy	9	3	5	2
Job Information	60	19	35	13
Lifelong Learning				
Adult Basic Education	22	7	15	5
Graduate Equivalency Diploma Classes	14	4	11	4
English as a Second Language Classes	19	6	11	4
Literacy Programs	59	19	61	22
Independent Learning Program	7	2	4	1
Education Brokering	6	2	3	1
Aging Awareness	5	2	6	2
Services for Older Adult Service Providers	10	3	9	3
Other	6	2	1	.3

For both the nominated libraries and the random sample, the provision of large print books tops the list. Delivery to institutions and the homebound, and the provision of talking books and magnifying devices are also among the most highly cited. Films are the basis for most of the group programming both within and outside the library among nominated libraries, but in the random sample films receive less attention. Oral history, an exercise leading to the integration of life experience, perceived by gerontologists as an important task of the later years, is available for elder participation in 16 percent of all Phase I libraries and close to the same amount—at 14 percent—in the Phase II libraries. Aging awareness and services for older adult service providers are at the lowest end of the scale. At the same time, most lifelong learning activities and information and referral are found less than 10 percent of the time in both cases; only literacy programs come anywhere near 20 percent. Thirty-two services not listed in the survey are also available. Except where enumerated in parentheses, offerings noted below are provided at only one site.

Special Resources

1. Closed-Circuit Magnifying TV Monitors
2. Closed-Captioned Films and Video Cassettes (four sites)
3. Multimedian, Multisensory Kits (six sites)
4. Books on Tape and Cassette (seven sites)
5. Large Print Newspapers and Periodicals (ten sites)
6. Braille Typewriters (three sites)
7. Braille Books (7)
8. Visual Tek Print Enlarger (eights sites)
9. Telephone Amplifiers
10. Large Print Bibliographies (four sites)
11. Large Print Bookmarks
12. Distribution of Aging Network publications (five sites)
13. Hearing Loops
14. Foreign Language Materials

Special Services

1. Library Skills Classes
2. Waiver of Fines
3. Income Tax Assistance (eight sites)
4. Day Care
5. Space for Community Programming (three sites)

Extension

1. Radio Reading
2. Hospital Deposit Collections (five sites)
3. Newsletters for Homebound Elderly
4. Storytelling (three sites)

Group Programs Outside the Library

1. Recreational Trips
2. Historic Walks
3. Information Booths at Senior Fairs, Exhibitions (four sites)
4. Library Service Talks (five sites)
5. Program Packages for Service Providers

Group Programs Within the Library

1. Library Tours (three sites)
2. Writers' Workshops
3. Arts and Crafts
4. Puppetry (two sites)

Table 2 compares the development of Extension, Special Resources, Group Programs, and Special Services since the *National Survey.* The categories measured in the *National Survey* have all shown increases in volume when compared to the *Update,* Phase I. Group Programs held outside the library have grown most, but Extension and Special Resources are still supplied by the highest proportion of libraries. Special Services, recognized within the last decade as important to the developmental and information needs of elders, although offered by the lowest proportion, are reported by the majority of libraries.

All service categories are supplied from fewer sites in the random sample than in the nominated libraries. Special Resources and Extension are once again the mainstay. Special Services are absent in the majority of cases, although they are offered at more sites than Group Programs.

When the number of older adults using each of the five types of service is tabulated as a percentage of the total elder population in the libraries'

Table 2. COMPARISON OF MAJOR PROGRAMS OF SERVICE.

Type of Services	NATIONAL SURVEY LIBRARIES ($n = 228$)		UPDATE PHASE I LIBRARIES ($n = 318$)		UPDATE PHASE II LIBRARIES ($n = 275$)	
	NUMBER	PERCENTAGE	NUMBER	PERCENTAGE	NUMBER	PERCENTAGE
Extension	209	86	265	83	163	59
Special Resources	200	82	291	92	216	79
Group Programs						
Within the Library	93	38	146	46	80	29
Outside the Library	98	40	194	61	63	23
Special Services	N/A	N/A	180	57	127	46

N/A = not applicable

collective service areas, the market penetration for Phase I libraries is on the average no greater than 7 percent; in Phase II libraries it is only a fraction more than the 4 percent reported by the *National Survey.*

ORGANIZATIONAL SUPPORT

A number of means to define current priority were employed in the *Update* as they had been in the *National Survey,* including the relative rank assigned for service development to four age groups—children, young adults, adults, and older adults—funding, staffing, administrative patterns for service, and the use of older adults as resources.

In 1971 the aging were most frequently accorded the lowest priority for service development; that fact has not changed much in the eighties. Currently older adults are given a rank higher only than young adults. Budgets show a similar pattern. While there is some improvement in funding from the .4 percent support found in the *National Survey,* the 2 percent and 1.2 percent respectively allocated by the Phase I and Phase II libraries do not constitute major growth. The same limited progress is apparent in staffing. Once again Phase II patterns are closer to those of the *National Survey.* Then staffing constituted about 1.3 percent of available workforce. At present, for the nominated libraries that figure reaches approximately 3 percent, but for the random sample it hovers around 1.6 percent.

The *National Survey* urged that to elevate library service for elders to a higher, more visible priority, the aging should be considered a distinct programmatic entity with a coordinator appointed to ensure that elders' special needs are identified and opportunities to serve them are met in a way that encourages orderly, systematic development and implementation. To date only one library in each of the two *Update* study phases has followed the recommendation. In fact, services are most frequently divided among several administrative units with no organizational mechanism in place to coordinate them.

One of the few bright spots discovered in the *Update,* however, is that public libraries are cooperating with other agencies to serve older adults. The *National Survey* and the *Update,* Phase I, both support the contention that about two-thirds of all public libraries do forge links, but that one-third do not. For the Phase II random sample, that figure is less than two-thirds but well over the majority.

To determine whether the library had joined the movement to recognize older adults as a valuable resource, the *Update* asked for specific numbers of elder employees and volunteers and found that the majority have both, although the proportion of employees is decreasing.

Volunteers present a more encouraging note. In the *National Survey* sixty-six libraries had 363 elder volunteers for an average of 5.5 per library. That number increased to 183 for Phase I libraries where a total of 1,861 volunteers are on roll, an average of 10.2 per library. In 227 Phase II libraries a total of 1,339 volunteers—an average of 5.9 per library—help with library tasks. It appears that elder employees are generally persons who have not as yet retired. There is little evidence that those aged sixty-five and up are hired by libraries; elder volunteers enjoy more popularity.

Measuring Progress

Evidence demonstrates that there has been limited progress in public library service for older adults; the attention they are receiving is not in keeping with the growth in the size of the elder population. The results of the *Update* are chillingly similar to those of the *National Survey*. The gains discovered are for the most part in Phase I libraries. Rather than representing the universe of public libraries, the nominated sites likely attract attention because they offer more exemplary service.

But progress is measured by more than an increase in volume of service, however slight. It also hinges upon whether the added offerings are responsive to the broadest current audience. Today's older Americans are the most self-reliant population in history: only 5 percent are in institutions; most live in communities. Their educational attainment is rising, although it is still lower than that of younger populations. On the other hand, services for older adults have not changed significantly, concentrating on the homebound, institutionalized, and impaired.

In spite of documentation from the Russell Sage Foundation that, next to financial reasons, lack of education is the most frequently cited barrier to older adults' sense of fulfillment, sparse attention is being paid to educational service.[38] For the future libraries must place a high priority on lifelong learning. Since the same strong case can be made for information services, it is equally disappointing that few libraries have instituted such programs for elders or their service providers, in spite of the recognition that better services for older adults depend on better informed service providers.

Even more disappointing, however, is the lack of attention paid to aging awareness. Kenneth Ferstl's research has shown that the attitudes of public librarians, like those of other professional service providers, are not significantly different from the common stereotypes of the American public.[39] Aging awareness is needed to disrupt the patterns that cause us to grow old prejudiced against ourselves.

More than a decade after the *National Survey,* elder services are still understaffed, uncoordinated, and scattered among many administrative locations. Not all libraries can afford a specialist in older adult services, but responsibility for their planning, development, implementation, and evaluation must be assigned to one highly placed administrator before elder services are considered a vital programmatic entity rather than a series of unrelated special events.

Funding issues are perhaps the most complex. Priorities within the library have prevented realignment of funding to allow a greater share for older adult services, no matter how rational the argument for such an approach might be. Building new services is an expensive business and frequently a duplicative one. Coordinated service delivery is one of the most cost-effective ways of creating fiscally spare programs. While libraries are cooperating with other agencies, in the main that cooperation depends on informal arrangements resulting from negotiations between persons who know one another. Collaborative mobilization requires working toward a formal structure for interaction and coalition building.

The low priority accorded to serving the older adult is most surprising, however. Librarians who perceive the importance of meeting the developmental needs of children, young adults, and adults fail to realize that such a perspective is as necessary for elders. Margaret Monroe has devised the framework for building services around gerontological tasks of development outlined in Figure 1.[40]

But too few libraries know about and use Monroe's framework, pointing up the need for greater attention to older adult services in library education. Librarians concerned with competent practice must be able to tie knowledge of gerontology closely to concepts of service, translating relevant theory into practice.

Gerontological Concepts to Professional Practice

The *Update* confirmed Kanner's earlier research findings that the library profession had failed to absorb and implement the insights of gerontology.[41]

It is not enough to know who the aging are: successful service demands an understanding of aging within the social and cultural setting in which it takes place. Disengagement theorists assert that aging is a process of receding from active participation in life.[42] Activity theorists enjoin that engagement is normal and necessary for continued satisfaction, self-esteem, and good health.[43] To account for those who remain active and those who disengage, Rose claims the emergence of an aging subculture that is growing into a powerful sociopolitical movement.[44]

Tasks of Major Change

> Role loss and change of status
> Social isolation
> Widowhood
> Orientation to aging
> Grief and grieving
> Death and dying

Tasks of opportunity

> Leisure
> Keeping current
> Community service
> Self-affirmation
> Self-actualization

Tasks of adjustment

> Family life and relations
> Companionship and friendship
> Intergenerational friendships
> Health
> Sexuality
> Housing
> Life review

Figure 1. MONROE'S DEVELOPMENTAL TASKS OF AGING.

Age stratification proponents attempt to bridge the gap between those that stress social factors and those that emphasize personal ones. According to them, aging is a process of becoming socialized to new or revised role definitions affected by the size of the aging population, the roles available, and differences in the timing of the individual and social needs.[45]

Continuity theorists contend that older adults respond to aging in ways that are consistent with their psychological makeup and personality. Responses developed over a lifetime do not alter with aging, though roles may.[46] To the concepts based on personality patterns, exchange theorists add that older persons continue to participate in social interaction only so long as the rewards are commensurate with the costs.[47] Social breakdown theorists maintain that control over the environment is necessary to ensure competence and self-esteem. Proponents of intervention attach the corollary that compensatory intervention on the part of older adults and agencies working with them can counteract declining control and self-esteem.[48] Currently, Woodruff is leading gerontologists who hold that not all older adults need intervention on their behalf. Instead many are national assets who possess faculties, such as wisdom and the ability to integrate experience, that have improved with aging.[49]

Knowing gerontological concepts can help librarians anticipate varying older adult responses to aging and to supply them with relevant services. To develop independent learner programs for older adults without adequate food or security is as foolhardy as offering information and referral services on survival needs to the growing number of those more affluent. *Update* findings suggest that too often we think of older adults as homogeneous with little uniqueness. As a result, services are planned for a nonexistent, amorphous mass. Disengaged, active, or compensating, older adults must all be considered in planning activities if they are to be attracted to public libraries in significant numbers.

Models for the Future

Finally, the *Update* reviewed services to find models for the future. Not all of the exemplary programs—those that showed evidence of gerontological linkages—are being offered currently; still, the nineteen described here can provide librarians with a range of starting points for their own service initiation.

Society needs older adults to occupy vital roles as much as older adults need to occupy them. In helping to combat psychological segregation resulting from role loss, some public libraries have emphasized purposeful activities, not exclusively recreational ones. For example, several Massachusetts libraries have instituted an information exchange for part-time employment of older adults in their communities. The Over 60 Service, a Milwaukee Public Library program to shut-ins, has involved older persons acting as community aides to identify and serve the homebound population. The aides canvassed neighborhoods to locate and interview prospective clients. Partly because of their closeness in age to the people they contacted, the aides were able to relate to many shut-ins who were previously unreceptive to library service.

As part of Project LIBRA under the direction of Kathleen Adams, the Monroe County Library System in Rochester, New York, has provided live entertainment to senior citizens. The entertainers included magicians, pianists, and a woman who displayed and talked about her extensive doll collection, and all were over sixty years old. The library has maintained information on the entertainers in the Visiting Artists' Program file so that other agencies could draw on their services on a fee or volunteer basis.

At the Schenectady Public Libraries, older adults have offered their expertise to others through the People-to-People Index in the library's Educational and Job Information Center. The elders listed in the file are ready to teach on an individual basis in a wide range of areas including crafts, home repair, music, and numerous hobbies.

Gerontologists have concluded that reminiscence can contribute to successful aging by supporting the concepts of self and individual identity even in times of role loss and other stress. Several programs have focused on the recollections of older persons. In Vermont, for example, a history project drew together senior citizens and teenagers as they worked to locate primary source materials in homes of community residents—letters, diaries, newspapers, photos, maps—to evaluate, photograph, and preserve. In seeking out elderly residents for taped interviews about an earlier era, students came to appreciate their contributions to the community and to the nation. The Oak Lawn (Illinois) Public Library has brought grandparents and children together to pass on family stories. The grandparents share incidents from their childhood—a favorite holiday, recollections about their own grandparents—by telling stories one-on-one to their grandchildren. The grandchildren, in turn, write a short story about the tale and illustrate it. These activities unite youth and elders who are otherwise separated by generations.

The stereotypical labelling of older adults and the tendency to deny their individuality are recognized as damaging throughout gerontological literature. Programs that create an awareness of aging as a continuity in the life span, not a rupture, lessen the fear of aging and thus ageism itself. The Chicago Public Library's services for aging, when under the direction of Jim Pletz, offered a seminar for branch librarians to help them better understand and interpret the aging process.

Psychological and physical segregation are not mutually exclusive but tend to aggravate and perpetuate each other. The integration of older adults with different age groups also facilitates breaking down stereotypes. The Newton, Massachusetts, Public Library, for example, has used older adults as expert resources for children's interest groups, mothers' discussion seminars, and adult literature groups. Those involved reported that the interaction was stimulating.

Eradicating illiteracy is a top priority in the national legislative agenda. Literacy volunteers, using the one-teach-one method, have an ever-increasing number of affiliates among public library systems. At the Brooklyn Public Library, the most comprehensive program of library and information services for older adults in the United States, literacy programs have drawn on older persons to train volunteers. There the Services for the Aging (SAGE) Program has provided more than one-third of the tutors for the literacy program from its constituents over sixty years of age. SAGE employs senior assistants to develop educational programs utilizing films and lectures on consumerism, legislation, housing, and other areas of interest to older adults as well.

Interagency cooperation has been incorporated in Williamsport, Pennsylvania's elder services in "Bringing Reading to the Aging through Volunteer Outreach (BRAVO)." Over fifty volunteers were mobilized to serve well over 300 homebound persons. To locate potential users the librarian accompanied the volunteers in the local home-delivered meals program and talked with the participants about their interest in a home visit system. When the program was started, local newspapers and radio stations gave time and space to publicize it and the librarians sought speaking engagements to spark organizational interests. BRAVO was also publicized at civic events and on billboards and city buses. Downtown stores made window displays showing the volunteers on their rounds and their contented patrons. Volunteers were solicited on the radio, in church bulletins, and in service clubs. Funds for continuing support have come from the Friends of the Library and from local foundations.

Some public libraries offer formal classes where older adults participate. The Los Angeles Public Libraries have hosted classes in English as a second language for Spanish-speaking and other ethnic groups. Library users, among them older adults, have received help in preparing for high-school equivalency examinations through courses and self-teaching tapes. The Cuyahoga Falls (Ohio) Public Library has drawn large audiences of older adults to educational programs on retirement planning and stress management. In Grand Prairie, Texas, librarians have taken materials on numerous subjects to persons attending nutrition sites where they would also present educational programs consisting of physical exercises, music, and education on preretirement and budget planning. From its branches the Cuyahoga County (Ohio) Public Library System has provided free monthly blood pressure checks as well as programs featuring experts on health.

Public library learning activities have also used new technologies and reached beyond traditional delivery systems. In an area of small towns and farms where no commercial television was available, the Tri-County Regional Library of Rome, Georgia, has broadcast daylong educational cable television programs. The programs have covered everything from news and recipes to college courses for credit and newspaper readings for the blind. Most of the shows were produced at the library's own studios; a heavy viewing population was found among older adults.

At the Westerville (Ohio) Public Library older adults have been introduced to microcomputers. Since it seemed that this age group was the most intimidated, least educated, and most ignored potential user group, Nancy Smith included a history of computing, an examination of everyday uses, and hands-on experience with the Apple IIe in her sessions.

With LSCA support, the Oklahoma Department of Libraries has funded a statewide Right-to-Read project, *News in Review,* which produced a weekly newspaper column written at a fourth-grade reading level with an adult interest level and printed in large type to meet the needs of the 18 percent of the state's population who cannot read local papers.

A research and demonstration project at the Dallas Public Library, funded by the U.S. Department of Education, Office of Libraries and Learning Resources, has used existing library print and automated resources to develop Special Information Services (SIS) on Aging. The SIS staff concentrated on information provision coupled with education to increase information literacy: the ability to differentiate among types of information and information resources, and the ability to use them. The dissemination activities undertaken combined reference services with computer-assisted searches on commercially available data bases.

User profiles were prepared from needs assessment and current awareness activities undertaken through the selective dissemination of information (SDI), in which information from pertinent reports, documents, and publications regularly received in the library was sent to those whose profiles was delivered to all participants; fact sheets on specialized subject areas, which repackaged information in a format that allowed rapid scanning, were also mailed.

SIS developed a bank of programs and speakers around subject interests determined from feedback. In addition, workshops in information on aging and resources available through the library were conducted on government documents; media orientation to library resources for programming; and humanities programs useful for elders, including the National Council on Aging's Humanities series. Over 841 service providers attended programs in the educational component. The fact sheets, guides for workshops, and other resources prepared during the project were disseminated throughout the library as well. The library also provided document delivery services through the mail or through delivery to branches for pick-up.

There are successful examples of public library information and referral services as well. In an expansion of its long-running I & R services, the Plainedge (New York) Public Library sought and received designation as the site for Project TOTE (transportation of the elderly) for its area. TOTE has provided free door-to-door transportation to those sixty years of age who were physically or financially unable to use other means of transportation. TOTE vehicles were operated by the American Red Cross under contract with the County Department of Senior Citizen Affairs. Funds came from Title III of the Older Americans Act. Door-to-door transportation was provided to obtain medical services, travel to nutrition sites, or for legal aid, financial aid, and other eligible trips on referral from agencies. The library requested the designation because many I & R calls were for repetitive transportation that volunteers could not supply.

The Baltimore County Public Library, through its Gray and Growing, has created a cost-efficient model to get information to elders through programming. Professionally produced films and slide shows are grouped into individual programs aimed at the expressed needs and interests of persons aged sixty and older. A manual with step-by-step guidelines accompanies each package and includes optional scripts, discussion questions, activities, and resources. Projectors and screens are made available for loan to registered senior groups. Organized groups are the target audience for the programs, in order to reach large numbers of seniors at the same time for a lower cost. The packages are also designed so that activity directors of senior groups can borrow them and present the programs themselves.

Conclusion

In the main, evidence from the *Update* challenges public libraries as they enter the 1990s. Today even exemplary libraries are not fully aware of their elderly client groups, not cognizant of the networks of agencies providing them service, and not reaching the maximum potential audience. Although the list of services compiled in the *Update* and the exemplary programs detailed here are a useful starting place for libraries that want to initiate services for older adults, only the more traditional are widely available. The accounts of innovative services, widespread in the professional literature, are more models for emulation and initiation than they are an accurate reflection of the current state of professional practice.

The road ahead includes greater older adult participation in planning and executing programs of service for their peers. It includes working closely with other organizations serving elders to coordinate services and their delivery. It includes initiating services for those who work with elders, and, most importantly, it includes dispelling the myths of ageism to all sectors of the community. It will take continuing resolve, on the part of older adults and all professionals who serve them, not only to change society's perspective to appreciate and utilize the resources of older adults, but also to change the perspective of older adults themselves, for whom society's current outlook has become a self-fulfilling prophecy.

The human condition allows us to move to what is expected. What is expected can become what we believe, which can affect what we are able to do. In the past too little attention has been paid by public libraries to the ways in which older adults serve as valuable resources in our society. That must be the emphasis to transform public libraries for the 1990s if we are to furnish the services elders deserve.

Notes

1. *A Profile of Older Americans* (Washington, D.C.: American Association of Retired Persons, 1987), pp. 2–4.
2. *Statistical Abstracts of the United States, 1987,* 107th ed. (Washington, D.C.: Bureau of the Census, 1987).
3. Cynthia M. Tauber, "America in Transition: An Aging Society," Current Population Reports. Series P-23, No. 128 (September 1983), pp. 1–28.
4. Muriel C. Javelin, "How Library Service to the Aging Developed," *Library Trends* 21 (January 1973): 377.
5. "Older Americans Act," One Hundredth Congress, First Session, *House of Representatives Report,* pp. 100–197.
6. Ronald E. Gelfand and Jody K. Olsen, *The Aging Network* (New York: Springer, 1980), pp. 29–31.
7. Eleanor Phinney, "Library Services to an Aging Population," *American Library Association Bulletin* 51 (September 1957): 607–609.
8. Pauline Binnick, "Serving the Seniors," *American Education* 14 (June 1978): 20.
9. *The National Survey of Library Services to the Aging* (Washington, D.C.: U.S. Department of Health, Education and Welfare, Bureau of Libraries and Educational Technology, 1972), ED 067-521.
10. Jean-Anne South and Henry Drennan, "The 1971 White House Conference on Aging," *Library Trends* 21 (January 1973): 452.
11. Virginia Mathews, *Libraries: Aids to Life Satisfaction for Older Women* (U.S. Department of Education, Office of Libraries and Learning Technologies, September 1981).
12. Betty J. Turock, *Public Library Services for Aging in the Eighties* (U.S. Department of Education, Office of Libraries and Learning Technologies, September 1981).
13. Connie Van Fleet, "Public Library Service to Older Adults: Survey Findings and Implications," *Public Libraries* 28 (March/April 1989): 107–113.
14. *The National Survey,* pp. 3,4.
15. Illinois State Library Task Force for Library Service to the Aging, *Service for the Elderly in Illinois Public Libraries: A Survey,* report no. 6 (Springfield: Illinois State Library,1981).
16. U.S. Offices of Libraries and Learning Resources, "Report on Public Library Activities for Older Adults," 1982 (unpublished).
17. Kathleen M. Heim, "Adult Services as Reflective of the Changing Role of the Public Library," *RQ* 27 (Winter 1986): 180–187.

18. M. Baykan and S. Collings, "Senior Citizens: A Bridge for Community Involvement," *School Library Journal* 31 (January 1985): 31–33.
19. D. Bedient and J. Angelis, "Meeting Information Needs of Older Adults," *Illinois Libraries* 69 (January 1987): 57–59.
20. A. Carpenter, "Springfield–Green County Library's Elderfest: Variety of Activities by and for Older People," *Show-Me Libraries* 33 (May 1982): 17–21.
21. Genevieve Casey, *Library Services for the Aging* (Hamden, Conn.: Library Professional Publications, 1984).
22. L. G. Denis and M. J. Nauratil, "Library Science Students' Commitment to Library Service for Older Adults," *Journal of Education for Librarianship* 24 (Winter 1984): 183–188.
23. C. K. Dobretz, "Sharing and Preserving Family Stories," *School Library Journal* 33 (Fall 1987): 40.
24. "Guidelines for Library Service to Older Adults," *RQ* 26 (Summer 1987): 444–447.
25. Celia Hales, "Planning for the Information Needs of the Aging: A Delphi Study," Ph.D. dissertation, Florida State University, 1982.
26. Judith Kamin, "How Older Adults Use Books and the Public Library: A Review of the Literature," Occasional Paper No. 165 (Urbana: University of Illinois, Graduate School of Library Science, 1984).
27. Elliott E. Kanner, "Library Service to Older Adults: Progress in Research Applications," *Public Libraries* 23 (Fall 1984): 93–95.
28. Alan M. Kleiman, "Brooklyn's SAGE Program: Providing Service to All the Elderly," *Library Journal* 108 (March 15, 1983): 556–557.
29. "Library Comfort Level, Checklist for Serving Older Adults," *American Libraries* 18 (September 1987): 690.
30. "Library Service to the Aging," *Bookmark* (Winter 1984): entire issue.
31. Linda S. Lucas, "Reading Interests, Life Interests and Life-Style," *Public Library Quarterly* 3 (Winter 1982): 11–18.
32. Bessie Boehm Moore and Christina Carr-Young, "Library/Information Services and the Nation's Elderly," *Journal of American Society of Information Science* 36 (November 1985): 364–358.
33. N. J. Smith, "Humanizing the Computer for the Older Adult," *Ohio Library Association Bulletin* 56 (April 1986): pp. 25–26.
34. Betty J. Turock, *Serving the Older Adult: A Guide to Library Programs and Information Sources* (New York: Bowker, 1982).
35. Catherine Ventura-Merkel, *Education for Older Adults: A Catalogue of Program Profiles* (Washington, D.C.: National Council on the Aging, 1983).
36. T. Watson, "Reading Aloud in Seattle," *Wilson Library Bulletin* 61 (Fall 1987): 20–22.
37. White House Conference on Aging, *Final Report: Toward a National Policy on Aging*, 2 vols. (Washington, D.C.: Administration on Aging, 1982).
38. White House Conference on Aging, *Strategies for Linking the Generations: A Report of the Mini-Conference* (Washington, D.C.: Department of Health and Human Services, 1982).
39. Roger DeCrow, *New Learning for Older Americans* (Washington, D.C.: Adult Education Association of the U.S.A., 1974).
40. Kenneth Ferstl, "Public Libraries and Services to the Aging: A Study of Attitudes," Ph.D. dissertation, Indiana University, 1977.
41. Margaret Monroe and Rhea Rubin, *The Challenge of Aging: A Bibliography* (Littleton, Colo.: Libraries Unlimited, 1983).
42. Elliott E. Kanner, "The Impact of Gerontological Concepts on Principles of Librarianship," Ph.D. dissertation, University of Wisconsin, 1972.

43. Elaine Cummings and W. E. Henry, *Growing Old: The Process of Disengagement* (New York: Basic Books, 1961).

44. George Maddox, "Fact and Artifact: Evidence Bearing on Disengagement from the Duke Geriatrics Project," *Human Development* 8 (1965): 117; Erdman Palmore, "The Effects of Aging on Activities and Attitudes," *The Gerontologist* 8 (Winter 1968): 259; George Maddox, "Themes and Issues in Sociological Theories of Human Aging," *Human Development* 13 (1970): 17–27.

45. A. M. Rose, "The Subculture of Aging: A Framework in Social Gerontology," in *Older People and Their Social World,* eds., A. M. Rose and W. A. Peterson (Philadelphia: Davis, 1965), pp. 3–16.

46. M. W. Riley, M. Johnson, and A. Foner, *Age and Society,* vol. 3 in *A Sociology of Age Stratification* (New York: Russell Sage Foundation, 1972).

47. B. L. Neugarten, R. J. Havighurst, and S. S. Tobin, "Personality and Patterns of Aging," in *Middle Age and Aging,* ed. B. L. Neugarten (Chicago: Univ. of Chicago Pr., 1968), pp. 173–177.

48. Jon Hendricks and C. Davis Hendricks, *Dimensions of Aging* (Cambridge, Mass.: Winthrop, 1979), pp. 200–201.

49. Ibid., pp. 201-202.

50. Diana Woodruff, "Aging and Intelligence: Changing Perspectives in the Twentieth Century," in *Libraries and Aging,* proceedings of the annual Alumni-Faculty Symposium, Rutgers University School of Communication, Information and Library Studies, ed. Betty J. Turock (Jefferson, North Carolina: McFarland, 1988), pp. 17–27.

CHAPTER 11

Service to the Handicapped

Janice M. Simpson

During the 1980s there was a surge of interest in identifying and meeting the needs of the disabled. The General Assembly of the United Nations designated 1981 as the International Year of Disabled Persons,[1] and the United States Congress declared 1982 the National Year of Disabled Persons.[2] Disabled persons are now encouraged by society to move into the mainstream and take part in educational, economic, cultural, and social activities.

Many programs now exist in the public library for disabled persons, and there is the possibility for the development of even more programs and activities that would benefit the disabled library patron. At the White House Conference on Handicapped Individuals in May, 1977, President Jimmy Carter estimated that over 18 percent of the total U.S. population is disabled in some way.[3] Ruth A. Vellman, in *Serving Physically Disabled People*, estimated that 36,000,000 people are disabled—either physically, emotionally, or mentally.[4] This represents a large number of people, many of whom are not making use of the public library's resources, facilities, or programming.

Definition of Terms

There is a controversy over whether "handicapped" or "disabled," should be used in reference to this group. Recent literature favors "disabled," agreeing with Vellman that while "handicapped" seems rather limiting, "disability is usually perceived as referring to a specific medical condition."[5] Whichever term is preferred, the federal government, in Part 713, subpart G of the *Code of Federal Regulations*, defined a disabled person as "an individual who has a physical or mental impairment that substantially limits one or more major life

372

functions, has a record of such an impairment, or is regarded as having such an impairment."[6]

Mandates for Service

In addition to offering a definition of "disabled," the federal government regulates library service to the disabled. Part B of the Library Services and Construction Act (LSCA) Amendment of 1966 provides "library service through public or other nonprofit libraries, agencies, or organizations, to physically handicapped persons (including the blind and visually handicapped) certified by competent authority as unable to use or read conventional printed material as a result of physical limitations."[7] The International Federation of Library Associations and Institutions specifies that "all public library services should be available to handicapped and housebound readers both adult and children."[8] The UNESCO Public Library Manifesto also suggests that the public library should be available to all community members, regardless of physical impairments.[9] Clearly, library service to disabled persons is mandated by international as well as federal guidelines, and is an important part of a library's function. The fact that these laws exist, however, shows a failure on the part of libraries to voluntarily provide services to the disabled and a lack of recognition of the information void that the public library could help fill.

Library service to disabled persons has a long history, and many of the services that are now common were originally begun as service to disabled patrons. These include bookmobile service, books-by-mail, circulating spoken records, and (to a lesser extent) library networking. Bookmobile services can trace their origins to an enterprising Springfield, Massachusetts, librarian who used a horse and buggy to make deliveries to the homebound in 1901. Books-by-mail began in 1904 when Congress authorized the free mailing of Braille books for the blind, while the Library of Congress network for the blind was, in 1933, the first to lend "talking" records. The first instance of library networking was reported in 1931 when the national library network for the blind and physically handicapped began.[10]

Barriers to Service

Even though library service to disabled persons has a long history and is required by law, many barriers to service still exist. Disabled people need access to library resources and services as well as to libraries themselves. Library access can be improved by the removal of architectural barriers that prevent the physically disabled from using the library, but often it is the attitudes of library personnel that present the larger obstacle. These nonphysical barriers are often the more difficult to overcome, since they are usually invisible and often hard to identify. While a physical barrier is fairly easy to identify and correct, attitudinal, cultural, and social barriers must also be removed. These barriers must be removed in order to make library service appealing to disabled and nondisabled alike.

Blind and Visually Handicapped

One of the largest groups of disabled persons, and the group with the longest history of library service, is the blind and visually impaired. According to statistics for 1984, 8.2 million people in the United States have visual impairments, and 1.4 million of these are classified as severely impaired.[11] Nearly 500,000 of this number are legally blind.[12] Many blind persons partake of library services and make use of the special programs offered.

The Boston Public Library established service to the blind in 1868 when it acquired eight Braille volumes. Soon other libraries followed suit. In 1894 the Chicago Library began services for the blind when it received a donation of Braille books from a women's club. The New York City Free Circulating Library for the Blind (which joined the New York Public Library seven years later) was established in 1896, the same year the Detroit Public Library began its service with 110 books for the blind.[13] In 1897 John Russell Young established the Library of Congress reading room for the blind, with over 500 books and musical items with raised type comprising the original collection.[14] The Pennsylvania Home Teaching Society and Free Circulating Library for the Blind was incorporated into the Free Library of Philadelphia in 1899.[15] Ushering in the new century, the San Francisco Public Library established a reading room for the blind in 1902.[16] As the above data shows, libraries were willing to offer services to and provide resources for the blind and visually handicapped in the nineteenth century. Although it has recently been in vogue to provide numerous opportunities and services for the handicapped, some public libraries have been providing just this type of service for over 100 years.

LEGISLATION

With the passage of the Pratt-Smoot Act in 1931, the Library of Congress National Library Service for the Blind and Physically Handicapped was established.[17] This law authorized the Library of Congress to provide books for the use of the adult blind residents of the United States. One hundred thousand dollars was provided for books, and the Librarian of Congress was authorized to arrange for circulation of materials with libraries judged appropriate to serve as local or regional centers.[18]

Since the passage of that act, the service has since expanded to include not only blind adults, but visually and physically disabled children as well as adults. Although only Braille books were furnished in the beginning, talking books and tapes are now available as well.[19] Special cassette and record players, with such accessories as speed control units, remote control switches, and headphones are also included in the list of items now furnished.

LIBRARY OF CONGRESS

Service to readers is provided on three distinct levels—federal, state, and local. Under Public Law 89-522, approximately 1200 book titles and 70 magazines are produced annually by the Library of Congress. These, plus equipment, publications, and catalogs, are distributed to more than 100 regional and subregional libraries throughout the country. At the state level, the goal is to have one cooperating regional library in each state. Subregional libraries provide more personalized services on the local level.[20]

Regional and subregional libraries act as storehouses of material for the Library of Congress and also distribute this material to libraries or patrons in their areas. The administering agency of a regional library may be a state library agency, a public library, a commission for the blind, a state department of education, or a private service agency. Each subregional library is a unit of a public library or library system.[21]

NATIONAL LIBRARY SERVICE

The National Library Service (NLS) offers accessibility to a quite extensive collection. The 56 regional and 101 subregional libraries now in operation, in addition to four multistate service centers, are responsible for storing and circulating numerous materials for the Library of Congress.[22] The National Library Service has also been responsible for many innovations in service to the blind and visually impaired. In 1934, talking books were added to the list of materials distributed by the Library of Congress. Funds for the replacement and maintenance of talking book machines already in use were appropriated in 1942, and use of those funds for the purchase of new machines was approved in 1946.[23] In 1966 services were extended to users whose physical impairments prevent the use of printed materials.[24] Cassette players and tapes were introduced to the Library of Congress program in 1969, their low cost, smaller size, and ease of use helping them to become quite popular.[25] Postage is not paid by the patron, so there is no cost involved in receiving these materials by mail. According to 1976 figures, about 478,000 people were served through the regional library system.[26] Only 19 percent or so of those eligible make use of this service, and almost 45 percent of those were not aware of its existence.[27] Even though this service has been in existence for quite a while, more attempts need to be made to make certain that those eligible are aware of its existence. Perhaps they would then take advantage of it.

The budget for the National Library Service increased from $6 million in 1969 to $34 million in 1979. In that same year, 1979, state and local governments added over $14 million to supplement reader services for the blind and physically handicapped. In addition to a budget increase, the National Library Service circulation for recorded books jumped from 5 million in 1969 to almost 14 million in 1978. The number of patrons utilizing the availability of recorded material also increased from 135,000 to 640,000 in the same time period.[28]

According to Francis St. John, who did a survey of library services for the blind in 1956, two of the most important functions of the Library of Congress are "stimulation and financing of mechanical research to produce better quality machines and embossed books."[29] Certainly the Library of Congress appears to be striving to assure the accomplishment of both these goals. A variety of "talking book machines" have been developed over the years, but quite a few of them are now obsolete. More books are now available on cassettes, and computers are making it easier to reproduce Braille books and other reading materials.[30]

TECHNOLOGICAL DEVELOPMENTS

The burgeoning technological advances of the past few years have played a large part in recent innovations in library service to the blind and visually impaired. One of the most intriguing developments in this area has been the development of reading machines. In 1970, the Optacon machine, which converts printed matter into tactile forms that can be felt instead of looked at with the eyes, was introduced. The user passes a small camera over a printed line while keeping one finger on a small tactile screen where the image is reproduced. The Optacon is light, battery-operated, and portable, and has several attachments to enhance its capabilities, including a visual display and devices for converting it to use with a typewriter, TV screen, or calculator.[31]

The Ealing Reader is designed for readers who are visually impaired or have a physical disability that precludes their holding a book or periodical. It consists of a magnifying box that measures approximately 11" by 11" by 6". A large-print book on a reel of paper is attached to a take-up spool and put into the box, somewhat similar to film being loaded into a camera. The reel can then be either advanced or rewound, and the machine can be adjusted so that only slight physical pressure is required to operate it.[32]

Perhaps the most exciting of the recent technological advances has been the development of the Kurzweil Reading Machine, which converts printed matter to sound. Designed by Ray Kurzweil, the machine uses an electronic scanner with a speech synthesizer to read printed matter aloud.[33] This computer-camera combination allows the user to control the rate of speech, and even have words spelled out individually. The Kurzweil Reading Machine has gone through various refinements and can now be used with a wide array of printed matter. The current models are much lighter and easier to handle than the original, and the price has also become more manageable.[34] More public libraries are now acquiring these as the price gets less expensive and the machine itself becomes less cumbersome.

RADIO PROGRAMS

Radio reading services are another area into which public libraries have expanded. In 1975 these programs were operative in 26 areas and offered local information services to persons with special radio receivers.[35] These special broadcasts include varied subjects, with the reading of newspapers, magazines, and books by volunteers and staff members being among the most popular. Discussions on areas of interest to the listening audience are also presented.[36]

MAGNIFYING DEVICES

In addition to large-print books, some visually impaired patrons benefit from magnification aids. Aside from the familiar magnifying glass, there are several devices available to aid visually impaired patrons. One of these is the Ednalite magnifier, which is mounted on arms that can be moved over the printed text. Some have internal lights for illumination.[37] Closed-circuit TV systems can also be helpful in magnifying some forms of printed material. The Apollo Lasa and the Visualtek systems are two examples that use a camera and TV receiver to enlarge the print anywhere from four to forty times. These systems both have the drawbacks of being bulky and rather expensive.[38]

Useful as they may be, technological devices do not satisfy all the library needs of the blind. Basic reference tools, as well as a broad range of materials for general reading, should be available for the blind. In 1980 the *World Book Encyclopedia* was produced on 219 cassettes contained in nineteen booklike volumes, needing about six feet of shelf space.[39] Although bulky and rather cumbersome, this tool is extremely beneficial. Other reference tools are available on tape, and tactile maps and atlases are also produced for libraries.

Programs designed for sighted patrons are often of interest as well to the blind and visually impaired. The need for book talks, lectures, and musical events, among others, exists for this group just as it does for the sighted, and many existing library programs do not require even slight adaptation. Other programs, such as a "Please Touch" art exhibit, can be of interest to the sighted even though designed for the blind and visually impaired.

According to the 1966 *Standards for Library Services for the Blind and Visually Handicapped*, only 25 percent of the blind actually patronize library services.[40] Each library needs to utilize and develop its resources to include a full range of materials and programs for the blind and visually impaired, in order to encourage increased library usage.

Deaf and Hearing Impaired

"Library service to the deaf and hearing-impaired population is still very much in its infancy."[41] While the problems the blind encounter with conventional library materials are obvious, the problems of the deaf have not always been as clear, yet over 13 million Americans have hearing problems.[42] Communication difficulties for the deaf and hearing impaired present problems in dealing with many public services. Too few public libraries have staff members literate in sign language, and many deaf people are reluctant to indicate a need for help. Failure to establish proper contact can result in problems for both the patron and staff. A reference problem, for example, might be simple to answer if the hearing-impaired patron could properly explain the question to the library staff member. A staff member fluent in signing might be able to quickly locate a desired book for a patron, once the request was understood.[43]

Hearing problems seem to encourage reading problems too. The 1965 Babbidge Report to the Secretary of Health, Education, and Welfare stated that many deaf students leave school with very poor reading skills.[44] The average deaf adult reads at a fourth-grade level and writes at an even lower level. The ability to read well seems to be related to the ability to hear: deafness seems to cause trouble understanding the fundamentals of grammar and syntax.[45]

People with no hearing problems gain information in many ways that are unavailable to the deaf and hearing impaired. Radio and television programs impart large quantities of information daily, and "word of mouth" is still an important way of passing information on. With these avenues closed to the deaf and hearing impaired, libraries play an important role in helping them learn what resources and services are available in the community as well as in the library. Libraries can also help the public become aware of the world of the deaf through programs, displays, and advertising of special events.[46] Librarians need to become aware of people who are not using the library due to communication problems and also need to identify resources already in the collection which would be of use to the deaf and hearing impaired.[47]

Since communication with the deaf can present some difficulties, libraries might consider having one or more staff members learn American Sign Language. This training could be useful not only for communicating with patrons, but could provide interpreters for programs that some deaf individuals might like to attend. Classes in sign language could also be taught at the library.[48]

Closed-captioned films and videotapes, art prints, slides, and silent films can all be used successfully with the deaf and hearing impaired. Materials written in high interest and low vocabulary format can also be utilized. Most of all, libraries should be certain to advertise programs, especially ones for which an interpreter will be available.[49]

TECHNOLOGICAL INNOVATIONS

Technology has also proven useful in helping libraries deal with the needs of the hearing impaired. Telecommunication devices for the deaf (TDDs) are electronic devices that provide video or printed communication over telephone lines. Although TDDs started out as bulky and expensive, they are now quiet, compact, and relatively inexpensive, making them accessible to most public libraries. Telephone reference service for the hearing impaired should soon be within the grasp of all but the smallest libraries. Personal computers can also be used as TDDs with a modem that is now available.[50] Once again, technology has greatly improved library service in only a few years.

Physically Disabled

While it is sometimes hard for a librarian to recognize a visually or hearing impaired individual immediately, the physically disabled are usually very easy to recognize, especially those in wheelchairs. However, not all physically disabled persons suffer from the same disabilities. Physical disabilities can be divided into three general categories: skeletal, muscular, and neuromuscular. Skeletal disabilities include such diverse conditions as dwarfism, rheumatoid arthritis, and amputations. Muscular dystrophy is included under the category of muscular disabilities.[51] Cerebral palsy and multiple sclerosis are included in the neuromuscular classification.[52] People who suffer from physical conditions may be unable to turn pages on printed matter; they can borrow talking books from the Library of Congress under the National Library Services for the Blind and Physically Handicapped.[53]

BARRIERS

Federal law makes it illegal for libraries to have barriers which preclude their use by the disabled. Under Public Law 90-480, the Architectural Barriers Act of 1968, "any building constructed or leased whole or in part with federal funds must be made accessible to and usable by the physically handicapped."[54] The Rehabilitation Act Amendments of 1974 also help to ensure compliance with these standards.[55] Additionally, Title 1 of the Library Services Construction Act offers money for special projects for the handicapped. Public libraries are able to apply for government monies this way.[56]

In order for disabled persons to take advantage of all a library has to offer, they must first be able to get into the building. Designated handicapped parking spaces should be available, near the building, with curb cuts nearby to help a wheelchair onto the sidewalk. If the ground leading to the library is not level, a ramp might be needed. A barrier-free route through the library is also important. Passages between book stacks should be of adequate width to accommodate a wheelchair, crutches, etc. Staff members might need to assist disabled patrons in removing articles from high shelves.[57]

Furnishings need to be selected with the disabled patron in mind. Tables should be of adequate height to accommodate wheelchairs. Such items as pencil sharpeners, typewriters, photocopiers, and magazine or newspaper racks should be readily accessible to handicapped patrons. Pay telephones, water fountains, and restrooms should all accommodate the disabled.[58]

In addition to insuring that the building is accessible by the handicapped, librarians must also be careful to assure that their programs are also accessible. Programs should be offered in a non-discriminatory manner, and disabled persons should not be denied access to or offered unequal services.[59]

Physically disabled persons can be encouraged toward more frequent library use in several ways. Handicapped persons can be included on library committees, especially those that consider architectural changes for the library. Programs of general interest as well as those conceived with the disabled in mind should be well publicized.[60] Some libraries have found that travel information is of special interest to the handicapped, since information on which areas are equipped for handicapped travellers makes planning trips much easier.[61] Many library programs already in existence would be of interest and useful to handicapped persons if these programs were publicized.

Developmentally Disabled

While library service to the preceding groups, especially to the blind, has a fairly long history, the developmentally disabled are a group whose library history is not quite so long. Although the Quaker Hospital for the Mentally Ill in York, England, did establish a library for its patients in 1796, most service to the developmentally disabled lagged far behind.[62] The 1935 *Florida Library Survey* reported that the State Hospital at Chattahochee, which housed 4,000 patients, had no books for patients' use, but a library was said to be under consideration and was "reported as desirable."[63]

Some institutions for the mentally ill did see libraries as desirable. The Pilgrim Psychiatric Center in West Brentwood, New York, opened

October 1, 1931 and established a library in 1933. This original library consisted of 700 volumes of fiction designed for both children and adults.[64] In 1944 a librarian was hired to oversee the collection. Unfortunately, libraries were not seen as desirable for most institutions. In 1956 the Association of Hospital and Institution Libraries was formed within the American Library Association.[65] Today most mental hospitals and institutions have some sort of library available for patients as well as for staff use.

Since the late 1960s, the trend has been for fewer developmentally disabled persons to be housed in state institutions. Budget cuts of recent years have resulted in many facilities releasing patients back into society, and fewer people are placed in these institutions at all. Developmentally disabled individuals are encouraged to lead so-called normal lives in the mainstream of society. Many are trained for different types of jobs and live alone or in groups, sometimes with counselors in residence. This group can greatly benefit from the many diverse resources the library has to offer.

Until the 1970s the term "mentally retarded" was used, but now "developmentally disabled" is generally preferred. A developmentally disabled individual is defined as one whose disability is found to be "attributable to mental retardation, cerebral palsy, epilepsy, or another neurological condition found by the Secretary of Health, Education, and Welfare to be closely related to mental retardation or to require treatment similar to that of mentally retarded individuals."[66]

The library can play an important part in helping this group become assimilated into society. Mental stimulation is important for the developmentally disabled since it enables them to overcome their limitations. Libraries can provide good learning experiences as a new patron obtains a library card, learns the rules governing the library, becomes familiar with circulation procedures, and so on.[67] Attendance at library programs can also be a positive learning experience as group interaction and the exposure to new ideas can both have positive effects on a developmentally disabled person.

The Altoona, Pennsylvania, Area Public Library initiated a program called Learning Is for Everyone (LIFE) that attempted to serve the developmentally disabled adult through a collection of multimedia materials, programming, and, probably the most important, interaction with other patrons.[68]

It is important to use a wide variety of materials in designing programs to appeal to the developmentally disabled adult. Photographs, films, music, art, dance, games, puppet shows, and group activities are all popular, as well as activities that involve different senses, such as drawing or crafts. High interest and low reading level material is needed, as are large-print books and items designed for the newly literate. The different levels of development must be considered, since no two people will be at exactly the same level. While some developmentally disabled patrons might be interested only in picture books, others are capable of reading for recreation and enjoyment as well as for information. Audiovisual materials can be useful, especially for those with short attention spans. Models, maps, tapes, records, toys, games, and puzzles are also effective. Some childrens' programs can be adapted for the developmentally disabled, but special care should be taken in attempting this. Even though this group might not have as high a reading level as others, their interests have usually progressed past the point of many childhood involvements. Story hours can be useful, but the stories must not be just rehashed childhood standards.

Bibliotherapy, "the use of selected reading materials as a therapeutic tool," is gaining interest among public librarians. As deinstitutionalization continues, the trend to make better use of library facilities for the developmentally disabled grows. There are many advantages in encouraging the developmentally disabled to explore the options available to them in the public library. It benefits society as well as the "mainstreamed individuals" themselves.

Some library staff members have attitudinal barriers that can be a hindrance in encouraging facilitation of the public library by developmentally disabled persons. As with all other groups of disabled persons, attitudes are of tantamount importance—both the attitudes of the group members as well as the attitudes of the library staff and even the attitudes of the community.

ASE Survey Findings

In looking at the ASE survey data that relates to library services for the disabled, several seemingly conflicting pieces of information emerged. On question 34C (Does your library organize programming for the handicapped?), only 15.3 percent answered "yes." While this response would seem to indicate that very few libraries provide services for the handicapped, other answers shed a slightly different light on the subject. For example, a total of 72.6 percent provided spoken records at no charge, and 69.5 percent also circulated spoken tapes for free. Films were offered at no charge by 45.1 percent, while 3.5 percent provided films for a fee. A total of 43.9 percent circulated videotapes, with 6.2

percent charging a fee for this service. Audiovisual equipment was circulated by 54.2 percent, while 59.4 percent provided this equipment for in-library use.

These other answers seem to show that services are being provided. Spoken records and tapes, audiovisual materials, films, and musical records and tapes are all utilized by the disabled, yet they are considered to be part of the standard library collection. By providing these as an integral part of library services, librarians are indeed meeting the needs of the disabled.

This conclusion is further borne out by the fact that when asked to list up to five adult service programs conducted by their libraries in 1985, respondents did not always include special programming for handicapped in their lists. A disabled person is frequently interested in a subject that is not considered to be "programming for the disabled." A genealogist in a wheelchair might make use of a program on tracing one's roots, while a deaf person might attend an exhibition of art prints. Programs on microcomputers, local history, travel, books, and income taxes are all varied in their appeal. They can be utilized by disabled as well as "able-bodied" patrons. Often no special programming is needed.

Several libraries did provide special programming for disabled patrons, and these programs included a wide variety of topics.

Teaching sign language proved to be one of the most frequently offered courses. The Ocean County Library in Toms River, New Jersey, offered signing classes in two of its branches, as did the Chattanooga-Hamilton County Library System in Tennessee. These were ongoing programs, having been conducted for at least one year. Professional instructors were used, and the programs were advertised by the media and flyers. An average of twelve people per session took part in these activities, conducted in the library. Signing courses were also offered in New York, Kentucky, California, South Carolina, Ohio, Maryland, North Dakota, Illinois, Indiana, Hawaii, and Pennsylvania.

The Broward County Division of Libraries in Fort Lauderdale, Florida, offered a tax assistance course with an interpreter. An annual event in cooperation with the Friends of the Libraries and United Hearing and Deaf Services. It is conducted in the library by a VISTA volunteer and an interpreter. Newspapers, fliers, posters, direct mail, and direct contact are used to advertise the event. An informal discussion is conducted after the workshop, where the opinions of both the speakers and the audience are solicited.

Captioned films for the hearing impaired were offered by several libraries. The Miami-Dade Public Library, Miami, Florida, averaged fifteen viewers for its closed-captioned films. Both Fullerton and Pasadena (California) offered captioned films. Pasadena has sponsored this activity for three years, while the Fullerton series has been ongoing for five years. Both libraries advertise these activities through newspapers and fliers.

A few libraries also opened their facilities for hearing screening tests. South Bend (Indiana) Public Library had 200 people take part in the free tests conducted by volunteers from the County Speech and Hearing Association. In a similar activity, the Palm Beach County (Florida) Public Library had a professional audiologist conduct a free hearing screening for its patrons. Radio announcements and posters were utilized to advertise these events.

Libraries in Mississippi, Alabama, Florida, Georgia, New Jersey, and California provided reading materials for the blind and physically handicapped, funded in part by the Library of Congress and LSCA grants. Large-print books were provided in conjunction with the Clarksville (Tennessee) Public Library and funded by the Tennessee Library Association. The program reached eighty to eighty-five people.

Movies for the handicapped have been provided for five years by the Hawaii State Library System. An average of thirty-three people from the Waimano Home Facility took advantage of the films offered, with patrons notified by phone. The Carnegie Free Library in Beaver Falls, Pennsylvania, provided films designed for the developmentally disabled adult. A similar film program was offered by the Cherokee Regional Library in Lafayette, Georgia.

Library tours for "Adult Day Activity Clients" have been provided for over twenty years by the Burke County Public Library in Morgantown, North Carolina. Sixteen developmentally disabled adults are brought in a group to the library in an attempt to expand their horizons as well as teach them to enjoy the library. This activity is not advertised in any medium.

Two Ohio libraries, Columbus and Middletown, offered programs that dealt with the role of handicapped in literature. These were offered once and were conducted by teachers. Newspaper advertisements as well as radio announcements were used.

Conclusion

Many library programs and resources are available for the disabled, and many existing resources can be better utilized in providing information, education, cultural, and social opportunities. Librarians need to become aware both of what their libraries can offer to disabled patrons as well as of changes they can make to facilitate the increased use of libraries by disabled. The opportunities exist, but we must be aware of them.

Notes

1. Donald John Weber, "Historical Overview," in *Library Services for the Handicapped Adult*, eds. James L. Thomas and Carol H. Thomas (Phoenix: Oryx, 1982), p. 3.
2. Ibid.
3. Ruth A. Vellman, *Serving Physically Disabled People* (New York: Bowker, 1979), p. 3.
4. Ibid., p. 4.
5. Kieth C. Wright and Judith F. Davie, *Library and Information Service for Handicapped Individuals* (Littleton, Colo: Libraries Unlimited, 1983), p. 34.
6. Earl C. Graham, "Public Library Services to the Physically Handicapped," *ALA Bulletin* 61 (February 1967): 170.
7. Ibid.
8. International Federation of Library Associations and Institutions, Public Libraries Section, *Standards for Public Libraries*, 2d ed. (Munich: Verlag Dokumentation, 1977), p. 18.
9. Della Pearlman, *No Choice: Library Services for the Mentally Handicapped* (London: The Library Association, 1982), p. 17.
10. Weber, "Historical Overview," p. 9.
11. "Counting Handicapped Clients for Library Services," *Library Journal* 111 (June 15, 1986): 20.
12. Alfred D. Hagle, "Information Access by Blind and Physically Handicapped Person," in *Advances in Librarianship*, 12 (1982): 249.
13. Robert S. Bray, "Library Services for the Blind and Physically Handicapped," in *Encyclopedia of Library and Information Service*, vol. 2 (New York: Dekker Marcel, Inc., 1969), p. 628.
14. Steven J. Herman, "Information Center Profile: Library of Congress Division for the Blind and Physically Handicapped," in *Library Services to the Blind and Physically Handicapped*, ed. Maryalls Storm
15. Bray, "Library Services," p. 628.
16. National Library Service for the Blind and Physically Handicapped, *That All May Read* (Washington: Library of Congress, 1983), p. 3.
17. Library Administration Development, *Standards for Library Services for the Blind and Visually Handicapped 1966* (Chicago: ALA, 1976), p. 2.
18. Hylda Kamisar and Dorothy Pollett, "Those Missing Readers: The Visually and Physically Handicapped," *Catholic Library World* 47 (May–June, 1976): 418.
19. Hagle, "Information Access," p. 251.
20. Francis R. St. John, *Survey of Library Service for the Blind, 1956* (New York: American Foundation for the Blind, 1957), p. 12.
21. Genevieve M. Casey, "Library Service to the Handicapped and Institutionalized," *Library Trends* 20 (October 1971): 360.
22. Hagle, "Information Access," p. 265.
23. Mona D. Werner, "Collection Development in the Division for the Blind and

Physically Handicapped, Library of Congress," *Catholic Library World* 47 (May–June 1976): 418.

24. Wright and Davie, *Libraries and Information Service,* p. 49.
25. Evenson and Levering, p. 37.
26. St. John, *Survey of Library Service,* p. 5.
27. Frank K. Cylke, "Library Services for the Blind and Physically Handicapped," in *The ALA Yearbook 1979* (Chicago: ALA, 1979), p. 61.
28. Wright and Davie, *Libraries and Information Service,* p. 45.
29. Cylke, "Library Services," p. 69.
30. Ruth Carol Chusman, "The Kurzweil Reading Machine," *Wilson Library Bulletin* (January 1980): 56.
31. Wright and Davie, *Libraries and Information Service,* p. 45.
32. Margaret E. Monroe, "Library Services for the Blind and Physically Handicapped," in *The ALA Yearbook 1976* (Chicago: ALA, 1976): p. 72.
33. Wright and Davie, *Libraries and Information Service,* p. 46.
34. Ibid., p. 44.
35. Ibid., p. 45.
36. Ibid., p. 47.
37. Library Administration Development, *Standards,* p. 25.
38. Kathleen Low, "Telecommunication Devices for the Deaf, "*American Libraries* 16 (November 1985): 746.
39. Suzanne F. Cohen, "United but Accessible System Meets Needs of Deaf and Hard-of-Hearing Individuals," *Illinois Libraries* 68 (November 1986): 557.
40. Wright and Davie, *Libraries and Information Service,* p. 58.
41. Ibid., p. 59.
42. Michele Freese, "Library Service for Deaf and Hard-of-Hearing Individuals," *Illinois Libraries* 68 (November 1986): 551.
43. Vellman, *Serving Physically Disabled People,* p. 53.
44. Ibid., p. 141.
45. Freese, *Library Service for Deaf,* p. 561.
46. Phyllis Dalton, *Library Service to the Deaf and Hearing Impaired* (Phoenix: Oryx Press, 1985), p. 236.
47. Low, "Telecommunication Devices," p. 746.
48. Vellman, *Serving Physically Disabled People,* p. 25.
49. Ibid., p. 26.
50. Ibid., p. 30.
51. Ibid., p. 56.
52. Ibid.
53. Ibid., p. 103.
54. Dale Brown, "Serving Disabled People in Public Libraries, "*Public Libraries* 23 (Spring, 1984): 8.
55. Robert T. Begg, "Disabled Libraries: An Examination of Physical and Attitudinal Barriers to Handicapped Library Users," in *The Mainstreamed Library: Issues, Ideas, Innovations,* eds. Barbara H. Baskin and Karen H. Harris (Chicago: ALA, 1982), p. 16.
56. Ibid., p. 12.
57. Vellman, *Serving Physically Disabled People,* p. 102.
58. William L. Needham and Gerald Jahoda, *Improving Library Service to Physically Disabled Persons* (Littleton, Colo.: Libraries Unlimited, 1983), p. 12.
59. Casey, "Library Service to the Handicapped," p. 351.

60. Helen V. Stelle, *Florida Library Survey 1935* (St. Petersburg: Florida Library Association, 1937), p. 18.
61. Aime Atlas, "Half A Century of Library Service at Pilgrim Psychiatric Center 1935–1985," *Bookmark* 44 (Winter 1986): 99.
62. Casey, "Library Service to the Handicapped," p. 352.
63. Thomas, p. 1.
64. Pearlman, *No Choice*, p. 17.
65. Anne Marie Forer and Mary Zazac, "Library Services to the Mentally Retarded," in *The Mainstreamed Library: Issues, Ideas, Innovations*, eds. Barbara H. Baskin and Karen H. Harris (Chicago: ALA, 1982), p. 56.
66. Pearlman, *No Choice*, p. 22.
67. Ibid.
68. Helen Elsen, "Bibliotherapy in Practice," *Library Trends* (Winter 1987): 647.

CHAPTER 12

Genealogical Reference Service in the Public Library

Chris E. Marhenke

Many public libraries in the United States do not offer services to genealogists and genealogical researchers. There are many reasons for the lack of assistance to this clientele. Development of genealogical services has a relatively short history. Understanding who genealogists are, where they come from, and the kinds of information they require is vital to adult service. The growth of interest in genealogy points to a need for further development of services to genealogists in addition to providing genealogical collections for these patrons. This chapter presents some of the beliefs of librarians about genealogical collections as well as types of services that might be expected of libraries.

Genealogy Defined

Genealogy has been defined in many ways, but the definitions are for the most part identical. One definition for genealogy, "people who trace their ancestry," is quite broad and nonspecific.[1] While this definition suffices for most purposes, a clearer definition must be pursued for greater specificity. The *Encyclopedia of Library and Information Science* defines genealogy as "the study of family history, the tracing of a line of descent through successive generations or a pedigree, the history of a family or group of families."[2] However, genealogy is slightly different from family history; while closely related, they are still separate lines of inquiry. A better definition comes from Richard Harvey, who states that genealogy is "the study of relationships between individuals, and of families composed of related individuals."[3] Both of these definitions define the term more clearly and with a greater degree of feeling for the potential of a sense of accomplishment. In other words, the last two definitions present a more "personal" meaning for the patron as opposed to the broad meaning given in the first definition.

Genealogy as defined by Harvey has existed since the time of the Old Testament, as shown by different biblical passages concerning family lineages and before, as characterized by the tradition of oral family histories. However, it is only within the last century, and really the past few decades, that an increase in genealogical popularity on a nationwide scale has occurred.

History of Genealogy

U.S. interest in genealogy was almost nonexistent in the 1700s as the country was becoming established, partly due to the belief that only members of the upper class had families whose histories were worth knowing. Before the American Revolution, Americans had a strong dislike for genealogy, since it reminded them of society in the old country where strong traditions of inheritance and caste existed. With the American Revolution, ties with the old country were not as strong as feelings of independence. As the country grew, Americans became increasingly mobile. This mobility made the gathering of family information increasingly difficult, since needed records were not all located in one place. On the other hand, this mobility assisted in the revival of genealogical interest because of the lack of knowledge people had of family background. People's desires to know why their greatgrandparents moved from one state to another show how this trend from disinterest to interest has been reversed. On a larger scale, relatives that came from other countries hold even more interest for the researching family member. In this sense, the melting pot tradition has played a role.[4]

Reasons for the continuous growth of genealogical inquiry are varied. Genealogy's popularity, as a hobby, has been steadily increasing through the years. The U.S. centennial in 1876 began a broad awakening of interest for Americans in the history of the United States and consequently in the histories of their own families.

This interest was a popular movement rather than a scholarly one. A popular movement can lead to a scholarly movement, however, as people enroll in history classes to obtain a better understanding of the events in which members of their families were involved. The opposite can be true as people begin to be curious about their families in relation to history. The Centennial Exposition in Philadelphia in 1876 helped to bring about the creation of the Daughters of the American Revolution (DAR) in 1890. Other genealogical organizations arose soon afterwards.[5] These organizations include the Genealogical Department of the Church of Jesus Christ of Latter-Day Saints (1894), the United Daughters of the Confederacy (1894), the National Society of the Children of the American Revolution (1895), the Sons of Confederate Veterans (1896), the General Society of Mayflower Descendants (1897), the National Genealogical Society (1903), and the National Society of Sons and Daughters of the Pilgrims (1908).[6] A few genealogical organizations existed before the DAR was formed, such as the General Society of the War of 1812 (1814), the Sons of Union Veterans of the Civil War (1881), the Daughters of Union Veterans of the Civil War (1885), and the Sons of the American Revolution.[7] The following organizations are among those that have formed more recently: the American Society of Genealogists (1940), the Genealogy Club of America (1969), the Federation of Genealogical Societies (1975), the Institute of Family History and Genealogy (1976), the Association of Professional Genealogists (1979), and the Society of Americans of Colonial Descent (1982).[8] These are only a few of the many organizations that have sprung from the growth of genealogical interest in the United States.

A look through *Meyer's Directory of Genealogical Societies in the U.S.A. and Canada* shows that 181 genealogical societies have been organized since 1954.[9] Most societies did not list their founding dates, and therefore these 181 societies are only a small portion of the total number of societies listed in the *Directory*. Of the 181, fifty-four were organized since 1980.[10] Additional genealogical societies exist that were organized before 1954, but the growth of the number of genealogical societies in recent years is obvious. Meyer states that in 1984 150 new societies were formed.[11] Although this number dropped in 1985 to only seventy-five new societies,[12] the growing interest in genealogy is clearly demonstrated by the many new societies being formed.

The period following World War II brought about new changes to the average American lifestyle with the establishment of the five-day work week, the expansion of Social Security benefits, and the practice of forced retirement. All of these changes combined to cause the development of a new leisure class of Americans who had the time to develop new interests and hobbies.[13]

Reasons for the Popularity of Genealogy

The biggest impact on the recent growth of genealogy was the immense popularity of Alex Haley's book *Roots*, which was further boosted by its being televised in 1977. This story of one man's search for his antecedents had an unbelievable impact on Americans and their interest in genealogy. Examination of the *Readers' Guide to Periodical Literature* shows a substantial increase in the number of citations under the term "genealogy" after 1976. The increase of citations in 1977 alone shows that the largest increase in the number of citations corresponds to the showing of *Roots* on television.

There are many reasons for the rise of popularity of genealogy, including increased affluence, earlier retirement, intellectual interest, excitement, curiosity, delusions of grandeur, religion, and the pursuit of genealogy as an occupation (professional genealogist).[14] One overlooked cause is that while entertainment prices have been rising along with the cost of living, use of the library has become more attractive and economical compared to the expenses incurred with many other hobbies.[15] Another more general reason is that interest in genealogy can arise independently of any knowledge or experience.[16] The desire for an authentic family crest may lead many people into the genealogical web. (The purchase of an "authentic" crest should be approached with caution, since many crests are simply created "out-of-the-blue" and sold for an exorbitant amount to unsuspecting buyers who believe the crest to be authentic.)

People interested in genealogy today are frequently younger than those of a decade ago. Young people's interest has been encouraged by many means, such as a merit badge for Boy Scouts and courses in genealogy in the elementary grades.[17] Education and encouragement of young people have led to the development of a broader spectrum in the range of ages of people interested in genealogy.

Records of the National Archives reflect an increase in genealogical inquiries from approximately 3,000 a month in 1954 to 2,300 inquiries a week in 1982.[18] The increase in the number of articles and books being published is also an indicator of the growth of genealogy. *Subject Guide to Books in Print,* under "genealogy" and related headings, listed only four books in 1957. By 1985–1986, this number had increased by approximately 4,000 percent to 161.

The Effect on Public Libraries of Interest in Genealogy

This increase in popularity has affected libraries of all types, but especially public libraries. The first professional literature on genealogy consisted of hortatory and how-we-do-it articles and manuals primarily designed for researchers. In the 1960s standard bibliographies for genealogical use began appearing.[19] Until then librarians did not have many sources to rely upon for assisting patrons. Patrons were generally amateur genealogists who used the library for one of the four following reasons:

1. To join a patriotic society
2. To prove descent from nobility
3. To satisfy curiosity about their antecedents
4. Because they were active members of the Church of Jesus Christ of Latter Day Saints.[20]

The burden or joy of helping these patrons falls mainly on public libraries. Academic libraries and special libraries are often more restrictive in their policies regarding service to the general public and the types of services they offer. Along with the popularity of genealogy have come the problems that arise with any rapid increase in the popularity of a service. Among the problems that affect public libraries directly are the absence of a genealogical collection, lack of knowledge or avoidance on the part of librarians, and problems caused by the patrons themselves. Patrons create problems by their perseverance and determination to find information, even if the library has no materials that meet their needs. Many patrons, for instance, believe that a family genealogy book for their own family must already exist in a library. The various and multiple needs of patrons cause various and multiple demands on a library's collection, needs that the library may not find possible to meet.

Despite the presence in most states of state or private historical societies and other specialized libraries that have genealogical collections, "every city should have a public library with enough basic books of genealogy and heraldry to meet ordinary demands".[21] A 1967 article in *RQ* stated that most libraries do not have a genealogical collection nor do librarians have any knowledge of or training in genealogical research.[22] New graduates of schools of library and information science programs usually have no knowledge of genealogy and the associated research processes, and more experienced librarians tend to avoid the subject of genealogy altogether.[23] Experienced librarians avoid genealogy primarily due to the bad reputation of amateur genealogists in public libraries. This avoidance can be attributed to lack of knowledge of the subject on the part of librarians and their frustration in being unable to assist genealogists, failure of the library to collect genealogical resources, genealogists' expectations being too high for the library and the librarians, the dogged persistence of many genealogists, and the inability of each side to understand the other.

Preying on this lack of understanding gives rise to a number of fraudulent genealogists who do a minimal amount of research and other activities for clients strictly as a moneymaking venture. To combat this problem, the Board for Certification of Genealogists was created in 1964 "for the purpose of formulating standards of genealogical research and the establishment of a register of persons who are deemed to be qualified for this type of work."[24]

The lack of knowledge of genealogy sources and research methods on the part of librarians appears to be attributable to a lack of available professional training in these areas. A review of 1986–1987 catalogs of ALA-accredited library education programs showed no classes offered regularly on genealogy. Most library and information science school curricula probably include some mention of genealogy with history in the basic reference classes or in their resource classes for the social sciences. Some schools may offer genealogy under the rubric of either "Special Topics" or "Independent Study." One school, the School of Library, Archival and Information Studies at the University of British Columbia in Vancouver, British Columbia, does offer a class that specifically mentions genealogy in its course title. However, this class is part of the curriculum for the Master of Archival Studies Program rather than the master's degree in library and information science.[25] Four universities other than Schools of Library and Information Science offer courses in genealogy. All four offer correspondence courses that cannot be taken for credit. These universities are Brigham Young University, Oklahoma State University, the University of Texas at Austin, and the University of Wisconsin Extension.[26] Brigham Young University offers an Associate of Arts degree in genealogy, requiring from twenty-five to thirty-one credit hours of study.[27]

Deterrents to Building Genealogical Collections

It is not surprising that problems have arisen in the public library with the growth of interest in genealogy. But should every library have a genealogy collection? J. Carlyle Parker, in his book, *Library Service for Genealogists,* says that not every library should, but that librarians should at least know about genealogy research techniques and where some materials may be located to serve the patron better.[28] The diversification of patrons' backgrounds and interests creates even more difficulties.

If genealogy materials were not useful for research in areas such as local history, it would be relatively easy to justify their exclusion from public library collections.[29] Since genealogical materials have some usefulness for special collections of local interest materials, they present problems for libraries that already have such collections or are in the process of developing them. As a result of the highly specialized nature of genealogical materials, many librarians are opposed to maintaining collections devoted to genealogy. The main difference between genealogy and history, however, may be only the degree of professionalism and research experience of the patron.[30]

Since genealogical patrons come from such a wide variety of backgrounds, assistance given them must necessarily be of an assorted nature. Each individual search or reference question is unique. The particular family members being researched further expand the quality of uniqueness, since each member is also a unique individual with a unique history. Assisting a patron can be potentially difficult and may require many sources to answer questions.[31]

Genealogical patrons bring a number of other problems into consideration. As discussed by Mary Sherard in the *Mississippi Library News* in 1967, these patrons "demand more advisory service," talk to the librarian too much about their research, don't understand why materials can't be checked out, expect the library staff to do their work for them, and are incredibly persistent.[32] From the viewpoint of the librarian, it seems as if there is never enough staff and that once a genealogy collection is begun there is no end to purchasing new materials.[33] Some of the problems specifically associated with having a collection arise in the areas of acquisitions, interlibrary loan, reference, preservation of materials, and location of the collection. The Genealogy Committee in the History Section of the Reference and Adult Services Division was established in 1968 as one approach to helping librarians address problems in these areas.[34] This committee has recently prepared and published guidelines for editors of publications relating to genealogy as one step in assisting libraries.[35]

Many, perhaps most, libraries do not have formal policies concerning genealogical materials and collections. The establishment of such policies, especially circulation, interlibrary loan, reference, and acquisitions policies is essential to the provision of consistent, high-quality service.

Selection of genealogical materials may be difficult in that priorities and criteria are frequently different for genealogical materials than for other library materials. Most genealogical materials must be evaluated on the basis of potential for extended future rather than for immediate, current use.[36] This archival function may conflict with the policies of libraries that deliberately emphasize the provision of popular, high-use materials. Genealogical materials are changing rapidly and will continue to change in nature, availability and accessibility.[37] These changes also include the information contained in the materials, the quality of this information, and the type of information desired by the patrons.

A very new resource for genealogical research is the computer. Computers are useful for genealogists, and many software packages are available for most microcomputers.[38] Preparing publications of family histories, organizing research findings, sharing and finding family information, providing a base of information (so that others can look at the information and see what has been gathered and what needs to be located), consistency in performance (the software will run the same each time it is used), speeding up repetitious tasks, and minimizing the labors of the genealogists are a few of the useful reasons for utilizing computers to store family information.[39]

Reference Service to Genealogists

Reference librarians have had a tendency to view genealogists with dread. The reference librarian should provide the same type of help given to other types of patrons, suggesting possible sources, making use of interlibrary loan, providing referral to other libraries or historical societies, and providing the names of professional or amateur organizations.[40] In many instances referral to courthouse records and local genealogical researchers is one of the most valuable services that librarians can provide to genealogical patrons.[41]

There are several points for reference librarians to consider. First, it is important to try to understand who genealogists are and what motivates them. Reference librarians should attempt to gain firsthand knowledge of the research involved, perhaps by researching their own families. It is essential to thoroughly learn the basic tools. Utilizing local genealogists and genealogy organizations can be of immense benefit. Reference interviews should be informal. The library's genealogy and local history collection can and should be enhanced by the use of interlibrary loan.[42]

Interlibrary Loan of Genealogical Materials

Interlibrary lending of genealogical materials has been a major problem area for public libraries. Most libraries do not lend genealogical material because much of it is rare, heavily used locally, and expensive or impossible to replace. Until recently the National Interlibrary Loan Code was another major deterrent to the lending of genealogical materials.[43] The code adopted in 1968 specifically identified genealogical materials as being among those resources libraries should not request through interlibrary loan.[44] This may not have been a matter of direct discrimination towards genealogists so much as it was a reflection of speculation concerning the amount of materials genealogists may want to put their hands on and the potential for overwhelming interlibrary loan offices.

Every month new genealogical publications enter the market. Many of these are oriented towards a specific locale, or are book reviews that genealogists become aware of. Some of these book reviews can be located in magazines such as *The Genealogical Helper*, the *Newsletter* of the National Genealogical Society, and others. Because of the amount of new materials and the fact that genealogists quickly become aware that these publications are available, genealogists frequently want to obtain this new information, usually through interlibrary loan. The genealogist typically wants just a glance at the index or a brief glimpse of a publication to determine if it is of some interest. After this brief look the patron is finished with the material, returns it, and then asks for more. This rapid turnaround of interlibrary loan materials probably contributed substantially to revision of the code, removing the specification of genealogical materials.

The Church of Jesus Christ of Latter-Day Saints (LDS) began extensive microfilming of genealogical materials shortly after the development of microfilm technology in the 1930s.[45] Two main advantages the church leaders saw were:

1. The creation of durable copies of original records
2. Distributing microfilm copies to genealogical researchers in remote locations.[46]

A wide variety of records are routinely microfilmed by the LDS, including birth, marriage, and death records; the total number of microfilm reels has now grown to over 1.4 million reels.[47] Since many normally unavailable items have been microfilmed by the LDS, a very great amount of information is potentially available for genealogical research. Access is limited, however, because most libraries do not lend microform materials.

Handling Genealogical Materials

Since genealogical materials come in various physical forms and may not have been created with long-term storage and use in mind, they frequently need special handling and storage procedures. The differing physical formats of these materials may also create problems with storage. Paper materials of widely varying sizes and shapes must be accommodated, as must a variety of microformats. For many libraries the problem of where to house the collection in the library may be difficult enough, without the additional difficulties of purchasing and maintaining storage facilities and viewing equipment for microform materials. Allied with this problem is that of preservation. Keeping valuable items from deteriorating is a growing concern for all library materials and is a very major issue for genealogical collections. The solutions, including microfilming and making new printings on acid-free paper, are expensive and of as yet undetermined value.

The formation of cooperative agreements among libraries is another method of insuring preservation and duplication of original sources. Two libraries that made such an agreement are the Newberry Library of Chicago and the Fort Wayne and Allen County Public Library of Fort Wayne, Indiana. In the mid-1960s, the staff of the Fort Wayne Public Library "photocopied thousands of the most deteriorated volumes from the [Local and Family History Collection of the] Newberry collection, keeping one copy to add to the Fort Wayne collection and returning another copy to the Newberry to replace the worn-out book."[48] This project saved the Newberry materials "for at least another generation and formed the nucleus of the distinguished collection of genealogy materials at Fort Wayne."[49]

The usual treatment of genealogical materials as special collections often makes total patron access difficult. For example, if the special collection has closed stacks, patrons will have to rely on library employees to select and retrieve the proper material. The increasing popularity of genealogical research and the concomitant demand for access to genealogical collections may make the use of a closed shelves system unfeasible for most libraries. Even if the stacks are open, patrons may have to sign in so that librarians know who has used the collection. This procedure may help librarians locate patrons in the event that damages have occurred to materials in the collection, but it is an uncertain security device and may arouse resentment in some patrons. This conflict between the need of the patron to have ready access to genealogical materials and the desire of the library to maintain careful control over fragile and irreplaceable items is a difficult one to resolve.

Another frequently overlooked problem is that there is no single widely used organizational scheme for genealogical materials. The standardized classification systems used for ordinary library are poorly matched to the nature of genealogical materials and the needs of genealogists. Normally, if any special scheme is used it is one the library has developed locally based upon topographical arrangements.[50] This lack of standardization may lead to a considerable amount of patron frustration, since familiarity with the approach used in a given library is not generally transferable to the use of other libraries' collections.

Why Public Libraries Should Provide Genealogical Services

All of the above arguments may be presented in opposition to having a genealogical collection. While many of the points have validity, there are ways to counter these problems, and genealogical collections can be seen as being appropriate and beneficial in several ways.

One main reason for having a genealogy collection is to support the study of local history, a goal that fits well with the purposes of most public libraries. Historians interested in particular events, places, or people may be able to locate major pieces of information or even crucial minor pieces by going through material that has been maintained at the local public library. Records of past events in the area and related material should be preserved for future use. Many important pieces of information have been found in libraries that accepted material as donations or made it a practice to purchase local interest material.

Libraries wishing to establish a genealogical collection should think small and should probably concentrate on local history first.[51] From these basics they might expand to include materials pertinent to state and then regional history and genealogy. This gives an order to the collection process and provides a strong foundation. The genealogy and local history collection can then be promoted and used to develop an interest in the library.[52] The most important factor in justifying the existence of a genealogy collection should be its level of use.[53] In some cases, it may be necessary to spur use through promotional and informational activities. Perhaps the problem lies in the knowledge or the lack of knowledge of patrons. If they were better acquainted with the collection it is possible that they would utilize it more fully and increase the average attendance of the library.

A genealogy collection can also provide an avenue for instilling incentive and motivation in patrons and act as a method for broadening their reading interests to other fields.[54] Broadening the patrons' reading interests can be accomplished in several ways. If patrons are able to trace their family lines to other countries, perhaps they will want to read about those countries. Reading about other countries can focus on the present—what the country is like now, or on the past—what the conditions were in that country at the time of emigration. Other ways that readers are attracted to genealogy are through the study of specific events, professions, or occupations. One benefit springing from such an increase in reader interest is that these people may very well go out and spread good will for the library. If patrons are happy and satisfied with services they have received, they will naturally inform others of their positive experiences. A positive public image for the library could be very important in times of budget cutbacks, openings or closings of branch libraries, or other times when there is a need to rally public support for the library.

Services Related to Genealogy

The decision whether to maintain a genealogical collection must be made on the basis of local needs and resources. The same considerations determine the types and ranges of services to be provided. The quality of service, however, depends on the librarians in each situation. If librarians view genealogy as a burden, this view will be communicated to the patrons. Genealogical service can be a burden if librarians attempt to shirk their duties to patrons, make finding information difficult for the patrons, and dislike helping people, regardless of the assistance these people need. If, on the other hand, librarians consider genealogy and related services an enriching experience, their patrons will too. The whole issue rests on the sentiments of librarians concerning genealogy, the services associated with genealogy, and especially librarians' views on assisting patrons with genealogical research.

There are many services that can be performed by librarians to assist genealogists. Reference service is almost always available in varying degrees. Assistance by mail or telephone indicating if the library has a particular source is another type of service in addition to doing the research for the patron if time permits. This aspect is not very common and could involve charges. Librarians could arrange library tours and exhibitions and sponsor programs or offer classes on genealogy. Workshops are an extension of this idea and should also be considered. Compilation and publication of guides to genealogical sources are another way of offering services to genealogy patrons.[55] Developing notebooks of various information such as the names of families being researched or cemeteries in the surrounding area would be useful.[56] A file could be developed that refers requests for information and assistance to other people who might have knowledge pertaining to the request.[57] These people might be genealogists, historians, or archivists. Special indexes could be developed: for example, a surname index of families whose histories and genealogies are in the library's collection.[58] General services that should be provided, possibly as part of the general library services to all patrons, are a reading room, a map collection, copying services, and a microforms area.[59]

The range of services offered to genealogists will necessarily vary according to the nature, needs, and resources of the library, the size of the population being served, and the quality of the collection. The most basic service in any library is reference, or showing the user the proper pattern of information gathering to follow. At the other extreme, is not a single, definable service, but rather many services, including reference. Basic reference should be the same throughout all the libraries serving genealogists. It is the upper and middle sections of the range of services that will differ. The upper range will usually be the direct provision of information to the user, whereas the middle range depends on the type of user and the information they need.

For small libraries, the basic service is reference; some small libraries will be hard pressed to provide even this basic service and will be unable to go further. The middle range consists of services such as general library use instruction, introduction to the use of basic genealogical tools, and other relatively simple tasks. The upper range of services may include interlibrary loan services, locally published in-house guides to the collection, or other documents of general genealogical information.

For medium-sized libraries, the basic service level includes reference services and basic library use instruction. The middle range includes the distribution of in-house guides to what types of services are provided and how to use the collection. The upper range involves limited use of interlibrary loan. This limited use is generally the result of restricted funding available for interlibrary loan and consequently the user may have to be willing to pay for interlibrary loan services.

For large libraries, the basic services are reference and more extensive library use instruction, including instruction in the use of the genealogy collection. The middle range consists of detailed workshops and tours of the collection and interlibrary loan services. The upper range, or the range providing the most services, consists of compilations of guides, a comprehensive obituary file from the local newspaper, development of indexes to state census records, and other such projects prepared by the staff. Services provided at this level have far-reaching effects that may affect genealogists in other states.

A potentially valuable extended service for any library is the development of programs for youth interested in genealogy. Teaching youth about basic genealogical tools and general research techniques at an early age may alleviate some future difficulties, since they will have a knowledge base to rely upon. They can be taught some of the basic procedures and be provided with some materials and resources to get them started.[60]

A Look at the ASE Data

Findings from the ASE survey show that 853 of the 4,214 responding libraries (20 percent) reported that they do provide services to genealogists. Only eight libraries said that they provide genealogical services for a fee.

The most helpful data for the topic of genealogy came from the third page of the survey which asked for the following information: title of programs offered, the purpose of the programs, the cooperating agencies involved in the programs, whether the programs are ongoing, how long have they been operational, the type of participants involved, and the estimated number of participants.

The most common response to the question concerning the purpose of the programs was education. Other answers were more specific, stating that the purpose was to teach users how to begin genealogical research, to familiarize users with library resources, to introduce users to local resources, or to help users develop good research skills. Recreation and personal interest were also given as responses. One other response that is more library-oriented than user-oriented was that the program was designed to attract users.

The majority of the programs were conducted by local genealogical societies, genealogy clubs, or historical societies. The LDS, professional genealogists, experienced volunteers, DAR members, and even a mental health association were other named cooperating agencies. In some instances the library, either alone or with another public library or college, was the sponsoring agency for the program.

Perhaps the most interesting information from the survey data was whether or not the activity was an ongoing one. Most of the respondents replied that their programs were ongoing. Of these ongoing programs, many had been active for several years. One library's program had even been active for twenty-five years! The programs differed in regard to time of offering from one extreme to the other. Some were only offered on an annual or biannual basis, while others were given as courses that lasted for several weeks. Public demand was the primary determinant in deciding if a genealogical program was offered.

A wide variety of people participated in these programs. Many of the answers were men and women, adults, senior citizens, etc. The

Table 1. REGIONAL PROVISION OF SERVICES TO GENEALOGISTS

REGION	PROVIDE		DO NOT PROVIDE		FEE CHARGED		TOTAL	
	NUMBER	PERCENT	NUMBER	PERCENT	NUMBER	PERCENT	NUMBER	PERCENT
Central	200	20.2	786	79.6	2	0.2	988	100
North	108	16.8	533	82.8	3	0.4	644	100
South	347	22.0	1,231	77.9	2	0.1	1,580	100
West	198	19.8	803	80.1	1	0.1	1,002	100
Total	853	20.2	3,353	79.6	8	0.2	4,214	100

lack of answers specifically stating minority groups is perhaps an indication that non-Europeans are ignored as well as a reflection of the amount of genealogical services and resources available to them. On the other hand, these individuals could have been represented as men and women and other answers as given above.

A great assortment of answers was given in response to the question asking how many people attended the programs. Attendance ranged from four to 200. This response may not be truly reflective of the real attendance since in many cases the answers may represent the average attendance weekly, monthly, or yearly, may be an estimate, or may be a total for the month or year.

Table 1 shows the numbers and percentages within each region for those libraries providing special programming for genealogists, not providing the service, or providing the service for a fee. There appear to be no great regional differences, although libraries in the south were somewhat more inclined to provide programming for genealogists than libraries in the other regions, with libraries in the north being the least likely to provide such programming.

Conclusion

The number of genealogical publications being published, the number of people interested in genealogy, and the range of ages of people doing genealogical research have all increased substantially in the last few years. While the number of libraries providing services to genealogists has also increased, this number is still small. The ASE study shows that only 20 percent of the libraries that responded to the questionnaire indicated that they provided programming for genealogists. The increases mentioned above seem to indicate a need for an increase in the number of libraries serving genealogists and genealogical researchers. Many librarians may not realize the advantages and benefits that can be achieved by having a genealogical collection. More libraries should explore the possibilities of having genealogical collections to serve patrons interested initially in researching their families and ultimately researching the history of their families in relation to the United States and the many other countries represented by the patrons' ancestors.

In addition to increasing numbers of libraries with genealogical collections, an increase in qualified persons to assist these patrons is needed. Although many of these people will come in the form of volunteers, professional genealogists, or special groups, a need persists for trained personnel from the schools of library and information science. Until these needs are met, growth in the number of libraries providing genealogical services will be minimal.

Another area of service that needs to be addressed by genealogical libraries is that of service to nontraditional groups identified in this paper as those groups with non-European roots. A greater demand for resources of these types will continue to be evident in the years to come. All of these factors and others must be addressed in order for progress to be made in providing services to genealogists.

Notes

1. Allen Gardiner, "Genealogy and the Librarian: Hope and Help for the Librarian's Frayed Nerves," *Show-Me Libraries* 35 (September 1984): 25.
2. *Encyclopedia of Library and Information Science*, s.v. "Genealogical Libraries and Collections," by Gilbert H. Doane
3. Richard Harvey, *Genealogy for Librarians*, (London: Clive Bingley Limited, 1983), p. 8.
4. Russell E. Bidlack, "Genealogy Today," *Library Trends* 32 (Summer 1983): 9.
5. Gilbert H. Doane, *Searching for Your Ancestors* (Minneapolis: University of Minnesota Pr., 1973), p. 2.
6. *Encyclopedia of Associations* (Detroit, Mich.: Gale, 1987), pp. 1590–1607.
7. Ibid., pp. 1591–1612.
8. Ibid., pp. 1598–1601.
9. *Meyer's Directory of Genealogical Societies in the U.S.A. and Canada,* 6th ed. (Mt. Airy, Md.: Mary Keysor Meyer, 1986).
10. Ibid.
11. Ibid., p.v.
12. Ibid.
13. Doane, *Searching for Your Ancestors,* p.3.
14. P. W. Filby, "This Librarian Asserts: Genealogy Is Reference," *RQ* 6 (Summer 1967): 164.
15. Tom Bonanno, "Turning the History Crisis Around," *Ontario Library Review* 65 (June 1981):119.
16. Harvey, *Genealogy for Librarians,* p. 10.
17. Russell E. Bidlack, "Genealogy as It Relates to Library Service," *The ALA Yearbook* (Chicago: ALA, 1978), p. xxiii.

18. "Quest for Identity: Americans Go on a Genealogy Kick," *U.S. News & World Report* 77 (July 29, 1974): 41; Peter Andrews, "Genealogy: The Search for a Personal Past," *American Heritage* 33 (August/September 1982): 10.
19. Rick J. Ashton, "Curators, Hobbyists, and Historians: Ninety Years of Genealogy at the Newberry Library," *Library Quarterly* 47 (April 1977): 149.
20. Filby, *RQ,* pp.164–165.
21. Ibid., p. 166.
22. Ibid., p. 165.
23. Ibid.
24. Bidlak, *Library Trends,* p. 15.
25. School of Library, Archival and Information Studies, *Master of Library Science Program and Master of Archival Studies Program* (Vancouver, British Columbia: by the author, 831-1956 Main Mall, [n.d.]), p. 13.
26. *The Macmillan Guide to Correspondence Study,* (New York: Macmillan, 1985), p. 607.
27. *Brigham Young University Bulletin,* 83 (March 6, 1986): 160.
28. J. Carlyle Parker, *Library Service for Genealogists* (Detroit: Book Tower, 1981), p. 15.
29. Harvey, *Genealogy for Librarians,* p. 11.
30. Wagenknecht, *Illinois Libraries,* p. 465.
31. Harvey, *Genealogy for Librarians,* p. 8.
32. Mary Sherard, "Genealogy—a Growing Problem?" *Mississippi Library News* 31 (March 1967): 37.
33. Ibid.
34. M. Ann Reinert, "The Challenge of Genealogical Reference Services: Introduction," *RQ* 23 (Winter 1983): 159.
35. "Guidelines for Editors of Historical and Genealogical Bulletins and Family Newsletters," *RQ* 27 (Winter 1986): 169.
36. Harvey, *Genealogy for Librarians,* p. 12.
37. Ibid., p. 9.
38. Paul A. Andereck and Richard A Pence, *Computer Genealogy: A Guide to Research through High Technology* (Salt Lake City: Ancestry, 1985), pp. 98–100.
39. Ibid., pp. 28–36.
40. Robert E. Wagenknecht, "Genealogy Reconsidered," *Illinois Libraries* 58 (June 1976): 458.
41. Doris Roney Bowers, "Genealogical Research in the County Courthouse," *Illinois Libraries* 70 (September 1988): 480.
42. Brent L. Kendrick, "History Section Program," *Library of Congress Information Bulletin* 41 (September 3, 1982): 279.
43. J. Carlyle Parker, "Resources in the Field—Genealogy: Part I: Discrimination against Genealogists," *Wilson Library Bulletin* 47 (November 1972): 255.
44. "National Interlibrary Loan Code, 1968," *RQ* (Fall 1968): 44.
45. Ted F. Powell, "The Miracle of Microfilm: The Foundation of the Largest Genealogical Record Collection in the World," *Microfilm Review* 14 (Summer 1985): 148.
46. Ibid.
47. Ibid., p. 149.
48. Ashton, *Library Quarterly,* p. 159.
49. Ibid.
50. Harvey, *Genealogy for Librarians,* p. 13.
51. Willie Nelms, "Using Local History and Genealogy to Build Library Support," *Library Journal* 104 (March 15, 1979): 686.

52. Ibid., p. 687.
53. Dorothy M. Lower, "Should the Local Library Provide a Genealogical Collection?" *Library Occurrent* 22 (May 1968): 250.
54. Ibid., p. 249.
55. Harvey, *Genealogy for Librarians*, pp. 16–17.
56. Bonanno, *Ontario Library Review*, p.121.
57. Richard L. Barclay, "Access to Information with a Genealogy and History Referral File," *RQ* 18 (Winter 1978): 153.
58. Patricia Chadwell, "Discrimination against Genealogists," *Wilson Library Bulletin* 47 (March 1973): 566.
59. Laureen R. Jaussi and Gloria D. Chaston, *Fundamentals of Genealogical Research* (Salt Lake City: Deseret Book Co., 1977), p. 108.
60. Henry C. Dequin, "Leading Young Adults into Family History," *Illinois Libraries* 68 (June 1986): 361–363.

CHAPTER 13

Parent Education

Lolah Giamalva

Although pamphlets and treatises advising parents on child rearing have been printed since the seventeenth century and local clubs, reading circles, and social gatherings have held seminars on child rearing since the 1800s, the concept of parent education actually developed during the 1920s as an outgrowth of child behavior studies and research. These studies radically changed the view of parent-child interaction from a one-way, parent-to-child communication mode for impressing values to a multidirectional mode of communication affecting each member of the family unit. Parents, as facilitators of this process, were seen as requiring education and guidance to become "whole" parents producing "whole" children. This need broadened the scope of parent education.[1]

Origins

Parent education began as a focused movement during the late nineteenth century. "Advice to Parents" periodicals and self-help groups were an outgrowth of the social clubs of the time.[2] By 1897 these groups coalesced into the National Congress of Mothers, now known as the National Parent-Teachers Association (PTA).[3] The objectives of the early PTA were to provide parents with the newest in "scientific" childcare, to provide mothers with a support group of peers, and to extend information on childcare developments to poor and deprived families.[4]

These programs began making an impact at the turn of the century. The PTA used strong political advocacy to provide a supportive environment for child development before World War I.[5] Libraries began providing services to children at this time, and by 1915 children accounted for a third of the total circulation in many libraries.[6]

In 1913, under the auspices of home education, the U.S. Office of Education conducted a parent education project. After two years, the project underwent reorganization to provide advisory service on the education of parents, caretaking of children, production of pamphlets for distribution, and further research.[7]

World War I provided a demarcation between Victorian values and emergent twentieth-century values. Before World War I, adults had been inoculated by societal values of the Victorian era and "gilded age" of the 1890s to the 1900s. During this period, G. Stanley became a popular theorist of child behavior, the Dr. Spock of his time. His theories on child rearing were that children should be free to explore and develop until the age of six. At that age, it was incumbent upon the parent to shape the child to fit current societal mores and values.[8] By the 1920s Hall's methodologies were discounted as unscientific and sentimental.[9]

Servicemen returning from World War I found that the homefront had changed during their time away: adolescents and women had entered the labor force, and higher wages during the war's boom years had increased the quality of life.[10] Compulsory public education had begun mid-decade, but public backlash at progressivism caused major changes within the educational profession. Scientists enjoyed large public esteem as science made increased life expectancy a reality. The most popularized scientific field was psychology as Freud's theories captured the attention of the general public.

The democratization process that provided the impetus for formalized parent education groups was also a guiding force for public libraries of the period, since the library was often viewed as the great leveler between the elite and the poor.[11] The libraries and the child study movement shared a common denominator at this juncture: both originated from egalitarian ideals but were later considered to have promoted middle-class values.

Parent education underwent a radical transition by the twenties. Leading behavioral scientists claimed that their research bore no relationship to earlier, discredited studies. Non-PTA parent education programs stated that their goals and philosophy were unrelated to the earlier PTA-sponsored research.

The enormous popularity that parent education programs enjoyed in the twenties was due to extensive changes in societal values. Many who came of age during the twenties possessed a cynical and flippant attitude toward social conventions and adult authority. Youth peer groups carried more weight than parental dictates.

The fabric of American life was seen as being eroded by the antics of "flaming" youth, and behavioral changes occurred in the urban middle class, particularly among young women. Speech had become blunter, and certain modes of behavior were looked upon with great disfavor by parents. Social commentary by the media focused on the ailing middle-class family. Popular opinion concluded that mistakes made in middle-class child rearing were responsible for the moral decline of youth. However, the new child sciences would provide tools to prevent this breakdown of societal adjustment (and parental dictates) with the next generation.[12]

Amidst these upheavals of societal mores, parent education gained the championship of the Laura Spelman Rockefeller Memorial Fund. This fund had previously given block grants to established organizations, such as the Boy Scouts and the YMCA, to further child welfare.

The fund's administrators desired a different philanthropic direction while retaining the foundation's commitment to improving the quality of life for children. Lawrence K. Frank reshaped parent education by devising a policy model still employed today: a program of child study to be conducted by universities or research centers and disseminated by scientists to parent educators at the local level.[13]

By 1924–25 the Laura Spelman Rockefeller Memorial Fund had provided over a million dollars for parent education. These monies not only attracted new researchers, but also enhanced the academic status of child development programs. The Child Study Association was formed to promote scientific child developmental research untinged by sentimentality.[14]

The transitions in parent education were also marked by the library's changing role during the twenties. ALA's program of direct book services to soldiers during World War I led in part to the proposal of ALA's Enlarged Program[15] that included library extension services, services to immigrants and the handicapped, adult education, and institutional library development.[16] The intervention of the Carnegie Corporation and the creation of the American Association for Adult Education aided in the development of these educational services. Libraries during this period served as an intermediary through which informal adult education continued.[17]

ALA's direct involvement with parent education originated from the Reading With a Purpose series. This program targeted the general reader and was used by other adult education reading programs.[18] A meeting of the National Committee on Home Education in 1928 promulgated the following:

> The American Library Association will (a) continue the preparation and publication of its Reading With a Purpose Series, and (b) use its good offices in urging local libraries, state libraries, and library commissions regarding the desirability and importance of cooperating in making available to readers the books required for the successful pursuit of these courses.[19]

The professionalization of librarianship also underwent radical changes during this time. The Williamson Report reflected concerns and increasing criticisms of other professions that felt librarians encroached upon their territorial interests.[20] Most professionals involved in parent education held doctoral degrees in psychology, education, or child development. These people usually were administrators while coworkers either held lesser degrees in the same fields or were non-degreed. Carter maintained that "although libraries are thought of primarily in relation to book circulation, many of their services reach out of that realm."[21] The issue revolved on what services were offered. Librarians and parent education professionals debated whether the librarian should be trained in parent education or whether larger libraries should have a trained parent educator on the staff. Numerous library publications during the late twenties attest to the increased importance of trained professionals.[22] However, libraries were largely ignored in the professional or popular literature of the period as a positive influence on the cognitive development of young children (ages one through five). The revitalization of the library's role in adult education and the Carnegie Corporation funds provided the springboard for the libraries' involvement in parent education. Parent education was relegated to "Services to Groups," a part of community activities maintained by the public library.

The Depression

The Depression had a profound impact on American life. More families moved to single-family dwellings and separated further from the overall community as relatives were unable to provide assistance to the entire family network.[23] Yet the Depression produced one unexpected benefit. Despite the fact that Americans preferred pastimes that cost money, lack of funds for leisure activities spurred greater use of the public libraries. ALA estimated that public libraries acquired 4 million new borrowers from 1929 to 1933 and that book circulation increased by more than 40 percent.[24]

Decreasing funds available to public libraries during this time prompted Alvin Johnson and Carleton B. Joeckel to suggest consolidation of readers' advisory librarians with group services. In 1938 the Joint Committees of ALA and the National Council of Parent Education held a meeting at the national ALA conference in Boston. The U.S. Office of Education, through its Extension Home Economics Service, introduced the library's part in the Community Organization for Family Life.[25]

The Joint Committee determined that librarians should consult with parent educators on book selection. "As for librarian qualification to participate in the program, the librarians were cautioned that they were not experts and furthermore in any specific instance were not in a position to know family situations."[26]

Public librarians' increased involvement with parent education stemmed in part from New Deal federalism. Some libraries, mainly in metropolitan areas, provided some parent education (bibliographies, pamphlets, books), but most did not. The Laura Spelman Rockefeller Memorial Fund, which provided the original impetus, was exhausted by 1935, and Carnegie funds were severely reduced by this point in the Depression. The federal government allocated funds for parent education in the states through the Federal Emergency Relief Administration,[27] but federal mandates concerning human well-being were minimal until the Social Security Act of 1935 was enacted.[28]

The 1940s and 1950s

During the 1940s and 1950s ALA shifted the emphasis of its adult education commitment to the preservation of democracy and its meaning to Americans. The parent education movement was supported but somewhat submerged as an ancillary service. Nevertheless, Elizabeth M. Smith, library authority on parent guidance, advocated the establishment of a family life section in public libraries in her 1946 article, "The Public Library Contributes to Parent Education." The collection she proposed would be comprised of childcare, child development and health, family living, marriage, and homemaking while incorporating the storytelling hours, games, and read-aloud books already offered. Librarians were advised to become subject specialists in these areas while providing reader's advisory and community information referral services. As Smith stated, "Such complete programs were rare if not non-existent."[29]

Family life in America underwent massive changes during this period 1940 to 1960. In 1946, the annual birthrate was 3,426,000. This rate increased steadily until its peak in 1961 of 4,268,000 births.[30]

The population shifted with urban inflight, a rapid population movement from rural areas to urban centers. America had become a mobile society, and the post–World War II family unit was typified as the nuclear family, deprived of interaction with kin or nonkin within the home environment.[31] Education during the fifties enjoyed more prestige and support than at any period in American history. Prosperity and the presence of a parent, usually the mother, provided an atmosphere conducive to "good" child development in the middle class.

The nationwide prosperity after World War II provided libraries with their greatest expansion, due to the Library Services Act (now LSCA) enacted in 1957. Yet the fifties provided a narrower interest in childcare despite the increased birthrate. Piaget's theories were being published in the early fifties, and the only major change in childcare was the increased use of the childcare center. Little parent-child interaction occurred at these centers.[32] The same held true for children's library services. Parent education was not considered a major concern, nor were parents encouraged to participate in the story hours at the public library. These programs were child-librarian oriented and did not provide child-parent-librarian interaction.[33]

The 1960s

The Great Society was launched in the mid-sixties. Government reforms were enacted to offset cultural deprivation caused by racial and sexual discrimination. The main benefit of direct government intervention in childcare was revitalized interest in lower income families. The better known programs to offset cultural deprivation were: Title I of ESEA (Elementary and Secondary Education Act), Head Start, and Title XX of the Social Security Act.

Passed in 1965, ESEA Title I was established within public school jurisdictions to provide remedial education services for children from preschool to high school, with the heaviest emphasis within the elementary school. This program constituted the second largest federal contribution to the public schools after the school lunch program. Its goal was primarily academic remediation to offset the effects of culturally disadvantaged backgrounds.

Head Start, begun in 1965, was a comprehensive childcare program for preschoolers covering concerns for health, nutrition, cognitive development, and social skills. Essentially community based, it required substantive parent participation. Head Start provided socialization, reading competence, and shared acculturalization.

While such programs were offered by public agencies other than libraries, their services directly impacted library services. Many of the early preschool efforts of the sixties had not focused on the parental role, an omission rectified by specialists in the late sixties. The results of many of the early intervention efforts indicated a relationship between high parent involvement and positive results.

This correlation reinforced parent education as a viable component of programs during the 1970s. The evaluation of these same programs was based on earlier methodology: cognitive development.[34] Many researchers felt that the home environment was the single most influential factor on the socialization and cognitive development of children.[35]

The National Advisory Commission on Libraries Study, *Libraries at Large,* reported that elementary school children were the heaviest users of public libraries. Further, parents with two children were equally distributed among light and moderate users of the public library. These parents were likelier to check out materials while accompanying a child to the library.[36] The inclusion of parents within the research literature had reintroduced the adult factor into childcare.

The 1970s

Changing societal mores (the higher divorce rate, sexual revolution, unwed motherhood) during the seventies brought the family as a unit under observation. The breakdown of the traditional family unit caused policymakers to take more than a casual interest regarding public policy and the family.[37]

A number of groups, such as the National Research Council's Advisory Committee on Child Development and the Carnegie Council on Children, advocated the development of a national family policy. Numerous other groups opposed such policies, claiming that "it would impose a single set of standards" on family life. The Child and Family Services Act of 1975 was defeated (S.626 and H.R.2996), partially because of fears that the government would interfere with the family's privacy. The stance taken during the War on Poverty in the sixties was to initiate the program first, then to establish research methodology for evaluative results.[38] Unfortunately, this approach did not anticipate evaluation of intrusive effects from direct intervention programs.

One model to provide diversity within parent education programs was the community compatible ideal. Communities would be asked to be responsible for the support and nurturance of families within the existing parameters of the local area. The PCDC (Parent-Child Development Centers) experiment provided the framework for this program. The program was born in the early seventies under the auspices of the Office of Economic Opportunity (OEO). The difference with the PCDC was that adult development and growth was a core concept, emphasizing the fact that parents may change their styles and beliefs over time to suit their needs. The program was comprehensive in nature, focusing on the entire family environment instead of the child. Service referrals to other professionals (i.e., doctors and counselors) were provided.[39]

A 1978 NCLIS user study evaluated needs for parents, homemakers, and women. Marcia J. Bates reported that the objectives outlined were in order of expected implementation: information and referral service and dissemination of "life information" as prepared by the appropriate agencies.[40] Public libraries, by and large, met these needs. At the time of the survey no statistics had been compiled on the ratio of parents to total library clientele.

Services to parent groups became identified as the province of the children's librarian or school librarian. Benne noted that children's and adult librarians used different methods to attract users.[41] The adult services librarian used community analysis to determine collection development; the children's librarian used the library program. Children's librarians needed to readjust their perception of the parent as an integral part of the child served.[42] This particular aspect of parent education, parents and their impact on offspring, had been submerged for more than twenty years by researchers and policy-makers alike.

Due to the results of child intervention programs initiated during the latter part of the sixties, public libraries reinstituted services geared for young children (aged three to five) and their parents during the seventies. Many early childhood programs were offered in public education facilities. An early childhood specialist program for librarians was developed at the University of North Carolina at Greensboro during 1971/72, designed to teach librarians to aid parents as facilitators of their children's cognitive (learning) and social skills. The parent involved was usually a young mother of eighteen to twenty-five years of age.[43]

Title XX of the Social Security Act, mandated in 1974, provided funding for states to plan and support various social services, including childcare and parent education. Title XX was intended to enable welfare families to become self-sufficient.[44]

A central goal of children's services is to encourage reading at a young age, and several federal efforts reinforced reading programs for young children. Storytelling, book use, and library visits were an important part of the Head Start program.[45] The prime objective of the Right to Read program (1970s) was to promote reading as a lifelong activity through the cooperative efforts of librarians, parents, and schools. The Reading Is Fundamental (RIF) program was another service designed to offset cultural and economic deprivation while providing books to youngsters and adults alike. RIF was targeted at the school-age child, but materials used at home were intended to foster reading readiness by other family members.[46]

RIF and Head Start were aimed at preventing illiteracy. Intervention methods progressed from child-oriented to parent-child-professional— oriented. The evaluations of these programs supplied the impetus to integrate parent education with the established child intervention programs already in place within communities.

The U.S. General Accounting Office concluded in 1979 that parent and family education programs that focused on illiteracy prevention would be a good investment.[47] However, Florin found that when parent education programs were evaluated, the most numerous group served was the middle class.[48]

Parent education has been considered a nonformal education program. In *Learning to Be Parents*, Harman and Brim asserted that a lack of systematic effort to identify and assemble data on the numerous parent education activities has created great difficulty assessing and determining the characteristics of participants.[49]

Adult education programs are the framework of parent education programs. Most participation in adult education is job-related, but the second largest category is in personal or family interest areas.[50] Harman has stated that among this group parent education could be assumed significant. Of 11 percent of all adults who participated in adult education activities, nearly 15 percent were enrolled in activities concerned with family and personal issues. A majority of parents capable of reading at appropriate levels had access to relevant print sources on childcare and family. The largest group of participants consisted of people who read printed, distributed materials.[51]

The provision of books to parents constitutes a major contribution to parent education, so that parents have a variety of information sources available on child rearing. Several different approaches were used by social service workers to provide a basis for parent information needs. A survey undertaken by Sparling and Lowman on parent information needs used several related concepts: preference in information sources and interest in information topics became two categories.[52] Under preferred sources, books rated third in the percentile of first-choice options after (1) families and friends, and (2) nurses and doctors. Books were in the top percentile rating for second and third choice as an information source. The source versus content question (preferred sources depending upon content of information need) showed that among sources on child development, doctors and nurses received a 39 percent rating and books received a 20 percent rating, making these the primary information sources. The "how to teach children" content area was split evenly between "books" and "family and friends" as second choice. Knowledge of preferred information access modes, and not just the types of information needed, is imperative for effective library service and programming.[53]

Lowell A. Martin stated,

> Will libraries anticipate needs growing out of social trends and while holding to their essential role, organize and focus special programs for identified groups? Libraries should long have had separate and vital home and family sections—treating a fundamental institution in the society as a unit—and the need, if anything, is greater.[54]

The 1980s and the ASE Data

As we have seen, the family unit has changed since the beginning of the century. The fastest growing family type currently is the single-parent (usually the mother) household, and frequently these are poor households. Children, particularly preschoolers, have become the largest disadvantaged age group in the United States. In 1984, more than 20 percent of all U.S. children, 13.3 million children, were living in poverty. The 1984 child poverty rate of 21.3 percent was higher than that of 1964, and for young black children it was the highest rate ever—over 51 percent.[55]

Social indicators show that the number of parents who are not able to cope financially, physically, or mentally is on the rise.[56] Many parents experience loss of control with family decisions while experiencing "information overload" from varied sources.[57]

Both Title XX and ESEA Title I programs had funding levels reduced significantly after early evaluations of the programs. ESEA Title I received numerous criticisms related to implementation and effectiveness during its first five years of operation. The federal government's intrusion into education usurped state and local prerogatives. Title I's main fault was ineffectual parental participation. Title XX was a cash assistance program and encouraged the broadening of its scope of services. In 1981, when Title XX became the Social Services Block Grant, the program changed to a revenue sharing base and states were no longer required to provide 25 percent matching funds to receive federal funding. As a result, thirty-two states cut their funding base for Title XX services.[58] By 1983, childcare funding was reduced to $623 million and an additional $200 million earmarked for training and development of caregivers was eliminated.[59]

The continuation of Head Start through the 1980s provided a comprehensive child development program geared for low income families.[60] Parent education was targeted as an integral part of Head Start almost since its inception. Head Start grew from a $96.4 million program in 1964 to a $1.1 billion program in 1985. Despite Head Start's program innovations, not all children eligible for these services participated in the program. Estimates placed the total number of children served at 2.7 million, or 20 percent of those eligible. The freeze placed on many federal program monies reduced the number of children served by 19,000 during the 1986 fiscal year.[61]

According to the evidence of various researchers, the previous programs did not warrant establishing a federally supported program.[62] The conclusion given by Clarke-Stewart stated:

> Before we expand our parent education efforts in this era of scarce resources, I suggest we make sure we've got our facts straight. Support for parent education will inevitably come at the expense of other social programs; we need to make sure we make the most of our limited opportunities for social change. We will not get away for long with promising outcomes we can't deliver. . . .[63]

This radical shift of funds has become dubbed the New Federalism. According to Ornstein, what evolved were four basic and broad trends in federal education policies: (1) a shift from human and social or educational concerns to business and military interests; (2) a reduction in federal funds for education; (3) the growing demise of egalitarianism as a national policy; and (4) an increase in federal programs that coincide with national need.[64] The continuation of the family unit has been a major concern of policymakers. Their concern rises from the interlinking of families with occupation, education, government, homes, and the economy. Acknowledgment of this concern caused the formation of the U.S. House of Representatives Committee on Children, Youth, and Families in 1983.

The Public Library Association established an ad hoc committee for Preschool Services and Parent Education in 1972 that soon became an official committee. Other divisions of the American Library Association that focus on children include: Association for Library Service to Children (ALSC—formerly Children's Services Division), American Association of School Librarians (AASL), and Young Adult Services Division (YASD). These divisions relate to the varying age groups served by parent education as part of the total library community services.[65]

The 1981 symposium *Reading and Successful Living: The Family-School Partnership* listed numerous principles and recommendations for service professions.[66] The seventy-two numbered recommendations targeted actions for the local community and at state levels.

Nine national recommendations for implementation followed. These proposals were aimed at increasing interaction and cooperation between families, schools, and public institutions such as the library. Verne Duncan also stated,

> With the importance of the parent and family firmly established in the educational process, attention must be turned to harnessing the immense influence of the home to a positive educational end—teaching the parent to teach.[67]

Clarke-Stewart's surveys determined that young women with relatively high levels of formal education expecting their first child or engaged in infant care formed the bulk of library users of childcare literature.[68] Harman and Brim stated, "libraries and books in general could hardly expect to attract parents who cannot read with sufficient ability or for whom reading is not a customary activity."[69] Jonathan Kozol's illiteracy estimates reinforce these concerns. According to Kozol, 37 percent of adults under age twenty-one do not read books at all. He also states that many parents, due to reading deprivation, are unable to conform to societal mandates regarding their offspring's educational needs.[70]

Recent popular periodicals of 1988 reinforce the importance of parent education upon the lifelong reading habits of their children. Literacy, adult education, and parent education are so closely interwoven that programs for one group directly affect another group.

The librarian's service to the child provides a rationale for total family programming in the library. The value of lifelong learning is impressed on children when they accompany their parents or caregivers to the library.[71] In fact, several public libraries provided exemplary family service programs.[72]

Efforts to address the needs of parents for education on how to help their children learn have centered on workshops for parents of very young children with the aim of fostering interaction among parents, children, and library professionals. Examples of such efforts have been documented by the Middle Country Public Library (MCPL) in Centereach, New York,[73] and the Ames, Iowa, Public Library.[74]

The Ames Public Library program is designed to help parents read aloud effectively and provide educational experiences for their children. Puppetmaking and effective reading skills for parents are just two of the workshop topics. In addition, the staff wrote a parent education booklet with information on resource guides and an annotated list of recommended children's books for sharing with their youngsters. This program also involved a wide variety of community groups.[75]

The MCPL effort, involving numerous community groups, service organizations, and nine other Suffolk County libraries in the Librarian's Alliance for Parents and Children serves almost 1500 families per year. Their workshop is conducted in five-week sessions, one session per week, and is limited to twenty-two families per session. The reasons cited for the success of the MCPL program are "room design and environment, a willing staff, access to community resource professionals, and enough financial support to properly initiate and continuously run the program."[76]

Many public libraries have several factors inhibiting their participation in such services: diminished funding base, lack of trained personnel, reduced information and referral services, and duplication of programs offered by other agencies. However, according to the following data from the Adult Services in the Eighties (ASE) survey, over one-third offer services with parents as the primary targeted audience.

Question 37g of the ASE Survey, "does your library organize programming for parents?" found 1,587 positive responses (37.7 percent). Table 1 demonstrates regional dispersal.

The ASE survey confirmed findings conducted by other professions. Based on demographic information, the white population was the group best served. Although a state-by-state breakdown for parent education was compiled from survey results, it was determined to be statistically inconclusive for comparative purposes.

Specific programs were listed by respondents on the third page of the survey. The programs provided tended to center on motivating parents to encourage children to read, but there was also a great variety of others. The majority of parent education programs took place during scheduled story hours for children, and the usual participants were listed as young mothers.

Some of the types of parent education offered included effective parenting workshops, day care information exchanges, family nutrition workshops, baby sitter referral centers, child abuse prevention and awareness films and seminars, and parental stress management classes. These programs appear to make use of community resources

Table 1. REGIONAL PROVISION OF PARENT EDUCATION SERVICES.

REGION	PROVIDE	
	NUMBER	PERCENT
North	314	48.8
South	503	31.8
Central	410	40.6
West	396	36.8

such as mental health centers, county extension services, and many others. One such program listed by the Newport, Rhode Island, Public Library was called "Magic Years—Information Fair for Parents." It is an ongoing effort in cooperation with various family service agencies, providing information, brochures, and programs to an average 353 attendants.

Conclusion

It appears from recent additions to the literature that parent education efforts are being revived as a result of the media attention devoted to widespread adult illiteracy. Many experts feel that the only successful program to address illiteracy is to stop it before it starts. But parenting is more than teaching children an appreciation for books. Parents need more and different kinds of information to be successful parents. The Public Library Association (PLA) gives the following list of information needs of parents that should be addressed by public library programs and services:

1. General parenting information
2. Information on food, shelter, jobs, and medical care
3. Survival skills information for their children
4. Information on child care and afterschool activities for their children
5. Information on ways the library can and cannot help them.[77]

To meet these needs, PLA has challenged librarians to be creative and innovative in trying to reach parents with hectic lifestyles. Some of their recommendations include collections for parents in the children's section, mailing information directly to homes, sending brochures to schools for children to take home to their parents, distributing brochures at shopping malls or in churches, librarians giving speeches outside the library, and providing information through print or broadcast media.[78]

The need for parent education is evident every day in news stories about child abuse, latchkey children, children living in poverty, poor school performance, drug abuse, illiteracy, and runaways. Professionals in fields such as psychology, medicine, and education have long tried to convey the message that education in these areas is the key to prevention. Given that the library is in a unique position to coordinate information providers with public needs, libraries and librarians should play a vital role in parent education.

Despite some obstacles such as funding, libraries do have resources to work with and facilities in which to provide parent education services using available resources and proper planning. The nineties should provide the public libraries with a renewed purpose and focused service.

Notes

1. Jean Carter, *Parents in Perplexity* (New York: George Grady Pr., 1938), p. 9.
2. Steven Schlossman, "Formative Era in American Parent Education," in *Parent Education and Public Policy*, eds. Ron Haskins and Diane Adams (Norwood, N.J.: Ablex, 1983), pp. 8–9.
3. Carter, *Parents in Perplexity*, pp. 45-48.
4. Steven Schlossman, "Before Home Start: Notes toward a History of Parent Education, 1897–1929," *Harvard Educational Review* 46 (August 1976): 452.
5. Schlossman, "Before Home Start," pp. 450–451.
6. Robert Ellis Lee, *Continuing Education for Adults through the American Public Library, 1833–1964* (Chicago: ALA, 1966), p. 42.
7. U.S. Department of Interior, Bureau of Education, *Parent Education*, Bureau of Education Bulletin no. 15 (Washington, D.C.: GPO, 1929), pp. 1–4.
8. Paul R. Florin and Paul R. Dokecki, "Changing Families through Parent and Family Education: A Review and Analysis," in *Changing Families*, eds. Irving E. Siegel and Luis M. Laosa (New York: Plenum, 1983), p. 31.
9. Ibid.
10. David A. Shannon, *Twentieth Century America: The United States since the 1890s* (Chicago: Rand McNally, 1963), pp. 256–257, 273, 285.
11. Sidney H. Ditzion, "Democratic Strivings–Arsenals of Democratic Culture: A Social History of the American Public Library Movement in New England and the Middle States from 1850 to 1900," in *Public Librarianship: A Reader*, ed. Jane Robbins-Carter (Littleton, Colo.: Libraries Unlimited, 1982), p. 56.
12. Schlossman, "Formative Era," p. 11.
13. Ibid., pp. 13–14.
14. Ibid.
15. *ALA Bulletin* 15 (January 1921): 18.
16. Margaret E. Monroe, *Library Adult Education: The Biography of an Idea* (New York: Scarecrow, 1963), pp. 28–32.
17. Lee, *Continuing Education*, p. 40.
18. Monroe, *Library Adult Education*, pp. 28–32.
19. U.S. Department of Interior, *Parent Education*, p. 19.
20. John Chancellor, *Helping Adults to Learn* (Chicago: ALA, 1939), p. 153; Monroe, *Library Adult Education*, p. 42; Carter, *Parents in Perplexity*, p. 117.
21. Carter, *Parents in Perplexity*, p. 117.
22. John J. Dempsey, *The Family and Public Policy: The Issue of the 1980s* (Baltimore: Paul H. Brookes Publishing, 1981), p. 21.
23. U.S. Congress; House Committee on Children, Youth, and Families, *The Diversity and Strength of American Families* (Washington, D.C.: 99th Congress, First Session, 1986), p. 32–37.
24. Shannon, *Twentieth Century America*, p. 394.

25. American Library Association, "Parent Education Joint Committee," *ALA Bulletin* 35 (October 1940):128–131.
26. American Library Association, "Parent Education Round Table," *ALA Bulletin* 35 (October 1939):144–148.
27. Ellen C. Lombard, "Parent Education's First 10 Years," *School Life* 21 (1936): 148.
28. Dempsey, *The Family and Public Policy*, p. 21.
29. Elizabeth M. Smith, "The Public Library Contributes to Parent Education," *Library Journal* 71 (October 1946): 1427–1432.
30. Don Lacy, "Social Change and the Library, 1945–1980," Libraries at Large (New York: Bowker, 1969), p. 3.
31. Marguerite Baechtold and Eleanor Ruth McKinney, *Library Service for Families* (Hamden, Conn.: Shoe String, 1983), pp. 37–38.
32. Irving E. Siegel and Luis M. Laosa, *Changing Families* (New York: Plenum, 1983), p. 35.
33. Ann D. Carlson, *Early Childhood Literature Sharing Programs in Libraries* (Hamden, Conn.: Shoe String, 1983), pp. 5–7.
34. Florin and Dokecki, *"Changing Families,"* p. 38.
35. Nicholas Hobbs et al., *Strengthening Families* (San Francisco: Josey-Bass, 1984), p. 134.
36. National Advisory Commission on Libraries, "Insight into Adult Public Library Use and Nonuse as Suggested by a Social Survey of Attitudes," in *Libraries at Large* (New York: Bowker, 1969), pp. 69–77.
37. Hobbs, *Strengthening Families*, p. 134.
38. Ibid.
39. Paul R. Dokecki, Edwin C. Hargrove, and Howard M. Sandler, "An Overview of the Parent-Child Development Center Social Experiment," in *Parent Education and Public Policy*, eds. Ron Haskins and Diane Adams (Norwood, N.J.: Ablex, 1983), pp. 80–83.
40. Marcia J. Bates, "Library and Information Services for Women, Homemakers, and Parents," in *Library and Information Needs of the Nation*, Proceedings of the National Commission on Libraries and Information Science (Washington, D.C.: NCLIS, 1978), pp. 129–140.
41. Mae Benne, "Educational and Recreational Services of the Public Library for Children," *Library Quarterly* 48 (Winter 1978): 500–501.
42. Ron Haskins and Diane Adams, eds., *Parent Education and Public Policy* (Norwood, N.J.: Ablex, 1983), p. 356.
43. Tommie M. Young, "Libraries and Parent Education Programs," in *Start Early for an Early Start*, ed. Ferne Johnson (Chicago: ALA, 1976), pp. 128–140.
44. Hobbs, *Strengthening Families*, pp. 183–184.
45. Jane Granstrom, "Families in Reading," in *Start Early for an Early Start*, ed. Ferne Johnson (Chicago: ALA, 1976), p. 120.
46. Hobbs, *Strengthening Families*, p. 196.
47. D. A. Duffy, "Findings of a National Study on Early Childhood and Family Development," as presented to Congress and cited by Irving E. Siegel and Luis M. Laosa, *Changing Families* (New York: Plenum, 1983), pp. 57–58.
48. Paul R. Florin, *New Models, New Modes*, Vanderbilt University: unpublished manuscript, 1980, as cited by Irving E. Seigel and Luis M. Laosa, *Changing Families* (New York: Plenum, 1983), p. 57.
49. David Harman and Orville G. Brim, Jr., *Learning to Be Parents* (Beverly Hills, Calif.: Sage, 1980), p. 99.

50. Ibid., pp. 100–101.
51. Ibid.
52. Sparling and Lowman, "Parent Information Needs," in *Parent Education and Public Policy*, eds. Ron Haskins and Diane Adams (Norwood, N.J.: Ablex, 1983), pp. 317–320.
53. Ibid.
54. Lowell A. Martin, "Demographic Trends and Social Structure," *Library Trends* 27 (Winter 1979): 273–281.
55. Sylvia Ann Hewlett, Alice Ilchman, and John J. Sweeney, eds., *Family and Work: Bridging the Gap* (Cambridge, Mass.: Ballinger, 1986), pp. 1–5.
56. Baechtold and McKinney, *Library Service for Families*, pp. 34–35.
57. Ibid., p. 65.
58. Hobbs, *Strengthening Families*, p. 192.
59. Hewlett, Ilchman, and Sweeney, *Family and Work*, pp. 70, 106–115.
60. Hobbs, *Strengthening Families*, p. 196.
61. Hewlett, Ilchman, and Sweeney, *Family and Work*, pp. 106–115.
62. Haskins and Adams, *Parent Education*, pp. 351–369.
63. K. Alison Clarke-Stewart, "Exploring the Assumptions of Parent Education," in *Parent Education and Public Policy*, eds. Ron Haskins and Diane Adams (Norwood, N.J.: Ablex, 1983), p. 257.
64. Allan C. Ornstein, "The Changing Federal Role in Education," *American Education* (December 1984): 4–7.
65. Dorothy M. Broderick, *Library Work with Children* (New York: Wilson, 1977), pp. 112–123.
66. Lester Asheim, D. Philip Baker, and Virginia Matthews, *Reading and Successful Living: The Family-School Partnership* (Hamden, Conn.: Shoe String, 1983), pp. 127–131.
67. Ibid., pp. 15–16.
68. Clarke-Stewart, as cited by Harman and Brim, *Learning to Be Parents*, p. 107.
69. Harmon and Brim, *Learning to Be Parents*, p. 110.
70. Jonathan Kozol, *Illiterate America* (New York: Plume, 1986), pp. 17, 57–71.
71. Baechtold and McKinney, *Library Service for Families*, pp. 155–156.
72. Sandra Feinberg, "The Parent/Child Workshop: A Unique Program," *School Library Journal* (April 1985): 38–40; Gail Teriwillinger, "A Sampling of Parent Education Programs," *Public Libraries* 23 (Summer 1984): 54–55; Kathy Sheehan, "Family Library Service through Programming—Suffolk's Way," *The Bookmark* 43 (Fall 1984): 3–7.
73. Sandra Feinberg, "The Parent/Child Workshop: A Unique Library Program for Parents and Babies," *Public Libraries* 24 (Winter 1985): 143–145.
74. Carol Elbert, "Parents, Kids, and Books: A Literature Workshop for Parents of Preschoolers," *Illinois Libraries* 67 (January 1985): 80–82.
75. Ibid.
76. Feinberg, "The Parent/Child Workshop," p. 143.
77. Service to Children Committee, Public Library Association, "Latchkey Children" in *The Public Library: A Position Paper* (Chicago: ALA, May 1988), p. 37.
78. Ibid.

CHAPTER 14

The Role of Public Access
Microcomputers in Adult Services

Anthony E. Barnes

The provision of microcomputer services to adult users of public libraries is an area of rapidly growing importance and concern. Unfortunately, the recency of the development of microcomputer technology makes it difficult to provide the depth of analysis that is possible in assessing the role of the public library in providing other services to the adult community. Beyond growth in isolated instances, a mature body of knowledge, agreement on needs, and outlook for future programs are limited. The forces that shape the role of public access microcomputers are continually shifting, and the future can be expressed in numerous and differing scenarios.

Within a comparatively short time, society has accepted the computer as a basic tool for serving an extensive range of needs. A new age of information has evolved; this age is inextricably tied to the computer, and for many individuals the means to unlock new information resources is the microcomputer. The need to provide microcomputer services in public libraries is easily defendable. Figures from 1985 indicated that 12.5 percent of U.S. households owned microcomputers, with another 10 percent identified as prospective buyers in the near future.[1] These figures were probably underestimates, and current figures would surely indicate a much higher incidence of personal ownership of personal computers. Availability of microcomputers in schools and work places must raise the number of households for which a microcomputer is in some way accessible to a substantial majority of the U.S. population.

Despite continual expansions of computer capability and growth of use, there is a substantial segment of society to whom the technology is not available and who are not directly benefiting from microcomputers. This segment consists primarily of adults whose line of work does not necessitate or allow contact and training in microcomputer technology and

424

applications, and who do not have the financial resources necessary for acquiring their own computers. The children of these same people probably have access to microcomputers and receive education in their use in the school environment, and accept the computer as just another tool. Adults with adequate financial means or who work with computers as part of their work will not be left behind, for they may meet and acknowledge the technology in work or on their own time, perhaps at the insistence of their computer literate school children.

Those left behind by a lack of access to new technology are those the public library can best serve. If the library can establish programs that allow these adults the opportunity to gain that initial experience with a computer in an environment that is open, educational, supportive, and nonthreatening, the good that may result will be of immense and immediate value. A further extension of the same ideal is of even grander design: assisting patrons in learning a new technology may allow them to apply the newly gained skills to better their own lives. This is a lofty and presumptuous thesis, but not without substantiation in the present library setting.

In addition to the value of service to the community, public access microcomputers are beneficial to the library itself. The news media is still in a stage of great fascination with computers, and will usually provide valuable public exposure, particularly if the library appears to be doing something unusual or innovative. As a reaction to this publicity, a segment of the community who have not made use of the public library before will find reason to visit, and may be introduced to other services previously available but overlooked.

The goals of a public access microcomputer project can be divided into three general classes. Computer literacy, a term difficult to define to any precise degree, is an important objective. A second broad goal is to allow access to computers, perhaps for the first time, as an introduction that may inspire patrons to continue learning about microcomputers and perhaps encourage them to invest in microcomputers for themselves. A third goal is allowing patrons access to a circulating software collection that can be used to perform specific tasks on computers either in the library or for use at home on the patrons' own equipment.[2] This third goal may be accompanied by the availability of microcomputer hardware for circulation to patrons.

Within this statement of goals, a number of factors exist that make such services difficult to develop for the typical community made up of very different people with very different microcomputer needs. Unlike many library programs, the provision of microcomputer services must represent an ongoing, constant commitment: "a micro project never 'ends' in the same way that a series of movies, a book talk, or a lecture end."[3] Julien has presented a review of some of the factors that will need to be addressed before attempting to offer such services to the public.[4] One factor is community needs, which involves the many differing computer literacy skills that can be identified. These skills can include programming skills (the creation of computer instructions to perform a task), expertise on a variety of different machines and their very different operational languages and commands, and the use of a variety of major commercial applications packages for complex tasks.[5]

Another factor has to do with the limitations of the equipment made available in the library. Any microcomputer system may seem excessively complex and beyond the needs of a beginner, just as a small beginner's system will not satisfy the advanced user.[6]

The site at which hardware, software, and training are provided will greatly influence success in reaching the greatest segment of the community. Julien has suggested that nonlibrary sites may be better than libraries in some instances,[7] and includes a list of sites where public access microcomputer programs have been conducted, including computer stores, museums, and other nonlibrary sites.[8]

In closing his arguments, Julien states firmly the necessity of planning and evaluating the need for a public access program and accurately assessing the extent to which the library can offer useful assistance.[9] The pressure from within the library and from the outside may be strong enough to cause the administration to say "yes" to a program when a careful examination of what the library is capable of offering would result in a decision of "no".[10] The opposite, of course, is also possible. The emphasis in deciding on a public access microcomputer project should be on making the decision that is most useful and most practical from the point of view of the library's constituency, not on bending to political pressures.

An Evolutionary History of the Microcomputer

The microcomputer is the product of a remarkably short evolution. Computers of any kind have been commercially available for only about thirty-five years. The UNIVAC I in its role as the first commercial mainframe computer led to later generations of mainframes by Honeywell, General Electric, Burroughs, IBM, and Sperry Rand.[11] In 1961, Digital Equipment Corporation produced the first sixteen-bit minicomputer, somewhat slower than the mainframes, but at much lower cost, allowing its application to smaller tasks. Solid state components in 1965 led to a much more serviceable and dependable technology.

The microcomputer became possible with the 1971 introduction of the microprocessor by INTEL Corporation.[12] These early four-bit processors were not very powerful, but brought some computing power into the hands of people who could not afford the very high costs of "real" computers. As the technology of the microchip developed, the microcomputer became smaller, better, cheaper, and, most important, common. During these times, the microcomputer was viewed by society as a device capable of what they were most used for: powering handheld calculators and video games.

Four-bit processors were replaced by eight-bit units by the late 1970s. The added power and speed were critical in the acceptance of microcomputers as serious business tools.[13] The Apple II computer is often regarded as the first serious microcomputer. Although the Apple was certainly not the first commercially available microcomputer and had rivals from the outset, its packaging and marketing produced a position of great market strength. The introduction of the Apple and its rivals fostered a vision of the microcomputer as something far beyond a simple calculator or game-playing device.[14] The first commercially available microcomputers had considerable appeal in environments that had suffered from a lack of access to larger computers, and quickly became nearly ubiquitous in some settings, such as elementary and secondary schools.

The acceptance of the microcomputer within the library community has lagged behind much of society and certainly has lagged far behind the educational and academic communities. The role played in the automation of library processes by such institutions as the Library of Congress, bibliographic utilities, large university libraries, and vendors of turnkey system automation equipment has encouraged individual libraries to avoid developing their own in-house computerized systems.[15] In libraries with budget cutbacks and additional pressure for services, however, manual systems of library operations have been studied for ways in which micros can be efficiently utilized. Resistance was perhaps overcome in 1981 with the introduction of new microcomputers by mainstream computing corporations such as IBM, Xerox, and DEC.[16] With the entry into the market of names known and respected by librarians, a new optimistic outlook developed about the role of microcomputers in libraries.

Financing Computers in the Library

The costs involved in establishing a public access microcomputer center are not small. The list of needed supplies is extensive and includes not only the computer itself, but also expansion equipment, furniture, cables, peripheral equipment (disk drives, modems, printers), security systems, documentation, literature on computing, and more. Continued funding will also be needed as maintenance and repair costs need to be considered. In addition, a successful program will result in the creation of a base of computer users who will expect the library to move with them into more complex computer procedures. Broader ranges of software will be desired by patrons as their level of skill increases. Also, as microcomputer technology continues to evolve, patrons will expect to see technological improvements reflected in public access equipment in such areas as increased memory capacity and faster computing speed.

The state of budgets in most public libraries has been such that a substantial percentage has not been available for microcomputers. For many libraries, the best means of procuring funds for the establishment of services has been through outside agencies. An approach that has worked for a number of libraries has been to request funding from a Friends of the Library group. A request for a complete system plus maintenance and costs over time is a large request to most Friends organizations, however, and a library operating at less than optimum funding may prefer to exploit its Friends group for continuing existing basic services rather than for investing in a new and uncertain endeavor. Furthermore, libraries with poor budgets are frequently found in communities with poor resource bases, and the availability of funds from a Friends group in such a community may be as limited as the availability of funds for the library's regular budget.

A second source for equipment is donations by corporations or private individuals. The best example of corporate support and donations is the story of ComputerTown USA!, in Menlo Park, California, which led to a very successful national computer program.[17] Apple Computer, Tandy Corporation, and Atari have all supported public access programs. Betty Costa and Marie Costa offer suggestions and strategies for approaching these companies with innovative educational projects.[18]

It may be possible to enter into agreements with local computer stores and arrange for a public access system to be set up free to the library. Individual contracts may be needed in such instances, dealing with signs indicating the donor corporation and also clauses dealing with sole rights to display equipment in the library.[19] The benefits and problems of such an arrangement need to be examined on an individual basis.

Software can be defined as the coded instructions to the computer on how to interpret information, and can be contained in different physical forms such as cartridges, cassette tapes, and most often, floppy disks. Software may be procured on a similar basis to that of computing hardware. Public domain software that is available for duplication at no cost can be located easily, but a serious evaluation and debugging program may be needed before entering it into the software library.[20] Patrick Dewey presents a valuable list of public domain software package producers, consisting of bulk high-quality programs that may do much to round out a software collection at a reasonable cost.[21] Requests may be issued to commercial software producers, with prominent mention made of the public service purpose of the donation. Many producers will gladly agree to contribute software, especially if the result will be exposure to potential customers.[22]

LSCA

A primary source of funding for public access microcomputers can be found through Title I funding (Public Library Services) of the Library Service and Construction Act program (LSCA). Substantial amounts of money have been allocated either on a statewide or systemwide basis for adult microcomputer education.[23] These grants have been the driving force in establishing many of the larger public access microcomputer programs in the country. The New York State Library announced a total of $100,000 of LSCA funds available to local systems for innovative adult computer literacy projects in 1982.[24] The California State Library was involved in sizable LSCA Title I grants to the ComputerTown USA! project.[25] Other major funding sources have also awarded grants for microcomputer projects. The National Science Foundation, for instance, contributed funding for microcomputer projects in the early 1980s.[26] A major impediment to seeking grants for supporting microcomputer projects is that many librarians are unfamiliar with the process of preparing and submitting grant proposals. To that end, Dewey has offered a model grant proposal for public access computer projects.[27]

COIN OPERATED AND PAY SYSTEMS

When the library feels the need to offer a public access microcomputer but does not have the supporting funding, several options exist that will involve a good deal of debate. The cause of this debate can be expressed in one word: fees. The continuing debate over the role of fee-based service in public libraries has not lessened. If the public library's mandate is to provide services to all members of the community on an equal basis, is it acceptable to charge a fee for a public library activity? Does the equal access concept become one of equal access to all that can afford to pay?

The core of the problem in this area is the definition of how important public access microcomputer services are, and whether the need is regarded as so necessary as to allow fee-based equipment into those libraries unable to absorb the full cost of the service. John Smith defines three levels of service. First are profitable enterprises that can pay for themselves (private business). Second are those deemed as socially important enough to be supported by taxation upon the local community (the public library). Third are services within the middle ground involving both subsidies and user fees. Public libraries have entered into service areas of this middle ground.[28]

The paths available to libraries for fee-based systems fall into several categories. The first involves the library purchasing a system and charging a nominal fee for use. The fees charged will be determined by the library, presumably based on expenses involved in the provision of the service, volume of use, and other budgetary factors. A small fee may be assessed that will support the project at a minimal level, or a higher charge that will help the library recoup more of the costs. A survey of the literature reveals usage fees ranging from $1 to $5 per hour for usage, with $3 per hour being the average charge. Patrick Dewey suggests the nominal charge of $1 an hour to prevent discouragement of the disadvantaged patron who needs exposure to the service the most.[29] At this level, the library and the patron more or less split the cost of the system.[30]

One alternative to the library-developed pay system is entering into agreement with a vending company for microcomputer equipment. The agreements fall into two categories. The first involves a leasing arrangement whereby the library is not required to pay at all. A complete outfit will be installed under an arrangement much like that of a vending system photocopier.[31] The vendor receives a high percentage of the collected fees with a minimum monthly guarantee.[32] A library in such an arrangement may adjust the fees with expected usage to generate the needed amount. A second arrangement involves the library either purchasing outright or leasing a fully equipped vending system that can be operated at an hourly cost set by the library.[33] The library can apply the money collected towards the monthly bill from the vending company.

Patron access to any of these systems can be handled by various means. Systems that accept coins and dollar bills offer the least involvement of the library staff in everyday operations, but will offer problems such as vandalism of the equipment. Token-operated systems may ease vandalism problems, but the circulation or reference desk staff takes on the responsibility for issuing tokens and handling cash if a token machine is not in place. Encoded time cards can be used in such systems as those offered by Maxwell Library Systems, whereby cards are purchased and inserted into the timekeeping controller of the microcomputer.[34] The clock keeps track of usage in the session, and any leftover time is available for future use.

With all of these vendor systems, the library is generally given an override function that allows free use of the equipment for library staff.[35] Using the free time, the library staff can become comfortable with the equipment, conduct training classes, become familiar with new software, and do library-oriented tasks.

Microcomputer Equipment Used in Public Libraries

The first reported public use of a microcomputer in a public library occurred in 1977 when a Wang personal computer was connected to a coin operation system from a launderette.[36] Tandy and Apple equipment appear to have been used most often in public libraries, although the dominance of the microcomputer market by IBM-compatible machines has undoubtedly had a substantial impact in recent years.

The Radio Shack TRS-80 line of microcomputers led the market in sales until 1981.[37] Software availability was greater for Tandy equipment than for many early microcomputers, but documentation for earlier Tandy systems was regarded as weak and confusing.[38] Apple Computers assumed sales leadership in 1981.[39] The Apple II series of computers became the most popular computer of its time and continues to dominate some segments of the computer market, although it has been losing ground to other computers, including IBM compatibles and Apple's Macintosh.

The IBM PC was introduced in 1981, and quickly gained great popularity in the business world. IBM has allowed for the licensing of its technology by other manufacturers, a practice not pursued by Apple, and the widespread acceptance of the IBM standard by the business community quickly led to the development of "PC clones" that provide compatibility with the IBM standard, usually at a greatly reduced price. The worldwide product recognition of the IBM name has made it possible for IBM to maintain a firm base in the midst of dozens of immitators, and IBM has continued to set new standards by introducing new product lines.

Apple introduced its innovative Macintosh series in 1984 in an effort to regain ground lost to the IBM compatibles. Promoted as being more "user friendly" than other personal computers, the Macintosh offers an approach to operations that relies on constant visual clues and is very easy to learn. The Macintosh does not as yet appear to have made significant inroads into the general business community, but has become a frequent replacement for older Apples in education and has been

widely accepted for special purposes such as computer-assisted design
and desktop publishing.

The brands of computers most used in public access programs can be
examined by several different methods. The instances of projects reported in the library literature of the last decade can be assumed to be a
reflection of most public access programs. From published reports over
time, there is a nearly even division of reportings of Apple and Radio
Shack usage. The small percentage using neither of these systems is
divided among equipment made by Texas Instruments, Kaypro, Wang,
Apple Macintosh, and IBM. Smaller portable systems are addressed
below in the discussion of the practice of circulating microcomputers.

A second indication of equipment used can be found in a survey of
libraries concerning microcomputer applications conducted by Knowledge Industry Publications in 1984, in which 220 libraries of all types in
the United States and Canada received questionnaires. Of these, twenty-five usable responses were received from public libraries.[40] The poll
revealed information concerning library microcomputer applications in
all fields of usage, including both administrative and public access. The
results indicated that 84 percent of the libraries used Apple equipment,
48 percent used the TRS-80, and 24 percent used IBM.[41] In response to
the question "Is your micro available for public use?" nineteen of the
twenty-five libraries (76 percent) responded "yes."[42] The small number of
responses does not allow any generalizations, but this breakdown of the
computer equipment market seems to be in line with the expected
results.

A third indication can be seen in the program titles listed in the third
page of the ASE survey. The computer-related projects reported were
dominated by introductory classes for use of the Apple IIe computer
system. Other systems mentioned include the TRS-80, the Texas Instruments 99/4a, and the VIC-20.

Use of Microcomputers in Public Access Projects

The potential applications for microcomputers in public access projects
form a lengthy list, and new ideas are developed and implemented daily.
From reported uses in the library literature, an overview of activities
and operating procedures around the country can be developed.

The first application of a public access microcomputer usually is not in a
public place. If a library will be offering a system for public use, the public
service staff first needs a period of training in which to become comfortable
in the operation of the equipment and software. The attitudes of the staff

involved with overseeing operations of the microcomputer are critical. Robert Walton classifies staff attitudes into several categories. The first is indifferent or negative staffer, characterized by open hostility or complete indifference to the project.[43] The second is the positive or normal staffer, who looks forward to learning about the new technology.[44] Third are staffers who are extremely positive.[45] The zeal of this group may lead to unrealistic expectations of the system, and they may sour the program by grumbling about not offering services at a high enough level. It is important in the preaccess program training to get the staff in the proper frame of mind for assisting patrons unfamiliar with systems, without either a negative attitude or an overly exuberant demeanor. A helpful and reassuring attitude fosters an atmosphere for learning a new skill that is frightening to those patrons who have not encountered it before.

Staff training can be conducted by three basic methods. A first method involves training provided by the equipment dealer.[46] A second is the use of persons from within the community who will, either on a volunteer or hired basis, provide more intense personal training of staff.[47] Third, a staff member may possess the expertise to conduct staff classes. Walton states that plenty of hands-on time is what matters the most in staff training.[48] No amount of lecturing on the operation of the microcomputer can take the place of getting comfortable at the keyboard and becoming familiar with basic commands and operations. Walton also offers valuable suggestions on developing staff training programs, including: scheduling training of staff members in pairs for support and help; giving staff plenty of time for keyboard familiarization; avoiding classroom-type lectures; distributing a glossary of the most important computer terms to the staff; and staying away from programming at the early stages.[49]

IN-LIBRARY EQUIPMENT ACCESS

The primary purpose of public access microcomputer services is to provide hardware and software in an environment that will encourage their use by the community. A first consideration in promoting public access is location within the library. Two factors work against each other in deciding whether to place the microcomputer in an open and secure location, or in an isolated, unobserved, but comfortable enclosure. For security and monitoring purposes, an observable location offers the best results. Even in such a location, some security measures should be taken. Locking bolts or harnesses may prevent complete removal of the system, but expensive components (cables, circuit boards) may still be removed if not somehow secured.[50] In addition, the location of the equipment should never be visible from the street.[51]

A second consideration deals with locating the equipment in the most educational setting possible, where it is isolated in an enclosure so that outside distractions will be limited. A centrally located computer may become a gathering point for people who wish to watch, and often disrupt, the user's attention. By placing the equipment in an enclosed area, the noise produced by most computers (software messages, printers) will not interfere with patrons who seek the quiet of the library for study and reading purposes.[52]

In either case, consideration must be given to dealing with the physical design of the library. The system must be located near properly wired (and surge-protected) electrical outlets, away from overpowering sources of glare, and accessible to telephone connections if any online operations are to be used.

Rules and procedures for patron use must be well developed before operations begin. Most libraries demand a brief first-time test of the patron's skill or a brief demonstration or tutorial program to verify basic knowledge of how to operate the system. After passing such a test, the patron often gets a stamp on his or her library card allowing unsupervised access in the future.[53]

Scheduling procedures need to be developed and enforced. Many libraries allow scheduling a week in advance on systems that are popular, and these schedules must be strictly enforced to allow access for all interested parties and for preventing domination of the system by just a few people. Many libraries limit the time each patron may use a system each week if the number of users justifies a limit. Scheduling may also be used to reserve the microcomputer for certain targeted age groups at various times of the week.[54] Quieter times in most public libraries, such as weekday mornings and afternoons, can be utilized to hold adult classes in a more peaceful and relaxed environment.

The cost of use will probably determine demand for the system. When a fee-based system is employed, use will probably be less than on a free system. On the other hand, free systems are frequently overwhelmed with patrons interested in trying them out. Dewey lists eight rules for scheduling that should make the scheduling process more workable.[55] Included are using an official, substantial appointment book for scheduling, noting first-time users who may need personal help in starting out; making appointment cards to prompt patrons to remember their reserved time; enacting penalties for chronic appointment missers; and having a user agreement form signed by the patron acknowledging rules and regulations of the user program.[56] The effort to fill out a form may be enough of a deterrent to keep those patrons not seriously interested in using the equipment (i.e., simply playing with whatever is available) from taking up time that could be used by others who are truly interested in more productive use of the equipment.

Reports of library public access microcomputer experiences are highly favorable, with patron enthusiasm generally very high at the program's inception and remaining reasonably high thereafter. Only a few cases of unenthusiastic public response can be found. Suffolk County, New York, reported good public relations value from the microcomputer, but little adult use of the system.[57] Denver Public Library installed a fee-based system in several branches that failed to generate enough response to please either the library or the vendor.[58]

IN-LIBRARY SOFTWARE ACCESS

The ASE study found that 20.1 percent of public libraries provided software for in-house use. The choice of computer equipment, while not an easy decision, is generally viewed as a one-time process, although there will be an inevitable need to upgrade and replace equipment. The development of a software collection is, however, an ongoing process, and decision factors that accompany it are more problematic. At the start of the software collection procedure, it is necessary to establish a software collection policy. Dewey offers a list of selection criteria that include the following: compatibility with hardware, well-documented support material, value, and instructional soundness if for educational purposes.[59]

A problem that inevitably arises concerns the role of computer games in the library setting. Arcade-type games may promote loitering, noise, and other activities not compatible with the goals of the public access program.[60] One library reports allowing a maximum time for game playing of one half-hour at a time, while other applications receive a full hour.[61] Dewey offers guidelines on selection criteria for games in the software library.[62]

The collection policies for public access libraries run the entire range of treatment of games. One report discusses a strict no games policy.[63] The other side is represented in a report from Liverpool, New York, where the argument is given that since recreational reading and audiovisual materials are collected, recreational software should not be shunned and is allocated one-third of the software budget.[64] Two microcomputers are located in the library, with one machine designated as a no-games station.[65]

The types of software a library collects will vary with the types of patrons expected to use the service. Basic types of software a library will probably collect include programming languages, database management packages, word processors, spreadsheets, and computer literacy instruction programs.[66] This range of offerings is reflected in the findings of a 1984 survey of libraries, which indicated that the top three microcomputer software programs owned by public libraries were Typing Tutor (educational), Bank Street Writer (word processing), and VisiCalc (spreadsheet).[67] Although these specific packages may no longer be the most popular, they represent categories of software of enduring popularity. Librarians may collect a preview software collection, where patrons with home computers can try out new software offerings that they are interested in purchasing for home use.[68]

With the wide range of software available and the unique operational characteristics of each, it is unlikely that all members of the staff will be completely knowledgeable about each piece of software within the collection. It is a good idea, however, for staff to have some exposure to help beginners get started and to solve minor procedural problems as they arise.[69] It may also be wise to have staff members who specialize in certain applications packages who can be referred to for special problems when they arise.

A well-planned use policy governing the in-house use of software is essential. Dewey recommends allowing only three pieces of software to be checked out during any one session, and a deposit of a driver's license or other identification (other than a library card) at the checkout desk to ensure return of the software after use.[70] It is necessary, however, to give some care to such policies so that they are not out of line with policies for other library materials and so that they do not act as an excessive deterrent to use of the software.

Policy must also be set concerning patrons' in-library use of their own software. The same "games or no games" policies developed for library-owned software must be applied to patron-owned software. Damage and theft are constant problems. To limit damage and help prevent theft, some libraries have repackaged software and supporting documentation in more durable packages, with all items except disks security stripped.[71] It is imperative that libraries keep a master copy of each piece of software in an archival collection and circulate only copies, so that if the copy is damaged or lost, another is available. It is also important to educate patrons and staff in the proper handling and use of diskettes and other electronic media.

CIRCULATING HARDWARE

The circulation of computer hardware is an ambitious program that a small number of libraries have chosen. The ASE study indicated that 3 percent of responding libraries offered microcomputers for home use.

An early driving force behind these programs was the introduction of small and relatively inexpensive microcomputers that often sold for less than $100, such as the Timex Sinclair 1000, the Commodore VIC 20, and the Texas Instruments 99/4a, which were frequently chosen for library circulation.[72] These bargain basement computers are no longer available, but the idea of circulating microcomputers has endured, and has even been made somewhat more practical by the introduction of a new breed of laptop microcomputers that are very portable, require no peripheral devices for operation, and are frequently battery powered.

There are several benefits to be gained from the circulation of microcomputer systems. It allows people who cannot come into the library access to equipment. Patrons who would be uncomfortable using a system in the library, perhaps afraid of not being able to deal with the equipment, may show more initiative working on one at home, where failure will not result in the need to admit their inabilities to the library staff. A second factor may work to the library's advantage. If patrons can make use of a small system at home, it will likely result in their desire to work on a more complex machine or additional projects or tasks. Most of the libraries that circulate microcomputers have larger in-house public access systems, and circulating small systems may lead to an increase in in-house equipment use. Another potential use of circulating micros is to reinforce computer lessons taught within the library. This may allow patrons in computer literacy classes to practice what they have learned on home units.

Several programs of this type have been reported, and all work basically the same. The "fee or free" dilemma exists here, also. One library circulated a complete package of needed equipment (computer, TV hookup, joysticks, manual, and two programs) at a charge of $25; $15 is refunded with the return of the equipment after the twelve-day loan period.[73] A second library provided a seven-day loan of a similar package, but without fees.[74]

Reports indicate that the programs have worked well, with little mention of damage or problems. One library reported from completed survey cards that of patrons borrowing the Timex Sinclair 1000 (by far the most popular circulating system at the time), 76 percent indicated a desire to check out the system again.[75]

The same library, along with others, reported decline in circulation of systems over time, which was assumed to be indicative of the success of the program: many of the patrons first exposed to the home computers through the library programs had begun to buy computer systems of their own.[76]

CIRCULATING SOFTWARE

A public library with a collection of circulating software is of value only to those with home computers (unless the library also circulates hardware). Patrons may use software to perform specific tasks with applications packages, to play games, and to make use of instructional programming. The circulation of software may also assist the patron to decide whether or not to purchase similar software.

Two problems need to be addressed at this time. The first is the matter of physical protection for the fragile software. Floppy disks must be gently cared for, and the rigors of circulation are demanding. Thomas Smisek suggests a need for separate return procedures to be developed, because disks returned to book drops will not last long.[77] Doreen Cohen offers suggestions on how to create circulation packages that hold disks and documentation together.[78] A more critical issue in software circulation deals with copyright and piracy of programs. When a patron borrows a valuable piece of software and makes an illegal copy, who is responsible for possible penalties? Dewey states his feelings as "only public domain software can be considered for a software circulation program."[79] When popular and expensive programs are circulated by libraries, the library either needs to reach an agreement with the software producer about the situation or take upon itself the chances of litigation if a patron ignores the "do not copy" label on the software.[80] The legal questions in this matter have not yet been addressed in court, but they will inevitably arise if licensed software is circulated. A detailed discussion of copyright legislation as it pertains to software can be found in a 1984 article in *Louisiana Law Review* by Mary Brandt Jensen.[81] She includes a suggested "softwrite act" as an appendix and a section on distribution rights and obligations as they pertain to libraries.[82]

Computer Classes

The most widely reported programs dealing with public access microcomputers are the teaching of computer classes. The form, size, and construction of these courses vary widely, depending on the goals of each program and the community being served. There are basically three types of computer instruction offered. The first is informal instruction on how to operate the machine. Instruction of this nature is frequently one-on-one at the keyboard, where the basic operations of a computer are discussed and often takes less than fifteen minutes. Frequently, the patron needs to run through a tutorial program, such as "Apple Presents Apple," as part of this introduction.[83]

A second approach to instruction is more organized classroom instruction that, if successfully completed, will allow the patrons to use the system's public access microcomputer. Classes of this nature usually last from one to several hours, but some do require more time. One library reports a six-hour course (four weekly meetings of one-and-a-half hours each) before accrediting the patron for free public access time.[84] Frequently covered topics include microcomputer background information, terminology, capabilities of the system to be used, and actual demonstration. Classes of this nature are generally held at scheduled times, and require registration for attendance.

The third range of services deals with specific programming and applications. Programming languages (particularly BASIC) are often taught in classes, with students taking circulating microcomputers home to practice ideas discussed in class.[85] One library reported signing up and training 300 people in eight weeks of free classes on microcomputer applications for business and home use.[86] The majority of these programs are free, but some lessons offered for fees have been reported. Denver Public Library offered classes in more advanced applications (VisiCalc, PFS:Report) at a cost of $20 per session.[87]

While most courses are taught in the library, there are several reports of efforts to take computers to other locations to teach computer literacy programs. A rural computer literacy program in New York State developed a traveling computer show that sent trained staff to smaller libraries, bookmobile stops, nursing homes, and small businesses to demonstrate computer technology.[88] A similar rural program involves rotating equipment among rural libraries with an option to buy the equipment; if not purchased, the equipment moves to another setting.[89]

There are several approaches to staffing computer courses. In some cases, LSCA funding has included funds set aside for conducting classes.[90] Other methods of instruction reported in the ASE study and the literature include using knowledgeable staff members, guest lecturers from local businesses (frequently salespeople from computer stores), and members of computer clubs who enjoy sharing their knowledge of computers. A computer expert may be hired to train the library staff, if adequate funds are available.[91]

Another approach to computer orientation is to conduct classes targeted at groups that the library feels are at a disadvantage in a large group setting. Westerfield (Ohio) Public Library conducted orientation courses just for older adults, who may be more intimidated by the technology than younger people.[92] Special classes have been conducted in "women only" groups as a result of findings that women tend to be lagging behind in computer literacy, and that a "same sex" class would result in a more relaxed environment.[93] Finally, ethnic groups have been targeted as needing computer exposure, and Lorraine Public Library (Ohio) has placed computers at sites determined to have the greatest contact with ethnic communities.[94]

Assistance to Special Groups

Many special groups can be served well by microcomputer services. One such group deals with literacy, a high priority item for the public library since its inception. Simple educational programs may help an adult learning to read. The verbal capabilities of some newer machines offer the adult a new approach to literacy training. A report in the literature reveals that both the Apple IIe and Macintosh, with voice synthesis programming, can be used effectively to teach the adult patron writing skills through interactive teaching that does not demand an instructor or printed instructions.[95] Libraries have had an important role in assistance to adults in mastering remedial programs, especially GED and Civil Service exams. Several systems report making use of computer programs to help patrons prepare for exams of this type.[96]

A very specialized service has been offered in Rockville, Maryland, to handicapped patrons. Two TRS-80s were dedicated for handicapped users with the use of Handiwriter software and other programs designed for nonverbal and severely handicapped patrons who cannot operate systems in the same manner as other patrons.[97]

Local Databases

Local databases of information that can be effectively searched with a microcomputer have been created on a variety of subjects. Manual files can be transferred to a computerized format that will allow easier access, upkeep and updating functions for the files. A good example is the Native American Information and Referral Center at the Chicago Public Library.[98]

Similar types of information can be purchased in ready-made databases for local access by the patron. An example is the Coordinated Occupations Information Network, a database produced for local access by Bell & Howell and used in the Chicago Public Library by patrons for an assortment of information: school courses, careers, college majors, and an "interest profile" to help the patrons realize possible careers matched to their interests and abilities.[99] A similar database was constructed by the Adult Continuing Education Department at the Forsyth County Public Library in Winston-Salem, North Carolina.[100]

Sponsoring Computer Clubs

A computer club is a group of people who share an interest in computer activity. There has been a trend in the last few years for public libraries to offer their facilities as sites for these meetings. Several advantages to library support and participation can be found. Such cooperation will help to build up a pool of computer-oriented individuals who regularly visit the library. If this pool can be used as volunteers in the public access program, perhaps in exchange for meeting rights, both the library and the club will benefit.[101] The volunteers can be used as computer assistants and for projects such as workshops, classes, and seminars.[102]

A secondary type of computer club is the users group, people bonded together by devotion to a similar type of computer. A users group may be formed from the patrons of the public access computer within the library. An example is the Public Access Microcomputer Users Group (PAMUG) in Illinois, formed in 1983.[103] Two databases are being created by the Public Library Association's Microcomputing Task Force: one will be a directory of libraries' user groups, and another of names of individuals wishing to form groups in their own areas.[104]

Bulletin Boards

An electronic bulletin board is a computer-based system that operates much like a typical bulletin board: participants may place comments, stories, or anything else on the bulletin board for other people to use. It is a means by which the computer owners of a community can communicate with each other using their computer equipment and a central switchboard as a means of linking.

The electronic bulletin board is such a switchboard. Microcomputers link with telephone lines and a central linking microcomputer, the contact point of the bulletin board, which is tended by the systems operator (sysop). The central computer must have some special features: an automatic answering device for incoming communications from users, messaging software, and at least one dedicated telephone line.[105] Due to the potentially high volume of communications, a sizable memory capacity is desirable.

The first step in operating a bulletin board is to find a home for the system. The public library has acted as host on several occasions with great success. A library microcomputer and the appropriate software can be dedicated to this purpose, but it should be recognized that if the bulletin board succeeds, the microcomputer will not be available for other functions. Part-time bulletin boards have been implemented, but usually without much success.[106] Such a system allows the library a powerful, previously untapped avenue for information dispersal. Library information, book reviews, and civic events can all be entered daily into the system.[107]

Dewey discusses the potential services a bulletin board system may provide. A user can read existing messages and leave new messages, either to all registered users or just to specific people. Feature materials and articles can be read. Public domain computer programs can be uploaded and downloaded, or copied by users for their own use. Games, if allowed, can be played online or downloaded.[108] These services allow many potential uses for computer owners. A participant can send a program from his or her computer to the bulletin board, where it can be disseminated to anyone who wishes it. Articles of interest can be submitted for other users either to read online or to download for their own use later. Solutions to common problems can be discussed in a forum atmosphere to reach solutions.

Any electronic bulletin board requires systematic, daily maintenance. Messages to the host from users have to be read and responded to, older material removed, and backup copies of the data made.[109] Maintenance is generally not a difficult task, but it can be quite labor intensive. The role of sysop should be a regular part of an employee's work assignment, not an unscheduled task to be done when time is available.

The number of libraries providing bulletin board systems appears to be expanding rapidly. The best documented system is probably the North-Pulaski (Chicago) Branch Library's People Message System software system, which has evolved into the LINCOLNNET system. Patrick Dewey has been involved with the program and has published numerous articles documenting the effort. His 1986 book describing approaches to creating bulletin boards is titled *Essential Guide to Bulletin Board Systems*.[110]

Other benefits of library bulletin boards include the ability to conduct surveys of system users in an automated mode. The survey form can be entered into the message board. Then the form can be completed by a user online and sent in electronically, or downloaded by the user who can then print any number of copies and distribute them with instructions requesting their return to the library when completed.[111] New library programs can be announced, and registration for such events can be conducted online.[112] Even an online reference service using a bulletin board has been successfully implemented. The Liverpool Public Library in New York implemented an online reference librarian, "Aunt Libby." The goal of Aunt Libby was to answer questions left on the bulletin board within twenty-four hours.[113] The bulletin board system was reported to have been very successful, averaging over 1,000 uses a month.[114]

Online Searching by Library Patrons

Online searching involves accessing a commercially available database for information of the type provided by indexes, abstracting services, directories, or other reference materials. The database itself may be mounted on a large remote access computer located across country and reached via long distance telecommunications, or it may be in the form of a laser disk mounted on a player connected to a microcomputer. Recent developments in online retrieval system design have focused on enhancing ease of use, and many newer searching systems have been designed with the personal computer user in mind.[115] The role of online searching in public libraries has been growing rapidly, and much of the growth has been in the area of end-user searching, in which the patron conducts the inquiry rather than having a librarian act as an intermediary.

Carol Tenopir breaks end-user searching into four approaches: end-user searching systems, front-end software, gateway services, and local databases.[116] The end-user searching systems include BRS/After Dark and DIALOG'S Knowledge Index. These are both scaled-down versions of well-established systems that offer a sampling of the parent system's immense collection of databases. Knowledge Index uses a simplified command language, while BRS/After Dark achieves ease of use through a set of menus.[117]

Front-end software, such as Sci-Mate, ProSearch and Grateful Med, allows the formation of a search strategy before logging onto the system and allows the capture of the information on disk for printing offline.[118] For general purpose searching, the savings achieved through limiting online connect time may pay the cost of such a system over time.[119]

The third type of service is the gateway. These systems connect a user through a host computer to the desired vendors, often with the before-mentioned front-end capability.[120] EASYNET is a prominent example, in which the cost of a search is $8 for up to ten citations in one database.[121] Unlike front-end and end-user searching systems, the library does not need an account with each database used with EASYNET.[122]

Finally, microcomputers can be used to access local databases on floppy disks or compact optical disks (CD-ROM). Floppy disk retrieval systems constitute a failed experiment, but CD-ROM is a rapidly expanding field, and many subject areas are being indexed with CD-ROM systems. CD-ROM systems are particularly appealing to libraries because they replace the widely varying costs associated with online remote access with fixed subscriptions, do not require the use of complex telecommunications routines and passwords, and eliminate telecommunications costs.[123]

The four types of systems Tenopir discusses are basically electronic reference tools. Another approach to online services can be seen in consumer networks, such as CompuServe and The Source. The services available from these systems are basically leisure activities and include booking of airline flights, shopping services, and electronic mail.[124] User profiles can be developed to match people of similar interests, who can then communicate with each other using electronic messaging routines.[125]

Two Model Programs

The microcomputer has been a part of public libraries for a decade now, and a somewhat common public access fixture for the last five years. A great deal of the credit for the spreading of the idea comes from two public access projects that have acted as the role models for other projects. These two programs are ComputerTown USA! and the Personal Computing Center.

COMPUTERTOWN USA!

ComputerTown is a project of the Peoples Computer Company, a non-profit organization.[126] The program had its beginnings in 1979, when two educational authors and computer experts started a program in Menlo Park, California, to allow people access to their computers at local restaurants, bookstores, and the Menlo Park Library.[127] The positive response resulted in the selection of the public library as a permanent site.

Access to the equipment was free to anyone who had received training in how to work the computers. Local computer stores contributed additional computers for the project.[128] After operating for eighteen months on a volunteer basis, the project was awarded a National Science Foundation grant of $224,000 to expand the scope of the project.[129] The goal behind the grant was to allow a model program to be created and the idea disseminated to other locations. A monthly publication, *ComputerTown News Bulletin,* shared successful ideas, events, and projects for other libraries to try.[130] ComputerTown affiliates are all local volunteer organizations operating under loose affiliation with the national organization for support.[131]

After several years of operation and study, a guide based on the Menlo Park experiences was released. The guide offers suggestions on how to best initiate a project and details the best methods to use. The guide was distributed in package form, and later published as *ComputerTown: Bringing Computer Literacy to Your Community.*[132]

The Menlo Park project went through several changes over the years. The levels of noise from the programs caused the game-playing hours from 2:00 to 6:00 p.m. to be eliminated.[133] The ComputerTown Project has expanded to other sites in this country, as well as to England and Germany.[134] The Menlo Park project has been the model project for the West, while the Upper Arlington (Ohio) Public Library has been the model for the East.[135]

In 1984, the Peoples Computer Company and the California State Library received LSCA funding of $500,000 for a statewide computer literacy project.[136] The money was intended to be used to train staff, establish adult computer centers in libraries, and to establish regional resource centers to assist in the training of personnel on equipment funded for in the grant.[137]

NORTH-PULASKI PERSONAL COMPUTER CENTER

A second program that has been highly publicized in the literature is the Personal Computer Center at the North-Pulaski branch of the Chicago Public Library. Patrick Dewey was the librarian there during the beginning of the project in 1981 and has documented the project extensively, giving libraries approaching a public access microcomputer project an idea of the scope of the project and potential pitfalls to be avoided.

The Personal Computer Center was started in 1981, based on a single Apple II + system and accessories supplied by a Friends of the Library grant.[138] The Center continued to grow and developed new services, such as a public domain software collection for users to copy, a software library built largely on donations of over 2,000 programs available for patron use, and seminars on specific applications and programming languages.[139] The computer served double duty by operating the library's electronic bulletin board system during the night and on weekends.[140]

Statistical Information on Public Access Microcomputer Projects

The history of public access microcomputers in public libraries is a short one, and efforts have been made on the national and state level to identify reliable data concerning public access programs. Several states have conducted surveys of public library use of microcomputers, including surveys in Georgia.[141]

Two national surveys that offer some limited data on patron microcomputer usage include the *Knowledge Industry Publications Survey of Microcomputer Use in Libraries* and the *Bowker National Library Microcomputer Usage Study, 1984*. Both surveys dealt primarily with the use of microcomputers in all types of libraries, with some general questions that dealt with public libraries and public access, but the reported figures do not correspond well to the data developed from later surveys. The Knowledge Industry survey involved only twenty-five public libraries.[142] The only public success question asked was, "Is your micro available for public use?" and 76 percent of the public library respondents answered "yes." The survey did not present data dealing with the percentage of libraries that offered public access services.[143]

The Bowker Study was a much larger effort involving 3,500 libraries of all types.[144] This comprehensive study offers an excellent overview of the role of microcomputers in all types of libraries, including the predominant brands of equipment in different types of libraries, future hardware purchase plans, and software application packages most often purchased.[145] Information concerning public access services is represented in the findings, but only in a few instances.

The data gathered from two other surveys, however, allow an excellent statistical study of the range of public access microcomputer programs offered in public libraries in the United States. The first set of data comes from the Adult Services in the Eighties survey, which specifically asked whether libraries offered in-house library microcomputers, in-library software, circulated microcomputers, and circulated software for the public, and whether fees were charged for each service. Over 4,500 public libraries responded, allowing for a national overview of services. With the use of cross-tabulated demographic factors such as community racial makeup, income levels, and population incorporated into the data, services offered by public libraries can be statistically studied.

A second set of data is found in a survey conducted by the Office of Educational Research and Improvement (OERI) "Survey of Patron Use of Computers in Public Libraries."[146] It was conducted during the winter of 1984/85, and results were published in a *Bulletin OERI* format in March 1986. It was conducted using the *Fast Response Survey System,* which used a probability sample of 900 public libraries selected to proportionally represent the public libraries of the nation, and was designed to take a minimum of effort by respondents, resulting in a 99 percent response rate.[147] From the survey responses, all specifically covering public access microcomputers and including demographic information, a set of data that supplements the ASE responses regarding microcomputers is developed.

IN-HOUSE USE OF MICROCOMPUTERS

According to the ASE study, approximately 20 percent of public libraries offered public access microcomputers for use within the library; the OERI study reflected a fairly similar figure of 15 percent. The ASE breakdown of regional responses found a reasonably constant figure in all areas of the country (22 to 24 percent) except for the South, which lagged behind at 13.9 percent. States that offered more in-library microcomputers included Iowa (65.4 percent), Wisconsin (37.7 percent), and New York (65.4 percent). Lower than average responses came from Mississippi (8.2 percent), Louisiana (5.5 percent), and Tennessee (0 percent). OERI regional figures, based on different geographic areas, indicated more libraries offer public access microcomputer services in the West and Southwest (18 percent), with the North Atlantic region lagging behind (13 percent).[148]

Data concerning public access microcomputer projects and population size of the community served by each library are presented in both surveys, but again the divisions are dissimilar, with the ASE study using a four-tiered division (0–25,000; 25,000–40,000; 40,000–80,000; over 80,000) based on library systems rather than on independent library responses. OERI used three levels of population (0–10,000; 10,000–99,999; over 100,000). Such divisions do not make for easy comparisons except for the top end of the scale. OERI figures reveal the tendency for more services to be offered in the highest population ranges (41 percent offering services), compared to the middle population group (23 percent) and the smallest group (10 percent).[149]

Metropolitan status figures are presented throughout the OERI report, defined in terms of rural, suburban, and urban areas. Dramatic differences again appear in this data in regard to population. Urban areas offered by far the most public access microcomputer services (41 percent). Suburban libraries trailed behind (19 percent), and rural libraries were lower still (11 percent).[150]

CIRCULATION OF MICROCOMPUTERS

Approximately 4 percent of the nation's public libraries circulate microcomputers, based on the ASE figure of 3.8 percent and the OERI figure of 4 percent. Regional breakdowns from ASE show a much higher figure for the North (8.1 percent), with approximately constant figures for the remainder of the nation. States responding at higher levels included New Jersey (14.5 percent), West Virginia (11.6 percent), and New York (10.4 percent). Significantly lower rates were found in such states as California (.6 percent), Florida (0 percent), and Maryland (0 percent). OERI reflects a similar trend, with the North Atlantic region figure much higher than any other region (9 percent).[151]

Population size factors indicate that microcomputer circulation occurs more often in communities of a medium size (10,000–100,000). The ASE study reported that the highest figures for libraries offering such services occurred in areas with a population of less than 40,000. The OERI report indicated that 6 percent of medium population libraries offered such services, with institutions serving the smallest population group at the 4 percent level and larger libraries at 3 percent. The metropolitan status reflected the same trend, with suburban libraries offering the services more often than both rural and urban libraries.[152]

SOURCES OF FUNDING

The sources of funding for microcomputer projects, as discussed earlier, can include state funds, gifts (Friends groups, donations), federal funds, etc. From the "programs" page of the ASE study, sources of funding most often mentioned are LSCA grants and Friends gifts. Statistical data on this matter are available from the OERI report. The dominant sources of funding reported were local or state funds and grants (47 percent) and gifts and benefactor donations (34 percent), with federal funds and grants the only other sizable source (10 percent).[153]

Sources of funding differed by size of the community. Smaller libraries (less than 10,000) were much more reliant on local and state funds than the national average, while larger libraries (over 100,000) used federal funds and grants at twice the national average, with less funding from state or local grants and funds than the average.[154] Regional breakdowns reflected the national average with the exception of the Southwest, where state and local funds and gifts were both well below the national average, with a much heavier usage on federal funding (41 percent).[155]

COMPUTER SKILLS TRAINING SESSIONS

The results of the ASE study indicate that sessions designed to teach computer use to adults were a very popular program. These classes were most often taught by staff, businesspeople, and volunteers. The OERI study reported that 48 percent of libraries with public access microcomputers offered some sort of training. Both rural and small libraries (less than 10,000) offered significantly less training than average. Regionally, the Southeast offered training much more often than the rest of the country.[156]

SOFTWARE AVAILABILITY

The ASE study shows that the figures for in-library and circulating hardware are nearly identical to those for software—20.1 percent of the libraries offered software to be used on an in-library computer, and 4 percent allowed circulation of the software within the community. The OERI report did not differentiate between in-house and circulating software, but did report a total figure of 17 percent of the libraries offering some software service, and indicated no great regional differences between levels of service.[157] The ASE study, however, indicated that the West offered far less circulating software services than the rest of the country.

Population size and metropolitan status again offered some definite trends. The OERI study reported a much higher percentage of urban community libraries offering software services (40 percent). Similarly, large communities (over 100,000) offered the services much more often (42 percent). Rural and small communities were well below the national average.[158]

PATRON USE OF SOFTWARE

The OERI report contains a chart detailing different types of software and indicates whether demand for the type is heavy, moderate, or light. Applications packages such as word processors and spreadsheets received moderate to light usage. Adult literacy software received light usage in 53 percent of the libraries. Video entertainment games were available in only 31 percent of the libraries, and of those libraries, 56 percent reported heavy usage, 30 percent moderate, and 14 percent light. Few libraries reported heavy usage by patrons bringing in their own software (18 percent).[159]

PLANS TO INITIATE OR EXPAND PUBLIC ACCESS MICROCOMPUTER PROGRAMS

The OERI report details plans of libraries to increase or initiate various components of their microcomputer projects (number or variety of software, number of computers, etc.) and correlates the data by size of population, metropolitan status and regions. On the national average libraries responded that variety or number of software was first on the list of increased or initiated services (26 percent), followed by promotional efforts for patron use of the computer (22 percent). A recurring theme can be seen in all areas in terms of population size and metropolitan status. The larger and more urban areas responded in much higher numbers with plans to increase or initiate a project. The regional breakdown for plans to expand or initiate are fairly consistent with only minor deviations.[160] Of those libraries that already had a microcomputer project in place, 75 percent placed emphasis on increasing software holdings and variety. The second highest priority of such libraries was in the area of increased promotion of public use of library microcomputers.[161]

Conclusion

As society continues to move toward a greater acceptance of automation, the microcomputer and its applications will become more pervasive in all aspects of life. The ability to interact successfully with new technology will not be a skill for adults to choose to study, as it is now; but rather the inability to do so will be a handicap. The need for a source of education and training for the adult user who has not mastered the technology is obvious. The source of this training, however, is not yet clear.

The number of public access microcomputer projects in this country is growing at a fairly rapid rate, but the spread of projects reveals some problems that will need to be addressed. The availability of such services is much more predominant in urban, high population areas. Rural areas tend to have much less access to the new technologies. These unintentional inequities need to be corrected if the public library intends to pursue the ideal of assisting adult citizens in their effort to cope with a rapidly changing society.

The public library has made the effort through many different projects and approaches to meet the public's needs. The differing levels of computer literacy make it difficult to judge whether any success has been achieved. The results will perhaps be more noticeable in the very near future when the technologies now offered as recreational become necessities.

Notes

1. "Silver Lining among PC Market's Clouds," *Sales and Marketing Management* 135 (March 1985): 37.

2. Patrick R. Dewey, *Public Access Microcomputers: A Handbook for Librarians* (White Plains, N.Y.: Knowledge Industry Publications, 1984), pp. 4–5.
3. Patrick R. Dewey, "Public Access Micros: An Overview of Options," *The Electronic Library* 4 (1986): 50.
4. Don Julien, "Expanding Service: Public Access Microcomputers," *Wilson Library Bulletin* 59 (February 1985): 381–385.
5. Ibid., p. 382.
6. Ibid.
7. Ibid., p. 384.
8. Ibid., p. 383.
9. Ibid., p. 385.
10. Ibid.
11. Betty Costa and Marie Costa, *A Micro Handbook for Small Libraries and Media Centers* (Littleton, Colo.: Libraries Unlimited, 1983), p. 19.
12. Ibid., p. 4.
13. Howard Fosdick, "Microcomputers in Libraries: How Useful Are They?" in *Microcomputers for Libraries: How Useful Are They?* ed. Jane Beaumont and Donald Krueger (Ottawa: Canadian Library Association, 1983), p. 9.
14. Lawrence A. Woods and Nolan F. Pope, *The Librarian's Guide to Microcomputer Technology and Applications* (White Plains, N.Y.: Knowledge Industry Publications, 1983), p.4.
15. Costa and Costa, *A Micro Handbook*, p. 5.
16. Fosdick, "Microcomputers in Libraries," p. 4.
17. Barbara Harvie, "Out of the Arcades and into the Library," *American Libraries* 12 (November 1981): 602–605.
18. Costa and Costa, *A Micro Handbook*, pp. 184–185.
19. Kent Oliver, "Leading the PACC: Public Access Computer Center," *Show Me Libraries* 36 (May 1985):34–36.
20. Dewey, *Public Access Microcomputers*, p. 43.
21. Ibid., p. 44.
22. Ibid., p. 43.
23. Ibid., p. 124.
24. "New York Challenge: LSCA for Micros," *Library Journal* 107 (October 1, 1982):1804.
25. Dewey, *Public Access Microcomputers*, p. 74.
26. Ibid.
27. Ibid., p. 125–128.
28. John Smith, "A Conflict of Values—Charges in the Publicly Funded Library," *Journal of Librarianship* 13 (January 1981):3.
29. Ibid., p. 62.
30. Patrick R. Dewey, "Public Access to Microcomputers: Thoughts from the North-Pulaski Experience," *Reference Services Review* 11 (Fall 1983):23.
31. Dewey, *Public Access Microcomputers*, p. 27.
32. "Microcomputers for Rent at San Francisco Public," *Library Journal* 108 (March 15, 1983):538.
33. Dewey, *Public Access*
34. Ibid., p. 27.
35. "Gaylord Offers Vending System to Make Computers Pay Their Way," *Library Journal* 107 (October 1, 1982):1804.
36. Harold M. Shair, "Coin-in-a-Slot Computing at the Public Library," *Creative Computing* 3 (May/June 1977):36–38.

37. Mark E. Rorvig, *Microcomputers and Libraries: A Guide to Technology, Products, and Applications* (White Plains, N.Y.: Knowledge Industry Publications, 1981), p. 98.
38. Ibid.
39. Ibid.
40. Jim Milliot, compiler, *Micros at Work: Case Studies of Microcomputers in Libraries* (White Plains, N.Y.: Knowledge Industry Publications, 1985), p. 11.
41. Ibid., p. 12.
42. Ibid., p. 22.
43. Robert A. Walton, *Microcomputers: A Planning and Implementation Guide for Librarians and Information Professionals* (Phoenix: Oryx Press, 1983) p. 79.
44. Ibid., p. 81.
45. Ibid., p. 81.
46. Ibid., p. 55.
47. Dewey, *Public Access Microcomputers,* p. 55.
48. Ibid., p. 56.
49. Ibid., p. 56–57.
50. Walton, *Microcomputers: A Planning and Implementation Guide,* pp. 76–77.
51. Dewey, *Public Access Microcomputers,* p. 52.
52. Walton, *Microcomputers: A Planning and Implementation Guide,* p. 76.
53. Dewey, *Public Access Microcomputers,* p. 57.
54. Ibid., p. 86.
55. Dewey, *Public Access Microcomputers,* p. 60.
56. Ibid.
57. "Micros for the Public Get Mixed Reviews," *Library Journal* 111 (October 1, 1986):26.
58. Milliot, *Micros at Work,* p. 31.
59. Dewey, *Public Access Microcomputers,* pp. 38–40.
60. Ibid., p. 35.
61. Milliot, *Micros at Work,* p. 89.
62. Dewey, *Public Access Microcomputers,* p. 36.
63. Bonnie S. Fowler and Duncan Smith, "Microcomputers for the Public in the Public Library," *Information Technology and Libraries* 2 (March 1983):49.
64. Jean Armour Polly, "Burning In: Four Years at the Public Library's Microcomputer," *Small Computers in Libraries* 5 (September 1985):14.
65. Ibid.
66. Dewey, *Public Access Microcomputers,* pp. 31–34.
67. Terri Mitchem, "The Bowker National Library Microcomputer Usage Study, 1984," *Bowker Annual of Library & Book Trade Information 1985* (New York: Bowker, 1986), p. 432.
68. Julien, "Exanding Service," p. 385.
69. Dewey, *Public Access Microcomputers,* p. 62.
70. Ibid., p. 60.
71. Doreen Cohen, "The Software Library," *Small Computers in Libraries* 5 (October 1985):27.
72. David S. Bryant, "Circulating Personal Computers," *Library Journal* 110 (November 1, 1985):162.
73. Dewey, *Public Access Microcomputers,* p. 80.
74. Ibid.
75. Bryant, "Circulating Personal Computers," p. 163.
76. Ibid.
77. Thomas Smisek, "Circulating Software: A Practical Approach," *School Library Journal* 31 (May 1985):138–139.

78. Cohen, "The Software Library," p. 26.
79. Dewey, *Public Access Microcomputers,* p. 64.
80. "Circulating Software or Let the End User Beware," *Technicalities* 4 (December 1984):1.
81. Mary Brandt Jensen, "Softwrite: A Legislative Solution to the Problem of Users' and Producers' Rights in Computer Software," *Louisiana Law Review* 44 (May 1984):1413–1483.
82. Ibid., p. 1461–1462
83. Dewey, *Public Access Microcomputers,* p. 58.
84. "ComputerTown, OK!," *Oklahoma Librarian* 32 (May/June 1982):1.
85. Carol S. Duncan, "COMPULIT: Computer Literacy for Tacoma," *Library Journal* 109 (January 1984):53.
86. "Microcomputers Take Off in Tacoma COMPULIT Program," *Library Journal* 108 (August1983):1414.
87. Milliot, *Micros at Work,* p. 31.
88. Elaine Baker, "From Victrola to Microcomputer: Rural Libraries and New Technology," *Library Journal* 109 (July 1984):1289–1290.
89. "Use of Micros in Rural Libraries Focus of Illinois Pilot Project," *Library Journal* 108 (February 15, 1983):339.
90. "Community Development Dollars Buys Computers for Lorraine, Ohio," *Library Journal* 107 (October 1, 1982):1904.
91. Baker, "From Victrola to Microcomputer," p. 1289.
92. Nancy L. Smith, "Humanizing the Computer for the Older Adult," *OLA Bulletin* 56 (April 1986):25.
93. Phillip E. Rose, "Microcomputers: One Library's Approach," *Online* 8 (January 1984):31.
94. "Community Development," p. 1804.
95. Susan Rappaport, "Literacy and Computers," *Library Journal* 110 (October 1, 1985):74–75.
96. Steve Freemen, "The 'Apple Corps' at St. Louis," *School Library Journal* 31 (May 1985):140–142.
97. "Computers for the Handicapped," *American Libraries* 14 (February 1983):108.
98. Dewey, *Public Access Microcomputers,* p. 119.
99. Ibid., p. 119.
100. Fowler, "Microcomputers for the Public," pp. 46–52.
101. Dewey, *Public Access Microcomputers,* p. 89.
102. Ibid.
103. Ibid., p. 90.
104. Ibid.
105. James LaRue, "Sending Them a Message," *Wilson Library Bulletin* 60 (June 1986):30.
106. Gene Williams and Chris Mitchell, "Setting Up a Library BBS: A Step-by-Step Guide," *Wilson Library Bulletin* 61 (February 1987):12.
107. Dewey, *Public Access Microcomputers,* p. 112.
108. Ibid., p. 104.
109. Polly, "Burning In: Four Years at the Public Library's Microcomputer," p. 14.
110. Patrick R. Dewey, *Essential Guide to Bulletin Board Systems* (Westport, Conn.: Meckler Publishing, 1987), 205 pp.
111. LaRue, "Sending Them a Message," p. 33.
112. Ibid., p. 33.
113. Dewey, *Bulletin Board Systems,* p. 141.

114. Ibid., p. 141.
115. Dewey, *Public Access Microcomputers*, p. 87
116. Carol Tenopir, "Four Options for End User Searching," *Library Journal* 111 (July 1986):56.
117. Ibid., p. 56.
118. Ibid., p. 57.
119. Ibid.
120. Ibid., p. 57.
121. Ibid.
122. Ibid.
123. Ibid.
124. Dewey, *Public Access Microcomputers,* p. 116.
125. Ibid.
126. Ibid., p. 74.
127. Harvie, "Out of the Arcades," p. 602.
128. Ibid., p. 603.
129. Ibid.
130. Ibid., p. 605.
131. Barbara Harvie and Julie Anton, "Is There a Microcomputer in Your Future? ComputerTown Thinks the Answer Is Yes," *Top of the News* 39 (Spring 1983):275.
132. Liza Loop, Julie Anton, and Ramon Zamora, *ComputerTown: Bringing Computer Literacy to Your Community* (Reston, Va.: Reston Publishing Company, 1983), 160p.
133. Doreen Cohen, "Public Access: Micros—ComputerTown USA!," *Access: Microcomputers in Libraries* 2 (October 1982):5.
134. Ibid.
135. Dewey, *Public Access Microcomputers,* p. 74.
136. Ibid., p. 70.
137. Ibid.
138. Milliot, *Micros at Work,* p. 77.
139. Patrick R. Dewey, "Public Access Micros," *American Libraries* 15 (November 1984):704.
140. Ibid.
141. Betsy Curry, Edward R. Moeller, and Vicki L. Williams, "Microcomputers in Public Libraries in Georgia—Survey 1983—Summary," *Georgia Librarian* 21 (May 1984): 36–37.
142. Milliot, *Micros at Work,* p. 11.
143. Ibid., p. 17.
144. Mitchem, "The Bowker National Library Microcomputer Usage Study, 1984," pp. 426–443.
145. Ibid., p. 428–431.
146. Department of Education, Office of Educational Research and Improvement, Center for Statistics, *Patron Use of Computers in Public Libraries*, Bulletin OERI (March 1986), 17pp.
147. Ibid., p. 5.
148. Ibid., p. 7.
149. Ibid.
150. Ibid.
151. Ibid.
152. Ibid.
153. Ibid., p. 9.
154. Ibid.

155. Ibid.
156. Ibid., p. 10.
157. Ibid., p. 11.
158. Ibid.
159. Ibid., p. 12.
160. Ibid., p. 13.
161. Ibid., p. 14.

CHAPTER 15

The Public Library as a Social/Cultural Institution: Alternative Perspectives and Changing Contexts

Connie Van Fleet and Douglas Raber

The library's role as a social/cultural institution has been the subject of extensive discussion and heated debate. Much of the literature is characterized by ambiguous definition of the terms *social* and *cultural* and by the conflict resulting from varying conceptions. While specific perspectives may be identified, it is impossible to clear away all ambiguity, since definitions and subsequent actions tend to overlap and become diffuse. The first of these perspectives is clearly sociological and institutional in nature, while others more specifically relate to role definition and library activities pursued in fulfilling those roles.

The social/cultural nature of the public library is inescapable when defined in terms of its sociological context. The public library, by its very nature, is a socially mandated and supported institution. Its continued existence is representative of communal decisions and priorities. The library's underlying and fundamental purpose—the preservation of recorded history and the cumulated knowledge of society—is cultural by definition, in that it preserves and extends the values and wisdom of the society by which it is supported.

While the fundamentally cultural nature of librarianship is universally accepted when viewed from this broadest perspective, operational definitions are open to wide interpretation and controversy. Stevenson describes the general policy implications by noting "what is communicated, why, to whom, and how it is communicated are questions which, when answered, place the public library in the larger cultural fabric."[1] The perspective of the public library as a purveyor of high culture and low culture is an extension of the underlying sociological perspective, but focuses on different issues and activities.

On one end of this spectrum, the library as a preserver and provider of the human record is closely associated with the broad mission of acculturation and socialization—in short, the sociological and psychological role of helping individuals define their place in society and in aiding society in recognizing and preserving its various components. This socialization role is sometimes made manifest in activities designed to place the individual in contact with governmental and service agencies, giving rise to the view of the library's social/ cultural role as one of a social service agency. Attempts to fulfill this mission have frequently centered on the disadvantaged and alienated and consequently often led to the characterization of the public library as a social welfare agency.

Toward the other end of the spectrum is the narrowly circumscribed concept of *social* as synonymous with the recreational function, and *cultural* as synonymous with the arts and humanities. Recent trends towards legitimating popular culture have tended to fuse these concepts of social and recreational.

For the purposes of this discussion, five basic definitional perspectives have been identified. These roles move from the broadest context with general philosophical guidelines to more narrowly defined areas with specific policy implications.

1. The library as a social-cultural agency in the most fundamental sense acts to preserve and organize the artifacts of an advanced literate society.
2. The library as an agency of socialization and acculturation serves to help the individual relate to society on a basic level.
3. The library as a social service agency functions to bring the individual into contact with opportunities and services afforded by governmental and other social service agencies.
4. The library as a cultural agency brings the individual into contact with the arts and humanities.
5. The library as a social agency affords opportunities for recreation and use of leisure time.

Delineation of these perspectives is important to the analysis of the social/cultural function. As Stevenson has observed, "Culture, no matter how you define it, is what libraries are all about, but how it is specifically defined makes all the difference in what librarians actually do, for whom they do it, and how they do it."[2] Inherent in these arguments is the controversy over the nature of services the public library should offer (educational, informational, recreational, or cultural) and whether any service may be defined exclusively in any one of these terms. Perhaps the greatest strength of the library has been its ability to offer services without narrowly prescribing the intended purpose of these services. Individuals are then free to decide upon the use and value of services from personal perspectives. It may be that definitional ambiguity has been a necessary device that allows librarians to fulfill a role that "fluctuates with a variety of social policies and with the economic needs of society."[3]

Additional argument centers on the form of service and format of materials, particularly in fulfilling the social/cultural role as most narrowly defined above. While some argue that librarians should stick to what they know best (books), others view this restriction as an unnecessary limitation to access. This seemingly trivial argument over whether nontraditional services (generally live programming and activities) should be offered is a critical issue in the definition of the profession. Does the librarian preserve recorded history to provide access to the records per se or to the knowledge and experience found within those records? Stemming from this debate is the issue of the nature of nonbook activities. Should programming be employed only as a stimulation to further use of the library's collection, or is the activity sufficient in and of itself as a means of bringing people into contact with the human record?

This chapter approaches the discussion of the public library as a social/cultural agency from two perspectives. First, it delineates the underlying sociological foundation of the public library as a social and cultural agency. Second, it traces the development and evolution of the library's social/cultural role in terms of the more operational definitions listed above and in light of debate over nonbook and other stimulation activities.

Sociological Foundations of the Public Library

LEGITIMATION FOR THE LIBRARY'S ROLE

Libraries, as social structures, were invented and designed to solve certain problems associated with the need to save and provide access to records of human activity. From this perspective, the library's cultural role is indisputable.

> It is not likely that anyone would challenge the proposition that libraries of all types are properly categorized as cultural institutions. They are products of advanced and emerging literate societies which need to store, organize and control graphic records. These records, and in fact all records, whether they need to be stored for some utilitarian purpose or not, are clearly cultural products; and one way or another, no matter how profound or mundane their use, they contribute something to the totality of a culture.[4]

The solution that libraries provide to these problems can be considered their social function. Weber, however, has warned that modern social structures are not concrete entities, but organizations of individuals each pursuing individual goals.[5] The maintenance of the structures is associated not only with an abstract function, but also with the legitimacy of organizations. Legitimacy is created by an authority formed from an appropriate combination of rules and force that bind individuals to collective goals.[6] Functions themselves are legitimate in the sense that they represent needs defined by goals and values common throughout a society.

Davis and Harris, in their history of libraries, point out that early libraries were associated with state, religious, and commercial orders.[7] It is important to remember that often no clear distinctions existed among these orders. All, however, eventually demonstrated a necessity for recordkeeping to know what had gone before, assuming it would continue into the future. The development of this temporal focus beyond the present is a prerequisite for the development of the rational authority that characterizes the social legitimacy of libraries. The existence of libraries is a sign of a society already developing structures whose legitimacy is associated with bureaucratic, rational authority. Libraries, their collections and services, no matter how simply defined, are symbols of the particular social order that sustains them and which they sustain by solving the problems of recordkeeping and access.

THE COLLECTIVE NATURE OF LIBRARY HOLDINGS

At an early stage in their existence, libraries clearly demonstrate social functions and characteristics. Materials as diverse as their creators are collected and organized for a social purpose. No one individual is responsible for the production of a library collection. These items represent the collective production of communication necessary for social activity. Library purposes are defined by purposes of social activity, and it is in terms of this activity that individual items collected by a library are fused into a meaningful whole. All libraries are, to an extent, collective creations. Even privately owned libraries, other than those that contain only the works of their owners, can be conceived in this way.

Public libraries are collective creations in a second sense. Their existence depends upon a distinctly social contribution. They may not be tax supported or necessarily accessible by right, or even useful to all members of society in equal measure. Those developments are signs of industrially developed societies. Nevertheless, the financial resources, administration, materials, purposes and uses of public libraries are all related to some social end, the achievement of which benefits all who are members of the social order that maintain such libraries.

> The most frequently stated purpose [of public libraries] is "to serve the needs of the people." A need for some sort of information exists, and the library supplies it. But behind this lie larger national purposes (e.g., the state's need for an informed electorate, a literate working class, paths to upward mobility, intellectual freedom, etc.).[8]

Public libraries that fail to provide this benefit will not be sustained. Likewise, as social orders decay, so do their libraries.

Early public libraries were, according to Davis and Harris, primarily concerned with preservation, as if the social order were so fragile that a concrete symbol of its existence was a necessary part of its claim to legitimate authority.[9]

At excavations of ancient Greek palaces that date before 600 B.C., special rooms were discovered that contained large numbers of clay tablets bearing government and business records.[10] Evidence gathered from excavations of the Assyrian library of King Assurbanipal (668–627 B.C.) suggests a collection of some 30,000 clay tablets containing written records of all kinds. Although religious texts were prominent, archaeologists also found tax records, laws, contracts and deeds, and early scientific treatises. The library was open to scholars, both official and unofficial, as well as to government bureaucrats.[11]

The earliest Roman libraries were often collections of historical records and laws. The power of libraries was demonstrated by Roman conquest. Collections of materials were often taken as spoils of war, and to a great extent these spoils were responsible for the Hellenization of Rome. The beginning of this process is often dated from the arrival in Rome of Crates of Mallos, then librarian of Pergamum, in about 160 B.C. His public lectures and private discussions stimulated interest in Greek culture.[12] Of course, the greatest working library of ancient times was that of Alexandria. Founded by the Ptolemies of Egypt in about 300 B.C., it served as a center of Hellenic culture and learning for all of the Mediterranean world for nearly 200 years.[13]

ACCESS ISSUES AS REFLECTIVE OF THE SOCIAL NATURE OF PUBLIC LIBRARIES

The focus of this chapter has been on the social character of the public library in terms of its structure and social function, but it has not been possible to delineate that focus without alluding to notions of access, use, and purpose. A library can serve a social function in a wide variety of historical, political, and social settings. Rational bureaucracy is not a structure unique to industrially advanced democracies. So it is precisely issues raised by problems of access, use, and purpose that further reveal the social nature of public libraries. Their purpose depends upon their public and the particulars of time and place that define the public and why it needs libraries. Publics define themselves socially by means of conflict and consensus, creating a social order out of the needs and passions of individuals. Public library purposes are social in the sense that they are related to the outcome of the political contests among and between groups that constitute the social order.

Issues related to the right of access to use a collection of materials have been among the leading issues of public library development and are directly related to larger issues concerning rights to political and social participation. The modern public library has evolved to become a structure whose primary purpose is to provide a means, unimpeded by social, cultural, or physical barriers, by which individual members of society can pursue personal enrichment and social participation. Given caution about the cultural relativity of the concept of social participation, this statement holds true for all industrially advanced societies, socialist or capitalist. The "public" of the modern public library has been expanded, by the course of politics linked to the values of the Enlightenment and the material resources of industrial development, to include the populations of entire nations.

It is at this broadest level of definition that the public library can clearly be seen to have a social purpose and character. Public libraries, by fulfilling a need identified by legitimate social and political processes, achieve their own legitimacy and develop structures, collections, and rules of use appropriate to their socially defined functions. The particulars of historically defined public libraries depend to a great extent upon how the public is defined by the same social and political processes. The social character of the public library is defined further, then, by the fact that its purpose is responsive to social change. The modern public library, for example, is a manifestation of the library appropriate to a public comprised of citizens.

Finally, the social character of public libraries is also defined by the nature of the library's relation to its culture. A very early specific purpose of libraries was the preservation of culture and cultural artifacts, especially those with religious significance. Some of the earliest libraries were associated with temples, mosques, and monasteries. As societies developed, however, religion did not remain the only source of culture, and libraries—particularly scholarly libraries—responded by expanding their collections. Works that were expressions of the values, morals, and nature of humanity as conceived by a given society were sought out regardless of their secular or religious origins. Increasingly these works included absurdities and contradictions as well as rules and identities.

This cultural role of libraries has developed and expanded as social change has created new libraries and defined new publics. Preservation is still an important function, but values of participation have helped to create public libraries whose goals include extending culture, both elite and popular, to all citizens to be used as they choose. Personal enrichment, entertainment or social status all may be motives for use.

Two questions have conditioned the relationship of public libraries to their cultures. First, and most significant, is the question of who has the right to access to what culture? Societies are complex and fractioned by subcultures and misunderstandings that serve as barriers to consensus. These divisions are sometimes used deliberately to achieve ends of discrimination and exploitation that can result in harm on all sides. In nineteenth-century Britain, the working class was denied access to elite education and culture, both of which were necessary to participate in a parliamentary power structure. The working class developed a language and subculture unique to its own conditions that excluded the elite, often while masquerading as deference. Both attitudes stood in the way of a resolution of the issues of social justice and participation that fundamentally separated the classes of a Britain experiencing the Industrial Revolution. The promise of the twentieth-century public library is that it can, by judicious and representative collections and services, bridge the gaps that separate subcultures in complex modern societies. To achieve this goal, the public library must also act to preserve the integrity of those separate subcultures and then guarantee free access to all members of all subcultures. Debate on the issues raised by this goal continues to define the course of modern public library development.

The second question that has conditioned the relation of the public library to its society is, who has access to the resources necessary to create culture, that is, to participate in the cultural life of their society? The modern public library deals with this issue by attempting to provide sources, primary cultural documents, to any who would use them as models to emulate or reject as they create their own cultural artifacts. This is an issue of participation linked to the historical movement of people to participate in the definition of their world and its destiny.

The issues of cultural conflict and social participation are not unique to the past. Modern industrial societies, regardless of the principles and values that serve as their foundation, have not solved these problems. Violent conflict over these issues has not been banished from the world. Public libraries are in a position to both document these problems and provide a means to their solution. Libraries are, nevertheless, subject to the same social forces that contribute to the struggle for consensus and participation and demonstrate a wide variety of social and cultural activities relative to those forces at particular times and places.

PUBLIC LIBRARIES AND FEDERAL POLICY

The public library's evolution as a social and cultural institution has also been influenced by the recognition of its potential to serve as an instrument of national social and cultural policy. Although federal government support for public libraries is a relatively recent development in the United States, it is in many ways a logical extension of a government commitment to social welfare that began with Progressivism and revealed its typical form in the welfare programs of the Roosevelt administration of the 1930s. The goals of these programs represented political consensus at the national level, but in the American context their achievement had been entrusted to local authority. Federalism is a particular democratic structure that values rational self-government over rational bureaucracy. One result has been local control over a wide range of essential services, governance, and taxation. Although the federal government does provide some direct services, national social and cultural policies have been realized through the federal financial support of local institutions. In effect, federal tax dollars have been used as an incentive to motivate local authorities to pursue policies developed at the level of national government.

The influence of these policies has been direct in the sense that funds have been provided for services to be administered at local levels of government and indirect in the sense that they have affected local choices of what services ought to be offered. Public libraries have been influenced by national social and cultural policy goals primarily through the Library Services Act (LSA)—later the Library Services and Construction Act (LSCA), and the National Endowment for the Humanities (NEH). As we examine the way in which the public library developed its social and cultural role in American society in terms of values and specific services, we will also examine the federal legislation that influenced that development.

The origins of federal government support can be traced back to the Progressive movement of the early twentieth century. Hofstadter has described Progressivism as a broad social movement not linked to any particular party or organization.[14] It was characteristically a middle-class movement associated with the rise of the professions and the idea that education and rationality should and could be in the service of society. Progressivism's self-assigned adversaries were the dominating corporations and corrupt politics, but it must be admitted that the goals of this movement were vague and often contradictory. America's transformation from a rural agrarian society to an urban industrial society provided the social and economic dislocations in which Progressivism grew.

The library profession in America was distinctly affected by the values of Progressivism. Although some historians see such gestures as Andrew Carnegie's library endowments as a capitalist response to pressures for reform and a discontented working class, it is nevertheless true that his gifts represented a commitment to the possibilities of self-help and self-improvement.[15] Through self-education, public libraries offered a means to middle-class status and cultural participation. The values of Progressivism are more explicitly presented in the Johnson Report (1919) and the Williamson Reports (1921, 1923) to the Carnegie Foundation that criticized the endowment for creating libraries without librarians and adequate collections.[16] Many of the newly established libraries failed to obtain the local support needed to continue operating.[17] A solution to the survival problem of public libraries, especially those in rural areas, was not to be found until after World War II, but throughout the 1930s librarians such as Carl Milam and Carleton Joeckel began to focus their efforts on the federal government.

Depression and war led the United States to reconsider the role of the federal government in civil society. If not exactly welcomed, wide-scale government social and economic intervention became a necessity.

It made itself apparent first as municipal reform and the development of the notion that city government had some responsibility to its citizens to solve urban social problems.[18] The first signs of a modern federal role in the support of public libraries emerged from the American Library Association with the publication of *A National Plan for Libraries* in 1938.[19] What began with the Harrison-Thomas-Fletcher bills in the 75th Congress (1937–1938) was finally realized with the passage of the Library Services Act in 1956.[20] To a great extent the LSA and the LSCA were programs that defined public libraries as agents of social policy. This will be examined in greater detail. Although developing much later and on a smaller scale, public libraries also figured in the rise of a federal role in culture and its politics, particularly after the establishment of the NEH in 1965.

These developments are more problematic than those stimulated by the LSA/LSCA. Compared to the appropriations for those programs or the total appropriations for the NEH, the funds available through the Humanities Projects in Libraries program of the NEH have been and remain negligible. Only $2.9 million was granted in 1987, and the estimated grants for 1988 totaled only $1.89 million. According to the *Catalog of Federal Domestic Assistance,* in 1990 an estimated 90 applications will be received and only 23 grants will be made.[21] The importance of this program is perhaps not so related to the level of spending and activity as it is to the recognition in federal law that public libraries are cultural institutions whose goals extend beyond preservation and include the active dissemination of culture. The purpose of the library program is to

> encourage public understanding of the humanities, an interest in academic and public library humanities resources through thematic programs, exhibitions, publications, and other library activities to stimulate the use of the resources.[22]

The issue of the appropriate federal role in the development and stimulation of culture is far from resolved, and the debate parallels in many ways that over the role of cultural programming in public libraries. One former director of the NEH, Ronald Berman, feels that national resources should be concentrated on scholarly activities. He argues that the humanities represent an end of human endeavor and cannot be used as a means to solve problems, social or otherwise.[23] In his comments on the Rockefeller Foundation report, *The Humanities in American Life,* Berman quarrels with the notion that books "enrich our experience . . . . I think it plain that the function of some books—those by Swift, Kafka, Hemingway—is to wound. They deride our 'human potential'."[24] Berman is generally opposed to the public programs of the NEH and objects especially to the state programs. The NEH authorizes state humanities agencies to dispense grant money in much the same way as state library agencies dispense LSCA funds.

Even a scholar who supports the NEH public programs suggests that these programs have been unnecessarily limited. Stephen Miller believes that stimulation is possible but doubts that public libraries are an appropriate mechanism and concludes that the NEH has not been of much help to libraries.[25]

> Given the nature and the facilities of most libraries, it is doubtful that they will ever become popular places for exhibits or discussion groups. NEH's program is well meaning, but it encourages libraries to become involved in activities—such as the creation of materials for exhibits and the staging of exhibits—that are extraneous to their main purpose and of only limited helping alleviating their financial woes.[26]

Despite these arguments, there are also those like former Congressman John Brademas, now president of New York University, who played a crucial role in the development and passage of NEH legislation. In the keynote address to the 51st Council and General Conference of the International Federation of Library Associations and Institutions, Brademas approvingly quotes Charles Coffin Jewett, who declared that an important mission of libraries was "to provide for the diffusion of a knowledge of good books and for the enlarging of the means of public access to them."[27] Brademas argues that this mission must be a part of federal educational and cultural policy.

> Providing funds for libraries and for learning generally is not a wasteful expenditure, a frill, but an indispensable investment in our future.[28]

In addition,

> A recent report from the National Endowment for the Humanities on the state of American culture calls libraries . . . a kind of "parallel school" providing humanities programs outside established educational institutions.[29]

In the report *Humanities in America,*[30] "growth in book buying and attendance at museum exhibitions and library discussion groups" are cited as evidence of a resurgent interest in the humanities at a grassroots level.[31]

It is beyond the scope of this review to examine in detail the activities of individual libraries. It is possible, however, to look at the types of programs funded by the LSCA and the NEH in public libraries to determine at least the outlines of federal social and cultural policies in libraries in the context of public library development.

This essay examines the way American public libraries have realized the goals and coped with the issues of their social and cultural purposes. To a great extent it will be seen that American public librarians have conceived of their purpose in terms of a mission that has motivated an activism devoted to the provision of social services and cultural programming. Some question has been raised about the extent to which this kind of activity should be pursued by public libraries, but broad principles of social and cultural service still dominate American librarianship. It is recognized that it is this service that secures for the public library a legitimate place in American society.

Evolution of the Library's Social/Cultural Role

The library profession's perception of its role as a social/cultural one has been marked by diverse and often conflicting viewpoints. The priority of the social/cultural role among those of education, information, and recreation has fluctuated, and even among those who have steadfastly supported a cultural role there has been disagreement as to appropriate services and activities. Generally, however, the broadest socialization-acculturation role was recognized as an appropriate one from the founding of the U.S. public library, though specific activities and services related to the role of the library as a social service agency and as a provider of social and cultural activities have been more gradually accepted. A gradual evolution of perspectives and goals may be seen from a study of library documents and the professional literature.

Among the most profound changes has been a shift from the goal of elevation of tastes to aesthetic appreciation. Implicit in this change is an essential egalitarianism. Rather than trying to absorb individuals into a dominant and elitist culture, librarians have moved toward a recognition of the value of the diverse and unique cultures that make up U.S. society. The study of popular culture and its subsequent legitimation in the 1970s provided the academic recognition and scholarly foundations to support the profession's natural inclination toward egalitarian service evidenced by the outreach programs of the 1890s and 1960s. The ASE project findings indicate that many of the reported programs that librarians classify as "most successful" reflect the cultural role in its most egalitarian form, presenting not only a wide variety of subject matter on varying levels, but employing diverse, easily accessible formats.

Some examples of such programming from the ASE survey include: "The Human Experience: Confronting Adversity," a discussion and presentation of humanitarian issues from the Sioux Falls (South Dakota) Public Library; "S.O.S. Consumer Education on Wheels," from the St. Louis County Library; "Censorship: Law, Art and Journalism," from the Providence Public Library; and a multimedia effort called "Appalachian Humanities Education Program to Promote Understanding," from the Fort Loudoun Regional Library in Athens (Tennessee).

The recreational role of libraries has grown in status but shifted in focus. We have defined provision of recreational materials and activities as part of the narrower social role, but this may be seen as an instrument of socialization as well. While in the early years the provision of recreational reading materials was often seen as a guard against sin and crime, sociologists in more recent times have underscored the need for leisure and recreation in ensuring personal well being and offering an escape from a stressful environment.

The provision of popular recreational materials has gained support from studies of popular culture and its functions. The recreational role is apparently widely accepted in public libraries in the 1980s. ASE findings revealed that librarians often perceive of programming as having a dual purpose, combining recreational elements with educational and informational presentations. This thinking is reflected in the Halley's Comet Watch sponsored by the Tacoma (Washington) Public Library, the "Tea for Tuesday" discussion at the Adams Library in Chelmsford, Massachusetts, and the Charles County (Maryland) Public Library's presentation of a combination history and craft program called "The Tradition of Quilting." Such multiple purpose programming may be either a conscious or an intuitive acknowledgment of the highly individualized benefits of public library services.

The use of multiple formats has received support in national documents for some years, but nonbook programming still creates some issues for discussion. Though there appears to have been an acceptance of programming, it is still often regarded as peripheral to the library's purpose, and is often funded only through external sources. At the heart of the programming controversy is the question of purpose: do live programs serve as stimulation to further use, or are they self-justified independent activities?

BROADENING THE SOCIAL/CULTURAL ROLE (1890–1929)

By the 1890s, librarians had become concerned with services other than the collecting and preserving of books. Changing sociological contexts forced a more active role upon the profession. America in the late nineteenth century was changing from a predominantly rural, agricultural society to an urban industrial one marked by increased diversity in its ethnic composition. The resultant change in value perspective from the individualist to the corporate created "social problems that the traditional social and governmental structures either would not or could not deal with effectively."[32] Pressure on U. S. educational institutions grew as a result of the need to create a trained, literate workforce from a previously agricultural and not necessarily literate population.[33] The library's focus on its socialization and acculturation roles sharpened in response to the converging social forces of urbanization, industrialization, and immigration. These shaped the public library's most basic philosophical perspectives, often leading to controversy and contradiction manifested in debate over operational decisions about specific activities.

ATTITUDES TOWARD SOCIALIZATION

Dain enumerates three viewpoints toward Americanization that were prevalent in the late nineteenth and early twentieth centuries.[34] Her classification is worth noting, since these attitudes not only reflect turn-of-the-century attitudes towards immigrants but serve to clarify perspectives in the treatment of many ethnocultural groups throughout the history of the American public library. The division is made on the basis of attitudes towards preservation of minority culture. The first group, Angloconformist, adhered to the position that white Anglo-Saxon culture was superior, and that immigrants should be forced to completely abandon their native culture and assimilate the dominant culture. The second group, melting pot advocates, felt that all cultures would contribute to one uniquely American and homogenized product without distinct subcultures.[35] Finally, cultural pluralism, which developed in the 1920s in response to the first two schools of thought and became widely accepted only much later, upheld the "belief that a democratic society should preserve the integrity of its constituent groups."[36] Dain contrasts practices of the public school system that required nearly total conformity and those of librarians of the New York Public Library, who recognized the dominant Anglo-Saxon culture and encouraged assimilation, but who eventually developed respect and appreciation for the non-Anglo culture.[37]

Ditzion noted that the provision of foreign language materials and participation in neighborhood activities may have grown from practical reasons as well as a genuine appreciation of foreign cultures. Early leaders recognized the political power of the masses, and the subsequent need for Americanization and education. Librarians realized that "if you would educate people with books, you must ease the way for them by removing barriers which in the past had made libraries unapproachable."[38] It was from this mixture of idealism and pragmatism that librarians began to conduct outreach programs and provide foreign language books.

Despite a relatively liberal outlook, the library profession generally perceived its role as one of elevation of taste of the growing urban population, whether it was comprised of immigrants or the previously rural and generally poorly educated native born American. In analyzing early library thought, Monroe sees a basically schizophrenic, "dual role of the public library in cultural matters."[39] On one hand, the cultural role of the time was based on an elitist philosophy of instilling in people an appreciation for high culture, while at the same time subscribing to a basically democratic philosophy of providing opportunity for improvement and cultural growth for everyone.[40] In general, political leaders saw the public library and public education system as a way to "allow the masses to emulate the qualities of the middle class, to act and think in conformity with accepted proprieties."[41]

THE SOCIAL UTILITY RATIONALE

The conflicting values and perspectives of the library's ultimate goal became evident in the debate over provision of high culture versus recreational reading, and fact versus fancy—in short, whether the public library was an opportunity for personal growth and development in every sense, or an agency designed to train workers for the greater economic good.[42] It is clear that for early trustees and founders

> Reading for amusement, for delight, for the enjoyment of life was not high among their priorities. Imbued with a desire to diffuse utilitarian knowledge, the early public librarians placed a heavy emphasis on serious works that were to be read for edification.[43]

Lacy noted that the need for a literate populace for an industrial society presented the conservative upper classes with "a dilemma. You've got to make people literate so they can learn mechanics, and you want to exclude them from access to the kinds of liberal arts material that is likely to be enfranchising."[44] It is necessary to confine workers to utilitarian, practical education to make them more useful employees "while keeping them away from troublemaking liberal arts ideas."[45]

Public librarians quickly diverged from this strictly economic utility point of view. The 1896 ALA manual justified the inclusion of fiction in libraries by asserting that "to the masses of people—hard worked and living humdrum lives—the novel comes as an open door to an ideal life, in the enjoyment of which one may forget for a time the hardship or tedium of the real."[46] This is not to suggest that librarians flew in the face of convention and alienated civic leaders by discarding all notions of social utility. Rather, there was an attempt to combine functions (education and recreation) and to shift the focus of the social benefit. Librarians began to argue that "not all fiction was recreational," and that the purposes of readers might vary.[47] They "tended to be humanistic in a cultural sense," asserting that "culture stood for both imagination and fact; people needed both. Novels could be as truthful and even more so than a biography, or a work of philosophy, science, or history."[48] This humanitarian aspect was reinforced by an appeal underscoring the social-economy aspect of public libraries. Recreational reading was seen as better than no reading at all, and the recreational activities of libraries as an alternative to poverty, crime, and baser forms of entertainment. Ditzion observed that "this general stress on the preservation of virtue by providing wholesome forms of entertainment appeared in practically every major declaration made during the infancy of the library movement."[49]

STIMULATION THROUGH NONBOOK ACTIVITIES

A changing cultural role based on an acceptance of diverse cultures, sensitivity to access issues, recognition of varying benefits to users, and an increasingly humanistic perspective emerged. It was evidenced in the growth of more diverse collections that included fiction as well as traditional educational materials, and in outreach services and nonbook activities.[50] This move towards a more egalitarian, proactive philosophy is demonstrated by a librarian who, in 1910, declared that "it is the function of the library to make accessible to every individual in the community that printed matter which is of value to him."[51] Bostwick was an active proponent of the "modern library idea" and urged librarians to become more active in using various means to introduce readers to the library and to promote access and "coordination of work [with other agencies] through lectures and exhibits."[52]

The uses of meeting rooms were expanded to programming, including live performances for both children and adults, meetings of civic organizations and municipal departments, and neighborhood gatherings.[53] Interaction with local organizations was seen as an opportunity for outreach, as well as a way of better understanding the nature of the neighborhood and its needs.[54] The emphasis on community activity and interaction foreshadowed outreach services of the 1960s as well as the community planning perspective that underlies recent library planning models.

SUMMARY

The changing social context of the late nineteenth and early twentieth century shaped the social/cultural role of the American public library. The first social/cultural role, the preservation and organization of artifacts, served as an unquestioned foundation from which the profession began to expand the role of the public library as an agent of socialization and acculturation. This role evolved from simply providing opportunities for the education of a desperately needed literate working class to include provision for social stability in the form of wholesome leisure activities. By the 1920s public librarians began to incorporate the roles of the library as a cultural agency bringing the individual into contact with the arts and humanities, and that of the library as a recreational social agency affording opportunity for entertainment and use of leisure time. "A product of mid 19th-century America, the public library was originally viewed as a repository of useful, even vocationally oriented material to aid a growing mercantile, artisan, and professional class. By the close of the century, the public library was seen as a cultural corrective to the burdens of a materialistic age."[55] While there had been some move towards the acceptance of cultural diversity and individual preference, the elitist notion of ultimately elevating the taste of the masses persisted. Collections had become more diverse, and nonbook stimulation activities were accepted as dynamic means of bringing the library and potential users together, as well as strengthening library and community ties.

Public Libraries as a National Resource (1930–1959)

The decades between 1930 and 1960 were marked by an attention to civic responsibility, solidarity, and appropriate use of leisure time.

Americans were forced to examine and reflect on their personal and national values as they were confronted with the Great Depression and World War II. The library profession's guiding documents echoed the concerns of the nation. Librarians saw their institution as fundamental to the well-being of America, asserting that "the achievement of the goals of a democratic society depends in large measure on the enlightenment of the people and on the vitality of their social and cultural ideals."[56]

FEDERAL SUPPORT FOR PUBLIC LIBRARIES

The American Library Association developed its own abilities to participate in political life during the 1930s and intensified its efforts to secure federal support for public libraries. ALA wavered between a call for general federal aid to libraries and support for the development of rural public libraries. Molz describes this course as an attempt to "link rationality with pragmatism."[57] Joeckel, especially, envisioned a national library network composed of all types of libraries, but as ALA political activity in Washington became more sophisticated, it became apparent that such a goal was beyond immediate achievement. The sympathies of Congress and the Roosevelt administration reflected a typical and still current attitude of strong but vague general support for libraries, combined with lukewarm financial commitment and a lack of specific goals.

By the late 1920s and throughout the Depression, America began to focus on the problems of rural areas. To some extent the rise of cities and the development of industry had left rural America behind. For a time, it seemed as if the country had two distinct cultures, one of which had been denied the benefits of the twentieth century but nevertheless suffered from its upheavals. As the attention of intellectuals and national planners focused on rural America, ALA planners began to see a clear need that could provide a means of entry for federal library support onto the national agenda. Federal aid to rural public libraries where they existed, or grants to establish them, fit with an emerging U.S. welfare state ideology not of egalitarianism, but of equality of opportunity. The complete lack of public library service in rural areas was a clear denial of such opportunity.[58]

The first significant ALA expression of this strategy appeared in the 1936 publication *The Equal Chance: Books Help to Make It*.[59] This document pointed to the fact that 45 million Americans were without library service of any kind and that the national per capita spending for library service was only thirty-seven cents. Two states spent as little as two cents per capita. In *The Equal Chance* the ALA attempted to link the notion of equality of opportunity with the educational advantage that public libraries could provide.[60] This strategy still provides the basis for arguments by librarians for both federal and local support.

One of the main issues raised at the time within the library profession was the possibility of the loss of local control to a dominant federal bureaucracy. Some librarians accused Milam of wanting to run an ALA dictatorship from Washington.[61] There are still sources of resistance within the library profession to an expansive federal role in library support and they resonate with recent political developments that suggest that there is a limit to what government can achieve.

Nevertheless, the obvious rural need was a pragmatic base on which the ALA could build a case for the Library Services Act. Joeckel realized that ALA library goals had to be transformed into goals that the federal government could adopt as part of a national agenda.[62] In 1956, during the 82nd Congress, this was finally achieved. The LSA specified that all federal money was to be administered by a state library agency, that the states had to match federal funds on a formula basis, that the amounts were to be a function of the state's percentage of rural population compared to the national average and that aid was to be limited to communities of 10,000 or less.[63] State governments were relieved of the burden of raising new funds at the state level by counting already existing local tax levies as part of their share for matching funds.

Priorities for programs were established by local or state agencies. The U.S. Office of Education administered the program, but had only very broad requirements under which states qualified for funds. States retained control in determining how these funds were spent.[64] This provision, which was retained in the Library Services and Construction Act, has led some evaluators to conclude that the states, lacking federal direction, have developed programs of "varied purposes and worth."[65] This criticism of a lack of cohesiveness can be directed not only at the state library agencies, but also at the federal government's denial of responsibility for public libraries as a national resource and at the library profession for failing to take a unified and consistent position with regard to the issue of federal support.

In 1956, however, the Library Services Act represented a breakthrough that had been sought after by librarians since the early 1930s. Public library service had become part of the national agenda. Congressmen such as Carl Elliot of Alabama guided the LSA through the legislative process with arguments that stressed the nation's responsibility and the public library's role in providing the information needed by a literate public for self-governance. As social policy the LSA was to give public libraries a means to diminish the sense of loneliness and isolation, especially among the young, that often characterized rural America. The public library was described in debate as a potential means of providing all Americans with an equal opportunity to participate in their common culture. The values of relief from boredom, the stimulation of the intellect, and the enrichment of lives were the ground from which the arguments for the passage of the LSA emerged.[66]

Absolutely crucial to success, however, was the retention of state and local control of the actual expenditure of LSA funds, and the fact that it was offered as a temporary measure.[67] ALA felt confident that the problems of rural library service could be solved within the five-year time limit on the authority of the legislation. The administration and Congress could afford to be generous when they were promised a concrete result of social spending and a guaranteed limit. Ironically, the temporary quality of the LSA may have contributed to the more permanent quality of the Library Services and Construction Act (1964) despite attempts by the administrations of Nixon and Reagan to remove libraries from the list of federal responsibilities. In any case, the cause of the LSA was not harmed by the fact that it was cheap. First-term Congresswoman Edith Green from Oregon, who sponsored the bill in the House, compared the per capita national cost of the LSA to the price of "a five-cent piece of chewing gum."[68]

EMPHASIS ON CITIZENSHIP

The theme of preparation for citizenship and preservation of the democratic way of life recurs in virtually every major American Library Association public library planning document between 1933 and 1956. It is reflective of the social/cultural role implied by the second definition—that the library functions as an agency of socialization and acculturation, serving to help the individual relate to his or her society. The 1938 *National Plan for Libraries* proposed two objectives directly related to the citizenship goal: "To improve their [public library users'] ability to participate usefully in activities in which they are involved as citizens," and "To maintain the precious heritage of freedom of expression and a constructively critical attitude toward all public issues."[69]

By 1943, these goals were more explicitly stated. The *Post-War Standards* suggested that by aiding parents in childcare, nutrition, health, budgeting, and recreation, libraries were helping to maintain "a democratic way of life," and that introducing young adults to "the stabilizing influence of books" encouraged them to become "responsible citizens."[70] This economic utility perspective echoes back to the 1920s when books were seen as a palliative for undesirable social behavior. By 1956, the responsibilities of the public library included assisting people to "become better members of home and community" and to "discharge political and social obligations."[71]

AESTHETIC APPRECIATION

A continued and strengthened concern for cultural development and appreciation is indicative of the acceptance of the fourth definition of the library's social/cultural role—bringing the individual into contact with the arts and humanities. During this thirty-year period, the language of ALA documents evolved from the goal of elevation of taste to aesthetic appreciation. This should not be seen as a completely egalitarian shift. Although there is some evidence of goals related to the enablement of minority cultures, there nevertheless persisted the notion that patrons should be helped toward higher standards of taste (presumably those recognized by the dominant culture.) "A National Plan for Libraries" was the first document to mention not only the need for libraries to enhance the individual's capacity for aesthetic appreciation, but also the capacity for "production in cultural fields."[72] Patrons were not seen as passive recipients, but as dynamic beings capable of contributing to "the educational and cultural objectives of the nation and community."[73] Yet the 1948 *National Plan for Public Library Service* did not specifically mention the user's potential contribution, referring instead to "the full development of . . . intellectual, social, and cultural capacities."[74] This same document reposed in the librarian the responsibility for providing "recreational and cultural materials of high aesthetic and moral value."[75] The value judgment is implicit, and would seem to imply a return (or perhaps a never very dramatic shift) to an attempt to impose dominant culture standards.

LEISURE AND RECREATION

The standards and goals created during the period of 1930 to 1960 demonstrate that librarians appeared not only ready to accept but to embrace the fifth perception pertaining to the library's social/cultural role, that of a social agency affording opportunities for recreation and use of leisure time. The trend toward the provision of recreational reading, begun in the 1920s, carried over and gained strength during the following decades. The 1933 standards, the first public library standards published by the American Library Association, asserted that the "public library is maintained by a democratic society in order that every man, woman, and child may have the means of self-education and recreational reading" and "opportunities for constructive use of the new leisure."[76] This goal was specifically reiterated over the following years in "A National Plan for Libraries" (1938), *Post-War Standards* (1943), and the 1956 *Public Library Service*.[77]

PROGRAMMING AND NONBOOK MATERIALS

While an increased attention to stimulation activities and an acceptance of live programming and nonbook formats evolved, these activities were clearly specified as a means of introducing potential users to the library collection.[78] Lee describes the growth of such group programs and the decline of individualized services such as the reader's advisor.[79]

The *Post-War Standards* advocated collection of a variety of materials, including pictures, films, and recordings.[80] These also described the uses and guidelines for meeting rooms. While rooms were

> Desirable for such educational activities as discussion and book review groups, film forums, radio and record listening, and story hours, . . . less closely related activities as a general rule should be included only when . . . the administration of such activities will not divert time and attention of the library staff from its primary responsibility.[81]

Here again, as in the earlier decade, is the charge that the library has an obligation to "integrate its services with the work of other social and cultural agencies."[82] This cooperative role persists to the current time, and was specifically identified and discussed by Monroe as part of the public library's cultural role in the 1970s.[83]

The notion of the library as a community center was specified in the 1948 *A National Plan for Library Service*.[84] In the plan, Joeckel and Winslow asserted that the library served "as a community center to which the citizen turns as he seeks expression of his interests and desires through group affiliation," and which might include such activities as children's programming, film forums, poetry readings, and symphony performances.[85] The 1956 plan *Public Library Service* asserted that "the library should facilitate the use of materials by verbal, visual, or other interpretive means," but nevertheless stipulated that "all group activities sponsored or co-sponsored by the library should be clearly related to the further use of library materials."[86]

SUMMARY

The thrust of documents produced between 1930 and 1960 can be summarized by Joeckel and Winslow: "The objectives of the public library are many and various. But in essence they are two—to promote enlightened citizenship and to enrich personal life."[87] The standards and goals demonstrate an acceptance of the library's social/ cultural role in its several facets. The first library role, as organizer and preserver of the human record, continued to serve as a consistent foundation, and while it has not been specifically discussed in this section, pervades all of the documentation.

During these thirty years, librarians strongly emphasized the role of the library in preserving American culture and in socializing citizens. Perhaps it was the environment of adversity created by economic depression and world war that created the need to assimilate, to form a solid, unified nation. This urge toward uniformity led again to the imposition of the dominant culture and the neglect of provision for diverse subcultures. This dual role of the public library in the service of both democracy and elitism was noted by Monroe.[88] Certainly, the *Public Library Inquiry* demonstrates the contradiction. While the *Inquiry* found that most librarians were in agreement with the democratic objectives of the *Post-War Standards,* the *National Plan,* and the *Four Year Goals,* it nevertheless argued that public library professionals should focus energies and resources on delivering service to the already well-served community elite.[89] For whatever reason, the emphasis on special groups that prevailed in earlier decades and reemerged in the 1960s is not found during this time.

The role of the library as a cultural agency that provides the opportunity for contact with the arts and humanities is reinforced throughout the entire period (1930 to 1960), as is the role of a social agency, providing for recreational reading and constructive use of leisure time.

Finally, the acceptance of these roles led to dynamic policies providing for stimulation activities through a variety of means. While these continued to be linked to further use of library materials, their value was established in providing access for a wide variety of individuals.

Social Responsibility and Federal Support (1960–1979)

The complacency of the 1950s was shattered by the social unrest of the 1960s. Recognition of social and economic inequality brought a new focus on the rights of individuals and previously neglected minorities. The federal government implemented a far-reaching slate of social welfare programs under the Great Society agenda of Lyndon Johnson. As in earlier decades, education was a panacea expected to provide answers to a vast number of social and economic problems.

The LSCA grew from this context and the general recognition that libraries had a legitimate need for federal aid because the nation had a legitimate need for libraries. The success of the LSA led librarians to believe that they had the political skills necessary to keep libraries on the national agenda. Extensions of the LSA survived into the Kennedy administration and as policy goals became prominent in the Johnson administration, ALA went to work in Washington again. In Johnson's state of the union address of January 8, 1964, libraries were associated with the war on poverty, urban renewal, civil rights, and improved health care as a means of equalizing the life chances of all Americans.[90] Congressman John Dent of Pennsylvania, arguing for the passage of the LSCA, said that public libraries were in a

> Strategic position to play an important role in the fight on poverty and its cause . . . the public library is now recognized as a vital cultural and economic resource, as well as a fundamental educational institution.[91]

REALLOCATION OF LIBRARY RESOURCES

Gans has observed that

> In heterogeneous societies, the struggle between diverse groups and aggregates over the allocation of resources and power are not limited to strictly economic and political issues, but also extend to cultural ones.[92]

It certainly appears that librarians of the sixties responded to social injustice by attempting to reallocate resources to bring cultural advantages to those previously exempted. Outreach services, community centers, storefront libraries, and other innovative means were used to extend the library to the community.

An account of an NEH public library program, for example, first appeared in the annual report of the NEH in 1968. A grant was provided to the Tulsa, Oklahoma City-County Library for a program entitled "Change: Discovery, Discussion and Decision." The Board of Trustees and directors of the library viewed their institution "not simply as a collection of books, but as a cultural service institution."[93] The library had already been involved in activities such as film presentations, lectures, exhibits, and providing information on cultural matters to the local press. The new program was designed to bring scholars, materials, and the public together to consider the rapidly changing social world of the late 1960s.

In a document sponsored by the Public Library Association, Peggy O'Donnell and Patsy Read described a plan of action for getting, implementing, and evaluating NEH library grants. The authors justified this activity on the grounds that it could attract new users, increase the community's awareness of library services, help the library become a cultural and information center and provide a public forum for consideration of current events.[94] The public library's universal accessibility and essential neutrality made it a "perfect" place for such events to occur.

Exposure to culture as a means of social understanding can be seen at work in the NEH grant program of the 1970s. The Houston Public Library presented a program of lectures, films, discussions, and walking tours entitled "City Images of Urban Life." The Indiana Library Association received a grant to establish a "Humanist in Residence" Program. The humanist was responsible for local programs on specific subjects and for organizing seminars on program planning.[95] To a great extent these programs focused on explicit consideration of values and the social goals these values implied.

Dain has drawn a parallel between the public library philosophy of the late nineteenth and early twentieth century and that of the 1960s. She suggested that unacceptable social conditions existed in both times that resisted effective treatment by existing social institutions, and that in such cases Americans were likely to turn to education as an "ameliorative, stabilizing, or egalitarian force."[96] She observed that modern librarians assumed an activist role under such circumstances, and that "librarians, like progressive reformers [of the turn of the century], believed that the public library had a mission to bring knowledge and culture to the masses."[97]

Although the document *Minimum Standards for Public Library Service* (1966) has been criticized for failing to provide dynamic leadership and promoting a more activist philosophy, it was clearly egalitarian in nature and focused on services to all groups and to every individual.[98] The *Standards* states that all library functions have meaning "only as they reach all people . . . and that a standard is not achieved if its provisions are met for one part of the population but not for another."[99] Objective 26 of the *Standards* stated that "the library system serves individuals and groups with special needs," and listed examples of such special groups, including those who are "economically, educationally, and culturally disadvantaged, the physically handicapped . . . and

Newcomers with limited knowledge of the language or customs of the area."[100]

A *Strategy for Public Library Change,* published in 1972, also stressed the need for reaching the unserved.[101] The disenfranchised were mentioned specifically at least twice in the document. The public library was charged with the responsibility "to play a role in the reintegration into society of groups now largely isolated and excluded by their lacks in education and training" and "to serve as both the motivator and supplier of aspirations for the dispossessed and disorganized."[102]

The *Public Library Mission Statement* (1979) moved even further toward the democratic ideal of individual worth and enablement.[103] After upholding individual rights to self-determination and civic participation, the statement asserted that "society needs an agency that can actively bring every person, regardless of age, education, language, religion, ethnic and cultural background and mental and physical health, into effective contact with the human record."[104]

LEGITIMATION OF POPULAR CULTURE

Concerns of ethnic minorities shifted somewhat during the 1960s. Although there was of course the demand to share in the rights and responsibilities of the dominant culture, there was also a growth in ethnic pride and demand for cultural recognition. Slogans such as "black is beautiful" were demonstrative of growing pride and demands for dignity. While there existed a struggle for economic and social equality, the need for cultural definition and acceptance was recognized as well. The struggle over "which culture and whose culture should dominate society" was a critical one.[105] The study of the phenomena of cultural pluralism gave rise to an academic discipline and subsequent legitimation of popular culture.[106]

Gans, a proponent of this cultural relativism, based his analysis of popular culture on two value judgments. First, that "popular culture reflects and expresses the aesthetic and other wants of many people," and second, that "all people have a right to the culture they prefer."[107] He observed that society is made up of an aggregate of varying taste cultures that reflect the class and educational background of the groups that adhere to them. Because of this, it is entirely appropriate and predictable that poorly educated citizens would have different aesthetic standards than better educated ones. The policy implication for U.S. institutions is simply this: until this nation can establish true cultural mobility by providing each individual with the educational

and economic resources that are prerequisites of access to and enjoyment of high culture, it is the responsibility of social institutions to
engage in subcultural programming that provides access to all taste
cultures.[108]

While the manifestations may be completely different, the urge to
bring beauty into their lives drives adherents of both low culture and
high culture. The choices people make, whether indicative of high or
low culture, are appropriate if they reflect the values and standards
meaningful to them. It is true that viewed in isolation, apart from the
people whose lives they serve, some cultures may seem superior to
others in their scope and depth, but cultures evaluated apart from
their consumers are meaningless. Not "all taste cultures are of equal
worth, but . . . they are of equal worth when considered in relation to
their taste publics."[109]

A truly democratic culture must be driven by an appreciation of
cultural relativism. The demand for recognition by minority groups
in the sixties has greatly influenced the nation's character and its
acceptance of alternate aesthetic standards. Nevertheless, controversy arose at the time and continues to exist. As cultural relativism has
moved into the mainstream, its genesis in class conflict and social
unrest has been somewhat forgotten. Generally, the conflict over
popular culture in the 1970s and 1980s focuses on aesthetics, and it
"has obscured the ideological and class origins of the criticisms and of
the very roots of the controversy."[110]

CULTURAL ROLE OF LIBRARIES

The conflict over the issue of cultural pluralism profoundly affected
the library profession. One faction opposed the use of many innovative
stimulation techniques as inappropriate and ineffective. Davies, author of a seminal work on the public library as a social and cultural
agency, echoes Berelson's earlier advice to focus library resources on
the well-educated elite who are most likely to use the library.[111] For
Davies, high culture and popular culture exist in separate realms for
different kinds of people. They could not be mixed, and by implication,
should not be. The proper audience for public library services is
composed of educated users capable of participation in high culture.

> If libraries confined themselves to books and reading it would
> certainly be true that their public would be narrower, as would their
> field of endeavor, but it is difficult to see why such a change would not be
> for the better.[112]

Davies's reasoning is reminiscent of Rosenberg, an outspoken critic of mass culture, who wrote,

> My position is that the antidote to mass culture is high culture, that high culture means art and learning and that these goods are potentially accessible to every person not suffering from extreme brain damage."[113]

Apparently, neither society as a whole nor the library in particular is accountable for access barriers and neither has the responsibility to provide opportunities for personal enrichment, since failure to take advantage of dominant cultural opportunities lies within the individual.

White, in rebuttal to Rosenberg, asserts that participation in high culture activities is not merely a matter of socioeconomic background and that "in reality, high culture is not so easily attained."[114] Of course, this is the crux of Gans's argument and the reason for his advocacy of subcultural programming.[115] Stevenson called for libraries to reevaluate the cultural role to accommodate the diversity made apparent by studies of popular culture.[116]

The number and variety of programs and services initiated during the sixties indicate that most librarians, guided by a heightened sensitivity to access issues, accepted the provision of popular culture as an appropriate function for the public library. Viewed in the context of cultural diversity and the acceptance of popular culture, policy implications were clear. While each individual might have personal standards that were sometimes at odds with those of the clientele, many librarians appeared to accept Gans's call for a separation of personal preference from public performance. He charged that

> Critics of mass culture . . . have translated their own private evaluations into a public policy position which not only ignore other people's private evaluations, but seek to eliminate them altogether.[117]

Librarians, in an attempt to avoid this type of cultural dictatorship, worked not to change the tastes of clientele, but "to widen exposure, to provide alternative cultural models, to expand life experience."[118] The role of socialization was accepted in its fullest sense. Individuals would not only locate themselves relative to their society, but would be able to make unique contributions to that society. Society would not assimilate and obliterate its diverse cultures, but nurture them for the qualities and perspectives they represented.

Monroe's truly fundamental work on the cultural role of the public library provides a useful conceptual framework.[119] As a result of her interviews with librarians in major library systems across the United States and her subsequent analysis of their programs and environmental context, Monroe described manifestations of the cultural role, documented professional attitudes and interpretations of the role, and delineated functions actually performed in pursuit of the role. She found that librarians tended to view culture in two ways: in the anthropological sense of total life environment and in the arts and humanities sense that encompassed folk, ethnic, and mass culture as well as high culture.[120] The services and programs studied relate most clearly to the arts and humanities perspective of the cultural role. All forms of culture appeared to be equally acceptable, and most of the systems studied tended to provide a variety of services. High-culture programming tended to be located in central libraries, while folk and ethnic culture were frequently found in branches of the same system.[121]

This division of service was reinforced by representatives of other agencies who saw the neighborhood branches as cultural outreach centers scattered throughout the community.[122] The implications for access issues are obvious: libraries were most often accepted as cultural centers in cases where no other agencies were offering service and where the limited mobility of the population prevented their participation.[123] In her study Monroe identified six functions of the library in fulfilling the cultural role:

1. To serve the arts information needs of the community [including the needs of artists and scholars]
2. To provide a showcase for the arts in the local community
3. To facilitate arts program coordination among community organizations and groups.
4. To provide a network of cultural outreach centers for the community.
5. To stimulate the consideration of public issues in the light of humanistic values, building such values into the everyday culture of our society.
6. To provide the fundamental cultural literacy needed for experience of the arts. [This includes literacy training as well as the removal of access barriers.][124]

Functions defined by Monroe reveal that library practice in the systems studied reflected the democratic principles of the standards documents as well as the operational manifestations of the stimulation function. The variety of functions and the flexibility with which they were applied foreshadowed the community planning emphasis of later documents, and it will be shown that all of these functions may be readily subsumed in one or more of the roles specified in the 1987 guide, *Planning and Role Setting for Public Libraries.*[125]

LEISURE AND RECREATION

The library profession continued to recognize the value of recreational reading and the importance of constructive use of leisure time. The *Minimum Standards* asserted that materials must be selected to assist people to "develop their creative and spiritual capacities, appreciate and enjoy the works of art and literature," and "use leisure time to promote personal and social wellbeing."[126] This theme was reiterated in all planning documents between 1960 and 1979, although it did not receive the same emphasis as other roles. Nevertheless, it is clear from a perusal of the literature and from the continued inclusion of the recreational role in subsequent planning documents that this was a function that most librarians viewed as integral to full library service. Increasingly, it had been recognized that "recreation has value as an end unto itself. Many individuals have little desire to 'improve' themselves and librarians must honor this choice."[127]

NONBOOK MATERIALS AND PROGRAMMING

Perhaps one of the most radical conceptual shifts has been that away from the view of nonbook formats and live programming as mere enticements to further use of the library's book collection. In 1979, the *Public Library Mission Statement* declared, "Access now implies innovative, imaginative delivery techniques which overcome geographic, educational, physical, and psychological barriers, as well as convenient location and schedule."[128] The value of live programming was clearly stated: "Information includes not only the sum total of recorded human experience . . . but also the unrecorded experience which is available only from human sources . . . ."[129]

Monroe noted that many librarians no longer saw the need to relate stimulation activities to collection use, preferring to offer "a wide range of traditional or innovative aesthetic experiences for the sake of the humanizing experience itself."[130] Increased attention was placed on the need to expand the librarian's concept of professional responsibility. A 1974 conference entitled "Differentiating the Media: A Focus on Library Selection and Use of Communication Content" focused on "shift[ing] librarians' interests from media packages to media contents."[131] Many activists felt that "we need to place less emphasis on cultural objects (books, sound recordings, or whatever) and more emphasis on the function of these objects in people's lives."[132]

SUMMARY

During the 1960s and 1970s, the library profession adhered to the socialization role but shifted its focus from the general citizenry to the individual and to minority groups. Issues concerning popular culture and access came to the fore and were manifested in the growth of innovative services aimed at reaching the disadvantaged.

Policy decisions were viewed in the context of larger philosophical and sociological implications. It was apparent, as articulated in the *Public Library Mission Statement,* that

> The cultural role of the public library has shifted from the nineteenth-century view of the public library as an agency of acculturation, Americanization, and standardization of life style and values, to an agency which recognizes cultural and ethnic differences and encourages self pride and appreciation of different cultural heritages.[133]

The implementation of a wide variety of programs demonstrated the acceptance of the library social/cultural role in several of its perspectives: that of a social welfare agency (through job-related and community information services), as a social agency (through the provision of recreational reading and leisure activities), and, most visibly, as a cultural agency (through the provision of numerous programs sponsored by NEH and NEA). Ultimately, the library profession saw public libraries as highly flexible institutions that could provide a wide variety of services to groups and individuals. Librarians accepted the responsibility to

> Accept the individual as an individual and to provide spiritual nourishment, intellectual stimulation, cultural enrichment, and information alternatives to him at the neighborhood or community level.[134]

Retrenchment and Renewed Commitment (1980–Present)

The global recession of the late 1970s strongly affected public libraries in diverse ways. Most directly, special funding for innovative programming has been greatly reduced, and many library budgets have not been able to sustain programs implemented in the past two decades. Perhaps more pervasively, scarcity of federal resources has led to a new emphasis on program evaluation in all fields at all levels of government, and the library profession appears to have whole-heartedly embraced the new emphasis on quantitative measurement. Economic scarcity has contributed to a new federal outlook on information dissemination, often to the detriment of accessibility. A conservative administration has attempted to impose increased restrictions on information in the name of national defense. Technology has brought to the fore issues concerning privacy as well as access to information. These factors have served to refocus the library profession's commitment on its most fundamental social/cultural role—the preservation and dissemination of information—not just for diverse minority groups, but for the citizenry as a whole. Nevertheless, many librarians recognize the special needs of minorities, and library services to those groups continue to be of major concern.

PROGRAM EVALUATION EMPHASIS

The expectations for federal involvement and support created by the Great Society Program of the 1960s followed by the scarcity of the 1970s has lead to increased emphasis on program evaluation.[135] Social scientists have been quick to realize that evaluation research not only is valuable for assessing current programs and planning future ones but may be used in highly political ways to effect the distribution of funds.[136] Weiss has observed, "Evaluation has always had explicitly political overtones. It is designed to yield conclusions about the worth of programs and, in doing so, is intended to affect the allocation of resources."[137] Rich has argued that "the probability of information being used is less a consequence of the appropriateness of the information to the substantive policy than it is of the utility of the information to bureaucratic interests."[138]

The library profession has accepted the pragmatism and political realities of the 1980s. *A Planning Process for Public Libraries* (1980), *Output Measures for Public Libraries*(1982), and the Public Library Development Project volumes (*Planning and Role Setting for Public Libraries* and *Output Measures for Public Libraries,* 2nd edition) are all intended as specific management and planning tools, not as inspirational statements of the public library's mission and responsibilities.[139] Librarians are for the most part well aware of the political uses of program planning and evaluation. Speakers at library conferences have emphasized the value of quantitative measurement and sustained evaluation research, not just as a way to improve library service, but as a means of gaining political leverage and additional resources.[140]

These planning volumes are also reflective of current political thought that advocates a return to federalism by encouraging local planning and funding and a diminished central involvement. Library planners have reinterpreted and elevated this focus as a means of better serving the needs of the immediate community. The local planning focus reveals the library as a social institution in the broadest sense. The emphasis on planning based not only on objective data but on interaction with community members is a reminder of the library's commitment to the society it serves. The focus on political use of the data is an implicit recognition of the library as part of a larger social structure. This focus serves as a reminder that the library competes for resources with other social institutions and that the library's existence depends on continued recognition of its value to the larger society.

FUNDING: LSCA AND NEH

The Library Services and Construction Act as it now stands authorizes both a library and a social program. State library agencies still retain control over local spending decisions and must still match federal funds on a formula basis. The Act is composed of four titles:

> Title I—Public Library Services
> Title II—Public Library Construction
> Title III—Interlibrary Cooperation
> Title IV—Older Reader's Services

Titles I and IV are of particular interest as social policy. Title I still provides funds for equalizing library opportunities between geographic areas, but is no longer limited to rural communities. It also specifies four social service policy goals. Funds will be provided to public libraries to provide services to patients or inmates of state supported institutions, the physically handicapped, disadvantaged persons in low income areas and persons of limited English speaking ability.[141] Title IV has never been funded. In general, the current purpose of Title I is to stimulate public library development in the direction of serving as a means of equalizing opportunities for participation by individuals at the margin of society. Titles II and III tend to provide funds to libraries as libraries regardless of the intended audience for services.

Although tailored to the needs of social policy and politics of the late twentieth century, federal public library policy still carries the values of its Progressive roots. It is still a vaguely conceived and somewhat contradictory reform oriented policy. One evaluation of the LSCA has noted its similarity to many other American federal social service policies in that it appears to be more a tax redistribution scheme than a goal-oriented aid system.[142] Recent ALA and Public Library Association activities to promote the use of the Public Library Development Project techniques seem to indicate that librarians now believe that state and local governments could be a source of new financial support. Rational planning, cost effectiveness, and measurable public good are values behind this project and are not unrelated to a new drive toward municipal reform stimulated by the transfer of many government functions from federal to local levels during the Reagan administration. For libraries, this may be a successful short-term strategy, but until attention returns to Washington, Milam and Joeckel's vision of a national system encompassing libraries of all types will go unrealized.

In the 1980s, the focus of library NEH programs changed to encourage cooperative and cost-effective efforts, but the themes of public library activities still focused in general on the relationship between values and actions. The latest *Catalog of Federal Domestic Assistance* offers three programs as examples of recently funded grant applications as a guide to NEH priorities. In the first case, two county library systems were awarded a grant to develop a reading and discussion program, called "Literary Reflections of the New South." A regional consortium of northeastern public and academic libraries was awarded a grant to present a series of programs on the framing of the Constitution and the character and values of eighteenth-century New England society. In the third example, a public library and an antiquarian society joined forces to make the resources of both institutions more accessible to a general audience. Reading lists were distributed in libraries and bookstores. Exhibitions and lectures were given at both the library and the society to allow the general public to become aware of how they might use humanities resources. In all three programs, there was a strong presence of the scholarly and a focus on what might be considered "timeless" rather than "topical" social concerns.[143]

Since its inception, the NEH has played a rather small part in the development of public libraries as cultural centers. The programs funded seem to have more the character of demonstration projects than continuing commitment, but most public libraries would not be able to offer such programs on their own budgets. Joeckel once made the argument that this condition was not a sign that libraries had no role in a national policy of cultural development. Rather it demonstrates the need for cooperative efforts and funding from federal, state, and local governments to develop libraries as a national resource. Each level of government bears a responsibility for library support appropriate to its unique capabilities and resources. The NEH effort may be absolutely small and the LSCA relatively so compared to other federal programs, but together they represent an ideologically powerful precedent for federal support of libraries.

CONCERN FOR MINORITIES

Service to minorities continues as a major social/cultural role of the public library. While *Planning and Role-Setting* does not specifically delineate the need for services to special groups, one may expect that this is implicit in the community planning model.[144]

The 1986 ALA conference theme, "Diversity," demonstrated on-going concern for the library's responsibility for serving the needs of ethnic and cultural minorities by spotlighting exemplary programs geared to the needs of culturally diverse groups: American people of color, the illiterate, the disabled, and new Americans.[145] A number of ALA units are specifically devoted to improving library service to a wide variety of minorities.[146] The commitment to equal service for ethnic minorities and the culturally disadvantaged that had resurged in the 1960s continues, and it has expanded in the 1980s to include two previously neglected minorities: the handicapped and the aging. Officially, the public library profession remains committed to the socialization and acculturation role of helping individuals interact with the society in which they live and preserving the unique contributions of cultural minorities. Evidence of formalized concern notwithstanding, there is some argument as to whether libraries truly represent all aspects of popular culture.

Harris asserts that libraries and librarians continue, consciously or unconsciously, to cater to the dominant culture and reinforce some points of view to the exclusion or minimization of others.[147] Serebnick found that while few librarians engage in overt censorship, they tend to select materials reviewed in national review sources, and that these sources tend to overrepresent larger, mainline publishing houses.[148] One of the potential hazards of a planning model that is exclusively community-based and not supported by a broader professional mission statement is that community pressure may have undue influence on material selection. Curley and Broderick have discussed the strength of community influence and noted that "there is enough censorship in the selection process in most libraries to make us vulnerable to attacks that proclaim that *we* are the real censors."[149]

SOCIAL/CULTURAL ROLE REFLECTED IN *PLANNING AND ROLE SETTING FOR PUBLIC LIBRARIES*

The 1987 *Planning and Role Setting for Public Libraries,* produced by the Public Library Development Project, does not prescribe specific services to which every American citizen is entitled. It asserts instead that "no library has a large enough budget, staff, or collection to meet *all* the service needs of its community. No library can fulfill all roles with excellence, so each library must focus its resources on a *limited* number of roles."[150] The manual then outlines eight suggested roles from which libraries may choose: Community Activities Center, Community Information Center, Formal Education Support Center, Independent Learning Center, Popular Materials Library, Preschoolers' Door to Learning, Reference Library, and Research Center.[151] While a specific social/cultural role is not discussed, the five perspectives of the public library's social/cultural role as delineated earlier are embedded in the specific roles described in *Planning and Role Setting*.

As suggested by our classification of social/cultural roles, the first and most basic social responsibility of the public library is the preservation and organization of artifacts of an advanced literate society. The research center role fulfills this fundamental charge by collecting exhaustively in a particular area and providing information and access for local scholars.[152] The human record is thus preserved and serves as a stimulus for further growth and knowledge production. Closely related is the role of a formal education support center, as it serves much the same purpose, though on a less elevated plane.[153] Sociologists and students of popular culture have suggested that the library as a popular materials center provides important documents and materials for their studies of modern society and may serve as the only readily accessible and formalized archive for this type of material.[154]

The socialization-acculturation facet permeates several *Planning and Role Setting* role definitions and may be most clearly seen in the "Benefits" section that accompanies each role description in the manual. The community activities center provides a meeting place for neighborhood activities and services and works in conjunction with community groups and other social agencies. The primary benefit of this role is that "Community members have opportunities to explore their common heritage, discuss their divergent views on issues and current topics and receive some social services."[155] The aim is to provide a "coordinated program of social, cultural and recreational services."[156] Here is the combination of the socialization and recreational roles first seen in the settlement houses of the 1890s and several of the library's cultural roles in the 1970s as delineated by Monroe.[157]

The community information center role combines the broad socialization role and some aspects of the library as a social welfare agency. In performing this role, the library provides information on community organizations, issues, and services.[158] One of the benefits of this role is that "access to this information helps individuals to become self-sufficient, control their lives, and better understand community issues."[159] This role echoes the earlier commitment to developing skills for citizenship and as such may be seen as a socialization role for the public library.

Three of the roles, formal education support center, independent learning center, and preschoolers' door to learning, relate directly to education and lifelong learning and are conceptually linked. As was noted in earlier sections, the socializing effect of school systems and education has often served as a rationale for school and library support. The importance of this socialization and acculturation process is made most explicit in describing benefits of the independent learning center. The library helps users "to 'get ahead,' to do better in their work, to clarify their values, to learn something new, or to adjust to changes in life and work . . . ." [160] The social economy justification is again called into play as McClure points out that one of the benefits of the independent learning center role is that "the library supports an educated, self-reliant, and productive citizenry, thus contributing to the stability, attractiveness, and economic well-being of the community."[161]

The perception of education (and hence, the library's support of education) as the ultimate panacea for social problems persists. Public education is prized for its supposed capacity for developing individual ability and directing it into socially useful channels. The political impact of serving any of these educational roles is clearly spelled out for each. The formal education support center role "closely associates the library with education, and benefits taxpayers by supplementing, not duplicating, other educational collections."[162] The independent learning center makes "powerful allies" of those who use the library, and the preschoolers' door to learning not only promotes lifelong use of the library, but "generates visibility, popularity, and support for the library in the community by reaching children unserved by any other community agency."[163]

The fulfillment of the library's social welfare agency role is clearly stated in the description of the community information center. Provision of information about social issues such as high unemployment, teenage pregnancy, and drug abuse is given high priority. The description asserts that "access to this information helps individuals to become self-sufficient, control their lives, and better understand community issues. For the community, the library helps link those in need of services and resources with an appropriate provider."[164]

The library acting as an "independent learning center" aids individuals in setting their "own learning objectives to meet such concerns as citizen education, self-improvement, job-related development, hobbies, and cultural interests."[165] Again we see the combination of the socialization role (citizen education, self-improvement), the social and recreational role (hobbies), and the social and cultural role (cultural interests). It may be the acceptance of popular culture in the previous decade that has led to the overlapping of two previously distinct roles: recreational and cultural. As argued in another section, this fusion is probably appropriate given that recreation and culture may be viewed respectively as low culture and high culture and so address similar needs for diverse groups.

The popular materials library role again fuses the previously distinct recreational and cultural roles, stating that the benefit of this role derives from its "support for cultural and leisure activities [which] make the community an inviting place to live and visit."[166] The value of this service is defined in terms of its social and economic benefit to the community as well as in terms of its contribution to individual well-being, again placing personal development in the context of a larger societal benefit.

While *Planning and Role Setting* does not address the importance of the library's social/cultural role, it provides multiple avenues for fulfillment of that role in its various aspects. As analyzed above, some facet of the social role is fundamental to each of the suggested roles. Certainly, while some public library observers are arguing for a return to basic service and a suspension of nonbook programming and other stimulation activities often seen as integral to the social/cultural role, *Planning and Role Setting* supports these as appropriate within the context of public library service.

SUMMARY

Librarians in the 1980s have been forced to reassess basic goals and priorities. Tightening budgets, a call for fiscal accountability, and the dominance of quantitative evaluation have lead to retrenchment. Planning documents of the era emphasize quantitative measures and the importance of limiting, not expanding, the library's service mission. While the basic role of preservation and organization has been accepted as fundamental since the inception of the U.S. public library, it has gained increasing attention in the face of threats from technology, the lack of a national information policy, and an adversarial federal administration. The traditional concern for minorities and the disadvantaged is interwoven with broader access concerns. While many in the profession are still working towards equalization of opportunity for special populations, these special groups are not singled out for attention in the planning and role setting manual.[167] Although the philosophical foundations of library service are not addressed in the planning documents of this decade, the social nature of the public library is implicit in the community planning model. While the social/cultural roles delineated in this essay are not specifically addressed, they are nevertheless integral to the more operationally specific roles suggested by the planning manual.[168]

Conclusion

The public library of today has evolved over the past hundred years to fulfill several social/cultural roles. It preserves the culture of the past and present and organizes it for current and future use. This is its most fundamental social role: it preserves and makes accessible the knowledge that defines our society. Only recently, with the advent of electronic technology for information storage and transfer, has it been necessary to reexamine the library profession's defining function. The need for a national information policy assuring preservation of information and equality of access is evident. Librarians will need to assume a leadership role if this policy is to be implemented.

The priority of other social/cultural roles has fluctuated over time. The target populations of socialization functions and social welfare type services have changed from the immigrants and newly urbanized groups of the 1890s to ethnic populations in the 1960s to the economically disadvantaged, the handicapped, and the aging in the 1980s. While these groups change, the underlying role of the public library in regard to them has not.

The division of social (recreational) and cultural services has become less distinct since the early debates. The work of popular culture theorists in the 1960s tended to reinforce the functional similarities of the two. The library profession has now accepted the role of providing the opportunities for meaningful use of leisure time, as well as for self-discovery and expression.

Some debate still exists as to the appropriateness and the function of nonbook materials and programming. Nevertheless, nonprint materials have gained increasing acceptance, and many libraries offer live programming, not simply to encourage use of the library but as a means of sharing the knowledge found there.

Finally, there is tacit recognition at the federal level that libraries are a national resource. While fiscal support has been minimal, an ideological precedent has been established for a national library policy.

The roles suggested in this essay demonstrate the broad impact of the public library as a social/cultural institution. The library sustains individual growth while preserving the knowledge that defines society. Acceptance of the social role of librarianship carries with it enormous responsibility. In acknowledging the value of the library to society, librarians obligate themselves to preserve and increase the influence of this institution. Threats to their fundamental role in preserving, organizing, and providing equal access to information must serve to renew professional commitment.

Notes

1. Gordon Stevenson, "Popular Culture and the Public Library," *Advances in Librarianship* 7 (1977): 181.
2. Ibid., p. 180.
3. Dan Lacy, "Discussion" (following R. Kathleen Molz), in *The Role of the Humanities in the Public Library,* proceedings of a conference sponsored by the School of Library Science, University of North Carolina at Chapel Hill, March 5–7, 1978, ed. Robert N. Broadus (Chicago: ALA, 1979), p. 61.
4. Stevenson, "Popular Culture," p. 181.
5. Max Weber, *The Theory of Social and Economic Organizations,* trans. by A. M. Henderson and Talcott Parsons (London: Oxford Univ. Pr., 1947).
6. Peter L. Berger and Thomas Luckman, *The Social Construction of Reality* (New York: Doubleday, 1966), pp. 93–94.
7. Michael H. Harris, *History of Libraries in the Western World,* compact textbook ed. (Metuchen, N.J.: Scarecrow Press, 1984), pp. 80–95.
8. Stevenson, "Popular Culture," p. 199.
9. Harris, *History,* pp. 48–60.
10. Ibid., p. 33.
11. Ibid., pp. 16–17.
12. Ibid., p. 48.
13. Ibid., pp. 38–42.
14. Richard Hofstadter, *The Age of Reform: From Bryan to FDR* (New York: Knopf, 1966), pp. 5–7.
15. Page Smith, *America Enters the World: A People's History of the Progressive Era and World War I, vol. 7* (New York: McGraw-Hill, 1985), p. 81. See also George S. Bobinski, *Carnegie Libraries: Their History and Impact on American Public Library Development* (Chicago: ALA, 1969).

16. Alvin Johnson, *A Report to the Carnegie Corporation of New York on the Policy of Donations to Free Public Libraries* (New York: Carnegie Corporation, 1919); Charles C. Williamson, *The Williamson Reports of 1921 and 1923,* including "Training for Library Work" (1921) and "Training for Library Service" (1923) (Metuchen, N.J.: Scarecrow Press, 1971).
17. Bobinski,*Carnegie Libraries*
18. Smith,*America Enters the World,* p. 86.
19. "A National Plan for Public Libraries, Revised and Adopted by the A.L.A. Council, December 29, 1938," *ALA Bulletin* 33 (February 1939): 138.
20. Redmond Kathleen Molz, *National Planning for Library Service, 1935–1975* (Chicago: ALA, 1984), pp. viii–ix.
21. United States Office of Management and Budget, *Catalog of Federal Domestic Assistance* (Washington, D.C.: GPO, 1990), p. 805.
22. Ibid., p. 704.
23. Ronald Berman, *Culture and Politics* (New York: Lanham, 1984), pp. 157–165.
24. Ibid., p. 159.
25. Stephen Miller, *Excellence and Equity: The National Endowment for the Humanities* (Lexington: University of Kentucky Pr., 1984), pp. 125–154.
26. Ibid., p. 147.
27. John Brademas, *Washington D.C. to Washington Square* (New York: Weidenfeld Nicolson, 1986), p. 115.
28. Ibid., p. 114.
29. "NEH: 'Libraries Are Schools'," *American Libraries* 19 (October 1988): 747.
30. Lynne V. Cheney, *Humanities in America* (Washington, D.C.: The National Endowment for the Humanities, 1988).
31. "NEH: 'Libraries Are Schools'," p. 747.
32. Phyllis Dain, "Outreach Programs in Public Libraries," in *Milestones to the Present: Papers from Library History Seminar V,* ed. Harold Goldstein (Syracuse, N.Y.: Gaylord, 1978), p. 257.
33. Lacy, "Discussion," pp. 59–60.
34. Dain, "Outreach Programs," p. 270.
35. Ibid.
36. Ibid.
37. Ibid.
38. Sidney Ditzion, *Arsenals of a Democratic Culture: A Social History of the American Public Library Movement in New England and the Middle States from 1850–1900* (Chicago: ALA, 1947), p. 75.
39. Margaret Monroe, "The Cultural Role of the Public Library," *Advances in Librarianship* 11 (1981): 2.
40. Ibid.
41. Ditzion, *Arsenals of a Democratic Culture,* p. 55.
42. R. Kathleen Molz, "The American Public Library: Its Historic Concern for the Humanities," in *The Role of the Humanities in the Public Library,* p. 1.
43. Ibid.
44. Lacy, "Discussion," p. 60.
45. Ibid., p. 61.
46. Ditzion, *Arsenals of a Democratic Culture,* p. 109.
47. Robert Ellis Lee, *Continuing Education for Adults through the American Public Library, 1833–1964* (Chicago: ALA, 1966), p. 27.
48. Dain, "Outreach Programs," p. 265.
49. Ditzion, *Arsenals of a Democratic Culture,* p. 98.

50. For an excellent discussion of the evolution of the stimulation function, see Kathleen M. Heim, "Stimulation," in *The Service Imperative for Libraries,* ed. Gail A. Schlachter (Littleton, Colo.: Libraries Unlimited, 1982), pp. 120–153.

51. Richard N. Current, "Response," (Following R. Kathleen Molz, in *The Role of the Humanities in the Public Library,* p. 52.

52. Dain, "Outreach Programs," p. 258.

53. Ibid., p. 268.

54. Ibid.

55. Molz, "The American Public Library," p. 39.

56. American Library Association, Committee on Post-War Planning, Carleton Bruns Joeckel, chairman, *Post-War Standards for Public Libraries* (Chicago: ALA, 1943), p. 21.

57. Molz, *National Planning for Library Service,* p. 65.

58. Ibid., pp. 70–71.

59. *The Equal Chance: Books Help to Make It* (Chicago: ALA, 1936).

60. Ibid., p. 20.

61. Molz, *National Planning for Library Service,* pp. 76–79.

62. Ibid., p. 103.

63. Ibid., p. 97.

64. Ibid., p. 98.

65. Jean B. Wellisch et al., *The Public Library and Federal Policy Sponsored by the System Development Corporation under a Grant from the United States Office of Education* (Westport, Conn.: Greenwood, 1974), p. 203.

66. Edward G. Holley and Robert F. Schremser, *The Library Services and Construction Act: An Historical Overview from the Viewpoint of Major Participants* (Greenwich, Conn.: JAI, 1983), pp. 15–18.

67. Ibid., pp. 19–20.

68. Ibid., p. 23.

69. "A National Plan," p. 138.

70. American Library Association, *Post-War Standards,* p. 23.

71. American Library Association, Public Libraries Division, Coordinating Committee on Revision of Public Library Standards, *Public Library Service: A Guide to Evaluation with Minimum Standards* (Chicago: ALA, 1956), p. 31.

72. "A National Plan." p. 138.

73. Ibid., p. 140.

74. Carleton B. Joeckel and Amy Winslow, *A National Plan for Public Library Service,* prepared for the Committee on Postwar Planning of the American Library Association (Chicago: ALA, 1948), p. 130.

75. Ibid., p. 131.

76. "Standards for Public Libraries," *Bulletin of the American Library Association* 27 (November 1933): 513.

77. "A National Plan;" American Library Association, *Post-War Standards;* American Library Association, *Public Library Service.*

78. Heim, "Stimulation."

79. Lee, "Continuing Education," pp. 82–83.

80. American Library Association, *Post-War Standards,* p. 21.

81. Ibid., p. 64.

82. Ibid., p. 26.

83. Monroe, "The Cultural Role," pp. 7–11.

84. Joeckel and Winslow, *A National Plan*, p. 130.

85. Ibid., pp. 130–137.
86. American Library Association, *Public Library Service,* p. 29.
87. Joeckel and Winslow, *A National Plan,* p. 1.
88. Monroe, "The Cultural Role," p. 2.
89. Bernard Berelson, *The Library's Public* (New York: Columbia Univ. Pr., 1949); Robert Leigh, *The Public Library in the United States: The General Report of the Public Library Inquiry* (New York: Columbia Univ. Pr., 1950).
90. Lyndon B. Johnson, "First Annual Message. January 8, 1964," in *The State of the Union Messages of the Presidents, 1790–1966,* ed. Fred L. Isreal (New York: Chelsea House, 1966), pp. 3156–3161.
91. *Congressional Record,* 88th Congress, 2nd Session (1964) CX pt. 1, p. 770.
92. Herbert J. Gans, *Popular Culture and High Culture: An Analysis and Evaluation of Taste* (New York: Basic Books, 1974), p. 3.
93. United States National Endowment for the Humanities, Barbara C. Keeney, chairman, *Third Annual Report, FY 1968* (Washington, D.C.: GPO, 1969), p. 25.
94. Peggy O'Donnell and Patsy Read, *Planning Library Programs* (Chicago: PLA, 1976), pp. 2–5.
95. United States National Endowment for the Humanities, Division of Public Programs, *Public Library Program Guidelines, 1978–1979* (Washington, D.C.: NEH, 1978), pp. 10–11.
96. Dain, *Outreach Programs,* p. 258.
97. Ibid.
98. American Library Association, Public Library Association, Standards Committee, *Minimum Standards for Public Library Systems, 1966* (Chicago: ALA, 1967).
99. American Library Association, *Minimum Standards,* p. 9.
100. Ibid., p. 33.
101. American Library Association, Public Library Association, Allie Beth Martin, project coordinator, *A Strategy for Public Library Change: Proposed Public Library Goals—Feasibility Study* (Chicago: ALA, 1972).
102. Douglas M. Knight and E. S. Nurse, eds., *Libraries at Large,* quoted in American Library Association, *Strategy,* p. 20.
103. American Library Association, Public Library Association, PLA Goals, Guidelines and Standards for Public Libraries Committee, Peter Hiatt, chair, *Public Library Mission Statement and Its Imperatives for Service* (Chicago: ALA, 1979).
104. American Library Association, *Public Library Mission Statement,* p. 3.
105. Gans, *Popular Culture,* p. 3.
106. Frank W. Hoffman, *Popular Culture and Libraries* (Hamden, Conn.: Library Professional Publications, 1984), pp. 8–9.
107. Gans, *Popular Culture,* p. vii.
108. Ibid., p. xi.
109. Ibid., p. 128.
110. Stevenson, *"Popular Culture,"* p. 192.
111. D. W. Davies, *Public Libraries as Culture and Social Centers: The Origin of the Concept* (Metuchen, N.J.: Scarecrow, Inc., 1974); Berelson, *The Library's Public.*
112. Davies, *Public Libraries,* p. 125.
113. Bernard Rosenberg, "Mass Culture Revisited I," in *Mass Culture Revisited,* eds. Bernard Rosenberg and David Manning White (New York: Van Nostrand Reinhold, 1971), p. 9.
114. David Manning White, "Mass Culture Revisited II," in *Mass Culture Revisited,* eds. Bernard Rosenberg and David Manning White (New York: Van Nostrand Reinhold, 1971), p. 16.

115. Gans, *Popular Culture,* pp. 128–29.
116. Stevenson, "Popular Culture," pp. 219–220.
117. Gans, *Popular Culture,* p. 121.
118. Ibid., p. 123; Monroe, "The Cultural Role," p. 6.
119. Monroe, "The Cultural Role," p. 5.
120. Ibid.
121. Ibid., pp. 5–6.
122. Ibid., p. 7.
123. Ibid.
124. Ibid., pp. 11–13.
125. Charles R. McClure et al., *Planning and Role Setting for Public Libraries: A Manual of Options and Procedures,* prepared for the Public Library Development Project (Chicago: ALA, 1987).
126. American Library Association, *Minimum Standards,* p. 36.
127. Hoffman, *Popular Culture,* pp. 15–16.
128. American Library Association, *Public Library Mission Statement,* p. 5.
129. Ibid.
130. Monroe, "The Cultural Role," p. 3.
131. Stevenson, "Popular Culture," p. 222.
132. Ernest Van den Haag, "Of Happiness and of Despair We Have No Measure," in *Mass Media and Mass Man,* ed. A. Casty (New York: Holt, Reinhart and Winston, 1961), p. 53, cited by Stevenson, "Popular Culture," p. 222.
133. American Library Association, *Public Library Mission Statement,* p. 5.
134. American Library Association, *Strategy,* p. 47–48.
135. John P. Blair and David Nachmias, eds., *Fiscal Retrenchment and Urban Policy, Urban Affairs Annual Reviews, vol. 17* (Beverly Hills, Calif.: Sage, 1979), p. 8.
136. Charles O. Jones, *An Introduction to the Study of Public Policy,* 3rd ed. (Monterey, Calif.: Brooks/Cole, 1984), pp. 200–203.
137. Carol H. Weiss, "The Politicization of Evaluation Research," *Journal of Social Issues* 26 (Autumn 1970): 58, quoted in Jones, *An Introduction to the Study of Public Policy,* p. 202.
138. Robert F. Rich, *Social Science Information and Public Policy Making: The Interaction between Bureaucratic Politics and the Use of Survey Data* (San Francisco: Jossey-Bass, 1981), p. xi.
139. Vernon E. Palmour, Marcia C. Bellassai, and Nancy V. De Wath, *A Planning Process for Public Libraries* (Chicago: ALA, 1980); Douglas L. Zweizig and Eleanor Jo Rodger, *Output Measures for Public Libraries* (Chicago: ALA, 1982); Charles R. McClure et al., *Planning and Role Setting for Public Libraries: A Manual of Options and Procedures,* 2nd ed., prepared for the Public Library Development Project (Chicago: ALA, 1987); Nancy Van House et al., *Output Measures for Public Libraries* (Chicago: ALA, 1987).
140. Note, for example, these programs offered at the Public Library Association Conference, Pittsburgh, Pa., April 27–30, 1988: "Generating Support Through Statistics," "Playing the Numbers with YA's: Program Planning and Evaluation for Young Adult Services," and "Answers from Managers: New Data for Decision Making."
141. Marilyn Gell Mason, *The Federal Role in Library and Information Services* (White Plains, N.Y.: Knowledge Industries, 1983), pp. 60–62.
142. *Alternatives for Financing the Public Library,* a study prepared for the National Commission on Library and Information Services (Washington, D.C.: GPO, 1974).
143. Mason, *The Federal Role,* p. 72.

144. McClure, *Planning and Role Setting,* et al.
145. Regina U. Minudri, "Diversity: The Challenge to America's Libraries," ALA President Inaugural Address, July 2, 1986, ALA Annual Conference, New York.
146. *ALA Handbook of Organization 1987/88* (Chicago: ALA, 1987).
147. Michael H. Harris, "State, Class, and Cultural Reproduction: Toward a Theory of Library Service in the United States," *Advances in Librarianship* 14 (1986): 238–41.
148. Judith Serebnick, "An Analysis of Publishers of Books Reviewed in Key Library Journals," *Library and Information Science Research* 6 (1984):289–303, cited in Harris, "State, Class," pp. 244–45.
149. Arthur Curley and Dorothy Broderick, *Building Library Collections,* 6th ed. (Metuchen, N.J.: Scarecrow, 1985), p. 150.
150. McClure, *Planning and Role Setting,* p. 28.
151. Ibid.
152. Ibid., p. 39.
153. Ibid., p. 34.
154. Janet K. Schroeder, "Studying Popular Culture in the Public Library: Suggestions for Cooperative Library Programs," *Drexel Library Quarterly* 16 (July 1980): 65–72.
155. McClure, *Planning and Role Setting,* p. 32.
156. Ibid.
157. Dain, *Outreach Programs,* p. 268; Monroe, "The Cultural Role," pp. 11–13.
158. McClure, *Planning and Role Setting,* p. 33.
159. Ibid.
160. Ibid., p. 35.
161. Ibid.
162. Ibid., p. 34.
163. Ibid., p. 37.
164. Ibid., p. 33.
165. Ibid., p. 35.
166. Ibid., p. 36.
167. Ibid.
168. Ibid.

Contributors

Lolah Giamalva and Joyce Meadows

Anthony E. Barnes was involved with the Adult Services in the Eighties project while working on his MLIS at Louisiana State University, School of Library and Information Science. Upon graduating in 1987, he joined the staff at New Orleans Public Library in the Reference and Information Division. In 1988, he assumed the duties of interlibrary loan librarian in addition to continuing his reference duties. Before attending the School of Library and Information Science at LSU, he worked in the Children's Department of the Lafayette (Louisiana) Public Library.

Bert R. Boyce is dean and professor at Louisiana State University, School of Library and Information Science since 1983. He has received the ASIS Outstanding Information Science Teacher Award presented at the 52nd Annual Meeting in Washington, D.C. on November 1, 1989, and the American Library Association Shera Research Award for 1988 with Danny P. Wallace for a paper entitled, "Holdings as a Measure of Journal Value." Bert Boyce holds a BA from Marietta College in Marietta, Ohio, and a MSLS and PhD from Case-Western Reserve University, Cleveland, Ohio.

Judith I. Boyce is director of the Jefferson Parish Public Library. She was previously a library consultant with the State Library of Louisiana, Baton Rouge, where she received a John Cotton Dana Award for the State Library of Louisiana for its summer reading program, "Summer Safari," in 1989. Judith Boyce holds a BA Degree from Baldwin-Wallace College, Berea, Ohio, and a MSLS from Case-Western Reserve University, Cleveland, Ohio. The Boyces have jointly written several papers on bookmobiles and were the coinvestigators of a Council on Library Resources Cooperative Research Grant, "The Bookmobile, a Service Mechanism for the Nineties?" which ran from January, 1989, through May, 1990.

Charlene C. Cain received a BA in history from Nicholls State University in Louisiana in 1977. From Louisiana State University she received an MA in history in 1980 and an MLIS from the School of Library and Information Science in 1986. Before receiving her MLIS she was the lead archivist at Louisiana State Archives and Records Service. She is currently the government documents librarian at Southeastern Louisiana University in Hammond. She also serves as chair of the Louisiana Library Association's Government Documents Round Table.

Michele M. DeLorme received her MLIS from Louisiana State University School of Library and Information Science in August of 1987. She returned

501

to her position at Northfield Public Library in Northfield, Minnesota. In December of 1988 she accepted a position at Ramsey County Public Library as librarian coordinator of children's programming. Ramsey County Public Library is a six-branch system outside St. Paul, Minnesota.

Lolah C. Giamalva graduated from Louisiana State University with a BA in applied design and an MLIS from the School of Library and Information Science. She has worked in reference positions at the Louisiana State University, Middleton Library, and the State Library of Louisiana in Baton Rouge. She was employed as a cataloger for the Computer Company in Richmond, Virginia, and is now employed as an Adult Service librarian for the Gloucester County Library System in Sewell, New Jersey.

Kathleen M. Heim is dean of the Graduate School at Louisiana State University. She was dean of the School of Library and Information Science from 1983 to 1990. She was the author of the ALA Goal Award on behalf of the RASD Services to Adults Committee that funded the Adult Services in the Eighties project and was principal investigator. Heim edited the Reference and Adult Services Division journal, *RQ,* from 1982 to 1988 and the Public Library Association journal, *Public Libraries,* from 1988 to 1990. She has written several *ALA Yearbook* entries on adult services, the adult services entry for the *ALA Encyclopedia of Library and Information Services,* and a background paper on the ASE project, "Adult Services as Reflective of the Changing Role of the Public Library" for *RQ.* Heim holds the BA degree from the University of Illinois at Chicago, MA degrees from the University of Chicago and Marquette University, and the PhD from the University of Wisconsin.

Chris E. Marhenke is currently a government documents librarian at the Broward County Main Library in Fort Lauderdale, Florida. He was the 1986 recipient of the Frederick Winthrop Faxon scholarship. Marhenke holds the BS degree in computer science from the University of Arkansas at Monticello, and the MLIS from Louisiana State University.

William E. Moen is a network system research analyst in the Network Development and MARC Standards Office at the Library of Congress. He was selected to participate in the Library of Congress intern program in 1988-1989. His MLIS was awarded at Louisiana State University in 1988. Prior to enrollment at the Louisiana State University School of Library and Information Science, Moen was a bookseller in Butte, Montana, and served on the Montana State Library Advisory Council. He is the coauthor with Kathleen M. Heim of *Librarians for the New Millennium* and *Occupational Entry: Library and Information Science Students' Attitudes, Demographics and Aspirations Survey.*

Douglas Raber has recently been appointed to the faculty of the School of Library and Information Science at the University of Missouri. His research interests include public libraries, American library history, and American popular culture. He has contributed articles to *Indiana Libraries* concerning public library politics and has presented workshops on marketing reference services, and presenting online catalogs to the public. Raber holds BA and MA degrees from Indiana University, and the MALS from Northern Illinois University. He is currently a candidate for the PhD in library science at Indiana University.

Gary O. Rolstad presently directs the St. Bernard Parish Library in Chalmette, Louisiana. He worked for over fifteen years in Hennepin County Library in Minnesota; on the ASE project for one year; for two years as assistant dean at the Graduate School of Library and Information Science at the University of Illinois; and as adult services consultant in Queens Library in New York. He has written on adult services for *RQ, Bookmark,* and the *ALA Yearbook of Library and Information Services.* He has taught classes for Queens College and as adjunct assistant professor for the Louisiana State University School of Library and Information Science. Rolstad has served two terms on the Services to Adults Committee in the Reference and Adult Services Division of ALA, including one year as chairperson. He has completed a BA program at the University of Minnesota, an audiovisual skills institute at Mankato State University, and a MLS at Louisiana State University. He began doctoral studies at the University of Illinois in 1987.

D. W. Schneider served four years in the Navy and worked in production planning for Eastman Kodak. He worked as an intern at Indiana University while obtaining his library degree, holding positions in the business library, in Latin American bibliography and in government documents. He has served as head of the Business Administration and Social Science Division, as undergraduate librarian at the University of North Carolina at Chapel Hill, and was associate director for Public Services at Louisiana State University from 1975 to 1990. Currently he is acting director of libraries at LSU. Schneider holds an AB in economics from Kalamazoo College and an MBA in finance and MA degrees from Indiana University.

Janice M. Simpson is director of the Cullman County Public Library in Alabama. Previously she was director of the Winn Parish Library in Winnfield, Louisiana. While a student at the School of Library and Information Science at Louisiana State University, she became involved with the Adult Services in the Eighties project and served as project coordinator in 1987–1988. Simpson wrote several "ASE Updates" for *RQ* and coauthored an *ALA Yearbook* article on adult services. She has a BA in English from Southern Benedictine College in Cullman, Alabama, and the MLIS from Louisiana State University School of Library and Information Science. Simpson is a member of the ALA Notable Books Council.

Betty J. Turock is chair of Library and Information Studies at Rutgers University, where she also coordinates and teaches in the management curriculum. Before her career in library education she held posts in school, college, and public libraries in Illinois, Arizona, North Carolina, New York, and New Jersey. She was assistant director, then director of the Rochester and Monroe County (New York) Library System. During the 1988/89 academic year she was a senior associate and advisor in the United States Department of

Education, Office of Educational Research and Improvement, Library Programs. Turock is a frequent lecturer and consultant to libraries and is the author of over forty publications centering on public libraries. She is the founding editor of *The Bottom Line: A Financial Magazine for Librarians.* Her book, *Serving the Older Adult: A Guide to Library Programs and Information Sources* from Bowker has been called the definitive work on this topic. She is currently completing a book, *Creating a Library Financial Plan* for Neal-Schuman. Two publications are also forthcoming from the U.S. Department of Education: *Beyond Output Measures: Models for Evaluation* and *Evaluating Federally Funded Library Programs.* A magna cum laude graduate of Syracuse University, Turock did graduate study in clinical psychology at the University of Pennsylvania before receiving her MLS and PhD degrees from Rutgers University.

Connie Van Fleet is an assistant professor at the Louisiana State University School of Library and Information Science. Her work as ASE project coordinator (1986–1987) led to a number of presentations and publications about the ASE project. She has discussed ASE findings at the Library Research Round Table research forum at the ALA annual conference in 1987 and at a 1988 Conference program cosponsored by the ASCLA Library Services to the Impaired Elderly Forum and the RASD Committee on Library Services to an Aging Population, as well as at several state and local conferences. She has written a number of articles based on the ASE project, including "Public Library Services to Older Adults: Survey Findings and Implications" *(Public Libraries,* March/April 1989). Van Fleet serves as chair of the PLA Research Committee and is a member of the Louisiana Advisory Council for the White House Conference on Library and Information Services. In 1991 she will become co-editor, with Danny P. Wallace, of *RQ,* the official journal of Reference and Adult Services Division of ALA. She holds a BA degree from the University of Oklahoma, a MLIS from Louisiana State University, and a PhD from Indiana University.

Danny P. Wallace, currently associate dean of the School of Library and Information Science at Louisiana State University, has also held faculty positions at the University of Iowa and Indiana University. His articles have appeared in *Journal of the American Society for Information Science* (for which he is associate editor for book reviews), *Information Processing and Management, Library Trends, American Libraries, Library Journal* and other library and information science periodicals. His paper "Holdings as a Measure of Journal Value," written with co-author Bert R. Boyce *(Library and Information Science Research* 11 (1989): 59–71), was the winner of the 1988 ALA Library Research Round Table Jesse Hauk Shera Award for Research. In 1991 he will become co-editor, with Connie Van Fleet, of *RQ,* the official journal of RASD. Wallace holds a BS in education from Southwest Missouri State University, an MA from the University of Missouri, and a PhD in library and information science from the University of Illinois.

Index

Compiled by Kathleen J. Patterson